Beginning
Xcode®

Beginning
Xcode®

James Bucanek

WILEY

Wiley Publishing, Inc.

Beginning Xcode®

Published by
Wiley Publishing, Inc.
10475 Crosspoint Boulevard
Indianapolis, IN 46256
www.wiley.com

Copyright © 2006 by Wiley Publishing, Inc., Indianapolis, Indiana

Published simultaneously in Canada

ISBN-13: 978-0-471-75479-4
ISBN-10: 0-471-75479-X

10 9 8 7 6 5 4 3 2 1

1B/RW/QT/QW/IN

Library of Congress Cataloging-in-Publication Data:

Bucanek, James, 1965–
  Beginning Xcode / James Bucanek.
     p. cm.
  Includes index.
  ISBN-13: 978-0-471-75479-4 (paper/website : alk. paper)
  ISBN-10: 0-471-75479-X (paper/website : alk. paper)
  1. Mac OS. 2. Operating systems (Computers) 3. Computer software—Development. I. Title.
  QA76.76.O63B826 2006
  005.4'46—dc22
                        2005037953

Credits

Acquisitions Editor
Katie Mohr

Development Editor
Adaobi Obi Tulton

Technical Editor
Michael D. Trent

Production Editor
Michael Koch

Copy Editor
Kathryn Duggan

Editorial Manager
Mary Beth Wakefield

Production Manager
Tim Tate

Vice President and Executive Group Publisher
Richard Swadley

Vice President and Executive Publisher
Joseph B. Wikert

Project Coordinator
Ryan Stefffen

Graphics and Production Specialists
Carrie A. Foster
Lauren Goddard
Denny Hager
Jennifer Heleine
Barbara Moore
Alicia B. South

Quality Control Technician
John Greenough

Proofreading and Indexing
TECHBOOKS Production Services

This book is dedicated to Deborah and Doug
for two decades of friendship and support.

About the Author

James Bucanek has spent over 25 years programming and developing microprocessor systems. He has experience with a broad range of computer hardware and software, from the smallest embedded consumer products to robotic control of silicon wafer deposition furnaces used in integrated circuit manufacturing. His development projects include the first local area network for the Apple][, distributed air conditioning control systems, a piano teaching system, digital oscilloscopes, and collaborative writing and assessment tools for K-12 education. James holds a Java Developer Certification from Sun Microsystems and was awarded a patent for optimizing local area networks. He has been the technical editor and a contributing author for several recent books on Mac OS X. James is currently focused on Macintosh software development, where he can combine his deep knowledge of UNIX and object-oriented languages with his passion for elegant design. James holds an Associates degree in classical ballet from the Royal Academy of Dance.

Acknowledgments

This book wouldn't have been possible without the patience, experience, and guidance of my editor, Adaobi Obi Tulton. Ms. Tulton spent countless hours reviewing the manuscript, correcting my grammar, suggesting changes to make it more readable, keeping me on schedule, and handled the countless administrative and technical details required to publish a technical book. If my knowledge of Xcode is communicated to you, it is Adaobi's knowledge of publishing that made it possible.

Standing just behind Adaobi Tulton is the fantastic staff of Wiley publishing. From the acquisition editor to the production staff, every individual I've worked with has been friendly, professional, and stunningly easy to work with. I would also like to thank my agent, Laura Lewin, and the other talented individuals at StudioB, for all of their help.

Having been a technical editor myself, I am uniquely qualified to appreciate the contribution of Michael Trent, the technical editor on this book. Michael painstakingly reviewed each detail and procedure, making sure everything presented was correct, consistent, and unbiased. Michael, who is also an accomplished book author and professional developer, made many suggestions; often pointed out features, shortcuts, and practices that I was unaware of. Michael substantially influenced the breadth and richness of this book. I take full responsibility for any inaccuracies herein, but Michael is largely responsible for its precision.

I would also like to acknowledge Kirk McElhearn and Dan Frakes. Kirk is a prolific and entertaining author of many fine books on the Macintosh, iPod and other topics. Dan has written the Mac OS X Power Tools book and is senior writer for *MacWorld* and *PlayList* magazines. Kirk is the one who recommended me when Wiley publishing was searching for an author for this book. I've work with both Kirk and Dan on several writing projects in the past. If one learns by example, these two gentlemen have been my greatest teachers.

Finally, this book would not even exist if it weren't for the imagination, skill, and hard work of the Xcode development team. I would particularly like to thank Chris Espinosa, Eric Albert, Jim Ingham, and Scott Tooker at Apple for answering my numerous technical questions about Xcode over the past six months. A very special thank you goes to Chris Hanson, who spent a considerable amount of time patiently explaining the inner workings of Xcode's unit test framework.

Contents

Contents

Contents

Contents

Contents

Contents

Contents

Contents

Contents

Introduction

Welcome to Xcode. Xcode is Apple Computer's integrated development environment (IDE) used for writing, building, and testing programs to run on the Mac OS X operating system. Using Xcode, you can create a wide variety of applications, plug-ins, drivers, and frameworks using different technologies and languages. It includes tools to design, edit, analyze, debug, test, package, and distribute your projects. It can be used by an individual developer or to collaborate with a group of developers.

An IDE is the "glue" that gathers together and helps you manage all of the little pieces that are needed to produce modern software. It is entirely possible to edit, compile, link, bundle, and test your software without using an IDE. In fact, that was how software used to be developed—and still is, occasionally. You can edit your files with an editor, save them, run a compiler to compile the source, run a linker to link the object files into a program, and then start a debugger to test it. Most of these tools have little or no user interface, being driven almost exclusively from the command line. As applications become more complex, however, so do the tools needed to produce them. Even a "simple" project might employ a dozen different tools to create a working application. Using the correct tools, running them in the correct order with the correct arguments, managing the hundreds of intermediate files produced during this process, and doing this repeatedly and consistently becomes a huge burden on the developer—sucking most of the joy and spontaneity out of your life.

Enter the IDE. The Xcode IDE puts a convenient, friendly, and graphical face on all of the tools you need to develop your project. Instead of dealing with individual folders and files, Xcode presents you with a project window filled with icons representing its constituent parts. Instead of maintaining macros and compiler rules, Xcode gives you a list of build settings. Instead of wrestling with the complex syntax of debugger commands, Xcode highlights the line in the source that your application is executing and shows you the state of its variables, conveniently formatted in a scrollable table. By simply dragging icons, you can make complex structural changes to your projects.

Despite its complexity, and the length of this book, it's interesting to consider that Xcode doesn't really "do" much of the actual work in producing your finished product. It doesn't compile your source code, it doesn't build your NIB files, it doesn't link your code, it doesn't assemble your application bundle, and it doesn't control your code during debugging. What Xcode does is bring together all of the tools that actually do this work and make them appear to be a single application. It's a facilitator that smoothes out the wrinkles between all of the parts, leaving you with a seamless, comfortable, and productive working environment.

Who This Book Is For

This book is for anyone who wants to start using the Xcode IDE to write Macintosh software, or who wants to develop a deeper understanding of the Xcode application and its capabilities. This includes C, C++, Objective-C, AppleScript, and Java developers. It includes anyone who wants to create simple command-line tools, Java applications that employ Macintosh-specific technologies, AppleScript Studio authors, and any kind of application with a graphical user interface. The latter includes any application that uses the Cocoa or Carbon APIs. Xcode can also produce kernel extensions, hardware drivers, and application plug-ins. WebObjects development also relies on Xcode. Although this book doesn't explicitly cover WebObjects development, a thorough knowledge of Xcode will benefit any WebObjects developer. In short, Xcode is the preeminent IDE for producing any kind of executable program written specifically for the Mac OS X operating system.

For a few development targets, however, Xcode may be a less-than-optimal choice. Java programmers who want to develop "pure" cross-platform Java applications have several IDE choices beyond Xcode. Although Xcode is certainly capable of producing any kind of Java application, Java IDEs like Eclipse (www.eclipse.org/) offer many more Java-specific features. If your goal is to download and build, but not really develop, open source projects, then Xcode can be somewhat superfluous. Most open source projects have self-contained make files that will build the project for you. While it's possible to integrate these projects into Xcode, you may find very little advantage in doing so unless you plan to extensively explore or alter those projects.

Having said that, Xcode is unmistakably the most comprehensive development environment available for Mac OS X. Although it might not be the perfect choice for every kind of development project, there are very few kinds of programs that it can't produce. If you only want to learn one development tool for Mac OS X, Xcode is it.

What This Book Covers

Xcode means different things to different people. The ambiguity arises from the use of the term "Xcode" to refer to both the entire suite of developer tools available from Apple Computer as well as the name of the Xcode IDE application itself. This book describes the latter. It focuses exclusively on how to create, configure, edit, and control projects using the Xcode application. Whenever I generically refer to *Xcode*, I mean the Xcode IDE application, not the entire set of developer tools.

The Xcode Developer Tools package includes a huge collection of tools, including Xcode itself. Some of these tools are integrated with the Xcode application and some are not. Tools that are not integrated are not covered here, and the ones that are integrated are only discussed in terms of how those tools are used from within Xcode. For example, the entire debugging interface is thoroughly discussed in Chapter 15. Everything you will do while debugging, from setting conditional breakpoints to editing memory, is ultimately preformed by the gdb debugger under the direction of the Xcode application. Although the full range of capabilities provided by Xcode's debugger interface is explained, I make no attempt to teach you how the gdb tool works or its command syntax. The same thing goes for the compilers, linkers, and other tools employed by Xcode.

In some ways, this is the point of using Xcode in the first place: so you don't have to deal with the complex, and often arcane, details of tools like gdb. You'll be amazed at how little you need to know about the tools that work behind the scenes. I've been developing Macintosh applications for years, and never once have I had to run the compiler or linker directly from the command line. And even if you do want to dig down in the details of these tools, Xcode is still the place to start. If nothing else, Xcode will show you how these tools are nominally used and how they fit into the overall development picture.

What this book doesn't cover is how to program. You may find it ironic that a book about software development has very little in the way of actual code or programming advice. The code and projects used throughout this book are minimal and written explicitly to demonstrate the features and concepts being explained. The breadth of Xcode is partially to blame—that, and the fact that my publisher won't let me write a 4,000-page book. Xcode supports development in C, C++, Objective-C, Java, and AppleScript, using Java, Carbon, Cocoa, and UNIX APIs, and can be extended using bash, tcsh, perl, python, awk, and other scripting languages. An introduction to any *one* of these topics is a book on its own, and you'll find many well-written books have already been published on all of these subjects. If you want to get started developing applications for Mac OS X, consider Xcode one half of your journey. Choose your language and programming API, and then let this book show you how to build your product using those technologies.

How This Book Is Structured

This book is organized in, more or less, the steps you'll take when developing any program. The initial chapters explain how to set up and control your working environment, create a project, and add source files to it. You will then learn how to edit your source files and alter the structure of the project itself. Later chapters cover how to configure the project to build your product and how to start and control the build process. Towards the end, this book shows you how to run and debug your application and how to construct automated test suites for it. Along the way, you'll be introduced to a variety of editing, documentation, design, and analysis aides.

While this order follows the typical edit-compile-run sequence of development, we all know that development rarely happens in exactly that order and is never a purely linear process. Although the project you will be working on six months from now might include three targets, your first project—from start to finish—will probably only use the one preconfigured target that was set up automatically for you. This may predispose you to skip over the sections in Chapter 13 that explain how to create new targets. Read enough of the chapter to understand targets and what role they play in your project, and then move on. You can always come back to those sections when you need to create a target yourself.

Along the way, this book introduces concepts and technologies that you may be completely uninterested in. Chapters 8, 10, 16, 18, and 17, for example, are self-contained and don't introduce any concepts that will prevent you from understanding the other chapters in this book. That's not to say that you shouldn't at least take a quick peek. Some of the technologies presented in these chapters are down right amazing. Try some of them out—you'll be glad you did.

What You Need to Use This Book

To develop applications for Mac OS X you need a Macintosh computer running Mac OS X 10.4 or later and a copy of the Xcode Developer Tools. Chapter 1 explains where you can obtain the Xcode Developer Tools and how to install them. You also need sufficient RAM and disk space to accommodate the operating system, the development tools, and your projects. Don't be stingy with RAM. Development tools are notorious memory and resource hogs, and Xcode is no exception.

You need to know how to program. If you are just starting out, begin with an introductory programming book for the language of your choice. If you want to develop "real" Macintosh applications, start with Objective-C and Cocoa. If you want to learn to program in a language more applicable to other platforms, learn Java. If you are already an accomplished C/C++ programmer and want to stick with that language, find a book on Carbon (Mac OS X's C interface). Ideally, try to use a book that is written specifically for the

Macintosh. These include programs, examples, and even Xcode projects that you can build and run without translation. These are very general recommendations—use your own experience and goals to guide your choice. After you are comfortable with the language you want to develop with, return to this book to learn how Xcode can help you turn your programming ideas into reality. Alternatively, keep this book alongside your others and learn Xcode as you go along.

Many examples in this book use entire projects to demonstrate a feature. See the "Source Code" section, later in this introduction, for information on how to download the projects and source files used throughout this book.

Conventions

To help you get the most from the text and keep track of what's happening a number of conventions are used throughout the book.

Try It Out

The "Try It Out" sections are exercises you should work through, following the text in the book. For instance:

1. They usually consist of a set of steps.
2. Each step has a number.
3. Follow the steps through with your copy of the database.

How It Works

After each "Try It Out" section, the code you typed is explained in detail.

Additional Information

> **Boxes like this one hold important, not-to-be forgotten information that is directly relevant to the surrounding text.**

Tips, hints, tricks, and asides to the current discussion are offset and placed in italics like this.

Text Styles

The following style conventions are used in the text:

❑ Keyboard strokes are shown like this: Ctrl+A
❑ URLs and code within the text are in monofont, like this: `persistence.properties`
❑ Code is presented in two different ways:

```
In code examples, new and important code is highlighted with a gray background.
```

The gray highlighting is not used for code that's less important in the present context, or has been shown before.

Source Code

As you work through the examples in this book, you may choose either to create your projects manually or to use the projects that accompany the book. All of the projects used in this book are available for download at www.wrox.com. When you are at the site, simply locate the book's title (either by using the Search box or by using one of the title lists) and click the Download Code link on the book's detail page to obtain all the projects for the book.

Because many books have similar titles, you may find it easiest to search by ISBN; this book's ISBN is 0-4717-5479-X (changing to 978-0-4717-5479-X as the new industry-wide 13-digit ISBN numbering system is phased in by January 2007).

Alternately, you can go to the main Wrox code download page at www.wrox.com/dynamic/books/download.aspx to see the code available for this book and all other Wrox books.

Bonus Sections

Due to length constraints, a few topics didn't make it into this edition of the book. These have been collected and are available for download at www.wrox.com as bonus sections. Follow the links to download the projects files, as described previously.

Errata

Every effort is made to ensure that there are no errors in the text or in the code. However, no one is perfect, and mistakes do occur. If you find an error in one of our books, like a spelling mistake or faulty piece of code, we would be very grateful for your feedback. By sending in errata, you may save another reader hours of frustration, and at the same time, you will be helping us provide even higher quality information.

To find the errata page for this book, go to www.wrox.com and locate the title using the Search box or one of the title lists. Then, on the book details page, click the Book Errata link. On this page, you can view all errata that has been submitted for this book and posted by Wrox editors. A complete book list including links to each's book's errata is also available at www.wrox.com/misc-pages/booklist.shtml.

If you don't spot "your" error on the Book Errata page, go to www.wrox.com/contact/techsupport.shtml and complete the form there to send us the error you have found. We'll check the information and, if appropriate, post a message to the book's errata page and fix the problem in subsequent editions of the book.

p2p.wrox.com

For author and peer discussion, join the P2P forums at p2p.wrox.com. The forums are a Web-based system for you to post messages relating to Wrox books and related technologies and interact with other readers and technology users. The forums offer a subscription feature to e-mail you topics of interest of your choosing when new posts are made to the forums. Wrox authors, editors, other industry experts, and your fellow readers are present on these forums.

At http://p2p.wrox.com, you will find a number of different forums that will help you not only as you read this book, but also as you develop your own applications. To join the forums, just follow these steps:

1. Go to p2p.wrox.com and click the Register link.

2. Read the terms of use and click Agree.

3. Complete the required information to join as well as any optional information you wish to provide and click Submit.

4. You will receive an e-mail with information describing how to verify your account and complete the joining process.

> *You can read messages in the forums without joining P2P, but in order to post your own messages, you must join.*

After you join, you can post new messages and respond to messages other users post. You can read messages at any time on the Web. If you would like to have new messages from a particular forum e-mailed to you, click the Subscribe to this Forum icon by the forum name in the forum listing.

For more information about how to use the Wrox P2P, be sure to read the P2P FAQs for answers to questions about how the forum software works as well as many common questions specific to P2P and Wrox books. To read the FAQs, click the FAQ link on any P2P page.

Installing Xcode

Xcode is part of the Xcode Developer Tools suite developed and distributed by Apple Computer. If you haven't installed it already, read this chapter to find out how to do so. If the tools are already installed, you can skip to the next chapter.

> If you've already installed Xcode, be aware that the default installation choices do not include all Xcode components. Features described in some chapters may require you to reinstall the omitted packages before you can use them. Return to this chapter to reinstall, upgrade, or remove the Xcode Developer Tools in your system.

The Xcode Development Tools encompass a huge amount of material: dozen of applications, scores of utilities, hundreds of sample projects, and tens of thousands of pages of documentations. Despite its scope, the developer tools team at Apple has made it remarkably easy to install this wealth of tools in only a few minutes.

The Xcode Installer

To install the Xcode Developer Tools, you must be running Mac OS X and have access to an Xcode Developer Tools installer. At the time this book was published, the current version of Xcode was 2.2, which requires that you be running Mac OS X 10.4 or later. This entire book was written with, and assumes you are using, Xcode version 2.2.

The Xcode Developer Tools installer is included on every Mac OS X 10.4 installation and upgrade DVD. So if you have a Mac OS X 10.4 installer DVD, you should already have a copy of Xcode. However, the copy of Xcode on the original release of OS X 10.4 is Xcode version 2.1. Although you can successfully use this book with Xcode 2.1, there are numerous small differences between 2.1 and 2.2. Download and install Xcode 2.2 if you can.

You can download a disk image of the latest Xcode Developer Tools from the Apple Developers Connection at http://developer.apple.com/. Anyone with an ADC account can download the latest development tools, software development kits, and example code directly from Apple.

Online ADC accounts are free and require only that you create an ADC account and agree to the nondisclosure agreement that covers all Apple development technologies. Student, Select, and Premier accounts can be purchased and include many additional benefits. One of these is the monthly ADC mailing, which ships current copies of the tools and reference material to you on CD or DVD. Other perks include discounts on hardware used for development and direct access to Apple engineers for technical questions. If you are serious about developing software for Mac OS X, you should invest in a Student or Select membership.

Running the Installer

Open the Xcode Tools folder found on the Mac OS X install DVD, shown on the left in Figure 1-1 or open the Xcode Developer Tools disk image, shown on the right in Figure 1-1 — whichever you are using. To begin the installation process, open the Xcode Tools.mpkg package. This launches the installer utility.

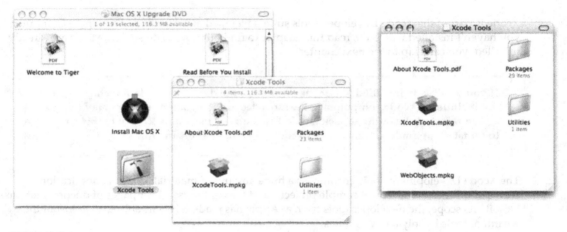

Figure 1-1

The installer presents a simple greeting screen. Click the Continue button. It next presents the software licensing agreement that accompanies the use of all of the developer tools provided by Apple Computer. The pop-up menu at the top of the window allows you to read the licensing agreement in English or Japanese. Review the document using the scroll bar. If you like, you can save it as a PDF file for review or for your records by clicking the Save button. The Print button prints the licensing agreement on any available printer.

After you click the Continue button, a dialog box asks you to confirm that you agree to the terms of the license. Click the Agree button.

Use the next screen, shown in Figure 1-2, to select the volume where the Xcode tools will be installed. The Xcode Development Tools can only be installed on the volume your operating system is currently booted from. In addition, the operating system you are running must meet the minimum requirements of the version of Xcode you are trying to install. If these conditions are not met, the volume has a red alert badge. Select the volume to find out why the tools can't be installed there.

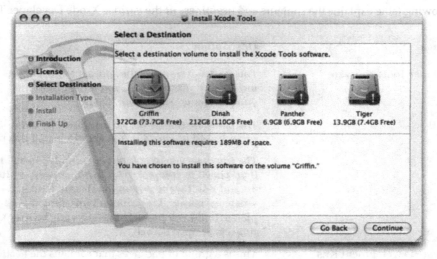

Figure 1-2

After selecting your boot volume, click the Continue button again. In the next screen, the installer offers to perform a basic installation or upgrade of the Xcode tools. This is suitable for most beginning developers. Remember that you can always run the installer again to install additional packages in the future.

If you want to expand or contract the set of software tools that get installed, click the Customize button. The pane changes to a list of packages, as shown in Figure 1-3.

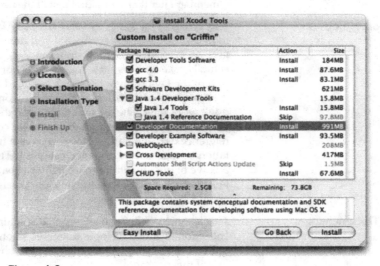

Figure 1-3

Each package is listed, along with an action and the estimated amount of disk space that package will consume on the volume. Select a package in the list for a brief description of what the package contains.

The following table explains the contents and usefulness of the various Xcode Developer Tools packages.

Package	Description
Developer Tools Software	This package contains the core set of development tools, including the Xcode IDE. You must install this package if you plan on working with Xcode.
gcc 4.0	The latest version of the gcc compiler. By default, all new projects will use gcc 4.0. You should install this package.
gcc 3.3	The previous version of the gcc compiler. Install this package if you need to compile programs that were written for gcc 3.3 and don't want to compile cleanly with gcc 4.0—for whatever reason. I recommend installing this package if you plan to build any pre-existing software, be that Xcode projects or open source.
Software Development Kits	This is a group of packages that contains the headers, libraries, and development tools needed to develop applications using these technologies. To write any kind of Macintosh software, you must install the Mac OS X SDK. To write any kind of command-line tool or to use any of the standard C libraries, you will need the BSD SDK. If you have no plans to write an X11 application or FireWire driver, you can save some disk space by omitting the more obscure packages. If you have *any* doubts, install them all. You could waste a lot of time trying to figure out why you can't use a particular set of APIs only to remember later that you didn't install the necessary SDK.
Java Developer Tools	This group of packages includes the basic Java developer tools and documentation. Even if you don't plan to write Java applications, install the tools package anyway. They actually take up very little space—most of the Java tools are part of the Java framework that's included in the OS—and it's just easier to install them now than wonder why things don't work later. The documentation, on the other hand, is a different matter. If you plan to write Java code, install the reference documentation. The size shown for the documentation is not accurate. The size listed is for the compressed archive of documentation that will be expanded when installed. On my system, the Java documentation occupies about 135MB of disk space.
Developer Documentation	This is the ADC Reference library. It contains an invaluable collection of core developer documentation, API documentation, articles, and technical nodes. You should definitely install this package.

Package	Description
WebObjects	WebObjects is a group of WebObjects-related development packages. This book doesn't cover WebObjects development. If you have a WebObjects license and are planning to write WO applications, then you will need to install these packages. Otherwise, skip them.
Cross Development	Cross-development is a means of writing a Mac OS X application that runs on earlier versions of the operating system. These packages include a complete set of SDKs from earlier versions of the OS. This allows you to compile and link your applications using these older SDKs, just as if you were developing your project on an older version of the OS and Xcode. By default, Xcode installs the 10.3.9 and 10.4.x SDKs. If you plan to write applications that will run on Mac OS X 10.2, install the 10.2.8 SDK package as well.
Automator Shell Scripts and Actions	This is a set of Automator actions that let you build projects, check them in and out of source control, and prepare finished applications for installation. Install this package if you plan to use Automator in your development workflow.
CHUD Tools	This package contains an advanced set of performance analysis and debugging tools, including the amazing Shark application that is used extensively in Chapter 16. The CHUD tools are often updated independently of Xcode and have their own installer. If you plan to use these tools, check the ADC web site for a more recent version.

If you decide against selecting a custom set of packages, you can return again to the default installation choices by clicking the Easy Install button.

After you choose what you want to install, click the Install button to start the installation process, shown in Figure 1-4. You will have to supply the account name and password of an administrator when asked.

The installer takes longer than what you would infer from observing the progress bar in the installer window. Most of the documentation gets unpacked from compressed archives. This occurs at the end of the normal installation process, so be patient. The installer may say that it has "less than a minute" remaining for ten or more minutes. *Do not panic and force the installer to quit!* You'll end up with a royal mess and have to start all over again.

The bulk of the installation occurs in the /Developer folder that is created at the root level of your boot volume, shown in Figure 1-5. Here you will find all of the Xcode applications, command-line tools, example code, and documentation. Do not attempt to move or rename this folder. The installer places support files in the system-wide /Library/Application Support/Apple/Developer Tools folder. It installs some special development frameworks, resources, and a few patches into the /System folder. Finally, it installs several UNIX man pages and a handful of tools into the /usr and /bin folders.

Figure 1-4

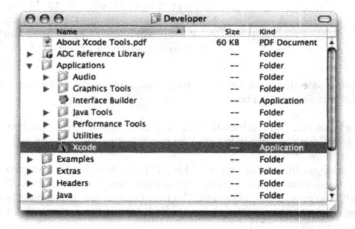

Figure 1-5

After the installer is finished, check out the About Xcode Tools.pdf document for an overview of the Xcode Developers Tool package and for any late-breaking news, additions, or corrections. The installer does not require you to restart your system afterwards. You can now skip to Chapter 2.

Upgrading Xcode

If you already have an older version of Xcode installed, you'll find some subtle differences when you run the installer again. The installer automatically detects the version of any package that you have previously installed. A basic installation upgrades any packages that need to be upgraded. The custom package selection, shown in Figure 1-6, displays which packages can be upgraded, installed, or skipped. An upgrade indicates that the installer has a newer version of the package to install. The size indicates the estimated amount of *additional* disk space required to upgrade the package. Skipped packages will not be upgraded or installed. If a package is disabled, Xcode has determined that the existing package does not need to be, or cannot be, upgraded. This is typically because you already have the most current, or a later, version of this software installed. The Xcode installer will never "downgrade" a package by attempting to install an older version over a newer one.

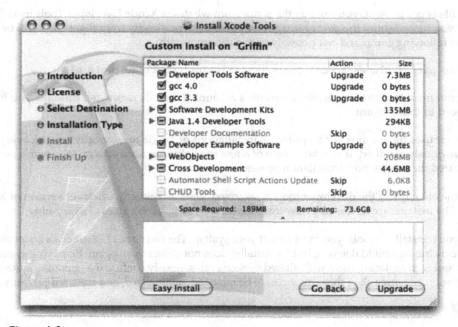

Figure 1-6

After you selected the packages you want upgraded, click the Upgrade button. The installer runs much as it does when installing for the first time.

Typically you won't have any problems using your upgraded tools as soon as the installer is finished. However, if you immediately start using some of the performance analysis tools or attempt distributed builds, you may run into problems. These facilities use daemons and system frameworks that may need to be reloaded. Restart your system after upgrading your Xcode tools.

Removing and Reinstalling Xcode

The Xcode Development Tools includes the means of completely eradiating itself — the entire suite of tools, support files, libraries, and frameworks — from your system. One really good reason to do this is the need to perform a clean installation of the tools. Apple often makes pre-release versions of Xcode available to ADC members. As a general rule, you cannot install a release version over a pre-release version even when that release version is newer. You may also have some need to downgrade your installation, something the regular installation process won't allow.

To remove your installation of Xcode, open a Terminal window and enter the following command.

```
sudo perl /Developer/Tools/uninstall-devtools.pl
```

If this file is not present, you can run the script from whatever Xcode Developer Tools install disc or image you have. Mount the disc or image and run the script directly from there. This will be something like the following command but possibly with a different path:

```
sudo perl /Volumes/Xcode\ Tools/Utilities/uninstall-devtools.pl
```

The script must be run from an administrator's account. The `sudo` command prompts you for the password to that account.

The script uses the receipts left by previous installations of Xcode to surgically remove everything that was previously installed. It also takes care of a few special cases, such as removing symbolic links that get created during the post-installation process.

After the old copy of the developer tools is removed, you can reinstall whatever version of Xcode you want. The installer treats this as a new installation, installing fresh copies of everything.

After you reinstall the tools, you must restart your system. The `uninstall-devtools` script stops processes like the distributed build daemon, but the installer does not restart them again. Removing system frameworks and then replacing them with altered versions can seriously confuse the operating system. Restarting your computer causes all of these resources to be reloaded, reinitialized, and restarted properly.

Summary

You're probably eager to start exploring Xcode, but installing the software first is a necessary evil. As you've seen, the process is relatively painless and quick.

Now, on to the grand tour.

The Grand Tour

Starting up Xcode is sort of like walking through the front gates of Disneyland for the very first time. It's vast. You have no idea where to go first. If you just start walking, you'll quickly be lost and disoriented. So you do what every first-time visitor does: You open the map.

Neither Xcode nor Disneyland has been intentionally designed to be cryptic or confusing. In fact, both go out of their way to be as friendly and accommodating as possible. However, the sheer size and complexity of what they offer cause them to be perplexing and frustrating at times. If you take a moment to get a feel for the scope and organization of Xcode, your initial forays will be much more enjoyable. So start down Main Street—I mean, with the project window—and get your bearings.

The Project

The central construct in Xcode, both physically and metaphorically, is the project. Everything you will accomplish in Xcode begins with a project. A project is stored as a document on your file system. The project window, shown in Figure 2-1, is the manifestation of that document in the user interface.

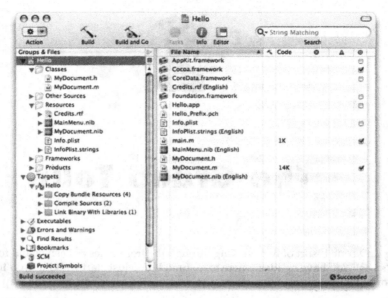

Figure 2-1

Try It Out   Open a Project

Locate the Hello project that accompanies this book. See the "Introduction" to learn how to obtain the projects and other resources for this book. Then follow these steps:

1. Open the folder that contains the Hello project. It should look similar to the folder in Figure 2-2.

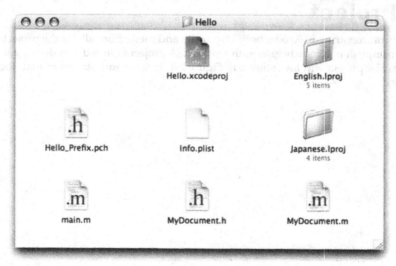

Figure 2-2

2. Open the Hello.xcodeproj document.

If you don't have ready access to the projects for this book, follow these steps:

1. From the Xcode File menu, choose the New Project command.
2. In the Application group, choose Cocoa Document-based Application. Click the Next button.
3. Enter **Hello** for the project name.
4. Click the Choose button to pick a location for the new project.
5. Click the Finish button.

How It Works

Each Xcode project is stored in a project document. The folder that contains that document is the project folder. The other items in the project folder are the project's source files and folders.

Use this project to explore the various groups in the project window. You can also build, run, and even debug this project. Explore the properties of source items, groups, and other objects by Control-/right-clicking them.

The Groups & Files pane is where everything that constitutes your project is represented and organized. This list consists of a hierarchy of groups, which should be instantly recognizable to anyone who has used applications like iPhoto. Click the expansion triangle to the left of a group's icon to explore its contents.

The right side of the window is a multi-purpose pane. It usually shows the details of a selection made in the Groups & Files pane, but it can also be used as an editor — or you may not even have a right side to your window. Xcode provides different window layouts to suite your work style. Chapter 3 explains these different styles and how to navigate your workspace.

Source Group

Broadly, there are two kinds of groups in the Groups & Files pane. At the top is the project group. This has the same icon and name as the project document. The project group organizes all of the sources used in the project, and is generically referred to as the source group. Sources are the files and folders used in your project. This could consist of program source files, headers, property lists, image files, dynamic libraries, frameworks, testing code, and even other projects. None of these constituent parts are stored in the project document itself. The files you will use to build your project exist elsewhere on your file system. The project group only contains *references* to those sources, not the sources themselves. Chapter 5 explains how to create, manage, and organize source references in the project group.

Double-clicking any source item will open it in an editor, assuming the item type is one that can be edited.

Smart Groups

The remaining groups are referred to as smart groups. Unlike the project group, which you may organize however you like, the smart groups each represent some specific kind of information about your project. These groups are self-organizing and update automatically to reflect the state of your project.

One of the most important smart groups is the targets group. This group shows the targets defined in the project. Each product your project produces, typically an executable program, is represented by a target. A target is organized into build phases. Each build phase performs a specific step in the build process, such as compiling all of the source files for a target or copying a set of files into the resource folder of an application bundle. A source is said to be a member of a target if the target includes that source item in any of its phases. Targets can depend on other targets. Targets are highly customizable and extensible. Chapter 13 explains the kinds of targets Xcode provides and how to create your own. It also shows you how to organize and customize targets to meet your needs.

The Executables smart group lists the executables (programs that can be launched and run) in the project. The executables in a project can be run or debugged from within Xcode.

Most of the remaining smart groups gather information about your project, collecting them into readily accessible locations. The Errors and Warnings group contains the current list of error and warning messages produced by the build process. As with many of the smart groups, this information is available in several other locations and in other forms as well. The Find Results smart group contains the history and results of recent searches. The Project Symbols smart group lists all of the symbols defined in your application. You can create your own smart groups that automatically collect source files that meet a certain criteria. If you've ever used smart playlists in iTunes, then you are already familiar with this concept.

Menus

The menus in Xcode are grouped by function. The File menu is where you'll find basic file and project commands. Use these commands to create new projects, files, and groups, close windows, save files, and print.

The Edit, Format, and Find menus deal primarily with the editing of source files. The View menu controls the visual appearance and layout of window and lists. It also contains a number of file and window navigation commands. The Project menu contains commands specific to the project and its targets.

The Build, Debug, Design, and SCM menus contain commands for building the project, debugging an executable program, class and data model design, and source control management respectively. Each of these topics is covered in its own chapter. The Help menu is the gateway to the ADC reference library and the programming documentation. It also provides a few shortcuts to commonly referenced topics.

The Window menu is one means of listing, and navigating between, the currently open windows. It provides access to a number of project windows that are oriented towards a particular activity — such as the build window or the debugger window — and other, more utilitarian, windows.

Editor

Xcode includes a sophisticated and flexible set of editors. The text file editor is shown in Figure 2-3. The text editor is syntax aware and capable of automatically formatting and highlighting text appropriately for recognized programming languages. It also has a context-sensitive, language-specific, auto-completion function. This feature presents you with an interactive list of the programming symbols valid at that point in your source code. The extensive editing and navigation features of the text editor are covered in Chapter 6.

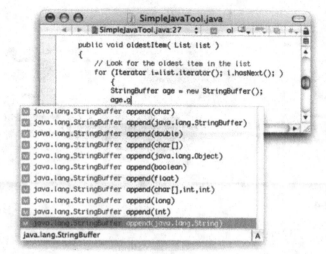

Figure 2-3

There are also many other editors, notably the property editors that appear in the numerous Info windows. More sophisticated documents, such as NIB files, have their own editor application that integrates with Xcode's environment. You can also tap your favorite text, image, audio, or resource editor to augment, or replace, the editors provided by Xcode.

Chapter 10 discusses the NIB file editor. Chapter 12 explains the data model editor.

Data Mining

Xcode includes a several tools for exploring the content and structure of your project. These are useful for finding something specific in your application or for understanding the structure of classes in the project.

The simplest of these tools are the various search commands. You can search a single file, or a group of files, for text patterns ranging from a sequence of characters to complex regular expressions. These commands are thoroughly covered in Chapter 7.

The Class Browser, shown in Figure 2-4, compiles the classes and data structures in your application into a structured table. Chapter 8 shows you how.

Chapter 11 introduces you to the class modeler. Like the Class Browser, it constructs a picture of your project's classes and their relationships. But unlike the Class Browser, the picture drawn by the class modeler is — well — a picture. The class modeler produces a graph of the classes in your application (see Figure 2-5). Models can be customized and are dynamically updated as you alter your code.

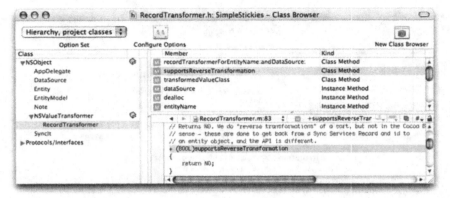

Figure 2-4

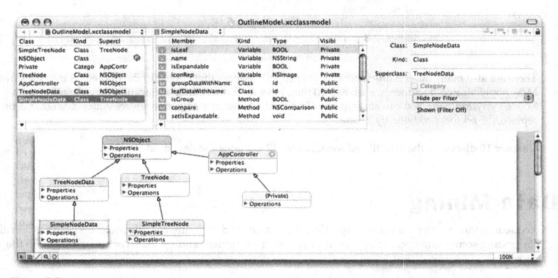

Figure 2-5

Getting Help

Someone once said, "It's not what you know, it's what you can find out." This sentiment is especially applicable to programming. It is impossible to remember every function name, every parameter, and every data type in the thousands of classes, headers, and libraries available to you. And often the question is not so much which specific function to call as it is "Where do I begin?"

Integrated into Xcode is the bulk of the Apple Developer Connection Reference Library, shown in Figure 2-6. This contains a vast wealth of introductory articles, examples, and programming guidance.

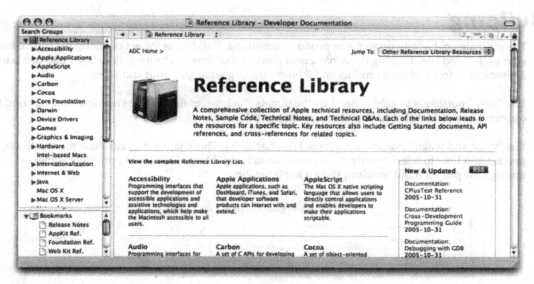

Figure 2-6

The Reference Library also includes a detailed, indexed, and searchable database documenting every major API in the Mac OS X operating system, an example of which is shown in Figure 2-7. You can instantly access the symbols in the Reference Library from within your source code or search for them interactively.

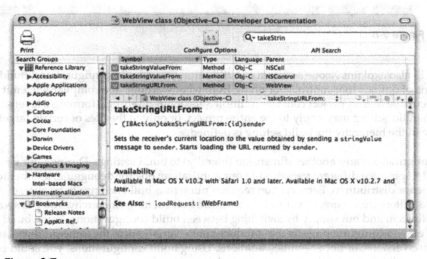

Figure 2-7

Being a productive programmer will largely depend on being able to quickly extract what you're looking for from this mountain of detail. Chapter 9 will help you find what you need.

Building

The ultimate goal of any project is to produce something. Building is the act of taking the source items in your project and transforming them into a final product. Building can be roughly divided into two activities: defining how to build each product and then controlling what gets built and when.

The "how" portion is largely defined by the targets. Each target defines the steps and sources used to construct its product. This is explained in Chapter 13.

The "what and when" portion is explained in Chapter 14. This chapter explains how to initiate a build process and how to select exactly what you want to build. Most of the build process is witnessed through the project build window, shown in Figure 2-8.

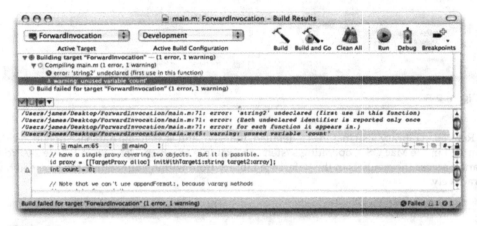

Figure 2-8

Chapter 13 also explains Xcode's system of build settings and build configurations. Build settings are collections of options that control everything from what warnings the compiler will emit to the names of your executable files. A project contains multiple sets of build settings, forming a layered hierarchy of values. A build setting may apply to the entire project, or only to the files of certain targets, depending on where in the hierarchy the build setting is defined.

Build configurations add another dimension (literally) to build settings. During your development, you will need to produce different versions of your application: one for debugging, another for analysis, and a final one for distribution. Each version requires numerous build settings to be altered. A build configuration is an alternate version of your project's entire build settings hierarchy. You can swap hundreds of build settings in and out simply by switching between build configurations. Using build configurations makes it easy to configure projects that produce subtle variations of the same products, such as debug and release versions, or not-so-subtle variations. Using build configurations, you could produce one version of an application for in-house testing, another version for use by the sales department, and a third variation for the field server engineers; all produced by a single project and target.

Getting It Right

After your project is built, you then have to verify that it performs the way you intended it to. If any bugs are found, you must locate and correct them.

Xcode is integrated with several debuggers. Launching your application under the control of a debugger, shown in Figure 2-9, enables you to step through the code in your application, view variables, and even fix bugs and data while it's running. The debugger facilities and commands are all explained in Chapter 15.

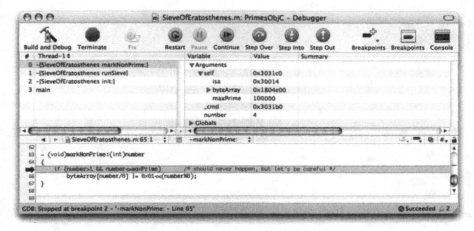

Figure 2-9

In addition to the debugger, you can employ unit testing and a cadre of performance and program analysis tools to help you identify, locate, and eliminate unwanted program behavior. Chapter 16 contains an introduction to the analysis tools. Chapter 17 outlines setting up your own unit tests.

Collaboration

You can share projects and project source with other projects and other developers. Chapter 18 shows you how to create common pools of project resources and how to integrate your projects with a source control manager.

Summary

This should give you some idea of the breadth and scope of the Xcode development environment. As you can see, there's a lot to cover in the subsequent chapters. You're probably anxious to get started, so move on to the next chapter to organize your workspace and learn your way around the interface.

3

Xcode Layout

Now that you have a bird's eye view of how Xcode is organized, drop a few hundred feet and look at the visual layout of Xcode. In this chapter, you'll learn how items are organized in the Xcode project window, how to reorganize them, how to customize your window layout, and how to get and control what information about your project is displayed.

The project window, shown in Figure 3-1, represents your project and is your home base in Xcode. All of the components that comprise your project are organized here. It is also the central means of browsing your project, allowing you to see the products that your project produces, symbols defined in your project, bookmarks you've saved, and other aspects. All other windows in your project are subordinate to your project window. Closing the project window closes the project. All other windows related to the project close as well.

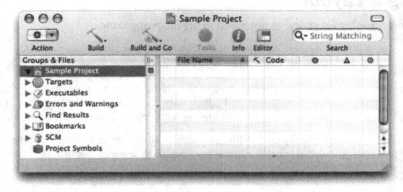

Figure 3-1

Editing windows edit the contents of source files, and are where you will be spending much of your time during development.

Info windows display detailed information about an item in your project. This is where you control the fine details and options for each item. You can usually open an Info window by choosing Get Info. The contents of an Info window vary depending on the type of the item, or items, being inspected. Figure 3-2 shows a typical Info window.

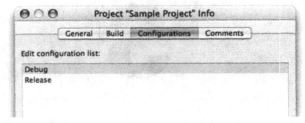

Figure 3-2

Reference windows contain documentation, help, and dynamic information about your project. These windows are for browsing and reference, and cannot be edited.

A number of Xcode commands have their own windows. Building, debugging, searching, and similar functions have windows customized for each purpose.

Project Layout

Xcode provides different strategies for organizing your windows and panes called layout styles. Choosing a layout style isn't a prerequisite for creating a project, because you can change the layout style again at any time. However, you do need to have a basic understanding of the layout styles offered by Xcode, because the layout affects how the project window is organized, and where information about its contents is displayed. It also affects Xcode's use of separate windows for various tasks.

Choosing a Layout

Xcode offers three layout styles, as described in the following table.

Style	Description
Default	All of the project groups and items are in a single browser shared with a combination details and editor pane. Source files may be editing here, or in separate windows. Build, debug, and other tasks open in separate windows.
Condensed	The project window contains only the project groups and items. All tasks, including editing, are performed in separate windows.
All-In-One	The project and most tasks are confined to a single window.

The Default layout style, shown in Figure 3-3, is the traditional Xcode windowing style. The project window contains all of the groups and items in a single browser. The window shares a split pane with a list and editing panes on the right side. You can view and edit source files immediately in the right pane, or you can open them in separate windows. Build, Debug, and similar tasks also appear in their own window. This is a good choice for general development on a moderate-sized screen.

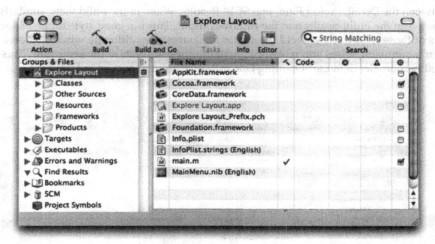

Figure 3-3

The Condensed layout style, shown in Figure 3-4, could also have been named the "Everything-In-A-Separate-Window" style. The project window contains only the project's group and items. The groups are further subdivided by a tab control at the top of the window. The tab selects between the source groups, the target groups, and all other types of groups. This chapter shows you how you can alter this organization a little later on. Everything else you work with, or open, appears in a separate window. This is a good style for complex projects and for developers with very large monitors.

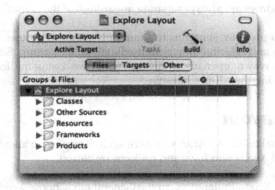

Figure 3-4

The descriptively named All-In-One layout style, shown in Figure 3-5, is essentially the opposite of the Condensed style. The project, editing, and all tasks are contained in a single window. You can switch which view you are working with using one of several tab controls. The tab control in the upper-left corner of the window switches the entire window between the project, build, and debugger views. While in the project view, another tab control above the right editor pane switches the upper portion of the pane between the Detail, Project Find, and SCM Results. When in the build view, similarly located tabs switch between the build results and the runtime output. This is a good style for developers with small monitors or those who want to avoid the clutter of having many different windows open. This can be particularly confusing when you're working with multiple projects at the same time. This problem is explained in more detail in the "Opening One or More Projects" section in Chapter 4.

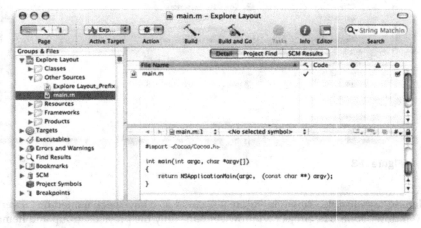

Figure 3-5

Despite its name, the All-In-One style does not force everything into a single window. There is nothing stopping you from opening some source files or reference documents in separate windows. And the Inspector and Info windows are always separate, regardless of the layout style you are using.

The View⇨Show menu provides shortcuts to commonly accessed groups. Select one of the groups from the menu and the view and selection moves immediately to that group. Similarly, the Window⇨Tools menu provides a quick way to open one of the tool windows. Using the Tools menu always opens a new window, even when using the All-In-One style.

Changing the Layout

The layout style is global to Xcode. After you have set it, it applies to all projects that you open. You can change it only when all Xcode windows and projects are closed.

Select the layout in the Xcode Preferences, in the General tab. Choose Xcode⇨Preferences, and then click the General (leftmost) icon at the top of the window (see Figure 3-6).

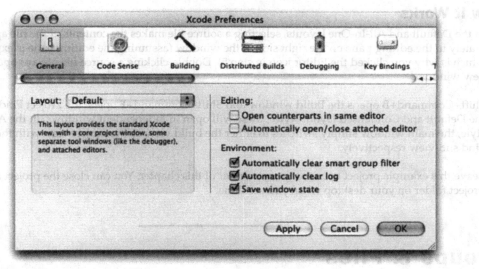

Figure 3-6

Try It Out   Exploring Xcode Layouts

Get a quick feel for the various Xcode layouts by trying them out. Follow these steps:

1. Create a new project using File⇨New Project. In the New Project assistant, select Cocoa Application under the Applications category and click Next. Name the project **Explore Layout**. Click the Choose button, select the desktop, and click Choose. Click Finish.

2. Close all Xcode windows.

3. Select a layout style in the General preferences.

4. Reopen the project by selecting its name in the File⇨Recent Projects menu.

5. Click the Editor icon in the toolbar of the project window (Default and All-In-One layouts only).

6. Expand the Explore Layout group in the Groups & Files tree. Expand the Other Sources group. Click the Explore Layout_Prefix.pch source file once. Click the main.m source file once. Double-click the main.m source file.

7. Press Shift+Command+B to open the Build window.

8. Press Shift+Command+F to open the Project Find window.

9. Repeat steps 2 through 8 with the other layout styles.

How It Works

In the Default and All-In-One layouts, selecting a source file makes the contents of the file appear immediately in the editing pane on the right side of the window (assuming the editing pane is expanded, which is why you clicked the Editor icon in step 5). Double-clicking a source file always opens it in a new window.

Shift+Command+B opens the Build window and Shift+Command+F opens the Project Find window. In the Default and Condensed layout styles, these will open in independent windows. In the All-In-One style, the main window simply switches to either the build view or the project view with the Project Find sub-view respectively.

Leave this example project open for the remainder of this chapter. You can close the project and trash the project folder on your desktop when you are done.

Groups & Files

All of the components of your project are represented as icons in the Groups & Files pane of your project window. Icons with a small grey "expansion" triangle next to them indicate a group of items. Groups contain items and sometimes other groups.

The very first group is the project structure group. This has the same name as the project and contains all of the source groups and assets for the project. The remaining groups are called smart groups that contain specific types of items. Smart groups automatically change to reflect the state of the project. Figure 3-7 points out the source and smart groups in a layout.

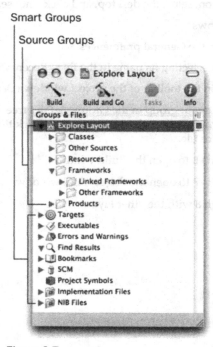

Figure 3-7

Compile a file that results in errors, and the list of errors will appear in the errors and warnings group. Fix the errors and recompile, and the items in this group disappear.

You can expand or collapse the contents of any group by clicking the small triangle next to the group's icon. Pressing the Option key when expanding or collapsing expands or collapses all sub-groups as well.

Project Structure Group

The most flexible group is the project structure group. Within this group, you add the source assets (program source, image files, documentation, and so on) that will be used to build your project. All of the groups in the project structure group are generically referred to as source groups. These can be organized into any arbitrary arrangement of subgroups that you like. When you created a Cocoa Application project, Xcode automatically created source groups for Classes, Other Sources, Resources, Frameworks, and Products. Within the Frameworks groups are subgroups for Linked Frameworks and Other Frameworks.

How many source groups you create, their names, and how you organize their contents is entirely up to you. Xcode does not impose any kind of organization or convention when it comes to the project structure group. You are free to put a movie file in the Classes groups. You are also free to rename the Classes group to "Wonkavator." You can just as easily move all of your assets to the top-level project structure group and delete all subgroups. This might not actually be a bad idea for very small projects, because too many groups just get in the way.

While this section has thus far emphasized that you have carte blanche to organize the source groups however you see fit, there is one exception. Products and the Products group are special. Products are the end result of targets (see Chapter 13). Products are also source files that can be used to build other products. As such, a product is both an output (of the target) and an input (source asset). You cannot delete or rename the Products groups or any of the products contained therein. You can rename products, but you must do this by editing the target, not the product.

Smart Groups

The remaining groups in the project window are collectively referred to as smart groups. If you have used iTunes or iPhoto lately, this concept will be immediately clear. A smart group contains items that reflect some property or information about your project, and have a fixed or restricted structure. Files or items that meet that criterion appear in the group automatically, and disappear as soon as they no longer qualify. Xcode defines several smart groups whose criteria are fixed, as listed in the following table. You can also create your own smart groups.

Smart Group	Contents
Targets	The targets defined in the project. Expand a target to reveal its build phases. See Chapter 13.
Executables	Executable programs produced by the project.
Errors and Warnings	Any errors or warnings produced by the most recent build.
Find Results	The results of the last several searches that were performed.

Table continued on following page

Smart Group	Contents
Bookmarks	Bookmarks you have created.
SCM	Pending Source Control actions for this project. See Chapter 18.
Project Symbols	The symbols defined in the project.
Breakpoints	The debugger breakpoints set in the project.

Altering Source Groups and Their Contents

The following applies only to source groups, because you never directly alter the content of smart groups. Thus, this section simply refers to them as groups.

You can create a new, empty, group using the File⇨New Group command. A new group with the name New Group is created inside the currently selected group, or in the same group as any currently selected file, as shown in Figure 3-8. Replace the name of the new group and press Return.

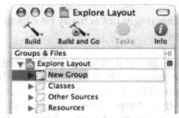

Figure 3-8

You can gather any arbitrary set of files or groups and place them inside a newly created group in a single step using the File⇨Group command. A new group is created, and all of the selected groups and files become members of the new group. You have only to name the new group and press Return.

You can rename any group or file by Option-clicking on the item's icon in the project window. You can also use this gesture to rename smart groups that you've created. As an alternative, Control-/right-click an item and choose the Rename command from the pop-up menu.

You can move almost any arbitrary selection of groups or items around the group hierarchy simply by dragging them to another location in the project structure group. The drop indicator tells you if are you about to drop the items alongside the group, or inside it.

On the left of Figure 3-9, two header files are being moved inside the Headers group. On the right, the same two files are being moved into the project's top-level group, and appear immediately following the Headers group.

Finally, you can delete a group in one of two ways. The first, and most obvious way, is to delete the group and its contents. Select a group, or groups, and choose Delete from either the Edit menu or the Control-/right-click contextual menu. This deletes both the group and the contents of the group. If the group contained file or folder references, you get a confirmation dialog box asking you if you want to delete just the references or the actual files. See Chapter 5 to learn about references.

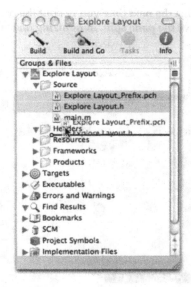 

Figure 3-9

You can also delete a group without deleting its contents. Select a group, or groups, and choose the Ungroup command from the Control-/right-click contextual menu (there is no main menu command for this). Ungroup dissolves the group and replaces it with the items it previously contained.

Showing and Hiding Groups

You are free to alter which top-level groups are visible in your project window. For instance, if you are not using source control you may want to hide the SCM group.

Control-/right-click any top-level group and drag down to the Preferences submenu. Here you will see all of the standard groups defined by Xcode and any Smart Groups that you've defined. Groups that are checked will be visible in your project window. Groups that are unchecked will not. You are free to check and uncheck whatever groups you wish.

When you're using the Condensed layout, you have three sets of groups, defined by the Files, Targets, and Other tabs above the groups list. Each set is independent of the other, and you can add or remove groups from any tab. I find it convenient to have the Bookmarks group in the Files tab, since most of my bookmarks are shortcuts to places in my source code. Add, or remove, the groups that make sense to you.

In the Default and All-In-One layout styles, you can also have multiple views of your groups. In these two layout styles, Xcode places a split-pane control just above the group list scrollbar.

Click the split pane icon, shown in Figure 3-10, to split the list into two lists. You can now alter which groups appear in the upper and lower panes independently. To return to one list again, click the join pane icon just below the split pane icon of the list you want to discard. Unfortunately, Xcode does not remember which groups were visible in the second list the next time you re-split the pane. So if you spend time customizing your groups, it's best to leave the pane split, minimizing one or the other as desired.

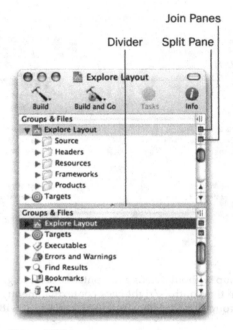

Figure 3-10

You can also, rather erroneously, select any top-level group and apply the Delete command as you would a source group. This does not actually delete the group. You can't delete any of the smart groups defined by Xcode. The Delete command merely hides the group and is equivalent to unchecking it in the Preferences submenu. Check the group in Preferences again and it reappears.

Reusing Your Layout

After you set up and customize the organization, panes, and column for a project, you can save that layout as the new default for all new projects. Here's how:

1. Customize the layout and organization of a project.
2. Choose the Windows⇨Defaults command.
3. Click the Make Layout Default button.

When you're using the same layout style, all new projects will have the same size, layout, and organization that your current project has right now. To reset the layout, execute the same command but choose the Restore To Factory Default button instead. Note that your changes only apply to new projects and when you are using the same Xcode layout style.

Creating Simple Smart Groups

You can create one kind of smart group yourself. This is limited to automatically collecting source files that match a particular pattern. Xcode comes with two of these "simple" smart groups pre-defined: The Implementation Files group and the NIB Files group.

Simple smart groups come in two flavors: Simple Filter smart group and Simple Regular Expression smart group. The Filter flavor matches files based on file name "globbing" used in the shell; *.c matches all C source files. The Regular Expression flavor matches files using regular expressions; \.[ch]p{0,2}$ matches file names ending in .c, .h, .cp, .hp, .cpp, or .hpp. See Chapter 7 for an extensive explanation of Regular Expressions. The "Searching Lists" section of that same chapter has a brief description of globbing patterns.

To create your own smart group, choose either Simple Filter smart group or Simple Regular Expression smart group from the File⇨New Smart Group menu. A new simple smart group is immediately created, and its Info window opens, allowing you to edit it. There is no opportunity to cancel here. If you didn't want to create the smart group, you will have to delete it (see the next section).

In the Info window, you can edit the name under which the group will appear in the project window and even provide something more evocative than the generic "gear folder" icon.

Start From chooses where the smart group looks for files that match the pattern. Project is the default, and refers to the top-level project structure group. You can also choose to restrict the search to a specific group within the project. The Recursively check box causes the Smart Group to search all subgroups of the Start From group for matches.

The Using Pattern field is either the Wildcard or Regular Expression pattern that will be used to match files. If you selected to create a Simple Filter smart group, Wildcard will be selected. If you selected to create a Simple Regular Expression smart group, Regular Expression will be selected. You can turn a Filter group into a Regular Expression group, and vice versa, at any time by selecting the other radio button.

The Save For menu determines if the Simple smart group you just created will appear in all projects opened on your system, or only the current project. The All My Projects setting is convenient for Smart Groups you plan to use over and over again, as you can elect to use in any project just by revealing it in the project's group list.

Be very careful when creating simple smart groups for all projects. There is no way to individually delete smart groups you've created. A procedure to delete all of the global smart groups is described in the next section. But if you want to delete some and preserve others, you will need to reconstruct them.

Also, be careful when saving a smart group for all projects that has a Start From location that is not the top-level project structure group. There is no clear rule for determining which group will actually be searched in other projects. Those projects might not have a group with that name, or they once did and the group was renamed, or the group has been moved to some other part of the group hierarchy. Any of these conditions can cause a global smart group to search the wrong group for files. When you're creating smart groups that you intend to use in other projects, stick to the top-level project structure group.

You can later open the Info window for any smart group and edit its definition.

One caveat about smart groups is that sometimes they aren't very smart. Although they will usually pick up files that you add to project, they often fail to update if you rename or remove them from the project. Closing and opening the project will refresh the list.

Deleting Simple Smart Groups

One unfortunate omission from the Xcode user interface is the ability to delete smart groups that you've created. Like the predefined smart groups, an attempt to delete them only hides them in the list. Even more irksome is that the data structures used to store smart group definitions are opaque, making it impossible to selectively delete smart groups. What you can do is delete all of the smart groups saved in an individual project, or all of the global smart groups available to all projects. If you have smart groups that you want to save and others that you want to delete, you will need to write down the settings for the ones you want to save and recreate them afterwards.

To delete all of the smart groups saved in an individual project, first close the project. Select the project's file icon in the Finder and use the Control-/right-click contextual menu to choose Show Package Contents. Inside the .xcodeproj package, you will find a series of files beginning with your account's short user name (Xcode preserves layout and window preferences individually for each user). The file <your_account> .pbxuser contains the smart group definitions that you've saved in this project. Open the file in a text editor, such as TextEdit or BBEdit, and delete the line that begins with com.apple.ide.PBXUser SmartGroupsKey. Alternatively, this could also be accomplished via the following command line in the Terminal:

```
james$ cd ~/Desktop/Explore\ Layout/Explore\ Layout.xcodeproj/
james$ mv james.pbxuser james.pbxuser.bak
james$ grep -v PBXUserSmartGroupsKey james.pbxuser.bak > james.pbxuser
```

To delete all of the smart groups saved for all projects, first quit Xcode. Using the Property List Editor (you will find this in the /Developer/Applications/Utilities folder), open the com.apple.Xcode.plist file in your account's ~/Library/Preferences folder. Look for an element with the key com.apple.ide.smrt.PBXUserSmartGroupsKey.ver10, shown in Figure 3-11.

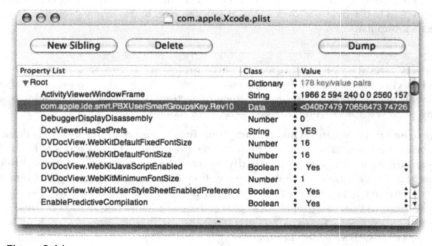

Figure 3-11

Delete this element and save the file. The next time you launch Xcode, it will recreate the default Implementation Files and NIB Files groups. All other user-created smart groups will be gone.

Details, Details

Now that you've learned to organize, customize, and navigate the top groups of your project, you're going to start digging into the details about the members of those groups. Details about the content of groups are displayed in a table called the details list. The columns of the table display properties about each item.

In the Default and All-In-One layout styles, the details list is displayed in a pane on the right side of the window (see Figure 3-12). The details pane can be displaced by an editor pane, so if the details list is not visible, click the Editor button in the toolbar to toggle between the two. You can also drag the divider between the details list and the editor pane to split the window between the two.

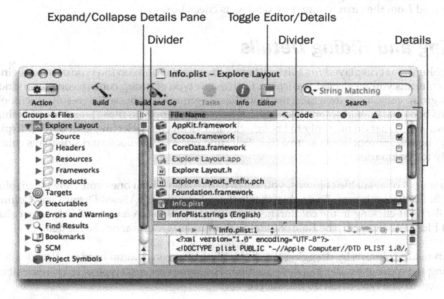

Figure 3-12

You can hide the details view and compact the window by double-clicking the expand/collapse control that sits between the Groups & Files list column header and the details list column header. You can also drag the divider bar. Double-clicking the divider completely collapses the Groups & Files pane, leaving only the details list.

The Condensed layout style does not include a details pane in the project window. You can view details for items by adding detail columns directly to the Groups & Files list (see "Showing Details in the Groups & Files List") or by opening a combined project and details view using the Windows⇨Tools⇨ Details command. In addition, when you double-click them, many groups will display their contents in a separate window, which contains much of the same information that would be displayed in the details pane.

The details list always consists of an aggregate of the items encompassed by the groups and items selected in the Groups & Files list. Selecting an item in the Groups & Files list lists the details of that item. Selecting a group lists the details of all of the items contained in that group and any sub-groups. You can view the details of any arbitrary set of items by selecting combinations of groups and items.

> *There are a few exceptions to this rule. For instance, the content of groups such as frameworks and bundles are not included in the details list unless the framework or bundle is explicitly selected in the Groups & Files list. This avoids accidentally mixing individual components of the framework, such as external headers, with other local source files you may have selected at the same time.*

The details list is typically used to see the status of an item; for example, to find out if there are errors in a file. Double-clicking an item in the list opens that item, and generally is equivalent to opening the corresponding item in the Groups & Files folder. A few columns in the details can be edited directly in the list; most notably, the Target column. An item with a check box in this column can be immediately added or removed from the current target by ticking its check box.

Showing and Hiding Details

What columns get displayed for a list of items is dependant both on the type of items being listed, and which columns you've elected to display. Each major type of group contains only one kind of item: The Project group contains source files, the Find Results group contains search results, the Bookmarks group contains bookmarks, and so on. There are properties that apply to files (Target membership, compiled size, and so on) that do no apply to bookmarks and vice versa. Selecting a set of files displays only the detail columns appropriate to source files. Selecting one or more bookmarks displays columns appropriate only to bookmarks.

Within the set of available columns, you are free to choose which ones you view by enabling and disabling individual columns. To do this, toggle the columns in the View⇨Detail View Column menu, or Control-/right-clicking in the column header of the details list. A few detail lists have columns that you cannot hide. For example, the Role column in the Targets group cannot be hidden.

You can resize columns by dragging the divider line between column headers. Reorder columns by dragging the column header to a new position. The layout for each type of list is remembered separately, so changes to one type of list do not affect others.

Showing Details in the Groups & Files List

In addition to choosing the columns for the detail list, you can add selected detail columns directly to the Groups & Files list. Choose the columns from the View⇨Groups & Files Columns menu. Not all details apply to all types of items. Ones that don't are blank.

This ability is particularly useful in the Condensed layout style, which does not have a details pane in the project window.

Info Windows

The Inspector and Info windows are the third, and finest, level of detail in Xcode. The details list shows simple properties about many items at once, but an Info window tells the whole story. It is where you can inspect and modify every aspect, property, and setting of each item. And for some items, that's a lot of information.

You can view the information about an item either in an Info window or in the Inspector palette. Info windows are regular windows. One is shown on the left in Figure 3-13. You can have multiple Info windows open at a time, which is particularly useful for comparing the details of two items. To open the Info window for an item, select the item the project window, or have an editor window active, and choose the File⇨Get Info command. You can also use the Command+I keyboard shortcut or click the blue *i* icon in the toolbar. Changing the properties of the project or a target is a very common activity, so Xcode provides an additional shortcut for these items. The top-level Project group, individual Targets, and individual Executables open an Info window when you double-click them, rather than expanding or collapsing their contents like other groups.

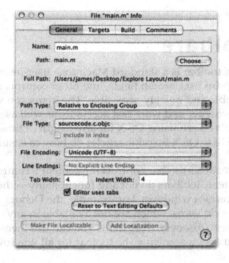

Figure 3-13

The Inspector palette, on the right in Figure 3-13, is always a single floating palette that shows the information for the currently selected item or active window. Getting information about a different item is as easy as selecting the item. The Inspector is always on top of all other windows and disappears when Xcode is not the active application. You can use both the Inspector and Info windows at the same time.

To reveal or hide the Inspector palette, hold down the Option key and select the File⇨Show Inspector or File⇨Hide Inspector command. The keyboard shortcut is Option+Command+I.

The Inspector and Info windows can display and alter the properties for more than one item at a time. Select one or more items, and the Info window presents all of the properties that are common to all of the items selected. If you select disparate items, the Info window may only present one or two properties that are common to all, such as changing the item's Comments. Radically different items result in an Info window that says "Nothing to Inspect."

For each common property, Xcode displays the value that is common to all of the items or it presents an indicator that the value of this property varies between the items. Changing the value of the property changes it for all of the items in the group. In some cases, the property cannot be consistently changed for all items and the control is disabled.

Changes made in the Inspector and Info windows are immediate. There is no opportunity to cancel the change and most changes are not tracked by the Undo facility. So be mindful about making changes that you might want to retract, although there are actually very few changes that you could make in an Info window that aren't easily reversed. The advantage is that you do not have to close the Inspector or Info window for the changes to take effect. This is particularly useful when you're changing values like build settings, because you can edit the setting and build without closing any windows. The only exceptions are some text entry fields. You may have to tab out of a field, or switch focus to another control or window, before any changes are applied.

Toolbars

The toolbar is a standard Macintosh user-interface element. Toolbars can contain command buttons, pop-up lists, search fields, and other controls right at the top of each window, making them immediately visible and quickly accessible. The items you want in your toolbar are those functions that you use repeatedly and want fast access to, as well as settings and conditions that you want to refer to quickly. If you've been using OS X for any length of time, you are undoubtedly comfortable using them. If not, see the Mac OS X help for articles on how to customize toolbars.

Almost all toolbar controls implement a command, setting, or function found elsewhere in the Xcode system. Toolbars do not add functionality — they merely add convenience. Some toolbar items are specific to certain windows. For example, the Debugger's toolbar can be populated with all kinds of debug specific items, which are not available in any other toolbars. So explore the toolbars for each window type to discover what items you can use there. When you customize the toolbar for a particular window, you are customizing the toolbar for all windows of that type.

Although most of the controls you can place in the toolbar are self explanatory, or are explained in the chapter containing those commands, the following table lists two that might need a little more explanation.

Toolbar Control	Function
Project	An oft-overlooked toolbar shortcut that simply brings you back to your project window. If you have a lot of editor windows obscuring your screen, it's the fastest way back home.
Task	The "stop sign" item is used to stop running tasks. Tasks include building, running, and debugging. Click once to stop the most recently started process or application. Hold down the button to reveal a list of running tasks and choose the task you want to terminate.

Status Bar and Favorites Bar

The thick portion at the bottom of the window's frame (which was visible in Figure 3-1) is not merely decorative — it's the status bar. The status bar displays various progress and status messages for processes like builds and multi-file searches. You can hide or show the status bar in most windows using the View⇨Hide/Show Status Bar command.

You can reveal the Favorites bar in the project window, shown in Figure 3-14, using the View⇨Show/Hide Favorites Bar command. Here you can place files and bookmarks that you want convenient access to. Drag a file or bookmark into the favorites bar to add it. Drag it out to delete it.

Figure 3-14

Clicking once on a favorites item selects that item in the project window. Double-clicking opens the file. In the case of a bookmark, it jumps to that bookmark location. If you add a source group to the favorites bar, click and hold on the folder to get a pop-up menu of the files in that group.

Activity Viewer Window

The Activity Viewer window is a bit of an odd duck. It's the only window that doesn't really belong to any specific Xcode function, tool, or item. It simply displays the internal status of the Xcode system. Open it using the Windows⇨Activity Viewer command. It displays the status of background processes, such as builds, re-indexing, predictive compilation, and similar behind-the-scenes activity. It is most useful for debugging Xcode itself. If you think files are not getting re-indexed, or they are and you don't think they should be, a quick trip to the Activity Viewer will tell you what's really happening. (Or maybe you just want something interesting to look at while building a large project.)

Summary

You should now have a good feel for how to get around in Xcode. You know how to choose the visual style that fits your needs, customize the interface a little, organize the items in your projects, and get varying degrees of information about items in a project.

You are now ready to create a working project.

Exercise

Create a new project based on the Java Swing Application template. See step 1 of the "Try It Out" section in this chapter for instructions on creating a new project. Name the project **Customized**. Make the following alterations:

1. Set the Xcode layout style to Default.

2. Create a new source group in the project structure group and name it **Default Package**. Move the Customized.java, AboutBox.java, and PrefPane.java files into that group. See if you can accomplish both of these steps using a single command.

3. Move the Customized.icns file into the Resources group.

4. Change the name of the Resources group to **Bundle**.

5. Hide the SCM group in the Group & Files list.

6. In the detail list, move the build (hammer) column so it is to the left of the file icon column.

7. Remove the Target column from the details list.

8. Add the Target Membership column to the Groups & Files list.

The Project

Now that you can navigate around the Xcode interface and organize your project, it's time to learn how projects are created, stored, opened, and closed.

There are two essential parts of every project: the project document and the project folder. The project document, Sample.xcodeproj in Figure 4-1, contains all of the structure, references, layout, settings, and other attributes that define the entire project.

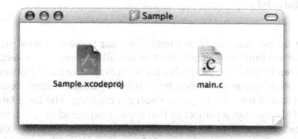

Figure 4-1

The folder that contains the project document is the project folder, in this case the Sample folder. This is the root location for the project. The project document and project folder usually have the same name, but that is not a requirement.

Creating a New Project

You create a new, empty, project using the File⇨New Project command. This opens the New Project Assistant, shown in Figure 4-2.

Figure 4-2

"Empty" is a bit of a misnomer. The New Project Assistant creates a new project using one of the many project templates that are built into Xcode. So this so-called "empty" project might actually have quite a lot in it before you even begin. The templates try to provide the basic framework—a main() function, an empty subclass of NSDocument, a menu bar with the standard items, required driver entry points, and so on—appropriate to the type of project you are creating. The templates also include dependencies on the libraries and frameworks a project of that type is expected to need. Some templates even go so far as to include libraries and frameworks that you *might* need. These frameworks are referenced in the project, but are not included in any of the targets. It's a trivial matter to add them to the target later, rather than forcing you to search through the scores of system frameworks trying to find the one you need.

The Xcode templates give you a "leg up" in getting your project going, because much of the basic groundwork is already done for you. But also remember that there's nothing done by the templates that will lock your project into a particular technology or configuration. Any project can be modified to produce any result, and you can obtain the same results as any of the templates by starting with an empty project. It's just a lot more work.

Choosing a Template

The first step in creating a new project is to choose the template that most closely matches the type of program or product you want to create. The templates are organized into groups. Scroll down the list and highlight a template that interests you. A brief description of the template appears in the pane below the list. In Figure 4-2, the Core Data Document-based Application explains, rather dryly, that "This project builds a Core Data application that uses Cocoa's NSDocument architecture." Sadly, many of the template descriptions tend to just state the obvious. Appendix B contains information to help you choose the template best suited to your project, a more detailed description of each template, what it produces, and why you might want to choose it.

If you have no idea where to begin, you might want to read more about what technologies Apple provides for creating applications at http://developer.apple.com/gettingstarted/, and more of this book to learn the implications of creating a project that uses, for example, internal versus external targets. Once you've decided what technology is most appropriate to your project, use Appendix B as a guide for choosing the closest template.

Naming the New Project

After you have selected a project template, click the Next button. The second, and final, screen prompts for two additional pieces of information: the name of the project and its location. Enter the name of your new project in the first field, which can be any valid file name. Although the name you choose is used for more than just the project's document name, as you will see in a moment.

To select the location for the new project, click the Choose button. Navigate to the location for the new project and click the Choose button. The path to the new project folder appears in the second field.

In Figure 4-3, Xcode appended the name of the project to the end of the folder's path as a new subfolder. By default, Xcode always creates a new project folder with the same name as the project, inside the folder you choose with the dialog box. The only exception to this rule is if you happen to choose a folder whose name is identical to the project name already entered. Xcode then assumes that you have already created the project folder and simply want to create the project documents inside it.

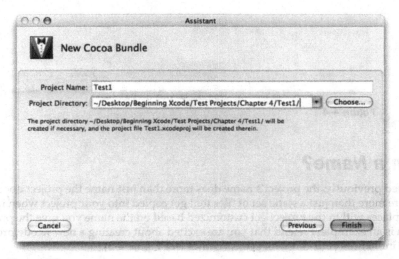

Figure 4-3

It doesn't matter if you name the project first and then select the location, or the other way around. Xcode automatically fixes the path so the last element is the name of the project. But what if this isn't where you want the project documents created?

After the project name is entered, you can freely edit the path field. You can delete the last path element, causing Xcode to create the project documents in the existing folder you chose earlier. You can rename the last element, causing Xcode to create a project folder with a different name than the project document.

The pop-up menu to the right of the project path field keeps a list of recently used project folder paths. You can select any of these to select a project path you have recently created. This is a convenient way of creating several project documents in the same project folder.

Xcode assumes that the last element in the path is the new project folder. It creates this folder, if it doesn't exist, without asking. The enclosing folder, however, is assumed to exist. If it does not, Xcode asks if you want to create it too (see Figure 4-4). Xcode will only create one, or both, of these folders. All other enclosing folders must exist before the project can be created.

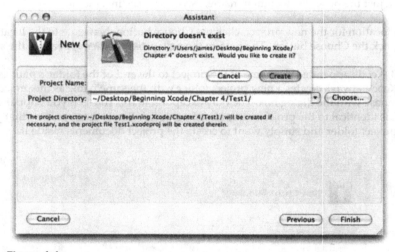

Figure 4-4

What's In a Name?

As mentioned previously, the project's name does more than just name the project document. Project templates are more than just a static set of files that get copied into your project when it is created. Numerous places within the project get customized based on the name you give the project. The easiest explanation is an example. Pretend that you are excited about creating a new Xcode project, and your exuberance influences your choice of project names (see Figure 4-5).

The project folder and documents are created from the Ant-based Web Start Application template. Opening up the newly created project folder, shown in Figure 4-6, everything looks exactly as one would expect.

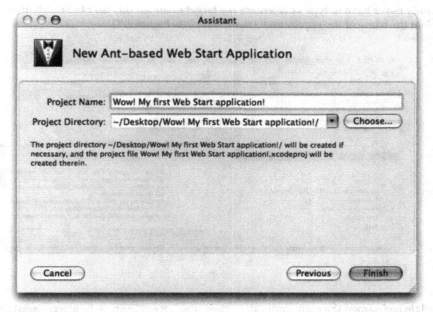

Figure 4-5

Figure 4-6

But when you open up the project, you discover some rather convoluted names. The project, shown in Figure 4-7, contains a target named `Wow__My_first_Web_Start_application_` that defines the variable `PRODUCT_NAME = Wow__My_first_Web_Start_application_`, that starts the Ant target in build.xml:

```
<project name="Wow__My_first_Web_Start_application_" default="jar" basedir=".">
   ...
</project>
```

You typically never have to type or reference the target name, so this isn't too much of an inconvenience. Now look at the name of the application's main class (see Figure 4-7).

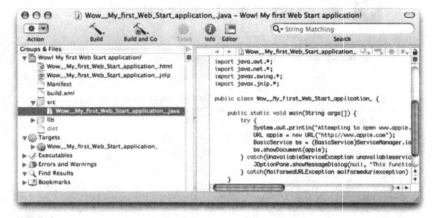

Figure 4-7

The template has named the main application class Wow__My_first_Web_Start_application_. This occurs in both the Wow__My_first_Web_Start_application_.java source file and the Manifest file. Even that might not be a problem, because most people never see Java class names in a Web Start application. But the project name was also used to generate the JNLP document names, Wow__My_first_Web_Start_application_.jnlp and Wow__My_first_Web_Start_application_.html. Which means that to try out your spiffy new web application, your friends are going to have to type the URL http://www.mydomain.com/Beginning_Xcode/Wow__My_first_Web_Start_application_.html.

If none of this bothers you, then go for it. Xcode, Java, and Web Start will happily use any valid document and symbol names you want to define. You may, however, quickly tire of seeing names like int minW = Wow__My_first_Web_Start_application_.MINIMUM_WINDOW_WIDTH; in my code.

When creating your project, consider what else you are naming, and what you might want to rename. Ultimately, the name of your project should describe what it produces. Because it is easier to rename products than classes, you may initially name your project for the principal or main class of your application and then rename the products, targets, and project document later. Or you can go the other route, naming your project after the application name it produces and then fixing up class and file names as needed.

Who's __MyCompanyName__?

Beyond just using the name of the project to name files and classes, Xcode uses a number of variables to fill in other values in the template. This doesn't apply just to templates used when you create a new project. Every time you create a new source file in Xcode, a template is used that may have variable fields. For a complete list of these variables, and how to alter the Xcode templates or define your own, see Chapter 19.

Right now, you're going to fix one of these variables so that new files in our template have nice comments. If you've just installed Xcode and created a project, you may find a comment like this at the beginning of your new source file.

In Figure 4-8, the name of the file, the name of project, my name, the date, and the current year have all been automatically inserted. (If you are curious, my name was obtained from the full name of the account under which I was currently logged in.) You can change the long name of your account in the Accounts pane of System Preferences.

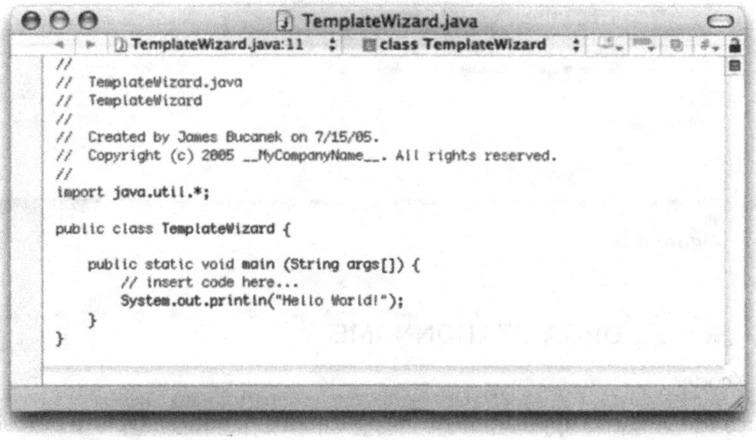

Figure 4-8

The anomaly is __MyCompanyName__. There is no system property that defines who you are working for. This value comes from a template macro definition named ORGANIZATIONNAME stored in Xcode's preferences file. Unfortunately, there is no user interface for editing these template macro definitions. They can be easily edited using the Property List Editor — after the macro definition dictionary has been created. But following a new installation of Xcode, this dictionary doesn't exist at all and creating it using the Property List Editor is tedious. Fortunately, the command line comes to our rescue.

ORGANIZATIONNAME is currently the only template macro definition that is defined or used by Xcode. You can create the dictionary of template macro definitions, and set the value of the one and only macro definition, all with one command.

First, quit Xcode. The Xcode application should never be running while editing its preferences file. Open a Terminal window and enter the following command, all on one line, substituting your real company name for My Company:

```
defaults write com.apple.Xcode PBXCustomTemplateMacroDefinitions -dict
ORGANIZATIONNAME "My Company"
```

If you want the copyright statement to include your name instead, use your full name.

To change this value again in the future, reissue the same command with a new value or just open ~/Library/Preferences/com.apple.Xcode.plist with the Property List Editor. Edit the value of any macro in the PBXCustomTemplateMacroDefinitions dictionary, as shown in Figure 4-9.

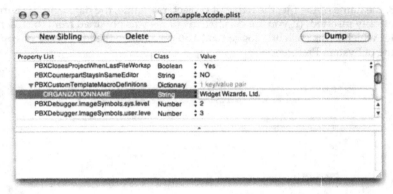

Figure 4-9

Try It Out   **Setting ORGANIZATIONNAME**

1.   Quit Xcode.

2.   Launch the Terminal application (in /Applications/Utilities). Open a new shell window.

3.   Enter the command `defaults write com.apple.Xcode`
`PBXCustomTemplateMacroDefinitions -dict ORGANIZATIONNAME "My Company"`.
Substitute your name, or your company's name, for "My Company." Press Return.

4.   Launch Xcode.

5.   Using the New Project command, create a new project named TemplateMagic based on the Java Tool template.

6.   From the project window, open the TemplateMagic.java source file created by the template. It should look something like this:

```
//
//  TemplateMagic.java
//  TemplateMagic
//
//  Created by Jane Doe on 2/1/06.
//  Copyright (c) 2006 My Company. All rights reserved.
//
import java.util.*;

public class TemplateMagic {
public static void main (String args[]) {
        // insert code here...
        System.out.println("Hello World!");
    }
}
```

How It Works

Whenever you create a new project, or a new source file, Xcode uses a template in /Library/Application Support/Apple/Developer Tool/Project Templates or /Library/Application Support/Apple/Developer Tool/File Templates to fill in some base content for each new file. In addition to some system variables, such as your account's full user name and today's date, these templates can also substitute any value defined in the PBXCustomTemplateMacroDefinitions dictionary in Xcode's preferences file.

Closing a Project

To close a project, close the project window or choose Close Project (Command+Control+W) from the File menu. Changes made to the project's structure or attributes are always immediate, so there is no confirmation dialog box asking if you want to save the changes to your project. However, if any source files in the project have been modified but not yet saved, you are prompted to save or discard the changes made to those.

Closing a project closes all of the windows associated with that project. Windows that directly refer to information in a project (editor windows, the build window, the class browser, and the debugger) are all closed when the project is closed. Generic windows (Activity Viewer and Help) that do not apply to a particular project remain open.

Opening One or More Projects

To reopen a project, open the project document in the Finder. If the Save Window State option in the General tab of the Xcode Preferences is checked, Xcode restores the position and size of all the windows that were open when you closed the project. Without this option, only the project window is reopened and any new windows open at default positions on the screen.

You can have several projects open simultaneously, but Xcode focuses on only one project at a time. Whenever a project window, or any project specific window, is the front (active) window, that project becomes the active project. Commands that act on a project, which include most of the commands in the Project, Build, and Debug menus, apply to the active project. You can (usually) tell which project is active by looking at the Window menu.

The Window menu in Figure 4-10 shows two projects — keyencoder and RegistrationDBQuery — open at the same time. All of the windows belonging to the keyencoder project are listed immediately under the project's name. This includes the project window itself and the main.c source file being editing in a second window. Note that if you are editing a file in a pane of the project's window, the name of the project window changes to that of the file. So the title of the project window may or may not be the name of the project depending on its state.

The check mark in the Window menu indicates the currently active window and, by inference, the currently active project. In this example, the main.c file is being edited. This file belongs to the keyencoder project, so keyencoder is the active project. Selecting a window from the menu brings it to the front, making it, and its project, active. Selecting the name of the project itself brings the project window to the front.

If the front window does not belong to any project, such as a window containing documentation or the Activity Viewer, things can get a little confusing. Some windows, like the Help window, cause Xcode to disable all project-specific commands. In effect, no project is active until you switch back to a window belonging to one of the open projects. Other windows, like the Activity Viewer and Single File Find windows, *don't* alter which project is active. The Windows menu doesn't indicate which project *was* active, so it is impossible to easily determine which project is still active. You might also become disoriented when editing a source file that is shared by two projects. A window belongs to the project you used to open the window, even if the file in that window is part of another project that is also open and active. When in doubt, activate the project window before starting a build or debugging session, or simply keep windows belonging to other projects closed when they are not the focus of your development.

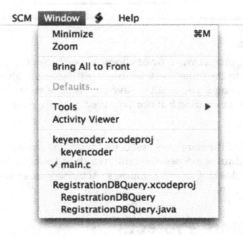

Figure 4-10

Try It Out   **Switching Projects**

In the resources for this chapter you will find a project folder named Hydra. Inside are two project documents: Hydra and Son of Hydra. Both projects use the same source file: Hydra.m. The Hydra project has two targets: Hydra and Hydra Two. The Son of Hydra project has one eponymous target. Follow these steps to switch between these two projects:

1. Open both of the project documents.

2. Bring the Hydra project window to the front. Expand the Source group and double-click the Hydra.m file to open Hydra.m in its own window. Examine the source. The build environment defines a preprocessor macro, HYDRANAME, that is set to the name of the target being built. The NSLog() function is used to output that name to stdout. Leave the window open; you'll come back to it in a moment.

3. From the Project menu, choose Set Active Target⇨Hydra. Choose Build⇨Build and Run to compile and run the tool. The tool runs and outputs a log message in the run console.

4. From the Project menu, choose Set Active Target⇨Hydra Two. Again, choose Build⇨Build and Run. The second variation of the tool runs and outputs a different message.

5. Bring the Son of Hydra project to the front. In the Project menu, make sure Set Active Target⇨ Son of Hydra is selected. (It should be—it's the only target.) Choose Build⇨Build and Run. The Son of Hydra tool builds. It compiles using the same source code as the Hydra project, and outputs its message to the run console.

6. Now try to edit the Son of Hydra project. Switch back to the Hydra.m source file window, or double-click the Hydra.m item in the Son of Hydra project window to bring the editor window to the front. Edit the first #define statement, changing the value of LOG_MORE_INFORMATION from 0 to 1. Select File⇨Save. Choose Build⇨Build and Run. What happened?

How It Works

In step 2, you brought the Hydra project window to the front. This made the Hydra project the active project. You opened the Hydra.m file, which also belongs to the Hydra project, so the project remained active.

Because Hydra is the active project, all project menus and commands apply to Hydra. The Project⇨Set Active Target menu lists the targets in the Hydra project, and no others. The Build and Run command built and ran the active target for the active project.

In step 3, you changed to a different target, but still within the Hydra project.

In step 4, you brought the Son of Hydra project window to the front. This caused the active project to change from Hydra to Son of Hydra. Accordingly, all of the Project menus now apply to the Son of Hydra project. The possible active targets consisted solely of Son of Hydra, which is the only target in that project. Selecting Build and Run compiled and ran the Son of Hydra project.

In step 5, you edited the Hydra.m file for the Son of Hydra project. But what really happened is that the active project switched back to the Hydra project because you originally opened that editor window from the Hydra project. As far as Xcode is concerned, that editing window "belongs" to the Hydra project, even though the source file is also used in the Son of Hydra project. Attempting to open the same file from the Son of Hydra project by double-clicking the Hydra.m source file does not solve the problem. Xcode is smart enough to know that this is the same file and merely brings the Hydra.m window to the front. Yet, the window still belongs to the Hydra project. The only solution is to close the editor window and re-open it by double-clicking it in the Son of Hydra project window.

You can see in the Windows menu, shown in Figure 4-11, that the Hydra.m window is now listed under the Son of Hydra project. If you edit the file and choose Build and Run, the Son of Hydra project will compile and execute.

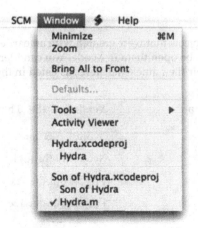

Figure 4-11

Renaming and Relocating Projects

You can easily rename the project folder or the project document after the project is created. To rename either, first close the project. In the Finder, rename the project folder or project document. Do not alter or remove the .xcodeproj suffix of the project document. Reopen the project by opening the project document. The Project Structure Group in the Groups & Files list reflects the new name of the project document.

The folder containing the project document is always the project folder. By definition, moving the project document changes the project folder. Renaming the project folder, or any folder that contains the project document, is considered a "move" because it changes the path to the project document.

The reason this is significant has to do with the way in which references to source files are kept. References to files used in your project can be relative to the location of the project folder. There are also other kinds of references, all thoroughly explained in Chapter 5. Changing the location of the project folder affects these references.

Moving the entire project folder to some other location is the safest relocation possible. This only breaks the project if it contains project-relative references to items outside the project folder, or absolute references to items inside the project folder. Both of these conditions are unlikely.

Moving the project document to some other location can be hazardous. The most significant thing this does is change the project folder. Absolute references outside the project folder won't be affected, but *all* project-relative references (both inside and out) will break.

Regardless, there are times when you will want to do this. There are very good reasons to have multiple project documents in the same project folder. See the "Build Location" section in Chapter 14 for some of them.

New projects are always created by first selecting a template. But if you have an existing project folder, creating a project document in that folder will try to write the template files there. You might not want this to happen. The solution is to create the project in a new folder, and then transplant the project document (and any template-created files that you want) into the existing project folder. Any references to files left behind can then be corrected or deleted.

Upgrading Projects

You must upgrade existing projects that were created with an earlier version of Xcode, or its predecessor Project Builder, before you can be open them in Xcode. You can identify project documents created with older versions of Xcode by their file name extensions, as listed in the following table.

Project Document Extension	Version of IDE That Created It
.xcodeproj	Xcode 2.1 or later
.xcode	Xcode 1.0 through 2.0
.pbproj	Project Builder 2.x
.pbxprog	Project Builder 1.x

When you open an older project, Xcode presents an upgrade dialog box, like the one in Figure 4-12.

Figure 4-12

If you elect to upgrade, Xcode creates a new project document and import, or translate, the contents of the old project into the new document format. It then presents a dialog box that asks where the new project document should be saved. You should save the new project document in the same project folder as the old one. Because the old project and the new one have different file extensions, Xcode doesn't overwrite the older project document. The project folder now has two project documents, as shown in Figure 4-13.

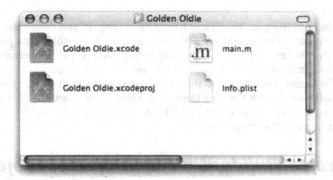

Figure 4-13

You can dispose of the older project document, Golden Oldie.xcode in this example. If you only upgraded the project to view it, dispose of the newer Golden Oldie.xcodeproj when you are done. It is unlikely that you will want to keep both project documents, unless you are willing to maintain them in parallel.

Old Project Templates

Xcode has a long history and its accompanying artifacts and antiques. Some of those antiques are templates you might have on your system. As you can see when upgrading a project, the format of the project document has changed over time, and a number of the project templates have lived through several format changes.

Project templates are stored in /Library/Application Support/Apple/Developer Tools/Project Templates/. When you upgrade Xcode, the installer adds new templates and updates old ones. The update process can leave artifacts, such as older versions of the project documents.

Figure 4-14 shows a new project created in Xcode 2.1 using the Standard Tool template. This template has been on my development system since the Project Builder days. Consequently, the template ends up with two project documents — the .xcodeproj document created by the current template, and a copy of the old .pbproj document from days gone by.

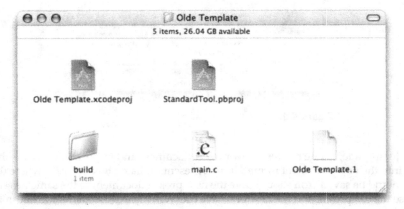

Figure 4-14

There are two ways of fixing this. The first is to just "live with it" and delete the obsolete .pbproj file after the project is created. The second is a little more involved, but solves the problem forever. Delete the Project Templates folder in /Library/Application Support/Apple/Developer Tools/. Open the Xcode installer package from the Xcode installation disc. When you get to the screen that says "Easy install on," click the Customize button. In the list of components to install, uncheck everything except Developer Tools Software. Check the Java Developer Tools if you want the Java templates, and check WebObjects Development if you want the WebObjects templates. Click the Upgrade button. The installer reinstalls fresh copies of all the templates.

Importing ProjectBuilderWO (WebObjects) Projects

Xcode finally unifies the development platform for WebObjects developers. In the past, WebObjects used a custom version of ProjectBuilder that understood WebObjects targets and components.

To migrate to Xcode, you need to import your ProjectBuilderWO projects into Xcode by following these steps:

1. Choose File⇨Import Project. This opens the import project assistant.

2. From the Import Project Assistant, choose Import ProjectBuilderWO Project and click the Next button.

3. Type the path to the ProjectBuilderWO project document in the ProjectBuilderWO Project field or click the Choose button to select the project document.

4. Type the name you want to use for the new Xcode project in the New Project Name field and click Finish. If you do not change the name, Xcode uses the name of the existing project.

Xcode imports the ProjectBuilderWO project and creates a new Xcode project file. Where possible, Xcode imports the targets defined in the ProjectBuilderWO project as native targets. If the WebObjects project contains target types that Xcode doesn't support, they are replaced with Jam-based targets.

Migrating from CodeWarrior to Xcode

With the introduction of Intel processors into the Macintosh lines of computers, Xcode is now a requirement for anyone developing software compiled for both PowerPC and Intel architectures. Developers who have been using CodeWarrior will want to import their existing projects into Xcode.

Xcode also provides some tools for converting a CodeWarrior project into an Xcode project. Before you can begin, however, there are some prerequisites that have to be addressed in the CodeWarrior project. Your CodeWarrior project must first be configured to build the same kind of product that Xcode produces.

Xcode only supports Carbon for C application development in OS X. Xcode cannot build applications for the older Toolbox routines in Mac OS 9 and earlier. So the first step is to update your application to Carbon. Apple engineers have prepared an extensive Carbon Porting Guide at `http://developer` `.apple.com/documentation/Carbon/Conceptual/carbon_porting_guide/`.

Secondly, Xcode does not support creating old-style applications that store their resources in the resource fork of the application binary. Your CodeWarrior project needs to produce an application that is stored in a package (bundle). In CodeWarrior, set the Project Type of the project to Application Package.

Finally, Xcode only builds applications in the Mach-O executable format. Xcode will not produce the now-obsolete Code Fragment binaries. Set the CodeWarrior project to produce Mach-O format binaries.

Just to be neat, delete any unnecessary targets from the project. You are now ready to import the project into Xcode. Follow these steps:

1. Choose File⇨Import Project. This opens the import project assistant.

2. Select Import CodeWarrior Project and click the Next button.

3. Click the Choose button and navigate to the CodeWarrior project file to import. You can also type the full path, if you wish.

4. Enter a name for the new project in the New Project Name field. If you don't, Xcode uses the same name as that of the CodeWarrior project. The new Xcode project will be created in the same folder as the existing CodeWarrior project.

5. If you want the importer to add any global source trees from CodeWarrior's preferences to the Source Trees list in Xcode, select Import "Global Source Trees" from CodeWarrior. (See Chapter 17 to learn about source trees.) When you import a CodeWarrior project, Xcode determines the location of the CodeWarrior root folder (referred to as {Compiler} in CodeWarrior's search path) and adds it to the Source Trees list in the Preferences window.

6. Select the Import Referenced Projects option to import any additional CodeWarrior projects referenced by the project you are currently importing.

7. Click the Finish button to dismiss the assistant and start the import. When the import is complete, the new Xcode project window opens.

Unfortunately, this is usually the beginning, not the end, of the migration process. There are many differences between the CodeWarrior development tools and Xcode's tools. For help, read "Porting CodeWarrior Projects to Xcode" at `http://developer.apple.com/documentation/DeveloperTools/Conceptual/MovingProjectsToXcode/index.html`. Of special interest is the section "After Importing a Project." This details a number of known migration problems and what to do about them.

Migrating from Anything Else to Xcode

Xcode provides automatic upgrading of Project Builder and earlier Xcode projects, and an assistant for importing CodeWarrior and older WebObjects projects.

With any other IDE you simply have to create a new project, add the source files to it, configure it, and fix anything that doesn't build. This often is not as difficult as it sounds. The C, C++, and Objective-C languages have matured over the years and are now amazingly uniform between platforms and compilers. Java is, and always has been, uniformly defined in all platforms. Often the only things that have to be fixed are compiler specific directives and determining equivalent compiler settings for gcc.

Project Attributes

Now that you can create projects, take a look at the attributes of the project itself. Xcode projects are organized into a hierarchy. Changes made to an individual source file, or the attributes of that file, affect only that file when the project is built. The attributes of a target affect only the items in that target. At the top of this hierarchy is the project itself. The attributes of the project apply to everything built by the project.

You can examine project attributes in an Info window or using the Inspector palette. To use the Inspector palette, select the project structure group in the project window. If the Inspector palette is already visible, the project's attributes will appear there. If not, hold down the Option key and select the File⇨Show Inspector command or press Command+Option+I.

To open the project attributes in an Info window choose Project⇨Edit Project Settings, or double-click the project structure group. Alternatively, select the project structure group and choose File⇨Get Info, press Command+I, or click the Info button in the toolbar.

The project's Info window has four tabs: General, Build, Configurations, and Comments. These sections are the same for all Xcode projects, even if some of the settings don't apply to the project you are building. The project Info window may have an SMC tab if the project has been configured to use source control.

The General section, shown in Figure 4-15, displays the name of the project document and the path to the project folder. See the earlier "Renaming and Relocating Projects" section to change either of these.

The next section controls where the final results of the build will be placed and where intermediate files generated during the build process are stored. See Chapter 14 for more information on relocating the results of a build.

The Cross-Develop Using Target SDK setting sets the SDK that all targets in the project will be built with. An SDK is a complete set of headers and libraries that are specific to a particular release of Mac OS X. If you need to develop an application for a specific version of OS X, select the appropriate SDK here. The default is Current Mac OS and will compile against the current framework of the OS you are running right now.

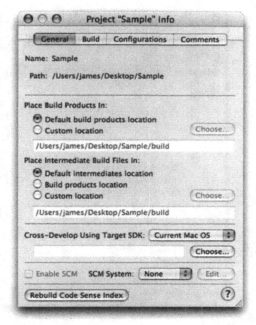

Figure 4-15

Cross-development only applies to native targets. It will not affect Java or other target types that don't link against the frameworks of Mac OS X. Selecting a different SDK for Java is done in the Java Target. To use Cross-development you must have installed the Cross-Development Tools using the Xcode installer. If you did not do this, run the installer again. After choosing the volume to install on, click the Custom button and select (just) the Cross-Development Tools. Click Upgrade to install the Cross-Development SDKs.

The SCM defines which source control system this project is using. See Chapter 18 for details on setting up source control.

Finally, the Code Sense indexes are stored in the project's build folder. Removing and renaming source files in the project can confuse Code Sense — the indexes get out of synchronization with the source code and need to be reset. The Rebuild Code Sense Index button causes Xcode to flush its cache of Code Sense indexes and rebuild them from scratch. See Chapter 6 for more information about Code Sense.

The Build tab is where you set build settings that will apply to everything built by this project.

The Configurations tab, shown in Figure 4-16, defines the named sets of build settings called Configurations. See Chapter 14 for a detailed explanation of build configurations and build settings.

That last tab is for comments (see Figure 4-17). The project, targets, and most other items in the project have a comments field. This is for your personal use. You can keep whatever information you find useful here — Xcode will store the comments in the project document. You might want to include build instructions for other developers, to-do lists, or just a general abstract about the project and why it exists.

Figure 4-16

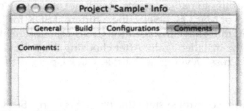

Figure 4-17

Summary

In this chapter, you learned how to create new projects. More important, you now know how to choose a project template that will get you started in the right direction. You can open, close, rename, relocate, and switch between multiple projects. Finally, you know where to set the project attributes — although most of those attributes won't make much sense until you get to the targets and build chapters.

But before a project can build something, the project has to contain something to build. These are the project sources and are the subject of the next chapter.

Exercise

Create a new project, make some minor modifications, and run it:

1. Create a new project that will produce a simple command-line tool written in Java. Name the project **Exercise4**.

2. Record a comment in the project attributes stating that the project was created as an exercise.

3. Build and execute the tool.

Sources

So far, you've learned how to create and reorganized projects. Everything you've learned so far deals exclusively with the project document. But project documents don't contain anything that generates code or anything else for that matter. To do that, you have to add sources—files that contain actual content—to the project.

> Except for the project structure and settings, everything used to build a project comes from source files stored somewhere else.

Program files, headers, folders, libraries, frameworks, window layouts, image files, Info.plist files, help files, documentation, QuickTime movies, you name it—every piece used to build your final product comes from separate files and folders stored somewhere else. They are not stored in the project document.

The information stored in the project document is a *reference* to those sources. Whenever Xcode needs the content of any source file in your project, it uses its reference to locate and access it. In this chapter, you will learn about the different kinds of references and how to create, organize, and maintain them.

References

Every file, folder, and framework that you see in the project group of your project window represents a reference to a file or folder in your file system. Each reference consists of two attributes:

❑ Path

❑ Reference type

The path attribute is a POSIX path, including its name, to the file or folder. The reference type determines from where the path originates. There are five reference types:

- ❑ Absolute
- ❑ Project relative
- ❑ Enclosing-group
- ❑ Source-tree
- ❑ Product

Absolute references are the easiest to understand. The path of an absolute reference specifies an absolute path to the source file or folder. Absolute references are usually used for referencing system components, such as libraries and frameworks, that never move. You would never use an absolute reference to a source file that you've created.

Project-relative references are also pretty easy to comprehend. A project-relative path is the path from the root folder of the project to the source file or folder. In the project pictured in Figure 5-1, the reference to the file libz.1.dylib is set to project-relative.

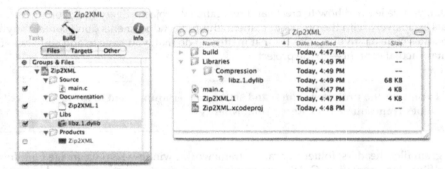

Figure 5-1

The path of the reference is Libraries/Compression/libz.1.dylib. That is the relative path from the project's folder to the library file.

Enclosing-group references are where references get complex. The basic definition is simple. In addition to defining a logical container in the project structure group, each source group has a reference to a real folder on the file system. Any item contained in that group can have a reference that is relative to the enclosing group's folder. This includes the folder references of subgroups. You can see the recursive nature of this definition. Any reference can be relative to the folder referenced by its enclosing group, which itself can be relative to its enclosing group, which can be relative to its enclosing group, and so on. You will see many more examples of enclosing group references as you read through this chapter.

The last two reference types are specialized types that are more fully explained in other chapters. They are mentioned here only for completeness. For most of your Xcode development, you will only be working with the first three references types.

Source-tree references are just like project-relative references, except that the starting location is defined by a named source tree folder. Source trees are ways of organizing folders of source files outside of the project folder. They can used to share source between projects or between developers. Source trees are discussed in detail in Chapter 18. For now, just know that source-tree paths are paths relative to some predefined location on the disk and otherwise act just like project-relative paths.

Product references are relative to the location of the active product build folder. The location of a product produced by a target is fluid because Xcode can produce variations of a target based on different build configurations. Xcode keeps these variations separate by outputting each variation to its own folder. The product folder reference changes depending on which build configuration is active. When Xcode creates references in the special Products group, they are automatically set to have product references. You would normally never need to create your own product references, but if for some reason you needed to add a product, or some piece of a product, to a special build phase, it should have a product reference. This ensures that the reference points to the version of the product that corresponds to the current build configuration.

You can examine the path and reference type of any source item in the project using the Inspector palette or an Info window. The General tab contains the reference attributes. Figure 5-2 shows the reference information for a C source file.

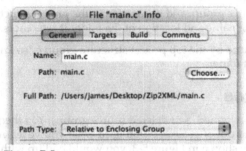

Figure 5-2

Organizing Sources

To illustrate how references can be used in a project, this section uses the very simple project pictured in Figure 5-3.

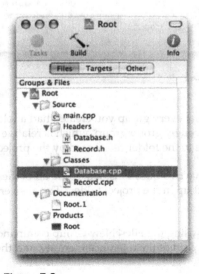

Figure 5-3

This project is, ostensibly, a C++ program built from three source files: main.cpp, Database.cpp, and Record.cpp. The two class files have matching header files, and there is a documentation file. Use this project to explore different configurations of source files and references.

This section organizes this project four different ways, using different kinds and combinations of references. Open the Root1, Root2, Root3, and Root4 projects as you work through this section to explore these projects at the same time. As you progress through these different reference schemes, keep the following in mind:

❑ Source *items* and *groups* are objects in the project. Source *files* and *folders* are the physical items in the file system.

❑ Every source item has a reference to its source file.

❑ Every source group references a folder.

❑ The name of a source group, and its location in the project structure group tree, is completely independent of the name and location of the folder it references.

❑ The folder referenced by the top project structure group (also known as the project group) is always the project folder.

Default References

In Chapter 3, you created, renamed, and deleted source groups. You then moved groups around and moved source files into and out of groups. If you used what you've learned in Chapter 3 to create the example project previously shown in Figure 5-3, you would end up with a project folder that looks like Figure 5-4.

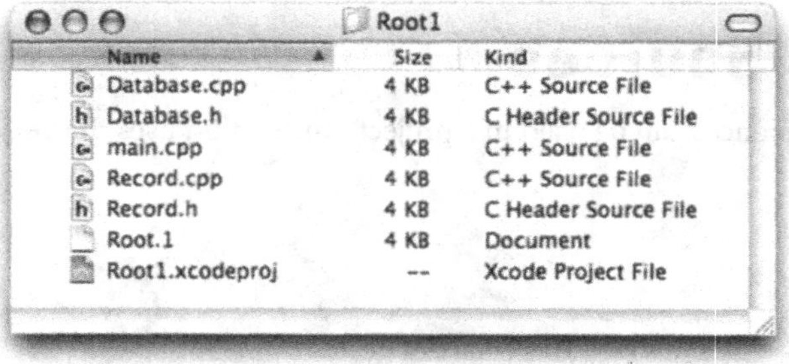

Name	Size	Kind
Database.cpp	4 KB	C++ Source File
Database.h	4 KB	C Header Source File
main.cpp	4 KB	C++ Source File
Record.cpp	4 KB	C++ Source File
Record.h	4 KB	C Header Source File
Root.1	4 KB	Document
Root1.xcodeproj	--	Xcode Project File

Figure 5-4

You were probably unaware that every group you created had a folder reference. The Database.cpp file is relative to the folder referenced by group group, which is relative to the folder referenced by the Source group, which is relative to the folder referenced by the project structure group.

At this point, you probably have two questions: where are all of these folders that are being referenced and why did all of the files end up in the project folder? The answer is explained by the default settings for new groups.

When you create a new group using the File⇨New Group command, Xcode creates a group with a kind of "null" folder reference. The path of the reference is empty, and the reference type is enclosing-group.

The net effect is that the group references the *same* folder as its enclosing folder. The Info window of the source group is shown in Figure 5-5.

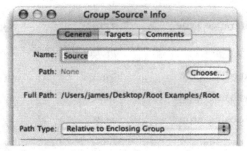

Figure 5-5

It doesn't matter how you reorganize the groups, every one will (indirectly) reference the folder of the top group. This is always the project structure group, and that always references the project folder.

Thus, the default organization of Xcode projects places all of the source files directly in the project folder. You are free to reorganize the hierarchy of your source groups and items to any depth you want; the organization of the actual files will remain flat. For small- to medium-sized projects that are self-contained and have no duplicate file names, this is the easiest organization. It is uncomplicated and shouldn't cause any surprises. Better yet, you don't have to worry about source group folder references. If your project falls into this category, feel free to skip ahead to the next section now and come back here when your projects get more complex.

However, if you want to control the physical organization of the files in your project, read on.

Sharing a Subfolder

Figure 5-6 shows a reorganization of the source files by type. All of the C++ source files in the Root2 project have been moved into the Source folder and the one documentation file has been moved into the Docs folder.

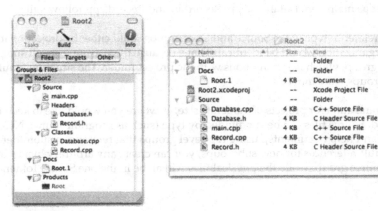

Figure 5-6

The folder references for the Source and Docs groups were changed from enclosing group to project-relative. The paths of those groups were set to Source and Docs, respectively. To illustrate the relationship between the items and groups, the references of the items are listed in the following table.

Item	Reference Type	Path	Complete Path
Root2	*fixed*	*project*	~/Root2
Source	Project-relative	Source	~/Root2/Source
Headers	Enclosing-group	*none*	~/Root2/Source
Classes	Enclosing-group	*none*	~/Root2/Source
Docs	Project-relative	Docs	~/Root2/Docs
main.cpp	Enclosing-group	main.cpp	~/Root2/Source/main.cpp
Database.h	Enclosing-group	Database.h	~/Root2/Source/Database.h
Database.cpp	Enclosing-group	Database.cpp	~/Root2/Source/Database.cpp
Record.h	Enclosing-group	Record.h	~/Root2/Source/Record.h
Record.cpp	Enclosing-group	Record.cpp	~/Root2/Source/Record.cpp
Root.1	Enclosing-group	Root.1	~/Root2/Docs/Root.1

In essence, this is a variation of the default references you looked at in Root1. The subgroups, Headers and Classes, are still relative to the enclosing group with empty paths. These groups, like all of the groups in the first project, refer to the folder of whatever group they are contained in, but instead of letting this percolate all the way up to the project group, the folder reference for the source group has been set to be the Source folder inside the project folder.

Likewise, the Docs group now references the Docs folder inside the project folder.

The main.cpp item is relative to its enclosing group, which is the Source group. Thus, the main.cpp file is in the Source folder. Database.h is also relative to its enclosing group, which is the Headers group. But as you just saw, Headers references the folder of its enclosing group, Source, which puts the Database.h file in the same folder as main.cpp. Database.cpp, Record.h, and Record.cpp follow suit.

Interestingly, the reference type of the Source and Docs groups could either be project-relative or enclosing-group, and the organization would be identical. That's because these groups are all subgroups of the project structure group, which is synonymous with the project folder. The situation would change if the Source or Docs groups were moved.

This is a good organization for projects of moderate size, or where you would like to keep the main project folder uncluttered. Source files can be subdivided by type (such as program source, NIB files, property lists, image files, and help documents), using top-level groups that reference a subfolder in the project. By using the default references for new subgroups, you can create any arbitrary hierarchy of groups and files within the source group, while the physical files will all be in the one Source folder.

Everything Is Relative

For large projects, the method most often employed for regaining some sense of control over the project's source files is to organize them into functional hierarchies. Java projects are naturally organized this way. The Java convention is to store each Java source file in a folder that has the same name as the package the class belongs in. The functional hierarchy of packages and classes parallels a hierarchy of folders and file names.

Figure 5-7 shows the reorganized project and folder structure. You'll have to use your imagination and pretend that there are scores of other source files, with base and subclasses in each group, and other groups like Query, Connection, and Utilities. In the real world, there would be little to gain in spending this much effort organizing a project containing only six source files.

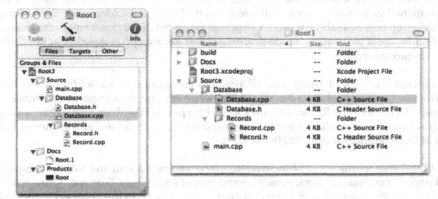

Figure 5-7

In this project, you really want the organization of the groups to parallel the organization of the folders on the disk. To accomplish this, all of the groups have enclosing group references. But instead of having empty paths, the path of each group references the subfolder immediately contained within the enclosing group's folder. The following table lists the modified references.

Item	Reference Type	Path	Complete Path
Root3	*fixed*	*project*	~/Root3
Source	Enclosing-group	Source	~/Root3/Source
Database	Enclosing-group	Database	~/Root3/Source/Database
Records	Enclosing-group	Records	~/Root3/Source/Database/Records
Docs	Enclosing-group	Docs	~/Root3/Docs
main.cpp	Enclosing-group	main.cpp	~/Root3/Source/main.cpp
Database.h	Enclosing-group	Database.h	~/Root3/Source/Database/Database.h

Table continued on following page

Item	Reference Type	Path	Complete Path
Database.cpp	Enclosing-group	Database.cpp	~/Root3/Source/Database/Database.cpp
Record.h	Enclosing-group	Record.h	~/Root3/Source/Database/Records/Record.h
Record.cpp	Enclosing-group	Record.cpp	~/Root3/Source/Database/Records/Record.cpp

The Record.cpp file is contained in the folder referenced by the Records group. The folder reference of the Records group specifies the Records subfolder inside the folder of its enclosing group. The enclosing group is Database, which references the Database folder inside the folder of its enclosing group. The Database group is contained in the source group that references the Source subfolder inside the folder of its enclosing group. That group is, thankfully, the project structure group that always references the project folder. Through four layers of indirection, Xcode determines that Record.cpp is stored at ~/Root3/Source/Database/Records/Record.cpp.

The core concept is the use of groups that all assume a corresponding subfolder relative their enclosing group. Why you do this will become more evident when it's time to reorganize the project. As an example, you may decide that the Records group should be a peer of Database rather than a subgroup. If the Records group was moved into the source group and the Records subfolder was moved into the Source folder, all of the references would still be valid.

You might think that setting up all of these references would be difficult and tedious—especially for the imagined project containing dozens, possibly hundreds, of source files. Fear not. Xcode has tools, which you will soon use, that create any number of nested groups exactly in this fashion with a single command.

Outside the Box

Conveniently, all of the references so far have been to folders inside the folder of the enclosing group or project. But this does not have to be the case. In Figure 5-8, the files in the Root4 project have been rearranged again. The Records folder containing Record.h and Record.cpp has been moved to the Source folder, making it a peer of the Database folder.

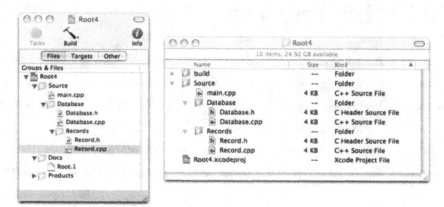

Figure 5-8

The Records group in the project has not been moved; it is still a subgroup of the Database group. This breaks the reference to the Records folder and to the files it contains, because those are both relative to the Records folder. To fix the reference, the path of the Records group was changed to ../Records. The following table lists the modified references.

Item	Reference Type	Path	Complete Path
Root4	*fixed*	*project*	~/Root4
Source	Enclosing-group	Source	~/Root4/Source
Database	Enclosing-group	Database	~/Root4/Source/Database
Records	Enclosing-group	../Records	~/Root4/Source/Records
Record.h	Enclosing-group	*none*	~/Root4/Source/Records/Record.h
Record.cpp	Enclosing-group	*none*	~/Root4/Source/Records/Record.cpp

Paths are standard POSIX paths that can refer to the current (.) and parent (..) folders. The path ../Records path starts at the Database folder, moves to the parent of that folder (Source), then to the subfolder named Records.

In a little more extreme example, the Docs folder has been removed from the Root4 project entirely, and the path of Docs group has been changed to ../Root3/Docs. The following table lists the new paths.

Item	Reference Type	Path	Complete Path
Root4	*fixed*	*project*	~/Root4
Docs	Project-relative	../Root3/Docs	~/Root3/Docs

The reference in the Docs group now points to a subfolder in the Root3 project, in the same folder as the Root4 project (see Figure 5-9).

Figure 5-9

The problem with relative paths like this is the danger of breaking the reference when project folders are moved or renamed. If the project folder Root3 is moved, the reference to the Docs folder in Root4 no longer works.

Bad References

It's just as important to know what kind of references you should *not* create. I left this last project open overnight, and some mischievous pixies snuck in and decided they would have a little fun with it.

At first glance, the Root Rot project looks pretty much like project Root4, as you can see in Figure 5-10.

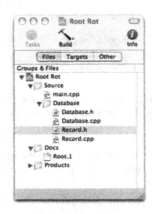 

Figure 5-10

All of the references are valid, and the project builds and runs. So things can't be all bad, can they? The following table lists the references in the project.

Item	Reference Type	Path	Complete Path
Root Rot	*fixed*	*project*	~/Root Rot
Source	Absolute	~/Root Rot/Source	~/Root Rot/Source
Database	Enclosing-group	Database	~/Root Rot/Source/Database
Record.h	Enclosing-group	../Records/Record.h	~/Root3/Source/Records/Record.h
Record.cpp	Project-relative	Source/Records/Record.cpp	~/Root3/Source/Database/Record.cpp
Docs	Project-relative	../Root3/Docs	~/Root3/Docs
Root.1	Enclosing-group	../../Root Rot/Docs/Root.1	~/Root Rot/Docs/Root.1

The source group has an absolute reference to the Source folder. If the project was renamed or moved, or any folder names that contain it were altered, this reference (and every reference that depends on it) would break.

The Database group references the Database subfolder relative to the Source folder. It and the references to Database.h and Database.cpp are as they were in the Root4 project.

Notice that the Records group was deleted, but the Records folder is still in the project. So how do the items Records.h and Records.cpp reference their respective files? The path to Records.h was changed to ../Records/Records.h. Being relative to the Database folder, the path traverses to the Database parent, and then into the Records subfolder. Using a slightly different approach, the reference of the Record.cpp item has been made project-relative with a path of Source/Records/Record.cpp. If the Database folder were renamed, the reference to Records.h would break, but the reference to Records.cpp would still be valid.

In the Docs group, you'll find true insanity. Like the Root4 example, the Docs group contains a project-relative reference to a folder outside the project folder. In a truly diabolical move, the reference to the Root.1 item has been made relative to the enclosing group, but with a path that traverses up the folder tree and back into the Docs folder of this project. So the project folder contains a file that is dependent on the name and location of not only a second project, but of this project as well.

It has been said that the difference between programming in BASIC and programming in C is the difference between using safety scissors and a surgeon's scalpel. You can't perform brain surgery using safety scissors, but you also don't have to count your fingers afterwards. Xcode, like many powerful tools, gives you great freedom in how you construct your projects, regardless of how ill-conceived that construction might be.

Despite its permissiveness, Xcode provides a number of tools for creating orderly and maintainable projects. It also has a few tricks for whipping projects like Root Rot back into shape.

Source Item Types

Xcode uses four different types of source items to organize and reference the files in a project.

Source Item Type	Reference
Source File	Any file used to build the project
Source Group	A folder that members of the group can refer to
Source Folder	A folder used to build the project
Framework	A folder containing a framework

A source file item is a reference to a data file on the disk. It can be a program source file, a header, a NIB file, an XML file, an image file, or a font—it doesn't matter. Every source file item references exactly one file.

You've already spent some time working with source groups. They are the logical containers of the project. Each source group references a real folder on the file system, but what the group contains (in the project structure group) may have little or no correspondence with the files in that folder. The folder it references is of primary interest to the items it contains, which can have references relative to that folder.

There are two more source item types that also refer to a folder but much more directly. A source folder item is very much like a source file item, but references a folder instead. The visual differences between a source group and source folder are very slight, but their behavioral differences are profound.

Figure 5-11 shows two projects. In the one on the left, the Help item is a source *group* containing three items (index.html, help.css, and background.png). In the project on the right, the Help item is a source *folder* containing three files. Do they look the same? In a black-and-white illustration, or if you're color blind, it's going to be hard to tell the difference. The source group (left) is yellow in the Xcode interface, while the source folder (right) is blue. Looking at the attributes of the two items in Figure 5-12 reveals that the item on the right is of type "folder."

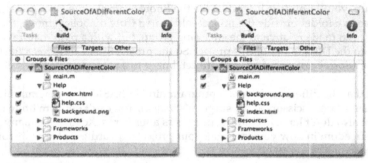

Figure 5-11

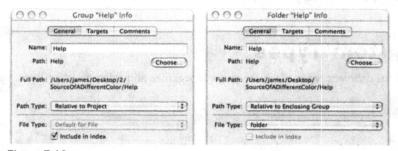

Figure 5-12

The key difference is that a source group is a logical container for other source items. A source folder *is* a source item. Although the interface lets you browse the contents of both, a source folder is treated as a single opaque object. The individual files in the folder are not treated as separate source items. Xcode does not compile any C source files in a source folder. The items in a source folder do not have any attributes or references.

You can see this difference in the interface. Look again at Figure 5-11. A target membership attribute appears next to the source folder, but not next to any of its items. The situation for the source group is reversed.

Like smart groups, the items in a source folder item dynamically reflect the contents of the folder on the disk. Add a file to the folder and it appears in the source folder item — well, sometimes. Xcode can be lazy about updating its display. Collapse and re-expand a folder item to see any changes made to the folder.

Finally, a framework item is yet another kind of folder item. The only difference between a framework item and a folder item is that Xcode automatically recognizes framework folders and integrates them into the project. It indexes the headers of the framework, includes symbols defined in the framework in auto-completion, and correctly links to the dynamic libraries in the framework. In the project, treat it as you would a single library that your project links to. Xcode takes care of the details.

Creating New Source Files

Unless your project is trivial, you will soon want to create new source files. The File⇨New File command creates a new source file based on a file template of your choosing, and adds that file as a source item to your project. The item is added to the currently selected group, or the group that contains the currently selected item. So the first step to creating a new source file is to choose the location in the project where you want it added. Then choose New File from the File menu.

Figure 5-13 shows the New File Assistant where you choose a file template. Most templates are self-explanatory, and simply produce skeletal files with some basic comments and sometimes an #include or #import statement. The C++, Java, and Objective-C templates will include an empty class definition with the same name as the file.

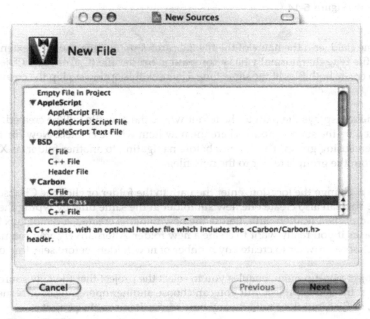

Figure 5-13

All of the templates produce a plain text file, except they are the Data Model and Class Model templates, which have their own assistant for creating the model files. Creating data and class models is covered in Chapter 11 and Chapter 12.

Click the Next button to accept your template choice. Xcode prompts for the name and location of the new file, along with some additional options as shown in Figure 5-14.

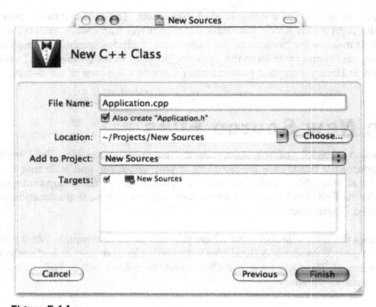

Figure 5-14

In the File Name field, edit the name of the file. Be careful not to alter the file's extension. If the template is for a source file type that normally has a companion header file (C, C++, and Objective-C templates), Xcode offers to create both files at the same time. Uncheck this option to skip the creation of the companion .h file.

The Location field displays the path to the folder where the new file will be created. This is always the folder referenced by the source group where the new item will be created. New file references are always relative to the enclosing group. Think twice before navigating to another folder, as Xcode will construct a relative path from the group's folder to the new file.

If you do need to change the location, enter the path to the folder or click the Choose button to select an existing folder. You can also create one new subfolder at the same time by typing the name of the new folder at the end of the Location path. Before the new folder is created, a dialog box like the one shown in Figure 5-15 asks if you really want to create a new folder. Alternatively, you can use the New Folder button in the Choose browser to create any number of new folders before selecting one.

The Add to Project pop-up menu enables you to select the project that the new source item will be added to. The default is the active project, but you can choose another open project or None. Selecting None creates the file, or files, but does not add any new source items to the project.

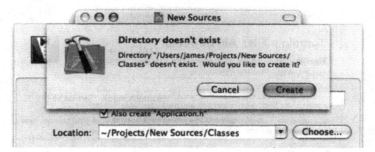

Figure 5-15

The Targets list shows all of the targets that accept the type of file being created. Only targets in the project selected in the Add to Project pop-up menu are considered. The list will be empty if the project is "none," or if there are no targets in the selected project that accept the type of file being created.

Each target in the list has a check box next to it. If checked, the newly created source item will be added to that target. If you are creating both a source file and its companion header file, checking a target will add both files to the target — unless the target only accepts one of the two types. This can actually be a hazard for targets that accept both types, because you often want to add the source file to a target but not the header. The "Ridding Targets of Unwanted Files" section has a trick for quickly getting unwanted headers out of a target.

Once the new file has a name, a location, a project, and a list of targets, click the Finish button to create the file and add the item to the project. The new file opens automatically in an editor window.

If you try to create a file that already exists, Xcode warns you with the dialog box shown in Figure 5-16.

You have three choices, obtusely explained in the dialog box. The first choice, which is probably the best, is to cancel the operation.

Your second choice is to check the boxes next to the files you want to replace and click the Overwrite Selected Files button. Despite the fact that the button reads Overwrite, the checked files are not overwritten. They are first moved to a new subfolder named with a numeric suffix and the extension .moved-aside, as shown in Figure 5-17. The folder will be in the same folder where the new files are being created.

The third choice is to click the Remove Old then Create button. The action of this button is equivalent to first checking all of the files listed and clicking the Overwrite Selected Files button. When the dialog box is first presented, all of the files are checked, making the action of the two buttons identical.

After the files are moved aside, new files are created in the same location from the template. If there were already source items for these files, you now have duplicate source items. You Find and delete these duplicate items.

The files that were moved aside are no longer referenced from the project. You can examine the files, recover what you want, and then trash them along with the spontaneously generated folder that contains them.

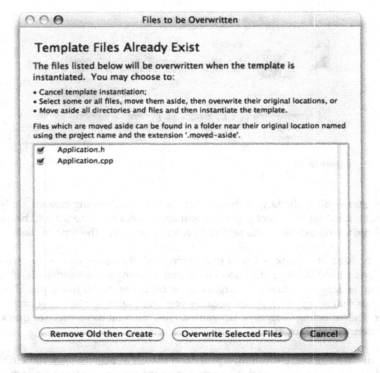

Figure 5-16

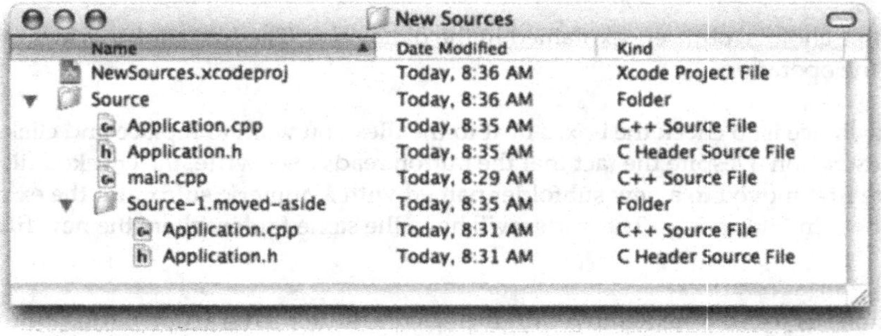

Figure 5-17

The File⇨New File command performs several common steps and can be a great time saver. But sometimes you just want an empty file that doesn't have a name, isn't based on a template, isn't added to a project, and isn't included in one or more targets. The File⇨New Empty File command (Command+Control+N) does exactly that. In fact, the New Empty File command is very similar to the New command found in most applications. It opens an empty, untitled, editor window. The content of the new window is not associated with a file until it is saved. The first time it is saved, Xcode kindly offers to add the new file to the active project, as shown in Figure 5-18. You can accept or decline.

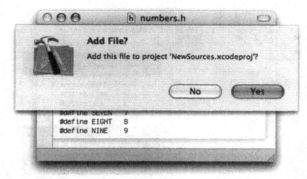

Figure 5-18

If you accept, you are presented with the same options you're given when you add any existing source file to a project. These options are explained fully in the next section.

Adding Existing Sources

Xcode projects can include many different types of files, well beyond the editable text files created by the New File command. At some point, you are going to need to add these files to your project. You may also want to import existing text files into a project.

Selecting the Items to Add

The process of adding one or more files that already exist can be started in one of two ways. The first is to use the Project⇨Add to Project command (Command+Option+A). As with the File⇨New File command, you begin by first selecting the source group that will contain the new source items, or an existing source item within that group. Then choose the Add to Project command from the Project menu. Xcode presents an open file dialog box to select the file to be added. This dialog box also permits you to select folders and multiple selections. Use the Command or Shift key while clicking items to select more than one file or folder. Xcode creates a new item references for every file and folder you select in the dialog box. Figure 5-19 shows six new source files being added to a project. Note that items already referenced in the project are disabled (grey) and can't be added again.

The second method is more direct. Select any group of files and folders in the Finder and simply drag them into the source tree of your project. A drop indicator shows you where in the source group the new item, or items, will be created — exactly as it does when you're dragging items around in the tree. Figure 5-20 shows two files and a folder being added to the source group.

One very useful advantage of using the drag-and-drop technique is that symbolic links and aliases are not resolved for the files being dropped. The source item created refers to the alias, not to the file or folder the alias resolves to. This is important if you need to add a dynamic library or framework that is actually an alias to the current version of that library. The only significant disadvantage of the drag-and-drop method is that Xcode permits you to create duplicate items to files that are already referenced in the project.

Figure 5-19

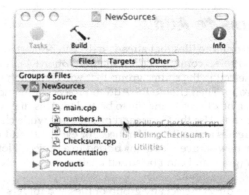

Figure 5-20

As soon as Xcode knows where to create the new source items in the project and what files will be used to create those items, it presents the dialog box shown in Figure 5-21.

This dialog box contains several controls that will determine what kind of source items are created, the type of references they will have, and where the final source files will reside. The effect of these options is often interconnected. Some options behave differently depending on the choices you make for other options.

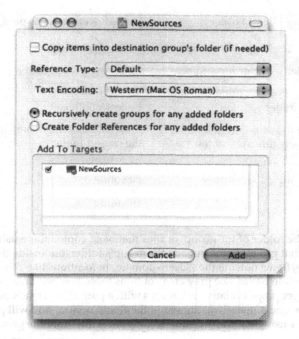

Figure 5-21

Copying Items into the Destination Group's Folder

Use the Copy Items into Destination Group's Folder (If Needed) option to make physical copies of the original files or folders inside the group's folder. The group's folder is the folder referenced by the group that the new source items are being added to. If you select this option, all of the files and folders being added are first copied into the group's folder. Each source item created references the copy made in the group's folder, not the original. Note that items contained inside subfolders of the group's folder are *not* considered to be in the group's folder. Files or folders in any other folder on the file system are copied, which could easily create duplicate source files inside your project folder. Use this option only to import sources from locations outside of the project folder.

The "(If Needed)" qualifier is there because this option is ignored if the files are already in the group's folder. Well, not entirely ignored. Due to a long-standing bug in Xcode, this works with files but not folders. If you check this option when you're adding a folder to a group whose folder already contains that folder, Xcode displays an error that it can't copy the folder to itself. No harm will come of this, but you will have to perform the operation again, this time turning the Copy option off.

Reference Type

The Reference Type option controls what type of reference each item will have. The choice you make will apply to all items being added. Choosing the special reference type of Default individually selects a reference type best suited for each item's location, as listed in the following table.

Location of Existing File or Folder	Default Reference Type
In the group's folder	Enclosing-group
Inside any subfolder in the group's folder	Enclosing-group, with a path into the subfolders
Anywhere inside the project folder but not inside the group's folder	Project-relative
Anywhere outside the project folder but within the /Users directory of the logged-in user	Project-relative, with a path that extends outside the project folder
Anywhere outside the /Users folder	Absolute
Another volume	Absolute

Files already inside the folder of the group, or files that were copied there using the Copy option, get a reference relative to that group. Items outside the group's folder, but inside the project folder, get a project-relative reference. Items outside the /Users domain, in locations like /System/Library/ Frameworks, get absolute paths. The grey area contains those files within /Users that are outside the project folder. These get project-relative references with a path that extends outside the project folder. Earlier in this chapter, one of these was shown in the Root4 project. You will probably want to fix those references, or consider using the Copy option to copy those files into the group's folder.

If you select any other type of reference, all items created will have that reference type regardless of their location. If you have source trees defined (see Chapter 18), each source tree will also appear in the menu.

Text Encoding

The Text Encoding option applies only to source items created for text files. It sets the text encoding for the file, which determines how the bytes in the file are translated into characters when the file is opened for editing. Normally, you wouldn't need to change this for regular program source files. The gcc compiler always assumes plain ASCII text, so all program source files must be ASCII text files. Change this option if you are adding things like XML files that are in UTF-8 or UTF-16 encoded Unicode, or text files in any other ISO encoding. You can always change the encoding later if you need to. See the "Source Attributes" section later in this chapter to find out how to change the encoding of a file.

Recursively Creating Groups and Creating Folder References

The two radio buttons, Recursively Create Groups for Any Added Folder and Create Folder References for Any Added Folders, determine if folders added to the project will create source groups or folder items.

With the Recursively Create Groups radio button selected, adding a folder creates a source group. Following that, every file and folder in that folder is recursively added to the new group using the same settings. The folder reference of the new group points to the folder that was added, using the reference type selected. The recursively added items get the same treatment.

If the reference type is Default — all of the recursively added items will (by definition) have enclosing-group references regardless of the reference type or location of the first new group. Does that organization sound familiar? Look again at the Root3 project. Each source group references a single subfolder in the folder of its enclosing group, and every source item references a file in the folder of its enclosing group. When you use these Add to Project settings, Xcode turns an entire folder hierarchy into an equivalent tree of source groups and source items with a single command. With the Create Folder References option selected instead, any folders added to the project create a single source folder item. No further processing of the files in that folder occurs.

At this point you may be wondering how framework folders are added. Xcode examines each folder being added to a project to determine if it is a framework folder. If it is, Xcode *always* creates a framework item and ignores the Recursively Create Groups and Create Folder References options.

Adding To Targets

At the bottom of the dialog box is a list of targets defined in the project. If you checking the box next to a target, Xcode attempts to add each source item created to that target. The key word is "attempt." Some targets only accept, or understand, certain types of source items. An item is added to a target only if the target accepts that type of item.

When everything is set, click the Add button to add the items to the project.

Adding an Open File

Xcode can open an arbitrary file into an editor window. The file does not have to first belong to a project. You can add the file of any open editor window to the current project by selecting the Project⇨Add Current File to Project command. A dialog box presents the same set of options that the Project⇨Add to Project command does.

Source Attributes

Now that you know how to create new source items en masse, take a look at the attributes of each to see how they can be changed individually or in batches.

Use the Inspector palette or an Info window to examine the attributes of a source item. Click the General tab to show the item's general attributes. Figure 5-22 shows a typical source file item.

The Name field contains the name of the item. If the item can be renamed, this field is editable. The name of a file, folder, or framework item is always the same as the actual item. Editing the name of a file, folder, or framework item also renames the file or folder it references. Renaming a source group merely renames the group and does not alter the name of the group's folder.

The Path and Path Type fields define the item's reference, and is what most of this chapter has been about. The Full Path field displays the ultimate path to the file or folder. This is how Xcode interprets the path using the given reference type. You can change the reference type using the pop-menu. Xcode recalculates an equivalent path. To change the path, click the Choose button. Select a file or folder from the browser. For file, folder, and framework items, the name of the item changes to match that of the selected file or folder.

Figure 5-22

> If you want to quickly see the file or folder that an item references, select the item in the project and choose Reveal in Finder from the Control-/right-click menu, or hold down the Option key and choose File⇨Reveal in Finder.

The next section in the Info window is the item's type. This is an internal categorization based on the file's file type and extension so that Xcode knows how to treat this item. It is used to determine if an item can be included in a target, and to what phase of the target the item belongs in. It determines how, or if, Xcode will display the item in an editor window and what language of syntax coloring should be used. You can change how Xcode treats an item by selecting a different type. But this type only extends to how Xcode treats the file. The operating system, external build systems, and compilers still interpret the file based on the file's type and extension. Changing the type of a .m file from source.c.objc to source.c.cpp will *not* cause the file to be compiled as a C++ file.

The File Encoding, Line Endings, and Tab attributes apply only text files and are disabled for all other types of source items. The File Encoding defines the binary format the characters in the file are expected to be in. Change this setting if the assumption is wrong. The Line Endings attribute is also an assumption, but one that is largely superfluous. Xcode determines what line endings are being used when the file is opened.

Changing the File Encoding for a text file presents the dialog box shown in Figure 5-23. The Convert button interprets the file using the previous encoding, and then rewrites the file using the new encoding. Use this option if the encoding of the file is correct, but you want to change the format of the file to a different encoding. The Reinterpret button simply changes the encoding attribute in the source item; it does not alter the file. Select Reinterpret if the encoding set for a file is incorrect.

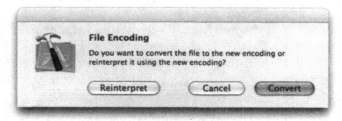

Figure 5-23

Returning to the General attributes (Figure 5-22), the Tab Width, Indent Width, and Editor Uses Tabs options are explained in the next chapter. Normally, you will want to use the same settings for all files, but you can change them for an individual file here, or by using the View⇨Tabs command while editing the file. Click the Reset to Text Editing Defaults button to restore the file's settings back to the defaults set in Xcode's preferences.

Many files can be localized so that the language and location specific information in the file can be customized for different regions and populations. File localization is covered in the next chapter.

The Targets tab lists the targets in the project. The item is included in targets that have a check mark next to them. If a target does not accept items of this type, the target is unchecked and disabled (grey).

The Comments tab is for storing comments about this item in the project document.

Changing Attributes for Multiple Items

In Chapter 3, you learned how to use the Inspector palette or an Info window to display the aggregate attributes for multiple items. Settings that are common to all of the items are shown. If all of the items have the same value for a particular setting, that value is displayed. If a value differs for some items, the value displayed is some kind of Mixed value, as shown in Figure 5-24. For check boxes, this displays as a dash. Changing any of the settings in a multi-item Info window changes that setting for all of the items to the same value.

Some settings require special handling when they are changed for multiple items. This is particularly true of the Path attribute. You wouldn't want Xcode to literally set the same path attribute for multiple items. All of the items would suddenly point to the same file or folder. Instead, the Choose button in a multi-item Info window allows you to choose the folder that *contains* all of the items. The name of each item is not altered, and a new path for each is constructed by combining the chosen folder and the item's file or folder name. This can cause item references to be broken if the folder chosen does not contain one or more of the items.

You're going to use this ability of Info windows in the next few sections. They will help you reorganize some large projects and fix the properties of targets.

Figure 5-24

Ridding Targets of Unwanted Files

It is very easy, when you're adding lots of new source files to a project, to end up with files in targets where they don't belong. This most often happens when you're adding source and header files at the same time. Targets that compile C source into object files (native targets) normally only accept C, C++, or Objective-C source files. Trying to add the companion header files to those targets at the same time does nothing. But some native targets have a Copy Files phase that accepts any kind of file. The end result is that all of the .h files get added to the target's Copy Files phase, and the target dutifully copies all of the headers files in your project into the final application. This is probably not what you want.

To fix this, select the project structure group in the Groups & Files list to display all of the files in the project in the details window (choose View⇨Details if you are using the Condensed layout style). In the details list, click the icon (file type) column to sort the items by type. Click the first header file in the list, then scroll down and Shift-click the last one to select all of the header files in the project. Now choose File⇨Get Info to get an aggregate Info window for all of the header file items. Switch to the Targets tab and uncheck all of the targets. This removes all of the header files from all of the targets in your project.

You can adapt this technique to make similar changes in other types of files.

Reorganizing Sources

This section walks you through reorganizing the files in a project. This entails rearranging the actual files and altering the source item references to agree.

When you're working with source item references, it's useful to know when an item's reference is valid and when it's broken. Whenever Xcode discovers that a reference no longer refers to a file or folder, the item in the source group turns red. Figure 5-25 shows invalid references for the main.cpp and NewSources items.

Figure 5-25

Again, this is hard to see in black-and-white. Red items are usually a clue that the item's reference needs to be fixed — but not always. Whenever you create a new project or target, a source item is created for the product that *will* be produced. Until you successfully build a target, its product doesn't exist and its product item in the source tree will be red. This is perfectly normal and expected.

There are two ways of fixing a reference: open the Info window for the item and correct its Path attribute, or put the file or folder the item is pointing to where the reference expects it to be. Xcode immediately recognizes that the reference is valid again, and changes the item's color to black.

The first example will be to relocate a couple of files from one existing folder to another.

Try It Out   Moving Files

Start with the ReorganizeMe1 project, shown in Figure 5-26.

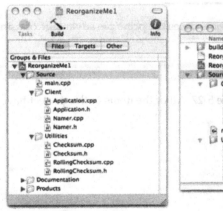 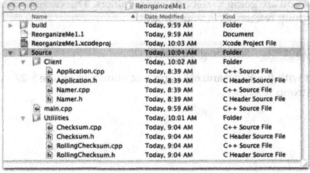

Figure 5-26

ReorganizeMe1 has two subfolders: Client and Utilities. You decide that the C++ files Namer.cpp and Namer.h need to be moved into the Utilities group and folder. Follow these steps:

1. Open the ReorganizeMe1 project.

2. Drag the Namer.h and Namer.cpp items from the Client group into the Utilities group.

3. Select the Source group. Control-/right-click the Source group and choose Reveal in Finder.

4. In the Finder window, move the two source files, Namer.h and Namer.cpp, from the Client folder into the Utilities folder.

5. Switch back to the project window. Notice that the two source items are now red. Select both items and choose File⇨Get Info.

6. In the multi-item Info window, click the Choose button. Select the folder Utilities and click Choose. The item references are now valid.

How It Works

Whenever you move a source item, Xcode adjusts the path of the item so the item continues to refer to the same file or folder. This is convenient in one sense, because it allows you to freely reorganize your source items without breaking any references. The disadvantage is that it permits you to quickly create convoluted item references and an organization that no longer agrees with the organization of the physical files.

All of the items in this exercise use enclosing-group references. When you moved the two source file items from one group to the other in step 2, Xcode recalculated new paths starting from the new group back to the old one's folder. If you had stopped and looked at the attributes of the two items after step 2, their paths would have been ../Utilities/Namer.h and ../Utilities/Namer.cpp. This also explains why the two items were still valid after the move.

In step 4, you moved the actual files. As a result, the files were no longer in the Client folder and the references broke. When you switched back to the project window, Xcode displayed the two items in red.

In steps 5 and 6, you examined the attributes of the two items and used the multi-item Info window to point both items to their respective files in the Utilities folder. The path for each was constructed using relative path to the Utilities folder (which is nothing, because the enclosing group's folder *is* the Utilities folder) and their respective file names. The references were once again valid.

Now you are going to relocate entire folders. This demonstrates the principle advantage of using enclosing group references in your project.

Try It Out   **Moving Folders**

Start with the ReorganizeMe2 project, shown in Figure 5-27. All of the items in this project have enclosing-group references.

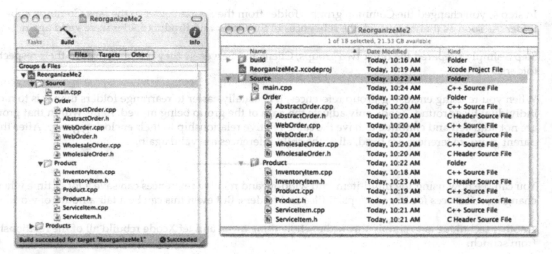

Figure 5-27

ReorganizeMe2 has two subfolders: Product and Order. The project is about to grow into a client and server. The source codes for the client and server need to be kept apart, and the common code moved into a shared tree. Follow these steps:

1. Open the ReorganizeMe2 project.

2. Select the Order group. Control-/right-click the Order group and choose Reveal in Finder. In the Finder window, create three new folders inside the Source folder: Common, Client, and Server. Drag the Product and Order folders into the Common folder.

3. Switch back to the project window. Select the Product and Order groups and choose File⇨Group to enclose them in a new group. Name the group **Common**. Use the File⇨New Group command to create new groups named **Client** and **Server** in the Source group.

4. Select the Common group. Control-/right-click the Common group and choose Get Info. In the Info window, click the Choose button and select the Common folder in the project. Click Choose to change the path.

5. Repeat step 4 for the Client and Server groups, choosing the Client and Server folders respectively.

How It Works

The Order and Product source groups refer to the Order and Product subfolders in their enclosing group's folder. Moving the Order and Product folders into the newly created Common folder broke the references to those folders, and the references of all of the items contained in them.

In step 3, the new groups Common, Client, and Server were created with relative references that referred to the folder in the source group (remember that this is the default for all newly created source groups). Although the Order and Product groups are now enclosed in the Common group, they still indirectly refer to the same location and are still broken.

In step 4, you changed the Common group's folder from the Source folder to the new Common sub-folder. As soon as that happened, the references in the Order and Product folder were valid again.

Step 5 simply prepared the other two groups, Client and Server, so they reference files in their respective folders.

When you're using enclosing-group references, it is usually easier to rearrange folders than it is to move individual files around. Xcode only adjusts the path of the group being moved. Items within that group are not adjusted and continue to have the same relative relationship to their enclosing group. After the parent group re ferences are fixed, all of the child references are valid again.

You can see how using the multi-item Info window and relative references can save a lot of time when changing references for large groups of files and folders. But even this can be a fair amount of work.

Another technique is to simply throw the whole thing away and let Xcode rebuild all of the relationships from scratch.

Try It Out   **Fast Reorganization**

Start with the ReorganizeMe3 project, shown in Figure 5-28. All of the items in this project have enclosing-group references.

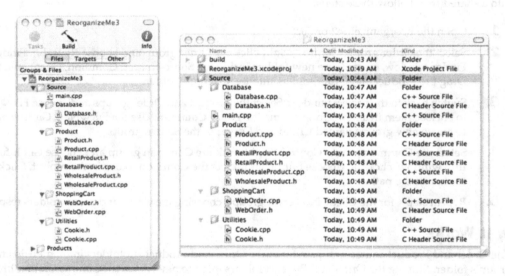

Figure 5-28

ReorganizeMe3 has several subfolders: Database, Product, Order, ShoppingCart, and Utilities. Create three new folders in the Source folder: Common, Client, and Server. Move the Database folder into the Server folder. Move the ShoppingCart folder into the Client folder. Move the Product, Order, and Utilities folders into the Common folder. The files structure should now look like Figure 5-29.

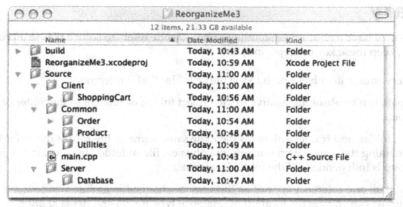

Figure 5-29

Now follow these steps:

1. Open the ReorganizeMe3 project.

2. Select the Source group. Control-/right-click the Source group and choose Delete. In the dialog box, choose Delete References.

3. Select the Project Structure group. Choose Project⇨Add to Project. Select the Source folder and click the Add button.

4. In the Add to Project dialog box, uncheck the Copy option, set Reference Type to Default, and select Recursively Create Groups for Any Added Folders. Click the Add button.

How It Works

Remember that the project document doesn't contain any of the source material for your project; just references to those files. In step 2, you deleted all of the references to the source files in this project — but just the references; the original source files are still in the project folder.

In steps 2 and 3, you used the Add to Project command to recreate new groups and source file items that match the reorganized folder hierarchy exactly.

If you have a major project reorganization, the fastest and easiest way to reorganize your groups and source items can be to simply start over. This might inadvertently include others files, or place files in targets that don't belong there, but these aberrations can usually be dealt with swiftly.

> Why you would *not* want to let Xcode rebuild all the groups and items? Deleting the source items also deletes any other attributes associated with those items. File encoding, custom tab settings, specific target membership, comments, and build options are lost when the source items are deleted. The newly created source items have default attributes. If you need to preserve attributes for a large number of source items, you probably have no choice but to reorganize the groups and folders "the hard way," as shown in the first two examples.

Summary

You should now have a clear understanding of how Xcode refers to source files in a project. As you work with Xcode, keep these key concepts in mind:

❑   Every source item has a path to the file or folder that it references.

❑   A path can be absolute, relative to the project folder, or relative to the folder of the enclosing group.

❑   File, folder, and framework items have the same name as the source file or folder they reference. Renaming the source item renames the physical file or folder. In contrast, the name of a source group is independent of the folder it references.

❑   The path and reference type of an item can be changed in an Info window. A multi-item Info window can change the location or reference type for several items at once.

❑   Moving an item in the source tree adjusts its path so that it continues to reference the same file or folder.

Now that you can add new and existing source files to your project, you will undoubtedly want to edit them. Editing text is the topic of the next chapter.

Exercise

The existing MakeMe folder, shown in Figure 5-30, contains three files: main.cpp, SieveOfEratosthenes.cpp, and SieveOfEratosthenes.h.

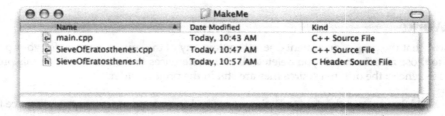

Figure 5-30

Turn these files into an Xcode project and then add a new Application class to the project:

1.   Create a new project.

2.   Create a source group and a matching Source folder. Put the three existing files into the source group and folder.

3.   Create two new source files named **Application.cpp** and **Application.h**. Add those files to the project and Source folder.

Editing Text

In the introduction, I mentioned that Xcode doesn't really *do* much of the actual development work. Most of the heavy lifting is performed by a suite of external tools—compilers, linkers, debuggers, and others—that are not part of the Xcode application. But Xcode does provide one critical tool that is integral to any developer's workflow: a text editor. You will spend far more time editing source files than doing any other single task while developing a program. Learning how to efficiently edit and quickly navigate your source files will greatly enrich your productivity.

Windows and Panes

Editing in Xcode occurs in an editor pane. An editor pane can be part of a multi-pane window, like the project window in the Default style, or it can be the sole content of a separate editor window. Figure 6-1 shows a file being edited in three panes: once in the project window, again in the editor pane of the project find window, and again in an independent editor window.

Editing Panes

Xcode editing panes are homogeneous. The features, functions, and capabilities are identical regardless of where they appear. This imparts one extremely useful feature: No matter where a source file appears in Xcode, you have the full power of the Xcode editor at your disposal. The text of a file that appears in a search window, the debugger, or the object browser can all be edited immediately without any need to locate the file or open a specialized window. The same file can appear in multiple editing panes at once. Changes made to one are reflected in all.

To edit a file in a separate editor window, double-click the source file item in the project window. If the file already appears in an editing pane of another window, you can force it to open in a new window by choosing the Open in Separate Editor command from either the View menu or the Control-/right-click contextual pop-up menu. This command is available whenever the file item is selected in a list, or any editor pane with that file is active. You can open several windows to the same file.

Chapter 6

Figure 6-1

Bringing the contents of a file into the editor pane of a multi-pane window is usually accomplished by some other selection in the window. Selecting a class in the Class Browser displays the source of the class' header in its editor pane. Clicking a line found in the Project Find window displays the file where the line was found in that window's editor pane.

The editor pane of the project window is no exception, but the behavior is a little more complex. When you're using the Default and All-In-One Xcode styles, the project source list shares a window with the details list and an editor pane. Figure 6-2 shows all three panes visible at once.

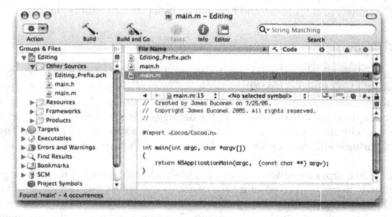

Figure 6-2

Selecting a single file in either the Groups & Files list or the details list immediately brings the contents of that file into the editor pane — that is, if the editor pane is visible. As you saw in Chapter 3, the details

88

list and the editor pane share the same area in the project window. You can adjust the division between the two by using the divider bar, the View⇨Zoom Editor In/Out command, or the Editor button in the toolbar.

All three configurations of the details list and editor pane are shown in Figure 6-3. On the left, only the details list is visible. On the right, only the editor pane is visible. In the center, both share the same area. The divider between them can be dragged to the top to fill the area with the editor pane, to the bottom to collapse and hide it, or anywhere in between. Double-clicking the divider alternately collapses the editor pane so it is completely hidden, or restores it to its previous location—which could be at the top, completely hiding the details list.

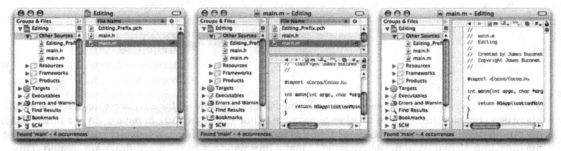

Figure 6-3

The Zoom Editor In/Out command (Command+Shift+E) is the complement to double-clicking the divider bar. Instead of alternately collapsing and restoring the details pane, it alternately expands or restores the editor pane. When the editor pane is hidden or shares the area with the detail window (left and center in Figure 6-3), the Zoom Editor In command expands the editor pane so that the details list is completely hidden. When the editor pane is expanded, the command changes to Zoom Editor Out and restores the previous position of the divider bar. The Editor button in the toolbar is equivalent to the Zoom Editor In/Out command in the menu.

Holding the Option key down turns the command into Zoom Editor In/Out Fully. When used in a multi-pane window like the project window, Zoom Editor In Fully collapses all other panes. This would be equivalent to expanding the editor, and then collapsing the Groups & Files list so only the editor pane is visible. Zoom Editor Out Fully runs the editor pane back down and re-expands the Groups & Files list. Using the All-In-One window style, this is a quick way of pushing everything else aside in order to see the code, and may be more efficient than opening the file in a separate window.

Normally, the division between the details list and the editor pane stays put until you change it. When the editor pane is collapsed, this requires two commands to edit the contents of a file. You must first select the file in a list, and then resize the divider or use the Zoom Editor In command before the editor pane is visible. As a convenience, Xcode includes the Automatically Open/Close Attached Editor option in the General pane of the Xcode Preferences. Checking this option causes the editor pane to automatically expand whenever a single source file is selected in the Groups & Files or details list.

Opening an editable file opens the file into the editor pane of the project window or a new editor window— which one you get is somewhat difficult to determine in advance. If Xcode has a project window open, Xcode may open the file in the editor pane of the project window. Otherwise, the file is opened in a new editor window. Opening any file that is already displayed in an Xcode window brings that window to the front.

Xcode can open a new window for every file, or restrict all files to a single separate editing window. This mode is only accessible through the toolbar Group/Ungrouped control, shown in Figure 6-4.

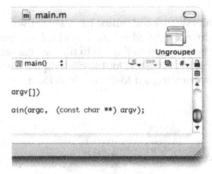

Figure 6-4

If the control shows as Ungrouped, opening a new file in a separate editor always creates a new window. There is no practical limit on the number of separate editor windows you can have open at a time. Clicking the button toggles the mode to Grouped. In this mode, opening a file in a separate editor simply changes the file being displayed in the active pane of that editor window. No new windows are created. This mode can be used to avoid window clutter. The setting of this mode does not affect any windows that have already been created. That is, changing from Ungrouped to Grouped does not close any windows. It merely prevents new windows from being created. In the Grouped mode, you can only open one new file at a time, and the Open in Separate Editor command is effectively useless.

Xcode opens files it is told to open. Open an Xcode file in the Finder and Xcode opens it. You can open any file that Xcode understands by dropping it on the Xcode application icon (see Figure 6-5), or by using the File⇨Open command. File⇨Open presents a standard open-file dialog box that allows you to choose one or more files to open. Although you can select multiple files in this dialog box, the side effect of some display rules, like the Grouped mode, can result in only one of the selected files being displayed in an editor pane.

Figure 6-5

The other command for opening a file is File⇨Open Quickly (Command+Shift+D). Enter the path of any file in the Open Quickly dialog box, shown in Figure 6-6, and Xcode opens that file. The path can consist of a complete Unix path or just the name of a file. If the latter, Xcode searches its recent file history, all of the folders in the active project that contain source files, and all of the folders listed in the Open Quickly pane of the Xcode Preferences. To open a file whose name is in a text file, first select the name of the file. Any selected text is placed in the Path field, providing quick access to header and other referenced source files.

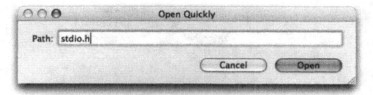

Figure 6-6

To make this even faster, the Skip Panel If Selection Is File Name option in the Open Quickly preferences bypasses the dialog box and immediately opens the file if the current selection is a valid file name.

Xcode has several editors and can also utilize other editor applications. Which editor is used when opening a file in Xcode is discussed at the end of this chapter in the "Using an External Editor" section.

Closing and Saving Editor Panes

Close any window using the File⇨Close (Command+W) command, or click the close button in the window's title bar. File⇨Close Project (Command+Control+W) closes the current project and all other windows that belong to that project. The File⇨Close File *filename* command closes all windows currently editing the current file and immediately prompts you to save any changes made to disk.

> **Hold down the Option key and click the close button of an independent editor window. This closes it and all other editor windows for that project, but not the project or any other type of window. This is really useful when you've been editing for a while and have dozens of editor windows piled up on the screen. The Option key does not modify the File⇨Close command, so you can't combine it with the keyboard shortcut.**

Because Xcode allows you to edit a source file in multiple windows simultaneously, there isn't a one-to-one correspondence between a window and a file. Unless you use the Close File command, closing a window does not necessarily force you to save the changes made to that file. Even closing all of the visible panes where a file was being edited does not force the changes to be written. The changes are held in memory until committed in response to another command. Files that have been modified but not yet saved appear grey in the project window. In Figure 6-7, the Manifest and SimpleJavaTool.java files have been edited but not saved.

The File⇨Save (Command+S) command immediately writes the changes made in the active editor pane to the file. The File⇨Save All (Command+Option+S) command presents a dialog box, like the one in Figure 6-8, that lists all of the unsaved files. Select the files to save and click the Save All or Save Selected button.

Some actions cause the Save All window to appear automatically. Closing a project forces you to save or abandon the changes made in all unsaved project files. You can configure the various Build commands in the Xcode Preferences to automatically save all unsaved files or prompt you for which ones to save before building.

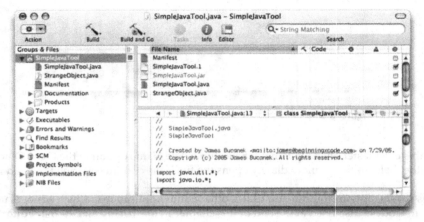

Figure 6-7

Figure 6-8

The Editor Pane

It's now time to take a detailed look at the Xcode editor pane, shown in Figure 6-9.

The editor pane has a number of controls and features. In the center, naturally, is the editor with the content of the file being edited. Across the top edge is the navigation bar, the various functions of which are explained later in the "Navigation" section. Across the right and bottom edges are the scroll bars and split pane controls. On the left edge is the gutter, explained later in the "Gutter" section. The line running down the right side of the main editing region is the page guide. Depending on your display preferences and the kind of file being edited, some of these features may not be visible. See the "Display Options" section to find out how to enable or disable them.

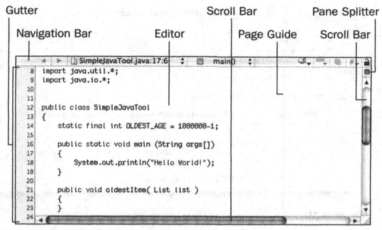

Figure 6-9

The active pane always has a blinking text cursor or a shaded text selection. You can change the color of the selection with the Highlight Color preference in the Appearance tab of the System Preferences.

> You might get the idea that the text insertion cursor and the current text selection mentioned throughout this book are separate concepts. In reality, they are usually equivalent. The blinking text cursor is logically a text selection of zero characters. Both indicate the current location in the file. There are times when the behavior of a command is different when the selection is empty (when the text cursor is visible). But unless stated explicitly to the contrary, if you read one assume it applies equally to the other.

Scroll Bars

The scroll bar controls are standard and shouldn't surprise anyone who has used a modern graphical user interface. Xcode enhances their basic behavior with a few extras.

Holding down the Option key when you click the arrow buttons scrolls the window a half screen's worth.

The editor is scroll-wheel aware, although a scroll-wheel is not an Xcode-specific feature. If your mouse, trackball, or trackpad has a scroll-wheel, the active editor pane will respond to it. I personally consider a multi-button trackball with a scroll-wheel an indispensable development tool.

The gutter, described in more detail later, indicates compiler errors and warning for the text that is visible in the window. Warnings and errors above or below the visible text are indicated as thin black (warning) or red (error) lines in the vertical scrollbar, as shown in Figure 6-10. This allows you to quickly scroll the window to reveal other warnings or errors in the file. If the Jump To Here option is selected in the system-wide Appearance settings for the scroll bar, clicking one of the bars jumps immediately to that point in the file.

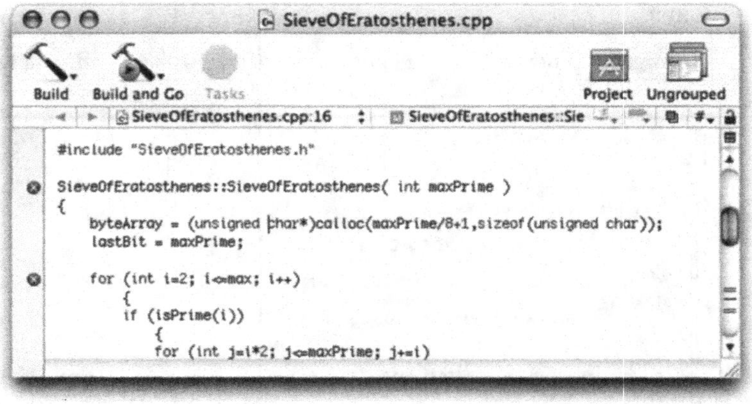

Figure 6-10

Split-Pane Editing

Above the scroll bar is the split pane button. Clicking it splits that editor pane into two independent panes, one above the other, separated by a divider bar, as shown in Figure 6-11.

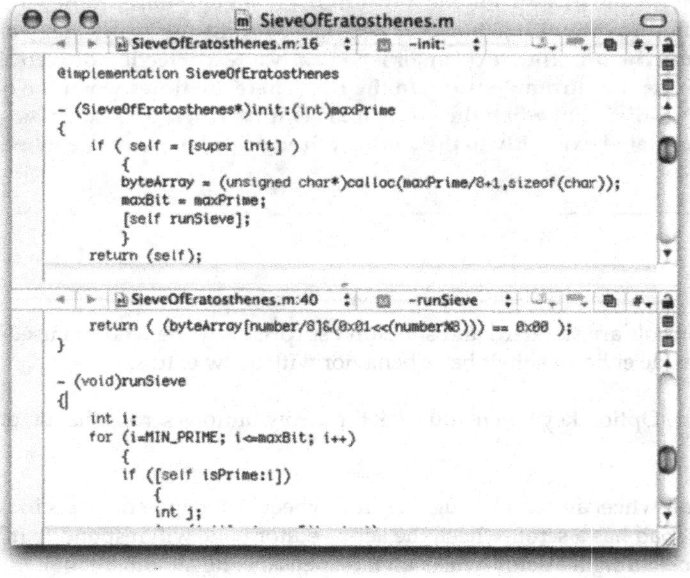

Figure 6-11

You can achieve the same effect using the View⇨Split *filename* Vertically command (Command+Shift+"), which splits the pane with the active text selection or cursor. Each new pane contains a split pane and a close pane button. The split pane button splits the pane again. The close pane button closes that pane; the adjacent pane assumes its space. The matching View⇨Close Split View command (Command+') accomplishes the same thing for the active editor pane.

Holding down the Option key splits the pane horizontally, as shown in Figure 6-12. This also works with the menu command, turning the Split *filename* Vertically command into the Split *filename* Horizontally command. However, choosing to split a pane horizontally or vertically only works for the first pane. After a pane is split horizontally, all subsequent splits are horizontal regardless of whether you select a horizontal or vertical split. The same is true of an initial vertical split. (This is considered a bug by the Xcode development team and may be fixed in a future version.)

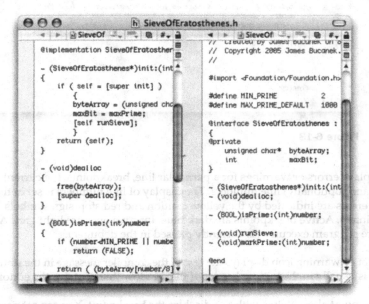

Figure 6-12

Unlike the pane divider between the editor pane and the details list, the divider between editing panes does not respond to a double-click. However, it is possible to drag the divider all the way to one edge if you want to hide a pane from view. Drag it back out to the middle again, or close the visible pane, to reveal the hidden pane.

The panes that result from a split are truly independent editing environments. The "Navigation" section will explain how to switch from one file to another in the same pane. You can do this with split panes, which allows you to edit two or more different files in a single editor window. Notice back in Figure 6-12 that the left pane is displaying the SieveOfEratosthenes.m file and the right pane is editing its companion .h file.

Gutter

The gutter is the shaded bar running down the left edge of the editor pane. If it is not visible, you can enable it by selecting Show Gutter in the Text Editing pane of the Xcode Preferences. The gutter, shown in Figure 6-13, can display a variety of annotations associated with specific lines of a file.

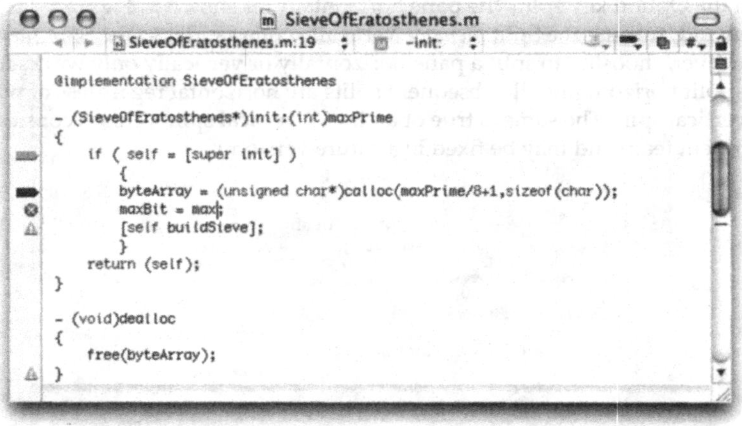

Figure 6-13

The gutter displays errors or warnings for a particular line, breakpoints, the current execution location of the debugger, and (optionally) line numbers. The display of line numbers is set in the Xcode Preferences. Warnings and errors are indicated by the yellow caution and red stop-sign symbols. Breakpoints show up as wide pointers. Active breakpoints are dark blue. Inactive ones are light grey. A large red arrow indicates where program execution is currently paused in the debugger.

Clicking an error or warning icon displays the text of the compiler message in the status bar of the window. The status bar is usually in the bottom border of the window that contains the editor pane.

Clicking a breakpoint alternately enables or disables the breakpoint. You can set new breakpoints by clicking anywhere in the background of the gutter. Breakpoints can only be set in file types that Xcode recognizes as program source (C, C++, Objective-C, Java, AppleScript, and so on). You cannot set a breakpoint in a property list or other types of non-program text files. You can relocate breakpoints to another line by dragging them there, or delete them by dragging them out of the gutter. You can also use the Control-/right-click contextual pop-up menu on a breakpoint, or anywhere else in the gutter, to add, remove, edit, or review breakpoints. Double-clicking a breakpoint opens the Breakpoints window. See Chapter 15 for more about breakpoints.

Navigation Bar

The navigation bar, shown in Figure 6-14, occupies the top edge of the editor pane and contains several status and navigation controls. You can hide the navigation bar of the active editor pane with the View➪Hide Navigation Bar command, and reveal it again with View➪Show Navigation Bar.

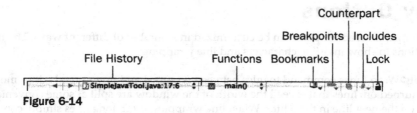
Figure 6-14

The following table lists the functions of the navigation bar controls.

Control	Function
File History	Jumps to a file that has been edited in this pane.
Functions	Jumps to a function, definition, or marker in the file.
Bookmarks	Jumps to a bookmark set in the file.
Breakpoints	Jumps to a breakpoint set in the file.
Counterpart	Jumps to the counterpart of this file.
Includes	Jumps to a file included by this file.
Lock	Locks or unlocks the file.

The Lock button toggles the lock (read-only) attribute of the file. If you lock a file, or the file was locked when it was opened, the editor will be in display-only mode. If you attempt to change the document, Xcode warns you that you cannot edit the file. You can override this mode in the dialog box and make changes to the document, but that does not change the permissions of the file and you will not be able to save changes until the file is made writable. Unlocking a file automatically switches the editor to its normal editing mode. See the option Save Files As Writeable in the "Display Options" section of this chapter.

All of the other navigation controls are explained in the "Navigation" section, later in this chapter.

Status and Toolbars

Although they are not part of the editor pane, a status bar and toolbar can be found in most windows that contain one. The description of an error or warning in the gutter appears in that window's status bar, and the Group/Ungrouped toolbar button can control if new editor windows are created. In most windows, you can control the visibility of the status bar with the Show Status Bar and Hide Status Bar commands found in the View menu.

> Hiding or showing the status bar sets the default for all new windows. Although these commands only hide or show the status bar for a single window, using either command sets the default for all new windows. So if you want to hide the status bar of one window, but want all new windows to have a status bar, you must open a new window and show its status bar. All subsequent windows will also have a status bar.

Display Options

The appearance of an editor pane can be customized in a number of different ways. The most immediate are the options to show invisible characters and line wrapping.

The Format➪Wrap Lines command toggles between wrapped and unwrapped editor modes. With line wrapping turned on, lines that exceed the width of the window are split at some convenient point and continued on the next line in the editor. When line wrapping is off, long lines simply continue off the right edge of the editor pane. If one or more lines exceed the width of the editor, a horizontal scroll bar appears at the bottom of the pane.

Control characters and the space character are normally invisible. Two more commands in the Format menu, Show Control Characters (Command+Shift+6) and Show Spaces, make those characters visible. Show Control Characters is particularly useful for finding gremlins, or illegal control characters in a source file. Normally, the only control characters allowed in a source file are the tab and line delimiters. Show Spaces marks the location of each ASCII space character with a diamond. Select either command again to toggle them back off. Tab and line delimiter characters are never visible.

The font and size of the text used for all editor panes are set in the Fonts & Colors tab of the Xcode Preferences, as shown in Figure 6-15. Click the Set Font button next to the Editor Font field to change the font or size of text.

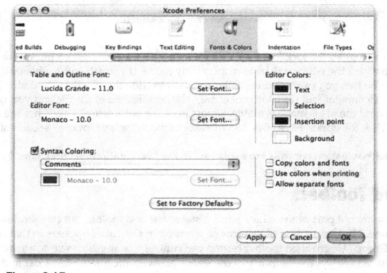

Figure 6-15

A font selection palette appears. Only the font face and size can be configured. Font styles and decorations, such as the text color or underline, are ignored in the font palette. To change the color of the editor's font, click the Text color well under the Editor Colors group. A color picker palette appears where you can choose a new color. You can also alter the color of the selected text, the text insertion cursor, and the background color. The color wells accept drops from other color sources. This includes other color wells and the palette of saved colors in the color picker.

You can also colorize language-specific elements of the text with the Syntax Coloring feature, which is described in detail in the "Syntax Coloring" section later in this chapter.

Several global settings control the appearance of editor panes for all windows. These are in the Text Editing tab of the Xcode Preferences (see Figure 6-16).

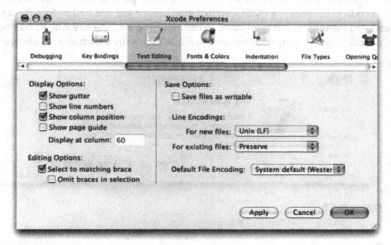

Figure 6-16

Show Gutter enables the display of the gutter in regular editor panes. Without the gutter, you cannot see or set breakpoints or find where the execution of the application is currently paused. Because of this, the gutter is automatically displayed whenever you start a debugging session, and is hidden again when the debugging session ends. The editor pane in the Debugger window always shows a gutter.

Show Line Numbers displays the number of each line in the gutter. The Show Gutter option must be enabled for line numbers to be displayed.

Show Column Position adds a column number to the file name of the current file in the history control of the navigation bar. The navigation bar must be visible for this option to have any effect. When this option is enabled, the name of the current file indicates both by the line and column number of the current insertion point or the beginning of the text selection. If the option is disabled, only the file's name and line number are displayed.

Turning on the Show Page Guide option causes a vertical line to be drawn at the column number specified in the Display at Column field. To the right of the guide line, the background color of the editor pane will be made slightly darker. If you have selected a background color other than white, the difference may be imperceptible. Some coding styles require all program text to fit within a certain number of columns. If you are adhering to such a coding style, or are formatting text for a fixed-width output device, the page guide will help you. Note that the page guide is based on the em-width of the font (traditionally, the width of a capital *M*) and is only accurate when you're using fixed-width fonts.

The Editing Options include a Select to Matching Brace option. This singular feature is most useful for C and Java programmers. When this option is enabled, double-clicking an opening or closing brace selects the entire block of text from that point to its matching brace. The Omit Braces in Selection option refines this feature by determining if the text selected will include just the text between the braces or the block and the braces.

The Save Options are an eclectic set of options that deal with file permissions and line endings. The Save Files as Writable option causes Xcode to set the POSIX write permission of a file when it is saved. With this option off, Xcode preserves the POSIX write permissions the file had before it was saved. That is, if the file was read-only it will be left read-only. When opening a read-only file, Xcode puts the editor pane in display-only mode. Any attempt to change the file is met with a warning, as shown in Figure 6-17.

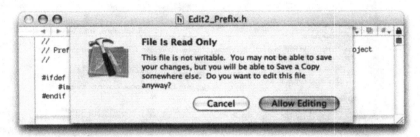

Figure 6-17

Clicking the Allow Editing button puts the editor pane in its normal editing mode, but it does not change the permissions of the underlying file. In this state, Xcode will refuse to save the file from the Save All window. However, you can save the file by using the File⇨Save command directly or by starting a Build with the Always Save option selected. Xcode temporary makes the file writable, write the changes, and then restore the read-only permissions of the file. The editor pane remains editable.

Set the Save Files as Writable option and Xcode will *not* restore the read-only permissions after a save, leaving the file writable. After the save, the file will behave like any other writable file.

This behavior applies to the POSIX write permissions for the file. The other method of making a file unwritable is to set its POSIX immutable flag. (On an HFS file system, this flag is synonymous with the HFS locked attribute.) You can set or clear this flag by using the Lock button in the navigation bar, or in the Get Info window for the file in the Finder. The POSIX immutable flag is never overwritten by Xcode, making it a more secure method of preventing changes to a file than merely denying write permission. A locked file behaves the same as a file that lacks write privileges, except that File⇨Save does not change the status of the immutable flag or write to the file. Instead, Xcode displays a simple error dialog box explaining that it cannot write to the file. To make changes to the file, you must first click the Lock control in the navigation bar to unlock the file.

The remaining options in the Text Editing tab deal with line endings and character encoding. Under Line Encodings, the For New Files option determines the line endings for files created in Xcode. The choices are to end each line with a single LF character (Mac OS X or Unix format), a single CR (Mac OS 9 and earlier format), or a CR+LF sequence (Microsoft DOS format). Unless you have some specific reason to use CR or CRLF line endings, all text files should be written using LF. The For Existing Files option determines the line encoding for files that are saved in Xcode. If this option is set to something other than Preserve, any file saved in Xcode will have its line encoding automatically converted into the selected format. The Preserve setting saves the file in whatever line encoding format it had when it was opened.

Use the Default File Encoding option to choose the character encoding that will be used for any file where Xcode does not know its character encoding. This applies to existing text files being added to a project, or any text file opened in Xcode that does not belong to an open project. If an open project contains a source file item that references the file being opened, the character encoding recorded in that source item is used.

Navigation Within a File

You'll probably spend more time moving around in your source code than you'll spend writing it. Programming just isn't a linear activity. One rarely sits down and types out a function of any consequence from start to finish. Knowing how to move around your source code quickly and decisively will greatly enhance your editing efficacy.

Cursor Movement

Let's start with just moving around in a single source file. First, the following table lists the key combinations that simply move the cursor around in the text.

> All of the key combinations in this chapter are based on the key binding set named "Xcode Defaults." This is the default set when Xcode is installed. Key bindings — the mapping of key combinations to actions — are extremely flexible and can be customized extensively. Xcode includes key binding sets that approximate the key combinations used in BBEdit, Metrowerks' CodeWarrior, and the venerable MPW system. You are also free to devise your own key binding sets. See Chapter 19 for a complete description of key bindings and how to alter them. If you have changed the key bindings in Xcode Preferences, you may want to set them back to the Xcode Default set while working through this chapter.

Key Combination	Cursor Movement
Right arrow, Control+F	Next character
Command+right arrow, Control+E	End of line
Option+right arrow	End of next word
Control+right arrow	End of next subword
Left arrow, Control+B	Previous character
Command+left arrow, Control+A	Beginning of line
Option+left arrow	Beginning of previous word
Control+left arrow	Beginning of previous subword
Up arrow, Control+P	One line up

Table continued on following page

Key Combination	Cursor Movement
Command+up arrow	Beginning of document
Option+up arrow	Previous beginning of line
Down arrow, Control+N	One line down
Command+down arrow	End of document
Option+down arrow	Next end of line
Option+Page Up	One page up
Option+Page Down	One page down

When you move the cursor vertically, Xcode tries to maintain the column position of the cursor. Until you move the cursor in some other direction, moving up and down positions the cursor as close to the column position that it was originally at when you first begin to move.

The word movement combinations allow you to quickly move to the beginning or end of symbol names. A word in Xcode is a run of letters, numbers, or the underscore character. A subword is a capital letter followed by a run of lowercase letters, a run of numbers, a run of uppercase letters, or a run of underscore characters between subwords. Leading and trailing underscore character do not count as subwords. Take the following source code as an example:

```
return [NSString stringWithUTF8String:extractUniString(buffer,128L)];
```

The words in this statement are: `return`, `NSString`, `stringWithUTF8String`, `extractUniString`, `buffer`, and `128L`.

The subwords in the statement are: `return`, `NS`, `String`, `string`, `With`, `UTF`, `8`, `String`, `extract`, `Uni`, `String`, `buffer`, `128`, and `L`.

If the correct name of the function was `extractUnicodeString`, not `extractUniString`, and the cursor was positioned at the beginning of the method name `stringWithUTF8String`, pressing Option+right arrow followed by pressing Control+right arrow twice would position the cursor between `Uni` and `String`. Type **code** to correct the function name.

Emacs

You may have noticed a few odd synonyms for some of the cursor movements, like Control+P to move up one line, or Control-E to move to the end of the line. Xcode key bindings emulate a number of the standard Emacs editor commands. If you're used to using Emacs, you will want to explore the key bindings in the Xcode Preferences to see what Emacs control sequences are supported. This book doesn't go into all of the Emacs commands that are supported by Xcode, but the following table provides a couple of examples.

Key Combination	Action
Control+Space	Set the mark from the current position
Control+X Control+X	Swap the current position with the mark

Emacs maintains the concept of a "mark" which is simply a saved location in the file, much like a bookmark. You can set the mark by pressing Control+spacebar. You can also "swap" the mark with the current cursor position or selection by pressing Control+X Control+X (that's Control+X twice in a row). The current cursor position or selection becomes the new mark, and the cursor position or selection is moved to the previous mark. This can be very handy when copying and pasting between two different sections of the same file.

Scrolling

Besides the scroll bar controls, there are also key combinations that scroll the text without changing the current cursor position or selection, as listed in the following table.

Key Combination	Scroll Movement
Page Up, Control+up arrow	One page up
Page Down, Control+down arrow	One page down
Home	To beginning of document
Command+Home	One line up
End	To end of document
Command+End	One line down
Command+J	Jump to Selection

These can often result in scrolling the text so that the current cursor position is no longer visible. Every cursor movement includes an implied request to scroll the window so that the new cursor position is visible. To scroll the window so that the current cursor or selection is visible again, use the Find⇨Jump to Selection (Command+J) command.

Jumping

The navigation bar provides several tools for quickly navigating to locations within the current file, as noted in Figure 6-18.

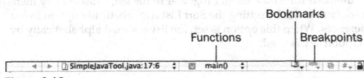

Figure 6-18

All of these controls are drop-down menus. Select an item in the menu and the cursor moves immediately to that location in the file. There are also keyboard shortcuts for the menus, as listed in the following table. Using one of the shortcuts drops the menu down. You can then navigate the menu with the up and down arrows or by typing the first few letters of the desired item. Press Return when the desired item is highlighted. Press Esc to dismiss the menu.

Keyboard Shortcut	Navigation Control
Control+2, Control+Option+2	Functions
Control+4	Bookmarks
Contorl+5	Breakpoints

Functions

The functions menu, shown in Figure 6-19, parses the definitions in the source file and dynamically builds a list of functions, classes, methods, types, and defines. This is one of the "syntax aware" editing features of Xcode and is only functional when you're editing file types that Xcode recognizes as being program source files.

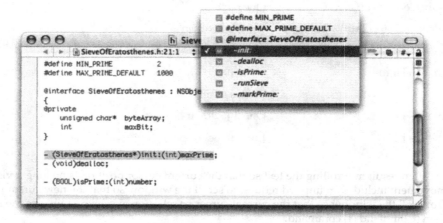

Figure 6-19

Normally, the menu is in the order that the declarations appear in the file. To sort the items in alphabetical order, hold down the Option key when clicking the menu or using the keyboard shortcut. Method names in Java and Objective-C classes are sorted as though their names were fully qualified (for example, MyReader::isEOF), so all of the methods for a class cluster together in the list, subsorted by method name. You can choose to switch the default order by setting the Sort List Alphabetically option in the Code Sense pane of the Xcode Preferences. When this option is set, the list is sorted alphabetically by default and in file order when the Option key is used.

The functions menu can also optionally include declarations as well as definitions. A declaration is a function prototype or method prototype in a class definition. Declarations are displayed in italics. With declarations enabled, the code in Figure 6-20 causes three entries to be added to the functions menu.

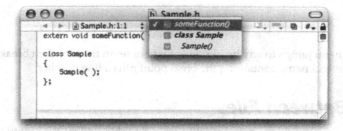

Figure 6-20

With declarations turned off, the functions menu would only include the Sample class.

The functions menu also includes any #pragma mark statements in the source code, which lets you customize the menu by adding categories or dividers in C and C-like source files. To add a divider, put a #pragma mark – line in the source file. Figure 6-21 show a source file with three mark statements.

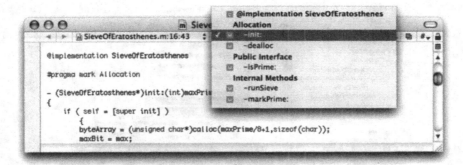

Figure 6-21

Finally, the function menu acts as a location indicator. Whenever the cursor or selection is in a definition or the body of a class, function, or method, the menu indicates the name of the current location. When the menu is popped open, the current location is indicated with a check mark. If the cursor position is not within any definition, the message "<No Selected Symbol>" is displayed.

Bookmarks

The bookmarks menu lists all of the bookmarks set in the file. It does not list bookmarks set in other files. Use the bookmarks window or the Bookmarks smart group in the project window to see those. Bookmarks are always listed in the order they appear in the file.

To set a bookmark, position the cursor or make a selection and choose the Add to Bookmarks (Command+D) command in the Find menu or from the Control-/right-click contextual pop-up menu. The selected text appears as the default name for the new bookmark. Edit the name of the bookmark as you see fit. Bookmarks are stored in the project document and cannot be set in files that do not belong to an open project.

Breakpoints

The breakpoints menu jumps to any breakpoints that are set in the file. Each breakpoint is displayed as the function or method name containing the breakpoint plus a line number.

Navigation Between Files

Just as important as being able to move quickly around within a file is the ability to move quickly between files. You've already seen how to open and browse file from the project window, but Xcode provides a variety of other ways to switch directly from one file to another.

File History

The file history menu in the navigation bar contains a list of the files that have been displayed in that editor pane, as shown in Figure 6-22. Select a file from the list and the pane switches to that file. The keyboard shortcut for the file history menu is Control+1.

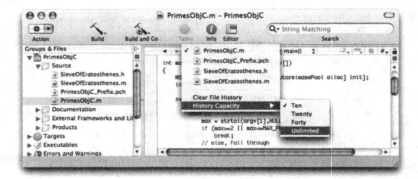

Figure 6-22

File history is maintained individually for each editor pane. Even multiple panes within the same window have their own history. For the editor pane in the project window, or when you're using the Grouped window mode, this can be quite a long list. For separate editor windows, it tends to be just the file that is being edited. All new panes have an empty history, and closing a pane discards the history for that pane. The only exception is when Xcode saves the state of a window in the project document. It always does this for the project window, and it saves the state of other open windows if the Save Window State option in the General preferences is set. Thus, the history of the project window's editor pane is always preserved and possibly the state of all open editor windows.

To limit (or not) how much file history is retained, the file history menu has two special items, as previously shown in Figure 6-22. The Clear File History item, or the View⇨Clear File History command, does just that. It forgets all previously visited files except the current one. The History Capacity item can limit the number of files in the list. The capacity defaults to Unlimited. For most editor panes, this isn't an issue because they rarely get past two. For editor panes, like the ones in the project window that are constantly being reused, you may want to limit the size of the history. Like the history itself, this setting is stored separately for each individual editor pane and is saved with the rest of the window's state.

The two buttons to the left of the file history menu move through the history list, like the previous and next buttons in a browser. The history menu lists each file in alphabetical order. But the history buttons are really a browser-like history of the files that have been visited, in the order that they were visited. Pressing the Previous button takes you to the file previously visited, not the file above the current one in the menu. Like the menu, files never occur more than once in the history. Visiting a file more than once only keeps its most recent visit in the list. The history and the menu are both limited to the number of items set in the History Capacity menu.

Aggregate History

Hold down the Option key when popping up the file history menu to see the aggregate file history. The aggregate file history is a combined list of the history items from every open window. This includes history items from the help window and any other open projects. Be careful about using the feature too liberally with multiple projects. You can easily open the project window for project A and switch to a source file that belongs to project B. This could be very confusing.

Adding an Arbitrary File to the History

Xcode windowing options tend to either open all files in a single editor pane, or every file in a separate window. Consequently, the file history consists of every file you've ever visited or just the file opened in that window. But there are some times when you'd like to work with a select number of files in a single, separate, editor window. There are two ways of accomplishing this.

The first method is to use the aggregate history menu to switch to a file that has been visited in some other editor pane. This is the simplest way of adopting a file that is, or has been, opened elsewhere.

The second method is to simply drag a file and drop it directly into the navigation bar, as shown in Figure 6-23. This switches the editor pane to that file and adds it to its history.

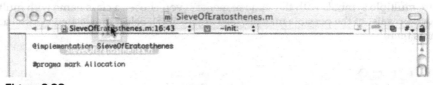

Figure 6-23

The source of the drag can be a source item in the project window, a file from the Finder, or the file icon in the title bar of a document window. This technique can only be used to add one file at a time.

Included Files

The included files menu is another syntax-aware feature for C and C-like language files. The menu adds an item for each #include statement that it finds. Selecting an item from the list, as shown in Figure 6-24, opens that file. Unlike the file history menu, you can open it in the same pane or a new window, just as if you had used the FileÍOpen command. The keyboard shortcut is Control+3.

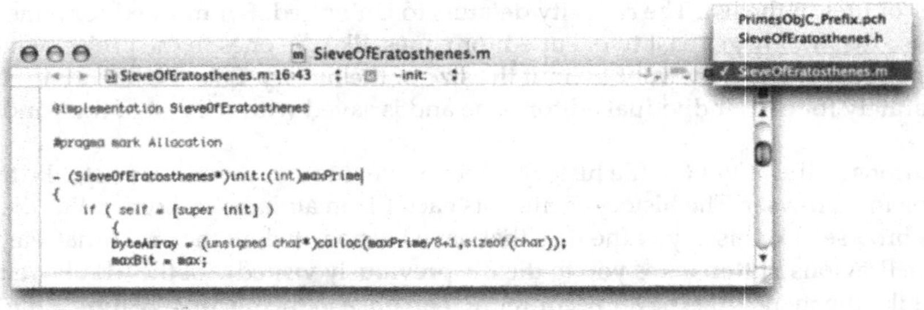

Figure 6-24

Switching to the Header or Source File

The convention for C, C++, and Objective-C languages is to place the declarations for functions and data types in a header file with a .h or .hpp file name extension, and write the implementation of those functions in a source file of the same name. If you use this convention, Xcode can help you quickly jump back and forth between the two using the View➪Switch to Header/Source File (Command+Option+up arrow) command. Your editor focus switches immediately to the companion header or source file, opening a new editing window if appropriate for your layout style.

Jumping to the Definition

One of the most useful navigation tools in Xcode is the Find➪Jump to Definition command. This command doesn't have a keyboard combination. To access it quickly, double-click a word in a source file while holding down the Command key.

Jump to Definition uses the syntax-aware symbols table to index all of the class, function, type, and constant names that are defined in your project. Command+double-clicking a word, or selecting a symbol name and choosing Find➪Jump to Definition, immediately jumps to the implementation of that function or method, or to the definition of that class, type, or constant. If the current selection *is* the function or method implementation, it jumps to the declaration of that function or method.

If there are multiple symbols with the same name, or if you choose a class name with multiple methods, Xcode pops up a list of the possible matches (see Figure 6-25). Select the desired symbol and the editor pane jumps there.

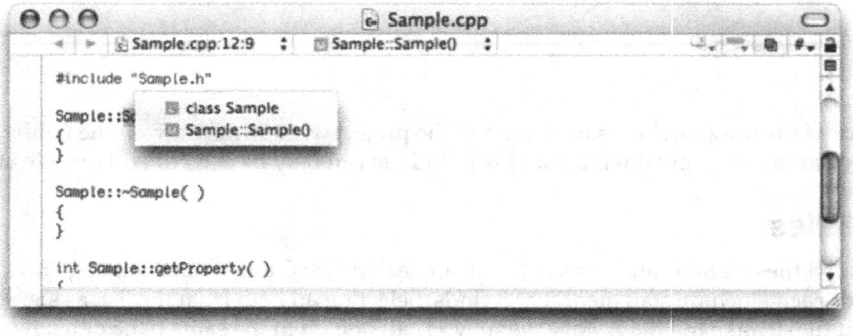

Figure 6-25

The database of symbols for a project is built by Code Sense. Code Sense indexing must be enabled for this feature to work.

Editing

All of the standard text selection and editing features supplied by the operating system's text editing framework work in Xcode. If you need a refresher on the basics, refer to the Mac OS X Help. The following sections highlight a few obscure features that are particularly useful when editing source code. In addition, Xcode adds its own set of features and commands.

Selecting Text

All of the standard text selection gestures work in Xcode. Click and drag to select some text. Hold down the Shift key to extend a selection. Selecting text by dragging is dependent on timing. See the "Drag and Drop" section later for an explanation.

While extending a text selection you may not have noticed that the editor is sensitive to word boundaries. When you simply click and drag, you create a selection exactly from the character closest to the starting location and that of the ending location. When you Shift-click to extend a selection, Xcode examines the other end of the selection (the end not being moved). If that end lies on a word edge, then the extended end includes the entire word under the cursor. If the stationary end is in the middle of a word or between non-word characters, then the extended end can be positioned at any character. This makes it very easy to extend a selection to include a whole word, because you don't have to select the edge of the word; clicking anywhere in the word will suffice.

Selecting Columns

One of the more obscure features of the editor is the ability to select columns of text. You can select all of the characters between two column positions across multiple lines by holding down the Option key and dragging out a selection. Figure 6-26 shows a column selection. Hold down the Shift and Option keys to extend or contract an existing column selection.

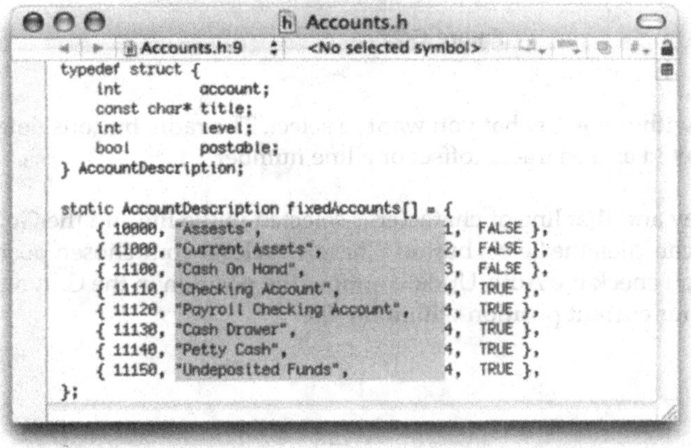

Figure 6-26

You can copy the selected characters to the clipboard or delete them. If you copy the selection, the clipboard will contain the selected characters of each line on separate lines. Lines that have no characters selected (lines shorter than the first column) are not included. You cannot, however, paste into a column or otherwise replace a column with multi-line content.

Selecting Blocks

The Balance command on the Format or Control-/right-click pop-up menu selects the contents of a C or Java style block, expression, or string. The command looks outward from the current selection to find the nearest block delimiter. Block delimiters include the brace, parentheses, bracket, single quote, and double-quote characters. After it determines what kind of block it is in, the command finds the matching character at the other end of the block and selects everything in between. It will correctly account for escaped quote characters and nested blocks.

When you choose the Select to Matching Brace option in the Text Editing pane of the Xcode Preferences, double-clicking a brace, bracket, parentheses, or quote character invokes the Balance command. The Omit Braces in Selection option determines whether the selection includes the matching delimiters, or just the text between them. Oddly, the setting of the Omit Braces option applies to the Format⇨Balance command regardless of whether the double-click shortcut is enabled or not. If you need to change the brace selection behavior, but have the double-click feature disabled, you need to enable it to change the setting. Ignore the fact that these options are worded towards the brace character. Both options apply to any of the matching block delimiters used in C and Java.

Selecting a Line or Character

The Find⇨Go To Line (Command+L) command lets you jump to a specific line or character position in a text file. Selecting the command opens the Goto window, as shown in Figure 6-27.

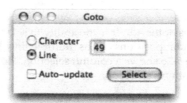

Figure 6-27

Enter the position within the file that you want to select. The radio buttons determine whether the position will be interpreted as a character offset or a line number.

Press the Return key and that line or character is selected in the file and the Go To window closes. Alternatively, you can click the Select button. This also selects your chosen position, but leaves the Goto window open. If you check the Auto-Update option, the position in the Goto window will continuously update to reflect your current position within the file.

Deleting Text

The text editor provides several useful variations when you're deleting text adjacent to the insertion point, as listed in the following table.

Key Combination	Deletes
Delete, Control+H	One character to the left of the cursor
Option+Delete	From the cursor to the beginning of the previous word
Control+Delete	From the cursor to the beginning of the previous subword
Delete-right, Control+D	One character to the right of the cursor
Option+delete-right	From the cursor to the end of the next word
Control+delete-right	From the cursor to the end of the next subword
Control+W	From the cursor to the current mark

The Delete key, just above the Return key (sometimes labeled ⌫), deletes to the left. The delete-right key (⌦) is typically found on extended keyboards near the Home and End keys, deletes to the right. Either can delete a single character, by word or by subword.

Control+H and Control+D are Emacs synonyms for Delete and delete-right, if you prefer using those or don't have a delete-right key on your keyboard. These control key equivalents cannot be combined with the Option or the Control key modifiers. The Emacs-centric Control+W command deletes from the current cursor location to the location of the mark, previously set with Control-spacebar or Control+X Control+X.

Drag and Drop

A text selection can be dragged around within a document, between documents, and between Xcode and other application.

A text selection and a text drag use the same gesture: click, move, and release. The difference is in the timing. To drag out a new text selection, press the mouse button and move the mouse immediately. The cursor remains a text cursor. To start a drag, press down the mouse button and wait. After a very short delay (less than a second) the cursor turns into an arrow. You are now dragging the text selection. You can customize this delay to suit your mousing speed. See the discussion of the NSDragAndDropTextDelay expert setting in Chapter 19.

Press down the Option key before dropping the text to make a copy. Dragging between documents always performs a copy. Dragging from other applications inserts the text equivalent of the object being dragged. Dragging file icons from the Finder or the project window inserts the URL of the file, not the contents of the file itself. To insert the contents of a file, open that file in Xcode, choose Edit➪Select All, and drag the text into your document.

Most lists, displays, and fields in Xcode can be the source of a drag even when they are not editable. How useful this is will vary, but keep it in mind before you reach for a yellow pad to write something down. You might be able to simply drag it somewhere to keep it. Drag any text selection to the desktop or an open Finder window to create a clipping file containing that text. This is a very handy way of saving or "setting aside" a chunk of code while you experiment.

Font and Text Styles

Use Xcode's plain text editor to edit source code. Plain text files do not store any font, style, color, or other typographic information. Logically then, the commands and tools in the View⇨Font and View⇨Text menus are inapplicable. The font and style used for the text is set globally, as explained earlier in the "Display Options" section.

When you use Xcode's RTF (styled text) editor, the commands in these menus perform as expected.

Saving Files

All editor panes, except for ones just created with the File⇨New Empty File command, are associated with a physical file. Editing only changes the copy of the text held in memory. A file is not actually altered until the editor pane is saved, which writes those changes back to the file. There are several variations of the Save command in Xcode, as listed in the following table.

Command	Action
Save (Command+S)	Writes the contents of the editor pane to its file.
Save As... (Command+Shift+S)	Allows you to create a new file and writes the text to that new file. The new file becomes the file associated with that pane. If the original file was referenced from a project, the path and name of that source item is also updated to reference the new file. The original file is not altered, and the project no longer has a reference to it. Use this command to rename a file while preserving a copy of the original.
Save a Copy As (Command +Shift+Option+S)	Like Save As, this command allows you to choose a new file, write the contents of the editor pane to it, and leave the contents of the original file untouched. But that's where it stops. The file associated with the editor pane is not changed, and it still refers to the original file. A subsequent Save command writes any changes to the original file. Nothing in the project is altered. This command is useful for making a snapshot of a file, or for quickly creating a new file that is a copy of an existing one without altering the project.
Save All (Command+Option+S)	This command presents a dialog box that lists all modified file buffers being held in memory. You can choose to save all, or only some, of them in a single command. The Save All dialog box was described earlier in this chapter in the "Closing and Saving Editor Panes" section.

The Revert to Saved (Command+U) command is the opposite of the various Save commands. Instead of writing the changes to the file, it discards any changes made since the file was opened or saved and re-reads the text from the file. Xcode presents a warning beforehand, shown in Figure 6-28, ensuring that you really do want to abandon all the changes you've recently made. You cannot recover these changes once the Revert to Saved command has executed.

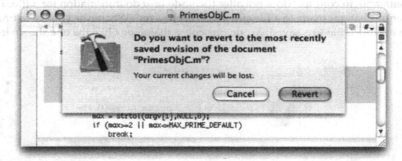

Figure 6-28

Undo

Although you can discard all of the changes made to a file with the Revert to Saved command, you would rarely want to do this. The Undo facility provides fine-grained control for reversing changes made to a file. Xcode provides multi-level undo and redo of actions taken in any editor pane. The undo history extends beyond the point that the file was last saved.

Undo history is maintained on a per-file basis. That means that closing an editor pane, even closing a project, does not discard the undo history for a file, and all editing panes showing the same file share the same undo history. Quitting Xcode is about the only way to forget a file's undo history, which is good because you usually need the undo when you've made a mistake. Being able to undo a change in a file hours later can be extremely useful.

Each atomic editing action is recorded as a step in the undo history. An "atomic" action would be typing some sequence of regular text characters, navigation, auto-completion, using the Tab key, deleting text, cutting, pasting, or any other menu command that changes the contents of the text buffer.

The Edit⇨Undo command reverses the effect of the most recent action recorded in the history. The original action is then remembered on the redo list. As you repeatedly use the Undo command, each change made to the file is undone, depleting the undo history and adding to the redo list.

> Undoing a Cut or Copy command does not restore the previous contents of the system's clipboard. It only restores the state of the editor pane prior to the Cut command.

The Redo command performs the complement of the Undo command. It takes the most recent action moved to the redo list, performs it again, and adds it back to the undo history. Together, the Undo and Redo commands are like a time machine, allowing you to step forwards and backwards through the history of the file's changes until you find the state of the file you want.

Any new change made to a file erases the redo list. If you go back in time and make a different choice, you can no longer visit the future that contained the original choice. The Revert to Saved command empties both the undo and redo information for a file.

The Save command, in contrast, does not alter the undo or redo information for a file. This means it is possible to undo changes made to a file *after* it has been saved. Whenever you try to undo the last action that occurred before a file was saved, Xcode presents a dialog box like the one shown in Figure 6-29.

Figure 6-29

Try It Out   **Undo and Redo**

Create a new document file using the File⇨New Empty File command. Use the File⇨Save command to save the empty file to disk. Save it to the Desktop, and give it any name you like. Then follow these steps:

1.   Type the text **Line 1**. Press Command+] to indent it once to the right.

2.   Press Return and type the text **Line 2**. Press Command+S to save the file to disk.

3.   Press Return and type the text **Line 3**.

4.   Choose Edit⇨Undo, or press Command+Z.

5.   Choose Edit⇨Undo, or press Command+Z, again. This displays a dialog box warning that you are about to undo past the point the file was last saved. Click the Undo Button.

6.   Choose Edit⇨Undo again.

7.   Choose Edit⇨Redo.

8.   Press Return and type the text **Line 4**. Check the availability of the Redo command in the Edit menu.

9.   Choose File⇨Revert to Saved and click the Revert button. Check the availability of the Undo and Redo commands in the Edit menu.

How It Works

You created a new file and performed several edit operations, saved the file, and then made one additional change. After step 3, the file should have looked like Figure 6-30.

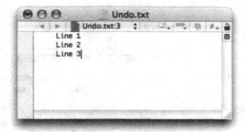

Figure 6-30

The first Undo command in step 4 simply reversed the last change. The next Undo reversed a change that occurred before the file was last saved, and presented a dialog box explaining that.

The command in steps 6 and 7 undid one more change, and then put it back again.

Making a new change in the file flushed the redo list. After you make a change, actions that have been undone can no longer be applied.

Reverting to the version of the file saved in step 2 restored the file to where it was then, and also cleared both the undo and the redo history.

Syntax-Aware Editing

Xcode provides editing aids that are "syntax aware." Simply put, the editor understands the basic syntax of the language you are programming in. It understands languages from ADA to XML. It uses this knowledge to highlight statements within your source and automatically indent lines for a consistent visual structure. Xcode looks up variable, class, function, and other symbols names and inserts them for you. It can also insert templates for constructors, comments, and commonly used control structures.

You've already encountered a few syntax-aware features. The Balance command, which will find a matching brace or parentheses, must understand the block structure, string format, comment syntax and other details of the programming language.

Syntax Coloring

The most passive of the syntax-aware editing features is syntax coloring. It uses a basic knowledge of a language's syntax to colorize the text of source code so that comments, literals, and language keywords are displayed in different colors. The intent is to make it easier to read the code by highlighting the function of elements in the source.

The colors that syntax coloring uses, or whether syntax coloring is done at all, is controlled in the Fonts & Colors tab of the Xcode Preferences, shown in Figure 6-31.

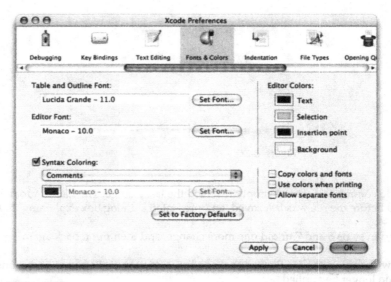

Figure 6-31

The check box next to Syntax Coloring enables syntax coloring (by default) in all source files. Below that is a pop-up menu of the various types of source code elements that can be colored. Below that is the currently chosen color, and optionally a font, for that element. The categories of elements are fixed and the same for all languages. The following table describes these elements. (Some elements don't apply to all languages.)

Code Element	Description
Comments	Comments in the source code. For C, Java, and similar languages this means text enclosed by /* and */ character sequences, and the text following a //. For property lists and shell scripts, comments are lines that begin with #. AppleScript denotes comments between pairs of (* and *) and after --.
Documentation Comments	Java's JavaDoc and Darwin's HeaderDoc tools scan source code files and generate documentation for a program or library. Both rely on specially formatted comments that begin with /** or /*! and contain annotations and keywords. The comments, along with the comment delimiters, are colored using this setting.
Documentation Comments Keywords	JavaDoc and HeaderDoc comments can also include any number of keywords that identify the different parts of the comment. For instance, the @param keyword is used to document a single parameter of a function call. These keywords can have a different color from the Documentation Comments color.

Code Element	Description
Strings	String literals contained between pairs of double quotes. Xcode interprets escape characters; it won't be confused by strings such as `"North Carolina (the \"Tar Heel\" State)"`.
Characters	Character literals contained between single quotes.
Numbers	Numeric constants. Xcode recognizes decimal, octal, and hexadecimal numbers that begin with `0x`. It does not recognize numeric Unicode constants.
Keywords	The standard keywords for the language. Obviously, this will vary wildly from one language to the next. For C-like languages, words such as `for`, `if`, `else`, and `then` are keywords. The word `register` is a keyword in a C++ source file, but not in a Java file. For shell scripts, the keywords are the bash built-in commands.
Preprocessor	C-based languages that use a preprocessor can have statement such as `#include` or `#define` colorized. The entire line containing the preprocessor statement is displayed using this color, regardless of whether it contains keywords or other types of elements. Xcode understands multi-line preprocessor statements.

To change the settings for a particular element, first select the element type from the pop-up menu. Then you can set the color of the element by clicking on the color well to display the color picker palette. As long as the color well remains selected, the color picker will alter its color. Alternatively, you can drop colors from other color sources on the color. Color sources include other color wells and the palette of saved colors at the bottom of the color picker.

Clicking the Allow Separate Fonts option permits syntax-colored text to be displayed in a font or size different than that of other text. Click the Set Font button to change the font for that element. This displays the standard Font palette, as shown in Figure 6-32.

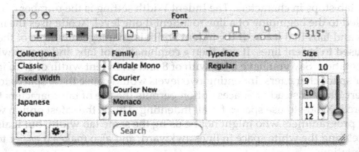

Figure 6-32

You can change the font and size, but you cannot alter the style, color, or other typographic decorations of the text. Here's a fun trick: set the font for Comments to Lucida Handwriting, 13pt. This might seem silly, but the basic principle is sound. Setting Comments to display in a proportional font makes them easier to read and visually sets them apart from the program code even more than colorizing.

Changing Syntax Coloring for a Single File

Normally, syntax coloring is determined by the file's type. You can use the Format⇨Syntax Coloring menu to have the text of a file interpreted using a different language, or to disable syntax coloring entirely. The normal setting is Default for file type, which allows Xcode to select the most appropriate language syntax automatically. When Default is selected, the language Xcode has chosen is displayed as a dash in the menu of available languages.

You can choose a different language or none. For files that belong to a project, this setting is stored in the project document and is persistent. For files that do not belong to an open project, the selection is lost when the editor pane is closed.

Indenting Text

Over the years, programmers have developed coding styles that visually reflect the structured nature of the languages they are programming in. One of these conventions is indenting. These conventions have become so common and consistent, that many can be automated.

Indenting is accomplished by starting a line with tab or space characters. Using spaces to indent lines is the most predictable method, but create unnecessary large files. Tab characters are more efficient, but are problematic because there is no standard that dictates how many column positions a tab character represents. If you decide that tabs stops should be every 4 columns and you open a text file from a programmer who thought tabs should be every 8 columns, the text won't line up correctly. You'll achieve the greatest compatibility by adopting 4-column tab stops, which seems to be the most common settings these days. You can also alter the tab width for individual files. The default tab settings for files are configured in the Indentation tab of the Xcode Preferences.

Xcode makes a distinction between the width of the tab stops and amount each line of code is indented. The two numbers do not have to be the same. The Tab Width setting, shown in Figure 6-33, determines the width of the tab stops in characters. The Indent Width setting is the number of columns worth of white space added to the beginning of a line to indent it one level. Xcode uses the most efficient combination of spaces and tabs that it can. If the indent width is an integer multiple of the tab width, then tab characters will used to indent lines. If not, then a combination of tabs and spaces will be used to achieve the desired indentation. Say you have a tab with of 8 and an indent width of 4. To indent a line one level will require four space characters. Indenting two levels would cause these spaces to be replaced by a single tab. The Insert 'Tabs' Instead of Spaces option permits the use of tab characters to indent lines. Turning it off forces Xcode to use spaces for all indenting. This is the safest option when you're sharing code with other programmers who might not be using the same tab width, but it also makes the file longer, makes deleting the white space in lines awkward, and also makes it easier to inadvertently align text at odd indentations.

"White space" refers to the non-graphic, printable characters in the Unicode character set. Practically that means the tab, space and end-of-line characters. But technically it also includes characters like the non-breaking space (Unicode A0). They get their name from the fact that they cause subsequent characters in the file to be shifted to new lines or column positions, but are not themselves visible. In other words, they just create space.

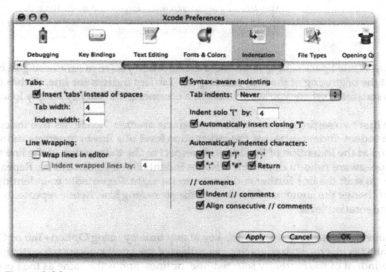

Figure 6-33

Automatic indenting occurs whenever you start a new line by pressing the Return key. The editor inserts the same amount of indentation on the new line as was present on the line above it. This feature is always active. To avoid this, press Option+Return at the end of the line. Option+Return starts a new line with no indentation. There is no simple option to turn this behavior off. It can be defeated only by changing the key binding for the Return key, as explained in Chapter 19.

Enable syntax-aware indenting in the Indentation pane of the Xcode Preferences. Turning it on collectively enables a variety of automatic indentation features. You can have Xcode automatically indent lines when you press the Tab key, automatically indent a block when you type the { character, automatically re-indent a line when you type one of several punctuation characters, or control the indentation of C++ style comments. Each feature can be independently disabled, if desired.

The Tab Indents option determines what action occurs when you press the Tab key. There are three settings, as described in the following table.

Tab Indents Setting	Tab Key Action
In Leading White Space	When the text cursor is at the beginning, in, or immediately to the right of any white space at the beginning of the line, pressing the Tab key will cause the entire line to be indented one level. When not in this leading non-white space portion of the line, the Tab key inserts a single tab character.
Always	Regardless of where the cursor position is within the line, pressing the Tab key will cause the line to be re-indented.
Never	Tab key inserts a tab character.

The In Leading White Space setting is the most useful when you're programming in block-structured languages. At the beginning of the line, pressing the Tab key indents the line. Within the line, typically at then end of a statement where you want to begin a comment, the Tab key simply inserts a tab character.

Note that the first two settings are not variations on one another. Xcode has two indentation functions: indent and re-indent. Indent increases the indentation level of a line by inserting more white space. Re-indention looks at the indention of the line with respect to the indentation of the line that precedes it, and uses syntax-aware rules to determine what its indentation level should be. Repeatedly indenting a line continues to shift the line further and further to the right. Repeatedly re-indenting a line does nothing. Until you change the contents of the line, or the preceding line, Xcode repeatedly reformats the text to the same indentation level.

You can circumvent the settings for the Tab key at any time by using Option+Tab or Control+I. Option+Tab always inserts a tab character, regardless of the syntax-aware tab settings. Control+I always performs a re-indent of the currently selected line, or lines, and is the same as the Format⇨Re-indent command.

Returning to the Indentations tab of the Xcode Preferences (see Figure 6-33), the Indent Solo "{" options determine what happens when you type an opening brace as the first non-white space character of a line. The first option determines how many characters the line will be indented. This is independent of the Indent width setting, but if used, it really should be the same value — or you will have some awfully odd-looking blocks. To have nothing happen, set the value to 0. The indentation amount is always relative to the indentation of the previous line, not the indentation level of the line before you typed the { character. In other words, if the setting is 4 characters and the line was already indented 4 characters more than the previous line, typing a { will do nothing. In fact, the indentation level could easily decrease if the current indentation amount is significantly more than the previous line.

The companion option is Automatically Insert Closing "}". With this checked, typing a { character does two things. It inserts a line with a matching } ahead of the cursor, then it advances to the next line as if the Return character had been pressed. The effect is simple: typing a { creates a balanced block with the cursor positioned at the first line of the block. Figure 6-34 shows an if statement before and after a single { character was typed.

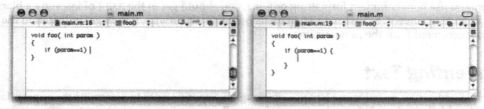

Figure 6-34

The Automatically Indented Characters work similarly to the Tab Indents Always setting. Whenever you type any of the checked characters, Xcode re-indents the line. Remember that this is a re-indent, not an indent. Xcode reinterprets the line using its syntax-aware rules and determines the appropriate indentation level for the line based on its new content. This may, or may not, change the indentation of the line. This re-indentation occurs *after* the character has been inserted. Thus, the Return key calculates the indentation of the new line it just created, not the line the Return key was pressed on.

The two // Comments options apply to C++ style comments when a line in re-indented. They are not applied when comments are being typed. The Indent // Comments option treats // comments like any other program statement and indent them to the same level as the surrounding code. If off, // comments are left at whatever indentation level the programmer typed them at. The Align Consecutive // Comments option indents a // comment that appears alone on a line to the same indentation level as the // comment in the previous line. This is most significant when // comments are started to the right of a program statement and continued in another // comment on the next line.

The following three listings illustrate the effects of the two comment formatting options.

No // Comment Formatting

```
int main (int argc, char * const argv[])
{
// Check the environment
    char * server_addr = getenv("SERVER");
    if (server_addr==NULL)
        exit(3);            // terminate immediately
                    // returning a status of 3
```

Indent // Comments Only

```
int main (int argc, char * const argv[])
{
    // Check the environment
    char * server_addr = getenv("SERVER");
    if (server_addr==NULL)
        exit(3);            // terminate immediately
    // returning a status of 3
```

Indent // Comments and Align Consecutive // Comments

```
int main (int argc, char * const argv[])
{
    // Check the environment
    char * server_addr = getenv("SERVER");
    if (server_addr==NULL)
        exit(3);            // terminate immediately
                    // returning a status of 3
```

When you use both comment formatting options, you should get in the habit of inserting a blank line before starting a new C++ style comment on its own line. Otherwise, it may get indented to the level of a trailing comment from the previous line.

Re-indenting Text

As explained earlier, re-indenting text uses the language-specific rules to determine the appropriate indentation level for each line. This can happen automatically, depending on which syntax-aware indentation options you have enabled, or manually when you use Control+I or the Format⇨Re-indent command. It also happens whenever text is pasted from the clipboard.

You can always manually alter the indentation level of a line, or lines, using the Shift Right (Command+]) and Shift Left (Command+[) commands in the Format menu. These do exactly what they say, and either increase or decrease the indentation of every line in the selection by one level. Lines that are already at the left margin cannot be decreased any further. This is just a manual adjustment of the amount of white space at the beginning of the line. A subsequent re-indent recalculates the appropriate indentation level based on the language rules, undoing any effect of Shift Right or Shift Left.

Tab Settings for a Single File

The global values for Tab Width and Indent Width set in the Xcode Preferences can be overridden for an individual source item. These settings are stored as one of the attributes of the source file item in the project. You can edit them for an individual source file using an Info window or the Inspector palette, shown in Figure 6-35.

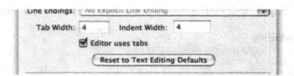

Figure 6-35

The three settings (Tab Width, Indent Width, and Editor Uses Tabs) correspond to the same three preferences in the Indenting tab of the Xcode Preferences. Change them for this file, or click the Reset to Text Editing Defaults to go back to using the global settings. Note that resetting the tab settings also resets the line and character encoding for the file.

Remember that these settings are attributes of the source file item in the project. These settings are not stored with, or in, the actual text file. Opening the file outside the context of the project reverts to using Xcode's global tab and indent settings. If the file belongs to multiple projects, you need to alter the source file item in each if you want to edit the file consistently.

Code Sense

The most sophisticated feature of syntax-aware editing is Code Sense, Xcode's auto-completion technology. Code Sense analyzes the context of the code you are typing and offers suggestions for completing the statement. It works by building a dynamic list of symbol names that would be appropriate at that point in your code. If you are starting a new statement, the appropriate symbols will include any global variable, function, class name, or language keyword. But if you typed a class or structure name, the appropriate symbols would be only the member function or instance variables in that class or structure. Figure 6-36 shows the available completions for the `java.util.Iterator` object defined in the `for` statement.

Figure 6-36

Code Sense understands the context, scope, and type of variables. It does this by relying on the actual compiler to periodically reinterpret the source file and update its index of symbols. Consequently, Code Sense is very accurate and is not easily fooled by name space, scope, or preprocessor symbols. The symbols included in Code Sense are the symbols interpreted when your project is built.

Code Sense supports the C, C++, Objective-C, Objective-C++, Java, and AppleScript languages. Because Code Sense must interact intimately with the compiler, it also requires that all the source items are members of a "native" target. Native targets are targets that Xcode knows how to build. And by extension, it knows what compilers will be used to compile each source file. External (non-native) targets defer the actual build process to some external program, like Make or Ant. Items in external targets cannot use Code Sense.

> If you would like to use Code Sense in a project that requires the use of an external target, you still can. Simply create an additional native target that includes all of the source files and libraries you want Code Sense to see. Code Sense indexes all of the native source files referenced in a project. You never have to build that target; it just has to be defined.

Invoking Code-Completion

After it has been enabled, Code Sense is available all of the time. There are two basic approaches for invoking code-completion. The most direct and interactive approach is to pop up the completion list. You can do this at any point in the code by pressing the Esc key (see Figure 6-37).

The list of possible class, variable, and function names that could be typed at this point in your code is ridiculously long. You need to narrow the possibilities considerably before code-completion will be useful. Fortunately, this is easy to accomplish — just keep typing. Type the first few characters of what you want, or think you want, and Code Sense instantly narrows the list to those symbols that begin with the characters you've typed. Figure 6-38 shows the list after the text `Buf` was typed. Code Sense responds with a far more manageable list of choices.

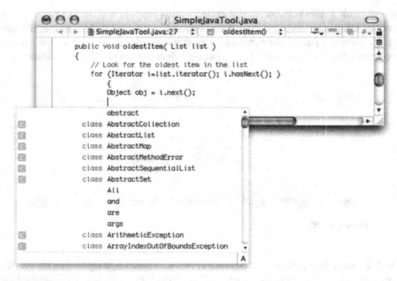

Figure 6-37

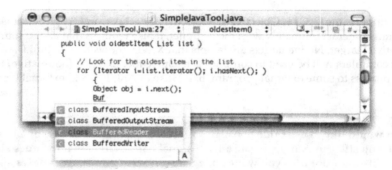

Figure 6-38

You can continue to type characters, further narrowing the list, or even delete characters to expand the list. At some point, you will want to choose one of the symbols from the list and insert that symbol into your code. You can do this via the keyboard or the mouse. If Code Sense hasn't preselected the symbol you want, use the Up and Down arrows to select the symbol in the list. If the list is very long, you can use the Page Up, Page Down, Home, and End keys to navigate. To use the mouse, simply click the symbol to select it, or use the scroll bar to scroll through a long list of symbols. After you select the symbol, press either the Tab or Return key. Code Sense inserts the desired symbol. Figure 6-39 shows that it also leaves the portion of the symbol that it completed highlighted in grey.

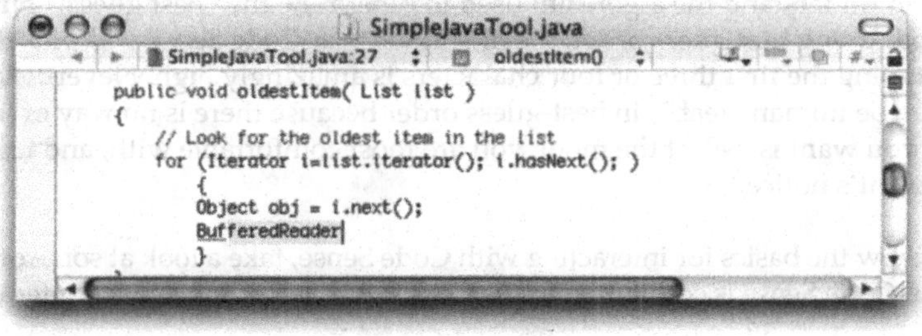

Figure 6-39

This is an indication that code-completion of this symbol is still active. While the symbol is active, you can change your mind and press the Esc key again to undo the completion. Code Sense removes what it just inserted and returns you to the completion list.

Which brings us to the second method for invoking auto-completion: the Edit⇨Next Completion (Control+.) command. Without bringing up the auto-completion list, or after a symbol has been inserted by Code Sense and is still highlighted, the Next Completion command selects the next auto-completion symbol from the available list and inserts it. This completely bypasses the Code Sense pop-up list. This is the command to use when you are reasonably sure that code-completion will choose the correct symbol on the first guess. For instance, the abstract java.util.Iterator class only has three methods: hasNext, next, and remove. If you wanted to insert a call to the hasNext method, for example, you would need only to type the letter **h** followed by Control+. Code Sense would insert hasNext, because that's the only possible choice.

After the Next Completion command has inserted a symbol, the portion of the symbol supplied by Code Sense is highlighted. This is the same state that follows inserting a symbol from the pop-up list. Press Control+. again, and the previously inserted symbol is replaced with the next choice in the list. Repeated use of Control+. cycles through all possible choices without displaying the pop-up list. Press Esc and the symbol is removed and Code Sense presents the pop-up list of choices.

It is important to note is that the list of choices is case-insensitive. For example, if you have a variable named "system" and you type **sys** and then press the Esc key, you will see the System class in the list. Selecting that will replace the entire name, replacing the lowercase *s* at the beginning with an uppercase *S*. Be careful when using code completion that you don't inadvertently change a variable name into a class name, or vice versa.

The order of the list is important. The further away the symbol that you want is from Code Sense's starting position in the list, the longer it's going to take to select the one you want. Code Sense provides two different list orders: alphabetical and best guess. You can tell which one is being used by looking at the lower-right corner of the pop-up completion list. An *A* indicates that the list is in alphabetical order. A pi symbol indicates best-guess order. Clicking the symbol toggles between the two orders.

I don't pretend to understand the algorithm used to determine the "best guess," but I can say that it's pretty darn good. Using best guess order, the likelihood that Code Sense will pick the symbol name that I wanted after typing the first three or four characters is amazingly high. Nevertheless, there are times when the list can be unmanageable in best-guess order because there is no way of telling where in the list the symbol you want is. Select the mode you are most comfortable with, and know that you can switch at a moment's notice.

Now that you know the basics for interacting with Code Sense, take a look at some of the ways that you can customize it. Code Sense is configured in the Code Sense tab of the Xcode Preferences (see Figure 6-40).

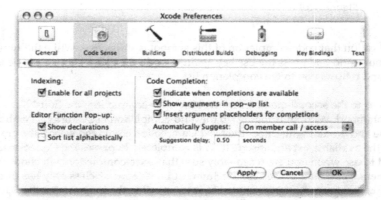

Figure 6-40

Code Sense relies on indexing. Indexing for the project must be enabled in order for Code Sense to function. Indexing is the engine behind many other Xcode features, such as the Class Browser and the Symbols smart group. Indexing, and by extension Code Sense and all other features that use the symbols database, is enabled here for all projects. Turning this off also discards the indexes for all open projects, which can be a significant amount of disk space.

> The two options underneath the Editor Function Pop-up apply to the Function menu in the navigation bar, not to the code-completion pop-up list.

On the right, the Code Completion options begin with the Indicate When Completions Are Available. Checking this option underlines text whenever Code Sense has a specific list of suggestions to make. This doesn't alter how you invoke or use Code Sense; it is simply a visual indication that there are one or more completions that match what you've already typed. You do not have to wait for Code Sense to indicate that it has completions before you invoke it.

The Show Arguments in Pop-up List option presents the arguments of methods and functions along with their name. Leave this on, especially in object-oriented languages that permit method name overloading (multiple methods that have the same name and differ only in the arguments they take). Figure 6-41 shows a completion list for a Java `StringBuffer` object. The method arguments are included in the list on the right and suppressed on the left.

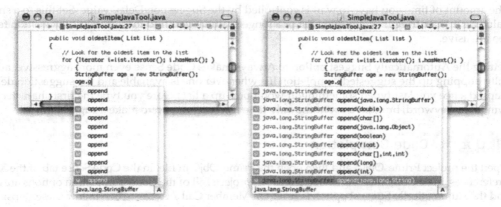

Figure 6-41

The complement to the previous option is the Insert Argument Placeholders For Completions option. Checking this inserts not only the name of a function or method, but also special placeholders for all of the arguments to the call (if any). Figure 6-42 shows the results of auto-completing a method call with this option turned on.

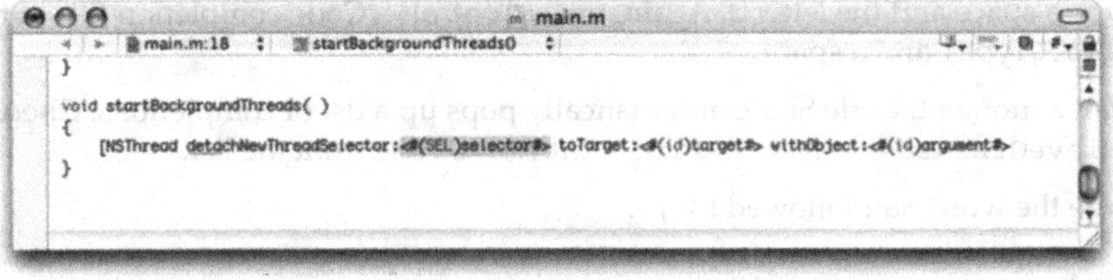

Figure 6-42

The first argument placeholder is selected automatically. Simply begin typing to replace it with the argument's value. The syntax of the placeholder is deliberate, and works with special Edit⇨Select Next Placeholder (Control+/) command. After you have edited the first argument, press Control+/ and Xcode selects the placeholder for the next argument. The Select Next Placeholder command is really just a specialized search function that looks for the placeholder pattern, and isn't even dependant on Code Sense. You can be anywhere in a file and use this command to jump to the next placeholder in the file. It wraps around the end of the file, so repeatedly using it cycles through all placeholders.

The last option in the Code Sense tab of the Xcode Preferences (previously shown in Figure 6-40) is the Automatically Suggest option. If this option is set to Never, Code Sense must be manually invoked in all situations. The On Member Call / Access setting causes the code-completion pop-up list to spring up whenever a completion is available for an object or structure. This includes instance variables and member functions. To make use of this feature, you must type the class, structure, or object name and whatever syntax the language uses to denote member access (. or ->, or just a space in Objective-C). Wait a moment, and Code Sense pops up the completion list for the class, object, or structure just as if you had typed the Esc key. If you begin typing the member name before the delay period expires, the feature is defeated and won't try again until you type another object or structure name.

The amount of time you have to wait is controlled by the Suggestion Delay value. Set this to a small value for a "hair trigger" suggestion list or a longer value if you find the automatic suggestion feature too intrusive.

Setting the Automatically Suggest option to Always makes Code Sense even more aggressive, automatically popping up the suggested completion list whenever one is available and the suggestion delay has elapsed since you last typed something. It won't pop-up a list before you type the first character of a symbol or keyword, but that's about the only time it won't jump in to make a suggestion.

Try It Out   **Code Completion**

Open the project PrimesObjC, and then open the PrimesObjC.m file. In the Code Sense tab of the Xcode Preferences, make sure indexing is enabled for all projects, all of the Code Completion options are checked, and the Automatically Suggest option is set to On Member Call / Access. Then follow these steps:

1. Position the cursor at the end of the commented line that begins `SieveOfEratosthenes*` `sieve`. Press Return to start a new line.

2. Type the letters **Sie** and press the Esc key. Choose `Class SieveOfEratosthenes` from the list, using the keyboard arrows or the mouse, and press the Return key.

3. Type **sieve = [[Sie** and press the Control+.. If Code Sense does not complete the text with `SieveOfEratosthenes`, continue to press Control+. until it does.

4. Type a space and the letter **a**. Again, press Control+.. Code completion fills in the method name `alloc`. Type] and a space.

5. Wait a moment. Code Sense automatically pops up a list of completions. Choose `(SieveOfEratosthenes*) init:(int)maxPrime` from the list.

6. Type the word `max` followed by `];`.

How It Works

Code Sense built an index of the classes and methods defined in the project.

In step 2, you invoked code completion directly using the Esc key. Code Sense compiled a list of all possible symbols within the current scope that start with the letters "Sie" as shown in Figure 6-43.

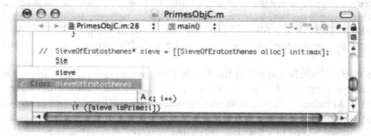

Figure 6-43

In step 3, you started to type **SieveOfEratosthenes** again. But this time instead of popping up the list of completions, you requested that Code Sense complete the name using its best guess. There were probably only two possible completions (SieveOfEratosthenes and sieve). If you didn't get SieveOfEratosthenes the first time, you probably got it on the second try.

By typing a space immediately followed by the letter **a** in step 4, you defeated the feature that would automatically make a suggestion for a member call or access. But code completion is still active, and Command+. completed the only possible class method that begins with the letter *a*.

In step 5, you waited before typing any portion of the method name. After the Suggestion delay expired, Code Sense popped up the list of possible method names for a SieveOfEratosthenes object. Selecting the init:(int)maxPrime method filled in not only the method name, but also a placeholder for its parameter. The parameter was preselected, so all you had to do is type the argument. If the method had more than one parameter, Control+/ would have selected the next placeholder in the argument list.

When you are all done, the line of code should look exactly like the comment line above it.

Rebuilding the Code Sense Index

Code Sense tries to keep up with the changes to your code, and keep its database of symbols current. However, changes in one file can affect code completion in another and Code Sense can get out of step with your project. There are several remedies to keep Code Sense up-to-date.

The simplest is to save your files. Code Sense incrementally re-indexes variable and function names near the code you are currently editing. This makes is possible for Code Sense to immediately provide the completion for a variable name you just typed on the previous line. But change the definition of a class in a header file and then switch back to editing another source file, and you may not see the new definitions in the completion list. Code Sense completely re-indexes a file whenever you save it to disk. A simple Save or Save All is often all that is necessary to make the symbols index current again.

But Code Sense can be fooled, especially when files in the project are renamed or removed. This usually results in stale symbol information in the database that is not cleared out by normal incremental re-indexing. To fix this, open the Info window for the project using the Inspector palette or the Project⇨Edit Project Settings command. At the bottom of the General tab is a Rebuild Code Sense Index button. Clicking this presents the warning in Figure 6-44.

Click OK, and the entire symbols index database for the project is discarded and rebuilt from scratch. This can be a time-consuming operation on slower machines or for very large projects. Code Sense functions, the Symbols smart group, and the Class Browser are unavailable until the re-indexing is complete. Open the Activity Viewer window from the Window menu if you want to monitor its progress.

Sometimes you may not want a file in your project included in the symbols database. In the General tab of the Info window for the source item, uncheck the Include in Index option under the File Type, as shown in Figure 6-45. The symbols indexer ignores this file in the future. None of its symbols or definitions appear in Code Sense or the Class Browser. Changing this option rarely updates the index, so you will probably have to rebuild the project's index before the change will have much effect.

Figure 6-44

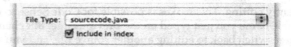

Figure 6-45

Text Macros

Text macros are another kind of auto-completion. These are text fragments that can be inserted whenever you need them. The text macros supplied by Xcode include a variety of common control structures and programming conventions, the kind that programmers tend to reuse repeatedly. This section discusses how to use text macros.

Text macros are organized by language in the Edit⇨Insert Text Macro menu. Select the desired macro, and its contents are inserted into the editor pane. When using the menu, you can choose any macro you want, but it really only makes sense to choose a macro that is appropriate to the language you're writing in.

Text macros can contain placeholders, just like Code Sense completions for method and functions. They may also contain a special placeholder that is replaced by the current selection in the editor. For instance, on the left in Figure 6-46 the statement `free(byteArray);` is selected. After you select Edit⇨Insert Text Macro⇨C⇨If Block, the text is replaced with the code on the right. If you don't select anything, the placeholder `<#statements#>` is inserted instead.

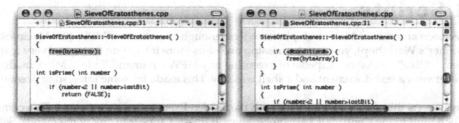

Figure 6-46

Like function arguments inserted by code-completion, the first placeholder in the macro is automatically selected. Use the same Select Next Placeholder (Control+/) command to jump to any other placeholders.

Code Sense can also insert text macros. Each text macro has a "command" name associated with it. These names appear in the Code Sense completion list. Unlike the menu, only those macros appropriate to your file's language appear. Selecting one inserts the entire text macro. Because you have to be typing the name of the macro to invoke Code Sense, you cannot simultaneously select text to replace the <#statements#> placeholder. If you want to use this feature, you have to invoke the macro by using the menu.

Macros can have several variations. Inserting the C⇨If Block macro inserts a simple conditional block guarded by a conditional. Without editing anything, select the macro from the menu again. The second time, this simple conditional block is replaced by a compound if/else statement with two blocks. The following code listing shows these two iterations. Some HTML macros have four or more variations for a single macro.

First Use of Edit⇨Insert Text Macro⇨C⇨If Block

```
int foo( int bar )
{
 if (<#condition#>) {
        <#statements#>
 }
}
```

Immediately Selecting Edit⇨Insert Text Macro⇨C⇨If Block Again

```
int foo( int bar )
{
 if (<#condition#>) {
        <#statements#>
 }
 else {
        <#statements#>
 }
}
```

In a similar vein, you can use the Next Completion (Control+.) command to cycle through similar text macros. There are several text macros that begin with the letters "if." Typing if and then repeatedly using Next Completion cycles through all of the symbols and macros that begin with "if."

Shell Scripts

If you've been around the Macintosh platform long enough to remember MPW (the Macintosh Programmer's Workshop), you may be missing one of its more intriguing features. Every text window in MPW was a "live" worksheet, capable of executing any MPW command. In fact, MPW made no real distinction between a text document and a shell window. This made for some interesting possibilities.

Xcode resurrects this ability, in a fashion, with the hidden Execute Script command. This command is normally bound to the Control+R key combination. It doesn't appear in any of the menus. Select any text and press Control+R. The selected text is executed in your default shell. The output of those commands is inserted into your text file immediately after the selected script.

The current directory is always set to the active project folder prior to execution, so you can reference project files using project folder–relative paths. A new instance of the shell is used for each invocation, so aliases and shell variables are not persistent. The shell's stdin is set to /dev/null, making it impossible to use commands that prompt for user input, such as sudo.

Spell Checking

Programmers are notoriously bad spellers. Thanks to the Cocoa underpinnings of Xcode, the editor inherits the standard OS X spelling checker. The spelling checker is great for correcting comments and documentation, thus avoiding the scorn and ridicule of the documentation department that is inevitably populated with English majors and spelling bee champions. The spelling checker is essentially useless for code. Avoid adding program symbols or language keywords to your user dictionary. Your login account only has one user dictionary, and filling it with programming symbols defeats its usefulness in other applications.

Interactive Checking

Start the interactive spelling checker with the Edit⇨Spelling⇨Spelling command. This opens the Spelling palette (see Figure 6-47).

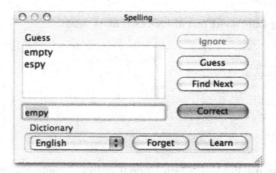

Figure 6-47

Checking starts at the text cursor or the beginning of the current selection. Checking is not limited to the text selection; it just starts there. The next word that the spelling checker suspects is misspelled is highlighted in the text and displayed in the entry field of the palette. Above the suspect word is a list of suggested corrections.

The Ignore button adds the suspect word to the temporary ignore list. The spelling checker ignores this word, and assumes that it is spelled correctly, until the next editor session. Use this to temporarily teach the spelling checker about correctly spelled words, without permanently adding them to the dictionary.

The Find Next button skips this word and goes looking for the next suspicious word. The spelling checker still considers the word to be misspelled.

You can immediately replace a word can be immediately replaced with a suggestion from the Guess list by selecting the suggestion and clicking the Correct button, or by double-clicking a guess in the list. You can replace the word with any arbitrary text by editing the contents of the text field before clicking the Correct button. Making any alterations to the suspect word tells the spelling checker that you intend to replace the word with those changes, rather than use the selected word in the Guess list.

If the spelling checker cannot guess the correct spelling of the word, you can help it by editing the suspect word and telling it to guess again using the Guess button. For example, the spelling checker cannot guess that you mean "exhaust" if you've actually typed "eghoust." Replacing the "g" with an "x" and clicking the Guess button, as shown on the right in Figure 6-48, gets the word close enough for the spelling checker to find the correct word.

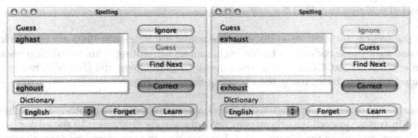

Figure 6-48

The Dictionary pop-up menu selects the main dictionary the spelling checker uses. The Learn and Forget buttons take the word currently in the entry field and either adds or removes it from your user dictionary. To remove a word you previously added, you have to type or paste it into the field before clicking the Forget button. Your user dictionary is shared by all incarnations of the Spelling Checker interface in all applications, so add to it wisely and sparingly.

Finding One Word

You can invoke the spelling checker without bringing up the spelling checker palette with the Edit⇨ Spelling⇨Check Spelling (Command+;) command. This command starts at the current location in the file and finds the next suspect word, which it highlights. That's it. Edit the word in the editor pane or use the command again to find the next suspect word.

This is probably the most useful spell checking command for programmers. After writing a long comment, position the cursor before the comment and press Command+;. The spelling checker will skip to the first suspect word in the comment. Once you've corrected all of the English words in the comment, simply go back to writing code.

Checking While Typing

The Spelling menu has an option to Check Spelling as You Type. If this option is selected, words that you just typed or edited will be spell checked and highlighted automatically. Note that this does not spell check the entire document, or text that you paste or drag. It only checks the word that your cursor was just in or adjacent to. The word that the cursor is currently in or adjacent to is *never* highlighted (because it is assumed that you are in the process of changing it.)

You may find this feature useless and annoying when you're editing source code, because practically every "word" in your program is going to be tagged as misspelled. However, if you are writing a large amount of documentation in Xcode, you might find it helpful to turn it on temporarily.

File Encoding

Chapter 5 showed you how to change the character and line encoding for one or more files using an Info window. You can also immediately alter the encoding for the file being edited by using the Line Ending and File Encoding submenus found in the Format menu. The source file item for files referenced in an open project is updated to reflect the new setting.

Changing the setting, by itself, does not alter the actual file. The encodings are used to interpret the bytes in the file and turn those codes into Unicode characters for editing. This translation uses the encoding set for the file when it is read. Conversely, when the file is later saved, the Unicode characters in the editor are translated back into bytes using the encoding that is set then.

Problems can arise when you change from one character encoding to another. Some characters cannot be represented in certain encodings or you may have the wrong characters in the editor because the encoding was mismatched when the file was read. For instance, the registered trademark symbol (®) appears in the Unicode, Mac OS Roman, and Windows Latin 1 character sets. But the binary code used to represent it in a text file is different for all three. If the file was written using Windows Latin 1 encoding and you read the file into the editor using Mac OS Roman encoding, the editor displays some other symbol because the value in the file is not the Mac OS Roman value for the registered trademark symbol.

When you change the encoding for a file, Xcode asks if it should convert or reinterpret the characters in the file (see Figure 6-49).

The Convert button actually does very little beyond remembering the new encoding for the file. The characters are already in their universal form in memory. The "conversion" doesn't actually occur until you save the file. The bytes in the file were read using the old encoding, and will eventually be written using the new encoding. Use this option if the characters in the file are correct and you simply want to write the file using a different encoding. The one thing the Convert button does do is to check that all of the characters in the file can be written using the new encoding. Xcode does not allow characters in an editor pane that cannot be encoded when it is saved. If the document contains characters that are illegal in the new encoding, the conversion is not allowed.

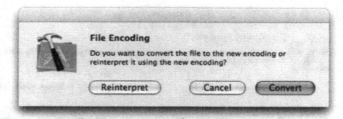

Figure 6-49

Use the Reinterpret button when the encoding is incorrect and the editor has misinterpreted the bytes in the file. If a file containing the registered trademark symbol is encoded using Windows Latin 1, and read using Mac OS Roman, the character that appears in the file is "Æ." To correct this, change the encoding to Western (Windows Latin 1) and click the Reinterpret button. The contents of the file are read again, this time using the Windows Latin 1 encoding, and the ® symbol appears instead. To save this file using Mac OS Roman encoding, change the encoding again — this time using the Convert button.

The Reinterpret button must re-read the bytes in the actual file. The binary encoding of characters is not maintained in memory — only the Unicode characters are. If changes have been made to a file, the Reinterpret button warns you that all unsaved changes will be lost when the file is reinterpreted (see Figure 6-50). You can choose to discard all unsaved changes or cancel. To preserve and reinterpret the file including all of the changes that you've made, cancel the reinterpretation, save the file using the old encoding, and change the encoding again.

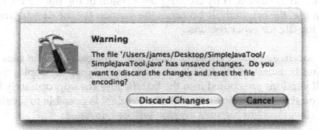

Figure 6-50

As mentioned earlier, Xcode won't allow you to convert a file if the resulting document would have characters that cannot be encoded. Likewise, the editor won't let you insert a character into a document if the file's encoding won't support it. If you try, you get a warning like the one in Figure 6-51.

You have the choice of converting your document to Unicode (really Unicode-16) or Unicode-8. Unicode-16 is the "raw" Unicode encoding used internally by the editor. Unicode-16 writes or stores each character as a 16-bit integer word. Most editors, compilers, and other ASCII-oriented programs are not compatible with Unicode-16. Unicode-8 writes the common ASCII (0-127) characters as single bytes and encodes higher-value Unicode characters using a complex system of escape values. Unicode-8 is compact, compatible with many applications, and backwards-compatible with plain ASCII text. If given this choice, convert your document to Unicode-8.

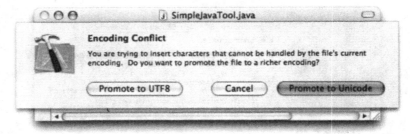

Figure 6-51

If you don't want to use Unicode-8 or Unicode-16, cancel the insertion. Convert the file to an encoding that supports the characters you are trying to insert, and insert them again.

Localizing Files

One of the hallmarks of the Macintosh is the ability of programs to adjust themselves to accommodate the language, currency, and time conventions of different countries and populations. This is generically referred to as localization. Xcode supports localization of individual source files. It does this by maintaining multiple copies of the file, one for each localization.

Your locale — the locale that your Xcode development system is currently set to — is called the development region. You should always start by creating the version of the file for the development region. When you localize a file, the original file becomes the version for the development region. You can then create variations of the file for other regions.

Normally, you only localize resource files like string lists, images, and NIB files. Localization requires run-time support, and is usually done for files that are copied into the deployment bundle. The bundle is organized so that all versions are copied into the bundle and the appropriately localized version of the file is loaded based on the locale of the current user. While it is possible to localize something like a source file, only the development region's version will be compiled.

To prepare a file for localization, open the Info window for the file's item and click the Make File Localizable button. The file's source item is turned into a group and the existing file becomes the localized version for the development region. The group becomes a proxy for the development region's version of the file; opening the group opens the localization for the development region. To open or change settings of an individual version, expand the group and deal with the individual versions.

After you initially localize the file, you can add more localizations by opening an Info window for either the group or any specific localization and clicking the Add Localization button. Enter the name of the localization, or choose one from the pop-up menu, as shown in Figure 6-52. A new file is created by duplicating the current file. The new file becomes the localized version for that region.

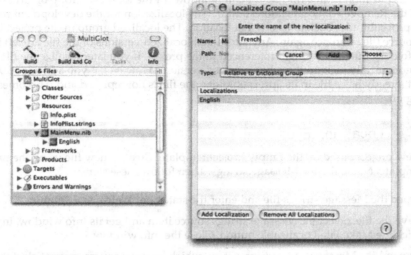

Figure 6-52

In the project folder, Xcode creates a .lproj subfolder for each localization. All of the files localized for English are in the English.lproj subfolder, all the files localized for French are in the French.lproj subfolder, and so forth. When the file is first localized, a localization folder for the development region is created in the same location, and the file is moved into the .lproj subfolder. The Multiglot project, shown in Figure 6-53, shows the organization of the project and project folder after the MainMenu.nib and InfoPlist.strings files have been localized for English, French, and Spanish.

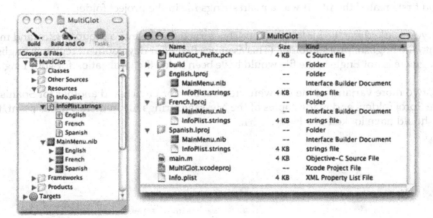

Figure 6-53

To remove localization from a file, get the Info window for the localized group or any specific localization. Click the Remove All Localizations button. The localization for the development region is moved from the .lproj subfolder back to its original location. The localized group in the project is replaced with a simple source file reference again. Any additional localized versions of the file are left in their respective .lproj folders, but are no longer referenced in the project. If you later localize the file again, Xcode will *not* automatically pick up the other localized versions. However, if you add a localization for a region that already has a file in its .lproj subfolder, the file is not replaced and it becomes the localization for that region.

Try It Out   **Localizing Files**

Create a new project based on the Empty Project template. Create a new file using the Empty File in Project template. Name the file **Message.strings**. Then follow these steps:

1. Open the Message.strings file and enter the statement **Welcome = "Hello"**.

2. Save the file. Select the Message.strings source item and get its Info window. In the General tab, click the Make File Localizable button. Close the Info window.

3. Expand the Message.strings source item, which is now a source group. Select the source group again and open its Info window again.

4. Click the Add Localization button, choose French from the list, and click Add. Click the Add Localization button again and enter the name **Spanish**. Click Add.

5. Open the French variation. Change the "Hello" text to **"Bonjour"**. Open the Spanish variant. Change the "Hello" text to **"Hola"**. Save your changes.

How It Works

When you first created the file, it was a plain strings file in the project folder.

In step 2, you marked the file for localization. This turned the file into a group of files, and moved the original file into the English.lproj subfolder. (This assumes that your development region is English. If your native language is not English, the file would have been made the localization for your language instead.)

In step 4, two more variants of the file were created, one for French and another for Spanish. This created two more .lproj folders and made copies of the Message.strings file in there. At this point, the project and the files should have looked like Figure 6-54.

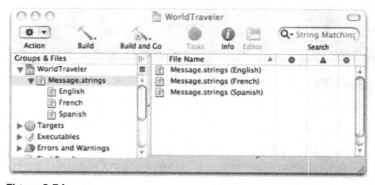

Figure 6-54

Finally, you edited the files so that the localized versions each had language-specific messages.

Printing

Rudimentary printing of editor panes is provided through the Page Setup (Command+Shift+P) and Print (Command+P) commands. Use the Page Setup command to specify the orientation, size, and scale of the printed page. The Print command prints the contents of the editor pane, using the editor's font. The gutter, page guide, and other annotations are not printed. Lines wider than the page are always wrapped to the next line; the Wrap Lines setting of the editor pane is ignored. The Use Colors When Printing option in the Font & Colors tab of the Xcode Preferences controls whether editor and syntax coloring is applied to the printout.

The text is printed at 72 dpi, which means that it will probably be unacceptably large. Use the scaling feature of the Page Setup dialog box to reduce the size of the text. A scale between 50% and 75% makes for very readable and compact listings. For an even more compact listing, set the scaling between 80% and 100% and select a two-up page layout in the Print dialog box.

Services

Xcode, like all well-written Cocoa applications, has access to Services. Services are small functions provided by other applications that can be applied to the current selection within another application. To open the URL in the source file shown in Figure 6-55, simply select it and choose the Open URL command from the Services menu.

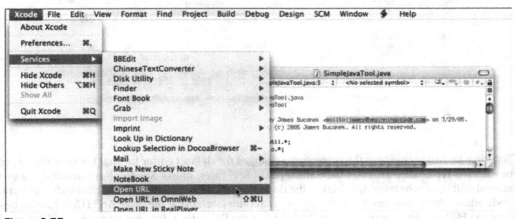

Figure 6-55

What services you have in your Services menu depends entirely on what applications and service plug-ins you have installed.

Using an External Editor

The editor built into Xcode has many useful and powerful features, and is tightly integrated with the rest of the Xcode environment. Still, it doesn't do everything an editor could. Or maybe you're just used to another editor that you've been using for years.

You can elect to use an external editor program, instead of one provided by Xcode, for some or all of your editing needs. Although Xcode's editors are powerful, Xcode has almost no specialized support for certain types of source files like XML. The ability to plug a dedicated XML editor into Xcode will add a powerful new dimension to your development environment.

Xcode has several different built-in editors. What you have been exposed to most in this chapter is the source code editor. But there is also a plain text editor, an RTF (Rich Text File) editor, an HTML editor, an Xcode Configurations Settings File editor, an AppleScript Dictionary editor, an image editor, and a few others. The editor that is used when you open a file is determined by the settings in the File Types tab of the Xcode Preferences (see Figure 6-56). Each file type that Xcode understands is associated with an editor. This can be one of the editors built into Xcode or a specific external editor, or the decision can be deferred to the Finder.

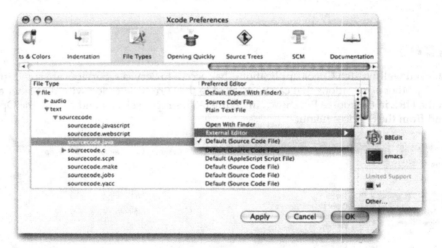

Figure 6-56

Changing an editor choice in the preferences changes the default editor for that file type for all projects. For each file type, there are essentially three possible choices: one of Xcode's built-in editors, a specific external editor, or whatever application the document file is associated with in the Finder. The choice of Xcode editors is always limited to the editors that understand that file type. An HTML file can be edited using the HTML editor or the plain text editor, but the RTF editor does not understand HTML and is not presented as a choice.

At any time, you can open a file with an alternate Xcode editor using the Open As command in the File menu or the Control-/right-click contextual pop-up menu. The menu contains the list of Xcode's internal editors that are capable of editing that type of file — the same list as in the Preferences. The Open With

Finder command opens the file just as if you had opened the file in the Finder. For Xcode source files, it's very likely that this will be Xcode itself. To force a file to open in another application, use the Reveal In Finder command to locate the file. Drag the file to an application in the dock or open it using the Finder's Open With command. Alternatively, simply switch to the other application and use its File➪Open command.

Specifying an External Editor for a file type causes Xcode to tell that application to open the file whenever Xcode would normally open the file in a separate window. The selection of an external editor does not affect single-pane operations, such as simply selecting a source file in the project window. The editor pane in the project window, the Class Browser, the Project Find window, and others will continue to use Xcode's internal editor to immediately display a file in the same window. Only double-clicking a source item or using the Open in Separate Editor command opens the file in the external editor.

External editors are not synchronized to the changes made in Xcode. Whenever Xcode is reactivated, it checks to see if any files were altered. Xcode cannot detect changes made in an external program before they are saved. Get in the habit of saving all of your changes before switching back to Xcode. If it detects changes, Xcode rereads the file and updates its display.

In the unfortunate situation where changes have also been made in both the Xcode editor and the external application, the dialog box shown in Figure 6-57 is presented. You can choose to keep the changes made in Xcode, ignoring the changes that were written to disk, or vice versa. Xcode does not have a merge function and cannot combine the changes made in two places. If you have inadvertently made important changes in both places, use the Keep Xcode Version choice. Reopen the file in the external editor, and then copy and paste the changes made there to the editor pane in Xcode. Save the file within Xcode to commit the combined changes. Another approach is to use Xcode's File➪Save a Copy As (Command+Shift+Option+S) command to make a new file of the Xcode version, then use a diff utility to compare and combine the changes.

Figure 6-57

Because of the hazard of editing source files in both the external editor and Xcode, use the Condensed layout or leave the editing pane in the project window collapsed. This reduces the temptation to make a quick edit in a file that might be opened elsewhere.

Xcode has full support for BBEdit, Text Wrangler, SubEthaEdit, Emacs, and xemacs, and has limited support for vi. Of this list, only the ones installed on your system will appear in the menu of choices. You can also select any other application, but Xcode will only provide limited support for it.

Full support means that Xcode communicates with the external editor and tells it to save files when appropriate. For example, when you build a project, you can have Xcode tell your external editor to save all of the unsaved files before compiling, just as it does for internally edited files. Similarly, closing a project saves all files in an external editor. The support for vi and other external editors is limited to opening the file. Once the file is open, Xcode has no more interaction with the application. It is your responsibility to save and close the file in the editor as needed.

External editors do not use the file and line encodings, tab, or indent settings of the source item. Some editors, like BBEdit, either automatically detect the format or store that information in the resource fork of the file. Use the external editor to change the encoding. Then change the settings in the project's source item to match.

Summary

As you can see, Xcode's editor provides a lot of features designed to make your editing sessions fluid and productive. Learning to use the various navigation controls will make moving around within a file, and between files, quick and efficient. After you get the feel for Code Sense, stopping to look up a function name or mistyping a local variable name should become a thing of the past.

You probably won't absorb all of Xcode's editing features in a single day. As you use Xcode to edit files, revisit this chapter from time to time to reacquaint yourself with some of the more esoteric features.

While the editor provides a number of navigation features that allow you to jump to predetermined or saved locations, sometimes you just need to go looking for something. The next chapter explains how.

Searching

A lot development is spent just looking for things: determining what code calls a certain method or uses a particular constant, or changing the name of a class or method name everywhere in your project. Xcode has tools to help you quickly find what you're looking for in a single file, the files in a project, and beyond.

Searching a Text File

The single file search tools are found in the Find menu. Find⇨Single File Find opens the Single File Find window, shown in Figure 7-1.

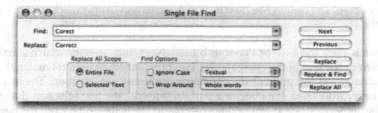

Figure 7-1

The Single File Find window contains all search and replace commands and options in a single window. The subject of the search is the file of the last editor pane that was active before you opened or switched to the Single File Find window. If you leave the window open, switch to a different editor pane, and then switch back to the Single File Find window, a search or replace occurs in the more recent file, not the one that was active when the window was originally opened. If you're ever in doubt, close the window, activate the editor pane of the file you want to search, and reopen the Find window using Command+F.

Enter the pattern you want to search for in the Find field. If you are going to replace multiple occurrences of what you find, enter the replacement text in the Replace field. Press the Tab key to move the selection from one to the other.

Searching for a Text Pattern

The Find Options control how the pattern in the Find field is used to match text in the file. The main control is the top pop-up menu, which allows you to choose between a Textual and Regular Expression. In Textual mode, the find function searches for the literal character sequence in the Find field. You can refine the search by requiring that a pattern be found on a word boundary. The options in the lower pop-up menu are described in the following table.

Textual Mode	Pattern Matches
Contains	Matches the pattern anywhere in the text. This option effectively turns off word boundary searching.
Starts with	Matches a pattern starting with the character immediately after a word boundary.
Ends with	Matches a pattern ending with a character immediately preceding a word boundary.
Whole words	Both the first and the last characters of the matched text must be on word boundaries.

The Ignore Case option causes case differences between the text and the pattern to be ignored. With this option on, the letters *a* or *A* in the pattern will match any *a* or *A* in the text, interchangeably. Likewise, the letter *ü* will match either *ü* or *Ü* in the text, but not *u*, *ù*, *ú*, or *û*. Matching is based on the Unicode rules for letter case. The option has no effect on punctuation or special characters. These must always match exactly.

To start a search, click the Next or Previous button. Next finds the first match starting at the current insertion point or the end of the current selection. Previous finds the first match that immediately precedes the current insertion point or the beginning of the current selection. The text within the current selection is never examined. If a matching pattern is found, the text selection changes to the text that was matched. The subsequent Next or Previous command starts its search from the new location.

You can also start a search by pressing the Return key. If the pattern is found in the text, the text is selected, the find window is closed, and your focus is returned to the editor pane. If the pattern could not be found, the single file find window remains open.

The Wrap Around option extends the search beyond the beginning or end of the file. Normally, this option is off. If there are no more matches in the remaining portion of the file, then the search fails. Turning this option on continues searching by "wrapping around" to the other end of the file. If you are searching forward with the Next command, the search continues, starting at the beginning of the file. The Previous search continues at the end of the file. With the Wrap Around option checked, the search only fails if there are no matches to the search pattern anywhere in the file.

Try It Out   **Search on Word Boundaries**

To demonstrate the effects of the word boundary options, open a new empty text document and type in the following text (note that there are *two* space characters between the words "one" and "two"):

```
one  two three done
```

Now follow these steps:

1. Open the Single File Find window. Select a search mode of Textual. Check the Wrap Around option.

2. In the Find field, enter the letter **o**. Select the Starts With option. Click the Next button. Click it again.

3. Replace the Find field with the letter **e**. Select the Ends With option. Click the Next button. Click it two more times.

4. Replace the Find field with the word **one**. Select the Whole Words option. Click the Next button. Click it again.

5. Replace the Find field with a space character followed by the letter **t**. Select the Contains option. Click the Next button. Click it two more times.

6. Select the Starts with option. Click the Next button. Click it again.

7. Delete the *t* from the Find field, leaving only a single space character. Select Whole Word mode. Click the Next button. Click it two more times.

How It Works

In step 2, you searched for the letter *o* at the beginning of a word boundary. Clicking Find found the *o* at the beginning of the word "one." But clicking Next again did not find the *o* in "two" or "done." Neither of these *o*'s immediately followed a word boundary.

In step 3, you searched for the letter *e* at the end of a word. This time, the Next command found the *e* at the end of "one," "three," and "done," but not the *e* in the middle of "three."

Step 4 demonstrated double-word boundary searching, otherwise known as Whole Word mode. The pattern "one" only matches the word "one" and not the text "one" at the end of the word "done." Both the *o* and *e* in the pattern are required to fall on word boundaries for the match to be successful.

In step 5, you turned word boundary matching off using the Contains option. The literal string " t" (a space character followed by the letter *t*) occurs in the text twice. The Next command found both.

Step 6 demonstrated one of the more subtle points of word boundary searching. Changing the search mode to Begins With and searching for " t" again only matched one of the two instances. The character sequence at the beginning of the word "two" did not match the pattern. The space before the word "two" follows another space, and therefore does not define a word boundary. The space before the word "three" is adjacent to the letter *o*, making the point between them a word boundary. You might naturally think of this as an "ending" word boundary, but Xcode makes no such distinction. All word boundaries are the same, and the Starts With rule requires only that the first character in the matched text immediately follow a word boundary.

Step 7 also demonstrated matching text between words. The single space character only matched the two spaces between the words "two," "three," and "done." Neither the space that follows the word "one" or the second space immediately before the word "two" are between word boundaries.

Searching for a Regular Expression

For those of you who have been living in a cave since the 1960s, regular expressions are strings of characters that describe patterns of text. Using a textual match, described in the previous section, the pattern "c.t" would match the literal text "c.t" in a file. The period character in a regular expression is instead interpreted as a pattern that means "match any single character." Thus, the regular expression "c.t" describes a sequence of three characters: The letter *c*, followed by any character, followed by the letter *t*. This pattern would match the words "cat," "cut," and "cot," as well as the text "c.t."

Regular expressions are an expansive topic. Entire books have been written on the subject. The following primer should give you a basic introduction to the most useful regular expressions. It should also serve as a handy reference to the patterns and operators supported by Xcode.

Regular Expressions

In simplified terms, regular expressions are constructed from patterns and operators. Patterns define a character to match, and operators augment how those patterns are matched. The key concept to keep in mind is that operators do not, by themselves, match anything. A pattern matches something and an operator must have a pattern on which to operate.

> When you're searching, or just practicing, with regular expressions, remember that regular expression searches are performed one line at a time and the search always begins on the line *after* the line containing the text cursor or selection. *No text within the current line will ever match an expression.* This also means that the expression only finds the first span of matching text in a line (because the next search starts on a new line). It can be very disconcerting to enter an expression that should match some text on the current line and have Xcode report that the pattern was not found.

Patterns

Every pattern in a regular expression matches exactly one character. There are many patterns that match a special character or one character from a set of possible characters. These are called meta-character patterns. The most common ones are listed in the following table. Any single character that is not a meta-character pattern, nor a regular expression operator, is a literal pattern that matches itself. The string cat is, technically, a regular expression consisting of three patterns: *c*, *a*, and *t*. This expression would match the word "cat." Which is a really long-winded way of saying that anything that doesn't contain any kind of special expression will match itself just as if you had used the Textual search mode.

Pattern	Matches
.	Matches any character.
\character	Quotes one of the following special characters: *, ?, +, [, (,), {, }, ^, $, |, \, ., or /.

Pattern	Matches
^	Matches at the beginning of a line.
$	Matches at the end of a line.
\b	Matches a word boundary.
\B	Matches a non-word boundary.
[set]	Matches any one character from the set. Sets are explained in more detail a little later.

The . pattern is used quite often with operators, but it can always be used by itself as was demonstrated in the previous "c.t" example.

Another useful pattern is the escape pattern. Most punctuation characters seem to have some special meaning in regular expressions. If you need to search for any of these characters — that is, use the character as a pattern and not an operator — then precede it with a backslash. The pattern \. will match a single period in the text. The pattern \\ will match a single backslash character.

The ^, $, \b, and \B are boundary patterns. They match the location between two characters. The first two match the positions at the beginning and end of a line, respectively. The expression ^# matches a single pound-sign character only if it is the first character on the line. Similarly, the expression ;$ matches a single semicolon only if it is the last character on a line.

The \b pattern matches the word boundary between characters. In Textual search mode, you used the Whole Words option to require that the first and last characters of the pattern "one" was found between two word boundaries. The equivalent regular expression is \bone\b. The \B pattern is the opposite and matches the position between two characters only if it is not a word boundary. The regular expression \Bone will match "done" but not "one."

The last pattern is the set. A set matches any character contained in the set. The set [abc] will match a, b, or c in the text. The expression c[au]t will match the words "cat" and "cut," but not the word "cot." Set patterns can be quite complex. The following table lists some of the more common ways to express a set.

Set	Matches
[characters]	Matches any character in the set.
[^set]	Matches any character *not* in the set.
[a-z]	Matches any character in the range starting with the Unicode value of character *a* and ending with character *z*, inclusive.
[:named set:]	Matches any character in the named set. Named sets include Alphabetic, Digit, Hex_Digit, Letter, Lowercase, Math, Quotation_Mark, Uppercase, and White_Space. For example, the set [:Hex_Digit:] will match the same characters as the set [0123456789abcdefABCDEF]. Named sets often include many esoteric Unicode characters. The :Letter: set includes all natural language letters from all languages.

The [,], -, and ^ characters may have special meaning in a set. Escape them ([X\-]) to include them in the set as a literal character. Sets can be combined and nested. The set [[:Digit:]A-Fx] will match any character that is a decimal digit, or one of the letters A, B, C, D, E, F, or x.

There are also a number of special escape patterns, as listed in the following table. Each begins with the backslash character. The letter or sequence that follows will match a single character or is shorthand for a predefined set.

Meta-character	Matches
\t	Matches a single tab character.
\n	Matches a single line feed character.
\r	Matches a single carriage return character.
\u*hhhh*	Matches a single character with the Unicode value 0x*hhhh*. \u must be followed by exactly 4 hexadecimal digits.
\U*hhhhhhhh*	Matches a character with the Unicode value 0x*hhhhhhhh*. \U must be followed by exactly 8 hexadecimal digits.
\d, \D	Matches any digit (\d) or any character that is not a digit (\D). Equivalent to the sets [:Digit:] and [^:Digit:].
\s, \S	Matches a single white space character (\s), or any character that is not white space (\S).
\w, \W	Matches any word (\w) or non-word (\W) character.

Operators

Although patterns are very flexible in matching specific characters, the power of regular expressions is in its operators. Almost every operator acts on the pattern that precedes it. The classic regular expression .* consists of a pattern (.) and an operator (*). The pattern matches any single character. The operator matches any number of instances of the preceding pattern. The result is an expression that will match any sequence of characters, including nothing at all. The following table summarizes the most useful operators.

Operator	Description
*	Matches the pattern 0 or more times.
+	Matches the pattern 1 or more times.
?	Matches the pattern 0 or 1 times.
|	Matches the pattern on the left or the right of the operator. A|B matches either A or B.
{n}	Matches the pattern exactly n times, where n is a decimal number.
{n,}	Matches that pattern n or more times.

Operator	Description
{n,m}	Matches the pattern between *n* and *m* times, inclusive.
*?, +?, ??, {n,}?, {n,m}?	Appending a ? causes these operators to match as few a number of patterns as possible. Normally, operators match as many copies of the pattern that they can find.
(regular expression)	Capturing parentheses. Used to group regular expressions. The entire expression within the parentheses can be treated as a single pattern. After the match, the range of text that matched the parenthesized subexpression is available as a variable that can be used in a replacement expression.
(?*flags–flags*)	Sets or clears one or more flags. Flags are single characters. Flags that appear before the hyphen are set. Flags after the hyphen are cleared. If only setting flags, the hyphen is optional. The changes affect the remainder of the regular expression.
(?*flags–flags*: *regular expression*)	Same as the flags-setting operator, but the modified flags only apply to the regular expression between the colon and the end of the operator.

The four repetition operators (*, +, ? and {n,m}) search for some number of copies of the previous pattern. The only difference between them is the minimum and maximum number of times a pattern is matched. As an example, the expression [0-9]+ matches one or more digits and would match the text "150" and "2," but not "one" (it contains no digits).

The ? modifier makes these operators parsimonious. Normally operators are "greedy" and match as many repetitions of a pattern as possible. The ? modifier causes repetition operators to match the fewest occurrences of a pattern that will still satisfy the expression. As an example, take the line "one, two, three, four." The expression .* matches the text "one, two, three," because the .* can match the first 15 repetitions of the . pattern and still satisfy the expression. In contrast, the pattern .*?, matches only the text "one," because it only requires three occurrences of the . pattern to satisfy the expression.

Use parentheses both to group expressions and to the capture the text matched by a subexpression. Any expression can be treated as a pattern. The expression M(iss)+ippi matches the text "Mississippi." It would also match "Missippi" and "Mississississippi." You can create very complex regular expressions by nesting expressions. The expression (0x[:Hex_Digit:]+(,\s*)?)+ matches the line "0x100, 0x0, 0x1a84e3, 0xcafebabe." Dissecting this expression, 0x[:Hex_Digit:]+ matches a hex constant that begins with 0x followed by one or more hex digits. The (,\s*)? subexpression matches a comma followed by any number of white space characters, or nothing at all (the ? operator makes the entire expression optional). Finally, the whole expression is wrapped in parentheses such that the + operator now looks for one or more repetitions of that entire pattern.

Finally, you can use the flag operators to alter one of the modes of operation. Flags before the hyphen turn the flag on; flags after the hyphen turn the flags off. If you're only turning one or more flags on, the hyphen can be omitted. The first version of the operator sets the flag for the remainder of the expression. The second version sets the flag only for expression contained within the operator. The only really useful flag is listed in the following table.

Flag	Mode	
i	Case-insensitive mode. If this flag is set, the case of letters is not considered when matching text.	

You can set or clear the i flag anywhere within an expression. When you set this flag, expressions match text irrespective of case differences. The case sensitivity at the beginning of the expression is determined by the setting of the Ignore Case option in the Find window. The expression one (?i)TWO (?-i)three will match the "one two three" text.

Finally, whatever regular expression you use, it must not match "nothing." That is, the expression cannot legitimately match an empty string. If it did, it would theoretically match every position in the entire file. The solitary expression .* will match any number of characters, but it will also match none at all, making it an illegal pattern to search for. If you try to use a pattern that matches an empty string, the Xcode warns you (see Figure 7-2).

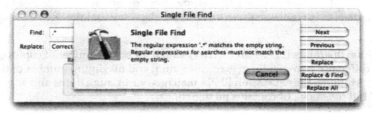

Figure 7-2

Try It Out   Search for Regular Expressions

Start with the following code fragment:

```
#define ONE    1
#define TWO    2
#if ONE+TWO != 3
    #warning "Math in this universe is not linear."
#endif

////////////////////
// Static data //
////////////////////

static Number series[] = {
        { 1, "one",    0x1 },
        { 2, "two",    0x0002 },
        { 3, "three",  0x0003 },
        { 4, "four",   0x0004 },
        { 5, "five",   0x0005 },
        { 6, "six",    0x0006 },
        { 7, "thirteen",0x000d }
```

```
    };

/////////////
// Methods //
/////////////

/*!
 * @abstract Establish the logical Set used by the receiver
 * @param set  The set to use. Will be retained by receiver. Can be null.
 */

- (void)setSet:(Set*)set
{
    [workingSet release];        /* release any old set we might still be using */
    workingSet = [set retain];   /* retain this set */
}


/*!
 * @abstract Get the set being used by this object.
 * @result The logical set used by this object. If none, an empty set is returned.
 */

- (Set*)getSet
{
    if (set!=null)
        return set;
    return [[[Set alloc] init] autorelease];
}
```

Open the Single File Find window, set the search mode to Regular Expression, clear the Ignore Case option, and set the Wrap Around option. Search repeatedly for the following regular expressions:

- ❏ one
- ❏ \bone\b
- ❏ \bSet
- ❏ \BSet
- ❏ [.*]
- ❏ \[.*\]
- ❏ /+
- ❏ /{2}.*
- ❏ /*.**/
- ❏ ^#\w+
- ❏ ".*"
- ❏ ".{3,5}"
- ❏ ".{1,10}",\t+0x[0-9a-f]{4}

151

- ❏   `".{1,10}",\s*0x[0-9a-f]{1,4}`

- ❏   ONE | TWO

- ❏   `(?i:ONE)|TWO`

How It Works

Searching for one found "one" and "done" but not "ONE." There were no special regular expression patterns or operators, making the search equivalent to a simple textual search. \bone\b required that the *c* and *e* start and end on word boundaries, making it equivalent to a textual search in Whole Word mode.

Using variations of the word boundary pattern, \bSet searched for text where the *S* starts a word, and is equivalent to a textual search in Begins With mode. \BSet specifies just the opposite and has no textual search equivalent. It only found the text "Set" when the *S* did *not* begin a word.

The expression [.*] matched any single period or asterisk in the file. Operators lose their meaning within a set and become just another character. In contrast, \[.*\] searched for an open bracket, followed by any sequence of characters, followed by a close bracket. By escaping [and] they are no longer treated as defining a set and instead are simple literal patterns that match a single bracket character. Now that they are not in a set, the . and * characters assume their more common meanings as a pattern and operator.

/+ matched one or more slash characters. Most would be C++ style comments, but it would also match a single '/'. The expression to match a C++-style comment is /{2}.*. This matches two consecutive slash characters followed by anything else up to the end of the line.

/*.**/ matched the more traditional C-style comments in the file. Note that the two literal *'s had to be escaped to avoid having them treated as operators.

^#\w+ matched a pound sign following by a word, but only if it appears at the beginning of the line. The pattern found "#define" but not "#warning".

".*" matched anything between double quotes. In the pattern ".{3,5}" this was limited to anything between double quotes that was between three and five characters long.

".{1,10}",\t+0x[0-9a-f]{4} is a complex expression designed to match statements in the Number table. If you opened the text file in the example projects, you'll notice that it failed to match the lines containing "one," "four," and "thirteen." It misses "one" because the 0x[0-9a-f]{4} expression requires exactly 4 hexadecimal digits following the "0x" and that line only has 1 digit. The line with "four" is missed because the white space between the comma and the "0x" turns out to be spaces, not tabs. And the line with "thirteen" is missed because there are no tabs at all between the comma and the hex number. The pattern ".{1,10}",\s*0x[0-9a-f]{1,4} corrects all of these shortcomings.

The expression ONE | TWO found either the text "ONE" or "TWO," but not both. The (?i:ONE)|TWO expression demonstrates altering the case-sensitivity of a subexpression. It matched "ONE," "one," and "TWO" but not "two".

More about Regular Expressions

Xcode uses the ICU (International Components for Unicode) Regular Expression package to perform its regular expression searches. This chapter explained many of its more common, and a few uncommon, features. But there is quite a bit more; although much of it is rather obscure. Should you need to stretch the limits of regular expressions in Xcode, visit the ICU Regular Expressions users guide at http://icu.sourceforge.net/ for a complete description of the syntax.

Replacing Text

Below the Find field is the Replace field. The contents of this field can be used to replace patterns found by the find command using the Replace command. The Replace field can be empty; in which case replacing the found text just deletes it.

The Replace button replaces the currently selected text in the file with the contents of the Replace field, if the currently selected text matches the current find pattern. If you find text using the Find command, and then alter the selection so that the text selected no longer matches the pattern, the Replace command no longer functions. So you can't use the replace function to change any arbitrary text selection.

The Replace & Find button replaces the current find with the replacement text, and then immediately initiates another search. Using Replace & Find with the Next button, you can selectively replace certain found text with the replacement and skip others. This is often more efficient than trying to get the "perfect" search expression that matches exactly the terms you want to replace. Use a close approximation to find all of what you are looking for, and then use the Next button to skip the ones you don't want to replace.

The Replace All button does just that. It replaces every instance of text that matches the current find pattern with the replacement text with a single command. The Wrap Around option is ignored. Instead, the current text selection and the Replace All Scope options are used to constrain the command. With one or more characters in the current text selection and the Selected Text option selected, only matching text within the current selection are replaced. If the Entire File option is checked, or if there is no selected text, every piece of matching text in the entire file is replaced. If these settings result in too much text being replaced, simply switch to the editor pane and use the Undo command to reverse the effects of the last Replace All command.

Replacing Text Using Regular Expressions

When you're using regular expressions, it is possible for the replacement text to contain portions of the text that was found. The parentheses operators not only group subexpressions, but they also capture the text that was matched by that subexpression in a variable. These variables can be used in the replacement text.

The variables are numbered. Variable 1 is the text matched by the first parenthetical subexpression, variable 2 contains the text matched by the second, and so on. The contents of these variables can be reference in the replacement text using the syntax \n, where n is the number of the subexpression. The variables in the replacement text can be used in any order, more than once, or not at all.

For example, take the text "one plus two equals three." The regular expression (\w+) plus (\w+) equals (\w+) matches that text. Because of the parentheses, the text matched by each \w+ sub-expression was captured and can be used in the replacement. The replacement text \1+\2=\3 replaces the original text with "one+two=three."

Try It Out   Replacing with Regular Expressions

Start with the following code fragment:

```
static Number series[] = {
        { 1, "one",      0x1 },
        { 2, "two",      0x0002 },
        { 3, "three",    0x0003 },
        { 4, "four",     0x0004 },
        { 5, "five",     0x0005 },
        { 6, "six",      0x0006 },
        { 7, "thirteen", 0x000d }
    };
```

Open the Single File Find window, set the search mode to Regular Expression, clear the Ignore Case option, and set the Entire File option. Then follow these steps:

1. In the Find field, enter the following regular expression: \{ ([0-9]+), (".*")

2. In the Replace field, enter the following text: { \2, \1

3. Click the Replace All button.

How It Works

The text of two subexpressions, ([0-9]+) and (".*"), were captured and used in the replacement text to reverse their order in the table. Note that the replacement text had to include the delimiters, which were outside of the subexpressions.

There are only nine variables. If the regular expression contains more than nine parenthetical subexpressions, those expressions are not accessible. Variables that do not correspond to a subexpression are always empty.

If parentheses are nested, they are assigned to variables in the order that the opening parentheses appeared in the expression. If a subexpression is used to match multiple occurrences of text, only the last match is retained in the variable. Take the following text:

```
one, two, three;
```

The regular expression ((, *)?(\w+))+ matches the three words before the semicolon. If you replace them using 1='\1' 2='\2' 3='\3', the result is as follows:

```
1=', three' 2=', ' 3='three';
```

Variable 1 contains the last occurrence of the outermost subexpression. Variables 2 and 3 each contain the last occurrence of their respective subexpression. The values of the first two occurrences are lost.

Search History

To the right of the Find and Replace fields are pop-up menus that keep a history of the search and replace terms you've used (see Figure 7-3). The history is global, but only lasts for as long as Xcode is running. Restarting Xcode clears the history.

Figure 7-3

New search and replace terms are added to the top of each list, but never duplicated in the list. Click the drop-down menu button to the right of either field to view the history. Use the mouse and click any previously used term, using the scrollbars to locate the item if necessary. Or after the list is popped-up, use the up and down arrow keys to select a pattern and then press the Return key.

Searching Multiple Files

Every project has a Project Find window. You can open the Project Find window for the active project using the Find⇨Find In Project (Command+Shift+F) command. The Project Find window, shown in Figure 7-4, consists of three principal parts.

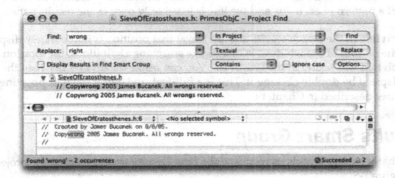

Figure 7-4

The Find and Replace fields are identical to those in the Single File Find window. The last search term used in any find window (project or single file) automatically appears in the Find field.

To the right of the Find and Replace fields are three pop-up menus. The top one determines the Batch Find Options set to use, which essentially determines which set of files will be searched. Normally, this is set to In Project, which searches all of the source files that are referenced in the project. The Options button lets you alter the batch find options or define new sets. (This chapter explores more about batch find options a little later on.)

The middle pop-up menu selects how the Find field is interpreted. The first two choices, Textual and Regular Expression, have already been covered at length in the earlier parts of this chapter. The additional choice of Definitions performs a textual search through the symbols defined in the project (you can't search the symbols using a regular expression). These are the symbols gathered when the project is indexed — the ones that appear in the Symbols smart group and are used by the Find⇨Jump to Definition command discussed in Chapter 6. Indexing must be turned on for a Definitions search to work. When you're searching Definitions, the batch find options are ignored.

The bottom pop-up selects between the four textual search modes: Contains, Starts With, Ends With, and Whole Words. It applies equally to Textual and Definition searches, and is disabled for Regular Expression searches. The Ignore Case option works the same way it does in the Single File Find window.

The Find button searches for every instance of the Find pattern in every file of the find set, or through all of the symbol names when you're searching Definitions. The results of the search are normally displayed in the middle pane of the window, as previously shown in Figure 7-4.

Every file that contains the search pattern is listed in the results pane as a group. The individual lines within each file that match the pattern are listed below the file. Use the disclosure triangle next to the file to collapse or expand the group, temporarily hiding all of the "hits" in a specific file. The text that matched the search pattern is displayed in bold text.

Textual finds search the file one character at a time. If a single line contains multiple occurrences of a pattern, that line appears multiple times in the results pane, with each successive match in bold text. Regular Expression searches search one line at a time. A Regular Expression search only finds the first occurrence of a pattern in each line and the line is listed only once in the results pane.

Select any text line in the search results and the file at that position is immediately displayed in the editor pane at the bottom of the window. When you're searching Definitions, the location is the definition or declaration that was found in the source file. You can resize the divider between the list and the editor pane, or collapse it by double-clicking it. This is a full-featured editor pane, supporting all of the built-in editing features described in Chapter 6.

Find Results Smart Group

Every find that is executed adds its results to the Find Results smart group in the project window, as shown in Figure 7-5.

Select an item in the Find Results smart group and the details pane lists the location (file name and line number) and the line or symbol definition that was found. Selecting a "hit" from the list displays that location in the project window's editor pane. You can also double-click the item or use the View⇨Open In Separate Editor command to open the file in a new window, at the location of the line or symbol. Selecting an item in the group and pressing the Delete key disposes of the search results.

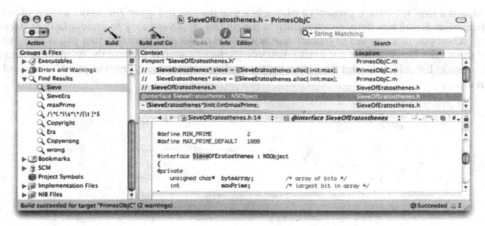

Figure 7-5

When you check the Display Results in Find Smart Group option of the Project Find window, the smart group interface becomes your primary means of browsing the results of a search. With this option checked, the results list in the Project Find window disappears. When a find is executed, the project window comes to the font and the results of the search are automatically selected. If you prefer to stay in the project find window and review the search results there, leave this option unchecked.

Project Search History

Like the Single File Find window, the Project Find window remembers the terms used for each find and replace. Each Project Find window maintains its own history. In addition to remembering the term that was searched for, the Project Find window also remembers the results of the find. Selecting a previously used term from the history pop-up button on the right side of the Find field not only restores the old term, but brings the results of that search back into the results pane. These are the same results kept by the Find Results smart group. The pop-up history in the Project Find window only retains the most recent result for each search term. The Find Results group keeps an individual record of every search performed.

The results — that is the individual locations that were found — remain the same long after the files have been changed. Recalling a previous search recalls the locations that were found when that search was executed. If you browse these locations, you may find that the text displayed in the results list no longer agrees with the contents of the file. To find the occurrences of the term as it exists now, you must run the Find command again.

Replacing Text in Multiple Files

The Replace button replaces some or all of the occurrences listed in the find results with the text in the Replace field. Regular Expression searches can use replacement variables. The selected text lines in the results list determine which occurrences are replaced. If no source lines are selected, all listed occurrences are replaced. If one or more text lines are selected, only those occurrences are replaced. Selecting a file group in the list has no effect and is not considered an occurrence. Use the Edit➪Select All command to select all lines in the results list. Select a subset using the Shift and Command keys while clicking lines in the list.

Clicking the Replace button presents a dialog box like the one in Figure 7-6. Make a habit of reading the confirmation dialog box before committing to the replace. It is very easy to accidentally replace all occurrences when you just wanted to replace one or a subset of the occurrences when you wanted to replace all of them. The latter usually happens when you perform a search, browse the results (leaving text lines in the results list selected), and then perform the replace—mistakenly thinking that Xcode will replace them all.

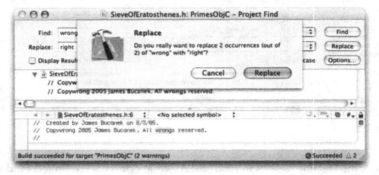

Figure 7-6

Also be careful about recalling old searches or editing files between the time you do the find and the replace. The history of search results remembers what the original occurrence was, and the original locations of those occurrences, even if the text in file is now different. Xcode will be more than happy to replace those locations with whatever you put in the Replace field; oblivious of what content is now at those locations. This is in stark contrast to the Single File Find window, which will refuse to replace anything that doesn't match the search term in the Find field.

Although this "feature" can save the day (if you make a mistake in the replacement text, you can perform another replacement to correct it even if the search won't find those occurrences any more), more often than not it creates a mess by replacing text that doesn't match the search term. When you're using the Project Find window, get into the habit of rerunning any search you recall. Use the Find Results group in the Project Find window to browse the results of old searches.

Batch File Options

Which files the Find command in the Project Find window searches for is determined by the batch file options. Batch file options are stored in sets. You select a set using the top pop-up menu control in the Project Find window. By default, the set is In Project. This set searches all of the files referenced by the project, excluding frameworks. Clicking the Options button presents the Batch Find Options window, shown in Figure 7-7.

The batch file options set you are modifying is controlled by the Find Sets pop-up menu at the top of the window. Be careful: the Find Sets selection does not automatically default to the set you have selected in the find window. After clicking the Options button, make sure you are editing the correct set before changing any of the options. Batch find sets are shared by all projects. If you want to define a special set of options, consider creating a custom set rather than redefining the default sets.

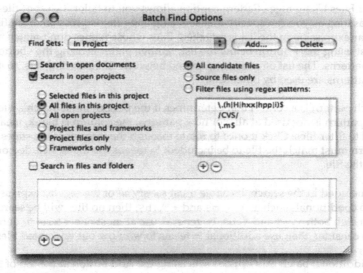

Figure 7-7

The Search in Open Documents option includes any file open in any editor pane.

The Search in Open Projects option includes files referenced in open projects. Which files, and from which projects, is defined by the next two radio button groups. The first group determines which files are included, and can be set to Selected Files in This Project, All Files in This Project, or All Open Projects. Normally, it is set to All Files in This Project and only searches the files in the current project. If you typically work with multiple projects that are related, using All Open Projects lets you search through all of the files in all of your projects. Selected Files in This Project requires that you first select the specific files you want to search in the project window.

The second radio button group controls which class of files is included in the search. Project Files and Frameworks searches all source files referenced in the project, including all of the source files in the project frameworks. Project Files Only excludes the headers and source files contained in frameworks. Frameworks Only searches only the headers and source files in the frameworks, ignoring the source files of the project itself.

Below these options are the Search in Files and Folders check box and a list. The list can contain any arbitrary file or directory that should be included in the search. Add a file or directory by clicking the plus (+) button below the list, or simply drag files and folders into the list. Remove items from the list by selecting them and clicking the minus (-) button or pressing the Delete key. Each set has its own list of additional files.

On the right are options that control which file types are searched. Use these options to exclude certain file types from the search. The All Candidate Files option doesn't exclude anything, and will search all of the text files defined by the other options. Source Files Only limits the search to files that contain source code. Text files like documentation, RTF, and HTML files will be skipped.

Finally, the Filter Files Using regex Patterns option allows you to tailor the set of files searched to any specific subset, as long as you can specify that set using a regular expression. Each file name that matches a regular expression in the list is searched. Files whose names don't match are ignored. Add a pattern to the list using the + button below the list; remove patterns using the - button. Double-click to edit one of the patterns. The list of patterns is shared between all batch find sets, so don't make arbitrary changes if the patterns are used by other sets.

To the left of each pattern is a control that determines if the pattern must match a file name, must not match, or if the pattern is not used at all. For new patterns, the column is blank, meaning that the pattern will not be used to filter files. Click it once to rotate through the three possible states. An equals sign (+) means the pattern must match the file to be included. != means the file is included only if the pattern does not match the file.

For a file to be included in the search, its name must satisfy *all* of the regular expressions in the list. If the list contains two conditionals such as = \.m$ and = \.h$, then no files will be searched. There is no file name that will match both \.m$ and \.h$. In general, use at most one = term to define the principle group of files to consider, then use additional != terms to winnow out unwanted files.

You can create additional batch find options sets using the Add button at the top of the window. Give the new set a name and then edit its settings as you see fit. Remember that editing a set doesn't alter the set selected in the Project Find window. After you've created a new set, remember to select that set in the Project Find window.

Use the Delete button to delete the current batch find options set. There is no confirmation; the set is deleted immediately and permanently.

Search Shortcuts

Searching and replacing text during development is very common, and often repetitive. A number of shortcuts are provided by Xcode to keep your keystrokes and mouse clicks to a minimum. Most of the Find menu commands, listed in the following table, apply to the active editor pane or the Single File Find window except where noted. Many of these same commands appear in the contextual pop-up menu in the editor pane.

> **Pressing the Return key in either the Single File Find window or the Project Find window executes the search.**

Command	Description
Find In Project (Command+Shift+F)	Opens the Project Find window, described in the previous section.
Find Selected Text In Project	Makes the currently selected text the search term in the Project Find window. The Project Find window is opened, the search mode is switched to Textual, and a find is executed. The other options in the window remain as they were.
Find Selected Definition In Project	Identical to the Find Selected Text In Project command, but the search mode is first changed to Definitions before executing the search.
Single File Find (Command+F)	Opens the Single File Find window, described at the beginning of this chapter.
Find Next (Command+G)	Executes the current single file find again. This command does not work in the Project Find window, but can be used in either the Single File Find window or an editor pane.
Find Selected Text	Makes the currently selected text the find term and executes a search. All of the other options and settings in the Single File Find window remain the same, including the search type (Textual or Regular Expression). It does not open the Single File Find window. This is equivalent to using the Use Selection for Find command followed by Find Next.
Replace	Replaces the currently selected text with the replacement text, but only if the currently selected text matches the current search term.
Replace and Find Next	Another combination command, this command performs a Replace followed by a Find Next.
Use Selection for Find (Command+E)	Takes the currently selected text and transfers it to the Find field of both the Single File Find and Project Find windows. A subsequent Find command will use the new text as the search term. The command does not alter the search mode, so if the search mode is Regular Expression, the selected text will be interpreted as a regular expression.
Use Selection for Replace	The companion command of Use Selection for Find, this command takes the currently selected text and makes it the replacement text in both find windows.

The states of the find windows are retained even if the windows aren't open. If you perform a find using the Single File Find window, and then use the Find⇨Find Next command, the same search is executed again. Likewise, if you use the Find⇨Find Selected Text command, all of the other options set in the Single File Find window apply.

Searching Lists

Another kind of search tool is located in the toolbar, as shown in Figure 7-8. This quick search field quickly winnows any details list to only those items that match the term in the search field.

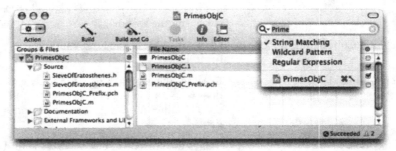

Figure 7-8

The list could be a list of files in the project, a list of bookmarks, the project symbols, or even the results of a project search. In short, whatever you have listed in the details pane can be filtered using this search field.

In most contexts, the search field operates in one of three modes — String Matching, Wildcard Pattern, or Regular Expression — as described in the following table. Select the mode by clicking the magnifying glass at the left end of the field. The current mode is displayed in grey when the field is empty, so you know what mode it is in before you enter anything.

Search Mode	Description
String Matching	Performs a simple textual search.
Wildcard Pattern	Wildcards patterns use the so-called "globbing" characters used by the shell. The characters * and ? will match any string or a single character, respectively. A set of characters can be defined with the set syntax: [chars]. For example, the pattern *.h will match all of the header files in a file list. Don't confuse wildcards with regular expression operators.
Regular Expression	The same regular expressions described earlier in this chapter.

In some contexts, the search field may have special modes specific to the type of list being displayed. The Project Symbols smart group displays the list of indexed symbols in the details list. When you're displaying the symbols list, the search modes change to Search All, Search Symbols, Search Kind, and Search Location. Choosing a setting other than Search All limits the search to a particular column in the table.

To use the search field, simply type something into it. Whatever you enter is immediately used to reduce the details list to only those items that match the search term. Figure 7-9 shows the effect of entering a simple term while the details list displays contents of the Project Symbols smart group. Notice that the search term "ma" found the symbol main, but it also found "Macro" symbols.

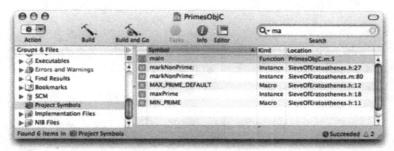

Figure 7-9

Erasing the contents of the search field, or clicking the X button at the right end of the field, cancels the search and restores the details list to its typically voluminous, uncensored, state.

Using the quick search field is particularly handy when digging through a large number of symbols or file names. It can also be extremely useful when you're browsing a search result. The results of a search can be further narrowed without the need to compose a more complex search, and the experiment doesn't require another search to be executed. Execute the broad search in the Project Find window, then switch to the Find Results smart group and enter a second search term in the search field. Only those lines that match both terms are listed.

Summary

You should now have at least a basic understanding of the file and project search tools. Regular expressions are a powerful tool, but using them is often more art than science. If you are new to using regular expressions, be patient. After you grasp the fundamentals of regular expressions, you will be in possession of a very powerful development tool. And don't forget the quick search field; it comes in very handy when you're wading through large projects.

The next chapter looks at yet another way of finding symbols in your project using the Class Browser.

Exercise

Open the version of the PrimesObjC project included with Chapter 7. Perform the following changes:

❑ You don't like seeing the message `warning: local declaration of maxPrime hides instance variable` when building. Change the name of the `maxPrime` parameter variable to `largestPrime`.

❑ Replace the C-style (`/* ... */`) comments at the end of a line with C++-style (`// ...`) comments.

Class Browser

In the previous chapter, you learned how to search for symbols in the Symbols smart group and the source code itself. Chapter 11 will show you high-level tools for designing and maintaining classes. The former only finds symbols by name, and the latter requires that you create special documents describing the classes you want to examine. The Class Browser sits right between these two extremes. It builds a structured picture of the project's classes that describes the methods, instance variables, and inheritance of each class.

The best part about the Class Browser is that it's free. You don't have to do anything special to your project beyond turning on indexing. Once the symbols index for your project is built, the Class Browser is ready to go.

Navigating the Class Browser

The Project⇨Class Browser (Command+Shift+C) command opens the Class Browser window, shown in Figure 8-1.

Figure 8-1

If a Class Browser window is already open, it is brought to the front. Normally, there is only one Class Browser window for each project. It is possible to open multiple Class Browser windows by clicking the New Class Browser button in the toolbar. This permits you to view different aspects of your classes simultaneously.

The toolbar contains the Option Set, Configure Options, and New Class Browser controls. The Option Set menu and Configure Options button work like the batch find options in the Project Find window. The pop-up menu lets you select the named set of browser options, and the Configure Options button allows you to alter the options in a set or create new sets. There are no menu or keyboard equivalents for these functions; you will have to use the toolbar to access them. This chapter will cover option sets and the browser options shortly.

On the left is the Class list. This lists all classes, interfaces, and protocols defined in the project. These can be organized in a hierarchy — each class becomes a group that contains all of the child classes that inherit from it. Expand or collapse groups using the triangle to the left of the class name. Hold down the Option key to recursively collapse or expand all subclasses. Alternatively, you can list the classes in alphabetical order. Java class names include the package so that similarly named classes in different packages can be easily distinguished. Classes defined in a source file of the project are displayed in a blue. Classes defined in a framework are black.

Selecting a class in the list displays the member elements of that class in the details pane on the right, and the definition of the class in the source code in the editor pane below it. The details pane lists the member elements, grouped by type. Members defined in the class are black, and members inherited from a superclass are grey. Member functions and methods are listed first, followed by data variables. Class (static) members are listed before instance members. You can reorganize and resize the table columns by dragging in the column headers, but you cannot change the sorting order.

Selecting any member in the details list displays the declaration of that item in the editor pane below it. Double-clicking either the class name or a member opens that location in a new editor window. You can resize, but you can't completely collapse, the editor pane using the divider bar.

If online documentation is available for a class, a small book icon appears to the right of the class name. Clicking the book displays the documentation page for that class in the editor pane. If an individual member is documented, that member has its own book icon in the details list. This is typically just a bookmark within the class documentation page, as shown in Figure 8-2, but it saves you the trouble of scrolling or searching to find that method. Double-click the book icon to open the documentation in a new window.

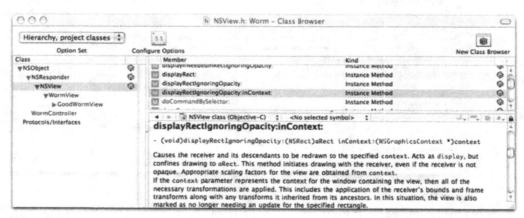

Figure 8-2

Browse Classes

Download the StickiesExample sample project from Apple's Developer Connection (http://developer.apple.com/samplecode/StickiesExample/StickiesExample.html). Open the SimpleStickies3_Final project, make sure project indexing is on, and then open the Class Browser. (If you download the disk image of the sample and you need to upgrade the project, you must first copy the project folders to a writable location.) Now follow these steps:

1.   Switch among the four predefined Class Browser option sets:

❑   Hierarchy, All Classes

❑   Hierarchy, Project Classes

❑   Flat, All Classes

❑   Flat, Project Classes

2.   Expand and collapse superclasses in the hierarchy list.

3.   Click different classes and members.

4.   Click the book icon for a class.

5.   Create a new option set and try out different combinations of the options.

How It Works

The Class Browser should automatically index and format all of the classes defined in the project and should appear like the Class Browser in Figure 8-3.

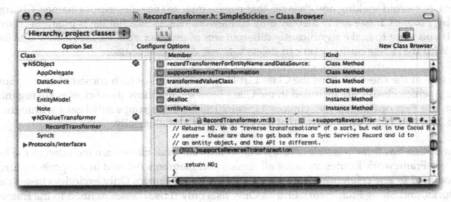

Figure 8-3

Class Browser Option Sets

The Class Browser comes preconfigured with four option sets. These four sets of options display just those classes defined in the project or all classes visible to the project. The classes can be organized in a hierarchy or listed alphabetically irrespective of relationships.

Click the Configure Options button to edit the configuration of a set. This displays the Class Browser options configuration sheet, shown in Figure 8-4.

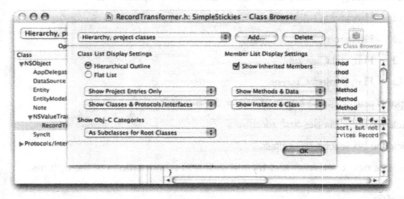

Figure 8-4

Select the set of options to edit using the pop-up menu at the top of the sheet. You can edit the prede-fined sets, but avoid making any changes that run counter to their descriptive names. Changing the Hierarchy, Project Classes set to display only framework classes in a flat list is guaranteed to cause con-fusion. If you want to make significantly different sets of browser options, create new sets using the Add button. With the delete button, you can delete sets you don't care to use.

The left side of the sheet contains the Class List Display Settings, which consist of four options that determine which classes are included in the Class Browser, and how those classes are organized in the class list. The first option has two choices: Hierarchical Outline groups subclasses within their superclass in a tree, and Flat List simply sorts all of the class names alphabetically.

The next option has three possible settings that determine what classes are included in the list. Show Project and Framework Entries includes all classes and members defined in the project source and any classes defined in any referenced frameworks. Show Project Entries Only excludes classes defined in the frameworks, and Show Framework Entries Only lists only those classes defined in the frameworks. When you use the Hierarchical Outline display, an exception is made for superclasses. Superclasses of a class, regardless of where they are defined, are always included in the hierarchical display as the parents of that class. This also affects the display of inherited class members. If a project class inherits a method or variable from a framework class, and Show Project Entries Only is selected, those inherited members are not listed.

The third option also has three possible settings: Show Classes & Protocols/Interface, Show Classes Only, Show Protocols/Interfaces Only. This control determines if only the class definitions, only protocols/interface definitions, or both are included in the class list. If both are included, protocols and interfaces are grouped together at the bottom of the class list. In the hierarchical view, they are listed under the title Protocols/Interfaces. In the list view, each is prefixed with the "Prot:" text.

The last option only applies to Objective-C and determines how Objective-C categories are organized in the class list. For those not familiar with Objective-C, a *category* is a way of defining a set of methods for a class where the definition and implementation of those methods is completely outside the definition of the class itself. In other words, it's a way of "attaching" methods to a class without subclassing, just as if those methods had been defined in the class itself. (If the C++ and Java programmers in the audience are scratching their heads wondering how this is possible, the magic occurs at runtime — all message dispatching in Objective-C is dynamic, so new method handlers can be added to any class during program execution.) The problem is that categories don't fit in the neat hierarchy of classes and interfaces, because they are neither.

The choice of As Subclass treats the category as if it was a subclass in the hierarchy. The category appears as a subclass of the attached class with a "Cat:" prefix. This makes it clear which class the category was written for, but is somewhat misleading because the category is *not* a subclass. The methods defined by the category are defined in that class and inherited by any subclasses — neither of which will be reflected in the Class Browser. If you're looking for the methods in a class, you have to browse not only that class but all of its categories, and any categories of its superclasses as well.

The second alternative is the As Subclasses for Root Classes option. This treats a category as though it was a subclass of the root object of the class it is attached to (almost invariably NSObject). Although this is also a fabrication, it has the advantage that categories are easy to find because they end up grouped together at the end of NSObject's subclasses. More important, the methods defined by a category correctly appear in the attached class and any of its subclasses. This is probably the most useful setting.

The final choice, Always Merged into Class, is the most accurate in that it merges the category methods into each class just as though those methods had been defined in that class. The categories themselves are not shown anywhere in the class list. To discover which methods of a class are defined by a category you must refer to the source declaration of each method.

On the right are three controls that influence the amount of detail presented about each class. The Show Inherited Members option causes the members of a class to include all inherited members. Inherited members are displayed in grey, and the members defined or overridden in the class are black. The Show Methods & Data, Show Methods Only, or Show Data Only options display all members of the class, or only methods, or only instance variables respectively. The Show Instance & Class, Show Instance Only, Show Class Only options further refine the class details such that it lists all class members, or only instance members, or only class members. The term *class* is really an Objective-C term, where it refers to messages that can be sent to the Class object, as opposed to regular messages that would be sent to an instance of that class. In C++ and Java, class refers to static members and variables. Note that so-called static nested classes are regular classes and will appear in the browser hierarchy within their superclass.

Browser Shortcuts

To quickly jump to a class or method in the class browser, select the symbol name in the source code and use the View⇨Reveal in Class Browser command. If the symbol is defined or overridden in several different classes, the first declaration found in the browser is selected. Use the Find⇨Jump to Definition (Command+double-click) command to quickly navigate between the similar declarations.

Summary

The Class Browser is a powerful tool, and learning to use it provides you with an important tool for viewing the class structure of any project. In some ways, it is both a search tool and a documentation tool. Object-oriented programs were once said to be self-documenting. Although this is rarely true, being able to visually navigate the class structure of a project can provide insights into its organization that code comments and documentation often fail to provide.

The position of this chapter is no accident. Conceptually, the Class Browser also sits somewhere between the generic search features of the last chapter and the documentation and help system described in the next chapter.

Help and Documentation

Modern operating systems are staggering in their size and complexity. The sheer quantity of application program interfaces (APIs) available to a developer can be overwhelming at times. There are scores of frameworks and libraries, each consisting of literally thousands of classes, methods, functions, and constants. Often, just finding the correct method or constant can be your most difficult programming task.

To help you navigate this jungle of symbols, Xcode provides integrated help and documentation. You can browse and search developer documentation All of the major APIs are indexed, allowing you to call up the documentation for any symbol almost instantly.

Help and Documentation Window

The main interface for all Xcode help is the Help and Documentation window, which this chapter simply refers to as the *help window*. There are various ways of opening it, but the simplest is to choose the Help⇨Xcode Help (Command+Shift+?) or Help⇨Documentation (Command+Option+Shift+?) command.

The help window, shown in Figure 9-1, has four panes. On the left are the Search Groups and Bookmarks panes. On the right are the search results list and the documentation browser. "Browser" is somewhat of a misnomer because the pane is really just an editor pane. But documentation is inevitably in HTML or RTF format and is not normally writable (notice the padlock icon in the upper-right corner). Consequently, the pane almost always displays HTML-formatted text that cannot be altered — making "browser" as accurate a term as any. The toolbar contains a Configure Options button and a Full-Text Search field, both used in searching the documentation.

Browsing the Apple Developer Connection Reference Library

The easiest way to use the help window is as a documentation browser. Every group and subgroup in the Search Groups list is a starting point in the Apple Developer Connection (ADC) Reference Library. Select any group in the list to display the overview for that topic, as shown in Figure 9-2.

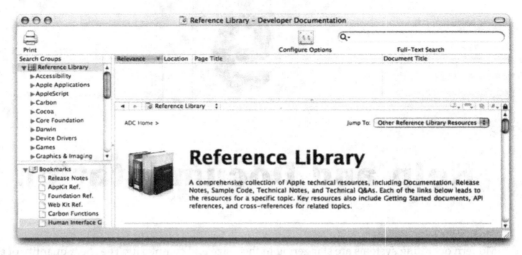

Figure 9-1

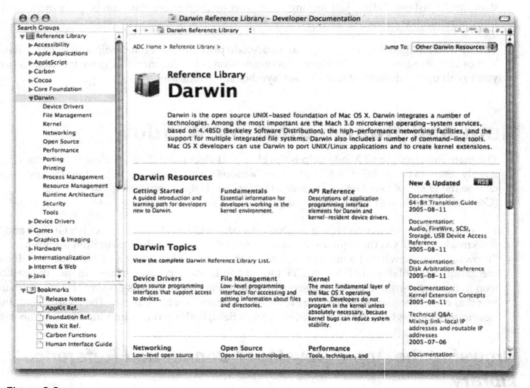

Figure 9-2

The Reference Library, the major groups within the Reference Library, and the Xcode help groups are all summary pages organized so that you can explore that particular subject or technology. Figure 9-2 shows the summary page for Darwin. As is typical for a summary page, it breaks down the various subtopics of Darwin programming with short abstracts about each one. At the top are introductory articles and technology overviews to help you get started.

Clicking any of the subtopic links takes you to a document collection, as shown in Figure 9-3. You can also jump to one of these document collection pages by selecting the corresponding subgroup in the Search Groups list. Figure 9-3 shows the documents for the Kernel subtopic, which was accessed by selecting the Kernel subgroup in the Search Groups list. (Clicking the Kernel subtopic on the summary page would have brought up the same page.)

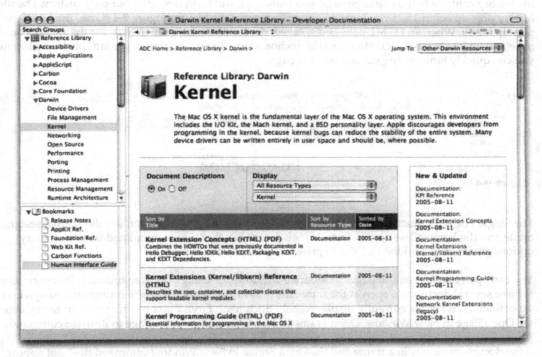

Figure 9-3

Document collection pages are simplified search engines. The articles listed are those that match the particular topic and subtopic of interest. Documents have a title, a description, a topic, a type, and a date. You can turn document descriptions on or off (for a more compact listing) using the Document Descriptions radio buttons. You can restrict the list of documents to a particular type by changing the top pop-up button under the Display title. Typical document types are Documentation, Sample Code, Technical notes, and Technical Q&As. For example, if you only want to see the sample code for this particular topic, change the Display option to Sample Code.

The pop-up menu below the resource type lets you quickly jump to other subtopics in the Kernel documentation tree. There is usually a Jump To pop-up menu at the top of the page that can take you back to the top-level Reference Library page or to other collections of documents in this topic. You will often find a list of related links and recently updated documents on the right side of the page.

Clicking the column headers above the list of articles allows you to sort the documents by title, type, or date.

Navigating Help Documents

Documents are web pages. For the most part, you navigate them by following the links on the page. The file history controls in the editor pane let you walk back and forth through your page history. The file history pop-up control lets you jump to a specific page in the history. Figure 9-4 shows the functions pop-up menu. When an HTML page is displayed, the functions navigation tools list the anchors on the page and let you jump directly to a specific anchor. Many documentation pages are constructed so that you can quickly jump to any subsection on a page.

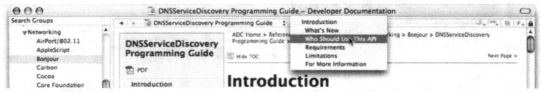

Figure 9-4

The Single File Find functions search through the contents of a page. You can use the Textual search mode and the Ignore Case option. In an HTML document, the Wrap Around and word boundary options are ignored, and the Regular Expression mode is nonfunctional.

You can open documentation pages in separate windows, or using your web browser. This permits you to have several documents open at the same time. Control-/right-click in the content area (anywhere other than a link) of the currently displayed help document. From the contextual pop-up menu, choose the Open Page in New Window, Open Frame in New Window, or Open Page in Browser command.

If the documentation is in a frame and the Open Frame in New Window command does not appear, make sure you don't have any text on the page selected.

The two New Window commands open the documentation in a new editor window. This is not a second help window, just an editor window with the contents of the HTML documentation. Similarly, the Open Page in Browser command opens the HTML document using your preferred browser.

Most of the ADC documents are organized using HTML frames with the chapter sections on the left and the documentation pages on the right. The two New Window commands either open just the documentation page alone, or the entire frame including the navigation links. The Open Page in Browser command always opens the entire frame.

Most ADC documentation pages have a link at the top of the page to Hide or Show the TOC. This link reloads just the documentation page (hiding the section links), or reloads the frame (showing the section links). These links work in Xcode's editor pane and should also work in your favorite browser.

You can also open up a link in a separate window or browser without displacing the document currently in the help window. To open the contents of a link in a new editor window, Command-click the link. To immediately open a link in your preferred browser, Option-click the link. To access additional options, Control-/right-clicking the link and selecting the Open Page in New Browser/Window, Open Link in New Browser/Window, or Copy Link command. The Open Link in New Browser and Open Link in New Window are the same as the Option-click and Command-click shortcuts. In an almost reversal of the terminology used in the previous commands, the two Open Link commands open just the document (link) that the link points to, and the Open Page variant opens the page in the chapter frame.

Bookmarks

Choose the Find⇨Add to Bookmarks command to create a bookmark to the current document. Many ADC documents are organized into chapters. You can always create a bookmark to an entire document, and often to a particular chapter, but you usually cannot create a bookmark to a particular page in a chapter. Select the Add to Bookmark command and Xcode creates the most specific bookmark it can. Bookmarks are added to the Bookmarks group in the lower-left corner of the help window (see Figure 9-5).

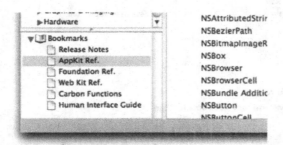

Figure 9-5

Click a bookmark to revisit the document. Select the link and press the Delete key to delete a bookmark. Documentation bookmarks are global and are independent of the Bookmarks group of the project. The title of the bookmark is the same as the title of the document or chapter. Unlike project bookmarks, you cannot edit the name.

External Links

Some links in the help window point to documents other than text, RTF, or HTML pages. These might be PDF versions of the documentation, disk images of example projects, or Internet links. These external links are handed off to the operating system for resolution outside of Xcode. The operating system responds in a predictable fashion. For example, a link to a local PDF document opens that document in your preferred PDF document viewer (typically the Preview or Adobe Reader application). It can be disconcerting to click a documentation link and suddenly discover that your web browser is downloading and mounting a disk image, but this is perfectly normal behavior.

Extended Documentation

The ADC documentation package provided with Xcode is expansive, but it's not everything. Apple's Developer Connection provides even more documentation and resources, both online and in the Developer DVD Series. Links in the documentation first look to the local documentation files installed with Xcode. If the document is not there, Xcode searches other sources. These extended sources are configured in the Documentation tab of the Xcode Preferences, shown in Figure 9-6.

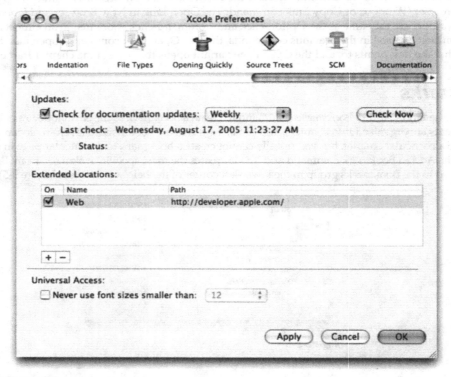

Figure 9-6

Xcode comes preconfigured to search the online documents on the ADC web site (http://developer .apple.com/). To access these extended resources, you must have an active Internet connection. You can also add the locations of additional copies of the ACD Reference Library by clicking the + button below the list and browsing to that location. The most likely source for an ADC Reference Library would be the copy distributed on the Developer DVD Series. This might be a permanently mounted DVD or possibly an image of the DVD on a file server being shared among several developers.

To remove a location from the list, select it and click the - button below the list. To ignore a location without removing from the list, uncheck the box in the On column.

Try It Out   **Add an Extended Documentation Source**

If you receive the Apple Developer DVD Series as a member of Apple's Developer Connection, insert the latest Developer DVD in your DVD drive. Then follow these steps:

1. Open the Documentation tab of the Xcode Preferences.

2. In the Extended Locations table, click the + button and navigate to the Developer DVD. Select the ADC Reference Library folder and click the Add button.

3. Drag the ADC Reference Library entry to the top of the list. The preference pane should now look like Figure 9-7.

Figure 9-7

4. Click OK. Open the help window.

5. Navigate to the ADC Reference Library⇨Darwin⇨Networking subtopic. Find the Network Kernel Extensions Programming Guide. Click the PDF link.

How It Works

Many of the alternate documentation formats (like the PDF versions of documentation) are not included in the Xcode package. The PDF link does not point to a document in Xcode's ADC Reference Library folder, so it went looking for an external source. The DVD was the first external source in the list, so the PDF document was opened from the DVD. This can be verified by looking at the path of the document in the Preview application, shown in Figure 9-8. If the DVD was not available, or did not contain the document, the search would have continued, trying to load the document from the ADC web site instead.

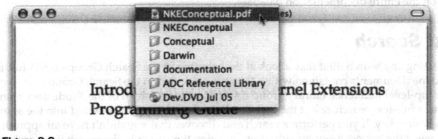

Figure 9-8

Controlling Text Size

You can adjust the size of text in the help browser pane with the Format⇨Font⇨Bigger and Format⇨Font⇨Smaller commands. You can establish a minimum size for text in the Universal Access section of Xcode's documentation preferences, as shown in Figure 9-9. Enable the Never Use Font Size Smaller Than option, and then select the smallest font size for documentation text.

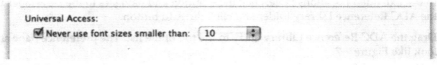

Figure 9-9

Searching Documentation

Browsing the ADC documentation is great way to get an overview of a technology or work through a tutorial. During actual development, however, you usually just want to find something specific — and you want to find it in a hurry.

The help window's search field is in the toolbar, as shown in Figure 9-10. It works in two modes, API Search and Full-Text Search, which you select using the magnifying glass icon at the left end of the field.

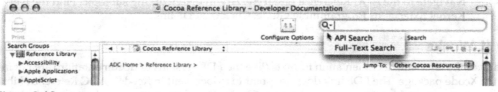

Figure 9-10

API Search mode searches only the Application Program Interface portion of the documentation. This mode will be discussed shortly. First, take a look at the Full-Text Search mode, which performs keyword searches on the entire documentation database.

Full-Text Search

Before starting any search, first take a look at the selection in the Search Groups list. A full-text search is limited to the documents contained within the group selected in the Search Groups list. For example, select the top-level Reference Library group if you want to search all of the Xcode documentation. Then to perform a full-text search, select the Full-Text Search mode, type a keyword into the search field, and press the Return key. If you perform a search and discover that you didn't have an appropriate group selected, select the correct group or subgroup, position the cursor in the search field, and press the Return key again. This reruns the search in the new group. You cannot select multiple groups at once.

The documents found are listed in the search results list. If necessary, you can adjust the divider bar between the results list and documentation browser — drag the divider to make the results list visible.

Each document found lists its relevance, location (local drive or Internet link), page title, and document title. The list is normally ordered by relevance, but you can sort it using other criteria by clicking on one of the column titles. Click the title a second time to reverse the order.

Click once on a line in the results list to open that document or link. Local HTML documents are displayed in the browser pane. Non-document resources and Internet links are passed to the appropriate helper application.

Search Expressions

Full-text searches are keyword searches. For example, a search for the word "oval" finds all documents that contain the word "oval" but not a document that only contains the words "ovals" or "oval's." A search for "oval button" finds only documents containing both the words "oval" and "button." More complex searches can be constructed using the operators listed in the following table.

Operator	Meaning
(...)	Logical group. Treats the terms between the parentheses as a single term.
!	Not. Inverts the sense of the search term.
&	And. Requires that the term on the left and the right are both true. This is the default when you're searching for multiple keywords.
|	Or. Matches if either the term on the right or the term on the left is true.
+	Required word. Equivalent to just searching for a keyword.
–	Unwanted word. Equivalent to excluding any document that contains the keyword.
*	Wildcard. Makes keyword matches variable.

You can use Boolean operators to refine the search considerably. A search for "oval & !(arc | line)" searches for all documents that contain the word "oval" but do not contain either the word "arc" or "line."

The shorthand - syntax specifies that the keyword must not appear in the document. The search "+oval -line" is equivalent to the Boolean "oval & (!line)" search term.

Use *either* the Boolean operators (!, &, |, (, and)) or the shorthand syntax of the + and – operators. Mixing the two can produce unexpected results.

The wildcard operator permits partial keyword matches. The * operator matches any string. The "window*" keyword matches "window," "windows," and "windowless." Wildcards can appear anywhere in the keyword. Wildcards at the beginning or middle of a keyword can result in slower search times.

The search technology used by the help window for full-text searches is part of the Search Kit framework. You can find out more about using Search Kit from within an application at http://developer .apple.com/documentation/UserExperience/Conceptual/SearchKitConcepts/.

API Search

Searching through the documentation is useful when you want to find high-level documentation, technical notes, example code, or tutorials. But when you get down to the nitty-gritty job of programming, most of the time you just need to look up the definition of a specific class or function. That's the time to reach for the API search tool.

Despite the visual similarity between the API Search and Full-Text Search modes, the two search technologies have virtually nothing in common. API searches are interactive, but you have to start full-text searches by pressing the Return key. An API search searches only the API symbols index; the full-text search searches the entire text of the ADC Reference Library. API searches are constrained to the languages selected in the search configure options; full-text searches are constrained to the selected Search Group. API searches are literal searches for the beginning of symbol names; full-text searches are whole word searches that can optionally use wildcards and Boolean operators. The only thing they really have in common is that you click a line in the results list to see the document found.

To start an API search, switch the search mode to API Search, place the cursor in the search field, and start typing. As you type, the results pane instantly updates to list only those symbols in the API documentation that begin with the letters typed in the search field, as shown in Figure 9-11. Case differences are ignored.

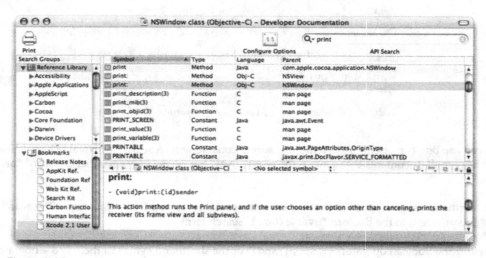

Figure 9-11

In API Search mode, the columns of the table change to Symbol, Type, Language, and Parent. You can sort, resize, and reorganize these as you please. The Parent field is the document name where the symbol was found. For instance variables and methods, this should be the class name where the member is defined. For many standard UNIX C functions, the document name is simply "man page."

You can limit the search to just those symbols defined for particular programming languages. Click the Configure Options button in the toolbar and check only the language, or languages, you are currently programming in, as shown in Figure 9-12.

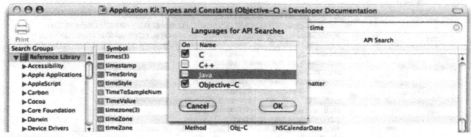

Figure 9-12

Man Pages

UNIX man pages are a source of documentation that is loosely integrated with Xcode. The C functions (section 3) of the man pages are included in the API Search index. Finding a UNIX C function displays the man page for that function. However, the man pages are not part of the ADC Reference Library, and therefore cannot be searched using the Full-Text Search mode, nor are any of the shell commands (sections 1 and 8), or file formats (section 5). To access man pages directly from within Xcode, choose the Help⇨Open man page command. This opens the dialog box shown in Figure 9-13.

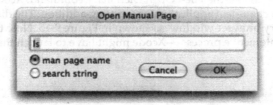

Figure 9-13

With the Man Page Name option selected, the command displays the named man page in the help window. One flaw with this interface is what happens if the name is ambiguous. Attempting to open the man page for "crontab" just beeps and does nothing. That's because there are two crontab man pages. You can resolve this ambiguity by including the section number after the name. Either "crontab(5)" or "crontab 5" opens the man page for the crontab file format, and either "crontab(1)" or "crontab 1" opens the man page for the crontab maintenance tool.

This is all well and good, as long as you know the exact page name and section of the man page you're looking for. If you don't know, select the Search String option in the dialog box and enter a literal search string. If the search string is found in one or more man page titles, the list of titles is displayed in the help window as shown in Figure 9-14. Click a link to display the entire man page. This is, more or less, equivalent to the apropos command.

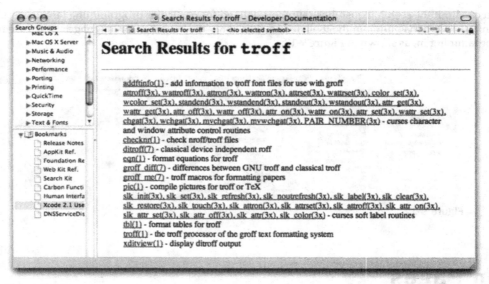

Figure 9-14

AppleScript Dictionaries

The AppleScript dictionaries provided by scriptable applications and scripting additions are another form of documentation. Choose the File⇨Open Dictionary command. Xcode presents an application browser where you can choose an application or scripting addition. The dictionary for the chosen item is displayed in a dictionary browser window, as shown in Figure 9-15. Note that obtaining an application's dictionary is often an interactive process — Xcode might have to launch the application before it can display its dictionary.

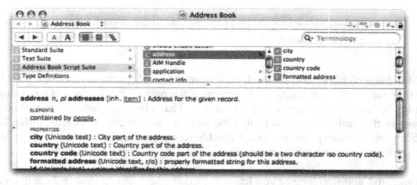

Figure 9-15

Three columns form a browser, with groups of classes on the left, classes and commands in the middle, and properties of classes on the right. The documentation for the selected item, or group of items, is displayed in the lower pane. To reduce the amount of detail in the pane, make a narrower selection in the browser.

Staying Up-To-Date

Anyone who has been programming for more than a year knows that code libraries are moving targets. As you read this chapter, the hardworking men and women at Apple and the open source community are adding new methods, new classes, new frameworks, and (hopefully) fixing bugs. Keeping up with these changes means keeping your internal documentation up-to-date.

Xcode defers to the ADC web site to resolve extended links. Assuming you have a live Internet connection, this information should always be current. An earlier section showed you how to add the latest Developer DVD Series reference library to your extended search path. As long as you keep your DVD and the link up-to-date, the content beyond the core documentation installed with Xcode will be current.

But sometimes the ADC Reference Library in the /Developer folder itself needs to be updated. You can accomplish this by downloading the latest documentation release from the Apple Developer Connection (ADC) web site. You must have an ADC member account to download the latest Xcode reference library. The free ADC membership at http://developer.apple.com/membership/ permits you access to the various Xcode downloads, so there's little reason not to sign up. Once you're logged in, you will find the latest documentation updates in the Download section. Look for "ADC Reference Library Update."

Xcode can automatically check for updated documentation for you. In the Documentation tab of the Xcode Preferences, enable the Check for Documentation Updates option, shown in Figure 9-16.

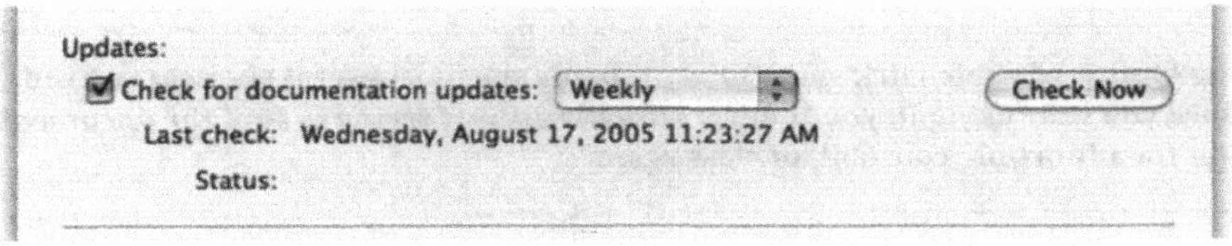

Updates:
☑ Check for documentation updates: [Weekly ◆]   (Check Now)
        Last check: Wednesday, August 17, 2005 11:23:27 AM
            Status:

Figure 9-16

You can specify the frequency of checking, and you can force Xcode to check immediately. This feature requires that you are periodically connected to the Internet while running Xcode. When Xcode discovers that new documentation is available, it spontaneously presents the message in Figure 9-17.

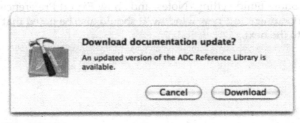

Download documentation update?
An updated version of the ADC Reference Library is available.

(Cancel)   (Download)

Figure 9-17

Clicking the Download button opens the update URL in your preferred browser. You have to log in using your ADC membership ID to obtain the update. The documentation can be rather large, as you can see in Figure 9-18. A high-speed Internet connection is highly recommended, unless you don't mind waiting 10 to 20 hours for the download to finish.

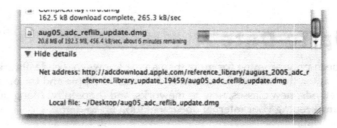

Figure 9-18

The update appears on your desktop as a disk image containing an installer package. Open the package to install the update. Quit and relaunch Xcode after the update is complete.

Documentation Shortcuts

Two menu commands, Help⇨Find Selected Text in Documentation and Help⇨Find Selected Text in API Reference, take the current text selection in any editor pane and use it to perform a full-text or API search, respectively. Option–double-click is the shortcut for the Find Selected Text in API Reference command. These commands are also available in the contextual pop-up menu in the editor. Select a symbol or text, Control-click the selection, and choose either command from the menu.

> **The Option+double-click shortcut is probably the most useful shortcut in Xcode. Once you start using it, you'll never stumble around trying to find the documentation for a function, constant, or class again.**

The Help menu also has a number of menu items that take you directly to some location in the documentation. Help⇨Documentation simply opens the help window — it does not alter the search mode or the current contents of the help window. Help⇨Xcode Help command opens the help window, switches to Full-Text Search mode, and opens the Xcode help topic.

The Help menu also provides four, somewhat superfluous, commands: Show Release Notes, Show Older Release Notes, Show Build Settings Notes, and Show Expert Preferences Notes. Each simply opens the respective document in a new window. It should also be noted that these tend to change from one release of Xcode to the next.

Adding Custom Documentation

The ability the Option–double-click a symbol, or click the book icon in the Class Browser, and instantly be transported to the documentation for that symbol is a huge boost to productivity. Wouldn't it be even better if Xcode would let you document, index, and look up symbols in your own projects? Well, you can — sort of — with a bit of work.

The ability to automatically link project-generated documentation into Xcode's API Reference library has been on the "wish list" of the Xcode development team for some time. With any luck, they will have added this feature by the time this book is published. In the meantime, know that you can hack in your own documentation. The effort would probably be worthwhile for large projects or for a team of programmers. Adding new API Reference documents to Xcode's help system requires these steps.

1. Generate HeaderDoc documentation pages. The normal process is:

    a. Add HeaderDoc or JavaDoc comments to your source code.

    b. Use the HeaderDoc tools to create HTML documentation files for each source file in your project.

    c. Gather all of your documentation files to a single location.

2. Add the new documentation location to the list of directories containing API Reference pages.

3. Rebuild the help indexes using the pbhelpindexer tool.

Using the HeaderDoc tools to generate documentation from your source code is extensively documented at `http://developer.apple.com/documentation/DeveloperTools/Conceptual/HeaderDoc/`. In brief, the headerdoc2html tool extracts the HeaderDoc or JavaDoc comments in a source file and produces HTML pages with the necessary tags, anchors, and format suitable for indexing by the Xcode help system. For a large project, you would probably want to turn this step into a target. See Chapter 13 to learn how to create a shell script target that runs the headerdoc2html tool.

The next step is to modify the Xcode help configuration files to include the location of your new documentation. In version 2.2 of Xcode that configuration file is /Developer/ADC Reference Library/ indexes/MacOSXDeveloper.pbHelpIndexerList. This is an XML file that typically looks like Listing 9-1.

Listing 9-1: MacOSXDeveloper.pbHelpIndexerList

```
<?xml version="1.0" encoding="UTF-8"?>
<!DOCTYPE plist SYSTEM "file://localhost/System/Library/DTDs/PropertyList.dtd">
<plist version="0.9">
<array>
    <string>/Developer/ADC Reference Library</string>
    <string>/System/Library/Frameworks/JavaVM.framework/Resources/</string>
    <!-- Add additional documentation locations here... -->
    <string>/Users/james/Development/Documentation/Projects/</string>
    -->
</array>
</plist>
```

The array of string tags contains the directories that will be included in the API Reference index. By default, it contains the API documentation files in the ADC Reference Library and all of the JavaDoc files from the Java2 SDK. In the example, the location of the HeaderDoc pages has been added to a Development folder. You only need to add the top-level folder to the list. The help file indexer searches every subfolder for documentation pages.

Finally, the help keyword database must be rebuilt with the pbhelpindexer tool. Because the indexes are written to a system-level directory, the tool must be run as root using the sudo command, like this:

```
sudo pbhelpindexer
```

Even on a fast machine, the tool will take several minutes to rebuild the index for the entire Reference Library.

As you've probably already gathered, there are several drawbacks to this procedure:

❑ There is only one help database. All symbols from all documented projects will show up in any project opened on your machine.

❑ The help database is not dynamic, nor is pbhelpindexer incremental. The entire help index must be regenerated from scratch to incorporate any changes made to the documentation. This can be a very time-consuming process, making it cumbersome to include as part of the project build.

❑ The pbhelpindexer tool must be run with root privileges, making it almost impossible to include in the project build.

Because of these limitations, here are a few suggestions:

❑ Only add the documentation for major projects that are your principle focus of development on a day-to-day basis. Don't fill your help system with obscure projects that just clutter the symbol space. When you move on to the next project, take that project's documentation out of the help system and insert the documentation for the project you are currently working on.

❑ Create a shell script target in your project, or projects, to generate the documentation and write it to a separate location. Build this target nightly or whenever you do internal code reviews or releases.

❑ Take a page from man (no pun intended) and add a script that will run the pbhelpindexer tool to the daily or weekly periodic process (see "man periodic"). Then, all you have to do is make sure your development machine is running each night and your Xcode documentation will be up-to-date every morning.

The Xcode Community

This chapter has focused on the help and documentation resources accessible through the Xcode interface. But one of the most valuable resources for Xcode users is *other Xcode users*.

In addition to the other developer information you'll find at Apple's Developer Connection web site, there are also a variety of mailing lists. You can see the complete list at `http://lists.apple.com/mailman/listinfo`. Of particular interest is the Xcode-users mailing list. This list is populated by Xcode users from all over the world and is a phenomenal resource for solving problems with Xcode. I tapped the talented and helpful individuals of this list several times while writing this book. I would strongly urge you to join the Xcode-users list.

As with many Internet discussion group, members contribute their time and knowledge as a courtesy to others and to support the community of Xcode users. Many are professional software engineers with busy schedules and none of them are obligated to help you. Be respectful of their time and efforts by adhering to these guidelines:

- ❏ The list does not exist to solve your problems for you. Post questions only when you've read all the available documentation (which should include this book), searched the list archives for similar questions, and tried all of the solutions you can think of.

- ❏ Be clear, concise, complete, and courteous.

- ❏ Give something back. The list is a community of members helping members. If you know the answer to a question, or have a helpful suggestion, take the time to post it. You can't expect others to help you if you never help anyone else.

- ❏ The list is not your personal soapbox. It's not a forum for rants and personal opinions.

- ❏ The list is not Apple support. If you need technical, sales, or developer support from Apple, contact the appropriate party through ADC. Apple engineers have been known to monitor and answer questions on the list, but they cannot provide you with any kind of official support through the list.

Summary

Xcode includes a massive amount of documentation, and several different tools for dealing with it. You've seen how to search for keywords and symbols, find API documentation from within the class browser and directly from within your source code. You can even add you own documentation, if you need to.

Eventually, you will still not find what you are looking for in the local documentation. Remember to avail yourself of the Apple Developer Connection web site (`http://developer.apple.com/`). Apple's online resources contain many more articles, documents, and sample code than could ever be downloaded and stored locally, and these resources are updated constantly.

Interface Builder

Interface Builder is a graphical user interface editor and the first of the specialized editors included in Xcode. Interface Builder and Project Builder (also known as Xcode) trace their lineage all the way back to NeXT, where they were originally conceived. The two work hand in glove, and can essentially be considered a single tool.

Interface Builder was originally designed for, and with, Objective-C. Much of the "magic" of Interface Builder is possible thanks to the dynamic nature of the Objective-C language. After being brought into the Macintosh-development fold, Interface Builder's role has expanded to embrace the C/C++, Java, and AppleScript languages as well.

NIB Files

Although this book isn't about Cocoa or Carbon programming, it's hard to discuss what Interface Builder does without a basic grounding in the technology that lets it work. Simply put, Interface Builder edits NIB files. A NIB file defines the placement, organization, properties, and relationships of objects like menus, windows, text, and buttons.

> NIB originally stood for NeXT Interface Builder, but Apple has officially rechristened it *Interface Builder* archive.

Unlike program source files, NIB files are not compiled. They are read at execution time by the application, which uses the information in the NIB file to create the objects or structures that will embody the interface you designed in Interface Builder. There are two very important concepts here. The first is that NIB files are interpreted at runtime. (The ramifications of this will be discussed later.) More importantly, *every object instance you define in a NIB file becomes an object (or structure) at runtime*. The objects created at runtime are identical to objects that you can create programmatically. There is no difference. Figure 10-1 (Interface Builder) and Listing 10-1 (Objective-C) both create a window containing some text fields and buttons.

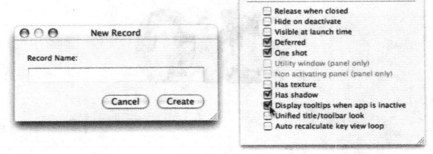

Figure 10-1

Listing 10-1: Objective-C

```objc
- (void)makeNewRecordWindow
{
    NSWindow* newWindow = [[NSWindow alloc]
        initWithContentRect:NSMakeRect(100.0,100.0,349.0,123.0)

styleMask:(NSTitledWindowMask|NSClosableWindowMask|NSMiniaturizableWindowMask)
                    backing:NSBackingStoreBuffered
                    defer:YES];
    NSView* windowContentView = [newWindow contentView];
    NSButton* okButton = [[NSButton alloc]
initWithFrame:NSMakeRect(253.0,12.0,82.0,32.0)];
    [okButton setTitle:@"Create"];
    [okButton setButtonType:NSMomentaryLightButton];
    [okButton setBezelStyle:NSRoundedBezelStyle];
    [windowContentView addSubview:okButton];
    NSButton* cancelButton = [[NSButton alloc]
initWithFrame:NSMakeRect(171.0,12.0,82.0,32.0)];
    [cancelButton setTitle:@"Cancel"];
    [cancelButton setButtonType:NSMomentaryLightButton];
    [cancelButton setBezelStyle:NSRoundedBezelStyle];
    [windowContentView addSubview:cancelButton];
    NSTextField* titleField = [[NSTextField alloc]
initWithFrame:NSMakeRect(20.0,90.0,130.0,13.0)];
    [titleField setStringValue:@"Record Name:"];
    [titleField setEditable:NO];
    [titleField setSelectable:NO];
    [titleField setBordered:NO];
    [titleField setDrawsBackground:NO];
    [windowContentView addSubview:titleField];
    NSTextField* nameField = [[NSTextField alloc]
initWithFrame:NSMakeRect(20.0,60.0,309.0,22.0)];
    [windowContentView addSubview:nameField];

    [newWindow makeKeyAndOrderFront:self];
}
```

It doesn't matter whether the program loads the NIB file containing the window in Figure 10-1 or calls the makeNewRecordWindow method in Listing 10-1; the end result is the same. The upshot of all this is that there shouldn't be any mystery about the objects you define in Interface Builder. A window in Interface Builder is an instance of the NSWindow class. If you wanted the window to display tool tips when inactive, you could send the [window setAllowsToolTips WhenApplicationIsInactive: YES] message *or* you could check the Display Tooltips When App Is Inactive option in the window's Inspector palette, as shown on the right in Figure 10-1. The effects are identical, and any questions about how this particular option will affect your application can be answered by looking up the documentation for NSWindow.

It should also be obvious in comparing the figure and listing that creating complex layouts in Interface Builder is easier than trying to write the same code in C or Objective-C. This doesn't mean that you won't ever need to create interface objects programmatically again. What it does mean is that you have an extremely powerful and flexible design tool that will let you create elegant and functional user interfaces, while saving vast amounts of programming time.

Serialization

Originally, all NIB files were archived Objective-C objects. Archiving is a technique in which a graph of objects (an object and all of the objects it references, directly or indirectly) are converted into data blocks that capture each object's type, member values, and any relationships to other objects. This *flattened* data can then be saved somewhere, typically in a file. This process is also called marshalling or encoding. In the slang of Cocoa, these are often referred to as "freeze-dried" objects. When the process is reversed, the data is read back. The recorded class information is used to create new objects with the same class. The value information is used to set the properties of the object, and the relationship information is used to reestablish any inter-object references. This is a protracted way of saying that objects can be saved to a file and later recreated, in tact.

> NIB files are actually packages (a folder containing multiple data files that acts like a single file in the Finder). Use the Finder's Show Package Contents command, found by Control-/right-clicking the NIB's icon, if you want to poke around inside.

Cocoa versus Carbon

When the role of Interface Builder and NIB files was expanded to accommodate the C APIs, collectively known as Carbon, the format of the NIB file was also redefined. Today, NIB files can be binary or XML representations of Cocoa objects. Or they can be XML representations of Carbon Human Interface (HI) elements. The content and format of Carbon and Cocoa NIB files are fundamentally different and are not interchangeable. Conceptually, they perform the same purpose, and share many of the same capabilities. Cocoa Java and AppleScript applications use Cocoa NIB files, because both are built on top of the Cocoa framework.

If you use Interface Builder to design both Cocoa and Carbon interfaces, you will notice significant differences between the attributes and capabilities of Cocoa and Carbon objects. These reflect the architectural differences between the two languages and their APIs. The most striking difference is how objects communicate with each other and with the application. Cocoa objects use dynamic Objective-C messages to communicate. C applications use Carbon events.

Still, there is a considerable amount of common ground between Cocoa and Carbon interfaces. A window in Cocoa is very much like a window in Carbon. The Has Shadow option of a Carbon Document window has the same meaning as the Has Shadow attribute of a Cocoa NSWindow object. The features and commands described at the beginning of this chapter generally apply to both Cocoa and Carbon equally. As this chapter delves into the details of editing objects, it will point out the differences between Cocoa and Carbon.

Xcode Integration

Interface builder works very closely with Xcode. Interface Builder files can be saved from within Xcode, or automatically saved before a build. Interface Builder knows which targets a NIB file belongs to and what image and sound resources are included in those targets.

Interface Builder's Interface

Let's start with a brief tour of Interface Builder's interface. One reason it will be brief, and also one of the reasons Interface Builder is so easy to use, is that there are basically only three interface elements: the NIB document window, the Inspector palette, and the Objects palette. All three are shown in Figures 10-2 and 10-3.

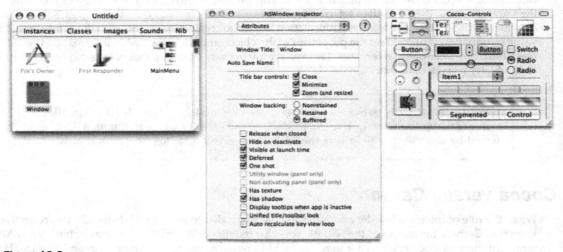

Figure 10-2

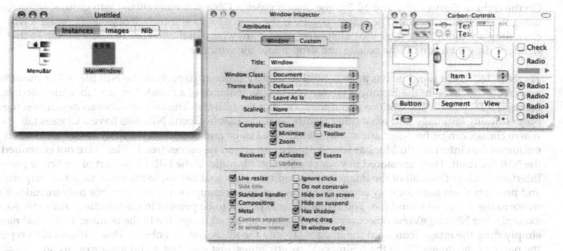

Figure 10-3

Figure 10-2 shows the basic windows for a Cocoa NIB, and Figure 10-3 shows the basic windows for Carbon. When you open a NIB file, the contents of the file are represented abstractly in a NIB document window, as shown on the left in Figures 10-2 and 10-3. NIB files contain objects, and those objects are shown here either graphically or hierarchically. You select which view you want to see, icon or list, using the small controls above the vertical scroll bar. Figure 10-4 shows the contents of a NIB file in list view and icon view. Only the top-level objects are shown in icon view.

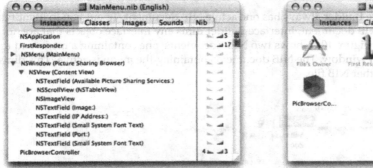

Figure 10-4

Shown in the middle of Figures 10-2 and 10-3 is the Inspector palette, sometimes referred to as the Info window. The Inspector palette shows the properties and settings of the currently selected object. Much of your time will be spent in the Inspector palette setting various attributes for your objects.

On the right in Figures 10-2 and 10-3 is the objects palette. Objects are organized into groups, selectable using the toolbar at the top. The objects palette is the source for new interface objects. To create a window, drag a window object off the palette and drop it anywhere in the screen. To add a button to that window, drag a button off the palette and drop it into the window.

The NIB document window has a tab control to display different aspects of the NIB file. All of the objects you create are listed in the Instances tab (an object is an instance of a class). The last tab is the Info tab. It contains information and options about the format of the NIB file. The tabs in between depend on the programming language and what other resources are available. Cocoa NIB files have a Classes tab where classes can be browsed and manipulated. The Image and Sound tabs display image and sound resources that Interface Builder has found. Image and sound resources (read "files") are not contained in the NIB file itself. They are stored in your application's bundle. If the NIB file is part of an Xcode project, Interface Builder finds all of the image and sound resources that belong to the same target, or targets, and presents them here for easy access. Using one of these resources in your interface only includes a *reference* to the image or sound file. The actual file is expected to be present in the bundle at runtime. As an example, the NSImageView object normally displays a named image file in the bundle. To set that name, simply drag the image icon from the Images tab into the NSImageView object. This is identical to typing the name of the image file in the NSImageView attributes, just a lot faster and less error prone.

Most of the other windows you'll be working with in Interface Builder will be layout windows: the actual window and menu objects that you are designing.

Multiple NIB Document Windows

Just as you break up large applications into multiple source files, complex user interfaces are often split up into multiple NIB files. This can be very confusing visually, because there's almost no way of identifying the NIB document that owns a particular interface element like a window or menu bar.

Like Xcode projects, Interface Builder always has one active NIB document. To aid you in identifying the elements contained in that NIB document, Interface Builder dims any interface objects that are not part of the active NIB document. Figure 10-5 shows two NIB documents: one containing a menu and the other containing a document window. The NIB document containing the menu is active. This dims the windows belonging to the other NIB file.

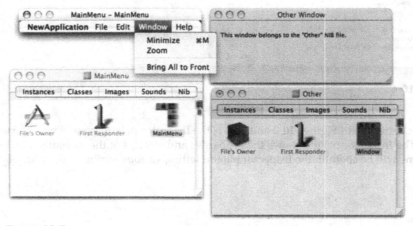

Figure 10-5

Another useful trick to clear out some window clutter is to minimize the NIB document window. This shrinks the document window into the dock and hides all windows that belong to it. Click the document's icon in the dock to restore the window to its original size and reveal all other windows that belong to it.

Building Interfaces

To create or edit an interface using Interface Builder, you must begin with a NIB file to store it in. If you created your project in Xcode using one of the standard templates, you probably already have a NIB file in the project. Open the NIB file in the source group and Xcode launches Interface Builder. If you need to create additional NIB files, launch Interface Builder. If Interface Builder is already running, choose the File⇨New command. Interface Builder presents the Starting Point assistant shown in Figure 10-6.

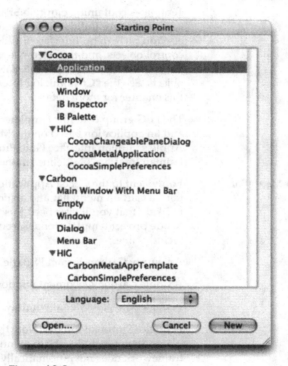

Figure 10-6

Choose a template from the list. The templates are organized into Cocoa and Carbon groups. All of the templates in the Cocoa group create a Cocoa-format NIB file; templates in the Carbon group create Carbon-format NIB files. You cannot change or convert between Cocoa and Carbon NIB formats, so make sure you choose the template from the correct group. The following table provides a brief summary of the templates.

Cocoa Templates	Contents
Application	A standard Cocoa application menu bar and an empty window. This template is appropriate for a "single window" (non-document based) application. However, you should rarely need this template — all Xcode project templates for Cocoa applications already include a NIB file containing the same thing.
Empty	Use this whenever you want a new, empty, Cocoa-format NIB file.
Window	A NIB containing a single NSWindow object.
IB Inspector IB Palette	Templates containing empty NSPanel objects suitable for use as Interface Builder inspector and custom control panels. You can extend Interface Builder with your own custom control objects, and these templates are here to help you build the Interface Builder interface for those custom objects. See the "Customizing Interface Builder" section in this chapter for more details.
HIG	The HIG group contains templates for preference panels and an application based on the Metal style that adheres to Apple's Human Interface Guidelines. See more about the Human Interface Guidelines in the "Guides" section.
Main Window with Menu Bar	Equivalent to the Cocoa Application template, this NIB contains a Carbon menu bar and an empty window. Again, it is unlikely that you'll ever need this template because the Xcode project template for a Carbon application already includes one.
Empty	An empty Carbon-format NIB file.
Window	A single Carbon Document window.
Dialog	A single Movable Modal window.
Menu Bar	A single Carbon menu bar. Note that Carbon menu bar templates do not include a Help menu because the Carbon framework does not automatically support Help.
HIG	Similar to the HIG group in the Cocoa group, these are HIG-compliant templates for a Metal-themed application and a preference pane written using the Carbon framework.

Below the list of NIB templates is the language selector. Choose your development region language. The NIB file you are about to create will be in the chosen language. If the NIB file needs to be localized, you must do that in Xcode *after* the NIB file has been added to the project. If you remember from Chapter 6, the pre-localized file becomes the version for the development region. So the NIB file's language should match your development region, lest you end up with a French menu on the English version of your application.

When you have made your desired template and language choice, click the New button. Alternatively, you can avoid creating a new file and open an existing NIB file by clicking the Open button. This option is here mostly because Interface Builder presents the Starting Point assistant whenever you start Interface Builder without opening a NIB file, or when you close all of the NIB document windows, thus providing a quick method to create a new NIB file or open an existing one. If you don't want to see the Starting Point assistant every time Interface Builder starts, you can turn it off in the General pane of the Interface Builder preferences.

Opening Existing NIB Files

In addition to the obvious File⇨Open command, Interface Builder has a couple of shortcuts for opening NIB files. The File⇨Open Recent submenu lists recently opened NIB files. Selecting one opens it again.

The File⇨Open Localizations menu lists all of the other language variants of the currently active NIB document. Interface Builder detects when a NIB file is located in an .lproj localization folder. It then finds all sister .lproj folders containing the same NIB file and presents them in this submenu. This allows you to quickly switch between localizations of the same file. An Open All command opens all localizations at once.

Importing Resources

If you are porting an old application from OS 9 to OS X, you may save some time by importing the window, menu, and dialog boxes defined in the application's resource fork. Choose File⇨Import⇨Import Resource Fork and choose an application or resource file containing the menu and window you want to import. Interface Builder presents a dialog box listing all of the importable resources, as shown in Figure 10-7.

Figure 10-7

You can select any arbitrary number of dialog box and window definitions. If you choose to import the menu definition and the resource file contains multiple menu bar definitions, you must choose the one menu bar you want to import.

Saving NIB Files

Choose File⇨Save or File⇨Save All to save the active NIB file or all NIB files. New NIB files are unnamed. You are prompted to name an unnamed NIB file when it is first saved. Use the File⇨Save As command to save an existing NIB document in a new file.

Saving a NIB file in the project folder of an open project in Xcode presents the dialog box shown in Figure 10-8.

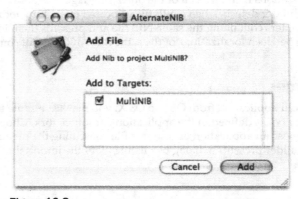

Figure 10-8

Select the targets that you want the NIB file added to. The NIB files are added as a single, non-localized, file. To localize the NIB you need to switch back to Xcode and localize the file in the project. Chapter 6 described how to localize a file.

> **Here's a timesaving tip.** If your project already has .lproj folders (because other files have been localized), you can save your new file directly into the .lproj folder of the appropriate language. Xcode treats the NIB file as if it has already been localized. You can skip the step of localizing the file, and jump right to adding new localizations.

If you save the file somewhere else, or if there is no open project in Xcode, the NIB file is not automatically added to a project. You need to add the NIB file to a project manually. Chapter 6 discussed different ways of adding a file to a project.

Making Backups

Whenever you save an NIB file, Interface Builder can optionally save a backup of the original file. The backup has the same name as the original appended with the tilde (~) character. If you find this unnecessary or just plain annoying, uncheck the Create Backup File When Saving option in the General tab of the Interface Builder preferences.

Creating Objects

In Interface Builder, you design your application's user interface by literally drawing it. The two user interface elements that you can design with Interface Builder are menus and windows. Window is used here in its most generic form. Document windows, dialog boxes, panels, sheets, palettes, and drawers are all windows in Interface Builder.

The tools and techniques for creating and editing menus and windows are significantly different, so they are covered separately in this chapter.

Creating Menus

To edit application menus, you must be editing a NIB that contains a menu bar object. There is no command in Interface Builder to directly create a new main menu bar. You must start with a NIB template that contains a MainMenu menu object, or copy and paste in a menu bar from another NIB document. The MainMenu object appears as a window containing a menu bar (see Figure 10-9).

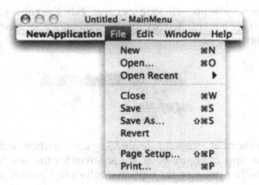

Figure 10-9

You can create additional NSMenu objects by dragging the menu icon in the lower-right corner of the objects palette into a NIB document. This creates an NSMenu object, but this object will not act like the main menu bar object for your application. You would do this if you needed to create menu objects that would be stored in a NIB for your application to load and use programmatically.

Click any menu to display its contents. Add menu items by dragging a new menu object into the menu bar window, as shown in Figure 10-10.

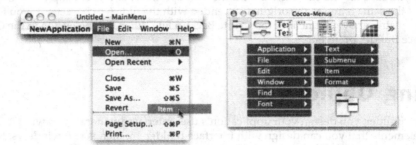

Figure 10-10

The menu palette contains standard submenu objects for the standard application menus defined in the Human Interface Guidelines: Application, File, Edit, Window, Find, Font, Text, and Format. The three remaining objects — the menu separator bar, Submenu, and Item — are the three generic menu objects you can use to create your application-specific commands and submenus. You can drag the Item and item separator objects into any menu, as demonstrated in Figure 10-10. You can drop the Submenu object into either a menu, to create a submenu item, or into the menu bar itself, to create a new top-level menu.

Drag items in a menu to reorder them. To delete an item, select it and press the Delete key or select Edit⇨Delete.

Edit the title of a menu item by double-clicking its name. Edit the name and press Return. You can also edit the keyboard shortcut for a menu item by double-clicking its shortcut, or the area where its shortcut would be, as shown in Figure 10-11.

Figure 10-11

After you've selected the shortcut, press the desired key combination, without the Command key, for that menu item. In the example in Figure 10-11, the shortcut for the new Save Copy As item was set to Command+Option+Shift+S by pressing the Option+Shift+S key combination.

Almost everything else you will want to configure for menu objects is done via the Inspector palette. Using the Inspector palette for menu objects is identical to using it for any other interface object, and is discussed at length in the "Editing Objects" section later in this chapter.

Creating Windows

To create a new window object, drag a window from the objects palette into the NIB document or any-where on the screen. Cocoa has three kinds of window objects: Window, Panel, and Drawer, as shown on the left in Figure 10-12. The fourth Cocoa object is just a combination of a Window with a Drawer already attached. The Drawer object doesn't have a visual representation; you have to drag it into the NIB document window to create it. Carbon has two window objects, shown on the right in Figure 10-12: Window and Moveable Modal Dialog.

Figure 10-12

Creating Other Objects

Most of the remaining objects in Interface Builder go into window objects. You create buttons, text fields, progress bars, and tables by dragging an object from the objects palette into a window (see Figure 10-13).

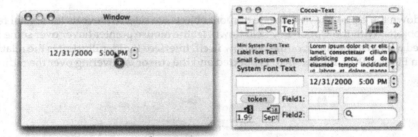

Figure 10-13

You can drag objects without visual representations, such as controller objects, into the Instances tab of the NIB document window. You can also create objects by duplicating existing object — select an object and choose the Edit⇨Duplicate command, or hold down the Option key while dragging an object. You can copy objects to the clipboard and paste them some place else.

Selecting Objects

You can select objects individually or in groups. Click an object in the NIB document (list or icon view) or its visual representation in a menu or window. A selected object is highlighted. If the object is resizable, Interface Builder draws resizing handles on its edges. Shift-click an unselected object to add that object to the selection. Shift-click a selected object to remove that object from the selection. You can select the window object itself by clicking any unoccupied region in the window. Select a group of objects by clicking an unoccupied region and dragging a selection box to overlaps the desired objects, as shown in Figure 10-14.

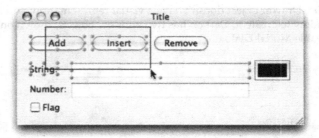

Figure 10-14

Some objects, like tab views and split pane views, are containers for other objects. Normally clicking an object selects the object, not the object that contains it. To select the container, click any unoccupied region within the container. Sometimes this is inconvenient or impossible (split views with an invisible divider might not have any unoccupied region on which to click). The General tab of the Interface Builder preferences has the Inside-Out Selection option. When this option is checked, clicking an object in a container selects the object, not the container. With this option off, clicking anywhere within a container selects the container, not any of the objects in the container. Change the option in the preference to permanently change the selection behavior. Hold down the Command key while selecting an object to temporarily reverse the preference setting.

Holding down the Option key while one or more objects are selected reveals the spatial relationship between objects. With the Option key held down, let the mouse pointer hover over some other object, the unoccupied area in a container, or the window itself. Interface Builder illustrates the relationship between the two. In Figure 10-15, the text field is selected and the cursor is hovering over the radio button.

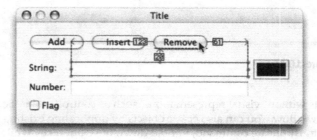

Figure 10-15

You can also select objects in the icon or list view of the NIB document. This is often the best way to avoid the ambiguity of trying to select objects visually. It is the only way of selecting objects that do not have a visual representation. It also lets you select objects that are in hidden views, behind other objects, and outside the window boundaries. In list view, the Command and Shift keys assume their normal list selection behavior. Command-click to arbitrarily add or remove objects from the selection. Shift+click to select all of the objects between the current selections and the target object. Double-clicking an object in the list view selects it and switches focus to the visual object in the window or menu. This is a very fast way of finding out which object in a window is represented by an item in the list.

Due to a long-standing bug in Interface Builder, selecting an object in the list view may not allow you to edit its attributes in the Inspector palette. Double-click the object, switching focus to its visual representation, and the Inspector palette will work correctly.

Deleting Objects

You can delete objects in an NIB by first selecting them and then pressing the Delete key or by using the Edit➪Delete command. If a selected object is a container for objects, for instance a window or a tab view, deleting that object deletes it and all of its subordinate objects. See the "Subviews" section, later in this chapter, to find out how to delete a container without deleting the objects it contains.

Testing an Interface

As you work through this chapter, and on your own projects, you want to see the results of changing layouts, sizes, and attributes. Many of these behaviors can be tested without running your application. In fact, you don't even need an Xcode project, let alone any working code.

The File➪Test Interface command starts a surrogate application that loads the current NIB file. Objects based on Cocoa framework classes (the menu bar, windows, buttons, text fields, and so on) will all behave exactly as they would in your application, assuming your application doesn't programmatically alter their behavior. No objects based on custom classes are created, and any connections to custom objects are not set. (See the "Connections" and "Custom Classes" sections for an explanation.) However, if you just want to see how a window will resize, or flip through a set of tabbed panels, the Test Interface command will save you a lot of time and guesswork.

To return to Interface Builder, quit (Command+Q) the surrogate application.

Editing Objects

Objects in Interface Builder wouldn't be much use if you couldn't bend and shape them to your needs. Most of your time in Interface Builder will be spent editing objects, and there are many different ways to do this. The overt aspects (visible text, placement, and size) of objects can be manipulated directly: drag an object around to reposition it; double-click the text of an object to change it.

Less obvious attributes such as formatting options and bindings are manipulated in the Inspector palette. There are also a few specialized commands just for grouping objects in containers.

Moving and Resizing Objects

An object, or a group of selected objects, can be repositioned simply by dragging it to another location. Depending on the layout, some objects may not be repositioned. For instance, an object in one half of a split view always occupies that entire space. It cannot be repositioned, because its location and size are determined by the split view. Altering the position of the split view or its divider is the only way to change that object's position in the window.

Interface Builder displays guidelines as an object is dragged. When the object is released, it "snaps" to nearest guideline. See the "Guides" section to find out how to control these automatic guidelines or create your own.

The arrow keys nudge the selected objects one pixel in any direction. Hold down the Shift key to nudge them 10 pixels at a time.

Dragging the handles on the edge of an object resizes it. Some objects cannot be resized, or can only be resized in certain directions. For example, the height of a button is fixed in Cocoa. You can only change its width. Using the resize handles, you can only resize one object at a time.

Try It Out　　**Create an Interface**

In Interface Builder, choose the File⇨New command and choose the Cocoa Application template. Then follow these steps:

1. From the objects palette, select the Controls tab. Drag some check boxes, a spinner, a slider, and a level indicator into the window.

2. From the Text tab, throw in an editable NSTextField and a date picker.

3. Choose File⇨Test Interface.

4. Play around with the controls, and then press Command+Q (Quit) to return to Interface Builder.

How It Works

Dragging objects from the objects palette into the window adds those objects to the window's visual hierarchy at runtime. The Test Interface command simply loads the NIB file you've created in a generic application. The application contains none of your project code or classes, so all functionality is limited to the default behavior provided by the Cocoa framework.

Shrinking Objects

Choose Layout⇨Size to Fit (Command+=) to shrink objects down to their minimum size. The Size to Fit command determines the minimum dimension required to display the object's content. A button or text field is shrunk down so that the object is exactly the size needed to display the title or text. A box is shrunk so that it is just larger than all of the objects it contains. Size to Fit does not apply to all objects.

Making Objects the Same Size

Use the Layout⇨Same Size command to set multiple objects to the same size. Start by selecting the object that is already the desired size. Shift+click to select additional objects to be resized. Choose the Same Size command. All of the additional objects are set to the size of the first object selected.

Aligning Objects

In addition to the automatic guides that appear when you drag or resize an object, the alignment palette and command provides numerous methods for aligning and distributing objects evenly. To display the Alignment panel, choose Format➪Alignment➪Alignment Panel (Command+Shift+A). The panel, shown in Figure 10-16, has three sections.

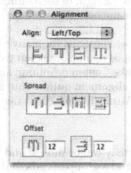

Figure 10-16

The Align section aligns multiple objects to each other. The Spread section spreads objects out so they fill a container. The Offset section distributes objects so they have some fixed amount of space between them.

The Align section has a pop-up menu that determines the anchor point for the alignment. It can be Left/Top, Center, Bottom/Right, or Baseline. The first three refer to the top left corner, dead center, or bottom right corner of the object. Baseline refers to the baseline of the text in the object. This can only be used to align objects with text, and only vertically. Selecting a mode changes the icons in the Align group to visually illustrate what they will do. The left two buttons align the objects so that all of their target points (corner or center) are aligned vertically or horizontally. The two buttons on the right are the column and row alignments. They perform the same alignment as the first two buttons, but also spread the objects out along the alternate axis so they are evenly spaced — a combination of align and offset operations. The offset is based on the current spacing of the first two objects (counting from top down, or left to right). In the example shown in Figure 10-17, setting the mode to Left/Top and choosing the Make Left Aligned Column (the third button) aligns the radio button's left edges while adjusting their vertical position so the space between the buttons is uniform.

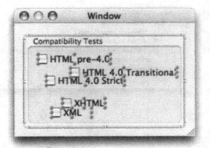 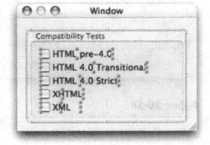

Figure 10-17

The Spread buttons distribute objects such that the space between objects is uniform. The two left buttons reposition the objects between the two outermost objects and require a section of at least three objects to have any effect. The right two buttons distribute objects evenly within their container, typically the window itself.

The two Offset buttons scatter two or more objects so the space between them is all the same. Set the amount of space using the text field to the right of each button. Be careful when using large values, as it is very easy to position objects outside the boundary of their container.

The Layout⇨Alignment menu provides shortcuts for many of the alignment palette functions. All of the Align commands are equivalent to choosing one of the left two buttons in the Align section with different anchor point settings. The two Make Centered Column and Make Centered Row commands should be equivalent to the column and row alignment buttons, but as of version 2.5.1, they appear to perform the same action as the Align Centers Vertically and Align Centers Horizontally commands.

Grouping Objects

You can group several objects so that they can be moved and aligned as a single unit. For example, you might want to treat a static text field and a group of radio buttons as a single object. Select Layout⇨Group to group the objects. Layout⇨Ungroup dissolves the group again.

Grouping is purely an editing convenience. It has no effect on the objects or their behavior at runtime.

Subviews

A number of interface objects types are containers for other interface objects, generically referred to as a subview. A subview is a visual container. It has its own coordinate system and can contain any number of other objects, including other subviews. This nesting of objects creates a hierarchy, which is reflected in the list view of Instances. When you create a new object by dragging an icon from the objects palette, Interface Builder indicates the container into which the new object will be inserted by drawing a border around the container's view. Figure 10-18 shows a new text field object being dropped into a tab view container. The Instances list view on the right shows the new object's location in the view hierarchy after it was inserted.

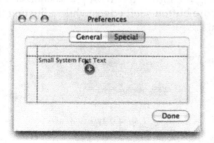 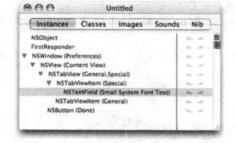

Figure 10-18

This only applies to inserting new objects into subviews that already exist. Some types of subviews can't be created from the objects palette, and dragging an existing object around never alters its relationship to its enclosing view. In other words, you cannot drag an object from one subview to another.

To move objects in and out of subviews, Interface Builder's Layout menu has the Make Subview Of commands and the Unpack Subview command (Command+Shift+Option+G). In Carbon, the Make Subview Of is named the Embed menu. To take one or more objects and nest them inside a subview, select those objects and choose the subview type from the Make Subview Of menu. The choices will be different for Carbon and Cocoa NIBs, and how the objects are organized in the new subview will vary depending on what type of subview is being created. For Box, Custom View, Scroll View, and User panes, all of the selected objects are placed inside the new subview. Split Views create one new subview for each object selected, which requires that you select at least two objects. Tab View creates a new tabbed view controller and places all of the selected objects in the subview of the first tab. You will have to populate the remaining subviews separately.

To delete a subview and release the objects it contains, select the subview object itself and choose Layout⇨Unpack Subview. The objects contained in the subview now belong to the view that owned the subview object.

You cannot move objects between subviews by dragging, but you can via the clipboard. Cut or copy some objects to the clipboard. Select the subview you want them added to, and then paste. When you're working with Tab View objects, all new objects and pasting of objects occurs in the subview of the currently selected tab. Use the tab control to switch between subviews. This works on every subview except the Split View. After they are created, you cannot alter the number of splits or subviews. The only way to change a two-split view into a three-split view is to unpack the view, select all three objects, and create a new split view.

Guides

Laying out a window or dialog box so that it is functional and visually pleasing is no small feat. To help you space and align items in your layout, Interface Builder provides two kinds of guides. A guide is a vertical or horizontal line at some ideal coordinate. Whenever you reposition an object by dragging, the boundary of the object "snaps" to that coordinate whenever it is near a guide. Aqua guides are relative to the edges of other objects, which include containers, in the layout. These distances are based on the Aqua interface design standard. The suggested distance between a button and the edge of a window is 20 pixels. Dragging the button, or resizing the window as shown in Figure 10-19, automatically places Aqua guides 20 pixels from the edges of the window.

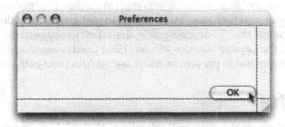

Figure 10-19

Aqua guides are very intelligent, but they don't know everything. You should still refer to the Human Interface Guidelines in making layout decisions. For example, the Human Interface Guidelines suggest that buttons that destroy data should be farther away from buttons that save data or cancel an operation. Interface Builder has no way of knowing what the buttons in your layout do, and therefore can't adjust its suggested spacing accordingly.

> You can find Apple's Human Interface Guidelines in Xcode's Reference Library under "User Experience" or "Getting Started," or online at http://developer .apple.com/documentation/UserExperience/Conceptual/OSXHIGuidelines/. There is also a small question mark button in the Inspector palette. Clicking it will take you to the relevant Human Interface Guidelines documentation for the selected object, if available.

You can turn off Aqua guides using the Layout⇨Guides⇨Enable/Disable Aqua Guides command. Holding down the Command key as you drag an object temporarily inverts the current Aqua guides setting.

User guides are another kind of guides. User guides are fixed guides that you can position anywhere in a layout. Objects dragged near a user guide snap to it just as they would snap to an Aqua guide. Add Horizontal Guide (Command+Shift+_) and Add Vertical Guide (Command+|) commands in the Layout⇨Guides submenu create a new vertical or horizontal guide in the current window. Position the cursor over the guide and drag it to the desired location, as shown in Figure 10-20. While you drag the guide, the distances to the opposite edges of the window are displayed on the guide.

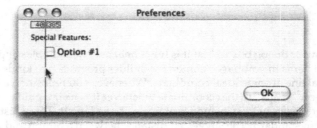

Figure 10-20

User guides snap to existing objects just as objects snap to guides. This makes it easy to position one object, snap a guide to that object, and then snap other objects to that guide. Hold down the Command key while dragging the guide to defeat this. To delete a guide, drag it off the edge of the window. You can hide or reveal user guides with the Layout⇨Guides⇨Show/Hide Guides command. Use the Layout⇨Guides⇨ Lock/Unlock Guides command to prevent or allow user guides from being repositioned.

Inspector Palette

The Inspector palette is where the nitty-gritty details of objects can be manipulated. The Inspector palette is a floating window that constantly shows the attributes for the currently selected object or objects. The palette is organized into different panels, selectable using the pop-up menu at the top of the palette. Cocoa objects generally have nine panels: Attributes, Connections, Size, Bindings, Custom Class, Accessibility, Help, AppleScript, and Sherlock. Carbon objects have five panels: Attributes, Control, Size, Layout, and Help. Use the Command+*n* (where *n* is a number) key combination to quickly switch between panels.

Each panel configures some aspect of the object. Most deal with runtime behavior and the programming model of the object. Correct use of these panels requires an understanding of the Cocoa, Carbon, or AppleScript frameworks you are using to develop your application. These topics are far beyond the scope of this book. However, the following sections briefly describe each of the panels and its purpose, how attributes are set, and where to find more information about what those settings mean.

Attributes

This panel is common to all object types and controls the "simple" attributes that can be configured for the object. The attributes that are available and what those attributes mean vary wildly from one object type to another. Figured 10-21 shows the attributes panel for different types of objects.

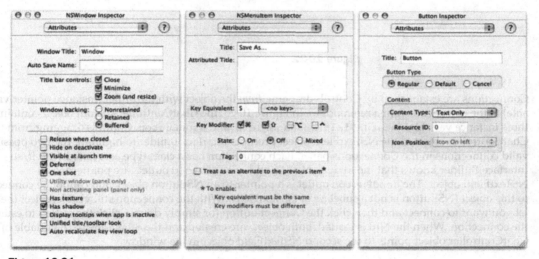

Figure 10-21

The best place to look for descriptions of object attributes is in the API documentation for that class or structure. The title bar of the Inspector changes to indicate the class of the object being inspected. For Cocoa objects, this is the object's class. In the left two examples, the documentation for the NSWindow and NSMenuItem classes should explain everything about the attributes for those objects. The pane on the right is for a Carbon Button object. Carbon objects are more obscure because the Carbon interface is C, not Objective-C or C++, so each object type doesn't have a simple one-to-one relationship with a class. The best place to start is the User Experience documentation collection in the Carbon group of the Reference Library. The *HIView Programming Guide* should give you an overview of the Carbon view model. The "Handling Carbon Windows and Controls" document explains how control events are handled in Carbon applications. In brief, the C interface that lets you control something about a window structure (like passing the `kWindowIgnoreClicksAttribute` constant to `CreateNewWindow`) will correspond to an attribute in the panel (the Ignore Clicks option).

209

Connections

Connections are a Cocoa-only feature and encompass Outlets and Target/Actions. Outlets are Cocoa-speak for object references that can be established in the NIB. An outlet is nothing more than an instance variable that contains a reference (pointer) to another object. When the NIB is loaded, the first object is "connected" by setting its instance variable so that it references the second object. A typical example would be to set the delegate for an object. Many Cocoa objects defer decisions to their delegate, if they have one. This allows the delegate to alter the normal behavior of an object without resorting to sub-classing. Figure 10-22 shows the delegate instance variable of an NSSplitView object set to a custom BrowserSplitDelegate object.

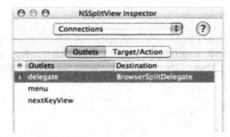

Figure 10-22

Connections are established by Control+dragging *from* the object with the outlet (instance pointer variable) *to* the object you want a reference to. In Figure 10-23, the ChatController custom object contains three instance variables: `statusField`, `messageField`, and `sendButton`. Control+dragging from the ChatController object to the NSTextField object prompts Interface Builder to highlight the two possible valid connections in the Connections panel. Each connection has a class type associated with it, so Interface Builder knows that the `statusField` and `messageField` outlets are pointers to an NSTextField object. The `sendButton` outlet is a pointer to an NSButton object, and cannot be connected to this object (NSButton is not a subclass of NSTextField). With the connection still visible, select the outlet you want to connect and then click the Connect button (or simply double-click the outlet) to establish the connection. When the NIB is loaded, both objects are created and the `messageField` variable of the ChatController object points to the second NSTextField object in the window.

The class of a connection may not be specified, or it may simply be Objective-C's undiscriminating `id` type. In either case, such a connection can be connected to any other object. It is up to you to ensure that the object connected is of the correct class.

To destroy a connection, select the connection and click the Disconnect button.

To visually see what a connection is pointing to, click that connection in the list. Interface Builder draws the connection between the two objects. Another way of viewing these connections is in the NIB document window. Switch to the list view of Instances, and look at the column on the right. It has a number of wedge shaped arrows, pointing to and away from each object. A black arrow pointing away indicates the object has one or more connections to other objects. A black arrow pointing towards an object indicates that some other object has a reference to it. Grey arrows mean there are no connections.

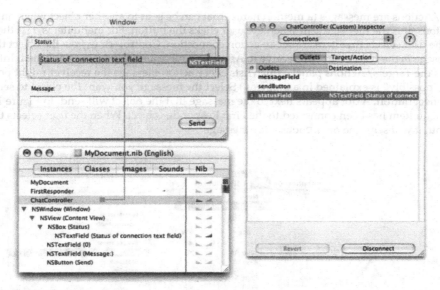

Figure 10-23

Click one of the black arrows and Interface Builder will draw a graph, like the one shown in Figure 10-24. On the left, it shows that the ChatController object has a connection to three other objects; the name of each connection is written above the line. On the right, an inverted graph shows all of the objects that have a reference to the NSButton object. In this example, there is only one object (ChatController), but to make the example interesting two connections were defined in ChatController and connected to the same object. Interface Builder shows that you are looking at connection 1 of 2. Clicking the (very) small buttons between the 1 and the 2 cycles through the connection names.

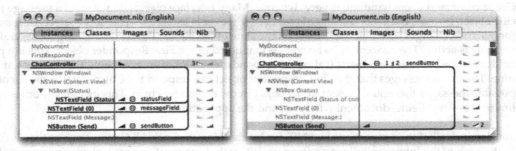

Figure 10-24

When you're Control+dragging between objects, you can choose any visual representation of that object you find in Interface Builder. You can Control+drag between two visible objects in a layout window, or between two objects listed in the NIB document window, or between an item in the NIB document window and an object in the layout window. All of these combinations are useful and are often necessary when you're connecting objects that do not have a visual representation in a layout window.

Targets/Actions are messages (a method name) that can be sent to another object when an event occurs. For buttons, it is the message sent when the user clicks the button. For menu items, it is the message sent when the user selects that item. To set an action connection, Control+drag *from* the object that will send the message *to* the object that will receive it. After the source and target are established, Interface Builder displays the Targets/Actions panel, which lists every action message the receiver might possibly understand. ("possibly" is explained in a moment.) Select the message you want the object to send and click the Connect button. A dot appears next to the message that the object will send. In Figure 10-25, the Open menu item has been connected to the First Responder object. When the user selects that item from the menu, it will send the openDocument: message.

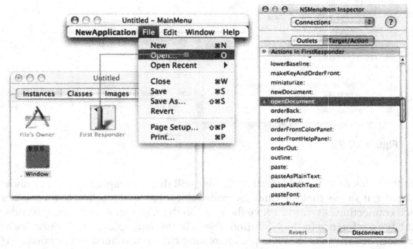

Figure 10-25

Cocoa command event handling is very dynamic. Many interface objects do not send a message to a specific object. Instead, the action message is sent to "whoever is listening." The Edit⇨Select All command, for instance, changes meaning depending on the state of the cursor, the current editing focus, and what window is active. The concept of "whoever" is embodied in the First Responder object. This is a placeholder for the list of active objects (called the responder chain) that an event will filter through at runtime. The list of messages that the First Responder object can respond to is, by necessity, the list of all possible messages that could be sent to *any* object in the responder chain. This includes — but is not limited to — text fields, document windows, and the application itself.

You can lock all of the connections in a NIB file by checking the Lock All Connections option in the Editing tab of the Interface Builder preferences. When these connections are locked, you cannot alter any connections or actions in your NIB files. Connections can be time-consuming to set up, and you don't want to accidentally alter them once you have them working. Before localizing a working NIB file and editing the new localization, first lock all of the connections.

The power of connections and actions really doesn't emerge until you define your own outlets and action messages. This is explained later in the "Custom Classes" section.

Size

The Size panel lets you set the position and dimension for most objects. Select the most convenient corner of the object for specifying its origin from the pop-up menu. Most objects have a definable height and width. Resizable objects often have minimum and maximum limits. Windows have auto-position options. Cocoa objects have auto-sizing springs that determine how the objects is resized and repositioned when the window dimensions change. For the auto-position and auto-sizing controls, click the "springs," both inside and outside the object. A "springy" spring indicates a dimension that will change, proportionally, when the window is resized. A straight spring indicates a fixed dimension.

The object on the left in Figure 10-26 will grow or shrink vertically, but not horizontally, when the window is resized. The object on the right will never change size. Instead, its distance from the bottom and right edges of the window will remain constant while its distance from the top and left edge of the window will vary. In other words, the right object will be anchored in the lower-right corner of the window.

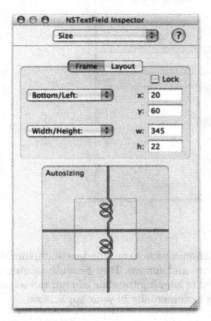 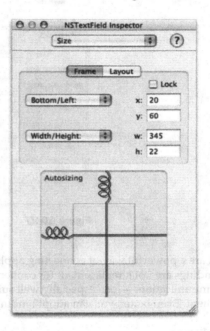

Figure 10-26

Bindings

Bindings are a relatively new addition to Interface Builder and Cocoa. You've seen how connections and actions can be created. You can use these to interact with interface objects and send events when something happens. But this still requires a lot of "glue" code that you must write yourself. A lot of programming in the Model/View/Controller paradigm is rote. Bindings attempt to alleviate much of that tedium (and bugs) by providing standard tools to connect model objects with their visual representations. These concepts are described in the documentation for Cocoa Bindings at `http://developer.apple.com/documentation/Cocoa/Conceptual/CocoaBindings/`.

The Bindings panel, shown in Figure 10-27, contains the properties of an object that can be bound to a controller. You bind objects to controller objects you create and add to the NIB. (See the Controllers tab of the objects palette for the standard controllers.) Controllers have no visual representation — drag them from the objects palette into the NIB document window to create a new one. Controllers use key-value binding. You must first define the value types a controller will control and then give those values a name (key). After the values are configured, you can bind a property of an object to a controller.

Figure 10-27

Bindings are a powerful way of connecting application objects to an interface with, literally, no programming. Bindings are not a replacement for connections and actions. They provide another form of inter-object communications — one especially well suited to keeping the state of your model and view objects in agreement. Even better, you can adopt bindings incrementally in your application.

Custom Class

The Custom Class panel allows you to change the class of a generic object to a more specific subclass (or vice versa). If you create an interface element using one of the generic objects from the objects palette and later decide that the object needs to be a subclass, change the object's class in the Custom Class panel. The visual representation of the object continues to use the generic object provided by Interface Builder. But at runtime, the object will be an instance of the custom subclass. The object gains or loses outlets and attributes as appropriate whenever you change its class.

Accessibility

This panel lets you set connections for a number of accessibility attributes. Just like a connection, first Control+drag to establish the direction between two UI objects. Then, switch to the Accessibility panel to set the connection. Read more about making applications accessible to users with disabilities at `http://developer.apple.com/documentation/Cocoa/Conceptual/Accessibility/`.

Help

The Help panel lets you set tool tips (pop-up windows with brief descriptions of what an interface element does or is used for) for Cocoa objects and help descriptions for Carbon objects.

AppleScript

AppleScript Studio applications (AppleScript programs with a Cocoa interface) can have AppleScript event handlers attached to individual interface objects. The handlers, shown in Figure 10-28, are all of the messages (or events) that can be sent to the selected object. If any of the messages are checked, the appropriate AppleScript handler is triggered whenever that message is sent to that object. For example, checking the clicked message of a button object will cause the on clicked handler to execute whenever the user clicks that button. To connect one or more AppleScript handlers to an object, check the messages you want the script to handle in the top portion of the panel. In the bottom, check the AppleScript file in the Xcode project that contains the handlers for those messages. You can only select one AppleScript file, and that file must contain the handlers for all of the messages you want to handle for this object. (The interface uses check boxes in the files list, where it really should use radio buttons.) Click the New button and Interface Builder assists you in creating a new AppleScript file and adding it to the project. Click the Edit button if you want to see or edit the selected AppleScript file.

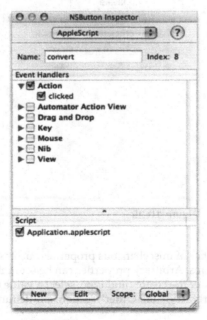

Figure 10-28

Sherlock

This panel is used exclusively for developing Sherlock channels. See "Introduction to Sherlock Channels" at http://developer.apple.com/documentation/AppleApplications/Conceptual/ Sherlock/ for an explanation of these attributes.

Control

This panel only appears for Carbon objects. In Carbon, control elements are addressed and identified by a signature and ID. Some can also send a "command" to the application when triggered. When the user clicks a button, a Carbon event containing the ID of the button and the command value is passed to your application. For control objects, the panel (shown in Figure 10-29) sets the signature and ID of the control, as well as the command that the control will generate. The signature is usually the creator code of your application, but in large and complex interfaces, the signature can be used to organize groups of objects. The ID is the numerical ID of the object, which is used to address the object at runtime. Choose from the list of predefined commands, or choose <other> and enter any arbitrary value. The command is a 32-bit value that can be expressed as a 4-character OS type or as an unsigned integer. Check the box next to the input field to select which.

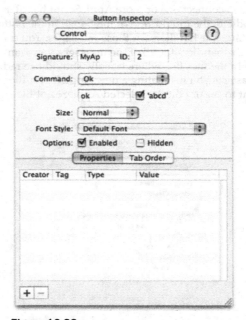

Figure 10-29

This panel can also set a number of miscellaneous properties such as the control's Size, Font Style, and the Hidden and Enabled options. Arbitrary properties can be set in the Properties tab. Click the plus button to add a new property. Enter the creator and type, select a value type, and enter a value. The - button will delete the selected property. The "Tab Order" section, a little further on, discusses the Tab Order tab.

Layout

Cocoa objects set their resize relationships in the Size panel. For Carbon objects, the layout settings are slightly different and are set in the Layout panel, as shown in Figure 10-30.

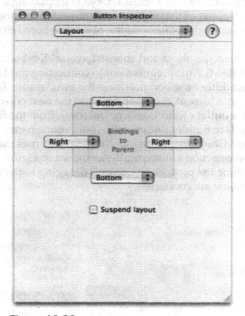

Figure 10-30

For each edge of the object, choose which edge of the object's container it will be bound to. Binding both the left and right edge of an object to the right edge of the window causes the object to slide to the right or left as the width of the window is changed. Binding the left edge to the left edge of the window and the right edge to the right edge of the window causes the object to be stretched as the window width changes.

Carbon events, controls, commands, IDs, and layouts are all explained in the "Carbon User Experience" documentation, found in the Reference Library. Carbon programming is an expansive topic. If you are just getting started, get an introductory book on Carbon programming. You can also learn a lot from the AppearanceSample example project provided with Xcode.

Tab Order

The tab order — that order in which the keyboard focus moves from one control to the next when the user presses the Tab key — is specified differently for Cocoa and Carbon applications. The tab order in Cocoa is controlled using the nextKeyView outlet (instance variable) of each interface object. A single object in the window is designated as the initial first responder. Starting at the initial first responder object, the objects connected using the nextKeyValue outlet form a linked list that defines the order of focus progression in the window.

You can explore the current tab order using the Layout⇨Keyboard Navigation⇨Show Keyboard Check (Command+K) command. When the Keyboard Check mode is enabled, the word "tab" appears in the lower-left corner of the layout window. In this mode, the Tab key will follow the tab order of the objects, changing the selection to the next object in the chain. The object designated as the first responder, the beginning of the tab order chain, display a small 1. Objects displaying a small red tab symbol indicate that that the nextKeyValue outlet of that object is *not* connected to another object. This is normal for the last object in the chain but usually indicates that the object has been left out of the chain.

To set the first responder, select the object and choose Layout⇨Keyboard Navigation⇨Make Initial First Responder (Command+Shift+M). This is equivalent to connecting the initialFirstResponder outlet of the window to that object. Either method produces the same result. To build the rest of the chain you simply connect the nextKeyValue outlet of each object to the next object in the chain. Make the connection as you would any other outlet connection. Control+drag from the first responder object to the next object in the tab order. Interface Builder presents the connections panel, exactly as it would for any other connection. But in Keyboard Check mode, Interface Builder assumes that you're setting nextKeyValue outlet and highlights that connection automatically, as shown in Figure 10-31. Click the Connect button to set the connection. Continue the process by Control+dragging to the next object. Repeat until all the desired objects in your window are connected.

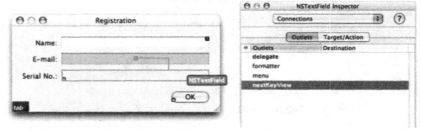

Figure 10-31

If you connect to an object that already has a nextKeyValue connection, you first need to disconnect it and then connect it to the new target. You can clear the initialFirstResponder and all nextKeyValue outlets using the Layout⇨Keyboard Navigation⇨Clear Keyboard Loop command. When you are done exploring or manipulating the tab order, select Layout⇨Keyboard Navigation⇨Hide Keyboard Check to disable the keyboard check mode.

For Carbon objects, you set the tab order in the Tab Order tab of the Control panel. Select a container, usually the window itself, and switch to the Tab Order list in the Control panel. To change the tab order of object, drag them around in the list.

Custom Classes

You've already seen numerous places where Interface Builder reflects and understands the class model of Cocoa objects. Connections, Actions, and Custom Classes methods all require knowledge of the object's class — its instance variables and methods, and where that class fits in the inheritance tree. By transferring the information about your own classes and subclasses, you extend Interface Builder's knowledge of your application.

The relationship between classes and instances in Interface Builder parallels the model of classes and objects used by Objective-C (and other object-oriented programming languages). A class is a template that defines the content and behavior of any number of like objects. An object is a single concrete instance that confirms to the definition of its class. This same model exists in the NIB file. Classes declared in the NIB file define outlets (instance variables), actions (methods), and inheritance. Every object in a NIB is an instance of a class defined in that NIB or is one of the Cocoa classes predefined in Interface Builder.

The key concept to keep in mind is that classes, like the class definitions in a language, don't get created at runtime. They are merely definitions. A class definition in a NIB file is used exclusively by Interface Builder. Class definitions don't produce anything when the NIB file is loaded. They are only used to guide the creation and editing of objects.

You can browse the classes defined in a NIB file using the Classes tab of the NIB document window, as shown in Figure 10-32. Classes are organized hierarchically according to their inheritance. You can view the browser as an expandable outline (the left window in Figure 10-32) or by using a column browser (on the right). Select between these two views using the control at the upper-left just above the list. Classes defined in the Cocoa framework are grey and cannot be edited. Classes that you have defined appear in black.

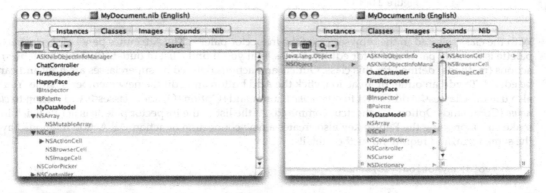

Figure 10-32

To the right of the outline/browser button is a pop-up menu that quickly jumps to one of the more common Cocoa classes. If you have defined your own classes, those appear at the bottom of the menu. On the far-right is a search field. Type the beginning of a class name, and the list jumps to the first class name that matches those letters.

There are two ways of defining a new class in Interface Builder: you can define the class directly in Interface Builder, or you can have Interface Builder import the declaration from your source file. Creating your class in Interface Builder is the most immediate and convenient method, but you run the risk of creating a class definition that is different than the class defined in your program. Regardless, it can be the method of choice when you're making some minor modification to a class or if you want to begin your class design in Interface Builder.

Creating Classes in Interface Builder

To create a class in Interface Builder, start by selecting an existing class in the class browser. Choose the Subclass *classname* command from the Classes menu or from the Control-/right-click contextual pop-up menu. Interface Builder also provides a shortcut: Select the superclass and press the Return key. A new, empty, subclass of the selected class is created and the name of the new class is selected, as shown in Figure 10-33. Edit the name and press Return.

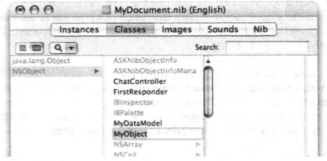

Figure 10-33

With the class selected in the browser, open the Inspector palette. The Attributes panel of the Inspector palette is the only panel useful for editing a class. In it you'll find a list of outlets (instance variables) and actions (methods) defined for this class. Outlets and actions defined by superclasses are grey and cannot be edited. To add an outlet or an action, click the Add button and edit the new member's name. You can also use the Classes⇨Add Outlet to *classname* (Command+Option+O) and Classes⇨Add Action to *classname* (Command+Option+A) shortcut commands. If the list in the Inspector palette is active (click in it to make sure), pressing the Return key also creates a new connection or action. All Action methods have the same form, and require no further details:

```
- (void)anyAction:(id)sender;
```

Outlets are instance variables and require a class type. If the outlet is indiscriminant and will accept a pointer to any object, set the type to id. If you want Interface Builder to be specific and only allow the outlet to be connected to a particular class (or subclass) of an object use the pop-up list to choose a known class from the list. You can also double-click the field and enter the class name directly. In Figure 10-34, a MyDataModel class is defined, which is a sub-class of NSObject. An outlet has also been added to the document class. That outlet takes a pointer to an object of the MyDocument class (a subclass of NSDocument, which was also created for this example).

> One very common reason to add actions to a class manually has to do with the First Responder class. As previously mentioned, the First Responder object is a surrogate for target/action connections that will be dispatched at runtime. The responder chain determines the actual recipient of the message when it occurs. But Interface Builder requires that a message be defined and a target specified before it can make a connection. If you have an object in your application that will respond to a message only when it's in the responder chain, add that action to the First Responder class and then connect your object to the First Responder object.

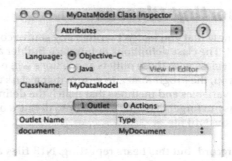

Figure 10-34

As previously explained, creating classes doesn't create objects. Nowhere (yet) is there an object of MyDataModel or MyDocument class in the NIB file. To create an object—a concrete instance of a class—select the class and choose the Class⇨Instantiate *classname* command. You can create as many, or as few, instances of a class as you need. At the beginning of this chapter, you were creating objects by dragging them from the objects palette. For objects without a visual representation, such as the NSController class, you could have just as easily selected the class in the class browser and created a new instance. The effect is the same.

Try It Out   Creating a Custom Class

In Interface Builder, create a new Cocoa NIB file using the Application template. Then follow these steps:

1.   Switch to the Classes tab of the NIB document window. Find and select the NSObject class.

2.   Choose Classes⇨Subclass NSObject command. Name the class **MyApplication**.

3.   With the new class still selected, open the Inspector palette to the Attributes panel.

4.   In the Outlets tab, create a new outlet named **mainWindow**. The type of the outlet is NSWindow.

5.   In the Actions tab, add an action named **openPreferences:**.

6.   With the class selected, choose Instantiate MyApplication.

7.   Switch to the Instances tab, and choose the list view.

8.   Control-drag from the MyApplication object to the NSWindow object and connect the `mainWindow` outlet.

9.   Find the MainMenu window, and click the NewApplication menu to reveal its items. Control-drag from the Preferences...item to the MyApplication object. Connect the `openPreferences:` action.

How It Works

Defining a class in Interface Builder defines the public member instance variables and action methods that an object will have a runtime. After they are defined, Interface Builder allows you to set those connections in the NIB file.

Importing and Exporting Classes

You've probably noticed by now that you haven't written any source code while defining classes and objects. And you'd be correct. The class definitions in Interface Builder are promises (or assumptions, if you like) that a MyDocument class with those outlets and actions will exist when the NIB is loaded at runtime. It is entirely up to you, the programmer, to ensure that a class named MyDocument is defined with a set of public instance variables and methods that match the definition in the NIB file. Creating these separately, it is very easy to forget to define a class or to define a method name that is slightly different from those defined in the NIB file.

This may sound like a broken record, but this bears repeating. NIB files are interpreted at runtime. The classes of objects, their instance variables and methods, are expected to exist exactly as they are described in the NIB file. If they do not, runtime errors occur. Objects for nonexistent classes do not get created. Nonexistent outlets don't get set. Nonexistent actions never happen. This is a very common source of bugs. If you think there is something wrong with Interface Builder or the objects in a NIB, first double-check all of your class definitions.

To help avoid these problems, Interface Builder provides two facilities that let you define your classes once and keep the class definitions in the NIB file synchronized with those in your source code. One imports a NIB class definition directly from an existing source file, and the other can be used to export a NIB class definition as a source file.

To use the import method, begin by defining your class in a source file. I prefer to stick to the convention of defining exactly one class per file, but you are free to organize your source anyway you like. In my application, I begin by creating a MyDocument.h file, shown in Listing 10-2.

Listing 10-2: MyDocument.h Source File

```
//
//  MyDocument.h
//  Chatter
//
//  Created by James Bucanek on 8/31/05.
//  Copyright James Bucanek 2005 . All rights reserved.
//


#import <Cocoa/Cocoa.h>

@interface MyDocument : NSDocument
{
  @public
  IBOutlet ChatController* chatter;       // controller for this chat session
  IBOutlet id             chatDelegate; // delegate for this session
}

- (IBAction)sendMessage:(id)sender;

@end
```

The source uses two important keywords: IBOutlet and IBAction. IBOutlet is a macro defined in the AppKit headers as nothing at all. So it makes no difference to the compilation. IBAction is defined as void, which is the required return type for action methods.

Saving the source file, I next switch to Interface Builder. I load the MyDocument NIB file, switch to the Classes browser, and choose the Class⇨Read Files (Command+Option+R) command. From the standard dialog box, I choose the MyDocument.h file and click the Parse button. Interface Builder reads the header file, discovers the name of the class and its superclass, and picks out all instance variables tagged with IBOutlet and all methods tagged with IBAction. It then constructs a compatible class definition in the NIB file. Examining the class in the Inspector palette shows that the class has two outlets and one action (see Figure 10-35). The third outlet was inherited from MyDocument's superclass.

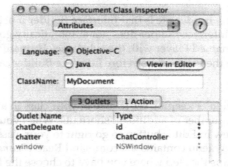

Figure 10-35

Inevitably, there will be changes to MyDocument as development proceeds. Simply repeat the process in the future to update the class definition to match that of the evolving source. If you add new actions or outlets, Interface Builder silently expands the definition of the class. If you rename or delete a member, Interface Builder presents the warning in Figure 10-36. You have the choice of replacing or merging the definition that's in the source with the one in the NIB. Replace will delete any outlets or actions that are no longer defined in the source. Merge will add any new outlets and actions discovered in the source, and leave all other existing members alone.

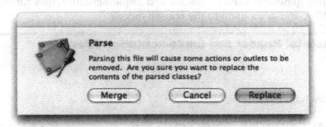

Figure 10-36

Renaming an outlet or action breaks all of the connections to it in the NIB. If you use Merge, the NIB is left with nonexistent outlets or connections to nonexistent actions. If you use Replace, all of the old connections are deleted. In either case, you must now go through your NIB and fix all of the connections to the renamed outlet or action.

The Read Files command, as the plural form implies, can parse multiple files in a single step. Use Command-click and Shift-click in the open file dialog box to choose more than one file to import.

> Each NIB file contains its own class definitions. If you use a custom class in more than one NIB file, you must update all of your NIB files when the class definition changes. As a rule, only define a class in a NIB that uses it.

One requirement for parsing a header file is that Interface Builder must already have a definition for the superclass of the new class. Interface Builder does not automatically go looking for superclass definitions. So if you have a class named Player with the subclasses HumanPlayer and MachinePlayer, you must first import and define the Player class before Interface Builder can import the HumanPlayer or MachinePlayer classes.

If you adhere to the convention of keeping the source of your class in a file with the same name, Interface Builder provides a number of additional shortcuts. When you're viewing a class in the Inspector palette, use the View in Editor button to go right to your class' source code. To update an existing class definition, the Class menu contains the command Read *classname*.h. This is the same as the Read Files command, but skips the step where you have to choose the file. These commands are only enabled when a file of the same name exists in your project. Interface Builder assumes that they contain a class of the same name, so don't try to confuse it.

The alternative to the import method is the export method. This time, you begin your class definition in Interface Builder. Define your class just as you did in the "Creating Classes in Interface Builder" section. After it is defined, select the class and choose Classes⇨Create files for *classname* (Command+Option+F). Interface Builder presents a dialog box like that one shown in Figure 10-37.

On the left is the list of files to create. You can choose to create just the header, just the implementation, or both. On the right is the list of targets in the project that the file will be automatically added to. Interface Builder then generates skeletal header and implementation files for the class, as shown in Listings 10-3 and 10-4, and adds them to the chosen targets.

Listing 10-3: Skeletal Header and Implementation Files

```
/* ChatController */

#import <Cocoa/Cocoa.h>

@interface ChatController : NSObject
{
    IBOutlet MyDataModel *usersBonjour;
    IBOutlet MyDataModel *usersLocal;
    IBOutlet MyDataModel *usersOnServer;
}
@end
```

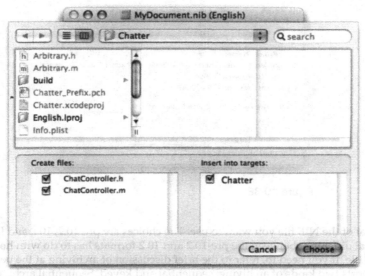

Figure 10-37

Listing 10-4: Skeletal Header and Implementation Files

```
#import "ChatController.h"

@implementation ChatController

@end
```

This code won't even compile — the definition for the MyDataModel class isn't included in ChatController.h. Also note that this method does not use the rich set of new file templates available through Xcode — there are no header comments or any other customized information. But it's a start, and it matches the class you are using in Interface Builder.

NIB File Formats

Cocoa has evolved over the years. The format of NIB files has changed to accommodate that evolution, adding new features, capabilities — and compatibility issues. The biggest change in Interface Builder has been the support for Carbon, which produces a completely different and incompatible form of NIB file. New features added to OS X can make newer Cocoa NIB files incompatible with older operating systems. As a program developer, you are left with the classic choice of using modern interface features or supporting older operating systems.

To inspect and change the format of your NIB file, switch to the Nib tab of the NIB document window (see Figure 10-38).

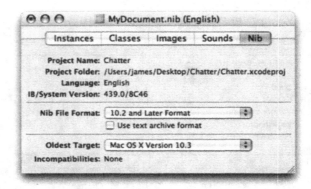

Figure 10-38

Select the format of the NIB file you want to use. The choices are pre-10.2, 10.2 and Later Format, or Both. The critical difference between the pre-10.2 and 10.2 formats has to do with how the objects are archived in the file. If you need to, refer to the brief discussion of archiving at the beginning of this chapter. Cocoa supports two kinds of archiving: sequential and keyed. Sequential archives contain only the raw values of each object. It is the responsibility of the object to understand those values and what order they are in. Keyed archives store each value with a type and a name (key). An object reads the values with the keys that it understands, and can ignore the rest. Sequential archiving is faster and more compact. But when new features and values are added to an existing class, those objects create archive data streams that older code can no longer understand.

The Both option archives the objects using both encoding techniques, storing both formats in the NIB file. The operating system will automatically choose the data format it is capable of reading at runtime. Choose the pre-10.2 or Both format only if your application *must* run on OS X versions 10.0 or 10.1. Otherwise, the 10.2 and Later Format is preferred.

The Use Text Archive Format saves a keyed archive NIB file using an equivalent XML representation. Normally, you would not use this format for application development, because the binary form of NIB encoding is much faster and more compact. It would be useful should you ever want to examine, manually edit, archive, or perform XSL transformations on the contents of the NIB file. Otherwise, leave this option off. Note that the XML produced is tightly bound to the internal logical of the NSCoder class and is not for the faint of heart.

Compatibility Checking

Keyed archiving is flexible because older classes can ignore newer values and still function. But those newer values still get ignored. As a developer, you must understand when new features were added and ensure that your application still functions acceptably when running in an older version of OS X.

To help you identify features that might be a problem, Interface Builder provides a compatibility checker. Choose File⇨Compatibility Checking, or click the Show button in the Nib tab of the NIB document window. The Compatibility Checking window, shown in Figure 10-39, lists the features or objects that may not function as intended when they're loaded by the operating system version you select in the pop-up menu at the top of the window.

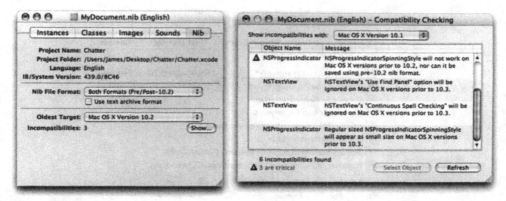

Figure 10-39

In this example, Interface Builder was asked to list all potential problems that would occur if this NIB file were loaded by an application running under Mac OS X 10.1. Most compatibility errors are minor, and represent special features or cosmetic differences that were introduced in later versions of the operating system. Interface Builder flags more serious problems as critical. These usually indicate major functionality that is completely absent in the older operating system. In this example, Interface Builder is warning that an NSProgressIndicator object was used in a window. This class does not exist in OS X 10.1. It can't even be written in the pre-10.2 NIB file format. Loading this NIB in OX 10.1 will not create this object, and any connections to it will be nil. Your application would have to deal with this possibility gracefully, or you should consider a different interface design that avoids using that class.

Customizing Interface Builder

Some basic features of Interface Builder can be tweaked in the Interface Builder Preferences (Command+,). The Preferences, shown in Figure 10-40, are divided into five tabs. Most of the options in the General tab are self-explanatory.

The Palette/Info Panel Are Utility Windows option changes the window type of the Inspector and objects palettes into regular windows. Regular windows can be layered behind other windows and remain visible with other applications are active. Normally, these are floating palettes, cannot be obscured by other Interface Builder windows, and disappear when you switch back to Xcode.

The Display Connection Warning Icons option alerts you to unconnected outlets in the Instances list view. Instances that have missing connections or Target/Actions have a little warning icon next to it. There are lots of situations where this is perfectly normal, so you many want to disable this feature if you find it annoying.

The first two options in the Editing tab have already been discussed in the "Connections" and "Selecting Objects" sections. The option to store images in a NIB is discussed in the "NIB Formats" section. The last option is the number of Undo steps that Interface Builder records.

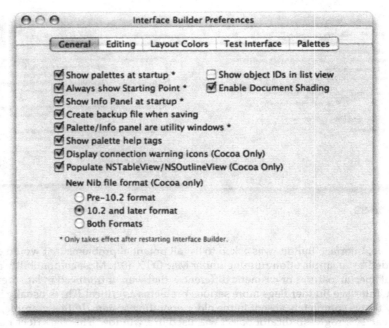

Figure 10-40

The Layouts tab lets you customize the colors used for Layout Rectangles, Guides, Measurement Lines, and Hidden views.

The Test Interface tab controls when the user defaults file belonging to the surrogate test application (the test application's preferences file) is deleted. Some Cocoa objects can automatically record their state in the user defaults file. You may, or may not, want these states preserved between test runs of your interface. You can read more about user defaults at http://developer.apple.com/documentation/Cocoa/Conceptual/UserDefaults/.

The Palettes tab lists the custom palettes currently loaded in Interface Builder. Most of the palettes discussed in this chapter are built into Interface Builder. The AppleTalk and Sherlock palettes are included with Xcode. You, or third-party developers, can define additional palettes. Add or remove these custom palettes using the Add and Remove buttons at the bottom.

Both the Inspector palette and the objects palette can be extended. You can create a custom object type — not just a custom class, a new object that appears in the objects palette — by building a custom IBPalette class. Likewise, you can add custom panels to the Inspector palette by writing an IBInspector.

How to create these classes is beyond the scope of this book, but Xcode includes several example projects in the /Developer/Examples/InterfaceBuilder folder that illustrate how. Other examples include projects, such as Clock Control and Reducer, that include custom Interface Builder objects. Unfortunately, there is no formal documentation for the IBPalette and IBInspector classes. You can gain some insight into these classes by reading the comments in the InterfaceBuilder/InterfaceBuilder.h header files. At the time of publication, Sun Microsystems was still mirroring the original documentation that was part of the OpenStep project (the predecessor to Cocoa) at `http://docs.sun.com/app/docs/doc/802-2110/6i63kq4uj#hic`. There you will also find a PDF version of the documentation, which you can download and keep.

Summary

Interface Builder provides a rich environment for designing menus and windows. But it goes beyond that, letting you define classes, create custom objects, and bind those objects together at runtime. All without having to write a single line of code.

You'll quickly become addicted to designing your application interfaces and object relationships using Interface Builder. And if you like seeing your interface design graphically, you'll enjoy the next chapter, where you'll learn how to visualize your classes graphically.

Exercise

Use Interface Builder to finish the NIB file for a simple application that lists manned spaceflights. Begin by opening the SpaceflightList project. Then open its MainMenu.nib file in Interface Builder and follow these steps:

1. The primary window contains two NSListView objects. Place these inside a split view.

2. Add a check box (NSButton) to the window. Title the check box **Solo-flights Only**.

3. Create a ListController class, with two outlets: `alphabeticList` and `dateOrderList`. Both are NSTableView objects. ListController has one action: `showHideSoloFlights:`.

4. Create a ListDataModel object. It has one outlet: `listController`. This outlet is a ListController object.

5. Create one instance of the ListController class and two instances of the ListDataModel class.

6. Connect the object outlets and actions as follows and as shown in Figure 10-41:

    a. Connect the two ListController outlets to the two NSTableView objects in the window.

    b. Connect the `dataSource` outlet of each `NSTableView` object should be connected to its own instance of the `ListDataModel`.

    c. Point the `listController` outlet of the two ListDataModel objects to the single ListController object. In addition, connect the `delegate` for the `NSApplication` (File's Owner) to the single ListController object.

    d. Send a `showHideSoloFlights:` action from the NSButton check box to the ListController.

7. Save the NIB, build, and run the application.

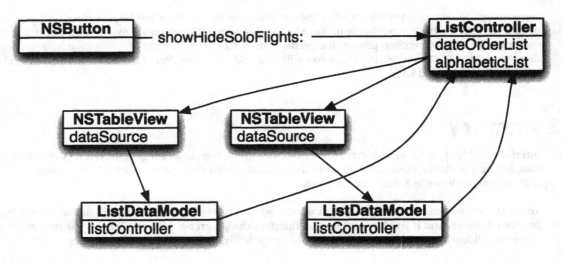

Figure 10-41

Class Modeling

To be an effective object-oriented programmer, you must have a clear mental picture of the classes in your application and their relationships. Sometimes this "picture" is hard to form, because class relationships can be both complex and abstract. The class browser, discussed in Chapter 8, uses the project's index to list the details and organization of your project's classes. While this helps, it still doesn't present a bird's-eye view of your application's structure. Enter class modeling. Class modeling, new in Xcode 2.1, performs the same function as the class browser — but in a much more visual and customizable way.

You can create a class model document from any group of classes. This could be your entire application or just a set of functionally related classes. Xcode then graphs those classes, as shown in Figure 11-1. The class model tracks, and instantly reflects, any changes made to your source files. Unlike data modeling, discussed in the next chapter, the class modeler is not an editor. You cannot design or alter the declarations in a class model and then transform that model into code. Maybe in some future version of Xcode, the class modeler will evolve into a full-circle UML-like design environment. But for now, class modeling is strictly a visualization and documentation tool.

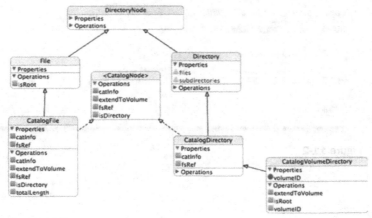

Figure 11-1

A class model is stored in a document. The documents themselves are extremely lightweight. Don't be too concerned about the amount of data required to define a class model document. The document really has very little information in it, beyond the list of source files included in the model. All of the information about the classes is gleaned from the project's symbol index. Think of a class model as just another "view" into your project.

This brings us to two very important requirements. First, your project must be indexed for class modeling to work. If indexing is turned off, turn it on in the Code Sense panel of the Xcode Preferences. If your project is currently being indexed in the background, class modeling starts working as soon as the index is complete. Secondly, class model documents cannot be used outside the context of the project. You cannot open a class model document unless the project that it references is also open. Although it is *possible* to create class model documents outside of your project, it is not advisable. If you are intent on keeping a class model, it should be stored in your project's folder and only opened when the project is open.

Creating a Class Model

You add a class model document to your project much as you would any other kind of source file, using the File⇨New File command. If you have any questions about this process, see the "Creating New Source Files" section in Chapter 5. Begin by selecting the Class Model document type from the list of file templates. Give the document a name and select the targets and the project the new model should be added to. Note that a class model doesn't produce anything, so adding it to a target is purely a cosmetic gesture. For class model documents, there's one more step in the assistant, as shown in Figure 11-2.

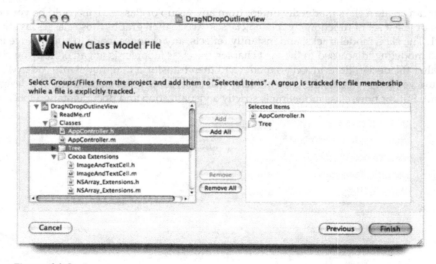

Figure 11-2

On the left are all the source groups and files defined in the project. On the right is the list of files, or groups of files, that will be tracked by the new model. Select the source files, or source groups, that you want to model on the left and click the Add button to include them in the model. You can do this all at once or incrementally. The Add All button adds every single source file *and* group in your project. This is excessive and is not recommended, for reasons that will be explained shortly. If you have added too many sources, select them in the list on the right and click the Remove button. Remove All removes all of the sources added, so you can start over.

You can add any kind of source file that you like, but the data model only uses source files that define a class. For Objective-C and C++, this can be either the header or the implementation file. In Java, the .java file that defines the classes should be added. The model will consist of the union of any classes defined in the selected source files and their superclasses. Other headers that contain only non-class declarations, libraries, and so on are ignored. There's no harm in adding those files to the model, but there's no point either. It also makes no difference how many source files define the same class. The class only appears in the model once.

Adding a source group to a model implicitly tracks every source file contained in that group. If the contents of that group changes in the future so do the source files in the model. You can add both a source file and the group that contains that source file to the model. One reason for doing this would be to avoid having a class disappear from a model if it were moved outside its current source group.

Frameworks can also be added. A framework is, logically, a source group that contains a number of headers files. All of the classes defined in those headers will be added to the model. Be judicious when adding system frameworks, as these typically defined scores, if not hundreds, of classes. This can make for an unwieldy model. If you want to include classes defined in frameworks, add the specific headers you want by digging into the framework group.

Don't fret too much about what files to include, or exclude, at this point. The list of sources for the model can be freely edited in the future (as will be explained in the "Changing the Tracking" section). After assembling your initial list of choices, click the Finish button. The data model document is added to the project and Xcode displays the new model.

Figure 11-3 shows a typical class model pane. Like any project document, a class model pane can appear in the project window or in a separate window. The top portion of the pane contains the class browser and the bottom portion shows the class diagram. The horizontal divider between the two can be resized to show just one or the other. As a shortcut, the Design⇨Hide/Show Model Browser (Command+Control+B) command quickly collapses or expands the browser portion of the pane.

Diagram

Browser

Tools   Functions   Details Pane

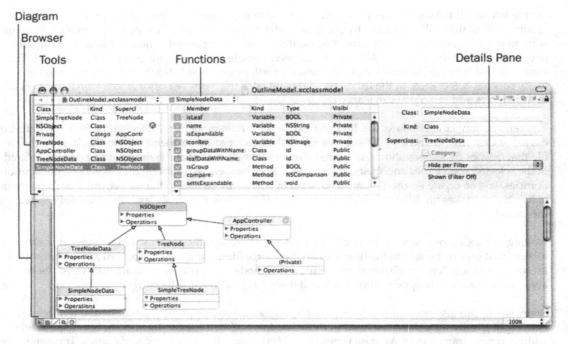

Figure 11-3

Creating a Quick Model

The Quick Model command is a fast way of creating an ephemeral model for a select group of classes, and is an alternative to the more formal procedure for creating class model documents that was just described. Select any number of source files or groups in the project window and choose Design⇨Class Model⇨Quick Model. A class model is immediately constructed from the selected sources — it does not have a model document, and is not added to the project.

Use this command to gain quick insight into the class structure of an application. When you are done with the model, simply close it. If you made no modifications to the model, it just goes away. If you did, Xcode treats it like any unnamed document window and prompts you to save it. As mentioned earlier, class model documents are useless outside the context of the open project. If you don't want to keep the model, discard the changes or just save the file as is. The document is a temporary file, so just saving the file doesn't preserve it — it will still be deleted once you're finished with the diagram. If you decide you want to save the class model document, choose the File⇨Save As command, write the class model document into your project folder, and then add the new document to the project. See Chapter 5 for one of the many ways of adding a source file to your project.

Try It Out   **Create a Quick Class Model**

Creating a class model is quick and painless.

Pick any Objective-C, Java, or C++ application; then follow these steps:

1. Start with any Objective-C, Java, or C++ project. For a robust example, open the /Developer/Examples/Java/Cocoa/BlastApp project.

2. Select the individual source files, or the group containing multiple sources files, in the project window. For the BlastApp demo, select the Classes group.

3. Choose Design⇨Data Model⇨Quick Model.

4. Explore the model. A fragment of the BlastApp model is shown in Figure 11-4. Save or discard the model file when you're done.

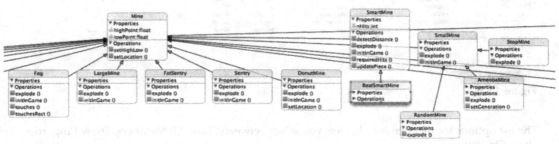

Figure 11-4

How It Works

A Quick Model takes the currently selected source files and diagrams the class relationships found in those files. The model is disposable and intended as a way to obtain quick insight into the organization of an application or module.

Class Model Browser

The upper pane in the class model is the class model browser. On the left is the list of classes being tracked by the model. Selecting a class displays the class's members in the middle list. Selecting an item in either list displays additional information about that item in the details pane area on the right. You can use the dividers between these sections to resize them, within limits.

> To avoid any confusion, the term "browser" in this chapter refers to the class model browser, not the Class Browser discussed in Chapter 8.

Class modeling can be used to model C++, Java, and Objective-C classes. The terminology used in class modeling tends to be neutral. "Properties" refer to instance or member variables. "Operations" generically refer to class methods, functions, or messages. Some terminology differs depending on the language. A Java Interface and an Objective-C Protocol are, conceptually, the same thing. Yet the class model uses the native term for each. Not all modeling concepts apply to all languages. Categories only appear when modeling Objective-C classes. Package names only appear when you're modeling Java classes.

You can customize the browser display a number of different ways. In the lower-left corner of both the class and member lists is a pop-up menu that will alter the list's contents. The choices for the class list, shown in Figure 11-5, are Flat List and Inheritance Tree. Flat List lists all of the classes alphabetically. Inheritance Tree lists the classes in a hierarchical browser.

Figure 11-5

The list options for the members list lets you select between Show All Members, Show Properties, and Show Operations.

You can resize and reorder the columns for both lists as desired by dragging the column separators or headers. Control+click the column title to control which columns the list displays. Check only those columns you want to see. Both menus include a Show All Columns command, which causes all columns to be displayed.

Class Model Diagram

In the lower portion of the pane is the class diagram (see Figure 11-6), and is class modeling's raison d'etre. The diagram presents a graphic visualization of the class relationships. Note that the browser and diagram show much of the same information, just in different ways.

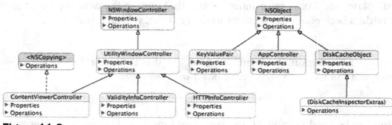

Figure 11-6

Nodes

Classes in the class model diagram are represented as nodes. At the top of each node is its title. Nodes may optionally show additional details below their title. The form and color of the title indicate its type, as listed in the following table.

Node Title	Color	Node Type
PlainTitle	Blue	A class
<TitleInBrackets>	Red	A Java interface or Objective-C protocol
(TitleInParentheses)	Green	An Objective-C category

The background color of framework classes is darker than that of classes defined in your application.

Lines between nodes denote inheritance. The arrow points to the superclass or interface from which the node inherits, adopts, or extends. The possible combination of arrows and lines is listed in the following table.

Line and Arrow Type	Relationship
Solid line with an open arrow between two classes	Arrow points to the superclass of the class
Solid line with an open arrow between a class and a category	Arrow points to the class that the category extends
Dashed line with an open arrow	Arrow points to the interface or protocol that the class adopts
Solid line with no arrow	Connects annotation node to any other kind of node

The compartments below the title detail the members of the class. The Properties member lists the instance variables and the Operations member lists the methods or functions. You can hide the details of a node by "rolling up" the node, and reveal them again by rolling it back down. You accomplish this by using the Roll Up Compartments and Roll Down Compartments commands in the Design menu. The command applies to the currently selected node or nodes and you can also access it by Control-/right-clicking a node. If no nodes are selected, the commands change to Roll Up All and Roll Down All.

The lists within the compartments can be individually expanded or collapsed. To affect this immediately for a single list in a node, click the disclosure triangle to the left of the compartment subtitle. To collapse or expand the lists in all compartments, select a node or nodes and choose either the Collapse All Compartments or Expand All Compartments command from the Design menu. When no nodes are selected, the commands change to Collapse All and Expand All. Figure 11-7 shows a node rolled-up, rolled-down, and with its compartment lists expanded.

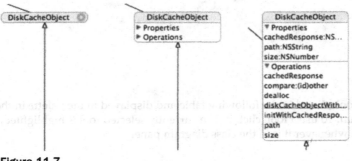

Figure 11-7

237

The members of a class may optionally display their visibility (private, protected, or public), type, return type, or method parameters. All of these display options appear in the General tab of the diagram's Info window. With the selection tool, click anywhere on the background of the diagram so that no nodes are selected, and then choose File⇨Get Info (Command+I). Switch to the General tab and the various display options appear at the top of the window, as shown in Figure 11-8.

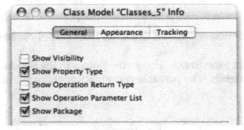

Figure 11-8

The Show Visibility option refers to the scope or accessibility of class members, indicated by a small icon next to each member. The possibilities are private, package, protected, and public. In the diagram these appear as a red circle, orange triangle (pointing down), yellow triangle (pointing up), or green square, respectively.

The Show Property Type option includes the variable type after each class property. Show Operation Return Type shows the return value type of each operation. This may appear before or after the operation name, depending on the language being modeled. The Show Operation Parameter List option includes the entire parameter list of each operation, and can make for some very wide class nodes.

The Show Package option only applies to Java. If you select this option, the package name appears below the name of the class or interface in the node's title compartment.

Figure 11-9 shows a diagram with all the display options turned off (left) and on (right). Static (also known as "class") members are underlined. This is one display option that is not customizable.

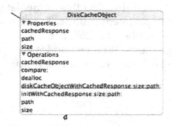

Figure 11-9

Tools

There are five tools, listed in the following table and displayed in the palette in the lower-left corner of the class diagram. To use a tool, click it. The currently selected tool is highlighted, and the cursor reflects the current tool whenever it is in the class diagram pane.

Tool	Description
Arrow	Selection tool. Used to select elements, move, expand, and resize nodes. This is the default tool.
Note	Note tool. Creates annotation nodes.
Line	Line tool. Connects nodes.
Magnifying Glass	Zoom tool. Enlarges or shrinks the diagram display.
Hand	Drag tool. Pans the diagram around in the window.

Choose the arrow tool whenever you need to select, move, resize, or otherwise manipulate the nodes in a diagram.

Use of the Note and Line tools are described later in the "Adding Annotations" section.

The Magnifying Glass and Hand tools are one way of navigating the diagram, and are described in the next section.

The entire class diagram is contained on a variable number of pages. The number of pages automatically changes to encompass the size of the diagram.

Navigation

Moving around the class diagram is pretty straightforward. You can use the scroll bars at the bottom and right side of the pane to scroll the diagram. You can also select the Hand tool and drag the diagram around.

Reduce or magnify the diagram by selecting a magnification amount in the zoom control in the lower-right corner of the pane.

Use the Magnifying Glass tool to incrementally zoom the diagram. Select the tool and click anywhere in the class diagram pane to increase to the next zoom magnification in the menu. Hold down the Option key and a minus sign (-) appears in the tool. Click with the Option key held down and the diagram is shrunk to the next zoom magnification level in the menu. To zoom the diagram to fit an arbitrary portion of the diagram, drag out a rectangle using the Magnifying Glass tool. The image zooms so that the approximate area of the diagram selected fills the pane.

The Zoom In (Command+Control+Shift+=) and Zoom Out (Command+Control+-) commands are equivalent to clicking, or Option+clicking, using the Magnifying Glass tool. To scale the display to fit entire diagram in the pane, choose the Zoom To Fit (Command+Control+=) command.

Selecting

You can select class nodes in a variety of ways. Selection is also closely tied to navigation. Selecting a class causes the diagram to scroll if the selected class was beyond the edge of the visible diagram.

Click a node to select it. Drag out a rectangle using the Arrow tool to select all of the nodes that intersect the area drawn.

Class selection in the diagram and browser are linked. Selecting a class in the browser selects the same class in the diagram, and vice versa. The Functions menu in a class diagram lists all of the classes in the model, as shown in Figure 11-10. Choosing one selects that class in both the browser and diagram, and scrolls to make both visible.

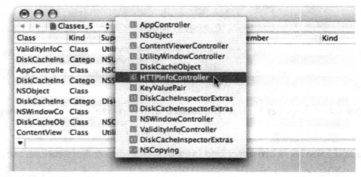

Figure 11-10

You can add class nodes to the selection by holding down the Shift key while clicking unselected nodes or dragging out a selection rectangle. Nodes can be individually removed from a selection by clicking a selected node while holding down the Shift key. It may be necessary to click the background area of the node; clicking the node's title or a member may not deselect the node.

You can also type the first few letters of a class name. When listed alphabetically, the first class that matches the characters typed is selected.

Quick-Jump to Source

Double-click any class or member in the browser, and Xcode jumps to its declaration in the source code.

In the class diagram, a small disclosure button, like the one pictured in Figure 11-11, appears whenever you hover the mouse over a class or member name. Click the button to jump to its definition. Note the subtle difference between "definition" and "declaration." Clicking a function or method name in the browser jumps to its prototype in the class definition. Clicking the disclosure button in the diagram jumps to its implementation. This distinction does not apply to Java methods, which do not have a separate declaration.

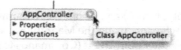

Figure 11-11

You can also explicitly choose to go to the declaration of the definition using the Go to Definition and Go to Declaration commands found in the Design⇨Class Model or Control-/right-click contextual menu.

Like the class browser, the class model browser and diagram are connected to the API documentation index. If a class or method appears in the API documentation, a small "book" icon appears next to its name in the browser. Click the icon to jump to its documentation. Alternatively, select a class or member in the class diagram and choose the Design⇨Class Model⇨Go to Documentation command.

Editing a Class Model

"Editing" a class diagram is limited to customizing its appearance. As mentioned at the beginning of this chapter, you can't alter the definition of a class in a class model. Class modeling is strictly a visualization tool. Any changes you make will be (mostly) cosmetic. That said, you can alter the layout and appearance of the class diagram significantly, which can profoundly influence its effectiveness as a programming aid.

Moving Nodes

The main point of class diagrams is to visually represent the relationship between classes. Creating a pleasing and readable distribution of class nodes is, therefore, paramount to creating a useful class model. Xcode provides a variety of tools and techniques by which you can reshape a class diagram. The inheritance lines between class nodes are permanent fixtures and will follow the nodes as you reposition them. In fact, organizing the diagram such that all of the inheritance lines are visible and unambiguous will be your biggest challenge.

You can move nodes individually, or in groups, by selecting and dragging them to a new position. You can also use the arrow keys on the keyboard to move selected nodes.

There are also a variety of alignment commands in the Design⇨Alignment⇨Align menu. Most of these are self-explanatory, and apply to the currently selected nodes. You must have at least two nodes selected for the alignment commands to work. These same commands are located in the Alignment submenu of the Control-right-click contextual menu in the diagram.

Automatic Layout

Xcode provides two algorithms for automatically rearranging class nodes: hierarchical and force-directed. Select the set of nodes you want laid out, and choose the appropriate command from the Design⇨ Automatic Layout menu. If no nodes are selected, the entire diagram is reorganized. Hierarchical layout, shown in Figure 11-12, produces graphs where sister nodes (two nodes that inherit from a common node) are distributed horizontally. For large collections of classes that all descend from the same class (NSObject, for instance), this can create very wide diagrams.

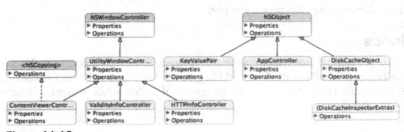

Figure 11-12

241

Force-directed layout tends to put progenitor classes in the middle of the diagram, with decedents radiating outward. Imagine that all of the nodes are negatively charged particles that are universally repelled by all other nodes. Imagine that the lines connecting the nodes are elastic bands. Now, pick up the root nodes of the model and let the remaining nodes hang like a mobile. This is, approximately, the effect of force-directed layout. The diagram in Figure 11-13 is the same diagram shown in Figure 11-12, reorganized using force-directed layout.

Figure 11-13

Hierarchical layout is the most predictable and produces extremely easy-to-see relationships, but it can produce unwieldy results for large collections of classes. Force-directed layout produces compact graphs but often not intuitive ones. The release notes for Xcode also warn that the algorithm used to generate force-directed layouts is "unbounded," meaning that it can take an indeterminate amount of CPU time to compute the layout of a large and complex diagram.

Xcode uses hierarchical automatic layout when a model is first created, and whenever the tracking for the model is changed. Automatic layout uses the current size of each node, and tries to create layouts such that nodes do not overlap. Locked nodes can interfere with this goal.

Resizing Nodes

You can resize nodes using the resize "handles" that appear on the edges of the node when it is selected. Choose the Design⇨Diagram⇨Size⇨Size to Fit command to resize selected nodes such that their height and width are exactly enough to show their entire names and all exposed members. The height of a node does this automatically whenever the compartments are rolled up, rolled down, expanded, or collapsed. The width, however, is never automatically adjusted. If you want to the width to be sufficient to show all members, have those compartments expanded before using the Size to Fit command.

You can also set the height or width of multiple nodes so that they are all identical. Begin by selecting a prototype node. Select additional nodes by holding down the Shift key. The Size⇨Make Same Width and Size⇨Make Same Height commands set the width or the height of all selected nodes so that they are identical to the dimension of the prototype node.

Locking Nodes

Locking a node prevents it from being moved or resized. To lock or unlock a node, or nodes, use the Lock and Unlock commands in the Design⇨Diagram or Control-/right-click contextual menu. Locking is very useful for preserving the layout of a subgroup of nodes, while you add, remove, or rearrange other nodes around them.

Grid and Grid Alignment

As an aid to positioning and sizing nodes, Xcode provides an optional grid. The grid is drawn in light grey behind the diagram, as shown in Figure 11-14.

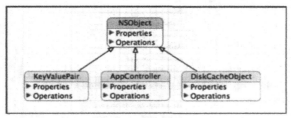

Figure 11-14

When you're dragging nodes around, their position will normally "snap" to the nearest grid line. To disable this behavior, choose the Turn Grid Off command from either the Design⇨Diagram menu or the Control-/right-click contextual menu. Choose the Turn Grid On command to restore it.

Use the Hide/Show Grid command to hide and reveal the grid. Grid snap is independent of the visibility of the diagram grid.

Page Layout

A class diagram occupies a series of pages. Like a WYSIWYG word processor or spreadsheet, Xcode extends the graph area in page increments to accommodate the size of the diagram. Drag a node off the edge of the page, and a new page appears. A solid gray line indicates the boundary between pages. If you plan to print a diagram, you can use the page guides to ensure that nodes don't straddle two or more pages. If they are unimportant, the page guides can be hidden use the Hide Page Breaks command in the Design⇨Diagram menu.

The size of a page is controlled using the File⇨Page Setup command. By default, Xcode sets the page magnification to 80% and the orientation to landscape. Smaller magnification values shrink the size of the node, allowing you to fit more nodes on a page. Consider passing out reading glasses if you reduce the page magnification below 50%.

Changing the Tracking

You can add or remove classes to and from a class model at any time. Click the diagram background, so that no nodes are selected, and then choose the File⇨Get Info command. This opens the Info window for the class model. Switch to the Tracking tab. In it, you will find the list of source files and groups the class model is tracking. To remove files or groups, select them in the list and click the - button at the bottom of the window.

To add new sources, click the + button. This presents the sheet shown in Figure 11-15. Select the additional sources you want added to the model and click the Add Tracking button.

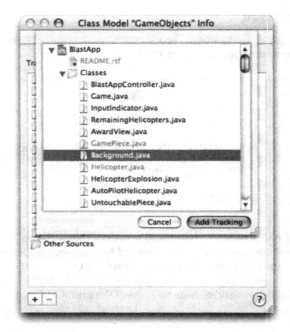

Figure 11-15

In its current incarnation, Xcode occasionally exhibits problems constructing class models. The symptom is missing inheritance between classes. If this happens, try removing the subclass and adding it back to the model following the classes and other nodes it inherits from. If that doesn't work, create a new, empty, model. Add classes in batches, starting with the superclasses, in such a way that you never add a class unless all of the superclasses and interfaces or protocols from which it inherits are already in the model. An easy way of accomplishing this is to keep the Class Browser window visible behind the diagram's Info window. That way, you can easily refer to the hierarchical arrangement of classes as you add them to the model.

Adding Annotations

Beyond altering its appearance, the only real content that can be added to a class diagram is an annotation node. Create annotation nodes by dragging out a rectangle using the Note tool, or by choosing the Design⇨Class Model⇨Add Comment command. An annotation node has a page-like, or PostIt-like, appearance (see Figure 11-16).

The content of the node is free-formed text. Double-click the node to enter text edit mode. All of the typographical formatting features in the Format⇨Font and Format⇨Text submenus can be used, which gives you an immense amount of formatting control. Even the text rulers and tab stops work, although they may seem a little silly in an area only 1 inch wide.

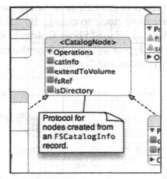

Figure 11-16

Annotation nodes can be connected to any number of other regular nodes, but not another annotation node. To connect an annotation node to a class node, use the Line tool to drag out a line between the two nodes. To remove a connection or an annotation node, select the line or node and press the Delete key or choose Edit⇨Delete.

Customizing Colors and Fonts

You can customize the text color, font, size, and style of nodes in the Appearance tab of the Info window. Choose File⇨Get Info with one or more nodes selected to alter the appearance of those nodes. With no node selected, the Info window allows you to set the default settings for new nodes. The default settings only apply to new nodes created by adding additional classes to the model.

Figure 11-17 shows the Appearance tab. The three categories — Name, Property, and Operation — address the three compartments of each node. Changing the color changes the color of the text. Changing the font, by clicking the Set button to the right of each sample, allows you to change the font face, style, and size of the text of each compartment.

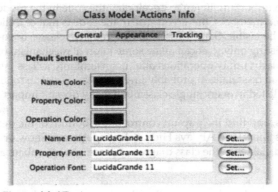

Figure 11-17

You can edit the background color used in the title to indicate the type of node, in a roundabout way. Drop a color from any color source onto a node to change its background color. Probably the easiest way to get a color source is to choose Format⇨Font⇨Show Colors to display the color picker. Dial a color, and then drag the color sample at the top of the picker into the node. Figure 11-18 shows a node with default (left) and customized (right) colors and fonts.

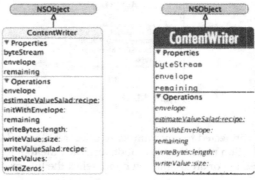

Figure 11-18

Hiding Classes and Members

One of the primary uses of a class diagram is to maintain a high-level vision of class relationships — but sometimes there can be so many classes, or class members, that its essence is obscured by the details. You can regain some perspective by selectively hiding superfluous classes and members. This can be done on a per-class basis or automated by using rules.

There are many reasons why you'd want to hide a class or certain members. Models are constructed by selecting files. Source files can define multiple classes, and the superclass of every class is always included in the model. Hiding classes lets you pair down the diagram to *exactly* the classes you want to see.

Your perspective is also important. If you're developing the code in the model, then you'll want to see all of the private and protected members. But if your use of the code is that of a client, then private and protected variables don't need to be visible. Some classes, like nested Java classes or so-called "helper" classes, are utilitarian in nature: existing only to encapsulate some internal mechanism or to avoid exposing private instance variables. Similarly, utility operations offer no insight into a class' reason for existing. Any Objective-C class that can be serialized probably implements initWithCoder: and encodeWithCoder:. Having these methods listed in every single class node really doesn't impart any useful information.

Select a class, or classes, and find the pop-up control at the bottom of the details pane. It has three settings: Hide per Filter, Always Show, and Always Hide. Selecting Always Show or Always Hide will fix the visibility of the selected classes in the class diagram. Classes and members are always visible in the class model browser.

Selecting Hide per Filter option shows, or hides, the class based on the model's Classes filter. When this option is selected, a line of text below the control indicates the visibility of the class based on the filter. Note that although you can manually override the visibility of individual classes, the only way to hide properties or operations is by using a filter.

There is also a Hidden column available in the class list of the browser. Control-/right-click the column titles to reveal the column; then click the check boxes to selectively hide, show, or filter each class.

You can set class, property, and operation filters in the General tab of the diagram's Info window. Make sure no nodes are selected, and then choose File➪Get Info to open the Info window. At the bottom of the Info window are three filter settings, shown in Figure 11-19.

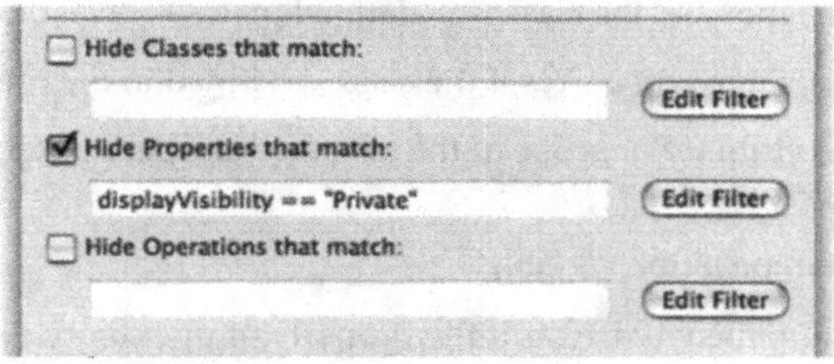

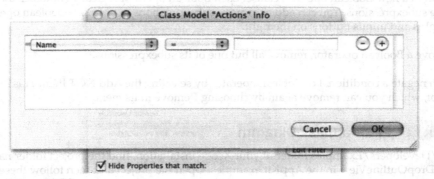

Figure 11-19

To enable a filter, check the box next to the desired filter. If disabled, the filter will not hide any classes, properties, or operations in the diagram. To edit the terms of the filter, click the Edit Filter button. Xcode presents the dialog box shown in Figure 11-20.

Figure 11-20

This is the predicate editor. It allows you to graphically create arbitrarily complex conditional statements. The predicate editor is described in more detail in Chapter 12, but here's the short version.

An expression is built from basic conditionals. A condition consists of three parts: variable, operator, and value. The variables are properties of each node or member in the class model, and the set of variables is fixed. For properties and operations, the variables are Name, Visibility, Type, and Static. For classes, the variables are Name, Kind, Superclass, Language, and Project Member. These variables are described in the following table.

Variable	Description
Name	The class or member's name.
Kind	The type of the class node in the diagram: Class, Protocol, Interface, or Category.
Superclass	The name of the class that the class or category extends.
Language	The language the class was defined in: C++, Java, or Objective-C
Project Member	This value will be Yes if the class is defined in the project.
Visibility	The visibility or scope of the property or operation: Public, Package, Protected, or Private.
Type	The type of the variable.
Static	This value will be Yes if the property or operation is a static or class member.

To configure a conditional, select the variable from the left side and an operation from the middle, and then enter a value or a select a constant on the right side.

You can insert a new Boolean operator into the expression by choosing the Add AND or Add OR item in either a variable or Boolean operator menu. Adding a Boolean operator makes the entire subexpression one term in a new Boolean operator clause. Each Boolean operator logically combines the results of two or more subexpressions. You can add or remove subexpressions to or from a Boolean operator using the round plus and minus buttons on the right.

To remove a Boolean operator, remove all but one of its subexpressions.

You can negate a conditional or Boolean operator by selecting the Add NOT item. This inserts a negation operator, which you can remove again by choosing Remove in its menu.

Try It Out   Filter a Class Diagram

In the /Developers/Examples folder of your Xcode installation, find the project folder named DragNDropOutlineView in the AppKit examples. Open the project and then follow these steps:

1. Select the Classes source group and choose Design➪Class Model➪Quick Model.

2. Choose Design➪Expand All to expand all of the compartments. Now choose Edit➪Select All, and then choose Design➪Diagram➪Size➪Size to Fit. Finally, choose Design➪Automatic Layout➪Hierarchical Layout.

3. Open the Info window for the diagram. Under the General tab, set class filter shown in Figure 11-21, the properties filter shown in Figure 11-22, and the operations filter shown in Figure 11-23.

4. Close the Info window and choose Design➪Automatic Layout➪Hierarchical Layout again.

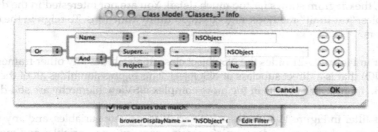

Figure 11-21

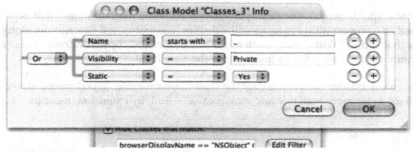

Figure 11-22

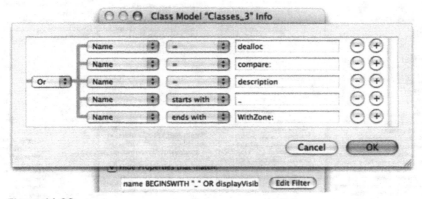

Figure 11-23

How It Works

The DragNDropOutlineView project contains only a few classes, but most extend from complex framework classes that contain numerous "off-limits" variables and methods. This Try It Out concentrated on just the essential classes, and only those member variables and methods applicable to your programming.

In steps 1 and 2, you quickly created a class model for all of the classes defined in the project. The model was expanded to show all of the details, and then reorganized. The resulting diagram is large and cumbersome. Even the largest monitor available today can't display the entire diagram at 100% magnification.

What's worse, the diagram shows far too much detail. You are not interested in the details of NSObject, private variables, "off-limit" methods, and common utility functions. To reign in the diagram, you created three filters.

The class filter in Figure 11-21 hides the NSObject class. It also hides any other framework class (Project Member == NO) that is a direct subclass of NSObject. This expression hides all of the "simple" objects in the framework. Framework objects in the more complex NSView hierarchy are still displayed.

The properties filter in Figure 11-22 hides static variables, private variables, and any variable that begins with the underscore character. Under Apple's naming conventions, variables and methods that begin with an underscore are "off-limits" and should not be used by application developers. It makes sense, then, that you don't want to see them in your class diagram.

The operations filter is similar. The filter you created will hide method names that begin with an underscore, as well as common utility messages like dealloc, compare:, and description, along with the family of methods that end in "WithZone:," such as initWithZone: and copyWithZone:. These are extremely common methods that rarely tell us much about the class itself.

After all that work is done, you can layout the class diagram again. The slimmed-down diagram, shown in Figure 11-24, is far more readable and manageable — and, by extension, more useful.

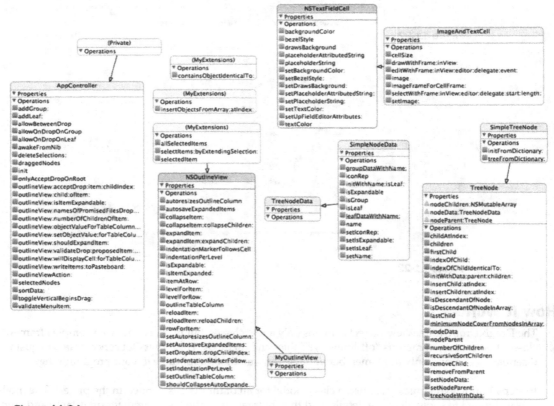

Figure 11-24

Summary

Class modeling is a powerful analysis tool. You can use it to quickly understand the structure of someone else's code, or classes that you haven't visited in awhile. Because class models instantly reflect changes in your code, class modeling is a great tool for watching as your own code develops and is a powerful aide when comes time to reorganizing a set of classes. Code model annotations are a convenient way of highlighting key concepts, and communicating them to other developers. Class and member filtering lets you tailor how much detail is revealed, keeping the focus on the important aspects of the class model.

In this chapter, you've seen how powerful visual modeling can be. In the previous chapter, you saw how easy and efficient visual editing of run time objects can be. The next chapter combines these two technologies, allowing you to visually design runtime data objects.

Data Modeling

Data modeling is a visual tool for defining data objects and their relationships, called a data schema. A schema defines entities that contain properties. Properties can be values or relationships to other entities. The data modeling tools in Xcode let you create and edit a data model. The data model then becomes a resource that can be loaded and used by your application at runtime.

> The user interface for data modeling is almost identical to the interface used for class modeling. The interfaces are so similar that discussion of the common features has been omitted from this chapter. If you haven't read the previous chapter, I strongly urge you to at least browse through the "Class Model Browser," "Class Model Diagram," and "Editing a Class Model" sections. For the most part, simply substitute the words "entity" for "class" and "property" for "member."

To use data modeling effectively, you need to have a basic understanding of Core Data. If you are not familiar with Core Data, a good place to start is the *Core Data Programming Guide*, which you can find in the Reference Library under Cocoa, Design Guidelines. Or you can browse it online at the http://developer.apple.com/documentation/Cocoa/Conceptual/CoreData/ web site.

Technology

Data modeling is the child of two parents: class modeling and Interface Builder.

The user interface for data modeling is essentially the same as the one used for class modeling, with one very important difference. In data modeling, you actually create and edit the objects in the data model. It is a true editor, not just a fancy visualization tool.

From a conceptual standpoint, data modeling is most like Interface Builder: you graphically define object definitions and relationships. These definitions are archived into a data file. That data file is included in the application's bundle. At runtime, the data is read and objects are created. In Interface Builder, the objects are Cocoa or Carbon objects that get written to a NIB file. In data modeling, the objects are all NSManagedObjects and the file is a MOM (Managed Object Model) file, produced by the Data Model Compiler.

Entities (the containers you define in a data model) are like a class definition: They define the form from which any number of instances are created. But unlike Interface Builder, you don't define the instances in the class model. The number of instances of the Employee entity that get created is entirely a function of how many employee records are read or created at runtime. A human resources application that tracks employees might create 50,000 Employee objects for a large company or none at all when used by a sole proprietor.

Every instance of an entity becomes an instance of an NSManagedObject at runtime. You can define your own class to be used instead, but it must be a subclass of NSManagedObject. The "Creating NSManagedObject Subclasses" section towards the end of this chapter introduces some tools for helping you subclass NSManagedObject.

Terminology

One of the things that can be immediately confusing about data modeling is the terminology. The interface and concepts are so much like classes and objects that it's hard to see why the same vocabulary isn't used. Nevertheless, they are different in very significant ways and the different monikers reinforce that. Furthermore, modern data models are the confluence of object-oriented programming and database design — two disciplines that, until only recently, have remained separate. Each brings its own vocabulary and terminology into the mix. The following table defines common terms used in Core Data and data modeling.

Term	Definition
Entity	An entity defines a container of properties. An entity can also contain other auxiliary data such as user-defined values and predefined fetch requests. Defining an entity is similar to defining a class or a table in a database. At runtime, instances of an entity are embodied by instances of NSManagedObject.
Property	The generic term for a member of an entity. The properties of an entity can be attributes, relationships, or predefined queries.
Attribute	A value in an entity. In a class, this would be an instance variable. In a database, this would be a field. Values store primitive, atomic, values such as strings and integers.
Relationship	A connection between an entity and other entities. Relationships can be one-to-one or one-to-many. A Person entity might have two relationships, mother and father, both of which would be one-to-one relationships. The same entity might have a cousin relationship. This would be a one-to-many relationship that connects that entity to all of its cousins — which might be dozens or none at all. Relationships can be defined in the actual storage using any number of techniques, but typical database tools would use foreign keys or junction tables.
Inverse Relationship	If entity A has a relationship to entity B, and entity B has a reflexive relationship back to entity A, these two relationships are considered to be the inverse of each other. The data modeler can recognize inverse relationships, and uses that to simplify the data model diagram and to highlight bidirectional connections.

Term	Definition
Fetched Property	A fetched property is like a relationship in that it connects an entity to some other set of entities. Unlike a regular relationship, fetched properties are based on a fetch request. A Person entity might have a relationship called "siblings." It might then define a fetched property named "sisters", which would be defined as all of the siblings where sex == "female".
Fetch Request	A fetch request is a predefined query, usually created with the predicate builder. A fetch request defines some criteria, such as person.age < 21, that can be used to filter entities.

Creating a Data Model

If you started your Xcode project using one of the Core Data application templates, then your project already has a data model source file. You can create a new data model and add it to your project using the File⇨New command. Choose the Data Model template, give the document a name, and decide what targets the model should be included in. Clicking Next presents a dialog box like the one shown in Figure 12-1.

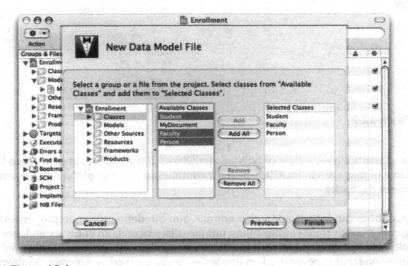

Figure 12-1

On the left are the project's source files and groups. Select a set of sources and Xcode scans those source files for class definitions. The classes it finds are listed in the center column. Click the Add All button to add them all to the data model, or select specific classes and use the Add button to add them selectively. Repeat this process until you've added all of the classes you want included in the model. If you add too many classes, select them in the right column and click the Remove button to forget them.

Click the Finish button to create the model and add it to the project. For every class added to the Selected Classes list, Xcode creates an entity with that class name and implementation. As mentioned earlier, entities based on classes other than NSManagedObject must be a subclass of NSManagedObject. The interface that lets you choose classes does not check or enforce this. It is entirely up to you to ensure that the classes chosen are valid managed data object classes.

All of the entities created from class definitions are empty. NSManagedObjects do not (normally) store attribute values and relationships in named instance variables or use accessor methods to access them. Consequently, there's no standard method for Xcode to determine what properties an entity should have, even if it has the custom class definition. In general, you should define your data object first, and then customize the class definition. See the "Creating NSManagedObject Subclasses" section for more details.

Creating Entities

The first thing to do is create entities, if you haven't already. Underneath the Entity list are a plus (+), minus (-), and disclosure button. Click on the plus button to create a new entity. Alternatively, choose Design⇨Data Model⇨Add Entity (Command+Control+E). A new entity is created and given a generic name. Edit the name in the details pane (see Figure 12-2). You can also double-click an entity name in the browser list, or double-click the title of an entity node in the diagram, and edit its name.

Figure 12-2

Newly created entities have a class of NSManagedObject. If the entity is implemented by a custom class, enter the name of that class in the Class field. At runtime, an instance of that class is created to represent each instance of the entity.

Like classes, entities can inherit from other entities. You can define common properties of several entities in a "super-entity," with child entities filling out the differences. If an entity extends the definition of another entity, select its parent entity in the Parent menu. A parent entity that exists only as a base for child entities — one that is never used on its own — can be marked as Abstract. Abstract entities are never created at runtime.

Properties of entities are not required to be stored as instance variables or implemented as methods. NSManagedObject can retain any property using key-value storage. Consequently, you have quite a bit of flexibility when it comes to mixing and matching classes and entities. For instance, you might have two entities, Customer and Vendor, that both extend the same base entity, Account. You might think that if custom classes were assigned to these two entities, they would have to be subclasses of the same class as well. But this is not the case. The class that implements the Customer entity can be completely unrelated to the class that implements Vender. This sort of situation might be unusual, but is completely valid.

To delete one or more entities, select them and click the - button, press the Delete key, or chose Edit⇨Delete.

Creating Properties

Entities aren't too interesting until they contain something. To add properties to an entity, begin by selecting the entity in the browser or diagram. The list of existing properties appears in the middle column of the browser. Click the + button below the Properties list and choose the Add Attribute, Add Relationship, or Add Fetched Property command. If you don't see this menu, choose Show All Properties from the disclosure menu to the right of the - button. Alternatively, you can choose the Add Attribute (Command+Control+A), Add Relationship (Command+Control+R), or Add Fetched Property command from the Design⇨Data Model menu.

> Interestingly, you can select multiple classes and add a new property to every one using any of the Add property commands. For example, selecting three classes and choosing Add Attribute adds a new attribute to all three classes. There probably aren't many instances where this would be particularly useful, but if you ever need it, it's available.

Adding any property creates the kind of property you chose and gives it a generic name. You can edit the name of the property in the Name field of the details pane. You can also double-click any property name and rename it in the browser list or in the diagram. All property names must begin with a lower-case letter.

Attributes

Attribute properties contain values. The types of data which Core Data supports are listed in the Type menu. Select the data type for the attribute from the list. Depending on which type you select, additional validation fields appear as shown in Figure 12-3. The validation settings are used to determine if the value stored, or attempting to be stored, in this attribute is usable.

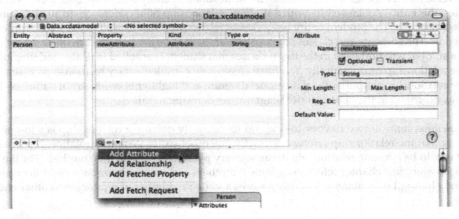

Figure 12-3

The scalar numeric types (Integer, Decimal, Float, and Date) define minimum and maximum values. String attributes can have minimum and maximum lengths. Alternatively, string attributes can be matched against a regular expression. If the regular express matches the string, the string is valid. Other types, like Boolean and Binary Data, have no constraints.

Attributes can be Optional. If this is checked, the attribute is allowed to be completely absent (nil) when stored. If not optional, a missing value will fail when validated. This is not to be confused with the value being merely zero or a zero-length string. Attributes that are *not* optional must be set, or have a default value, before they can be stored.

The Default Value is the value given to an attribute when a new instance of the entity is created. If left blank, the initial value will be absent (nil).

The Transient option is used for attributes that are not stored. As long as the instance of the entity exists in memory, the attribute will hold its value. But when the entity is stored for later retrieval, transient properties are not included. One reason for using transient attributes is to model data types that Core Data doesn't understand. A transient attribute can use the Undefined data type, allowing you to use any kind of value your application needs. In order to store the value, you also include one or more persistent attributes in the entity that the undefined type can be translated into. The persistent attributes retain the value, which can be converted back into the special type in the future. For example, you might define an application-specific class that represents a direction and speed (course, azimuth, and speed). Core Data does not know how to store your object, but your object can be easily converted into three Double attributes that Core Data can store. You can read more about non-standard attributes at `http://developer.apple.com/documentation` `/Cocoa/Conceptual/CoreData/Articles/cdNSAttributes.html`.

Relationships

Relationships relate an instance of an entity to some number of other entities. The Destination of a relationship is the kind of entity, or entities, the relationship returns. By definition, all entities stored by a relationship must be the same. The destination can be any other entity in the model, even itself. Self-referential references are common. For instance, a Person entity might have children and parent relationships, all of which are other Person entities.

The Inverse menu chooses the relationship in the destination entity that refers back to, or reflexively includes, this entity. A Class entity with a students relationship holds references to all of the Student entities enrolled in a class. The Student entity has a classes relationship that lists all of the Class entities a student is enrolled in. The students and classes relationships are said to be inverses of each other. Any class that references a student will find itself in the list of classes that student is enrolled in. Data modeling does not create inverse relationships automatically. You must create both complementary relationships yourself. Setting the inverse relationship simplifies the data model diagram and highlights symmetrical nature of the relationships, as described in the "Data Model Diagram" section later in this chapter.

Relationships come in two flavors: to-one and to-many. By default, a relationship is a to-one relationship, meaning that the relationship references exactly one other entity. A mother relationship in a Person entity would be a to-one relationship because every person has exactly one mother. (For the purposes of this discussion, this chapter refers to biological mothers and ignores boundary conditions such as adoption and cloning.) A to-many relationship stores a variable number of references to other entities. Define a to-many relationship by checking the To-Many Relationship option in the details pane, as shown in Figure 12-4. A children relationship in a Person entity would be a to-many relationship. A person could have none, one, or many children.

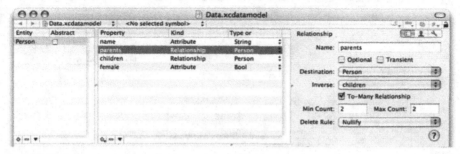

Figure 12-4

To-many relationships can be bounded, enforcing that the number of entities referenced does not fall outside a set range. Use the Min Count and Max Count fields to set these. An example would be a livingParents relationship, which would have a minimum count of 0 and a maximum count of 2.

Like attributes, relationships can be Optional. This means that the relationship may be empty when the entity is validated. On a to-one relationship, it means that that the relationship might be nil — logically equivalent to a to-many relationship with a minimum count of 0 and a maximum count of 1.

Relationships also have a Delete Rule. The Delete Rule determines what happens when an entity is removed from a relationship — or even if it is allowed to be removed. The meanings of the different settings are explained in the *Core Data Programming Guide*.

Try It Out   Create Entities

Create a new project based on the Core Data Document-based application template. Open the MyDocument.xcdatamodel file and then follow these steps:

1. Create a PhoneNumber entity. Create a Person entity.

2. In the PhoneNumber entity, add an attribute named `number` that stores a telephone number as a string. Add a to-one relationship named `owner` to a Person entity.

3. In the Person entity, create a string attribute named `name` and a date attribute named `birthday`. Create a to-many relationship named `phoneNumbers` to a PhoneNumber entity. Choose the owner relationship as the inverse of the phoneNumber relationship.

How It Works

You just created a data model that defines a Person entity with a name and birthday that can have any number of phone numbers. The phone number entity has an inverse relationship such that given a particular phone number, you can find out who its owner is. All of these properties and relationships are illustrated in the data model diagram, shown in Figure 12-5.

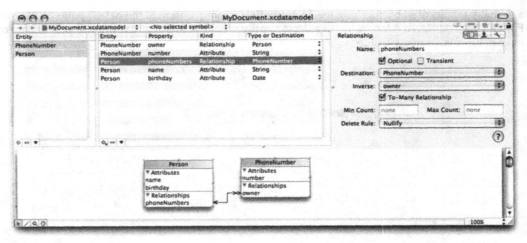

Figure 12-5

Adding Fetched Properties

Fetched properties are like relationships in that they define a set of related entities. Unlike relationships, they don't store actual references to other entities. Instead, they define a predicate (such as a rule or criteria) that determines what entities are included. Like relationships, you must select a destination entity. To define the predicate to use, click the Edit Predicate button. The predicate builder uses the context of the destination entity, so don't forget to select the destination before editing the predicate. The textual version of the predicate you define is displayed in the Predicate field but is not directly editable there (see Figure 12-6).

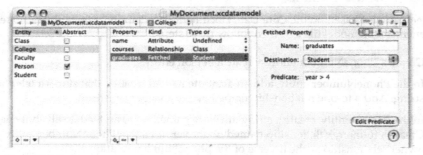

Figure 12-6

Adding Fetch Requests

Fetch Requests are simply predefined predicates. Your application can use them in a variety of ways. When you add a Fetch Request, the property list display changes from displaying regular properties to listing only fetch requests. To switch between two, select the desired view using the disclosure triangle at the bottom of the properties list. See the "Data Model Browser" section for more details.

260

Data Modeling Interface

The interface used by data modeling is so similar to the interface used for class modeling that it would be a waste to reiterate it all here. Instead, this section just points out the differences between class modeling and data modeling. Before reading this section, you should familiarize yourself with the class modeling interface if you have not already done so. Class modeling is described in detail in the previous chapter.

Data Model Browser

The data model browser displays the entities on the left, the entity properties and fetch requests in the middle, and the details pane on the right (see Figure 12-7).

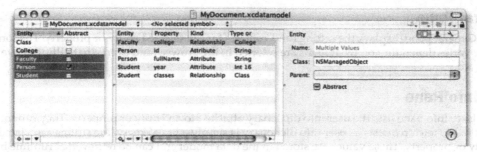

Figure 12-7

Selecting an entity in the Entity list displays the properties or fetch requests in the center list. Selecting multiple entities displays a combined list of all properties of the selected entities.

The use of the + and - buttons has already been described in the "Creating Properties" section.

The disclosure triangles below each list control how each list is displayed. Similar to the class browser, the Property list has the choices of Show All Properties, Show Attributes, Show Relationships, and Show Fetched Properties. These four choices let you display all standard property types, or limit the display to a single type. The fifth choice, Show Fetch Requests, shows only fetch requests. The formats of the fetch request and property lists are different and are mutually exclusive. The browser can't display both properties and fetch requests at the same time.

Detail Pane Views

The details pane shows the settings for the selected entity or property. If you have multiple entities or properties selected at once, the detail pane displays the settings common to all of those items, if any. Changing a setting that applies to all of the selected items alters all of those items at once.

The details pane has three displays, which you select using the small tabs in the upper-right corner of the pane. Figure 12-8 shows the three different panes, from left to right: General, User Info, and Configurations.

Figure 12-8

General Pane

The General pane displays the settings and controls for the selected entity or property. The format of this pane varies depending on what items are selected in the browser and even what settings have been selected.

User Info Pane

The User Info pane lists the user info dictionary attached to an entity or property. They cannot be attached to fetch requests. A user info dictionary is simply a list of key-value strings associated with the entity or property. These values are stored in the data model and can be retrieved at runtime by your application for whatever purpose you need.

Configurations Pane

The Configurations pane applies only to entities. Configurations are named collections of entities. Using configurations, a data model can contain many different combinations of entities. Your application can then selectively load a data model that contains only the set of entities that it needs. For example, an application for professional photographers might have entities for Image, Thumbnail, Keyword, ModelRelease, CopyrightOwner, and PriceSchedule. That same application, running in "amateur" mode, might only want a data model that includes Image, Thumbnail, and Keyword. This can be accomplished in a single data model by creating two configurations, "Pro" and "Consumer," and including all of the entities in the "Pro" configuration, but omitting ModelRelease, CopyrightOwner, and PriceSchedule from the "Consumer" configuration.

Create new configurations by clicking the + button at the bottom of the pane. Select one or more entities and put a check mark next to the configurations they belong in. To delete a configuration, select it and click the - button or press the Delete key.

Data Model Diagram

Nodes in a data model represent entities. The compartments of entity nodes are Attributes, Relationships, and Fetched Properties (see Figure 12-9). The Fetched Properties compartment only appears if fetched properties have been defined for the entity. Fetch requests are not visible in the data model diagram.

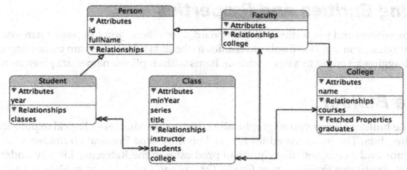

Figure 12-9

Lines between entities describe relationships and inheritance. The shapes of the arrowheads indicate the kind of relationship, as listed in the following table.

Line	Relationship
Single arrowhead	To-one relationship. The arrow points to the destination entity.
Double arrowhead	To-many relationship. The arrow points to the destination entity.
Hollow arrowhead	Inheritance. The arrow points to the parent entity.

If two relationships have been flagged as being inverse relationships, the data model diagram represents both relationships as a single line with two arrowheads. This greatly improves the readability of the diagram.

For relationships, the line begins at the name of the relationship and points abstractly at the relationships compartment of the destination entity. For inverse relationships, Xcode draws the line precisely from one complementary relationship to the other. Entities that inherit from other entities point abstractly from their center to the center of the parent entity.

Selecting a node, attribute, or relationship in the diagram selects the same in the browser. Selecting a relationship line in the diagram selects the relationship in the browser. If the line represents two inverse relationships, both relationships are selected along with the entities that contain them.

Like class modeling, you can customize the appearance of nodes. You cannot, however, filter the entities or properties that are displayed.

Tools

The Arrow, Magnifying Glass, and Hand tools work exactly as they do in the class modeling. There is no Notes tool in data modeling.

Use the Line tool to create relationships between entities. Select the Line tool and drag from one entity to another. A new relationship will be created in the entity where the drag began. To create a relationship between an entity and itself, click the entity. Follow the steps in the earlier "Relationships" section for editing its details.

Duplicating Entities and Properties

You can copy entities and properties to the clipboard. From there, you can paste them into the same or different data models. You can also duplicate entities in the data model diagram by holding down the Option key while dragging an entity to a new location. Items with duplicate names are given numeric suffixes.

Predicate Builder

The predicate builder allows you to graphically construct predicates — logical expressions used to find, select, or filter data. The predicate editor is based on the Cocoa Predicate framework. You can find both an introduction and a complete description of predicates in the Reference Library under Cocoa, Data Management, Predicates Programming Guide. Or you can find it online at `http://developer`
`.apple.com/documentation/Cocoa/Conceptual/Predicates/`.

You can invoke the predicate builder, shown in Figure 12-10, from a variety of places. It is even used in class modeling to determine what classes and members are displayed. The predicate builder is context-sensitive. That is, the pre-assembled set of values used to construct the expression will be garnered from the entity or its destination, as appropriate. Using the predicate builder will be easier if you have defined the entire context surrounding the predicate before you begin editing it. Specifically, you should define the types of attributes and any relationships between entities before trying to edit a predicate.

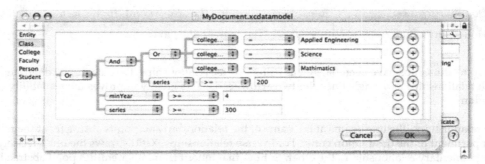

Figure 12-10

Simple expressions are constructed from keys (which specify the variable or attribute), operators, and values. You can combine simple expressions using logical operators. The textual form of the expression in Figure 12-10 is `((college.name == "Applied Engineering" OR college.name == "Science" OR college.name == "Mathimatics") AND series >= 200) OR minYear >= 4 OR series >= 300`.

Simple Expressions

The key menu selects the attribute you want to compare. The keys listed will be the attributes of the entity that the predicate is being built for. To select something more complex than a simple attribute, choose the Select Key item from the menu. This presents a key browser, shown in Figure 12-11.

The browser shows the same attributes, but also includes the relationships defined for the entity. A key is like a directory path, in that it can specify an attribute of an entity related to an entity. For example, in the university data model, students are enrolled in a class. That class is taught by a faculty member, who belongs to a college. The expression's key can specify the name attribute of the college of the faculty member that teaches the class the student is enrolled in.

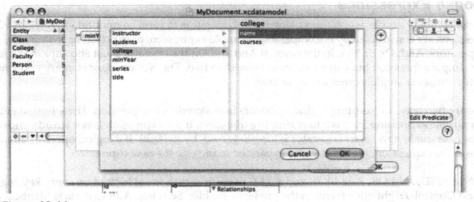

Figure 12-11

The type of the variable selected determines the operators and values that can be used in the expression. A Boolean variable presents only two operators (equals and does not equal) and two values (yes and no) to complete the expression. A string value presents numerous operators, all appropriate to matching string values. Select the desired operator from the operator menu.

The selected operator further refines the type of value that will be used in the comparison. Some operators, such as the "within" operator, have more than one value. Normally, the value is a constant. Type the value of the constant in the field. The text entered in the constant field must agree with the type of data on the other side of the operator. You cannot compare a Decimal attribute with the string "zero."

The value can also be another attribute (specified by a key) or a variable. Variables are values defined at runtime and exist in an environment space associated with the predicate. Variables appear as $VAR_NAME in a predicate expression. To change the constant field to a variable or key, Control-/right-click in the background of the expression and select Constant, Variable, or Key from the contextual menu, as shown in Figure 12-12. This is usually easiest to do by Control-/right-clicking just to the immediate right of the value field. Some choices may be disabled, depending on the data type of the key or the operator selected.

Figure 12-12

To compare the key with a variable, enter the name of the variable in the Variable field. Variable names cannot be verified in the data model, so make sure they are spelled correctly. You select a key value just as you would a key on the left side of the expression.

265

Compound Expressions

You can combine simple expressions using logical operators to form compound expressions. Compound expressions are constructed by encompassing a simple expression, or expressions, within one of the logical operators: And, Or, or Not. In the cases of And and Or, the operator must encompass at least one other simple expression but can encompass more than two. The Not operator is unary and simply negates whatever single expression it encloses.

There are two ways of inserting logical operators into a predicate expression. The + button at the right of every simple expression inserts a new simple expression. If the expression is not already enclosed in a logical operator, a new logical operator is inserted (And, by default). If a logical operator already encloses the expression, that operator is expanded to include the new expression.

The Add AND, Add OR, Add NOT, and Add Criteria commands are located on every key, logical operator, and Control-/right-click menu in the predicate builder. Selecting Add Criteria is identical to clicking a + button. The other three commands insert a new logical operator enclosing the expression. When you insert a new And or Or operator, a new simple expression is also created and inserted below the existing expression. Remember that And and Or operators must enclose at least two expressions. Add Criteria creates a logical operator only when it has to. The other three—Add AND, Add OR, and Add NOT—*always* insert a new logical operator. You can change a logical operator from And or Or and back again using its menu.

Drag expressions, even entire subexpression trees, to rearrange them in the tree. You can click and drag any portion of an expression's background, but it's often hard to miss the control areas of the pop-up menus. The most reliable drag point is the left end of the line that runs through the middle of the expression or at the root of an expression tree.

Figure 12-13 shows an Or expression being dragged to a different location in the expression tree. Dragging does not create new logical operators. However, if a logical operator contains only two expressions, dragging one of them to another subexpression deletes it—just as if you had deleted the expression.

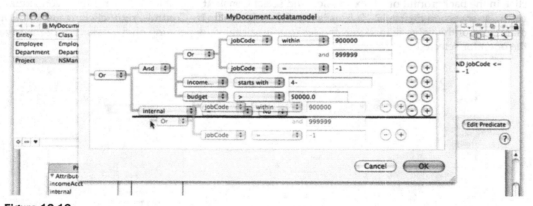

Figure 12-13

Use the - button to the right of the expression to delete it. You can delete expressions and Not operators by choosing the Remove command from any of the expression menus. You cannot delete the logical operators And and Or directly. To delete an And or Or operator, delete or remove all but one of the expressions the operator encompasses.

Build a Predicate

Start with the data model from the previous Try It Out exercise and follow these steps:

1. Select the PhoneNumber entity and add a new Fetch Request. Name the request **localCall**.

2. Click the Edit Predicate button to start the predicate builder.

3. Create a predicate expression that is true if the phone number contains only a 7-digit phone number in the pattern [0-9]{3}.*[0-9]{4}, or a 10-digit phone number matching the pattern [0-9]{3}.*[0-9]{3}.*[0-9]{4} and the first 3 digits are either 602, 480, or 623.

How It Works

Building predicates is easiest if you start from the leaf expressions and work up. You would probably start with an expression that was true if the number matched the pattern for a local call. You would then enclose that in an Or expression and add the next expression to test for long distance. That expression would then be wrapped in an And expression and the first of the three prefix tests, which would be expended into a three-way Or expression. Ultimately, you would arrive at something that looked like Figure 12-14.

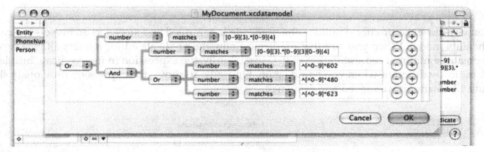

Figure 12-14

Alternatively, you might have been clever and combined the entire second half of the expression into a single regular expression resulting in something like number MATCHES "[0-9]{3}.*[0-9]{4}" OR number MATCHES "^[^0-9]*(602|480|623).*[0-9]{3}[0-9]{4}".

Textual Expressions

Every expression constructed by the predicate builder has a textual representation as well. It is this textual version of the expression that you see in the data model browser. You can also enter predicate expressions directly. You may elect to do this because entering the expression directly is often easier than building one graphically. This is especially true if you are pasting in an expression from the clipboard or if you just happen to be a good typist.

To enter an expression directly, select Expression from the key menu and then type the formula into the entry field, as shown in Figure 12-15. The expression must be a valid predicate expression. It must also be balanced — you cannot enter an unbalanced parenthetical expression. As long as the predicate builder is open, the expression will be displayed just as you entered it.

Be careful when pasting expressions that the predicate builder can't represent. It is possible to enter expressions, or later change the definition of an entity, resulting in an expression that cannot be edited. If you find yourself in this situation, copy the textual representation of the expression in the browser, delete the fetched property or request, and then create a new one by pasting the (modified) expression into the Expression field.

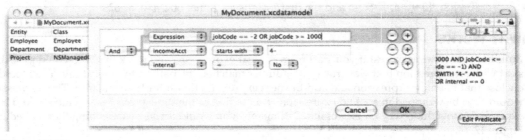

Figure 12-15

When you close the predicate builder, the predicate is compiled and stored as archived Predicate objects in the data model. When you edit that predicate again, the predicate editor reinterprets the expression and creates a minimal representation of it. Consequently, the expression in the predicate builder may look radically different when you edit it again. Figure 12-16 shows the expression previously shown in Figure 12-15 after it was saved and reopened.

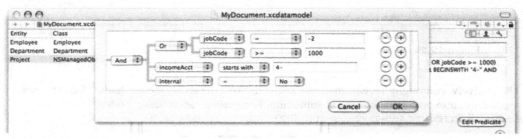

Figure 12-16

Creating an Instant Interface

Xcode can create an "instant interface" from a data model. This can be a huge time saver if you are just getting your application going. You often have some portion of a working data model, but no data and little or nothing that resembles an application. An instant interface produces a functional Cocoa interface that allows you to enter and edit data in your data model.

To create an instant interface, open a NIB file in Interface Builder that has a Cocoa window in it. Arrange the window so that it is visible on the screen alongside your data model window. Switch back to the data model window. Select the Pointer tool. While holding down the Option key, click and drag an entity from the data model diagram to the Interface Builder window. When you start the drag, a shadow of the entity with a + sign follows the cursor. If it does not, you are not dragging a copy of the entity. Drop the entity into the Interface Builder window. Xcode asks you if you want an interface that represents one or many entity objects. Entry fields are be created for each attribute. For a collection of entities, Fetch, Add, and Delete buttons are created along with a table listing all of the instances in the collection. Figure 12-17 shows the instant interface created for many Student entities.

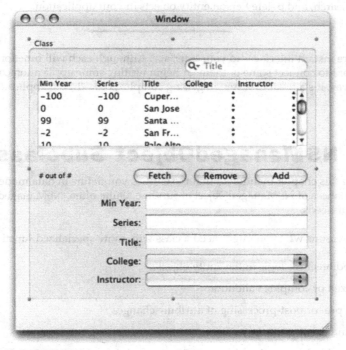

Figure 12-17

Amazingly, the entire interface is produced without any code. The interface is constructed using bindings and Interface Builder connections. If nothing else, it's a testament to the power of bindings. A little time spent exploring these bindings can be very educational.

Try It Out   Create an Instant Interface

Return again to the data model from the previous "Try It Out" exercise. Then follow these steps:

1. In the project window, open the MyDocument.nib file in Interface Builder. Delete any interface elements that might already be in the window.

2. Open the MyDocument.xcdatamodel file. Arrange that window so that does not obscure the NIB's document window in Interface Builder.

3. Hold down the Option key and drag the Person entity into the Interface Builder window. Choose Many Objects from the dialog box.

4. Switch back to the project window and choose the Build⇨Build and Run command.

5. When the application starts, click the Add button to create a new person. Edit their name and birthday. Repeat this step, adding as many people to the collection as you like.

How It Works

Dragging the Person entity into the Interface Builder window created an interface that permits you to create, list, edit, search, and delete Person entity objects in your application.

You can add more instant interfaces to your interface. Although each will function independently, you will probably want to connect some of them, or begin writing some application code to use the data entered. Either way, it's a great first step in getting complex, data-driven applications up and running quickly.

Creating NSManagedObject Subclasses

The beginning of this chapter mentioned that the entities you define in data modeling, and hence Core Data, exist as instances of NSManagedObject at runtime. Quite often, NSManagedObject is more than sufficient for your needs.

There are many reasons why you might need a class with more specialized functionality:

❑ Localized business logic in the entity object

❑ Specialized or complex validation

❑ Custom pre- or post-processing of attribute changes

❑ Non-standard attribute types

To create a custom implementation class for an entity, start by subclassing NSManagedObject. You cannot use just any arbitrary class; it must be a subclass of NSManagedObject. The easiest way to get started is to use the Managed Object Class file template. This template only appears when you have a data model open and (optionally) one or more entities selected prior to choosing the File⇨New command. Select the Managed Object Class template from the New File assistant and click the Next button.

Unlike every other new file template, the Managed Object Class does not ask for a file name. The file name is generated from the names of the entities. You do need to choose a location for the files and which targets the Objective-C source files should be included in. When you are done, click the Next button and Xcode presents the pane shown in Figure 12-18.

Check the entities that you want to create custom implementation classes for. By default, the entities that were selected in the model are already checked, but you are free to alter that here. The Generate Accessors option generates empty accessor methods for every property defined in the entity. Similarly, Generate Validation Methods define validation methods for every attribute defined. You can keep the ones you want and delete the ones you don't need to override. Core Data accesses the properties of NSManagedObject using a set of heuristics. If an object has an accessor defined for an attribute, that accessor is called to obtain or set the value. If not, the value is obtained using the default value method implemented in NSManagedObject. Only define accessor and instance variables for special cases, and omit any code for properties you want handled normally. See the Subclassing notes of the NSManagedObject documentation for more details.

Figure 12-18

After your custom implementation class is defined, edit the data model so that the new class name is specified in the Class field of the entity's details pane.

You don't have to use the Managed Object Class template. You are free to write your own subclass of NSManagedObject. It makes no difference to Xcode. Note that the accessor methods generated by Xcode include explicit calls to willAccessValueforKey:, didAccessValueForKey:, willChangeValueForKey:, and so on. This is because NSMangedObjects disable the normal automatic messaging for key-value access. You need to be mindful of this fact when implementing your own methods, which is another good reason to start with the methods generated by the template.

Exporting Class Methods

The Managed Object Class template is a great time saver, but it's a one-shot tool. You can't modify your entity and use the template again. Doing so will either overwrite or replace the previous class files — a dialog box warns you that Xcode is about to replace the class files and asks what you want to do with the old ones. You either have to replicate your previous customizations or copy and paste from the old implementation.

If you are simply adding new properties to an entity, there's an easier way. Xcode will produce the same accessor methods that the template creates, but copy them to the clipboard instead. It will do this for any selected property, or properties, in the data browser. Select one or more properties and choose either

Copy Method Implementation to Clipboard or Copy Method Declarations to Clipboard from the Design⇨Data Model menu. Switch to the implantation or header file for the class, as appropriate, and paste in the new methods.

Summary

Data modeling is a powerful tool. You can start incorporating the power of Core Data into your application in a matter of minutes, simply by creating an entity or two. Like class modeling, it is also a visualization tool, so you never lose sight of the "picture" of your data model throughout the course of your development. Instant interfaces make getting your application up and running quickly even easier.

Targets

Targets are the engines of Xcode. They define the steps that will transform your source code and resource files into a finished product. Targets can be very complex or ridiculously simple. Xcode comes with targets that automatically take care of the myriad of details needed to produce standard products such as application bundles. Or you can take complete control and choose a target that abdicates all of the responsibility for building a product to you.

The purpose of a target is to produce something. Most targets produce a product. There are different types of targets, depending on what kind of product is being produced. Each target references the source files and resources required to produce its product, along with the instructions on how those source files get processed, how the product is assembled, and the order in which all of those things have to happen.

Targets appear in the Targets smart group of the project window. Most project templates come with a target already defined, appropriately configured for that project type. If you stick to developing basic applications and tools you may never need to add a target to an existing project. Nevertheless, understanding what a target is and does is a prerequisite to customizing one and is fundamental to understanding the build process as a whole.

Target Components

Targets consist of several interrelated parts: build phases, build settings, build rules, dependencies, and a product, as listed in the following table. Different target types may include all, some, or only one of these parts. All of the parts are briefly described here, and each is described in detail later in the chapter.

Component	Description
Build phases	Defines the steps required to build a target. Each phase defines a procedure and the files involved.
Build settings	Variables available to the build phases that can be used to customize their behavior.

Component	Description	
Build rules	Rules that define how files of a particular type are compiled or transformed.	
Dependencies	The list of targets or projects that the target depends on.	
Product	The end result of the target.	

You edit most of these parts using various tabs in the target's Info window or via the Inspector palette. To open a target's Info window, select the target and choose Get Info from the File menu or the Control-/right-click contextual menu. For native targets (which are explained later), you can just double-click the target or select it and press the Return key. If the target you want to edit is the active target, use the Project⇨Edit Active Target '*TargetName*' command.

First of all, a target has a name. You can change the name of a target by selecting the target group in the project window and choosing Rename from the Control-/right-click contextual pop-up menu. You can also edit it in the General tab of the target's Info window.

A target can have one or more build phases. You can see a target's build phases by expanding the target's group in the project window, as shown in Figure 13-1. Build phases define the broad order in which steps will occur during a build. All of your C source files must be compiled into object files before those object files can be linked together. All of the object files must be linked together before the final executable can be copied into the application's bundle, and so on.

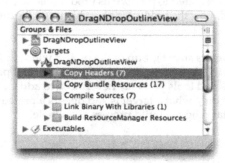

Figure 13-1

The order of steps *within* a build phase is entirely up to that phase. The order within some phases is fixed while others are very fluid. A build phase that compiles a gaggle of source files may compile them in alphabetical order or in the order in which they were most recently modified. It may compile them one at a time or two simultaneously on a dual-processor system. Intelligent build phases try to optimize the order whenever possible. Your only guarantee is that all of the processes within a phase will be completed before the next phase begins.

If a target includes build settings, you can edit those settings in the Build tab of the Info window or Inspector palette for that target (see Figure 13-2). The Collection pop-up menu, shown on the right in Figure 13-2, controls which category of settings are visible. If you are looking for a particular setting, limiting the scope keeps the list manageable.

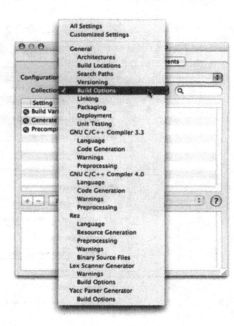

Figure 13-2

Targets can also have multiple sets of settings called build configurations. The project itself has multiple sets of build settings. Because build settings and build configurations are not unique to targets, the editing of build settings, the management of build configurations, and how they all interact with each other are explained in Chapter 14.

Targets that compile files have a set of build rules. Build rules tell a target what compiler or translator to use when building each source file. The build rules can be modified in the Rules tab of the target's Info window (see Figure 13-3). Each rule is a pairing of a file type, which you select using the Process menu, and a compiler, which you select using the Using menu. If necessary, you can define your own rules or redefine standard ones.

Each target also maintains a list of dependencies. An external dependency is a target or project that must be built before this target can be built. External dependencies are listed in the General tab of the target's Info window. A build phase may also maintain its own set of internal dependencies. These are the implicit dependencies between intermediate files and the source files used to produce them. Whenever possible, a target only recompiles source files that have changed since the last build. You can see the internal dependencies at work in the details pane of the project window. The small hammer column displays a check mark for files that need to be rebuilt.

Most targets produce a product. The kind of product produced is determined by the type of the target. Application targets produce applications, library targets produce libraries, command-line targets produce UNIX executables, and so on. A special type of target, called an aggregate target, doesn't produce anything itself. It exists solely to group other targets so they can be treated as a single target. In other words, it's a target that "produces" other targets.

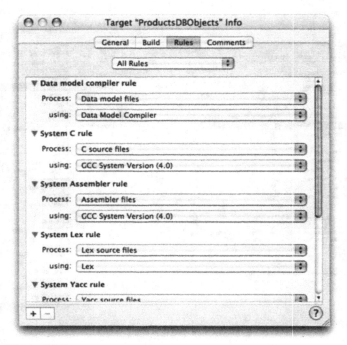

Figure 13-3

Target Types

It's difficult to neatly classify target types in Xcode, because the types form a kind of spectrum. However, the spectrum of target types can be roughly divided between the native and non-native targets. Native targets are at one extreme of the spectrum. They are sophisticated, are tightly integrated into Xcode, are highly configurable, have a flexible number of build phases, and produce complex products (like frameworks). At the other extreme is the non-native external target. An external target simply launches some external process with the understanding that said process will do whatever is necessary to build that target. Xcode doesn't know what an external process will do, what files it depends on, or even if it produces anything. An external target has no build phases and is not configurable. In between these two extremes are target types such as aggregate targets and the legacy Jam-based targets. The sophistication of these target types varies. They may have some of the same parts as native targets but are usually simpler and are not as tightly integrated into Xcode.

The type of a target is displayed in the General tab of the target's Info window. You cannot change the type of a target. If you find you are using the wrong target type, you must delete the target and create a new target of the correct type.

Native Targets

The native target types in Xcode are: Application, Command-Line Tool, Dynamic Library, Static Library, Framework, Bundle, Kernel Extension, and IOKit Kernel Extension. Native targets are easily identified by their colorful and emotive target icons. Application targets have a small application icon, Command-Line Tool targets are represented by a little terminal screen, Framework targets have a toolbox icon, and the remaining targets appear as plug-ins. Native targets usually have a full complement of parts (build phases, settings, rules, and dependencies). Native targets that include an Info.plist file in their product also include a set of properties. See the "Properties" section, later in this chapter, for more details.

Jam-Based Targets

Most of the non-native target types use the Jam build system and interface that Xcode inherited from its predecessor, Project Builder. Jam-based targets support legacy targets from Project Builder projects and targets that haven't (yet) evolved into native targets. The various Java targets are example of targets that might get native treatment in the future, but are still using the older Jam-based build system. The open-ended External target is also a Jam-based target.

All Jam-based, non-native targets appear as a red bull's-eye in the Targets smart group. Editing the details of some Jam-based targets is different than editing native targets. You configure native targets using the different panes in the target's Info window. Of the Jam-based targets, only the Aggregate target type is configured exclusively using the target's Info window. All other Jam-based targets are configured using a target editing window. See the "Jam-Based Target Editor" section later in this chapter.

Upgrading Jam-Based Targets

You can convert Jam-based targets that have an equivalent native target type into a native target using either the Upgrade to Native Target or Update All Targets in Project to Native commands located in the Project menu. These commands are especially useful for upgrading an existing project originally created with Project Builder or an old version of Xcode. These commands run a conversion process on either the selected Jam-based target or all non-native targets in the project, respectively. Not all Jam-based targets can be converted to native targets. If the conversion is unsuccessful, a report explaining why is produced. If successful, a native target with the same name plus the suffix "(Upgraded)" is created and added to the project. Ensure that the new target functions correctly before deleting the original target. The conversion process does not alter any project dependencies, so any targets that depended on the original target have to be edited.

The conversion also results in a report, an example of which is shown in Figure 13-4. In addition to making a new target, the conversion process may duplicate project files. The example in Figure 13-4 shows that a duplicate of the Info-StockMarketTicker.plist file was made and was named Info-StockMarketTicker__Upgraded_.plist. Delete the original .plist file when you delete the original target. You may also want to rename the new .plist file, which requires editing the new target's settings to match.

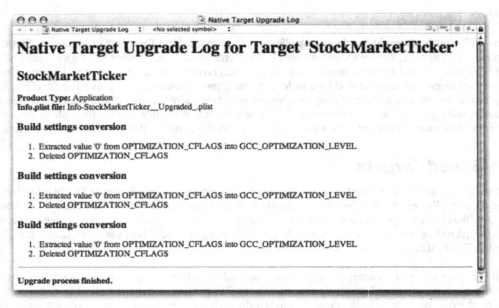

Figure 13-4

External Targets

An external target defines a build target that is produced by some external process. This was designed to permit Xcode to integrate with existing workflows based on build tools like Make or Ant. The target is little more than a placeholder. It specifies the tool that will perform the build and the arguments that are passed to it, as shown in Figure 13-5. Xcode has no knowledge of what files the process requires, what it does, or what it will produce. You cannot add project files or build phases to an external target.

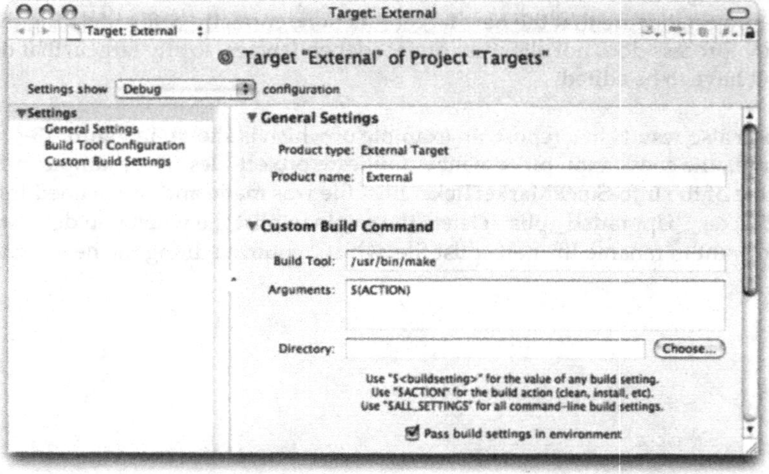

Figure 13-5

Aggregate Targets

Aggregate targets are another kind of placeholder. The name reflects its intended purpose of aggregating several targets together using dependencies. An aggregate target that depends on several different targets can be used to build all of those targets at once. Let's say you have developed a suite of BSD command-line tools, each produced by a separate target. To build all of these tools at once, you would create an aggregate target named "Tools" that depends on all of the Command-Line Tool targets. Now whenever you want to build all of the tools, you simply build the one Tools target. Likewise, you might have applications or other projects that depend on having all of those tools built. Making those targets dependent on the single Tools target is much easier to maintain than adding each tool target to every target that needs them.

Aggregate targets can also be used for utilitarian purposes. Aggregate targets don't produce a product, but they can still be made to do useful work by adding Copy Files or Shell Script build phases. These build phases are executed whenever the target is built, regardless of whether it has any dependencies. See the section "Build Phases" for more details about adding build phases to a target.

Creating a Target

Creating a target is much like creating any new file or project in Xcode. Choose the Project➪New Target command. Alternatively, choose the New Target command from the Add submenu in the Control-/right-click contextual menu in the Groups & Files list of the project window. Either method presents the New Target assistant, shown in Figure 13-6.

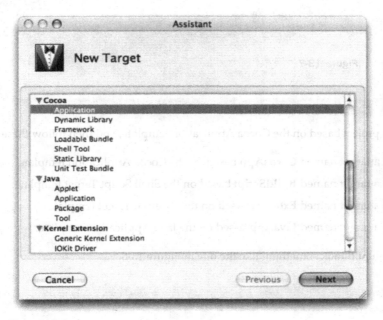

Figure 13-6

Choose a target template from the list. You'll immediately notice that there are far more templates than target types. Many of the templates produce the targets of the same type, but are preconfigured for different purposes. Choose a target template that is as close as possible to the type of product you want to produce. What is of utmost importance is to create a target of the correct type, because you cannot change the type of the target later. If you end up with a target of the wrong type, your only option is to delete the target and start over. The rest are just details. The Aggregate, Copy Files Target, and Shell Script Target templates all create an aggregate target with no build phases, one Copy Files build phase, and one Run Script build phase, respectively. Because build phases can be easily added or removed, the differences among these templates are trivial.

After you've selected the target template, click the Next button. The assistant presents you with a dialog box to enter a name for the target and select the project you want it added to (see Figure 13-7). The product produced by the target initially has the same name as the target. You can alter both the target name and product name later, but to avoid confusion, keep them the same whenever possible. If you have more than one project open, select the project that will receive the new target from the Add to Project menu. Click the Finish button.

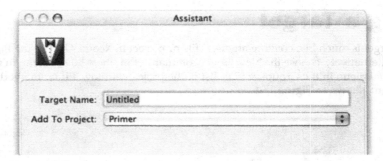

Figure 13-7

Try It Out   **Create a New Target**

Create a new project based on the Cocoa Application template, and then follow these steps:

1.   Add a target named **CocoaApp** based on the Cocoa Application template.

2.   Add a target named **BuildScript** based on the Shell Script Target template.

3.   Add a target named **External** based on the External Target template.

4.   Add a target named **JavaApp** based on the Java Application template.

Your project should look something like the one in Figure 13-8.

Figure 13-8

How It Works

Adding a target creates a new target based on the selected template to the chosen project. The templates define the target type and populate the target with an appropriate set of the build phases and settings. Use these targets to examine the various parts, properties, and settings of targets as you read through the rest of this chapter.

Target Template Groups

Target templates are organized into groups. Some templates are grouped by type (the BSD and Kernel Extension groups), and others are grouped by audience (the Carbon and Cocoa groups).

Special Templates

The special targets, listed in the following table, are the so-called placeholder targets. None of these targets produce a product, although the process launched by an external target is expected to build something.

Target	Description
Aggregate	An empty aggregate target.
Copy Files	An aggregate target with a single Copy Files build phase.
External	An external target. External targets run some external process (like make) to build the target. They cannot have build phases.
Shell Script	An aggregate target with a single Run Script build phase.

BSD Templates

The BSD templates, listed in the following table, create targets that produce flat BSD executable or library files.

Target	Description
Dynamic Library	A native Dynamic Library target that produces a .dylib library file.
Shell Tool	A native Command-Line target that produces a BSD executable binary.
Static Library	A native Static Library target that produces a static library file.

Carbon

The Carbon-based targets, listed in the following table, produce products built using the Carbon framework. Use these targets to produce applications, libraries, or shell tools that are built using C or C++. These templates produce targets of the correct type, already configured to link against the Carbon framework.

Target	Description
Application	A native Application target that produces an application bundle linked to the Carbon framework.
Dynamic Library	A native Dynamic Library target that produces a .dylib library file, itself linked to the Carbon framework.
Loadable Bundle	A native Bundle target that produces a generic bundle linked to the Carbon framework.
Shell Tool	A native Command-Line target that produces a BSD executable binary, linked to the Carbon framework.
Static Library	A native Static Library target that produces a static library file, linked to the Carbon framework.
Unit Test Bundle	A native Bundle target configured to produce a unit test written using the Carbon framework. See Chapter 18 for more information.

Cocoa

Use these targets, listed in the following table, to produce applications, libraries, or shell tools using Objective-C. These templates are almost identical to the Cocoa templates, except that all of the products are linked to the Cocoa framework instead of the Carbon framework. In fact, there is really no difference between the targets produced by the Shell Tool, Carbon Shell Tool, and Cocoa Shell Tool, except for the build settings that specify which framework and libraries your code should be linked against. With a little judicious editing, you could quickly convert a Carbon Dynamic Library target into a Cocoa Dynamic Library target, and back again.

Target	Description
Application	A native Application target that produces an application bundle linked to the Cocoa framework.
Dynamic Library	A native Dynamic Library target that produces a .dylib library file, itself linked to the Cocoa framework.
Loadable Bundle	A native Bundle target that produces a generic bundle linked to the Cocoa framework.
Shell Tool	A native Command-Line target that produces a BSD executable binary, linked to the Cocoa framework.
Static Library	A native Static Library target that produces a static library file, linked to the Cocoa framework.
Unit Test Bundle	A native Bundle target configured to produce a unit test written using the Cocoa framework. See Chapter 18 for more information.

Java

These templates, listed in the following table, produce Jam-based targets because there is no native target support (yet) for Java applications in Xcode 2.2.

Target	Description
Applet	A Jam-Based Tool target that produces a Java .jar archive. This template differs only slightly from the Tool template in that it includes a final Copy Files phase that copies the finished .jar file to the build directory.
Application	A Jam-based Application target the produces a Carbon application bundle. The application contains a stub that starts the Java VM and the Java application.
Package	A Jam-based Library target that produces a .jar archive.
Tool	A Jam-based Tool target that produces a Java .jar archive.

Kernel Extension

The two templates, listed in the following table, create the specialized targets used to produce kernel extension bundles.

Target	Description	
Generic Kernel Extension	A Kernel Extension target that produces a kernel extension bundle.	
IOKit Driver	An IOKit Kernel Extension target that produces a kernel extension bundle.	

Legacy

The legacy templates produce legacy Jam-based targets — the same target types that existed in older versions of Xcode and Project Builder. You can use these templates to create Jam-based targets that *might* be compatible with older versions of Xcode. You might, for whatever reason, prefer to use the Jam build system instead of the modern native target build logic built into Xcode. Projects that have been converted from Code Warrior, for instance, might require too many changes to make upgrading to native targets convenient. Legacy targets let you continue maintaining your project using Jam-based targets.

Duplicating Targets

You can also create a new target by duplicating an existing one. This is especially useful if you need a new target that is very similar to one that already exists. Select the target in the Targets smart group. In the Control-/right-click contextual menu choose the Duplicate command. A duplicate of the target is created with the suffix "(copy)" appended to the target's name. Note that the new target is an exact duplicate except, of course, for its name. If the original target produced a product, the new target will produce the same product. Assuming you want to build the target together, remember to edit the settings of the target so the two products don't overwrite one another.

Deleting Targets

To delete a target, select the target in the Targets smart group. Press the Delete key or choose Delete from the Control-/right-click contextual menu. Xcode presents a warning that removing a target will also remove the reference to it in any targets that depend on it. Click the Delete button to acknowledge the warning and delete the target.

Build Phases

Build phases define the steps that must occur in order to build a target. Build phases tend to paint with a broad brush. Targets typically have one Compile Sources build phase that compiles *all* of the source files for that target, even if that includes source files from many different languages. Consequently, targets rarely have more than three or four build phases.

Use the disclosure triangle next to the target's name in the Targets smart group to reveal the build phases for the target, as shown in Figure 13-9. The list of files that a build phase will operate on, or depends on, is referred to as the phase's input files. Selecting a build phase lists the input files in the details pane of the project window. Alternatively, you can use the disclosure triangle on a build phase to list the input files in the Groups & Files list. The number of input files is listed in parenthesis after the name of the build phase. Note that this only applies to build phases that process files using Xcode's internal build system. The input files listed for a build phase only include those source files which you have explicitly added to the build phase. Phases that use intermediate files produced by another build phase are not listed.

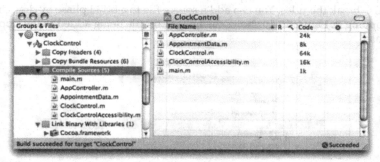

Figure 13-9

Build phases occur in the order in which they appear in the target. Build phases can be reordered by dragging a build phase to a new position in the target. Be *very* careful when doing this. The reason build phases exist is because build steps have to occur in a specific order for the build to be successful. You can't link code you haven't compiled yet. About the only time you'll find yourself reordering build phases is if you add your own build phase and need that phase to occur before or after another phase. You can also reorder the files that a build phase includes. For some build phases, this may be a significant change. For others, the order of files is superfluous. You cannot drag build phases into other targets, nor can you copy them via the clipboard.

New build phases are simple to add. Select a target and choose the new build phase from the New Build Phase menu found in either the Project menu or the Add menu of the Control-/right-click contextual menu. Not all build phase types can be added to all target types. An aggregate target can only contain Copy Files and Run Script build phases. The external target type cannot have any build phases. The New Build Phase menu lists only those phases appropriate to the selected target. After you've added the build phase, drag it to set its order in the target and then configure the new phase as desired.

To remove a build phase, select it and press the Delete key or choose Delete from the Control-/right-click contextual menu.

Files in a Build Phase

Every build phase has a set of preferred source file types. A Compile Sources phase prefers the source files it has build rules for (.c, .cpp, .m, .l, and so on). The Copy Bundle Resources phase prefers the resource files one typically copies into an application's bundle (.tiff, .icn, .nib, and so on). When you add a source file to a target, the file becomes an input file for the first phase that prefers that file type the most. If a target contains both a Copy Headers phase and a Copy Files phase, adding a .h file to that target adds the file to the Copy Headers phase. The Copy Headers phase is more specific than the Copy Files phase, and prefers headers more than the Copy Files phase does. If a target contains two Copy Headers phases adding a .h file adds it to the first Copy Headers phase in the target, because both phases prefer headers file equally.

You typically add files to targets via the targets list that appears when the file is created, added to the project, in the Info window for the file, or using the target check box column in the project window. This is usually foolproof and effective, allowing Xcode to automatically choose the appropriate phase to add the file to. If a target has no phases that prefer a source file's type, that file cannot be added to that target using any of the aforementioned dialog boxes.

Using the target group, you have more precise control over what input files are included in what phases, and you can also break the rules. You can add a source file to a build phase by dragging the file into that phase and dropping it. Figure 13-10 shows the Image1.tiff file being added to the Copy Bundle Resources phase.

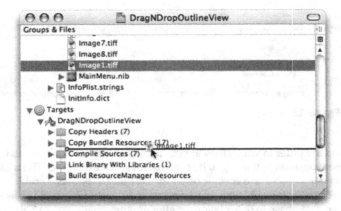

Figure 13-10

You can move or copy a file from one phase to another. In the previous example where there was both a Copy Files and a Copy Headers phase, you may really want a specific header file to be in the Copy Files phase, not the Copy Headers phase. But just adding the file to the target puts it in the Copy Headers phase. Grab the file in the Copy Headers phase and move it into the Copy Files phase. Hold down the Option key before dropping it, and Xcode duplicates the reference adding the file to both phases.

Using drag and drop, you can include a file in more than one phase and you can include it in phases that don't prefer them. Let's say you have developed a Java application that dynamically produces executable Java code by manipulating a source file template and then compiling it. You want the Java source file, GenericTransformTemplate.java, to be included in the application's bundle as a resource file. To accomplish this, drag the GenericTransformTemplate.java file into the Copy Bundle Resources phase. When the application is built, this Java source file is copied into the resource bundle of the finished application, something that would normally never happen.

You can remove a source file from a target by selecting it and pressing the Delete key or choosing Delete from the Control-/right-click contextual menu. You will receive a warning from Xcode asking if you want to delete the item. Don't panic. You are only deleting the phase's reference to the source file, not the source file itself.

If you have added a source file to any phase of a target, Xcode indicates that it is a member of that target. Removing (unchecking) a target in a target list removes that file from every phase it is included in. It's possible to paint yourself into a corner if you have manually forced a source file to be included in a target and that target has no phases that prefer that file type. The target for that source file will indicate that it is a member, but the check box control for the target will be disabled (because there are no phases that prefer that type). To remove a file from a target under these circumstances, you must delete the file directly from the build phase or phases.

Build Phase Types

There are nine build phase types: Compile Sources, Compile AppleScripts, Link Binary With Libraries, Copy Headers, Copy Bundle Resources, Copy Files, Build Java Resources, Build ResourceManager Resources, and Run Script.

Compiler Phases

The Compile Sources phase is the most sophisticated of the build phases. It is responsible for compiling any kind of source file. The kinds of sources files it will compile and what compiler it will use for each are determined by the build rules for the target. The Compile Source phase understands a vast array of build settings that apply to the compilers. It parses all of these and makes the appropriate adjustments to the parameters passed to each compiler.

The Compile AppleScripts phase is similar to Compile Sources, but it only compiles AppleScript source files. The Build ResourceManager Resources phase is another specialized compiler phase just for resource definitions files. It compiles and merges .r and .rsrc files to produce a resource file in the product's bundle, or inserts them into the resource fork of the product file.

The Link Binary With Libraries phase is the companion to the Compile Sources phase. It takes whatever intermediate files were produced by the Compile Sources phase and links them together, along with whatever libraries and frameworks they need. The input files to the link phase are the external libraries and frameworks that the object files need to be linked to.

Copy Phases

The Copy Headers, Copy Bundle Resources, and Build Java Resources phases are intelligent (or narrow, depending on your perspective) versions of the Copy Files phase. Their sole purpose is to copy files into the product's bundle. Copy Headers uses the "role" of its input files, be they public or private, and copies them to the appropriate location in the output project — which is assumed to be a plug-in or framework. The role of a header is set using the role column of the details pane with that file or phase selected. Copy Bundle Resources copies any input file into the Resources folder of the product's bundle. This is the phase to use if you want a literal copy of a file stored in your bundle's resource folder for access at runtime. This phase is also responsible for constructing and copying the Info.plist file into the product's bundle. (See the "Properties" section later in this chapter for more about how to configure the Info.plist file.) Build Java Resources is like Copy Bundle Resources, but it copies its input files into the bundle's standard Contents/Resources/Java folder.

The Copy Files phase is a utilitarian phase that copies all of the phase's input files or folders to the destination of your choice. That destination is set in the Info window of the phase, as shown in Figure 13-11. Control-/right-click the Copy Files phase and choose Get Info. The destination location can be either an absolute path or a path relative to the product's location. For targets that produce a bundle, predefined locations are provided that will target many of the standard locations in the product's bundle. An absolute path is just that. Use this to copy files to a particular installation or test location.

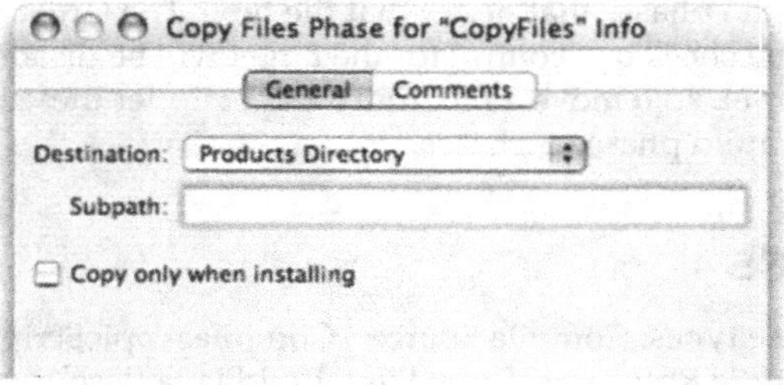

Figure 13-11

Relative paths require a bit of an explanation. The build location — the location where the product of a target will be written to — is unique for each build configuration. If you have two build configurations, Debug and Release, every target will produce two different products: a Debug product and a Release product. The remaining paths in the destination menu are all relative to the product's output directory. The choices are the output directory itself or one of the standard folders inside a bundle, assuming the target produces a bundle. (See Chapter 14 for a complete explanation of build locations and build configurations.) The path field can be left blank for any choice other than Absolute. Any folders that do not exist when the phase executes are automatically created.

The path can also contain build variables using the form $(BUILD_VAR). The macro will be substituted for its actual value when the build phase runs. By using build variables in the path, you can customize the normal destination location calculated by Xcode.

Speaking of build locations, remember when Chapter 5 mentioned that product relative references are based on the active build configuration and target? This fact is most applicable to product file references used as input files to a Copy Files phase. Product references also change based on the active build configuration, making both the source and destination locations of the phase variable. An example would be an application that includes a BSD executable in its bundle. A Copy Files phase could be used to copy the project-relative product produced by the BSD target into the resource bundle being produced by the application target. Both the source (product reference) and the destination (application bundle) are both variable. When built using the Debug build configuration, the Debug version of the BSD product is copied into the Debug version of the application bundle. When the Release configuration is active, the Release version of the BSD product is copied into the Release version of the application bundle.

If the Copy Only When Installing option is set, the copy phase is only executed when the build is being performed with the install option set. You can do this from within Xcode by turning on the DEPLOY-MENT_LOCATION build setting or passing the install option to the xcodebuild tool. Both of these are described in Chapter 14.

Script Phase

The Run Script phase is the "backdoor" by which you can insert virtually any custom build procedure. You configure a Run Script phase using the Info window of the phase (see Figure 13-12). The Shell field determines the shell, or interpreter, that will be used to execute the script. Below that is the shell script that will be executed.

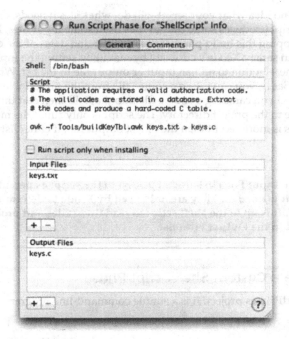

Figure 13-12

When the phase is built, the shell executable is put on a "she-bang" line and the remaining script is appended to it. The whole thing is written into an executable script file, as shown in Figure 13-13, and run using the sh shell. One side effect is that the zeroth argument to the script will be the path to the script itself.

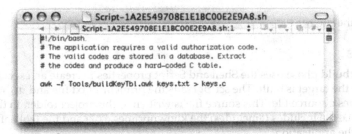

Figure 13-13

The Shell field, therefore, can be any valid interpreter. It could be perl, awk, or php. It doesn't matter, as long as the given interpreter can execute the script file. Most of the build settings are transferred into environment variables before the script is executed, so your script has free access to the build settings.

Checking the Run script only when installing option prohibits the script from running unless the DEPLOYMENT_LOCATION build setting is turned on or the install option was passed to the xcodebuild tool.

Xcode, of course, has no idea what your script will do, what files it needs, or what it produces. Assuming that the script produces some output files from some input files, Xcode would like to optimize the build by skipping this build phase if the modification dates of the output files are newer than the input files. You can satisfy Xcode's curiosity by manually setting the Input Files and Output Files for the phase. Click the + button to add an input or output file to the list. When the new entry appears, enter the file's path. (Sadly, you can't drag a source file from the project window into the list. However, once an entry is created you can drag a source file into the field then edit the path.) It can be an absolute path or a path relative to the project directory. The script is only run if the modification date of one or more of the input files is more recent than the oldest output file. If either list is empty, the script runs every time.

> The files in the Input Files list are *not* passed to the script as parameters, nor are they piped to it via `stdin`. They are only used by Xcode to determine if the script should be run. It is up to the shell script to read those files and produce all of the files promised in the Output Files list.

Try It Out   Write a Custom Shell Script Phase

Open the PrecompiledPrimes project. It is a simple command-line program that uses a static table of prime numbers.

Create a build phase to generate a C source file containing a table of prime numbers. How many prime numbers is controlled by a file named primelimit.txt. It contains a single number, which is the largest number in the table. The script will use primelimit.txt as an input file and produce a file named knownprimes.c. This file is included (#included) by the main.c file.

Start by adding a new Shell script build phase to the PrecompiledPrimes target. Move the build phase to the beginning of the target so that it is the first phase to execute. Open the Info window for the new build phase and configure it so it looks like Figure 13-14.

Build and run the project.

How It Works

The Run Script build phase uses the Shell and Script properties to create an executable script, which it runs whenever the target is built. The script reads the primelimit.txt file and uses that value to produce the knownprimes.c source file. This source file is written to the project folder. In the Compile Sources phase, the main.c file includes (#includes) the knownprimes.c file and the table of prime numbers gets compiled into the application.

The script is time-consuming (it isn't optimized), so you don't want it running on each build. By setting both an input and output file, Xcode will compare the modification dates of the two files before running the phase. If the knownprimes.c file exists and has a modification date later than primelimit.txt, then the phase is skipped. Thus, the table will only be regenerated if the primelimit.txt file is edited.

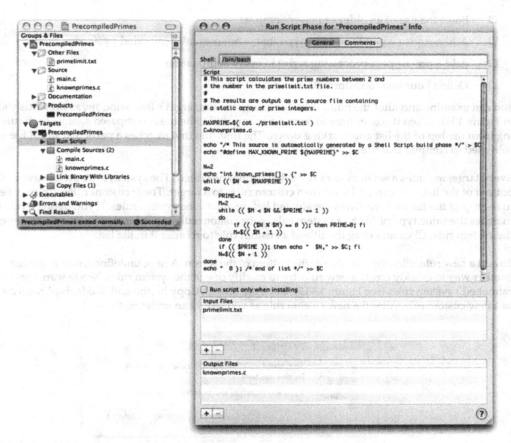

Figure 13-14

Build Rules

Build rules define the relationship between source files and their compiled results for the various compiler phases. The compiler phase uses the target's build rules to determine which compiler should be used to compile each input file. A build rule might specify that all C source files (C, C++, and Objective-C) are compiled using the gcc compiler. The type of a file is determined by its extension or the File Type assigned to that source file. A file's type is typically in agreement with the file name extensions, but it doesn't have to be. You can change the file type of a .java source file to sourcecode.cpp. The Compile Sources phase then tries to compile that .java file using the gcc compiler as if it were a C++ source file.

You'll probably never need to alter the build rules in Xcode. However, there are several reasons why you might want to:

❑ Force the use of an older or newer compiler

❑ Add a rule to compile a source type that is not normally compiled by Xcode

❑ Add a pre- or post-processing script to every compilation

❑ Define your own transformation

You can examine and alter the build rules for a target in the target's Info window, as previously shown in Figure 13-3. When it comes time to compile an input file, the file is compared against each rule starting from the top of the list and working down. The first rule that matches a particular input file is the rule used to compile that file.

Every target includes a set of system rules that cannot be edited. The system rules are always at the bottom of the list. You can add your own custom rules to a target. These custom rules can only be added to the top of the list and are always evaluated before any of the system rules. If you define a rule that matches the same type of file as a system rule, your custom rule is used instead — essentially overriding the system rule. Click and drag the title of a custom rule to reorder it in the list.

To add a new rule, click the + button at the bottom of the screen. A new, undefined, rule is created. There's another way to quickly create a new rule: try to modify one of the system rules. Xcode warns you that you cannot edit system rules (see Figure 13-15). Click the Make a Copy button and Xcode duplicates the system as a new custom rule. Alter the new custom rule as you would an undefined one.

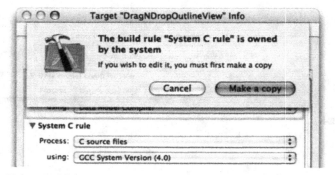

Figure 13-15

Choose the type of file that the rule will process from the Process menu. This can be one of the Xcode file types, as set in the source file's properties, or it can be a file name pattern. To match a file name pattern, choose the Source Files With Names Matching option at the bottom of the menu and a file name pattern field appears (see Figure 13-16). Enter the file name pattern, such as *.xml. This field is a globbing pattern like you would use in the shell; it is not a regular expression. The pattern is case-sensitive. By using file name patterns, it is possible to partially override system rules. For example, the "C source files" type encompasses C (.c), C++ (.cpp), and Objective-C (.m) files. By creating a custom rule that matches only *.c files, you can redirect plain C files to an alternate compiler while allowing C++ and Objective-C files to "fall through" and match the default system rule for compiling any kind of C file.

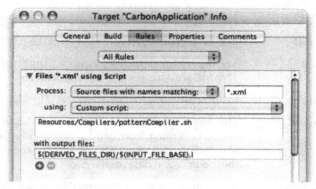

Figure 13-16

If you want to use a particular version of the compiler, say gcc 3.3 instead of gcc 4.0, create a custom build rule that overrides the system build rule for C files. There is a GCC_VERSION build setting that performed this same function for older versions of Xcode, but that setting has been deprecated and should not be used. Creating a custom build rule is the correct way of specifying an alternate compiler. Currently, there is no means by which you can edit the build rules for the entire project. You must create a new build rule in every target that compiles C source files. Modify the System C rule to quickly create a custom C rule, and then select the desired compiler.

A less refined approach is to use the `gcc_select` tool to change the default gcc compiler for your entire system. This will change the default compiler for *every* project you build on your system. See `man gcc_select` for details.

With the file type selected, choose the compiler that will process each file of this type with the Using menu. This can be one of the standard Xcode compilers or you can direct compilations to your own script by choosing the Custom Script item. When you use a custom script as the compiler two additional fields appear, as previously shown in Figure 13-16. The top field is the path and file name of the script to execute. The path to the script can be an absolute path or a path relative to the project folder.

When the script is executed, the current directory is set to the project's folder and environment variables are set by Xcode describing the file that Xcode wants processed. They also define where Xcode expects the output file, or files, to be written. Note that no parameters are passed to the script. The script must determine what to process by examining its environment variables. The following table lists the environment variables passed to a custom build script when it is executed.

Environment Variable	Description
INPUT_FILE_PATH	The full path, including the file name, to the source file being processed.
INPUT_FILE_DIR	Just the directory portion of INPUT_FILE_PATH, without the file name.

Table continued on following page

Environment Variable	Description	
INPUT_FILE_NAME	Just the file name portion of INPUT_FILE_PATH, without the directory.	
INPUT_FILE_BASE	The base name of the file; in other words, the value of INPUT_FILE _NAME without any file name extension.	
INPUT_FILE_SUFFIX	Just the file name extension of INPUT_FILE_NAME.	
DERIVED_FILES_DIR	The complete path to the directory where Xcode expects the intermediate files to be written. Intermediate files are kept between builds and used to determine if the source file needs to be compiled again by comparing the modification dates of the two.	
TARGET_BUILD_DIR	The complete path to the target's product directory; in other words, where the final product of this target is being constructed.	

The following is a simple shell script that demonstrates the use of a custom build script. In this example, the project includes XML files that define patterns of text. The project contains an SXL transform file that will convert that XML into a LEX file describing the pattern. The details are unimportant. The key ingredients are that there is some process that converts the input file into one or more output files and the shell's environment variables tell the script where the source and destinations are.

```
#!/bin/bash

# Xcode compile script
# Run the input file through the java XSLT transformer
# The KeyPatternToLEX.sxlt file contains a transform that
#  will convert the pattern record into LEX syntax.

XSLT = "Source/Transforms/KeyPatternToLEX.sxlt"
IN = "$INPUT_FILE_PATH"
OUT = "${DERIVED_FILES_DIR}/${INPUT_FILE_BASE}.1"

java org.mycompany.patterns.Transformer "$XSLT" "$IN" > "$OUT"
```

If the script produces intermediate output files, it should write those to the DERIVED_FILES_DIR directory. Intermediate output files are files that will be consumed later in this phase. If a script produces one or more intermediate output files, Xcode takes those files and runs them back through the build rules. It continues this process until no rule matches the files. This example defined a rule that takes an XML file and produces a LEX source file. When built, Xcode will run the XML file though the custom build script producing a LEX source file. That LEX source file will be run through the rules again. This time, it will match the LEX rule that will compile the LEX file into a C source file. That C source file is again run through the build rules, this time matching the System C rule, and ultimately producing an object file.

If the files produced by the script go into the target's product, then they should be written to the appropriate location in TARGET_BUILD_DIR.

This brings up an interesting conundrum. Xcode has no idea what a custom build script produces or where. You have to communicate that to the build rule by listing the files that the script will produce in the build rule. Under the With Output Files caption in the build rule, enter the file name that will be produced by the script. You can use any of the environment variables listed above. For this example, the output file is $(DERIVED _FILES_DIR)/$(INPUT_FILE_BASE).l, which agrees with the output file name in the script. The syntax for using environment variables in the output files list is $ (VAR_NAME), which may be different than the syntax required by your script's interpreter. If the script produces more than one file, say a matched pair of .h and .c files, add more files by clicking the + button immediately below the list. Delete a file by selecting it and clicking the - button. You can edit an exiting item by double-clicking it.

Try It Out   **Write a Custom Build Rule**

In the previous "Try It Out" section, you wrote a custom build script so that PrecompiledPrimes would generate its own knownprimes.c source file. The only "sloppy" thing about this solution is that known-primes.c is written into the project folder with the other source files, even though it is technically an intermediate file generated from another source file (primelimit.txt).

You can rectify that using build rules. Instead of a special build phase, make a rule in the Compile Sources phase that takes an input file containing a number and generates C source. The result of this rule is a C source file, which is fed back into rules where it gets compiled and linked into the application. main.c doesn't have to include the knownprimes.c file to get it compiled—it is already compiled. main() can now simply reference the global variable that has been linked into the application.

Follow these steps:

1. Open the PrimeRules project.

2. Open the build rules for the PrimeRules target.

3. Add a new rule to compile any file matching *.txt using the ./compilePrimeTable.sh script.

4. Add two output files for the rule: $ (DERIVED_FILES_DIR)/$ (INPUT_FILE_BASE).h and $ (DERIVED_FILES_DIR)/$ (INPUT_FILE_BASE).c.

5. Add the primelimit.txt file to the Compile Sources phase by dragging it into the build phase.

   Your project and build rules should now look something like the ones shown in Figure 13-17.

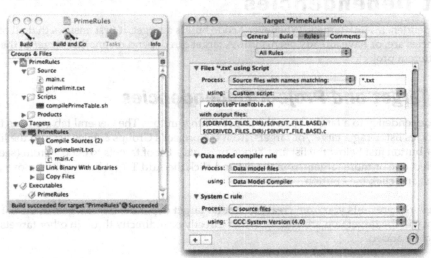

Figure 13-17

6. Build and run the project.

How It Works

Instead of defining a build phase to run a specialized script, you instead create a rule that takes the primelimit.txt file and turns it into the primelimit.h and primelimit.c files, which are then automatically compiled and linked into the application. These are intermediate files, and are not intermixed with the project's source files. If they were deleted or made obsolete, the build system would recompile them again automatically.

This works just fine, but there are two flaws. First, you've used up a very common file extension (.txt) for our rule. As long as the project (technically, this target) didn't include any other .txt files this shouldn't be a problem, but it could be for larger projects that include other kinds of .txt files. Because this rule was written specifically for this one file, you could make the pattern more specific, such as *primelimit.txt. Remember that the pattern has to match a full path name, so just primelimit.txt wouldn't match *any* source file. Or you could choose a different extension (.primemax, for example).

The other flaw is that your new "compiler" outputs two files: a source file and a header. It would be nice to include that header in main.c to get the MAX_KNOWN_PRIME definition and the table declaration. But you can't, because you don't know what order Xcode will compile the input files to the Compiles Sources phase. It might even be compiling them simultaneously in a multi-processor or distributed build system. Thus, you have no guarantee that primelimt.txt will be compiled before main.c, so main.c can't rely on primelimit.h being up-to-date when it is included (#included).

The solution to that problem is to compile primelimit.txt in a separate target or an earlier build phase, possibly outputting a static library that the main target could link to. A target dependency would ensure that primelimit.txt was always compiled before main.c. Target dependencies are discussed in the next section.

Target Dependencies

Target dependencies link targets. Whenever Xcode builds a target, it first ensures that all of that target's dependencies are, or have already been, built. A target can depend on another target in the same project or in a different project.

Adding Target and Project Dependencies

To add a dependency to a target, open the target's Info window. The General tab contains the Direct Dependencies list. Drag a target, or targets, from the project's Groups & Files list into the list. Or you can click the + button just below the list and Xcode presents a list of targets to choose from (see Figure 13-18). Select one or more targets from the list and click the Add Target button. To remove a target, select it in the list and click the - button.

Xcode, cleverly, prevents you from creating circular target dependencies. Targets in the list that contain a dependency to the target you are editing, either directly or indirectly through other targets, are disabled and cannot be added.

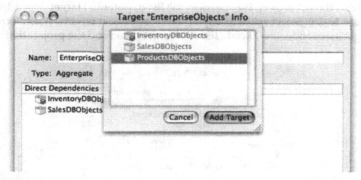

Figure 13-18

After you've added target dependencies, they also appear along with the other build phases of the target. You can also create target dependencies by dragging one target directly into another target's group. Logically, all dependent targets are built before any of the target's build phases begin, and the order in the target group reflects this. Just as you can reorder build phases, you can reorder dependent targets to control the order in which they are built. However, you cannot place a dependent target *after* a build phase.

You can also make a target dependent on a target in a different project. This is called a cross-project reference. Before you can start creating cross-project target references, you must first add that subproject to your project using any of the techniques described in Chapter 5. The easiest methods are to use the Project⇨ Add to Project command and choose the subproject's .xcodeproj file, or simply drag the .xcodeproj file from the Finder into the source group. The Add to Project dialog box prompts you to select the targets for the subproject, which you can ignore — regardless of which targets you select, the subproject are not added to any targets. What appears in your source group is a project reference group, illustrated with a small Xcode project icon. Expand the contents of the subproject group and you will find all of the products (not the targets) that the subproject produces (see Figure 13-19). These allow you to reference products produced by the subproject in your project.

Figure 13-19

After you've added the subproject, it appears in the list of potential target dependencies as a group of targets (see Figure 13-20). Select and add any of the cross-project targets. When a cross-project target is listed in the target's dependencies, Xcode lists the target name and the project that contains it.

Figure 13-20

There are some, potentially, important differences in how a project target and a cross-project target are built. The primary consideration is the build settings that will be used. Every target in the same project shares the same set of build configurations, so the Deployment version of one target always depends on the Deployment version of its dependent target. This is not necessarily true of cross-project targets, which might have a completely different set of build configurations. See Chapter 14 for a discussion on how Xcode handles build settings in other projects as well as shared build locations.

Strategies for Target Dependencies

Target dependencies serve a number of purposes:

❑ Modularize projects

❑ Control build order

❑ Aggregate targets

Projects can be organized into modules, or subprojects, by design or necessity. Large projects can be made more manageable by isolating common code into libraries or separate projects, which can be built using a single target. All of the other products that rely on that common code will have a dependency on that single target. Whenever any of those products are built, Xcode first makes sure that the common library target is built first.

Sometimes organizing your build into multiple targets is required by the nature of targets, which typically produce only one product. An application that includes two executable BSD command-line programs in its resource bundle requires three targets to build all of its components: an application target and two command-line targets. To produce the bundle, the application target depends on the other two command-line targets. In the application's Copy Bundle Resources phase, the products of the other two targets are added. Whenever the application target is built, Xcode first ensures that the two command-line tools are built first; then during the copy resources phase, it copies those products into the final product while constructing the application's bundle.

Target dependencies also imply an order of execution. All dependent targets must be completely, and successfully, built before a target begins to build. In the "Build Rules" section, you added rules to turn XML files into object files. The assumption was that the individual source files and their outputs are all independent of each other. It didn't matter which source files, or in what order, Xcode decided to build these files. Often, as in the case of C source files, this doesn't matter. But what if it did? What if source files in the target need to include header files produced by another rule, as was the case with primelimits.h file in the earlier "Try It Out" example? You could solve this by moving the compilation of the prerequisite files into another target, ensuring that these are all built before compiling the remaining source files. Aggregate targets depend on other targets, but don't build anything themselves. An aggregate target effectively groups other targets so that you, or another target, can build multiple targets by referring to a single target. When you build in Xcode, you always build the single active target. If your project produces several products, which aren't dependent on one another, you can create an aggregate target to build them all at once. Let's say you have a project that produces two applications, a client and a server. To build both the client and server at once, create an aggregate target that depends on both. Setting the active target to the aggregate targets will cause both applications to be built using a single build command.

Combining target dependencies, you can create large trees of targets. It would not be uncommon to have an aggregate target that builds five applications, each of which depends on a single common framework, which in turn depends on building several libraries. The Xcode build system is intelligent and attempts to eliminate excess building of targets. Building that single top-level aggregate target will only cause the common framework target to be built once. As Xcode progresses through the build, it knows what targets have already been built. Before the first application is built, Xcode first builds the framework target, which in turn builds its dependent targets. However, the other four applications can then be built without rebuilding the framework target.

Build Settings

Each target has at least one set of build settings. Build settings are a collection of named values (key/value pairs) used to customize a target's behavior. You can define your own variable names and assign them any value you choose. These variables are accessible by the target and all of its build phases. Xcode defines a large number of predefined build settings and the Xcode supplied build phases expect specific variables with strictly defined values. As an example, the INFOPLIST_FILE setting tells the Copy Bundle Resources phase where to get the Info.plist file for the bundle. The GCC_UNROLL_LOOPS setting tells the Compile Sources phase to pass the -funroll-loops flag to the gcc compiler. There are scores of predefined settings. This chapter explores some of them, some in the "Building Projects" section, and others in the "Debugging" section. Many are specific to the compiler or linker. For those, consult the gcc documentation for more details.

A target can have more than one complete set of build settings. Each set is called a build configuration. When you use different build configurations, you can use a single target to produce variations of the same product. In addition to targets, both the project and individual files define build settings. The build settings in the target form one layer of the build settings that will be used when the target is built. Because the build settings are part of a larger system of build variables, inheritance, and build configurations, using build settings is discussed in Chapter 14.

Jam-Based Target Editor

In the Jam build system, a target editor window performs the same functions as that of the build settings tab, the properties editor (see the next section), and the build phase Info windows found in Xcode. Double-click a Jam-based target or select it and press the Return to open its target editor window (see Figure 13-21). Jam-based targets still have an Info window, which you can open using the Get Info command, but it only permits editing of the target's name, dependencies, and comments.

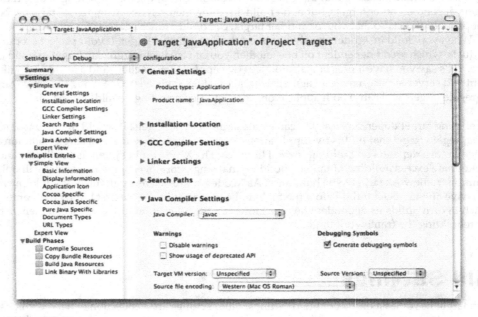

Figure 13-21

If you have used Project Builder in the past, this interface will look very familiar to you. In fact, it *is* the interface used in earlier versions of Xcode. The Jam-based settings window isn't quite as flexible, intelligent, or well integrated into Xcode as its native cousin. Nevertheless, most of the settings that you would find in the Info window of a native target are here, just in a different organization.

The settings that are available depend on the type of target. Generally, every target has a Settings group that controls the build settings for that target. Similar to the panes in the Info window, the settings are subdivided into groups for easier browsing. Selecting an individual setting or a group of settings reveals them in the right pane. Edit any of the settings as needed. At the bottom of each major section of settings is an Expert View group. This displays all of the setting in their raw form. You can also edit any of the settings here, or add your own build variables. The editing of setting in expert view is not intelligent, so be careful that the values you enter here are valid. A field that expects to be either "YES" or "NO" may not be happy if you set it to "1." Also, custom variables only appear in the expert view.

A build configuration menu has been added to the target editor to make the Jam-based settings compatible with the newer Xcode system of build configurations. Select the build configuration you want to work with from the Settings Show Configuration menu. All changes will be applied to that configuration.

However, the target editor interface is not really build-configuration savvy. Unlike the settings editor for native targets, it does not highlight settings that differ from the project build settings. You can't view a combined display of all of the build settings, nor can you set a build setting for all configurations at once. If you need to change a build setting in a Jam-based target for all build configurations, you must enter it separately for each configuration.

Also in this window are the target's build phases. You can manipulate the build phases of a Jam-based target in its settings window or from the project window, as described earlier in the chapter for native targets.

Finally, if the target produces a bundle the Jam-based target editor also defines all of the Info.plist settings for the product. You can define simple property values in the expert view, which become tagged values in the product's Info.plist file.

Properties

Native targets that produce an Info.plist file as part of their product have a Properties tab in their Info window (see Figure 13-22).

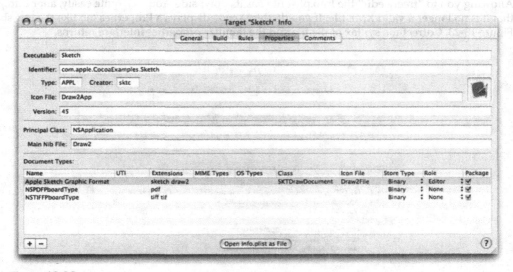

Figure 13-22

Each field in the Properties tab becomes one of the standard properties in the Info.plist file. For example, the Executable field becomes the CFBundleExecutable property in the Info.plist file. The Identifier field becomes the CFBundleIdentifier property, and so on. Make sure these values are correct, because Xcode does not check their validity. Depending on the type of product, any or all of these values may be superfluous. The Runtime Configuration Guidelines at `http://developer.apple.com/documentation/MacOSX/Conceptual/BPRuntimeConfig/` have more details.

At the bottom of the pane are the document types that your application creates, owns, understands, or works with. This information is used by Launch Services to relate document files with applications. Each line defines a single document type. You can add or delete document types using the + and - buttons at the bottom of the pane. Double-click any field in the list to edit it.

The Version field contains the version of your application, bundle, or framework. This is not, however, the version number that will appear to the user in the Finder's Get Info window. To set that, you need to define the CFBundleShortVersionString property.

Now you're probably wondering where to set the CFBundleShortVersionString property. Actually, there are scores of other properties that have meaning in an Info.plist file that do not have a convenient user interface in the Properties tab. To set any of the less common properties, click the Open Info.plist as File button at the bottom of the pane. This button opens the Info.plist file in an editor window. Here, you can freely edit the XML document that will become the Info.plist file when the bundle is assembled. As you will see in the next chapter, the Info.plist file can be processed by the gcc compiler. This allows you to use build setting variable names and conditional statements, making the Info.plist file that you are editing more of a template for the final Info.plist file. The values shown in the Properties tab are stored in, and extracted from, the source Info.plist file. A change to any of the standard properties made in the Info.plist file will be reflected the next time you display the Properties tab, and vice versa.

Allowing you to "freely edit" the Info.plist file has its downside. You can, quite easily, alter Info.plist so that it is no longer a valid XML file. If you do this, Xcode displays a Properties tab like the one shown in Figure 13-23. Correct the syntax of the file and the familiar properties interface returns.

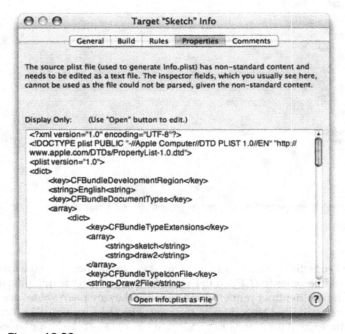

Figure 13-23

Products

Most targets produce a product. Targets that produce a product tell Xcode what that product is. Xcode then makes a product reference appear in the Groups & Files list under the Products group (see Figure 13-24). In this sense, the Products group is more like a smart group than a source group.

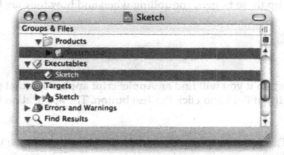

Figure 13-24

Like any source reference, the product reference turns red if the product that it refers to doesn't exist. Unlike source references, this isn't necessarily a bad thing. It just means that the product hasn't been built yet. As explained in Chapter 5, the path type of a product is relative to the build product. Each build configuration has a different product location, so the product references change whenever the build configuration changes. This means that if you use a product reference to refer to product, what the reference points to will change when you change the active build configuration. This is normally exactly what you want. When your build configuration is set to Debug, all product references refer to the Debug version of those products. You cannot change the reference type of a product reference, nor can you rename or delete a product reference. To change a product you must edit the target that produces it. To delete a product you must delete the target that produces it.

All native targets that produce a product have a Product Name build setting. This setting defines the name of the product the target will produce. Changing this build setting changes the name of the product, renames the product reference in the source group, and updates any other targets that reference it.

Executables

Targets whose products are executable programs also create an executable. Executables appear in the Executables smart group, which was also shown in Figure 13-24. Opening the Info window for an executable allows you to define the runtime environment used when the executable is launched from within Xcode. Executables, and custom executables, are explained in Chapter 15.

Summary

Up to this chapter, most of the organization of your project has been for convenience and clarity. Reorganizing your files and source groups has little impact on what your project builds, but the organization of targets literally shapes what the end result of your project will be. Targets define what your project builds, what sources are used, how those sources are compiled, and in what order.

Ironically, Xcode provides so many templates with preconfigured targets that you may never need to deal with targets much beyond tweaking a few build settings, but a keen understanding of targets, their component parts, and how they can be interlinked is critical to constructing and maintaining complex projects.

If targets are the engine of your project, then the build commands are the fire that drives them. The next chapter looks at firing up those targets, controlling when and how they are built.

Exercise

Open the Primer project. In it you will find an AppleScript application that puts up a simple window. Enter a number in the input field and click the Test button. The application tells you if the number is prime or not.

Here's how it works: The AppleScript attached to the Test button takes the value of the input field and passes it to a small BSD command-line tool named primetest. The result of the test is then returned to the AppleScript handler, which puts it in the results field.

The source for the primetest tool is in the primetest.h and primetest.c files. The programming of the project is complete, but targets to compile and bundle the command-line tool into the application's bundle aren't finished. Here's your mission:

1. Create a new target to compile primetest.c into a BSD command-line executable. The name of the product is "primetest."
2. Make the Primer target dependent on the target you just created.
3. Add the primetest product to the Copy Bundle Resources phase of the Primer target.
4. Choose Project⇨Set Active Target⇨Primer. Choose Build⇨Build and Run.

Building Projects

Building projects is Xcode's ultimate ambition. It might not be yours—you probably want your finished application to run flawlessly. Xcode does provide additional tools for debugging and performance analysis that are covered in subsequent chapters, but the principle objective of Xcode is to faithfully compile and assemble your finished product.

This chapter explains how to choose what you want Xcode to build and how to start and control the build process. This chapter also covers how to set and organize build settings, which are used to customize everything from compiler options to packaging, so your products come out just the way you want them to.

Starting and Stopping a Build

To build your project, choose the Build command (Command+B) from the Build menu. There are also two build commands that perform common combinations of commands. These are the Build⇨Build and Run (Command+R) and Build⇨Build and Debug (Command+Y) commands. These two commands perform a build and, if successful, immediately launch the finished product. In the case of Build and Debug, the executable is launched under the control of the Xcode debugger. These are typically the two most commonly used commands in Xcode.

These same commands can be invoked from toolbar buttons, if you find that more convenient. Xcode provides four build buttons for toolbars: Build, Build and Run, Build (menu), and Build and Go (menu). The Build and the Build and Run buttons are the Build⇨Build and Build⇨Build and Run commands, respectively. The Build buttons with drop-down triangles are combinations of a Build button and a drop-down menu of less commonly used build commands. Click it quickly to execute the Build command. Click and hold to select one of the other build commands.

The progress and results of the build are displayed in the build window for the project. See the "Build Results Window" section for all of the details. The progress of a build also appears in the Activity Viewer window. In the status bar—at the bottom of many Xcode windows—you will also see a one-line summary of the build's progress (see Figure 14-1). At the right end of the bar is a small round progress indicator with Xcode's estimate of how much of the build has been completed.

Figure 14-1

When the build is finished, a completion statement replaces the progress message. If the build was successful, the message "Build succeeded" is displayed. If not, the message indicates that the build failed, with possibly an explanation as to why. It may also include a count of the number of errors or warnings that were encountered.

You can only build one target in a project at a time, but you can build targets in different projects simultaneously.

Try It Out   Build a Project

You've probably done this a dozen times already, just working through this book. But let's do it one more time. Here's how:

1.   Open any project.
2.   Build it (Command+B).

How It Works

The Build command builds the currently active target using the currently active build configuration. It also, more than likely, opens the build window for the project. If it does not, use the Build⇨Build Results (Command+Shift+B) command to open the build window. Keep this window open as you work through this chapter. The build window, and the meaning of the active target and build configuration, will all be explained shortly.

A build normally stops when it is complete, either successfully building the target or terminating due to an error. Should you start a build and then decide that you don't want it continuing, press Command+. or use the Build⇨Stop Current Build command (Command+B). This menu item replaces the Build⇨Build command after a build starts. At the end of the build, the command again reverts to Build.

Clean Builds

A "clean" build is a build that constructs everything in the product based solely on the project's source files. You might think this would be true of every build, but it isn't. Xcode, like most Make systems, keeps all of the intermediate files that were produced during previous builds. A C source file is compiled into an object file, which is later linked to form an executable. The C file is the source and the executable is the product, but the object file is an intermediate file. Xcode normally only recompiles the source file when its modification date is later than the intermediate object file. Likewise, the executable is only re-linked if one or more of the intermediate objects are newer than the latest executable.

Xcode does this to avoid recompiling everything in the project and all of its libraries and frameworks every time you make a single change. For large projects the difference can be a 20-minute build versus a 5-second build. However, it's possible for Xcode to become confused. The classic example is to build a project and then retrieve an earlier version of a source file. The source file is different and needs to be recompiled, but its modification date is still earlier than the intermediate object file. Xcode does not recompile the file and much consternation ensues. Other actions, such as deleting or renaming components in a project, can also leave obsolete intermediate files behind.

Some build systems have a separate "build clean" command that simply ignores the state of intermediate files and recompiles everything. In Xcode, this is a two-step process using the Clean (Command+Shift+K) command or Clean All Targets command followed by a new build. These two commands run a script that deletes the product and all intermediate files generated by that target. The next time a build is executed, everything in the target will need to be rebuilt. The Clean command only applies to the active target. The Clean All Targets command cleans out all targets in the project. Both present the dialog box shown in Figure 14-2.

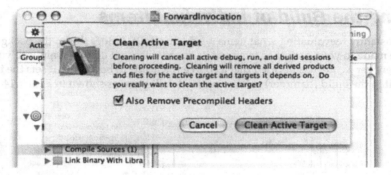

Figure 14-2

The dialog box warns you that the running application will be stopped before the target is cleaned. Remember that the product will also be deleted, and you wouldn't want to delete an application while it was still running. If you check the option to delete the precompiled headers, the precompiled headers for the target are also deleted. Precompiling the system headers is a lot of work, so saving the precompiled headers will save a considerable amount of time on the next build. Because the precompiled headers for most projects consist of *just* the headers from the system frameworks, they are also unlikely to have changed or be out of synchronization. On the other hand, it is also possible to include your own headers and symbols in your precompiled headers and, while rare, system frameworks do change from time to time. In any case, clearing the headers is the safest choice even if it adds a significant amount of time to the next build.

It's worth noting that running the Clean command is not equivalent to deleting the contents of your build folder, and is one reason that Xcode provides a command to do this. The build folder is also the repository for other project support files and possibly files from other projects. The support files are used to provide auto-completion, data modeling, predictive compilation, and other intelligent features of Xcode. Problems can arise if you delete a target, and then use the Clean command — the products of the target you deleted won't be removed, because they are no longer part of the project. If you want to ensure that everything in your project is clean, or you are just profoundly paranoid, follow these steps:

1. Close the project.

2. Trash the project's build folder.

3. Re-open and build the project.

Xcode automatically recreates any folder, index file, or build file that it needs. The build folder is normally the folder named "build" inside the project folder, unless you've relocated it. The "Build Locations" section explains how to change or identify a project's build location.

Controlling the Build of Individual Items

Xcode is constantly reevaluating what items need to be built. It does this in the background whenever changes are made to your project or to any of its source files — it doesn't wait until you start a build to decide. Whenever Xcode has decided that a source file needs to be rebuilt, it sets the item's build flag and marks it in the build (hammer) column of the details pane as shown in Figure 14-3.

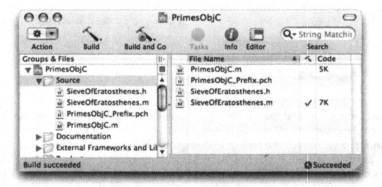

Figure 14-3

A check mark in the build column indicates that the source file will be built in the next build. You can manually uncheck that item, which tells Xcode to ignore the changes and treat the file as if it were up-to-date. Conversely, checking an unchecked item tells Xcode to rebuild the item anyway. The Touch and Untouch commands found in the Right-/Control-click contextual pop-up menus for source items, groups, and targets can also be used to set or clear the build flag of one or more source files.

You can use this ability as a more exacting alternative to a clean build. By checking a source file's build flag, you can force it to be rebuilt, even when Xcode is convinced that it doesn't need to be. The new state of the build flag persists only until Xcode decides to reevaluate the condition of the file. For example, clearing the build flag for a file and then modifying it causes Xcode to, once again, mark the file to be built.

Selecting the Active Target and Build Configuration

All build commands build the currently active target using the currently active build configuration of the currently active project. You can select the active target and build configuration from the Set Active Target and Set Active Build Configuration menus found in the Project menu. Each menu lists the targets and build configuration for the active project. Every open project maintains its own active target and build configuration. Switching between projects also switches the target and build configuration to match. (Chapter 4 discussed switching between open projects.)

The target and build configuration can also be changed from a number of other windows if you have the Active Target or Active Build Configuration menus added to the window's toolbar. You should include both in your build or project windows. It is a convenient way to switch between targets and configurations, but is also a visual indication of what you are about to build.

Changing the active target may also change the active executable. The active executable is the executable program that will be launched by any of the Run or Debug commands. (See Chapter 15 for more about executables.)

As you can see from the interface, you can only build one target at a time. If you regularly need to build two or more related targets—for example, if you have a project that builds both a client and server application—then create an aggregate target that depends on the targets you want to build as a group, and make that target the active target.

Building an Inactive Target

Although the build commands in the main menu and toolbar always apply to the active target, there is a shortcut for immediately building any of the other targets in your project. Control-/right-click a target in the target's smart group. In the contextual pop-up menu for the target you will find Build, Build and Run, Build and Debug, and Clean build commands. Selecting any of these is equivalent to making that target active, starting a build, and then switching back to the previously active target.

Partial Builds

There are a few facilities for compiling a single file without launching the entire build process. These are the Compile (Command+K), Preprocess, and Show Assembly Code commands found in the Build menu. Each is enabled whenever you are editing a program source file that belongs to the project. Selecting one of these commands compiles the file using the current, or only, target that compiles that file. The Compile and Preprocess commands are quick ways of checking that this source file compiles, without waiting for any other files or dependent targets to be built. The Preprocess command only runs the file though the compiler looking for errors. It does not replace the object code last compiled for the file, nor does it perform any other build-related steps, such as linking.

The Show Assembly Code command is a little different. It compiles the source file using flags that cause the compiler to output assembly source code for the file instead of a compiled object file. This can be instructive if you need to examine the actual machine code produced by the compiler. The assembly source file exists in the build directory and will be overwritten by the next Show Assembly Code command or the next time a clean build is run.

Xcode also includes a feature called Predictive Compilation. You turn this on in the Build tab of the Xcode preferences, explained a little later in this chapter. When this feature is enabled, Xcode quietly compiles sources files that you have, or are still, editing in the background. It does this to optimize the build process by trying to compile as many source files as it can *before* you request a build. Unless you've just made sweeping changes to a project, it's highly likely that all of your source files will already be compiled before the build begins.

While Xcode is precompiling your source files, it saves the precompiled object files in a temporary cache. Predictive compilation never overwrites any of the intermediate object files in your build folder until you start a build. When you do finally begin the build, Xcode makes one last check to see if each precompiled object file is still up-to-date. If it is, Xcode quickly replaces the intermediate object file in the build folder with the one it precompiled — skipping the need to compile the source file again. If the precompiled object file is not up-to-date, it is discarded and the build proceeds normally.

The Build Window

The build window is your central control for builds, as shown in Figure 14-4. Choose Build⇔Build Results (Command+Shift+B) to open the build window for the active project. From the build window, you can start and stop builds, monitor a build's progress, browse errors and warnings, read the detailed build logs, and even correct errors without switching to another window.

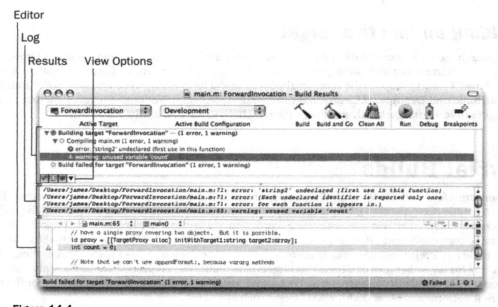

Figure 14-4

The build window's toolbar can contain a number of build-related buttons and controls. The more useful ones are the controls to display and change the active target and build configuration, the various Build buttons, and the Clean and Clean All buttons. Note that the Build button turns into Stop Build button whenever a build is in progress.

The build window is divided into three panes, some of which may be hidden or collapsed. From top to bottom, the build window consists of the build results pane, the build log pane, and an editor pane.

The build results pane shows a structured picture of the build's progress and results. The build target is shown as a group, which expands into the individual steps of the build, which themselves expand into a list of errors or warning resulting from each step. In the window previously shown in Figure 14-4, the ForwardInvocation target compiled the main.m file, which resulted in one error and one warning. The final result of the build is listed below the Building target group.

The contents of the build results pane can be filtered using two criteria, controlled by the small check mark and caution icon buttons found in the lower-left corner of the results pane. The check mark button is the "show build steps" button. When this button is selected (grey), the Building target group lists all of the steps that were executed during the build. When it is not selected, the Building target group shows only the steps currently being built and steps that resulted in errors or warnings. If the group has no steps to show — the build is finished and there are no errors or warnings to display — the group itself is hidden.

The "show warnings" button — the one with the small caution symbol — controls the display of warnings that occurred during the build. If this button is selected, both warnings and errors are displayed. If it is not selected, only errors are displayed.

The middle pane is the build log pane. It is only visible when the "show build log" button — the small text button to the right of the show warnings button — is selected. Clicking this button adds the pane and displays the detailed build log. This is the log of commands and their outputs that Xcode captures during the build. It shows exactly what tools were invoked and with what arguments. Normally this isn't of much interest because Xcode interprets the build results and organizes them for you in the build results pane. However, there are some errors that Xcode can't interpret, or possibly there are problems with the build tools themselves. Or maybe you just want to understand what Xcode is doing to build your project. Examining the build log can provide insights into exactly what happened, where, and what the results were.

Navigating Errors and Warnings

The bottom pane of the build window is a standard editor pane, exactly like the one in the project window. Selecting a line in the build results pane highlights the corresponding text in the build log, the editor pane, or both as appropriate. Clicking the warning shown in the build results pane selects both the warning message from the compiler in the build log and the line in the source file that the compiler is complaining about. Clicking the Compiling main.m line in the build results pane highlights the commands used to compile main.m in the build log. Double-clicking an error or warning jumps to the errant source file line in a separate window.

> The View⇨Zoom Editor In and View⇨Zoom Editor Out commands work equally well in the build window as they do in the project window. Double-clicking the divider bar between the editor and the rest of the build window also expands or collapses the editor pane.

The Build menu has two commands for quickly jumping to the next, or previous, build error. Build⇨Next Build Warning or Error (Command+=) selects to the next error or warning in the build results pane. If no error was selected, the first error is chosen. The Build⇨Previous Build Warning or Error (Command+Shift+=) command does the same, but in the opposite direction. As a consequence, the line in the build log and the source file line containing the error (if applicable) are also selected. If the build window is active and this is the first error selected, or if the editor pane of the build window is collapsed, a new editor window is opened with the offending line of source text selected. Otherwise, the source text is selected in the editor pane of the build window.

These two commands are especially useful because they are active outside of the build window, and even work when the build window is closed. From any project window they quickly transport you to the next, or previous, error listed in the latest build. If you are already on the last error, or first error, the commands do nothing but beep at you.

Try It Out   **Navigate Errors and Warnings**

Open a project. Make a few changes to the source code so the project does not compile: for example, comment out a semicolon at the end of a statement or rename a local variable. Build the project. Then follow these steps:

1. Show and hide the warnings in the build results pane.

2. Expand the editor pane in the build window. Click different errors and warnings.

3. Examine the contents of the Errors and Warnings smart group.

4. Double-click an error or warning.

5. Click the error or warning icon in the gutter of an editor pane (the editor's gutter must be visible).

6. Use the Next Build Warning or Error and Previous Build Warning or Error commands.

7. Correct the errors and build again.

How It Works

Errors and warnings are listed it the build results pane and in the Errors and Warnings smart group. Each compiler error and warning is a navigational link to the source code where the problem occurred.

In addition to getting you there, the editor highlights errors in the source code both in the gutter and in the scrollbar of the editor pane. Clicking an error or warning icon discloses the compiler's explanation of the error in the status bar of the window.

The Next/Previous Build Warning or Error command quickly skips to the next error or warning from the latest build, without having to navigate back to the build window or search through the source files.

Any errors or warnings generated by a build are also placed in the Errors and Warnings smart group in the project window. Selecting the entire Errors and Warnings group, or a specific file in the group, lists those errors and warnings in the details pane. Warnings in the Errors and Warnings group are not affected by the "show warnings" setting of the build window.

Xcode also displays the total number of errors from all build windows in its dock icon, as shown in Figure 14-5. This makes it practical to work in other applications while waiting for a long build to complete.

Figure 14-5

Opening and Closing the Build Window Automatically

You can set the build window to open and close automatically when a build is started or stopped. The disclosure triangle button to the right of the "show build log" button drops down a menu of choices, as shown in Figure 14-6.

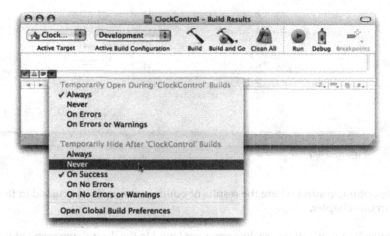

Figure 14-6

The top set of choices tells Xcode under what conditions to automatically open the build window when a build is started. The choices are Always, Never, On Errors, and On Errors or Warnings. Always causes the build window to open the instant any build is started. The two On Error choices cause the build window to open only when the first error or warning is encountered during the build process.

The second set of choices tells Xcode when to automatically close the build window again once the build has completed. On Success closes the build window only when the build completes successfully. On No Errors closes the build window after the build is complete and there were no errors. (Note that some build tools, like external build processes, may output an error message but still return a status of "success" to Xcode.) The On No Errors or Warnings only closes the window if the build completed without any errors or warning of any kind. These settings are specific to each build window. Changing them for one does not alter the behavior of other build windows.

The final option in the menu simply opens the Build settings tab in the Xcode Preferences window.

Common Build Preferences

The Build tab in the Xcode Preferences window is used to set a number of global and default build settings (see Figure 14-7).

Figure 14-7

The two Place options control where the results of builds occur and is discussed in the "Build Locations" section later in this chapter.

The Build Results Window options are the same ones found in the drop-down menu of the build window itself. The choices here are the defaults for new build windows and do not change the settings of any projects that are already open. These two options are not saved in the project document, so the next time you open a project and its build window, the Open During and Close After settings are set using these defaults.

A parallel set of options exists for the Errors and Warnings smart group in the project window. Independent of what the build window does, you can have the Errors and Warnings group automatically open or close based on the progress and success of each build. These are global settings that apply to all project windows. There is no interface for setting these options for a particular project.

The For Unsaved Files option, on the right, controls the automatic saving of source files in the project before a build begins. The Ask Before Building choice presents a standard Save All dialog box if there are any unsaved source files. (See Chapter 6 for information about the Save All dialog box.) Always Save automatically saves all open source files without asking. Never Save builds the project without regard to unsaved changed in source files. The Cancel Build choice simply blocks the build from starting if there are files with unsaved changes. Your only indication that a build has been stopped, besides the obvious fact that it didn't start, is a message in the status bar of your project's windows as shown in Figure 14-8.

You should use either the Ask Before Building or Always Save option — the Never Save choice is a very hazardous one and will inevitably result in your making a change to a file and then building your product *without* that change. This can be immensely frustrating during development.

Figure 14-8

> The automatic save options only save files belonging to the active project. This is a concern if your project contains cross-project target dependencies. If you have other projects open and have modified files in those projects, starting a build in your active project will *not* save the files belonging to those other projects. If you are using multiple projects with cross-project dependencies, you should cultivate the habit of manually saving all of your files before beginning a build.

The Continue Building After Errors option permits phases like Compile Sources to continue compiling source files even after one has failed. It's usually more efficient to concentrate on fixing the errors of just one file at a time, so stopping the build as soon as a compilation fails makes sense. However, there are rare occasions when an error in a second file is the root cause of the error in the first, in which case you'll want Xcode to show them all. Or maybe you simply prefer to fix as many errors as you possibly can before building again. For any of these cases, turn this option on. This is a global setting that affects all projects.

The Use Predictive Compilation option enables anticipatory compilation of source files while you are editing them, which was explained in the "Partial Builds" section earlier in this chapter.

Build Locations

When you start a build, Xcode (hopefully) begins producing a lot of files. The build locations determine where those files get written. There are two build locations. The product location is where the final products of a target are written. The intermediate files location is where all of the derived and intermediate files, like individual object files, are saved between builds.

Wherever the build location is, it has the same structure. Within the product location folder, Xcode creates one subfolder for each build configuration. Build configurations are discussed later in this chapter, but you should know that build configurations can produce variations of a single product. Xcode keeps each variant separate by creating a folder for each, as shown in Figure 14-9. In this example, there are two versions of the Sketch application: one built using the Deployment build configuration and a second using the Development configuration.

Within the intermediate files location, Xcode creates a single .build folder for each project. Within that folder are individual subfolders for each build configuration. Again, these are used to separate the intermediate files produced by a single target built with different build configurations. This location is also used by the project to store its project and symbol index files.

Figure 14-9

The product and intermediate files location can be the same location or different locations. As was shown in Figure 14-9, both the product and intermediate files locations are the same, so all of the build subfolders coexist in one place.

The default for a new installation of Xcode is to use a build folder within each project's folder as the location for both products and intermediate files. Technically, the build locations are set to $(SRCROOT)/build. This is a foolproof setting and works fine for all independent projects of any size or complexity. You many never have to change this setting.

However, there are some very good reasons why you might need to alter these locations. The most obvious one is to resolve cross-project product references. All product references in Xcode are relative to the product location. Within a single project this will never fail, because all of the targets in a project share a single build location. However, two projects that have separate build locations cannot reference each other's products.

Let's say you have two projects. Project A builds a static library that Project B needs to link to. In the target of the Project B you create a dependency on project A (to make sure it's up-to-date before linking), and then add the product of Project A to the link phase of Project B. With the default Xcode build locations, the link phase fails with a "library not found" error. Why? Because Xcode is expecting the library to be in the products location of Project B, along with the rest of the products. But it isn't. It's in the products location of Project A where it was produced.

This problem extends beyond Xcode. An application that loads plug-ins may be expecting those plug-ins to be in the same folder as the application. If the plug-ins are produced by a different project, they'll be somewhere else when you test your application. Or maybe your project source files are on a (relatively) slow network volume and you'd like your intermediate files written to your (relatively) fast local hard drive. The point is that there are lots of obscure reasons for moving your build locations.

The straightforward way of fixing these and similar dilemmas is to define a common build location, so the products from all projects are written to the same location. Products produced by Project A will be accessible to Project B just as if targets in Project B had produced them.

So where do you change the build locations for a project? The first option is to change the global build locations in the Build tab of the Xcode Preferences, as previously shown in Figure 14-7. The defaults are to use the project's folder for the products location and to use the products location for the intermediate files. You can specify a different location for the products folder by clicking the Customized Location radio button and entering an absolute path to the desired location, or click the Choose button and browse to the folder. The intermediate files location can be the same as the products location (wherever that might be), or it can be independent. Again, select the Customized Location and enter the absolute path to the folder. Unfortunately, you can't set a common location for the products while keeping the intermediate files location relative to the project.

The problem is that you just redefined the build locations for *every* project you open with this installation of Xcode. (That's not entirely true, but the caveat will have to wait a moment.) This may never be a problem, but there are some serious pitfalls to watch out for. The biggest problem is project and product name collisions. The intermediate and index files for a project are kept in a .build folder derived from the project's name. If you have two or more projects with the same name, they will all try to use the same index and intermediate build files. Just as bad is the situation of two or more projects that produce products with identical names. The product of one project will simply overwrite the product of the other project. These consequences can range from amusing to disastrous.

As an alternative, you can set the build locations for an individual project. This can be done through the Info window of the project, as shown in Figure 14-10.

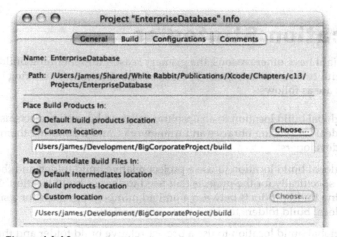

Figure 14-10

The choices for the Place Build Products In setting are Default Build Products Location and Custom Location. The default option refers to the setting in the Xcode configuration pane just examined. The custom option permits you to specify an absolute path by entering it into the field below the radio button, or by clicking the Choose button. Whenever you create a new project in Xcode, its build location is set to use the default products location. Changing the global preference changes the build location for all projects that use the default location, but it doesn't affect projects set to a custom location.

Similarly, the Place Intermediate Build Files In setting has three choices: Default Intermediates Location, Build Products Location, and Custom Location. The default location refers to the global default, which could be the product location or a custom location. The Build Products Location is whatever location was chosen for the products. Finally, the custom choice allows you to select an arbitrary location.

> You might think that the project build location settings would permit you to store
> your intermediate files in the project folder while redirecting the project's products
> to some other directory. But you would be wrong. Through a quirk of logic, overrid-
> ing the products location for the project overrides the product location for build,
> which also alters the intermediate files location.

In all cases, Xcode displays the path to the build location in the path field, even for derived paths, so
there shouldn't be any surprise as to where your files will end up.

> Whenever you change the build locations for a project, do a little housecleaning.
> Close the project and delete all of the project's build folders. This saves disk space
> and you won't have, potentially, thousands of orphaned files cluttering up your
> development folder. Xcode automatically recreates whatever build folders it needs.

Build Location Strategies

Although you might have other reasons, the primary reason for redefining build locations is to share a
single location with two or more projects. The three basic strategies for sharing build locations between
multiple projects are as follows:

❑   Set the global build location to an absolute path and have all projects use the default location.
    This is ideal for reusing libraries and frameworks, and for sharing them between multiple pro-
    jects or developers.

❑   Set the global build location to use a project relative build folder, and then override the build
    location specifically for the projects that need to share a build location. This is a good solution
    for sharing build products between a limited number of projects for a single user, without aban-
    doning local build folders for your remaining projects.

❑   Set the global build location to use a project-relative build folder and then share a single project
    folder. This is a handy trick for subdividing a single, self-contained, project into multiple projects
    while avoiding most of the build location issues inherit with the other two solutions.

The first solution is the simplest, and is probably the best choice when you're dealing with a large number
of projects or developers. You'll have to decide what a "large number" is, but keep in mind that many
professional software teams use a common build location to share built products. At the very least,
maintenance is easier if your projects don't override the build location defined in the Xcode Preferences.
Any change that needs to be made can be made in one place: the Xcode preferences.

The second solution sets the custom build location only in those projects that need to share built products.
Although this would appear to be the most concise solution, you are going to have problems sharing
those projects with other developers. Project-specific custom build locations are absolute paths stored in
the project document. Give that project to another developer, and the project won't build if the path to its
build location doesn't exist on their system. More than likely, it won't—unless you've colluded with the
other developer beforehand to ensure that it does. Using the single build location defined in the Xcode

Preferences (the first strategy) works because the only information stored in each project document is a flag to use the global build location defined by the current user—a location that can be different for every developer. This is, in a fashion, similar to the philosophy of source trees that is described in Chapter 18 and requires only that all of the developers have a custom build location defined in their preferences.

On the other hand, defining a centralized build location for all projects prevents any project from using the project folder for its build location. After you set the Xcode preferences to a custom build location, you lose the convenience of using the local build folder for all of your projects. If you have *just a few* projects that need to share built products, and you don't need to share those projects with other developers, consider setting the build location for those projects individually. The rest of your projects can continue to use their local build folder.

The third option is somewhat of a trick, but works well for small, self-contained, projects. When you place two or more projects in the same project folder, they all share the same local build folder without having to define a custom build location in Xcode or any of the projects. There's no configuration required and the projects build regardless of the current Xcode preferences.

When you're considering your options, think about *why* you need to break up your work into multiple projects. If the goal is to reuse libraries and frameworks or share projects with other developers, then one of the aforementioned solutions will meet your needs. However, if you are subdividing your project merely for the sake of organization, consider for a moment if you even need separate projects. You may be able to achieve the same goals using multiple targets, source groups, and build configuration files in a single project, eliminating all multi-project problems and complexities.

Build Settings

Other chapters mentioned build settings numerous times, so you'll probably be glad to finally be getting around to finding out about them in detail. At the risk of sounding monotonous, build settings are a set of named values used to customize the build process.

So what are build settings used for? Build settings are used by targets to determine what and how to construct their product, by the compile phases to control various compiler options, and by Xcode itself to control where files are written. Build settings are passed to compile scripts and external build processes, so those scripts and tools can make decisions and alter their behavior based on those settings. You can define your own settings, passing those values to the compiler and your own custom build scripts. A better question might be "what are build settings *not* used for?"

Later sections will enumerate some of the more important build settings and describe what they do. But for now, all you need to know is that build variables are named values, usually written as SETTING_NAME = value. To understand the interface for build settings, you need to understand how build settings are related to other build settings and how build configuration alter them.

Build settings form a layered hierarchy. Each layer has its own collection of build settings. A value in a higher layer overrides the value with the same name in lower layers. The layers, from top to bottom are: Command Line, Target, Target Configuration File, Project, Project Configuration File, Xcode Default, and Environment. Figure 14-11 shows the layers and their order.

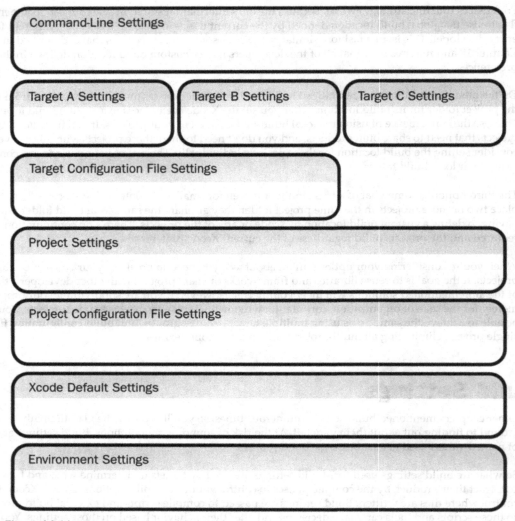

Figure 14-11

The top layer is formed by the command-line parameters passed to the xcodebuild tool. This is significant *only* if you are building Xcode projects from the command line. When you're building from within the Xcode application, this layer does not exist and can be ignored. "The xcodebuild Tool" section, later in this chapter, explains how to override build settings using the command line.

The next layer is the build settings for the current target. Most targets have a set of build settings. Aggregate targets do not have any configurable build settings — it is assumed that an aggregate target doesn't actually build anything.

Every target with build settings can also inherit a set of build settings from an Xcode configuration file. An Xcode configuration file is just another set of build settings, stored in a source file. (Creating and adding configurations file to your project is covered a little later in the "Configuration Files" section.) If a target is based on a configuration file, the settings in that file form the next layer in the hierarchy. If the target is not based on a configuration file, this layer is ignored. Multiple targets can be based on the same configuration file.

The next layer is the project layer. The project build settings are set in the project's Info window. As the name implies, there is only one set of project build settings. Like a target, the project itself can be based on an Xcode configuration file. If used, this configuration files forms another layer below the project build settings.

Below the project layer is a fixed set of build settings provided by Xcode itself. These are the default values for all projects, and comprises most of what you see when you go to edit build settings. At last count, there were over 150 default build settings. Build settings defined by Xcode also include more comprehensible names, descriptions of what each setting does, and type information that restricts the values you can set for it.

Finally, the bottom layer is the environment layer. These are values found in Xcode's or xcodebuild's execution environment. You can set these in the shell or as explained later in the "Environment Settings" section. Environment variables are a way of passing build settings to many or all projects.

For the most part, the important layers are the target and project layers. The remaining discussion often glosses over the other layers, like the command line layer, the environment layer, and the optional configuration file layers. Just remember that if those layers are present, they behave just like any other layer.

The Scope of Build Settings

Each set of build settings has a scope, or lifetime, as described in the following table. Build settings that are out of scope when a particular target is being built are inaccessible and irrelevant.

Build Setting Layer	Scope
Command-Line	Present for the duration of the build started using the xcodebuild tool.
Target Target Configuration File	Present whenever files are being processed by the build phases of the target.
Project Project Configuration File	Present when you're building a target in the project.
Xcode Defaults Environment	Always present.

Any build settings established using the command-line arguments passed to the xcodebuild tool exist for the duration of the build. This may span the building of many targets.

The build settings for a target only exist while files in that target are being processed. If dependencies cause another target to be built, the build settings used for the dependent target are the build settings belonging to that dependent target. Targets do not inherit, or in any way pass, their build settings to the build phases of other targets.

The project build settings exist whenever a target in that project is being built. If a dependency causes a cross-project target to be built, that target will be built using the project build setting belonging to the external project. Projects do not inherit or pass build settings to other projects.

Environment build settings are constant throughout a build. The environment settings used during a build are those that existed when Xcode or the xcodebuild tool was launched. When those build settings get created and their values are beyond Xcode's control.

> Custom build scripts and external build tools are free to alter any of the build settings that Xcode passes to them. However, changing them does not alter the build settings in the project. This is consistent with the UNIX model of shell variables. Altering a variable in a sub-shell does not alter that value in its super-shell. External build tools can pass modified build settings to other builds using the command line and environment layers.

Build Setting Evaluation

When a target begins to build, all of the build settings are first resolved. The basic rules for compiling the build settings are pretty simple. The build settings present during the build are the union of all sets of build settings that are in scope. If more than one set contains a value with the same name, the value defined by the top layer is used. Take a look at the build settings shown in Figure 14-12 as an example.

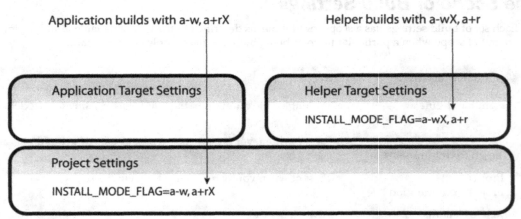

Figure 14-12

The INSTALL_MODE_FLAG setting is used to set the access permissions of executable product files. The default value of a-w, a+rX gives all users read and execute rights to the file, which is appropriate for most applications. However, this application includes a self-installing helper tool — an executable that will be copied to another location and executed there. For security purposes, you don't want the program file in the application bundle to be executable, because it should never be launched from within the bundle. To accomplish this, the INSTALL_MODE_FLAG build setting is set to a-wX, a+r in the HelperTool target. No corresponding build setting is defined in the Application target. When the

Application target is built, the four sets of build settings — Command-Line, Application Target, Project, and Environment — are combined. Only the project defines an INSTALL_MODE_FLAG setting, so the value used when building the Application target is a-w, a+rX. When it comes time to build the HelperTool target, the build sets that are in scope, which this time includes the HelperTool target settings but not the Application target set, are again merged together. Both the HelperTool target and the project define a setting named INSTALL_MODE_FLAG. The definition of INSTALL_MODE_FLAG in the target set is in a higher layer than the project, so the value from the HelperTool target is used. When it's all finished, the project produces an application that can be launched along with a BSD program file that can be read but not directly executed.

As you can see, the scope and precedence of build settings are pretty simple. That is, until build settings start referencing other build settings — which they can. This simultaneously makes build settings more powerful while complicating how build settings are resolved.

The $(VAR_NAME) syntax enables a build setting to reference any other build setting. For example, the GCC_PREPROCESSOR_DEFINITIONS build setting might be set to the value SECURE_MODE=$(SECURITY_SETTING). This build setting will cause the preprocessor macro SECURE_MODE to be defined whenever a source file is compiled using gcc. The value of the macro will be dependent on the value of the SECURITY_SETTING build setting. This setting could be defined differently, or not at all, in the project and various targets. So even though the GCC_PREPROCESSOR_DEFINITIONS setting is defined only once, its value will change whenever SECURITY_SETTINGS changes.

Figure 14-13 illustrates the order and rules used to resolve build setting references.

Figure 14-13

This project produces three applications: Problem Grapher, Algebra Solver, and Calculus Solver. Each application includes a copyright statement. Sharp Pencils wrote Problem Grapher and Algebra Solver, and Math Whiz wrote Calculus Solver.

The project defines a COMPANY setting containing a company name and a YEARS setting defining a span of years. It also defines a COPYRIGHT_STATEMENT setting that forms a complete copyright statement using the values of the other two build settings. When the Problem Grapher target is built, the value of the COPYRIGHT_STATEMENT setting is constructed by substituting the values of the YEARS and COMPANY settings where their references appear in the value. This is illustrated in Figure 14-14. Ultimately, the value of COPYRIGHT_STATEMENT is Copyright 2003, Sharp Pencils.

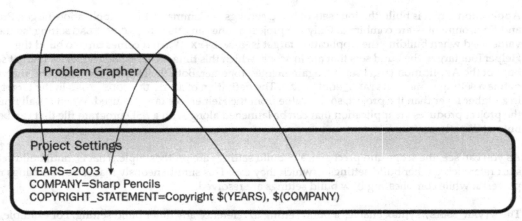

Figure 14-14

When the Calculus Solver target is built, things get a little more interesting. When Xcode resolves the references to YEARS and COMPANY, it finds values set in the Calculus Solver target (which is now in scope) that override the values in the project, as shown in Figure 14-15. Using those values instead, the COPY-RIGHT_STATEMENT setting now resolves to Copyright 2000-2003, Math Whiz. Notice how a value defined in a higher layer can alter a definition defined in a lower one.

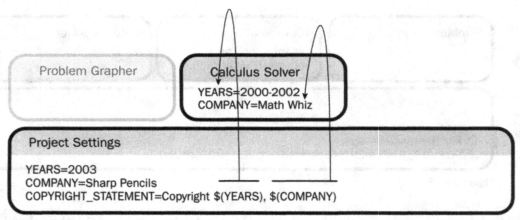

Figure 14-15

Next is the Algebra Solver target. This target is interesting because the YEARS setting contains a self-referential value. That is, the value of YEARS references the value of the YEARS setting. Xcode resolves self-referential references by obtaining the value of the setting from a lower layer of build settings. When the COPYRIGHT_STATEMENT setting references the YEARS setting, Xcode finds it in the Algebra Solver target setting. When Xcode constructs the value for the YEARS setting for that target, it finds a reference to the YEARS setting. Xcode recursively searches for another definition of the YEARS setting, but ignores layers at or above the layer containing the reference, as shown in Figure 14-16. Ultimately, the $ (YEARS) reference in the target's YEARS setting is replaced with the YEARS value set in the project, resulting in a value of 2003-2005.

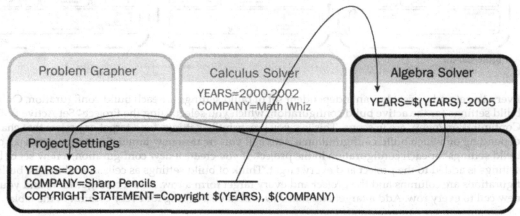

Figure 14-16

Recursive references are particularly useful for amending Xcode build settings. For example, the OTHER_CFLAGS build setting defines additional arguments that are past to the gcc compiler. If you defined just a set of flags in your target, it would override whatever the value of this setting might be in the project. Instead, you can define the value of this setting as $ (OTHER_CFLAGS) --myflag in the target. The argument --myflag is merely appended to whatever the project or environment setting was, rather than replacing it.

If there were no lower layers that contained a YEARS setting, then the reference $ (YEARS) would be replaced with an empty string. In fact, any reference to an undefined or out-of-scope build setting is replaced with nothing. Referencing an undefined build setting does not cause a build error or produce any kind of warning.

References to environment variables are treated like references to any other build setting. However, references *in* environment variables are a special case. References in an environment variable cannot refer to any non-environment layer build setting. In this example, the COPYRIGHT_STATEMENT setting could not be defined solely as an environment setting. If it was, the $ (YEARS) and $ (COMPANY) references would only be substituted if there were YEAR and COMPANY settings in the environment layer as well. Any values for YEAR and COMPANY in any other layer would be ignored.

Build Configurations

Build configurations are complete sets of build settings. Each named build configuration in a project represents a complete set of build setting for the project and all of the targets. The previous example had a project for four sets of build setting: one set for the project and three sets for the targets. If that project had three build configurations—named Alpha, Beta, and Release—then it would actually contain 12 complete sets of build settings, as shown in Figure 14-17.

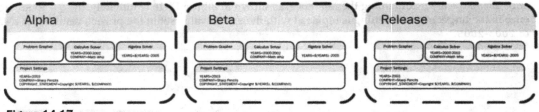

Figure 14-17

Every target and project has an independent set of build settings for each build configuration. Only the build settings for the active build configuration, which you select using the Project⇨Set Active Build Configuration menu, are in scope. This lets you create build settings for a target or project that change depending on which build configuration is active. If you create a new target, that target gets a set of build settings for each configuration in the project. If you create a new configuration, a new set of build settings is added to the project and every target. Think of build settings as cells in a table. The build configurations are columns and the project and every target form a row. Add a configuration, and you add a new cell to every row. Add a target and that row will have a setting for every column in the table.

> If you have used Xcode or Project Builder in the past (prior to Xcode 2.1), read this section carefully. Older versions of Xcode used a system of build settings and build "styles." There was only one set of build settings for each target. Each build style could then selectively override specific build settings. Although the two systems are effectively similar, the interface and conceptual structure of build styles and build configurations are significantly different.

You might be worried at this point that a complex project with five targets and four build configurations would have an unmanageable number of build setting — at least 25 complete sets of build settings, in all. Don't worry. Xcode provides several tools for visualizing build settings as a whole, editing multiple build settings at once, and moving build settings between layers. Each of these will be covered shortly.

The most common use of build configurations is to alter the compiler and linking options when producing an application for debugging versus deployment. For debugging, the application needs to be compiled with certain code optimizations turned off (code optimizations can interfere with source-level debugging) and with debug information included. Conversely, the released version of the application needs to be fully optimized, but does not need to include any debugger data (that the end-user should never need and which significantly increases the size of the application). You may also need to produce an application that's between these two extremes for performance testing. For that, you'll want an application that is fully optimized (just like the final version), but also includes all of the information used by the debugger to identify functions and variables.

This use of build configurations is so common that these are exactly the build configurations provided by Xcode templates. All Xcode project templates include two configurations, named Debug and Release. The default values for the build configurations set the compiler and linking options to those you would typically want. In the Debug configuration, optimization is turned off, ZeroLink (explained later) and debugging symbols are enabled, as are useful debugging features like Fix and Continue. The Release configuration has just the opposite settings. Optimization and normal linking are turned on, and all of the debugging aides are disabled.

Editing Build Settings

Now that you understand the hierarchy of build settings and build configurations, you should now be able to make sense of the interface for editing build settings.

Select a project or target and open its Info window, the easiest way is to double-click the project or target icon. Switch to the Build tab. A list of build settings is displayed, as shown in Figure 14-18.

Figure 14-18

The name of each setting is in the Setting column and its value is listed in the Value column. The Collection pop-up menu limits the display to only those build settings within the selected category. This in no way changes the build settings; it only limits the display to just the category of settings you want to focus on. There are over 140 default build settings in Xcode 2.2. If you're looking for something specific, this can save a lot of scrolling. Select All Settings to see them all.

Another way to quickly narrow down the list is to use the search field just to the right of the Collection menu. Enter some word or phrase in the search field. Only those settings in the current selection whose name or description contains that phrase are listed. Erase the contents of the search field, or click the small x, to restore the list.

Select one of the Xcode-defined settings and a description of the setting is displayed in the area at the bottom of the window. This is usually a brief description of what the build setting does and what its valid values are. Build settings all have names like GCC_WARN_UNUSED_VARIABLE. Some build settings are also gifted with a more comprehensible name, in this case Unused Variables. Xcode displays the friendlier name in the list, but the symbol that gets defined at build time will always be GCC_WARN_UNUSED_VARIABLE. Read the description of the build setting to learn what its actual name is. Settings that you invent do not have alternate names or description.

Try It Out **Peek at Build Settings**

Create a simple project that you can use to experiment with the effects of build settings. Here's how:

1. Create a new project based on the Command Line Tool / Standard Tool template. Name the project **Hello Build Settings**.

2. Rename the Hello Build Settings target to **First**.

3. Create a second Target using the BSD Shell Tool template. Name the target **Second**.

4. In the First target, choose Add⇨New Build Phase⇨Shell Script Build Phase. Open the Run Script build phase's Info window. In the General tab, set the shell to /bin/sh and enter the following script:

```
echo 'The build settings containing TEST:'
env | fgrep -i TEST
exit 0
```

5. Repeat step 4 for the Second target.

6. In the Project and Target build settings pane, create several different build settings that all contain the word TEST in their name or value.

7. Build a target and examine the build log (the middle pane of the build window). The script dumps the values of any build settings containing the TEST text to the build log, allowing you to easily see how Xcode ultimately defined each setting and its value.

How It Works

When Xcode runs a custom build phase script or external tool, it exports all of the current build settings for that target to the new process as environment variables. This simple script just picks out the environment variables you want to see and dumps them to stdout, which is captured in the build log pane.

As you progress through the build setting and configuration sections, use this project to experiment with editing and overriding build settings, referencing other build settings, and setting environment build settings.

As an example, I created a project build setting named TEST_VAR1. In the project, I also created TEST_VAR2=project and in the first target, I defined TEST_VAR2=$(TEST_VAR2)+target 'First'. There are also two other environment variables, TEST_ENV_VAR and TEST_LSENV_VAR, which were set globally and by hacking the Xcode application, respectively. Figure 14-19 shows the result of this build.

Figure 14-19

Edit the `fgrep` statement in the script to examine at other build variables.

The build settings editor always shows a composite view of the build settings, displaying all build settings starting with the layer that you are editing. When you're editing the build settings for a target, the Build tab lists all build settings set in this target, the target's configuration file, the project, the project's configuration file, and the Xcode defaults. If you were editing the project's build settings, it would display only the project, project configuration file, and default settings. By browsing the settings for a target, you can see what the value of every build setting will be when that target is built. Note that the Build tab never lists environment settings.

Xcode highlights build settings set in the target or project you are editing by displaying those settings using a bold font. In Figure 14-20, the Installation Directory and Strip Debug Symbols From Binary Files settings are both defined in the AlgebraSolver target. All of the other settings listed are inherited from the project and Xcode defaults. You don't have to open the project settings to see what the setting for Produce Unstripped Product will be when this target is built. Think of the Build tab as viewing a stack of transparent sheets. The view starts at the layer you are editing. Setting a value obscures your view of the same setting on a lower sheet. Settings not defined on a layer permit the setting from a lower layer to be visible. Settings in layers higher than the one you are editing are never visible.

Figure 14-20

If you want to see *only* the build settings defined in a target or project, choose Customized Settings from the Collections menu, as shown on the right in Figure 14-20. It still displays the value for the Installation Directory and Strip Debug Symbols From Binary Files settings, but all other settings from the project and Xcode are hidden. In other words, it only shows the top sheet of settings in the stack.

The remaining collection categories are broken down into groups and subgroups. Selecting the General group displays all build settings under the General category, which include all of the build settings in the Architecture subgroup through the Unit Testing subgroup. Selecting a specific subgroup displays only the settings within that subgroup.

Creating and Deleting a Build Setting

To create a new build setting, click the + button just below the list of build settings. Xcode creates a new build variable, creates a new setting entry, and places the cursor in the setting's name. Enter the name of the variable, as shown in Figure 14-21. The name you choose must be a valid build settings name. If the name you choose doesn't meet the requirements, Xcode presents a dialog box like the one on the right in Figure 14-21.

Figure 14-21

To delete a build setting, select the setting in the list and click the - button. You can only alter the layer of settings defined by the target or project you are editing. Thus, you can only delete settings that are bold — which indicate the settings defined in the layer being edited. All other settings belong to other layers, and must be deleted or edited elsewhere.

Build Setting Values

To edit the value of a setting, click or double-click the value field in the table, or select a setting in the table and click the Edit button. The one you use depends on the type of value allows for that setting. Constrained settings have controls (a check box or pop-up menu) in their Value column. To change these values, change the check box or make a menu selection. Most of the other settings are free-form string values. Double-click the Value field in the table to edit the raw string value. You can also click the Edit button or double-click the setting's name. The Edit button presents a small editing sheet for the value. The kind of sheet you get is dependent on the nature of the value. There are three common editing sheets (see Figure 14-22). There are some other specialty editing sheets and new ones are being added regularly.

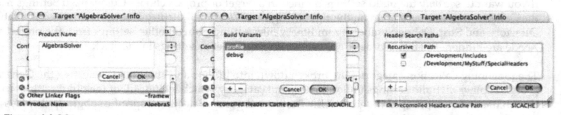

Figure 14-22

The simple string sheet, shown on the left, is for all free-form values — which include all user-defined values. Using the sheet editor for strings is more convenient when you're editing long string values, like parameter lists. Build settings that define a space-separated list of strings get the list editor, shown in the middle of Figure 14-22. Add entries using the + button and remove entries using the - button. Double-click a value to edit it, and drag values to reorder them. The setting's value is a concatenation of the individual entries in the list. Settings that are a list of paths get the path editor, shown on the right. It works just like the list editor with the addition of the Recursive column. If checked, a recursive path is appended with a **, which instructs Xcode to search the entire subdirectory tree starting at the given path. All of the specialized editors are just aides. You can easily edit the raw string value, separating list items with spaces and appending ** to the end of recursive paths, to achieve the same results.

Xcode allows you to edit the value of any build setting listed in the table. You can't actually edit the value of a setting in another layer. When you try to do this, Xcode automatically creates a duplicate setting in the current layer, and then permits you to edit its value. This is what makes editing build setting so transparent. Simply changing a setting automatically creates a new setting with the same name in the current layer with a different value, overriding the value established in the lower layer. When you do this, the build setting's name turns to bold indicating that you can now define that setting in the current layer.

To revert a setting to the previous value inherited from a lower layer, delete it. The setting's name is no longer bold and its value once again shows the value defined in the lower layer. Don't confuse "different" with "defined." Changing a build setting back to the value defined in a lower layer *does not* delete that setting. You just have a setting in a higher layer that causes the setting in the lower layer to be ignored. With a duplicate setting defined, changes to that setting in the lower layer are now ignored whenever the current set of settings is in scope.

You can also edit the name of any build setting defined in the current layer. Double-click the setting's name and edit it. Attempting to edit the name of a setting in another layer is either ignored or is equivalent to clicking the Edit button, resulting in a new setting in this layer.

Switching Between Build Configurations

Everything about editing and creating build settings to this point has assumed that that you only have one build configuration. A project with three build configurations means that there are three sets of build settings for each target.

You select which build configuration you are editing for the target or project using the Configuration pop-up menu at the top of the Build tab, as shown in Figure 14-23. To edit the build settings for a particular configuration, select that configuration from the list. You can also select the Active Build Configuration (*name*) item. The Info window always shows and edits whatever the active build configuration is. Changing the build configuration using Project⇨Set Active Build Configuration immediately changes the build settings in the Info window to match.

Figure 14-23

One of the most useful views is the All Configurations view. When you select this view, the Build tabs show a composite view of all of the settings from all configurations. It does this the same way items in a multi-item Info window are displayed (see Figure 14-24). Settings with values that are different between configurations are display as <Multiple values>. Binary options whose value is set with a check box show a hyphen.

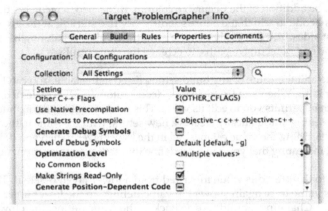

Figure 14-24

You can quickly scan the list to see which settings differ between configurations. More importantly, when you are in this view, any change you make to a setting sets that value in every configuration of the target or project. This mode is extremely useful for setting project and target settings in multiple configurations simultaneously. But it also requires some care. You can easily overwrite settings that were created for specific configuration. It is also easy to unintentionally create new build settings. In the All Configurations view, editing the value of a setting also creates that setting (with that value) in every configuration that did not previously contain that setting. Similarly, deleting a setting in the All Configurations view deletes that setting from every configuration.

As mentioned in the previous chapter, Jam-based targets do not have an All Configurations view. If you need to set a build setting for all configurations in a Jam-based target, you have no choice but to set the value individually for each configuration.

Editing Build Configurations

You manage build configurations in the Configurations tab of the project's Info window, shown in Figure 14-25. The Edit Configuration List shows the build configurations defined in the project. You can get to this by opening the Info window for the project. You can also jump there by selecting the conveniently placed Edit Configurations item from the Configuration menu of any build settings editor.

You create a new configuration by selecting an existing configuration and clicking the Duplicate button at the bottom of the pane. Remember that a build configuration represents a complete set of build settings for every target and for the project itself — you really wouldn't want to create a completely empty set of build settings. Select the configuration that is closest to the settings you want for your new configuration, duplicate it, and then go fix the differences in the build settings of the project and each target.

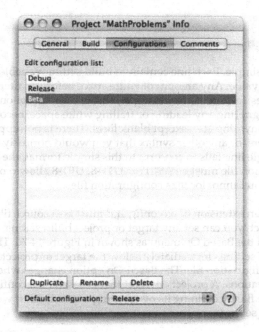

Figure 14-25

To delete a build configuration, select it in the list and choose the Delete button. A project must have at least one build configuration, so you can't delete them all. You can rename a build configuration using the Rename button or by double-clicking the configuration's name.

At the bottom of the pane is a Default Configuration selection. Use this to select the default build configuration for the project. This setting applies to cross-project targets and when you're building a project using the xcodebuild tool. When you're building a project directly within the Xcode application, the active build configuration unambiguously determines what build configuration will be used. However, subprojects and projects built with the xcodebuild tool are not as definitive. When a cross-project dependency causes a target in another project to be built, Xcode tries to use the build configuration in the external project with the same name as the one it is using for the current target. But what if a build configuration with that name doesn't exist in the other project? Furthermore, when using the xcodebuild tool, you are not required to specify which build configuration you want to use, forcing Xcode to choose for you. In both of these situations, Xcode uses the default build configuration you've specified. If the default configuration is set to "none" then the default build configuration is undefined and unpredictable. Resolve this by choosing a configuration in the menu.

Configuration Files

Target and project build settings can be based on a configuration file. A configuration file is nothing more than a specially formatted text file containing a collection of build settings. The following code demonstrates a configuration file that defines the same build settings using in an earlier example:

```
COMPANY = Sharp Pencils
YEARS = 2003
COPYRIGHT_STATEMENT = "Copyright $(YEARS), $(COMPANY)"
```

The format of the file is simple. Each line contains a build setting variable name, an equals sign (=), f
ollowed by the setting's value. Any amount of white space before or after the = and at the end of the line
is ignored. Placing quotes around values with special characters is optional. Everything between the =
and the end of the line, ignoring any leading or trailing white space, becomes the value for the setting.
The file cannot contain anything else, except blank lines. There is no support for comments, multi-line
values, escaped characters, or any other syntax that you would normally associate with a property list or
source file. If even a single line fails to conform to this simple format, the entire file is ignored. The
encoding of a configuration file must be ASCII or UTF-8. UFT-8 allows configuration files to contain
non-ASCII characters. You cannot localize configuration files.

A configuration file has an extension of .xcconfig and must be a source file in the project. After you've
added this file to a project, you can set any target or project build settings to be based on that configuration file by selecting it in the Based On menu as shown in Figure 14-26. The settings in the configuration
file form a layer of build settings immediately below the target or project. Each build configuration can
reference a different configuration file. The Based On option changes when you use the Configurations
menu to switch configurations. A project or target that is based on a configuration file can still override
any of the settings in the file by defining its own setting — exactly as it would override a setting from
any lower layer of build settings.

> The All Configurations view may not display a "mixed" value for the configuration
> file of the target or project. However, changing the Based On setting while you're in
> the All Configurations view dutifully sets the configuration file for all configurations
> to the new choice.

Figure 14-26

Adding a Configuration File

If you do not yet have a configuration file, you must create one. To create an empty configuration file and add it to the project, start by choosing the File⇨New File... command. Find and choose the Xcode Configurations Settings File template. Give the file a name and add it to the project. When asked, do not add the file to any target. Configuration files are not input files to the target's build phases; they are only used to populate the build settings.

If you already have a configuration file that exists but hasn't been added to the project, simply add it to the project like any other source file. See Chapter 5 for a quick refresher on adding source files. Again, do not add the configuration file to any targets when adding it to the project. Configuration files are part of the build infrastructure; they are not the thing being built.

Using Configuration Files

Configuration files are most useful when you have a number of targets or projects that each need to set a uniform, or at least very similar, set of build settings. Targets and projects can be based on a single configuration file. Configuration files cannot be linked to other configuration files, nested, or otherwise combined. So trying to create your own hierarchical structure of configuration files won't work. Configuration files are only an adjunct to the build settings layers defined by Xcode. Good uses of configuration files are as follows:

- ❏ Common build settings for similar product types. You might want to create a configuration for all Cocoa applications, for instance.
- ❏ Regularly used compiler or debug settings. All of your Debug build configurations in different projects could share a single MyFavoriteDebugSettings.xcconfig file.
- ❏ Build settings that are maintained externally or that can be generated programmatically. Build settings containing things like company product codes could be generated or updated by an external process.

Keep in mind the project or target can itself override anything defined in the settings file it is based on. Settings files don't have to contain exactly the values needed by all of the targets, projects, or configurations that are based on it. They only need to define the preferred values for the settings you regularly set. Think of them as your own layer of defaults, much like Xcode's default settings layer.

Moving Build Settings Around

Eventually, you'll discover that you have a build setting in a target that really needs to be in the project build settings or a build configuration file. Moving build settings around couldn't be easier, although it is not immediately obvious how.

The trick is to use the clipboard. You can cut, copy, and paste build settings between build settings panes and configuration files. When Xcode copies a build setting to the clipboard, it places a textual representation of the build setting in the clipboard using the format required by configuration files. Because of this, you can copy build settings from a build settings pane and paste them into another build settings pane, a configuration file, or vice versa.

Pasting in a build settings pane replaces any other settings defined with the same name. Cutting a build setting is equivalent to copying the setting to the clipboard and then deleting the setting. When you cut an inherited setting, only the setting's name is copied and the value is left empty. If you want to copy the value, you need to open the Build pane where the value is defined. Copying a value in the All Configurations view may result in copying the value <Multiple values>, which you'll have to edit.

Environment Settings

The environment layer of build settings must be set up outside of Xcode and they must be set before the Xcode application or xcodebuild tool are launched. Xcode uses any environment variable that conforms to the build settings naming convention. Specifically, a variable name must begin with a letter or underscore and contain only letters, numbers, or underscore characters. All letters should be uppercase.

Setting environment variable before launching the xcodebuild tool depends on the calling process. Shells such as bash and tcsh typically use some form of "export" command. For Perl, C, Java or similar programming languages, environment variables are usually assembled into a collection that is passed to the function that launches the tool. Regardless of how it is accomplished, whatever environment values are passed to the xcodebuild tool will be accessible to the build phases of each target built.

> The beginning of the build settings section stated that target and project build setting are never inherited or passed to other targets or projects. This may not always be true if your build involves shell scripts. Whenever Xcode starts an external process (a custom build script or external tool) all of the build settings for that target are resolved and passed to that process as environment variables. If that external process causes another Xcode target to be built using the xcodebuild tool, that build inherits *all* of the previous build settings as environment settings, regardless of their original scope. Thus, a setting that is defined as a target setting in one project can appear as an environment setting in a second if the second target was started by the first target using a custom build script or external build tool.

Setting environment variables for use with the Xcode application itself isn't immediately obvious. That's because you don't normally think of GUI applications of having an "environment" the way shell and BSD tools do. But, in fact, OS X provides a simple, albeit obscure, technique for defining whatever environment variables you want. These variables are available to all running applications. You can read more about it at http://developer.apple.com/qa/qa2001/qa1067.html.

The magic file is named ~/.MacOSX/environment.plist. The .MacOSX folder is an invisible folder in your login account's home directly. The environment.plist file is an XML property list file containing a list of key/value pairs. Each pair defines an environment variable that gets defined when you login. All applications you launch include these variables in their environment.

You can edit the environment.plist file using the Property List Editor or any good text editor. However, you might prefer to use a little utility called RCEnvironment, shown in Figure 14-27, which is available free from Rubicode at www.rubicode.com/Software/RCEnvironment/. It's a System Preferences panel that lets you edit your environment.plist file very much like you would edit build settings in Xcode. Remember that changes only take effect when you log in. After making changes, remember to save the file, log out, and then log back in again.

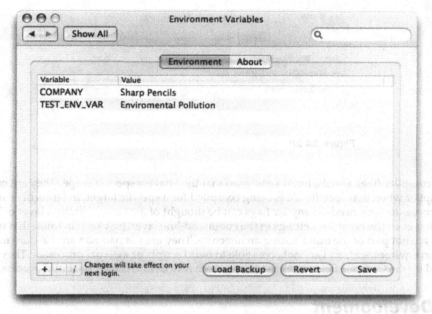

Figure 14-27

Customizing the Build

Using build settings, and a few specialized Xcode settings, it's possible to customize hundreds of details about your build. The next few sections cover various ways of customizing your build process and products. Some are special features of the Xcode application, but most are configured using build settings. The later sections will cover the more important build settings, especially ones that control the build process itself. But this book can't possibly explain them all — there are well over a hundred build settings at last count, and the number grows with each release of Xcode. The following sections hit the highlights and point you towards the documentation for the rest.

Per-File Compiler Flags

The per-file compiler flags setting is one of those "special" places where the compilation of a source files can be modified. These are literal command-line arguments, set for a particular source file and target, and passed to the compiler *only* when that source file is compiled. Each source file has a separate compiler flag for each target in the project, so you can specify one compiler flag when the file is being compiled for one target and a different compiler flag when it is compiled for another. There are no templates or documentation for these options in Xcode. You will need to consult the gcc documentation to compose your argument list correctly.

Open the Info window for a source file. If the source belongs to the active target, a Build tab appears in the Info window (see Figure 14-28). You can only edit the compiler flags for the active target. To edit the compiler flags for a different target, you must close the Info window, choose a new active target using the Project⇨Set Active target menu, and then open the Info window for the source file again.

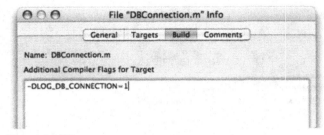

Figure 14-28

Per-file compiler flags are like build settings in that they have a specific scope. They are only passed to the compiler when that specific file is being compiled for a specific target. In terms of customizing the build process to your needs, compiler flags can be thought of as the very highest layer of build settings, overriding even the compiler settings in the command-line layer. Just keep in mind that compiler flags settings are not part of the build setting architecture. They are not named variables, are not added to the execution environment, and are not accessible to build scripts or external processes. They are a feature supplied by the Compile Sources phase as one more way of fine-tuning the build process.

Cross-Development

In Xcode, cross-development refers to developing a program for use in one or more different versions of Mac OS X. It does not mean cross-platform development, or writing a program that runs on a multitude of different operating systems or architectures. Cross-development allows you to produce a program that runs on a specific range of operating system versions (10.3.4 through 10.4.0 for example). You can also produce programs that run only on a specific version or a program that will run on any version that supports the features that application uses.

Before you can even think about doing cross-development, you have to install the cross-development SDKs. The cross-development SDKs are not part of the standard Xcode Developer Tools installation. If you did not install the SDKs when you installed Xcode, quit Xcode and run the latest Development Tools installer again. At the Install Type screen, choose the optional Cross-Development package. Or, open the Cross-Development group and choose the specific set of SDKs that you want to develop with. For example, if you have no intention of writing applications that will run on OS X system 10.2, you can skip the installation of the Mac OS X 10.2.8 SDK.

To use cross-development, you need to choose two boundaries. The end boundary is latest version of the operating system from which your application utilizes features. You might be writing and developing your application using 10.4, but your application only uses features and APIs that were present in 10.3, which should allow it run smoothly on both. This is called the Target SDK setting, and it's set for the entire project in the project's Info window as shown in Figure 14-29. When you set the target SDK, the compiler and linker will fail if you try to reference symbols, functions, or types that did not exist when that version of the operating system was released. Understand that this in no way prevents your application from running on later versions of the operating system. It simply means that Xcode will prevent you from producing an application that uses the features of newer operating systems — references that might cause your program to malfunction when run on older versions.

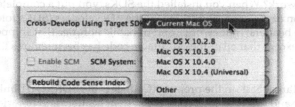

Figure 14-29

The beginning boundary is the deployment target, set using the Mac OS X Deployment Target (MACOSX _DEPLOYMENT_TARGET) build setting (see Figure 14-30). This sets the earliest version of the operating system your application will run on. Whereas the Target SDK setting is purely a compile time setting, the Deployment Target setting is both a development setting and a runtime setting. At compile time, this build setting flags certain framework and library references as "weak." So your application can link to a function that was introduced in 10.4, but still load on a system running 10.3. (Note that this doesn't mean you can successfully call that function in 10.3; it just means the program will load and start running.) This setting is also included in the Info.plist of your application bundle and tells the operating system not to allow your application to load if the minimum operating system requirement is not met. This may, or may not, have anything to do with what features your application uses. Maybe you have never tested your application on Mac OS X version 10.2 and you don't want anyone else trying.

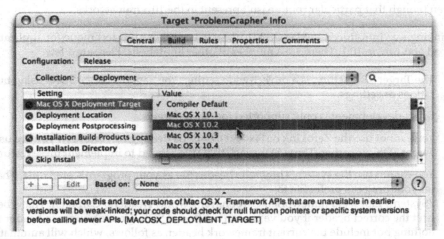

Figure 14-30

Both of these boundaries have defaults that are set for new projects. The default for the Target SDK is to compile and link against the operating system frameworks and libraries currently installed on your development system. This setting means that your program can use whatever APIs are currently installed on your computer. The default for the Deployment Target is Compiler Default, which really means "none." The operating system will do its best to load and link your application to the available APIs at runtime. This will fail if your application has "hard" links to APIs that don't exist.

So how does this all work? When you installed the SDKs, you put a complete set of system frameworks for each major version of the operating system in the /Developers/SDKs folder. Each folder contains a complete copy of the headers, frameworks, and dynamic libraries that shipped with that version of the operating system — except that all of the executable code has been removed. They are all "stub" libraries.

When you choose a Target SDK in the project, XCode sets the SDKROOT build settings. This is the path used by the compiler and linker to read all of the system headers and libraries your program links to. (Do not try to change its value using a build setting.) When you set the Target SDK for Mac OS X 10.3, it is just as if you were writing and compiling your program on a system running 10.3. The compilers and linkers know nothing about new features added in later versions of the OS, and won't let you use them. If you have an SDK installed in a non-standard location, use the Choose button below the Cross-Development Using Target SDK option in the project's Info window. Set it to the root path of the SDK you want to compile and link against. Note that if your project produces mixed architecture binaries, you must select one of the "universal" SDKs (see the next section for details).

The Deployment Target is a little more complicated. The headers in the SDK use the MACOSX_DEPLOY-MENT_TARGET setting to define special macros. These macros identify API symbols that did not exist in earlier versions of the operating system. The value of the build setting determines which symbols are affected. For example, say your application references a function that was added in 10.4. If run under 10.3, this function isn't present. Normally this would cause your application to fail before it even got started. By compiling your application with a deployment target of 10.3, it tells the compiler and linker to make a special "weak" reference to that symbol in the system framework. Your program will load and run, even though that particular routine isn't present in the 10.3 frameworks.

Weak linking was introduced in Mac OS X 10.2, so you can't use this technique for applications that must load and run on 10.1. There are a number of other limitations. Here are a few:

❑ The Target SDK setting is a project-wide setting. You cannot change SDKs using build configurations or settings.

❑ Cross-development is only supported for native targets.

❑ You cannot use the ZeroLink or Fix and Continue debugging features if you are using the 10.2.7 Target SDK, or earlier. These SDKs lack the APIs needed to implement these features.

❑ You cannot use the system's umbrella header file as your program's prefix file. That is, you can't set your project's prefix file to /System/Library/Frameworks/Carbon.framework/Headers/Carbon.h. That's because this isn't the correct header if you've chosen a different SDK. Create your own header that does nothing but include the current framework header, as follows, which will automatically include the Carbon.h header from whatever SDK you have selected:

```
#include <Carbon/Carbon.h>
```

There are a number of other, more obscure limitations and caveats. To find out about them, refer to the "Cross-Development Programming Guide." To locate this document, go to the *Xcode Reference Guide*, locate the Tools group, and then the Xcode topic. The "Cross-Development Programming Guide" is listed there. Also check out the SDKExample project. This demonstrates how to use weak linking for functions in a newer version of the OS, and then check to see if those functions are available at runtime.

Building Universal Binaries

Prior to 2004, Xcode only produced PowerPC executable binaries. That's because this was the only processor architecture that Mac OS X supported. Recently, Apple Computer has added two new architectures to the Mac OS X pantheon: 64-bit PowerPC and Intel. Xcode can compile your program for any or all of these architectures when you build your project. It does so by repeatedly compiling your application for each architecture and then storing all of the resulting versions in a single multi-architecture binary (MAB) file — a file format which Mac OS X has supported for a long time. Binaries that contain executable code for multiple architectures are referred to as Universal Binaries.

To determine which architectures you want to build, set the Architectures (ARCHS) build setting. You will find this in the Architectures collection. When you double-click the setting name, the architecture settings editor sheet appears (see Figure 14-31). Select the architectures you want to build.

Figure 14-31

The Architectures (ARCHS) setting is a space-delimited list of architectures to be built. The names of the architectures are ppc, ppc64, and i386 for 32-bit PowerPC, 64-bit PowerPC, and Intel respectively. Instead of using the editor sheet shown in Figure 14-31, you can edit the value of the setting directly by double-clicking its value. You will have to use this alternative method to add the ppc64 architecture, which is not included in the user interface.

The NATIVE_ARCH fixed-build setting defines the architecture of the system you are currently developing on. By default, the ARCHS setting is set to $(NATIVE_ARCH), which means that Xcode will compile your program to execute on the architecture of the computer you are currently using. If your project has build configurations for debugging or performance analysis, set the Architectures setting in those configurations to $(NATIVE_ARCH) — even if your Release configuration produces a universal binary. You can only debug code you can execute on your system — there's little point in building architectures for testing that you can't test.

The ARCHS setting is tempered by the VALID_ARCHS build setting. This setting does not appear in the Xcode interface, but defaults to ppc ppc64 i386 — in other words, all of the architectures that Xcode knows how to build. Xcode only builds the architectures listed in this setting. Setting VALID_ARCHS to ppc ppc64 would limit the project to producing only 32-bit and 64-bit PowerPC binaries, even if other project settings request the Intel architecture.

A number of build settings have _$(ARCH) variants. That is, some build settings have alternate names suffixed using the architecture being built. For example, the Other Linker Flags (OTHER_LDFLAGS) build setting contains flags for the linker. When linking a program built for the PowerPC architecture, the build actually uses the value found in OTHER_LDFLAGS_ppc. If OTHER_LDFLAGS_ppc is not defined, it uses the value of OTHER_LDFLAGS. By manually defining a build setting named OTHER_LDFLAGS_ppc, you can specify linker flags that will *only* be used when linking a 32-bit PowerPC program. The build settings that have $(ARCH) variants are as follows:

- ❑ SDKROOT
- ❑ OTHER_CFLAGS
- ❑ OTHER_LDFLAGS
- ❑ OTHER_LIBTOOLFLAGS
- ❑ MACOSX_DEPLOYMENT_TARGET
- ❑ LD
- ❑ LDPLUSPLUS

Here are a few other prerequisites to building universal binaries:

- ❑ To build non-native architectures, you must set your target SDK to one of the "universal" SDKs. (The previous "Cross-Development", section covered setting target SDKs.)
- ❑ The Architectures (ARCHS) build setting only works with native targets.
- ❑ You targets must be compiled using version 4.0, or later, of the gcc compiler.

Finally, recompiling your program for another architecture is no guarantee that it will work. Subtle differences in pointer sizes and byte order can cause your application to fail. Refer to the "Universal Binary Programming Guidelines" and the "64-Bit Transition Guide" in the ADC Reference Library for additional details.

Disallowing ZeroLink

Another special build setting is Build⇨Allow ZeroLink. Prior to Xcode 2.2, the only way to enable or disable ZeroLink was to change the ZeroLink build setting (see the "Linker Settings" section). This could be inconvenient in projects that have many separate definitions of the ZeroLink setting. As you'll discover in the next few chapters, there are many situations where ZeroLink interferes with the debugger and other analysis tools. Consequently, disabling ZeroLink is a common practice when testing.

If the Build⇨Allow ZeroLink item is checked, ZeroLink is controlled by the ZeroLink build setting in the project. This is equivalent to the behavior in Xcode 2.1 and earlier. If this item is unchecked, ZeroLink is forcibly disabled for all builds, ignoring all ZeroLink build settings in the project.

Build Settings in Detail

Many of the Xcode-defined build settings have more descriptive and easier-to-understand titles than the actual build setting variable names. Xcode displays the build setting title when you edit build settings, but it is always the actual build setting name that is used in scripts and by the Xcode tools. It is easier to read and understand Symbol Ordering Flags than it is to remember what the SECTORDER_FLAGS setting does.

When listing Xcode-defined build settings, this book uses the form "Full Title (NAME)" to describe each setting. Use the Full Title when you're looking for a setting in the Xcode interface. Use the NAME when you're referencing build settings in scripts or in build-setting values.

> Build settings fall roughly into two categories: modifiable build settings that alter the behavior of the build process and informational build settings created by Xcode. The latter are not intended to be changed. They are for use in other build setting values, custom scripts, and external processes and provide you with information about what is being built and how. Changing an informational build setting can lead to undesirable results.

Browsing the build settings in the Build tab of the target or project can be very instructional. The major build settings are described here. If you see a build setting that's not covered in this chapter, search the Xcode documentation for its name. The Xcode release notes cover most new and existing build settings.

Products

Product Name(PRODUCT_NAME)	This is, quit literally, the name of the product produced by the target. To change the name of your target's product, edit this build setting. Note that the final product name is actually a little more complicated if it includes an extension or is in a wrapper (bundle). See the EXECUTABLE_PATH settings.

Info.plist files

These settings control how the Info.plist file is generated for targets that produce bundles, as described in the following table.

Info.plist File (INFOPLIST_FILE)	This is the file in your project that will become the Info.plist file for your product.
Preprocess Info.plist File (INFOPLIST_PREPROCESS)	If this flag is set, then INFOPLIST_FILE is run through the gcc preprocessor. This allows you to use preprocessing macros and #if statements in your source Info.plist file.
Info.plist Preprocessor Prefix File (INFOPLIST_PREFIX_HEADER)	If your Info.plist file is preprocessed, this prefix file is read by the compiler first.
Info.plist Preprocessor Definitions (INFOPLIST_PREPROCESSOR _DEFINITIONS)	Space-separated list of macro definitions passed to the compiler when pre-processing the Info.plist file. Use this as an alternative to, or as an adjunct to, using a prefix file.

Search Paths

The search path settings determine where compilers and linkers look for headers and other files referenced only by their name or partial path. Each build setting is a space-separated list of paths. If a path itself contains a space or some other special character, it must be quoted in the list.

Each path specifies a specific folder to search. If the path ends in **, Xcode also searches any subfolders for the file it is looking for. Xcode always searches each folder for the file first, before looking in any subfolders.

Many of the paths in these settings refer to headers and libraries in the system framework folders. These would be paths that start with /System/Library/Frameworks. When you're building using a Target SDK, Xcode automatically prefixes any system framework path with $(SDKROOT) so that it correctly refers to the corresponding folder in the current SDK.

Header Search Paths (HEADER_SEARCH_PATHS)	The paths where the gcc compiler and other tools will look for included files. System paths are prefixed with $(SDKROOT).
Library Search Paths (LIBRARY_SEARCH_PATHS)	The folders where the linker will look for libraries. System paths are prefixed with $(SDKROOT).
Framework Search Paths (FRAMEWORK_SEARCH_PATHS)	Paths for frameworks, used mostly to locate framework headers. System paths are prefixed with $(SDKROOT).
Rez Search Paths (REZ_SEARCH_PATHS)	Paths for the Rez resource compiler.

Pre-compiled Headers and Prefix Headers

Pre-compiled headers are a saved compiler state containing all of the definitions defined in some source headers. It takes time to interpret and construct the type, class, and constants defined in a large group of headers. Yet, most headers do not change at all between builds. By saving the compiled form of a commonly used set of headers, the compiler avoids the need to repeat that work for every source file in your project.

You begin by creating what's called a prefix header with an extension of .pch. This is a source file that does nothing but include (#include) the headers you want access to in all of the source files in a target. A typical prefix header is shown in the following code:

```
#ifdef __OBJC__
    #import <Cocoa/Cocoa.h>
#endif
```

You can also include other global defines or headers which you expect every source file to need and you do not expect to change often. Xcode compiles this file first, and then automatically "prefixes" it to every source file it compiles. It is just as if you manually inserted #include "MyPrefixHeader.h" as the first line of every source file in your project. Most application project templates already include a prefix header, so look in your project before creating a new one.

Prefix Header (GCC_PREFIX_HEADER) The header to include at the beginning of every source file.

Precompile Prefix Header (GCC_PRECOMPILE_PREFIX_HEADER)   When set to YES, this causes the prefix header to be precompiled and saved between builds. If you use prefix headers, this should be turned on.

C Compiler

The gcc compiler is by far the largest consumer of build settings. Most apply to specific settings for the gcc compiler. You can browse them in the build settings editor under the GNU C/C++ Compiler category. Most are self-explanatory. You can refer to the gcc man page or the gcc manual at http://gcc.gnu.org/onlinedocs/ for more in-depth description of the various options and switches.

The following table describes some of the more generic C compiler build settings.

Preprocessor Macros (GCC_PREPROCESSOR_DEFINITIONS)	A space-separated list of macro definitions that will be predefined by gcc before each source file is compiled. Identical to inserting a #define MACRO value statement at the beginning of each file. The form for each definition in the list is either MACRO or MACRO=value. If the definition contains special characters, then it needs to be surrounded by quotes.
Preprocessor Macros Not Used in Precompiled Headers (GCC_PREPROCESSOR_DEFINITIONS _NOT_USED_IN_PRECOMPILED _HEADERS)	Just like Preprocessor Macros, but these are defined after the prefix file is included. If your prefixed headers do not need the definitions defined on the gcc command line, then they should be in this build setting. Otherwise, Xcode must recompile your prefix headers whenever these values change.
GCC_VERSION	This build setting is obsolete. It controls which version of the compiler to use. Don't use it. Change the build rules for your target instead. This build setting will probably disappear in the future, so you might as well use the correct configuration now, rather than having your project break later.
Other C Flags (OTHER_CFLAGS) Other C++ Flags (OTHER_CPLUSPLUSFLAGS, OTHER_CFLAGS_$(VARIENT), PER_ARCH_CFLAGS_$(ARCH))	These are open-ended build settings that let you pass whatever gcc compiler arguments you want. The Other C Flags are passed to the compiler when compiling C and Objective-C source. The Other C++ Flags are passed when compiling C++ and Objective-C++ source. The $(VARIENT) and $(ARCH) forms can be defined to pass a different set of flags when compiling a specific variant or architecture. See the "Building Universal Binaries" section for an explanation.

Java Compiler

These build setting are used only when compiling Java code, as described in the following table.

JAVA_COMPILER	The Java compiler that will be used to compile all Java source files. Normally, this is /usr/bin/javac.
JAVA_COMPILER_DEBUGGING_SYMBOLS	Set this option to include debugging information in the compiled .java file. This is necessary to debug Java applications using the Java debugger.
JAVA_COMPILER_DISABLE_WARNINGS	Turn this on if you don't want to see any Java warning. Turn on the deprecated warnings setting to suppress warnings about deprecated APIs.
JAVA_COMPILER_DEPRECATED_WARNINGS JAVA_COMPILER_TARGET_VM_VERSION	The target VM for the compiled Java code. It should be a major version number like 1.1, 1.2, 1.3, 1.4, or 1.5. This tells the compiler to produce byte code compatible with the specified version of the Java VM interpreter.
JAVA_COMPILER_SOURCE_VERSION	This setting tells the compiler which version of Java the source file was written for. Like the VM version setting, it should be a major Java release version number. This tells the compiler to prohibit use of features in newer versions of the Java language.
JAVA_MANIFEST_FILE	The path to the manifest file to be used when assembling a .jar file.

Other Compilers

Other compilers also use build settings. The two described in the following table let you pass arguments to the lex and yacc compilers.

LEXFLAGS	Command arguments passed to the lex compiler.
YACCFLAGS	Command argument passed to the yacc compiler.

Linker Settings

Linker settings control the ld linker, invoked for any compiler that produces object code files that need to be linked to create a binary executable. The following table describes these settings.

Library Search Paths (LIBRARY_SEARCH_PATHS)	See the earlier "Search Paths" section.

EXECUTABLE_PATH EXECUTABLE_NAME Executable Prefix (EXECUTABLE_PREFIX) Executable Suffix (EXECUTABLE_SUFFIX) Executable Extension (EXECUTABLE_EXTENSION)	The executable path is the complete path to the executable binary that will be produced by the linker. By default, it's constructed from the prefix, name, and suffix. The name is, by default, the product name (PRODUCT _NAME). The suffix is a period and the extension. By selectively redefining some of these settings, you can alter the extension, location, and name of the executable.
Zerolink (ZERO_LINK)	Turn this on to enable Zero Link. Zero Link is a technology that allows the linker to skip most of the work of linking the application to the dynamic libraries it needs at runtime. Instead, most of the work of linking to the individual symbols in a library is put off until the very last moment—when the application finally calls that function. The advantage is that it takes almost no time to link your application and start it running. This is a huge time-saver when you're debugging. Turn it off when you produce your final application, or if you suspect that Zero Link is causing other problems with your application.
Other Linker Flags (OTHER_LDFLAGS, OTHER_LDFLAGS_$(VARIENT), OTHER_LSFLAGS_$(ARCH), OTHER_LDFLAGS_$(VARIENT)_$(ARCH))	Like the "other" compiler flags setting, this set of settings let you pass whatever additional command-line arguments you need to the linker. The unqualified version passes these arguments to every link. The $(VARIENT) and $(ARCH) versions only pass their arguments when that particular variant and/or architecture is being linked.

Kernel Modules

If you're producing a Kernel module, you'll probably need to use some of the settings described in the following table.

MODULE_VERSION	The version declared in the module's stub.
MODULE_START MODULE_START	The names of the module's start and stop routines.

Deployment

Deployment settings control the deployment phase of a build. This is the final phase, where the finished products are cleaned up, polished, shrink-wrapped, and generally made ready to ship.

Deployment post-processing is performed whenever the DEPLOYMENT_POSTPROCESSING build setting is set to YES. This setting is also set to YES if you build a project using the xcodebuild tool and pass it the install argument. Deployment post-processing consists of:

❑ Stripping the binary of debugger symbols and unnecessary linkage information.

❑ Running any copy files or script phases that have the "only run when installing" flag set. (See Chapter 13 for more about copy file and script phases.)

❑ The ownership and permissions of the final product are set.

The following table describes the deployment settings.

Deployment Postprocessing (DEPLOYMENT_POSTPROCESSING)	If set to YES, deployment post-processing is performed.
DEPLOYMENT_LOCATION	If this is set, the products are built in the deployment location instead of the normal build location. See the INSTALL_PATH and related build settings to control where the deployment location is.
Installation Directory (INSTALL_PATH)	The path where the products for this target should be placed. This path is relative to $(INSTALL_DIR). For example, the install path for a BSD tool might be /usr/bin. The install path for a framework would be /Library/Frameworks.
INSTALL_DIR	The path where all of the project's products are installed. When running as a normal user, this path defaults to $(DSTROOT)/Users/$(USER). This causes all products to be installed in the user's local domain. Xcode does not run as root, so the local domain is typically the only location it can install into.
Strip Debug Symbols from Binary Files (COPY_PHASE_STRIP)	If this is set, the executable binaries are stripped of debugger information. Normally you don't have to set this, as stripping of deployed products should happen automatically. Set this if you are including code built by some external process or outside of Xcode altogether.
UNSTRIPPED_PRODUCT	If YES, the normal product stripping performed by post-processing is, instead, *not* performed.
Skip Install (SKIP_INSTALL)	If this and Deployment Location are both set, products are deployed instead to $(TARGET_TEMP_DIR)/UninstalledProducts. Use this for targets the generate products that are used by, but not included with, the final deployed products. This could include, for example, a static library.

DSTROOT	The destination folder for installed products. Products are "installed" within this folder using relative paths to their final location. For example, a BSD tool that installs a tool might be installed in $(DSTROOT)/bin. You might think that the normal value for DSTROOT would be /, but you'd be wrong for two reasons. It would be very surprising to novice Xcode users if in the process of building a project they started overwriting installed system components. Also, most of the locations in / are not writable unless root privileges are obtained, and Xcode does not normally run as root. Instead, this folder is a "picture" of what the final installation should look like. For normal builds, this is a temporary location or a folder within the build folder. To build and install a product directly in the system, set DSTROOT to / and run the xcodebuild tool as root.
Install Owner (INSTALL_OWNER) Install Group (INSTALL_GROUP) Install Permissions (INSTALL_MODE_FLAG)	When DEPLOYMENT_POSTPROCESSING is on, these settings determine the owner, group, and UNIX access privileges of the deployed product. These default to $(USER), $(GROUP) and a-w, a+rX, respectively.

Build Information

The rest of the build settings covered here are informational. That is, you shouldn't try to set these in the build settings in an attempt to influence how Xcode builds your product. Instead, most of these are build settings that are set by Xcode based on other information you have already configured in the project, or reflect specifically what Xcode is doing. For example, Xcode sets the TARGET_NAME build setting to the name of the target currently being built. You can use this information in custom scripts or external build tools, or reference it in other build settings. What you shouldn't do is try to redefine it.

Because of this, most informational build settings do not show up in the Build tab where project and target build settings are edited. The following table describes the informational build settings. (Also refer to Chapter 13 about the build settings that are defined when custom scripts or build rule wrapper scripts are executed.)

ACTION	This setting will be either build or clean, depending on what kind of build Xcode is performing.
PROJECT_NAME	The name of the project being built.
CONFIGURATION	The name of the build configuration that is active.
TARGET_NAME	The name of the target being built.
TARGET_BUILD_DIR	The path in the build folder where the products of this target should be written.

`TARGET_TEMP_DIR`	The path used for temporary files while building a target. Custom build scripts should write any temporary files they generate into this directory.
`PROJECT_TEMP_DIR`	A temporary folder for use by any build process in the project.
`SRCROOT`	The project folder.
`SDKROOT`	Described earlier in the "Cross-Development" section.
`OBJROOT`	The top folder where intermediate object files are
`SYMROOT`	The "symbol-rich" product location. This is where products are written before they are stripped.

Tools

To avoid having to hard-code the path of various build tools and to have the ability of redefining which tool to use for all phases of a build, the following build settings are defined:

ASM	GATHERHEADERDOC	MKDIR	REZ
CC	HEADERDOC2HTML	MV	RM
CD	JAR	NMEDIT	RPCGEN
CHMOD	JAVA_COMPILER	OSAC	SED
CHOWN	JAVACONFIG	OSAL	SH
CP	LD	OSAS	STRIP
DITTO	LEX	PBXCP	TOUCH
ECHO	LIBTOOL	RANLIB	UNZIP
EGREP	LN	REGGEN	XARGS
FIXPRECOMPS	MAKEPSEUDOLIB	RESMERGER	YACC
FIND	MERGEINFO	RESOURCE_PRESERVING_CP	ZIP

Each of these settings contains a path to the executable tool of the same name. Thus, if you wanted to invoke the Java compiler in a build script, use the statement `${JAVA_COMPILER}` instead of `/usr/bin/javac`. If at some point you decide to use a different Java compiler, both your scripts and Xcode will still be using the same one.

Standard System Locations

The build settings described in the following table may be useful for defining installation locations and for locating tools, plug-ins, templates, or other resources in your build scripts. Each gets defined with a path to one of the standard locations defined by the system or the current release of the Xcode tools.

SYSTEMS_APPS_DIR	/Applications
SYSTEM_ADMIN_APPS_DIR	/Applications/Utilities
SYSTEM_DEVELOPER_DIR	/Developer
SYSTEM_DEVELOPER_APPS_DIR	/Developer/Applications
SYSTEM_DEVELOPER_DOC_DIR	/Developer/Documentation
SYSTEM_DEVELOPER_RELEASENOTES_DIR	/Developer/ADC Reference Library/releasenotes
SYSTEM_LIBRARY_DIR	/System/Library
LOCAL_LIBRARY_DIR	/Library
USER_LIBRARY_DIR	~/Library
XCODE_APP_SUPPORT_DIR	/Library/Application Support/Apple/Developer Tools

The xcodebuild Tool

The development tools include an xcodebuild command-line tool for building Xcode projects. The xcodebuild tool is installed in your /usr/bin directory by the developer tools installer, so you do not have to add the /Developer/Tools directory to your shell path to use it. The installer also installs a man page for xcodebuild.

Having the ability to build Xcode projects via a command-line tool provides a great deal of flexibility in your development workflow. You can build complex shell scripts to build different product configurations automatically. You could schedule nightly builds of large projects. You can integrate Xcode projects into other make tools, like gnumake or Ant. Or maybe you'd just like to write an XcodeBuild Dashboard Widget.

Besides being able to drive the build process externally, you can also use xcodebuild to add a layer of intelligence inside Xcode. Using custom build scripts and external build targets, you can invoke scripts that make decisions, and then build another target or project using xcodebuild. Here's an example. One limitation of Xcode targets is that you can't change the input files to a target based on a build configuration. That is, you can't have a target that links to one library when built using one build configuration and a different library for another. But you could easily create two targets: MyApp-Release and MyApp-Debug. A custom script start can examine the build settings and build the appropriate target using something like xcodebuild -target MyApp-${CONFIGURATION}. The possibilities are almost limitless.

Using the xcodebuild Tool

To use the xcodebuild tool, the working directory must be set to the project folder. The tool does not accept a path to a project folder or document elsewhere. When you execute xcodebuild, you can optionally specify the name of the project, the target, and the build configuration to be built as arguments. If any are omitted, xcodebuild will choose a project, target, and build configuration for you.

> xcodebuild reads and respects the Xcode preferences you've defined. However, preferences are stored on a per-user basis. If you run xcodebuild under a different user ID, namely root, the Xcode preferences used will be those of that other user. Unless you've run and configured the Xcode application while logged in as that user, there will be no Xcode preferences file, and xcodebuild will use the defaults for all settings.

A project name can be specified using the -project projectname argument. This name is the complete file name of the project document, including its extension. If this argument is absent, xcodebuild finds and builds the one and only project document in the folder. If there is more than one project, xcodebuild throws an error and stops. This argument is only needed for project folders that have multiple project documents.

You can choose a target using the -target targetname argument. If this argument is omitted, the first target defined in the project is built. For projects you intend to build using xcodebuild, arrange your targets so that your top-level aggregate target is the first target in the Targets group. That way, you don't have to specify a target for your most common builds. Alternatively, you can use either the -activetarget or -alltargets switch. The -activetarget switch builds the last active target set in the Xcode application. The -alltargets switch builds all of the targets in your project; something you can't do in Xcode, except for clean builds.

The -configuration configurationname switch selects a build configuration to use. You can specify the build configuration or use the -activeconfiguration switch instead. These switches select either the named build configuration or the last active build configuration set in the Xcode application. If both are omitted, the default build configuration is used. Go to the Configurations tab of the project's Info window to set the default build configuration for the project.

There are two additional arguments used to modify the build. The first is the build action. This can be one of the values described in the following table.

build	Build the target or targets.
clean	Runs a clean build on the target or targets.
install	Perform a build, enabling all deployment post processing phases. This option sets the DEPLOYMENT_POSTPROCESSING build setting. You should define the DSTROOT location if you want the final products installed someplace other than the build folder.
installsrc	Copies the source of the project to SRCROOT. Rarely used.

If you don't specify any action, build is assumed. You can specify more than one action. The actions will be executed in order, just as if you had invoked the xcodebuild tool multiple times. For example, `xcodebuild clean build` first runs a clean build followed by a normal build.

You can also pass build settings to the xcodebuild tool. Build settings passed as arguments to xcodebuild supercede any other build settings defined elsewhere. See "The Scope of Build Settings," earlier in this chapter. The syntax for a build settings is `SETTING_NAME=value`. Each setting is a separate argument. The shell may require you to quote the contents of some build settings. You can include as many build settings as will fit on the command line. The following listing shows xcodebuild being passed two build settings: `DSTROOT` and `DEPLOYMENT_LOCATION`:

```
xcodebuild DSTROOT=/ DEPLOYMENT_LOCATION=YES install
```

There are three miscellaneous commands you can pass to the xcodebuild tool, as described in the following table.

`-version`	Outputs the version of the xcodebuild tool to stdout.
`-list`	List the names of the targets and the build configurations defined in the project. The active target and both the active and default build configurations are all noted. No build is performed.
`-help`	Outputs a concise summary of xcodebuild's argument syntax.

Compatibility

xcodebuild is capable of building .xcodeproj (Xcode 2.1 and later) documents as well as earlier .xcode project documents. If you run xcodebuild without specifying a project document name, it first searches for an .xcodeproj document and reads that if found. If there is no .xcodeproj document present, it looks for a .xcode document. In the latter case, xcodebuild upgrades the .xcode document, turning it into an .xcodeproj document, and then builds using that .xcodeproj document. This intermediate .xcodeproj document exists only in memory, and is discarded once the build is complete.

Distributed Builds

One of the more amazing features of Xcode is distributed builds. It's not so much the technology that performs it, which is sophisticated to be sure, but how incredibly easy it is to set up and use.

Distributed builds allow the compilation of source files to be distributed among a group of computers, where they can be compiled in parallel. Every build can call upon the resources of two or, if you have them, more than a dozen computers to simultaneously compile the files in your project. This allows a single developer to harness the power of other (probably) idle machines on their network, such as file servers. Teams of users can share and make more effective use of their resources. It's also a great equalizer. A team member editing programs on a MacMini can harness nearly the same power for their builds as the next developer, using a dual-processor G5.

Here are a few prerequisites and limitations to using distributed builds:

❑ All machines must be accessible via TCP/IP.

❑ All systems must be running the *exact* same version of the operating system and compiler. When you're upgrading your operating system or Xcode, perform the upgrade on all of your development machines simultaneously. This ensures that there is no difference between compilers and the system frameworks between distributed machines.

❑ All computers must be of the same architecture. PowerPC computers can only distribute builds to other PowerPC-based systems.

❑ Distributed building only distributes the Compile Sources phase of native targets for C language files. This includes C, C++, and Objective-C. Java, AppleScript, Link, Copy Files, custom scripts, and Jam-based targets can't be parallelized. Precompiling headers, linking, and product packaging are all performed on the local machine.

❑ To be effective, you need a fairly high-speed network. 100MB Ethernet is considered a minimum, with 1GB Ethernet or better preferred. You won't get much benefit from distributed builds over a wireless network. Remember that FireWire can be daisy-chained to create a very high-speed TCP/IP network.

❑ Firewalls can block distributed builds. Computers employing firewalls must allow traffic on ports 3632 and 7264.

Using distributed builds couldn't be easier. Every machine with Xcode installed can be a provider (will compile files for other developers), a client (will distribute builds to other providers), or both. Each client can also be selective about which machines it distributes builds to.

Open the Distributed Builds pane of the Xcode preferences of each development machine on the network. The Distributed Builds pane, shown in Figure 14-32, has essentially two settings: Share My Computer for Other Builds, and Distribute My Builds to Other Computers.

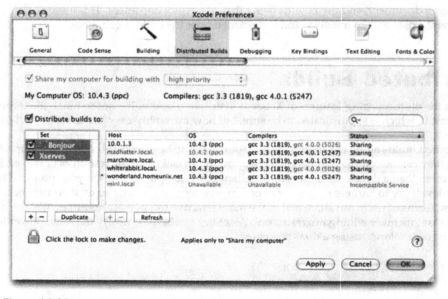

Figure 14-32

In order to share your computer (offer to compile files for other developers), you must first unlock the padlock in the lower-left corner. You are asked to supply an administrator user name and password. Authenticating as an administrator allows Xcode to install the background services that provide distributed building.

Check the box next to the Share My Computer for Building With option to make this computer available on the network to perform builds for other developers. The pop-up menu next to the option allows you to choose a process priority for the distributed build process. If you regularly perform time-sensitive, CPU intensive, tasks such as multi-media processing, you might consider setting this to medium or low priority. Lowering the priority also gives local builds an edge over builds for other developers. Remember that process priority only comes into play when two or more processes are competing to use the CPU. If the computer is idle, it doesn't matter what the priority is; the build will use all of the available CPU time.

In the lower portion of the pane is a list of computers you can distribute builds to. Available computers are organized into sets, listed on the left. The Bonjour set is a smart set that lists all active build providers on the local subnet. This set is assembled using the Bonjour (ZeroConfig) protocol, and automatically adjusts to reflect the available build providers on the local subnet. For most installations, this is the only set you will need.

The computers in the list display their status and suitability. The Host column contains the IP address of system. The OS and Compilers columns list the versions of the provider's operating system and compilers. You can only distribute a build to a computer with the same version of OS and compiler. The compiler in question will be the compiler required by the target being built. In the example in Figure 14-32, the computer whiterabbit.local has a compatible version of gcc 3.3, but an incompatible version of gcc 4.0. This computer could accept builds for targets that use the gcc 3.3 compiler, but not ones that required gcc 4.0. The computer marchhare.local, on the other hand, is running an older operating system and cannot accept any builds. Incompatible computers are listed in red.

If you want to limit the distribution of builds to a specific subset of local computers, or if you want to add computers that do not appear in the Bonjour list, then you need to create a custom set. Click the + button below the list of sets to create a new set, and then give the set a name. You can also duplicate an existing set. Selecting a set, or sets, lists only the computers in those sets. The list is always a union of the sets selected, so computers in multiple sets are only listed once. To delete a set, select it and click the - button. You cannot delete the Bonjour set.

To add a computer to a custom set, either drag a computer from the list into the set, or click the + button below the list with that set selected. Enter the IP address of the new system, using either a domain name or a numeric address. Xcode adds the new system to every set currently selected and automatically queries the system to discover its status and suitability. To remove a computer from a set, select it in the list and click the - button. You cannot add or remove computers from the Bonjour set. Consequently, having the Bonjour set selected disables both that add and remove buttons. To add or remove computers from the list, select only custom sets.

To distribute your builds to other computers, check the box next to Distribute Builds To, and then check the box next to each set that you want Xcode to include in distributed builds. The computers in all of the checked sets will be considered when Xcode distributes builds to other computers.

That's all there is to it. If you've elected to distribute your builds with other computers, your next build will employ distributed building. Figure 14-33 shows five different source files being compiled simultaneously.

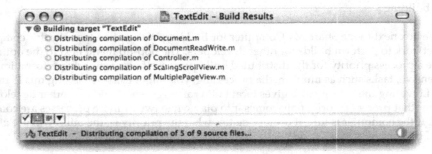

Figure 14-33

Summary

Controlling the build process is a critical step in any successful development project. You should now be able to start and stop builds at will, examine the results of the build, and locate errors that occurred while building. Using build settings and build configurations, you can customize many features of the compiler, linker, and Xcode itself. Using build setting layers and build configurations, you can create complex sets of build settings, allowing you to customize specific features of specific targets for specific variations.

Just as important as control is the speed of your development. By learning to enable such features as ZeroLink, prefix headers, and distributed builds, you can radically reduce the amount of time it takes to build and test your application.

Even after building your project successfully, you're still not quite done. The next chapter will show you how to run and test your application from within Xcode.

Exercise

Open the BuildPrimes project. This is a slight variation on the PrimesObjC project used earlier in this book. In it you will find a simple BSD command-line tool that counts prime numbers using a technique known as the Sieve of Eratosthenes.

The version you'll be using has been modified slightly. You'll be performing testing and performance analysis on it. This will require some build settings to produce different versions of the application. The code has been also changed to expect two C macro definitions to be defined while compiling, which can be configured from the build rather than editing the source code. MAX_PRIME_TO_TEST is the largest prime number to test in the debug versions. For testing, MAX_PRIME_TO_TEST can be different than

MAX_PRIME. A second compiler flag named BRUTE_TEST has been added. If this flag is set to YES, code is compiled that will correctly test prime numbers that are outside the range of the map (that is, when a number is larger than MAX_PRIME). Here's what you need to do:

1. Create a new build configuration named Performance similar to the Debug configuration.

2. This new configuration will be used for performance testing. It needs to have all of the debug settings enabled, but the optimization level for the Performance configuration needs to be set to Fastest, Smallest [-Os]. Change this in the BuildPrimes target settings.

3. While in the Performance configuration of the BuildPrimes target, create a build setting for TEST_PRIMES. Set its value to 1500. In the Debug configuration, create the same build setting and set its value to MAX_PRIME_DEFAULT.

4. In every build configuration of the BuildPrimes target, add the value MAX_PRIME_TO_TEST=$(TEST_PRIMES) to the Preprocessor Macros Not Used in Precompiled Headers setting. You can find this setting in the Preprocessing collection of the gcc 4.0 settings. Make sure this doesn't alter any other pre-processor macros defined in a lower layer of build settings.

5. Make the Performance build configuration active and build the project. Examine the build results. Make sure that warnings are visible.

6. Edit the project layer build setting for the Preprocessor Macros Not Used in Precompiled Headers setting. In Debug and Release configurations add the item BRUTE_TEST=TRUE. In the Performance build configuration add the item BRUTE_TEST=NO.

7. Build the project and examine the build results.

8. You don't like the compiler warning thrown by SieveOfEratosthenes.m. Suppress all compiler warnings (pass the compiler the -w switch) when compiling this file.

9. Build the project.

10. Switch to the Release build configuration. Build the project again.

11. Delete the Preprocessor Macros Not Used in Precompiled Headers setting in the Release configuration of the BuildPrimes target. Build again.

12. Locate the source line that produces the warning warning: #warning MAX_PRIME_TO_TEST is not defined and comment it out. Build again.

Debugging

Getting your project to build is sometimes only half the battle. OK, let's be honest: It's often less than half the battle. It's a cruel fact of programming that your application will have bugs, design flaws, and unexpected behavior. Object-oriented languages, modeling, good design, rigorous coding standards, and unit testing can reduce the number of bugs that creep into your code. But unless your application is trivial, it doesn't matter how careful you've been, how many code reviews you've done, or how many "best practices" you've employed. Someday your application is simply not going to work the way you want it to, and you'll have to find out why. The tool of choice to answer that question is the debugger.

The debugger is a magic window into your application. You can literally watch the internals of your program at work. You can stop your application at any point. You can examine the values of variables, the state of other threads, and much more. Xcode even allows you alter values and fix some code while your application is still running—the equivalent of performing a heart transplant on an athlete who's in the middle of running a marathon.

Running an Application

Before getting into debugging, this section covers the trivial case of simply running your application. You can launch your program, more or less as it would be launched from the Finder or shell, using either the Debug⇨Run Executable (Command+Option+R) or Build⇨Build and Run (Command+R) command. The latter performs a build of the active target before starting your program. This is the most common way of running an application—notice that it has the simpler of the two key combinations. It first ensures that any changes you've made are saved and the target is fully built before starting your program.

These two commands are also accessible via your toolbar in the form of the Run button and the Build and Go combination button, shown in Figure 15-1. The Run button is equivalent to the Run Executable command. Whenever the executable is running, this button changes into a Terminate button with a stop sign icon. You can unceremoniously terminate the running program (equivalent to a kill command or a Force Quit) using the Terminate button or by choosing the Debug⇨Stop Executable (Command+Option+R) command. The Build and Go button is a combination control.

If you simply click the control, Xcode performs the Build and Run command. If you click and hold down the mouse button, the button reveals a pop-up menu containing the different combinations of run and debug commands.

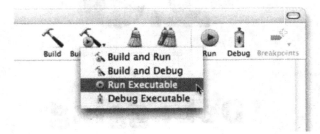

Figure 15-1

Running a program opens the run log window, shown in Figure 15-2. You can reopen this window at any time using the Debug⇨Run Log (Command+Shift+R) command. This window is connected to the stdout, stdin, and stderr pipes of the process. In Xcode, the run window is referred to as a Pseudo Terminal and acts as a surrogate shell for the process as it runs, capturing any output or error messages and supplying any keyboard input to the program's stdin pipe. For command-line tools, this is the main window for your application. For GUI applications, this window captures what would normally be sent to the System Console. For example, messages written using NSLog(. . .) are captured by the run log window when the application is started from within Xcode.

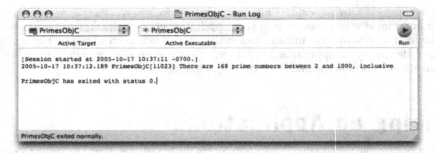

Figure 15-2

You can modify these I/O connections, along with many other aspects of your program's execution environment. See the "Custom Executables" section later in this chapter for more details.

Choosing the Active Executable

The active executable determines what program is launched when you choose any of the run or debug commands. You can change the active executable using the Project⇨Set Active Executable menu or using an Active Executable control that's been added to any toolbar. In each menu, there is an item for every executable your project produces. Normally, changing the active target also changes the active executable. If your project produces two applications, Client and Server, changing from the Client target to the Server target also switches the active executable from Client to Server.

There are a number of circumstances where this might not happen automatically. This is especially true when switching to or from an active target that does not produce an executable. Switching from an application target to an aggregate target (which produces nothing) or a framework target (that doesn't produce anything that can be executed on its own) does not change the active executable. In these circumstances, you need to choose the active executable yourself.

You may sometimes want to launch a different executable than the one produced by the target. Let's say you are working on the Server application, but need to test it using the Client application. Select the Server as the active target and then switch the active executable to the Client. When you Build and Run, the Server gets built but it's the Client that gets launched.

For the vast majority of projects, the executable produced by your application target is the executable that you want to run or debug. If you have a special situation, you may need to modify the environment in which your executable runs or create a custom executable. Both are explained towards the end of this chapter in the "Custom Executables" section. For now, you'll concentrate on debugging simple executables produced by application and command-line targets. Everything here applies to custom executables as well.

Built to be Debugged

How you build your application affects its ability to be debugged. The quintessential quality of a modern programming language is that it allows a developer to express procedures symbolically, letting the compiler deal with the ugly details of how to accomplish those procedures in machine code. Listing 15-1 shows just how obtuse the machine code for a few "simple" lines of programming source can be. The source code is shown in the listing, followed by the resulting PowerPC machine code. The debugger has the unenviable job of reversing this process — it must examine the raw machine code and translate that back into something that corresponds to the functions, methods, code blocks, classes, structures, and variable names defined in your source code. (You'll see this process at work later in Figure 15-6.)

Listing 15-1: Compiled Source Code

Source Code
```
- (void)dealloc
{
    free(byteArray);
    [super dealloc];
}
```

Compiled Assembly Code
```
    mflr r0
    stmw r29,-12(r1)
    mr r29,r3
    stw r0,8(r1)
    stwu r1,-96(r1)
    nop
    nop
    lwz r3,4(r3)
    bl L_free$stub
    lis r2,ha16(L_OBJC_CLASS_SieveOfEratosthenes+4)
    lis r4,ha16(L_OBJC_SELECTOR_REFERENCES_2)
    stw r29,56(r1)
    addi r3,r1,56
```

(continued)

Listing 15-1: Compiled Source Code (continued)

```
lwz  r2,lo16(L_OBJC_CLASS_SieveOfEratosthenes+4)(r2)
lwz  r4,lo16(L_OBJC_SELECTOR_REFERENCES_2)(r4)
stw  r2,60(r1)
bl   L_objc_msgSendSuper$stub
addi r1,r1,96
lwz  r0,8(r1)
lmw  r29,-12(r1)
mtlr r0
blr
```

To accomplish this feat, the debugger needs a lot of help. That help comes in the form of debugger symbols produced by the compiler. Debugger symbols are a kind of massive cross-index. They contain information like "the machine instruction at byte offset 12,738 corresponds to line 83 of the source file breakme.c." If you set a breakpoint at line 83 of breakme.c, the debugger knows it needs to stop your program at the instruction found at offset 12,738. If your program crashes at (or near) the machine instruction at offset 12,738, the debugger can tell you that your program crashed in (or near) line 83 of breakme.c.

The debugger symbols contain similar information about data structures, classes, automatic variables, and so on. You must request that these debugger symbols be produced when your application is compiled. If you have created your project using one of the Xcode templates, you should have a Release and a Debug build configuration. The Debug build configuration, shown in Figure 15-3, for your program's target has the following build settings:

- ❏ Generate Debug Symbols: On
- ❏ Strip Debug Symbols for Binary: Off
- ❏ Fix & Continue: On
- ❏ Optimization Level: None
- ❏ ZeroLink: On

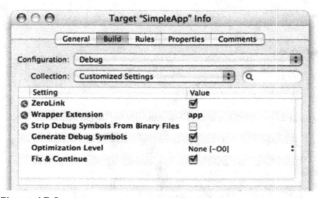

Figure 15-3

Generate Debug Symbols enables the full array of debugger symbols in the compiler, detailing every aspect of your code for the debugger. Without it, the debugger is close to useless. This information is produced when each source file is compiled. This process also takes extra time to compile and produces a lot of data (quite often more data than your actual program), which the debugger has to load. All of this slows down both compilation and debugging. If you are debugging a massive amount of code, you may elect to generate debug symbols only for some modules and not others. For example, you may generate debugger symbols for your main application code but not some well-tested library routines. This speeds up building and debugging, but limits your debugging to the portion of your code that has debugger symbols.

For obvious reasons, the Strip Debug Symbols build setting needs to be off. Even when Generate Debug Symbols is off, some rudimentary information about the function names and entry points to your code is still attached to your executable. This helps system facilities like the Crash Reporter to determine where your application crashed and what the calling chain was. For the final application you ship to customers, you'll probably want to strip off even this extra bit of information. That's what the Strip Debug Symbols setting does during a deployment build.

Fix & Continue is a feature, covered later in "The Magic Fix," that allows you to make limited code changes in your application while your application is running. That is, you don't have to stop your program, change your code, rebuild, and restart. You simply change your code and keep executing. To use this feature, your compiled object code must contain additional information that the Fix & Continue feature needs. If you turn this build setting off, you can still debug your code, but the Fix & Continue command is disabled.

While you're debugging, the optimization of your code should be set to None. The reason why goes back to how debuggers work. Optimization, by its very nature, is logic in the compiler that reorganizes, reorders, rewrites, and often eliminates code that it finds to be inefficient or redundant. Take the following code fragment as an example.

```
Line 100: int i=0;
Line 101: for (i=1; i<argc; i++)
```

With optimization turned on, the compiler eliminates the statement i=0 because the result of that assignment is never used. In the debugger, it now becomes impossible to set a breakpoint at line 100 because the code that corresponds to that line of source code doesn't exist in your compiled application. More advanced optimization techniques, such as loop unrolling or instruction reordering, can produce even more bizarre aberrations, such as programs whose statements execute out of order (for example, line 101, then 103, then 102). It might be impossible to stop an application at a certain point in your source code, or step through your code one line at a time. Skeptical readers are invited to enable full optimization and then attempt to debug their application.

ZeroLink isn't really a debugging aide as much as it's a development aide. It defers the actual linking of your applications until runtime, making the time it takes to build, link, and start your application much faster. Of course the application still gets linked, just incrementally and usually when you're doing something more productive then drumming your fingers on desk waiting for your project to build. ZeroLink can cause problems during development. The biggest problem is usually in referencing a nonexistent symbol in your program. If you use the regular linker, you'll get an error that says you have an invalid symbol. But because ZeroLink actually skips the formal linking process, you don't get any warning when you build. Executables prepared with ZeroLink only run in the environment where they were built. You can't ZeroLink a program and transfer it to another user or location. Turn off ZeroLink whenever you suspect symbol resolution issues might be a problem. This was discussed in the "Disallowing ZeroLink" section in Chapter 14. You might also want to refer to the ZeroLink release notes at `http://developer.apple.com/releasenotes/DeveloperTools/ZeroLinkReleaseNotes.html`, Technical Q&A #1322 `http://developer.apple.com/qa/qa2001/qa1322.html`, and the "Using ZeroLink" section of the Xcode documentation, all of which detail caveats and exceptional situations where ZeroLink can get into trouble, and what to do about it. Pay special attention to this if you are having problems getting your application to launch or if you can't set breakpoints.

The Release build configuration for new projects has the opposite build settings: no symbols, symbols stripped, normal optimization, no Fix & Continue or ZeroLink. If you have created your own targets or build configurations, you'll need to set them up accordingly.

Note that Xcode project templates have these options configured in the *target's* build settings. If you have a multiple target project, you can easily misconfigure the settings in one target and not realize it. For this reason, it's best to move these basic debug settings into the project build settings for multi-target projects, and then override these settings only in those targets that require something different (which is rare). This way, you can adjust the level of debugger symbols produced (for example) with a single build setting, rather than having to change this setting in every target.

> Here's a tip: If you think you're having problems getting your build settings right, create a temporary build configuration to experiment with. After you have everything working, you can compare that to the original, or just delete the one that doesn't work. If you've made a lot of changes and really want to know what the differences are, export all of your build settings by copying and pasting them into two separate text files. You can then compare them visually or using a diff tool.

Debugging Executables

With the preliminaries out of the way, you're ready to debug your application. Getting started is as easy as running your program. Choose either the Debug⇨Debug Executable (Command+Option+Y) or Build⇨Build and Debug (Command+Y) command to start your program under the control of the debugger. The time from which the debugger starts your program until it finishes is referred to as the debug session.

An alternative is available in the targets group if you would like to build and then run or debug a target's that is *not* the active target or executable. Control-/right-click on the target's icon in the target smart group and choose either the Build and Run or the Build and Debug command. The effects are the same as changing the active target to the one selected, issuing a Build and Run/Debug command, and then switching the active target back to what it was originally.

You can only have one debug session active for a project. However, you can have concurrent debug sessions from separate projects. A Client and a Server application, both built using separate projects, could each be running in separate debug sessions simultaneously.

Most of this chapter refers to the "the debugger" as a generic term, but in fact there are three debuggers: gdb, the Java debugger, and the AppleScript debugger. All of the features described here work when you're using the gdb debugger. gdb is the debugger you use to debug any binary executable. The Java debugger and AppleScript debugger are used to debug Java bytecode and compiled AppleScripts, and are far more limited in what features they support.

In general, most of the variable browsing, basic breakpoint, and program control features work in all three. The Java and AppleScript debuggers do not support expression evaluation, so any feature that depends on this is not supported. This includes conditional breakpoints and data formatters. Unfortunately, the Xcode interface does not communicate these limitations. Xcode lets you enter a conditional expression or a data formatter, and then ignore it.

Some features, like Fix & Continue and Shared Library browsing, are simply incompatible with the Java and AppleScript runtime architectures. These commands are appropriately enabled when they are available. It's impractical to innumerate all of the circumstances that allow or disallow these commands. Simply look in the Debug menu while debugging — if the command is enabled, it should work.

Attaching to Running Executables

Using the Debug Executable command or Build and Debug commands requires some forethought. You have to know that you wanted to debug the executable prior to starting it. Xcode compensates (a little) for this inability to see into the future with the Debug⇨Attach menu. This menu enables you to attach the debugger to any executable in your project that is already running. It doesn't matter what process started the executable — be that Xcode, the Finder, the shell, or even another process in your project. Select the process from the menu and Xcode starts a debugger session for it. If you don't see the process listed, you can choose the Debug⇨Attach⇨Process ID command and enter the ID of the process you want to attach to. Note that the debugger cannot attach to processes owned by a different user — an act that would violate the security model of the kernel.

Also see the "Custom Executables" section for the Auto-Attach Debugger on Crash option. This feature automatically attaches to any project executable that crashes.

The Debugger Window

When you start an application using the debugger, Xcode automatically opens the Debugger window, shown in Figure 15-4. Like the build window, the Debugger window is your central control center during your debug session. Each project has its own Debugger window. You can open the Debugger window without starting a debug session using the Debug⇨Debugger (Command+Shift+Y) command. You can also minimize or close the Debugger window, if only to get it out of your way, without upsetting the debug session. Open the debugger window again using the Debug⇨Debugger command and resume your debug session where you left off.

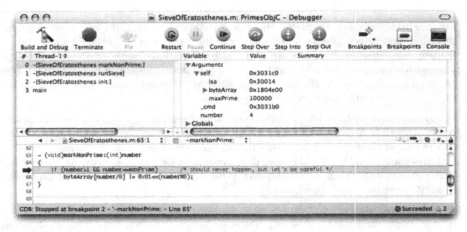

Figure 15-4

The Debugger window has three main panes: the threads pane, the variables pane, and the listing or editor pane. The debugger pane has an alternate layout to the one shown in Figure 15-4. Use the Debug⇨Toggle Debugger Layout command to switch between the two. The alternate layout splits the window vertically, with the threads and variables panes on the left and the entire vertical pane on the right dedicated to the listing or editor pane. Choose the style that you find most comfortable.

You can resize all three panes by clicking and dragging the small grey dot that appears at the nexus of the three panes.

The Threads Pane

The threads pane displays the stack state of the active thread. Each entry in the list represents a single stack frame. A frame contains the return address of the caller and all of the function's automatic variables. If the address of the function can be translated into a name, then the function's name is displayed. Otherwise the address of the function (in the current address space of the process) is listed.

When you stop an application in the debugger, the pane displays the call stack of the thread that hit the breakpoint. The left column indicates the relative depth of each function in the call stack. The name of the function currently executing is displayed at the top of the list and always has a stack depth of 0. The name of the function that called the currently executing function is listed underneath that and has a stack depth of 1, and so on all the way back to the function that started the thread.

> For the debugger, there are only functions, structures, and variables. Different languages refer to subroutines using various terminologies: procedure, function, member function, method, subroutine, or message handler. But ultimately, each becomes a block of code at an address in memory. When this book uses the words "function" or "subroutine," substitute the term of your preferred paradigm.

The contents of the variables pane and the initial contents of the editor pane are determined by the current selection in the threads pane. When you stop an application, the current (top) function in the call stack of the stopped thread is selected. Select another function in the call stack, and the variables and editor pane change to display the variables and calling location in that function. This allows you to examine not only the automatic variables of the current function, but also the data values and calling address of the functions that called the current function.

You can view another call stack by selecting a different thread from the pop-up menu at the top of the pane (see Figure 15-5). Change to another thread, and you can examine the local variables and calling address of any frame on that thread's stack. Depending on the language and runtime library used, threads may or may not have identifying names. In Java, the pop-up list of threads displays the name of each thread. In Objective-C, the threads are labeled Thread-1, Thread-2, and so on.

Figure 15-5

The Listing or Editor Pane

The listing or editor pane displays the source code of your application, a disassembly listing, or both. The latter combination is shown in Figure 15-6. The debugger chooses a view automatically when it needs to display a breakpoint or calling location. If the debugger can correlate the program location with a source file, it displays the source code in an editor pane. This is a full-featured editor pane, allowing you to edit your source code right in the debugger window. You can choose an alternate view using the Debug⇨Toggle Disassembly Display command. This command rotates through three display modes: displaying just the source code, a split view showing both the source and machine disassembly, or just the disassembly. If the debugger cannot determine a source file that corresponds to the program's location, it displays only the disassembly of the machine codes, and the Toggle Disassembly Display command has no effect.

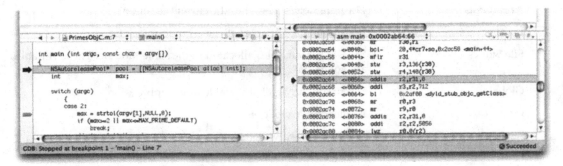

Figure 15-6

Java and AppleScript programs do not have a disassembly view of their byte code or tokens. The Toggle Disassembly Display command is ignored when you're debugging these languages.

Breakpoints and the current execution location are indicated in the gutter of the editor or listing. Breakpoints appear as dark or light grey markers, and the program counter (PC) indicator appears as a red arrow. The breakpoint and location indicators are so critical to the effective use of the debugger that the gutter display is turned on whenever you are in a debug session. If your Xcode preferences are set to not display the gutter in the editor, the gutters disappear again at the end of your debug session.

The program-counter indicator points to the current execution location for the selected thread and stack frame. In a source file, it points to the source line most closely associated with the program-counter position. In the disassembly listing, it points to the exact instruction. If the top (level 0) stack frame is selected, the arrow indicates where the current thread is executing. Select another stack frame in the list and it indicates the location where the stack frame above it was called.

> **Because the meaning of the PC indicator is relative, make sure you pay attention to what stack frame you have selected. If you choose another stack frame, the PC indicator points to where the current execution location was called from, not where it is. Using a command like Step Over does *not* step to the next instruction after the PC indicator. It steps to the next instruction in the top stack frame, where the program is actually stopped.**

The Variables Pane

The variables pane displays the known data variables for the selected stack frame. The key word here is *known*. The debugger *must* have debug symbol information that describes the structure for the selected stack frame. If there is no description available, it cannot interpret or display any data values on the stack and the pane is empty. You will encounter this most often when you stop an application in a system framework or library routine.

Variables in the display are organized into a hierarchy of groups. The top-level groups are listed in the following table.

Variable Group	Description
Arguments	The parameters passed to the current function.
Locals	The automatic variables allocated in the stack frame.
File Statics	Local static variables allocated in the same module. These variables are not global.
Globals	Potentially, any global variable in the application.
Properties	AppleScript properties.
Registers	The CPU's hardware registers.

If there are no variables of a given type, the group containing that type is not displayed. A simple C function with no parameters does not display an Arguments group.

Although the Arguments group is technically just more local variables, Xcode groups them for convenience. In object-oriented languages, the arguments include the implied automatic variables such as this or self. Expand the this or self object to view the instance variables of the current object.

The Locals group contains the local (also known as automatic or stack) variables allocated on the stack frame.

The Globals group contains any global variables you want to examine in the applications. Because this could, potentially, contain hundreds if not thousands of variables (remember that every library and framework that your application is linked to can declare globals), this group must be manually populated with just the symbols you want to examine. This is explained later in the "Global Variables" section.

The Registers group is exceptional in that it only appears when you are viewing a disassembly listing. If you want to look at the CPU registers while viewing source code, use the Debug⇨Toggle Disassembly Display to show both the source and disassembly simultaneously.

Variables are listed by name. Structures, arrays, and objects appear as groups in the listing. Expose the contents of a group to examine its member variables. The Value column shows the primitive value of the variable. For numeric types, it is the value of the number. For objects, arrays, and structures, it is the address or identity of the structure.

Pointers or references display the address or id of the object they are pointing to but act like the object they reference. Thus, you can expand a pointer to a structure so it shows the member values of the structure the pointer references. Change the pointerm and all member values change accordingly. Xcode dynamically determines the structure of objects, when it can. The most obvious example is a generic reference of an id or Object type. Variables of this type impart no information about the class or structure of the object they might reference. When Xcode displays an object reference, it examines the type of the object and adjusts its display to reflect the structure of the *actual* object. Thus, you will see the member variables of an id or Object reference change, depending on what type of object it references.

The Summary field is an "intelligent" interpretation of the variables contents. Using a system of data formatters, the field can display a more human-readable summary of the object or structure's contents. Xcode has numerous data formatters built in. A simple example is the NSCalendarDate object. Without data formatters, an NSCalendarDate reference would display as an object at a particular address. Exposing its member values would display several variables, shown on the left in Figure 15-7. The _formatString variable contains something cryptic, the _timeZone value contains a pointer to an opaque object, and the _timeIntervalSinceReferenceDate variable contains a big floating point number. Unless you can convert seconds-since-the-epoch to a calendar date in your head, none of these values are particularly informative. This is where data formatters come to the rescue. Xcode includes data formatter for strings, dates, and even the time zone object. Turn data formatters on and the display changes to something far more useful, shown on the right in Figure 15-7. The format string and time zone values are now easily readable, and the date object reference itself displays a practical representation of the date and time encapsulated by that object. You'll learn how to create your own data formatters, which is even more powerful, later in the "Data Formatters" section. You can enable and disable data formatters using the Debug⇨Variables View⇨Enable Data Formatters command.

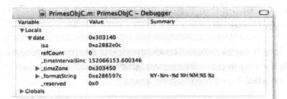
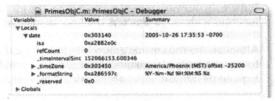

Figure 15-7

There is also an optional Type column that you can display using the Debug⇨Variables View⇨Show Types command. This column shows the type of the variable. For objects, this field shows the type of the object the debugger believes it to be, which is not necessarily the type of the reference. If the debugger cannot determine the type of the object, typically because the reference is invalid or set to NIL, the type displayed is the type declared for the reference.

There's a lot more to examining data in the debugger. This brief overview should give you some idea of what you're looking at while you progress to the more practical topic of controlling the debugger and setting breakpoints. Until you can stop your application, there's no data to examine.

Controlling the Debugger

One of the most elementary, and often most effective, methods of debugging an application is to simply stop it and examine its state. Look at the value of local variables and objects, and see what functions have been called and in what order. You may then want to step through the code one line at a time to witness its order of execution. This, rather passive, method of debugging is often all that's required to determine what your code is doing wrong or unexpected.

You control this kind of immediate and interactive debugging through a set of debugging commands. None of these commands (except the Pause command) are available until the debugger has suspended your application. This happens when the execution of your program encounters a breakpoint, some exceptional event, or when you use the Pause command. The most predictable method is to set a breakpoint. It's possible to stop your program using the Debug⇨Pause command, but it's rarely that useful. Pause stops your program wherever it is at that moment — usually in some framework or kernel call.

Breakpoints can do many sophisticated things, and there are a variety of ways in which you can set them, all of which is covered later in the "Breakpoints" section. For now, all you need to do is set and enable simple breakpoints by clicking in the editor pane gutter of any source file. A breakpoint appears as a black marker that indicates the position of the breakpoint in the source code. Clicking an existing breakpoint toggles its state between enabled (black) and disabled (grey). Only enabled breakpoints interrupt program execution. To delete a breakpoint, drag the breakpoint out of the gutter or use the Control-/right-click menu to select the Remove Breakpoint command.

After the execution of your program has been suspended, a set of execution control commands become available. These are listed in the following table.

Command	Shortcut	Description
Continue	Command+Shift+.	Resumes execution of your program. Your program will run until it encounters another breakpoint or terminates.
Step Into	Command+Shift+I	Executes one line of source code. If the line contains a call to another function, execution is stopped again at the beginning of that function, which is what gives this command its name — you are stepping *into* the function being called. If the source line does not call another function, this command is equivalent to Step Over.
Step Over	Command+Shift+O	Executes one line of source code and stops before executing the line that follows. If the line contains calls to other functions, those functions are allowed to execute in their entirety.
Step Out	Command+Shift+T	Resumes execution until the current function returns to its caller.
Step Into Instruction	Command+Shift+Option+I	Equivalent to Step Into, but steps through a single machine instruction rather than a full line of source code, which could represent dozens of machine instructions.
Step Over Instruction	Command+Shift+Option+O	Equivalent to Step Over, but steps over only a single machine instruction.
(*run to here*)	Option+click in gutter	Sets a temporary breakpoint and starts the program running.
Sync With Debugger		Returns the debugger window's view to showing the current thread, current stack frame, current function, and current PC indicator where the debugger is suspended.
Restart		Forcibly terminates your program's process, and then restarts it again under the control of the debugger. This is equivalent to choosing Debug⇨Stop Debugger followed by Debug⇨Debug Executable.
Pause	Command+Option+P	Immediately suspends execution of your program. This is the only command that will stop your program without setting a breakpoint.

The Pause and Continue commands are immediate and self-explanatory. Generally, the Pause command isn't very useful, especially for GUI applications, for reasons mentioned earlier. You will probably find it most edifying when your application is stuck in an endless loop. It can also be helpful to suspend your application while you think about your next move or contemplate where to set a breakpoint. You don't have to stop the program to set a breakpoint, but you don't necessarily want your application running amuck while you decide where to do this.

Step Over and Step Into are the two most commonly used debugger control commands. Step Over lets you walk through the logic of a single function, ignoring the details of other functions that it might call. Step Into traces the execution of the program one step at a time, regardless of where that leads. For both of these commands, you set a temporary breakpoint that will stop execution again after the current statement has executed. This is important because commands like Step Over permit called functions to execute in their entirety. However, if the source statement itself encounters a breakpoint or exceptional event, the debugger stops there instead. If a function exits abnormally (via a longjmp, by throwing an exception, or by terminating a thread), the program may never execute the code following the line you wanted to step over. The program avoids the breakpoint set by the debugger and continues running.

The Step Over command is intelligent about recursive functions. Stepping over a function that calls itself does not stop until all nested iterations of the function have executed and returned, even if that entails executing the same code position that you are stepping over.

If the source line contains multiple calls, the Step Into command steps into the first function called. This is significant if a function passes parameters that are obtained by calling other functions. The example in Listing 15-2 illustrates this. If the debugger first stopped at this line and you issued the Step Into command, the debugger would step into `getDefaultMode()`, not `setMode()`. That's because the `getDefaultMode` function is called first to obtain the value of `setMode`'s single argument.

Listing 15-2: Nested Function Calls

```
setMode(getDefaultMode());        // reset the mode
```

After you return from `getDefaultMode` (see the Step Out command), the debugger again returns to this line of source code. But the CPU's program counter is now poised at the call to `setMode`. This time the Step Into command steps into the `setMode` function. You can see this more clearly if you have the disassembly view visible, but it isn't necessary. Just be aware that Step Into is going to step into each function called, in the order they are called. You may have to step into and out of several functions before you step into the function you want to examine.

> If you have a very complex statement with many nested function calls, you may find it easier to set a breakpoint at the beginning of the function you want to catch rather than stepping into, and back out of, five or six you don't care about. Use this trick: Command+double-click the name of the function you want to trace, quickly jumping to its implementation in the source code. Option+click in the gutter next to the first line of the function (see the Run to Here command later in this section). Xcode creates a temporary breakpoint there and starts the application running. After all of the preliminary functions have been called, it stops again when it gets to the function you want to trace.

Step Into only steps into functions that have debug information and have local source files associated with them. You cannot step into library functions, framework APIs, or kernel code that was not compiled with full debug information. Attempting to step into such a function is treated like a Step Over.

Step Out is convenient for letting the current function complete its execution and returning again to the point where it was called. It's common to step into a function simply to examine the values of its arguments. After you are satisfied the function will behave correctly, you can then use Step Out to let the function finish and return to where it was called. The same issues about exceptional exits that apply to Step Over also apply here.

Try It Out   Step Through Code

Open the Stepper project and try the following:

1. Make the Debug build configuration active.
2. Set a breakpoint at line 24 of main.c.
3. Choose the Build⇨Build and Debug command.

The debugger should start your application executing, and then stop it again when it gets to line 24 of main.c. After it has stopped, try the various debugging commands:

- ❑ Step Over
- ❑ Step Into
- ❑ Step Out
- ❑ Continue

You can start the application again using the Restart or Debug commands.

How It Works

Figure 15-8 shows the application stopped at line 24. The outerCall function has called the function innerCall function, where the program is stopped. The innerCall function is about to call subroutine, as follows:

- ❑ The Step Over command will execute the subroutine function and stop again at line 25.
- ❑ The Step Into command will enter the subroutine function and stop at line 31.
- ❑ The Step Out command will finish executing the innerCall function and stop at line 18.

Try setting other breakpoints. Try a breakpoint at line 9 or 12. Set a breakpoint in subroutine at line 31 and try stepping over and out of the high-level subroutines.

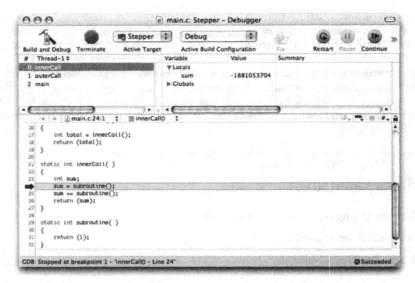

Figure 15-8

Step Into Instruction and Step Over Instruction are most useful when you're viewing the disassembly of your program's code. These two commands execute a single machine instruction. Because a single line of source code might translate into a score of machine instructions, you'd have to use Step Over Instruction 20 times to accomplish the same effect as a single Step Over. In the split view showing both the source and the machine code disassembly, you can watch the PC indicator advance as you execute each opcode. If you are only viewing the disassembly, the Step Over and Step Into commands become equivalent to the Step Over Instruction and Step Into Instruction.

The limitation of only stepping into functions that have source debug information for them does not apply to the Step Into Instruction command. If the function being called has no source code available, Step Into Instruction still steps into it, automatically switching to a disassembly-only view as needed.

The next command isn't really a command as much as a gesture. It isn't documented in Xcode, but it is often referred to as the "Run to Here" command. While holding down the Option key, click in the gutter of a source file just as if you were setting a breakpoint. This creates and sets a temporary breakpoint and starts your application running, just as if you had set a regular breakpoint and issued the Continue command. A breakpoint indicator is not visible in the gutter or anywhere else in Xcode, and the breakpoint is deleted as soon as it is hit. This makes it extremely easy to skip through blocks of code or around loops by simply clicking where you want to stop next.

The Sync with Debugger command reorients the debugger window back to the point where the program is currently stopped. By selecting different stack frames, navigating to other functions, switching to other threads, and so on, it's easy to lose your place. The Sync With Debugger command "snaps" the view back to the currently active thread, stack frame, variables, and PC indicator — the same view that was active when the debugger last stopped your program.

Debug Visualizer

The debug visualizer is a totally different way of tracing your program's execution. Instead of the traditional line-by-line approach of the debugger window, it presents an object-oriented view of your program's progress using a class model. Figure 15-9 shows the Debug Visualizer window on the left and the same execution location in the Debugger window on the right.

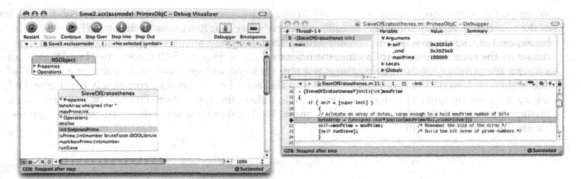

Figure 15-9

The Debug Visualizer highlights the function (`init` in this example) being executed. The toolbar of the Debug Visualizer has the same controls as the Debugger window, allowing you to control program execution right in the class diagram.

You can open the Debug Visualizer at any time. The Debug Visualizer always highlights the member function being executed in the currently selected stack frame. If the function is not a class function, the diagram is empty. The Debug Visualizer automatically chooses a class diagram in the project that contains the class being highlighted. If the project does not contain a class diagram for the executing class, the Debug Visualizer spontaneously creates a class diagram, much like the Quick Model command does. (Chapter 11 discussed creating class models and diagrams.)

Breakpoints

Breakpoints are locations in your program where you want the debugger to take control. Formally, a breakpoint is set at a particular address in memory. When the CPU's program counter matches the address of a breakpoint — that is to say at the instant before the instruction at that breakpoint's address is to be executed — the CPU stops executing your program and passes control to the debugger.

So far you've created only basic breakpoints. The default action of a breakpoint is to halt the execution of your program, hand over control to the debugger, and wait for instructions. But breakpoints are capable of much more.

Before getting into more advanced techniques for defining breakpoints, here's a quick review of the methods for creating a basic breakpoint — one that simply stops the program when encountered:

❑   Click in the gutter of a source file.

❑   Control-/right-click in the gutter of a source file and choose the Add Breakpoint command.

❑   Choose the Add Breakpoint At Current Line (Command+\) command when the active text cursor is in a source file.

❑   Option-click in the gutter to create a temporary breakpoint and start the program running.

When you're setting breakpoints graphically, Xcode allows you to set a breakpoint on just about any line of the source file. A lot of times this doesn't make any sense, but Xcode can't tell that. When you set a breakpoint in a source file, you're actually setting the breakpoint at the first executable instruction produced by the source file at, or following, the line you clicked. Figure 15-10 shows three breakpoints set in a source file. All three of these breakpoints point to the same address location. The first one is set on a declaration statement that produces no code, and the second one is set on a completely blank line. Only the source code on line 10 produces any executable code in the application. Ultimately, you could set a breakpoint on line 8, 9, or 10 with the same results. The breakpoint is set at the instruction that implements the switch statement.

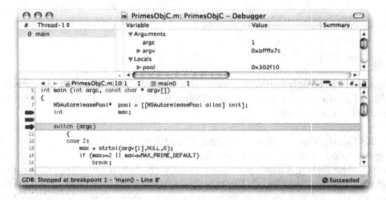

Figure 15-10

In a similar vein, source code that you might not think of as producing code often does. A good example is the closing brace of a C function. All functions have to return, and the closing brace of the function body produces code that destroys any automatic classes, pops up the stack frame, and returns to the caller. This happens even in void functions. Consequently, you can set a breakpoint at the closing brace of a function if you want to catch the function after the body of the function has executed, but before it returns to the caller (destroying the stack frame and all of the automatic variables).

Java can be frustrating because the HotSpot interpreter performs some optimizations automatically. For instance, it's sometimes impossible to set a breakpoint in an empty method. The HotSpot interpreter may detect that the method performs nothing, or something trivial, and either eliminate the call to the function or in-line the code. Either way, the function never gets called and the breakpoint is never hit. To combat this, you need to turn off the HotSpot run time compiler by passing the -Xint argument to the Java tool when the application is launched. See the "Custom Executables" section to find out how to accomplish that.

The caveat this section is trying to express is that there is not always a simple one-to-one correlation between the source code statements and the executable code that the debugger deals with. The debugger does its best to translate between the two, but inconsistencies do occur. Just be prepared for this and understand what's going on.

Breakpoint Types

There are two kinds of breakpoints: source breakpoints and symbolic breakpoints. So far, this chapter has only dealt with source breakpoints. Source breakpoints are associated with a particular line in a source file. You set and see source breakpoints right in the gutter of the source file's editor pane.

Symbolic breakpoints are breakpoints that have been created for a particular symbol—that is, at the address of a symbol defined in the program. There are two important differences between a symbolic breakpoint and a breakpoint set at a line in a source file. The most obvious of which is that you don't have to have the source file. Using symbolic breakpoints, you can set a breakpoint at the entry point of any library routine or framework API. For example, you could set a symbolic breakpoint at the free() function. Any code that calls the free(...) function would break into the debugger. The other important difference is that the breakpoint address is no longer tied to a line in a source file. You could cut the function from one file and paste it into another, and the breakpoint would still work.

You'll find out how to create symbolic breakpoints shortly.

Breakpoints Window

Breakpoint management gets far more interesting when you open the Breakpoints window (see Figure 15-11). This can be done using the Breakpoints (Command+Option+B) command, which is also available as a button in many toolbars. The toolbar button has an icon of a window containing a breakpoint (not to be confused with the *other* breakpoints button that has a + sign). You can also double-click any breakpoint you see in a source file.

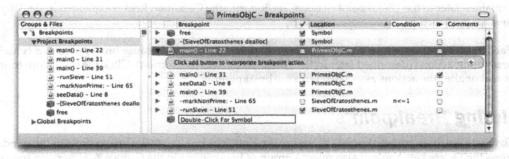

Figure 15-11

The breakpoint window has two panes: a Groups & Files pane containing the Breakpoints smart group and a details pane listing the breakpoints. It should be noted that this is really just an abbreviated view of your project window, without the editor pane. Everything you can do in the Breakpoints window can be accomplished in the Breakpoints smart group and details pane of your project window.

The Breakpoints smart group has two subgroups. The Project Breakpoints sub-group contains all breakpoints specific to this project. These breakpoints are saved for your user account in the project document. When you create a source file breakpoint, it's added to this group.

The Global Breakpoints group contains breakpoints that are available to all projects. This is particularly useful for complex symbolic breakpoints that you want to use in different projects. Or possibly, you could keep breakpoints in a common library that you use in several projects. Global breakpoints are stored in your Xcode preferences.

The list in the details pane shows the breakpoints selected in the Groups & Files window, or all the breakpoints contained in a selected group or groups. To limit the list of breakpoints to a particular subset, select only that subgroup in the Groups & Files pane. To see all of the breakpoints defined, select the top-level Breakpoints group.

Each breakpoint listed displays an icon, a name, an enabled check box, a location, a condition, and a continue option. By Control-/right-clicking the column header of the table you can optionally choose to display the Comments or Last Modified columns. You may also choose to hide columns that don't interest you.

The icon indicates the type of the breakpoint. Source breakpoints have a source file icon, and symbolic breakpoints have a 3D cube. The name of the breakpoint is really a description of its location. For source breakpoints this is the function name and line number within the source file, which is shown in the Location column. For symbolic breakpoints the name is the symbol of the breakpoint address, possibly with a qualifier to distinguish between similar symbols. Symbolic breakpoints are not associated with a source file and always display Symbol for their location.

The name or address of a symbolic breakpoint is editable — double-click the name to change the symbol. Source breakpoints are not. Double-clicking a source breakpoint in the list jumps to that location in the source file. This is the complement of double-clicking a breakpoint in a source file, which jumps to that breakpoint in the breakpoint window.

The Comments column contains a text field for recording your comments about, or a description of, the breakpoint. If you have a lot of comments, open the Info window for the breakpoint and edit the comments there. The last modified field records the last time the breakpoint was altered. The Continue column is explained later in the "Breakpoint Actions" section, and the Condition field is explained in the "Iffy Breakpoints" section.

Each breakpoint appears as a group in the breakpoints list. That's because breakpoints can contain breakpoint actions (described later in the "Breakpoint Actions" section). Click the disclosure triangle to reveal or alter the actions associated with the breakpoint.

Deleting Breakpoints

To delete one or more breakpoints in the breakpoints window, select the breakpoints in the window and press the Delete key. You can also select a group of breakpoints in the Groups & Files pane and choose the Delete command from the Control-/right-click contextual pop-up menu.

To delete a source breakpoint from within a source file editor, click and drag the breakpoint out of the gutter. You can also Control-/right-click the breakpoint and choose the Remove Breakpoint command.

Grouping Breakpoints

In addition to sorting breakpoints by clicking the list column titles, you can also organize breakpoints into groups and subgroups just as you organize source files. Use the File⇨Group or the File⇨New

Group command to create new breakpoint groups and subgroups. (Chapter 5 discussed creating groups in the Sources & Files pane.) You can drag breakpoints and groups around to reorganize them.

Enabling and Disabling Breakpoints

The check mark column in the breakpoints list shows whether that breakpoint is enabled or not. You can enable or disable an individual breakpoint by clicking its checksbox. This is synonymous with clicking the breakpoint's indicator in the source file. Enabled breakpoints are black; disabled breakpoints are grey.

Selecting breakpoints in the Groups & Files pane allows you to enable and disable breakpoints en masse. Select any combination of breakpoints and breakpoint groups in the Groups & Files pane. These commands do not work in the details list. Control-/right-click one of the selected items and choose either the Enable Breakpoints or the Disable Breakpoints command from the contextual menu as shown in Figure 15-12. Enabling or disabling a group sets the state of every breakpoint contained in that group. Hold down the Option key and the Enable Breakpoints command turns into the Enable Only These Breakpoints. This command enables the selected breakpoints, and then disables all other project breakpoints. If you organize your breakpoints into task-oriented sets, this is a quick way of switching the focus of your debug session.

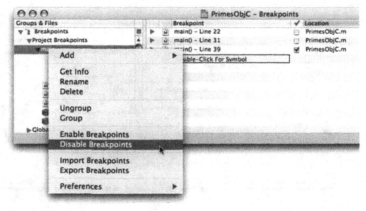

Figure 15-12

You may notice that some breakpoints display a - sign in their enabled check box. These are enabled breakpoints that the debugger can't set for some reason. Examine the debugger console output (covered later) to find out which breakpoints are having problems. This is most commonly encountered with symbolic breakpoints that the debugger can't resolve. Beyond the obvious reason that the symbol simply doesn't exist in the application's name space, it can also happen when you're using ZeroLink. ZeroLink defers the physical linking of functions until they are actually called, which means that the code for many functions won't be loaded into memory when the program starts executing. Until the debugger can turn a symbol name into an absolute memory address, it can't set a breakpoint.

Chapter 15

Creating Symbolic Breakpoints

To create a symbolic breakpoint, first select the Breakpoints gourp in which you want the breakpoint created. At the bottom of the details pane list is a special placeholder breakpoint with a border around the name Double-Click For Symbol. To create a new symbolic breakpoint, do just what it says, as shown in Figure 15-13.

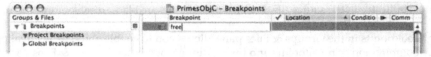

Figure 15-13

The symbol can be any function name known to the linker. This can be a function in your own application or any system API or library that your application is linked to. For C function calls, just the name of the function is sufficient. If there is any ambiguity, Xcode prompts you to choose the specific symbol that you meant. In Figure 15-14, a breakpoint is set on the free symbol, and Xcode wants to know which "free" it's referring to.

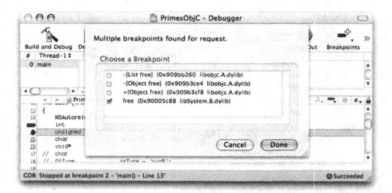

Figure 15-14

Objective-C and C++ methods must be expressed in their complete form. To set a symbolic breakpoint at the isPrime method of the SieveOfEratosthenes class, create a breakpoint for the -[SieveOfEratosthenes isPrime:] symbol. Note that the symbol must have a + or - sign indicating a class or member method. In this example, : indicates that the method takes a single parameter. Just like when you're using the @selector operator, isPrime and isPrime: are two different methods. If the method took a second BOOL parameter, the symbol would be something like -[SieveOfEratosthenes isPrime: ignoringMap:].

In C++, the symbol should be a complete, fully qualified, prototype of the method. If the NestOfBugs class contained a member function named catchMe that took a single integer as a parameter, the symbol to use would be NestOfBugs::catchMe(int i). Unlike the Objective-C symbol, the name of the parameter is included exactly as it was declared in the class statement. gdb will not find the function without a complete copy of its declaration. The return type of a function is not part of its name.

Symbolic breakpoints do not appear as breakpoint indicators in the gutter of the source file editor pane, even if the symbol identifies a function in your source code. Other than the visual differences, symbolic breakpoints are just like source breakpoints and share all of the same capabilities and traits.

Iffy Breakpoints

One of the first things you'll notice about breakpoints is that they always work. Although it might be gratifying to know that the technology is reliable, you may soon discover that it's curse as well. Setting a breakpoint in a function that gets called a million times is enough to wear out the button of any mouse if you have to click the Continue button 999,999 times. And it's quite often that the problem with a loop will be found at the end, not the beginning. Placing a breakpoint in the middle of a loop can be a study in tedium.

What you really want to do is break at the moment your application is doing something interesting or suspicious. For example, you want to break a loop on its *last* iteration or just when a parameter is NULL.

You can accomplish this by using a breakpoint conditional. In the Condition field of the breakpoint, enter any C Boolean expression. If the breakpoint is enabled and the conditional expression evaluates to true when the breakpoint is encountered, the breakpoint stops the program. Otherwise, the breakpoint is ignored and the program continues to run.

Try It Out   Set a Conditional Breakpoint

Open the Factor project, or create a new standard command-line project and enter the following code into main.c:

```c
#include <stdio.h>

static void long int factorial( long int n )
{
    if (n>=1)
        n *= factorial(n-1);
    return (n);
}

int main (int argc, const char * argv[])
{
    printf("10! = %ld\n",factorial(10));
    return 0;
}
```

Then follow these steps:

1. Set the active build configuration to Debug.
2. Build & Run the application.
3. Set a breakpoint at line 5 (the if (n>=1) statement).
4. Start the program in the debugger. Press Continue a few times.

5. Double-click the breakpoint on line 5 to open it in the Breakpoints window.

6. Add the conditional n<=1. Use the Continue command until the program finishes.

7. Debug the program again. Notice where it stops.

8. Fix the code and run or step though the program again.

How It Works

In steps 1 and 2, you built and ran the program. Examining the output, the code is clearly defective:

```
10! = 0
```

In steps 3 and 4, you walked the program through a few iterations of the recursive call to `factorial` using the debugger.

It shouldn't have taken you long to determine that the problem with the `factorial` function occurs when values of n are small, and to get to that point will require you to manually step into each iteration of factorial. What you really want to do is catch the factorial function at the point where n is 1 or smaller. In steps 5 and 6, you do that, setting a conditional on the breakpoint so that it is active only when n is less than or equal to 1.

Starting the program again in step 6 allows the program run, uninterrupted, until a call to `factorial` occurs when the value of n is 1 or 0. In step 7, you repeated the entire exercise from the beginning. But now the breakpoint is conditional and the programs starts and runs right up to the point where factorial is called with a value of 1 (see Figure 15-15).

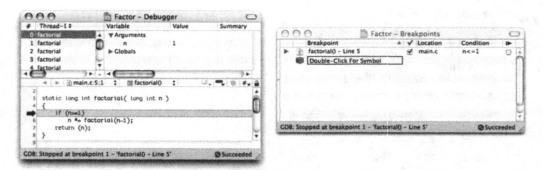

Figure 15-15

It should be obvious that the problem with the code is that the conditional n>=1 is incorrect and allows a recursive call to `factorial` with a value of 0 resulting in a zero result. The conditional should be n>1 or even n>2. The corrected program output is as follows:

```
10! = 3628800
```

The expression can contain only primitive C statements. It can't employ preprocessor macros or make use of any variables beyond what appears in the variables pane. In other words, it can only evaluate expressions based on what the debugger knows about your program. As an example, take the C variable `char string[MAX_LEN]`. Assuming `MAX_LEN` was 100, you could test to see if the string buffer contained a character near the end of the array using the expression `string[98]!='\0'`. However, you could not use the expression `string[MAX_LEN-2]!='\0'` (the debugger doesn't normally know about preprocessor macros)

If there is a problem with the expression, Xcode displays a warning symbol next to the condition in the Breakpoints window. Sometimes this is normal, because an expression might refer to local variables that aren't in scope when the condition is defined. The debugger reevaluates the breakpoint condition when the breakpoint actually occurs, but if the expression is still invalid, it is ignored and the breakpoint acts as if it has no condition. The debugger also notes the problem with a message in the debugger console like "warning: Error parsing breakpoint condition expression."

> **Be very careful about expression side effects.** The expression `i==0` activates the breakpoint when the value of `i` is zero, and ignore the breakpoint if it is any other value. The expression `i=0` *sets the value of i to zero* and continues executing. Assignment, increment, and decrement operations all have their normal effect on values. Be careful of expressions like `o[++k]!=NULL` that alter the value of `k` when the debugger evaluates them. The equivalent expression without side effects would be `o[k+1]!=NULL`.

Be conservative and defensive when you're using expressions. Don't make assumptions that will cause your expression to miss problems, or cause more problems itself. The following table describes a few examples.

Expression	Results
`i>1000000`	Poor. The variable is a signed integer. If the value exceeds `MAX_INT`, the value will be negative and the condition will never be true. If you're looking for a problem where this integer exceeds its nominal range of 0 to 1,000,000, this expression could miss it.
`!(i>=0 && i<=1000000)`	Better. The range of the integer is bounded at both ends.
`ptr->m!=0`	Poor. ptr is a pointer that could be NULL, causing the expression evaluation itself to throw an address error.
`(ptr!=0 && ptr->m!=0)`	Better. The member value m will not be tested if the ptr is NULL, avoiding possible access errors.
`(ptr==0 || ptr->m!=0)`	Best. If you really never expect ptr to be NULL, then the breakpoint should break on that condition as well.

If your condition requires something to be computed, consider adding some code to your application to help your debugging. Here's an example that assumes that you have defined a `DEBUGGING` macro and set it to a non-zero value when compiling your code for testing:

```
#if DEBUGGING
    int actualStrLen = strlen(str);
#endif
    strncpy(buffer,str,1024);
```

You can now set a breakpoint at the `strncpy` statement with the condition `actualStrLen>=1024`.

Breakpoint Actions

In addition to just stopping the program, breakpoints can also perform actions when they are encountered. When a breakpoint is taken, the program stops and control is passed to the debugger. If the breakpoint has breakpoint actions, the debugger immediately performs those actions.

To add or edit actions, expose the breakpoint's contents in the Breakpoints window. For source breakpoints, double-click the breakpoint in the gutter of the source file and Xcode takes you to that breakpoint in the Breakpoints window. Click the + button to add a new action. Click the - button to delete an action. You can't reorder actions, so when you're adding actions, use the + button above the point where you want to new action inserted.

After you've added an action, choose the type of action from the pop-up menu at the top. There are six kinds of breakpoint actions, as listed in the following table.

Action	Function	
Log	Logs a message to the system console.	
Sound	Plays a sound.	
Debugger Command	Executes a command in the debugger.	
Shell Command	Executes a shell command.	
AppleScript	Executes an AppleScript	
Visualize	Updates the Debug Visualizer (discussed later).	

The Log command enables you to receive a message when the breakpoint occurs. How you receive this message is controlled by the two check boxes in the lower-right corner of the action, shown in Figure 15-16. Log outputs the message to the debugger console, and Speak uses the Macintosh text-to-speech technology to say the message out loud. If you leave both unchecked, the action does nothing.

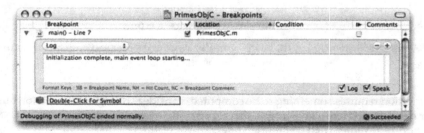

Figure 15-16

The message can contain any of three predefined variables using printf style escape codes. %B is substituted for the name of the breakpoint. %H is replaced by the number of times this breakpoint has been tripped. %C is replaced by whatever comments are attached to the breakpoint. In addition, the message can include any gdb expression — that is, any expression that would be suitable for use as a breakpoint conditional — by surrounding it between two @ characters. For example, the log message "main() called with @argc-1@ arguments" replaces the text "@argc-1@" with the value of the expression argc-1. To include a literal @ in an expression, escape it with a backslash character like this:

```
obj name is "@(const char*)[[obj getProperty:\@"name"] cString]@"
```

The Sound action plays the system sound selected from the pop-up menu.

The Debugger Command action is where the power of breakpoint actions really begins to reveal itself. This action enables a breakpoint to execute almost any other gdb command. There's a lot of potential here, but some all-time favorites are the print, backtrace, and breakpoint commands.

> **Two gdb commands that you should never use in a breakpoint action are** jump **and** continue. **Using** jump **or** continue **can interfere with Xcode's ability to execute other breakpoint actions. (See the "Breakpoint Continuation" section for information about the action you want your program to continue after hitting a breakpoint.)**

The gdb print command prints the value of an expression to the debugger console, similar to the Log action. The backtrace command dumps a summary of the call stack.

Try It Out   Breakpoint Actions

The power of debugger command actions can be illustrated using breakpoints that create and clear other breakpoints. One common problem is trying to debug the behavior of a function when it's called under specific circumstances. This kind of situation occurs often in complex object-oriented applications where seemingly innocuous methods get called under unusual situations, or at unexpected times. The reason these problems are so difficult to isolate is that the function encountering the problem might be called hundreds, if not millions, of times under normal conditions where the problem doesn't manifest itself; so simply setting a breakpoint at the problematic method is out of the question.

The following example illustrates this kind of puzzle. The object in question is the root for a tree of objects. It has a method that returns its name, appropriately named name, that is called from all over the program. When the root node is destroyed, it destroys the buffer containing the root node's name. If you run the application, it throws an exception and dies. It appears that something, somewhere, is sending the object a name message *after* the object is released. Here's the code fragment from the RootNote.m file in the project TreeHouse:

```
26: - (void)dealloc
27: {
28:     free(ASCIIName);
29:     ASCIIName = NULL;
30:     [super dealloc];
31: }
32:
```

```
33:  - (NSString*)name
34:  {
35:      return ([NSString stringWithCString:ASCIIName]);
36:  }
```

If you look at the program, you'll see that the name method is invoked many places, where it works just fine. The problem seems to be that something is calling the name method while the RootNode object is being deallocated. It isn't at all obvious from the source to RootNode where that call might be occurring.

This kind of problem can be trapped using breakpoints and breakpoint actions.

1. Create two breakpoints at lines 28 and 31.

2. Add a breakpoint action to the breakpoint at line 28. Set the action type to Debugger Command, and enter the following gdb command:

```
break 35
```

3. Add a breakpoint action to the breakpoint at line 31. Set the action type to Debugger Command, and enter the following gdb command:

```
clear 35
```

4. Build and start the program under the control of the debugger. Note where the program stops. Review the stack frame to find out who called the name method and why.

How It Works

When execution hits the breakpoint at line 28, the debugger automatically creates a new breakpoint at line 35. If any code calls the name method once the dealloc method has been entered, the debugger catches it and shows you where. After the call to [super dealloc] returns, the breakpoint at line 31 deletes the breakpoint created by the first one. Any further calls to name executes normally. If the breakpoint needed to be in another file, the line number of the breakpoint could have been qualified like this:

```
break RootNode.m:35
clear RootNode.m:35
```

When you debug the program, the call to name that occurred in the context of the RootNode's dealloc call is trapped. Walking down the stack frames, you discover that the releaseChildren method was sending the node a name message so that it could record its action in the log — an ironic case of debugging code getting in the way of debugging.

Note that the breakpoints don't appear in Xcode because Xcode didn't create them, but they are fully functional breakpoints nevertheless. Using the debugger command action requires an understanding of the gdb debugger commands and their syntax. Documentation for the gdb debugger is available online at www.gnu.org/software/gdb/documentation/.

The Shell Command and AppleScript breakpoint actions can be used to execute any arbitrary command line program or AppleScript program file. The usefulness of these actions depends entirely on what you're trying to accomplish. Let's say you have a database program that is corrupting record data. You could create a breakpoint action to execute a MySQL query statement that would dump the contents of suspect records at strategic points in the program. Another clever trick is to use Mac OS X's screen capture tool to take a snapshot of your display at a critical moment. The possibilities are almost endless.

The Shell command takes a command file and a list of arguments. This must be an executable command file—a binary program or an executable script. You can enter the path directly, or click the Choose button to browse for it. The path can be an absolute or project relative path. Arguments are space-separated, just as if you executed the command using the shell, and you can include gdb expressions enclosed between two @ characters just like the Log action. Normally, the debugger executes the command asynchronously. That is, it starts the command executing and immediately returns control to the debugger. If you want the debugger to wait until the command is finished before continuing, check the Wait Until Done option.

The AppleScript action accepts an AppleScript in the action pane. The script does not need to be in a handler block. You can compile your script and check to syntax errors using the Compile button and try out your script using the Test button. The AppleScript executes in the context of the gdb process, so interactive AppleScript commands like `display` can't be used. But commands like `delay`, `beep`, and `say` work just fine. The script can also contain gdb expressions enclosed between @ characters.

The Visualize action activates the Debug Visualizer. The debugger does not automatically open the visualizer. Unless you stop at a breakpoint (see the next section, "Breakpoint Continuation"), the debug visualizer does not automatically update its display. The Visualize action can cause these things to happen. The option Open Debug Visualizer forces the Debug Visualizer window to open whenever this breakpoint is hit. If the breakpoint continues without stopping, the Delay Continue For Some Number of Seconds option can be programmed to pause the execution of your application briefly so you can see the class method being executed in the diagram. Set several visualize action breakpoints at strategic points in your program and you can watch your class methods run like a pinball machine.

Breakpoint Continuation

The earlier example of using breakpoints to set breakpoints glossed over a serious problem in the earlier example. The breakpoints with the actions will still break. After the breakpoint has been hit, and all of its actions have been executed, the debugger still stops your program and waits for instructions. In the example of trying to trap a call that occurs during a destructor, this defeats the purpose of having breakpoints created and deleted automatically. What you really want is for the breakpoint to execute its actions and immediately resume execution of your program. This is exactly what the continue option does.

The continue option is the CD-player-style "play" column in the breakpoints list (see Figure 15-17). Checking this option for a breakpoint means that the breakpoint does not return control to you. The actions of the breakpoint are executed, and the program continues executing exactly as if you had clicked the Continue button.

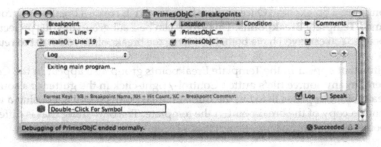

Figure 15-17

The continue option makes all manor of debug automation and checking possible. There are, however, some hazards. Debug actions are executed asynchronously. That is, the debug action merely starts the action. The debugger does not normally hang around waiting for them to complete. So be careful about creating breakpoints that will start, or queue up, hundreds of breakpoint actions. This can be particularly annoying when you're using audio feedback.

The Shell Script breakpoint action has the Wait Until Done option that suspends the debugger and your program until the shell command completes. The Visualize command has a delay value, allowing the Debug Visualizer to update its display, and for you to comprehend the change, before the program resumes execution.

Breakpoint actions can be combined with a breakpoint condition. The breakpoint and all of its actions are executed only if the condition evaluates to true.

Importing and Exporting Breakpoints

Pretend that you are working on a project with another programmer. You've isolated a problem using a complex set of breakpoints. How do you send those breakpoints to your team member so that they can reproduce the problem and fix it? Projects breakpoints are saved on a per-user basis in the project, so you can't just give them a copy of the project document. When they load the project, they won't see the break-points you've set. Scrawling breakpoint descriptions on napkins doesn't sound particularly efficient either.

The solution is to export the breakpoints to a file using the Export Breakpoints command. Select any set of breakpoints or breakpoint groups in the Groups & Files pane and Control-/right-click the selection. Choose the Export Breakpoints command to export the selected breakpoints to a text file. The Import Breakpoints command creates a new subgroup with the name of the breakpoint export file and populates it with its contents. Rename and reorganize the imported breakpoints as you see fit.

As a single developer, you can use these commands to archive a collection of breakpoints for some future purpose or move some breakpoints between projects without resorting to making them global breakpoints.

Breakpoint Templates

As you put more and more effort into breakpoints, you'll find that you want to use them over again. One very convenient way to do this is to create a breakpoint template.

Create and configure a breakpoint. Once you are happy with it, create a breakpoint group in the Groups & Files pane named **Template Breakpoints**. This group can be a subgroup of your project breakpoints or the global breakpoints. You can even have both. Now drag the breakpoints you want to reuse into this group.

Any breakpoints that appear in the Template Breakpoints group also appear in the Control-/right-click contextual menu in any source file's gutter. Control-/right-click in the gutter of a source file and choose any of the breakpoint templates listed in the Built-In Breakpoints menu. Choosing a template inserts a breakpoint that's a copy of the breakpoint in the template. The only thing that is different is the location of the breakpoint.

Xcode also includes a number of built-in breakpoint templates listed at the beginning of the Built-In Breakpoints menu.

Examining Data

Now that you've learned all about controlling the flow of your application while debugging, you can return to examining the content of variables. "The Variable Panes" briefly introduced the variables pane of the debugging window. Now look at that pane in a little more detail and look at other ways of examining the contents of memory.

To quickly review, the variables pane (previously shown in Figure 15-4) displays the known variables within the scope of the selected stack frame. Variables are organized into logical groups. Structures and objects appear as groups, forming a hierarchy of containers and values. These are described by the debug symbol information attached to your program.

As you step through your program, the debugger compares the values that were displayed when your program was last started against the values that appear when the debugger stopped it again (see Figure 15-18). Any values that are different are highlighted in red—you can't see this black-and-white illustration, but the value of variable i is red.

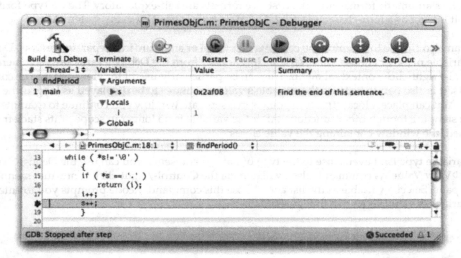

Figure 15-18

The code was stopped at line 17 where the value of i was 0. The Step Over command was issued. The debugger allowed one statement (the increment) to be executed and stopped the program again. The value of i is no longer 0 and Xcode highlights the change in the display. Using the Step Over command again returns the value to black again, because the next statement does not alter its value. It doesn't matter how much the program executes between stops. As long as the variables pane is showing the same set of variables at the next stop, Xcode highlights whatever values changed.

The Value column displays the primitive value of each variable. For scalar values, this is a numeric value. For structures and pointers to structures, it is the address of the structure or the value of the pointer. The default display format for scalar values is Natural. For signed integers and floating point numbers, the column displays a signed decimal value. Unsigned integers display an unsigned decimal number. Character types display both the decimal and Unicode representations of the value. Pointers and structures are shown as hexadecimal memory addresses. The natural format is usually sufficient, but you can manually choose a different representation. The choices are as follows:

❑ Hexadecimal

❑ Decimal

❑ Unsigned Decimal

❑ Octal

❑ Binary

❑ OSType

You can find these formats in the Debug⇨Variables View menu, or in the Control-/right-click contextual menu of the variables pane. Select one or more variables in the pane and then choose one of these fixed formats to force the expression of the value, or values, into the desired format. Choose Natural to return to Xcode's automatic formatting. The first five formats are self-explanatory. The OSType format displays a 32-bit integer as a four-character string. This data type is used by many system APIs.

You can also choose to examine the contents of a value or structure in a separate window. Double-click the variable name or choose View Variable In Window from the Debug⇨Variables View menu or the Control-/right-click contextual menu. This can be particularly useful for viewing large or complex objects. It is also handy because the variable's value continues to be displayed as long as the variable exists. You can place a local structure pointer in a separate window and continue to examine its value while stepping though other functions. After the variable is no longer in scope or its stack frame is released, the window containing the value closes.

If a variable type isn't even close to the type of data it represents, you can use the Debug⇨Variables View⇨View Value As command, also available via the Control-/right-click contextual menu of the variables pane. Select a variable in the list and choose this command. Xcode prompts you to enter a cast for the variable's value, as shown in Figure 15-19.

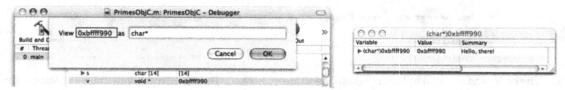

Figure 15-19

Xcode then attempts to interpret the value of that variable using the type cast. This is particularly useful for generic types such as void*. As shown in Figure 15-19, the pointer to a string was assigned to a void* variable. By using the View Value As command, you can coerce the debugger to interpret the void* value as if it was a char* variable, shown on the right.

Sometimes you just need to look at memory. Using the Debug⇨Variables View⇨View As Memory command, you can open the memory browser window shown in Figure 15-20.

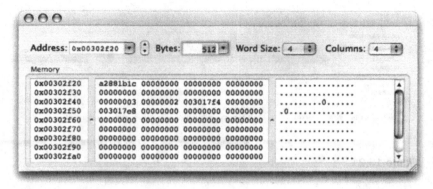

Figure 15-20

The browser displays a block of memory in hexadecimal and ASCII formats, much like the hexdump command. The Address field determines the starting address of the display. Initially, this is the address of the selected scalar, structure, or object in the variables pane. If the selected variable is a pointer or object reference, the address is the value of that pointer (a dump of what the pointer points to, not a dump of the pointer's value). The Bytes menu lets you select how much memory is disassembled in the window. Choose one of the preset values or enter your own. Use the up and down arrows between the Address and Bytes field to move one page of memory forward or backward. The Word Size and Columns menus control the number of bytes in each column of hexadecimal values, and the number of columns in each line, respectively.

There is only one memory browser window. Selecting a new address using the View As Memory command simply changes the address in the Address field. The Address field has a pop-up menu that keeps a short history of previously viewed addresses. If you need to follow a pointer to another address that you find in a block of memory, simply copy the address from the hexadecimal listing and paste it into the Address field (prefixing it with 0x).

If you try to view memory that is outside the address space of your application, the memory browser displays *A*'s for the bytes it can't access.

Viewing Global Variables

The Globals group in the variables pane contains a selected set of global variables that you want to examine. Normally, this group has nothing. It's impractical for this group to contain every global variable in your application's process space. The group could contain hundreds of variables, be impossible to navigate, and place a huge burden on the debugger display.

Instead, the group starts out empty. Use the global variables window, shown in Figure 15-21, to add variables to this group or merely browse the global variables in your application. You can open this window using the Debug⇨Tools⇨Global Variables command or by attempting to expand the Globals group when it is empty.

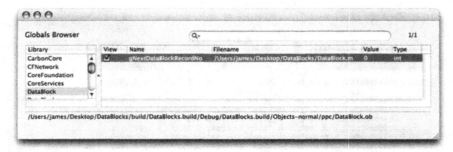

Figure 15-21

Figure 15-21

The global variables window is divided between a list of modules on the left and the list of global variables in each module on the right. Select a module, and Xcode lists all of the global variables that your application has access to on the right. To quickly search for a particular variable name, enter some fragment of the variable's name in the search field at the top of the window.

Figure 15-21 examines the global variables declared in a program named DataBlock. The listing tells you the file name the variable is declared in, its current value, and its type. By selecting the box in the View column, this variable is added to the Globals group in the variables pane. The viewed global variables are recorded in the user preferences of the project document. After these variables are added, they will always appear in the Globals group of your variables pane until they are removed or until the variable itself no longer exists.

Expressions

Another way to view variables is through expressions. Expressions appear in the Expressions window, shown in Figure 15-22. You can open this window using the Debug⇨Tools⇨Expressions... command. To add an expression in the window, type the expression in the input field at the bottom of the window, or select any variable and choose Debug⇨Variables View⇨View Variable As Expression.

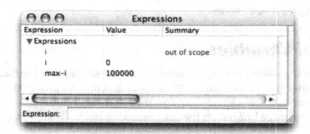

Figure 15-22

These are debugger expressions and are subject to all of the limitations and caveats of breakpoint conditions. In the Expressions window, each expression acts like a variable. You can alter its display format or open it in a separate window. You can also add type casts to an expression to coerce the interpretation of the expression's value.

Expressions are interpreted within the context of the currently selected stack frame, and those expressions retain that context. In the example previously shown in Figure 15-22, there are two expressions that resolve to value of the integer i. But these two variables are from different stack frames. Each was added to the window and a different stack frame was selected in the threads pane. The first one was added while a function was executing, but that function has now returned. Thus, the context that defined that variable no longer exists and the expression is marked as "out of scope."

To delete an expression, select it in the Expressions window and press the Delete key.

Expressions are very useful for examining the contents of array values. An expression like stack[1] examines the second element in the stack array. The expression buffer[index] examines whichever element the variable index references.

Data Formatters

You can use data formatters to summarize complex data structures and objects. A demonstration of the built-in data formatters was given in "The Variables Pane" earlier in this chapter. But the built-in formatters won't help with types or objects that you've defined, or to identify which Xcode doesn't include a formatter.

Creating your own data formatters is very easy. It is really nothing more than a format string with placeholders for values or expressions derived from the variable being summarized. Any regular text in the data formatter is displayed verbatim. There are two kinds of placeholders: references and expressions.

References are delimited by two percent characters (%reference%). A reference can refer to a single member variable by name. If the variable is contained in a sub-structure, then use the appropriate period (.) separated variable name. You cannot use operators such as pointer dereferences or array indexes. For that, you need to use an expression. Taking the class that's defined in Listing 15-3, the reference to the integer record_no of DataBlock class would be %header.record_no%.

Listing 15-3: Sample Class

```
typedef struct {
    int record_no;
    unsigned long checksum;
} BlockHeader;

@interface DataBlock : NSObject
{
    @public
        BlockHeader     header;
        NSMutableData*  data;
}
```

An expression is any debugger expression; the same kind of expression that you can add to the expressions window. In fact, it's good to think of an expression in a data formatter as an expression in the Expressions window, as you'll see in moment.

Expressions are contained between matching braces (`{expression}`). Unlike references, expressions do not assume the context of the value being examined. To refer to the object being examined, use the `$VAR` macro in the expression. `$VAR` will be replaced with the name of the variable when the data formatter is evaluated. Using the previous class as an example again, the expression to access the `record_no` value would be `{$VAR.header.record_no}`. If you're now guessing that you can reference other variables in the context of the current stack frame, you're correct. However, this isn't a good idea, which will be explained later. Limit your evaluation to the structure or object being examined.

The advantage of expressions over references is that they are more expressive. You can perform math, include conditionals, and even call member functions. Again using the class defined in Listing 15-3, here are some valid expressions:

❑   `{$VAR.header.record_no}`

❑   `{$VAR.header.checksum&0x0000ffff}`

❑   `{$VAR.data?(int)[$VAR.data length]:0}`

Combining these two techniques, you can now create a data formatter for the DataBlock object type. Start by running the program and stopping the debugger with an instance of the DataBlock class in scope. Make sure that Debug⇨Variables View⇨Enable Data Formatters is checked. Select the DataBlock variable in the variables pane and choose the Debug⇨Variables View⇨Edit Summary Format. The debugger lets you edit the data formatter for the variable. Now you can enter the data formatter string shown in Figure 15-23.

Figure 15-23

After it has been entered, this text becomes the data formatter used for every instance of the DataBlock class. The debugger resolves the references and expressions for each instance, creating the more informative summary shown in Figure 15-24.

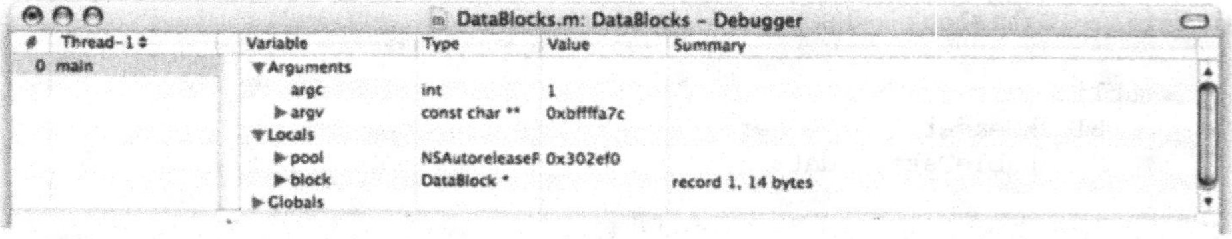

Figure 15-24

The syntax used for references and expressions can be extended to obtain other information about the value or expression. The final display value can be something different than the value that the expression evaluates to. The other types of information that can be extracted from an expression are chosen using one of the column selectors listed in the following table. The "column" you are selecting is one of the columns in the variables pane or the expressions window. In essence, the result of a reference or expression is treated as if it had been entered into the Expressions window. The column selector lets you choose which column in the window will be used as the result of the expression. You can think of an expression result as an object with four properties (value, name, type, and summary) — the column selector lets you choose which property to display.

Column Selector	Description
{expression}:v %reference%:v	The value of the expression — that is, the primitive numerical value that would appear in the Value column of the Expressions window. This is the default column. Omitting the column selector is equivalent to using :v.
{expression}:t %reference%:t	The type of the final data object the expression evaluates to. A numerical expression would result in a primitive data type, such as int or double. The type of an expression that references a member variable, or calls a function, will be the type of expression's result. For example, the expression {[$VAR owner]}:t would display the type of the object returned by the method owner.
{expression}:s %reference%:s	This selector results in the text that would appear in the Summary column of the expression. Because the Summary column can be formed using data formatters, this is a way of using other data formatters in portions of your data formatter. You can only use this on expressions that have a summary display. Expressions that result in primitive values do not have any content in their summary column.
{expression}:n %reference%:n	The name of the variable or expression that would appear in the Expression column of the Expressions window. The column is self-referential and not particularly useful.

The type column (:t) can be useful for displaying the type or class of a member value. For example, if you have a class that manages a collection of homogenous objects, a data formatter of collection of {[$VAR getFirstObject]}:t would tell you what kind of objects your collection contains.

The summary column selector is the most useful. You can use it to construct data formatters from other data formatters.

Try It Out   Create a Data Formatter

Open the DataBlocks project. The project contains both the DataBlock class described earlier, and a subclass of DataBlock called StampedDataBlock, shown in Listing 15-4.

Listing 15-4: DataBlock Subclass

```
@interface StampedDataBlock : DataBlock
{
    @private
        NSCalendarDate*    createdDate;
        NSCalendarDate*    modifiedDate;
}
```

Follow these steps:

1. Set the build configuration to Debug. Set a breakpoint in `main()` at line 13 of the DataBlocks.m file.

2. Build and debug the application. It should stop at line 13 and show the generic values for `block` and `trackedBlock` as shown in Figure 15-25.

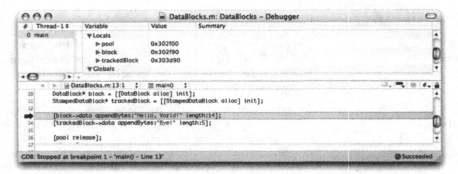

Figure 15-25

3. Set the data formatter for the `block` variable to `record %header.record_no%, {(int)[$VAR.data length]} bytes`.

4. Set the data formatter for the `trackedBlock` variable to `{(DataBlock*)$VAR}:s, created %createdDate%:s`.

5. Continue stepping through the program.

How It Works

The first data formatter created for the DataBlock class summarizes its contents by accessing its `record_no` and data instance variables. The debugger now presents a much friendlier summary of the object's state.

The StampedDataBlock formatter is a little trickier. The StampedDataBlock class does not inherit the data formatter for DataBlock. Data formatters for each type are independent of one another.

There are two problems inherent in creating a data formatter for the new subclass. First, you don't want to repeat everything you wrote for the DataBlock formatter. Secondly, you don't want to write a formatter for the NSCalenderDate member object. The summary column selector lets you avoid both of these problems by setting the data formatter for the StampedDataBlock class to `{(DataBlock*)$VAR}:s, created %createdDate%:s`. The first expression casts the object to an instance of its superclass and obtains text that would appear in its Summary column, effectively calling the data formatter you created for the DataBlock class. The second reference obtains the value of `createdDate` and inserts what would appear in its summary column. The final result, shown in Figure 15-26, is a data formatter that extends the data formatter of its superclass using a built-in data formatter supplied by Xcode.

Figure 15-26

Data formatters can be very useful during debugging. You can create data formatters that quickly summarize the state of complex objects. This allows you to concentrate on the high-level logic of your application, rather than spend all of your time digging through the member variables of objects trying to decode their content. Writing data formatters, however, can be a frustrating experience. If there is *anything* the debugger doesn't like about your data formatter, it won't use it. The following table lists some of the more common problems you can encounter while creating data formatters.

Type of Problem	Solution
Syntax	Be extra careful about the syntax of your expressions and references.
Quotes	Double quotes in the body of an expression must be escaped with a backslash. Example: `name "{[$VAR getProperty:\"name\"]}:s"`. Notice that the quotes inside the expression are escaped, but not in the text outside the expression.
Unknown types	The debugger often does not know the data type of values returned by functions. If you have any doubts, cast the result: `author {(NSString*)[$VAR authorName]}:s`
Execution problems	Expressions that call functions have to function perfectly. The formatter `name {[$VAR name]}:s` will fail if the method name throws an exception, tries to access a null variable, can't allocate memory, or any of a limitless number of similar runtime problems. The functions that you call using data formatters should be extremely defensive.
Null summary	You cannot use the `:s` column selector if the expression results in a data type that has no summary column content.
Invalid references	Expressions that use other variables in the current stack frame context will fail when interpreted in a different stack frame or execution context where those variables don't exist. Data formatters should concern themselves only with examining the contents of the structure or object.

Table continued on following page

Type of Problem	Solution
ZeroLink	This is yet one more situation where ZeroLink can trip you up. ZeroLink loads functions and type information on demand as your program executes. Expressions executed in the debugger will *not* cause unreferenced symbols to load. If your application hasn't caused a symbol or function to load yet, a data formatter that uses that function or type will fail.
Temporary Objects	(For Objective-C programmers) Be warned that creating autoreleased objects in your data formatters may result in memory leaks. An example would be `{ (NSString*)[NSString stringWithCharacters:$VAR .uStr.unicode length:$VAR.uStr.length] }:s`. The problem here is that the NSString object is created in the context of the debugger and has no autorelease pool. You will see a "leak" message in the debugger log.
Side Effects	Data formatters can call functions in your application. Side effects, such as altering instance variables or releasing objects, can have unexpected consequences in your application and your debugging efforts.

If you are having problems getting a formatter work, break it down into its individual components and subexpressions and try each one at a time. Slowly build up the expression until you get it working or find the element that thwarts your efforts. Try expressions without the column selector. Cast return values liberally. Replace macros and function calls with constants. Turn off ZeroLink. Add the same function call to your code and try debugging it.

Data formatters you define are stored in the `~/Library/Application Support/Apple/Developer Tools/CustomDataViews/CustomDataViews.plist` file. Data formatters are global to all projects and are not stored in the project document. Sharing data formatters with other developers will require some copying and pasting, or you may just want to exchange `CustomDataViews.plist` files.

Beyond Data Formatter Strings

Although data formatters can do a lot, they are limited to what can be expressed in a format string. If you need a data formatter that exceeds these capabilities, you can develop your own data formatter plug-in. The descriptions for doing so can be found in the `DataFormatterPlugin.h` file, buried inside the Xcode application itself at /Developer/Applications/Xcode.app/Contents/PlugIns/GDBMIDebugging .xcplugin/Contents/Headers/DataFormatterPlugin.h. This file contains detailed information about formatter strings, the format of CustomDataViews.plist, and how to create a data formatter plug-in, among other topics.

In brief, you create a data formatter plug-in by creating a bundle. The bundle contains its own CustomDataViews.plist file. Unlike data formatter strings that you type into the debugger window, the data formatter strings in the bundle's CustomDataViews.plist file can call any of the functions defined in the plug-in bundle. The sample ManagedObjectDataFormatter project produces a data formatter plug-in for managed objects and is available at `http://developer.apple.com/samplecode/ManagedObject DataFormatter/ManagedObjectDataFormatter.html`. You can use this project as a template for creating your own data formatter plug-ins.

Object Descriptions

Like data formatters, many object-oriented languages have adopted conventions for converting any object into a textual representation. In Java, this is the `toString()` function. Objective-C uses the –[NSObject description] method. If you are using an object that supports one of these standards, you can use the Debug⇨Variables View⇨Print Description to Console command. The debugger invokes the standard "to string" function on the object and sends the result to the debugger console.

Watchpoints

Watchpoints are breakpoints for data. You can make any variable a watchpoint. Whenever the debugger detects that the value of that variable has changed, it stops your application.

Watchpoints sound great, but they are fairly limited. The biggest problem is that your application can't execute any code where the watchpoint variable is out of context. So they are mostly useful for global variables that are always in scope and for catching state changes in a loop.

You set a watch point by first selecting a variable in the variables pane. Choose the Debug⇨Variables View⇨Watch Variable command. This places a magnifying glass icon next to the variable as shown in Figure 15-27. Start the program executing again, and it breaks at the point just before the variable is altered with a dialog box explaining what is about to happen, also shown in Figure 15-27.

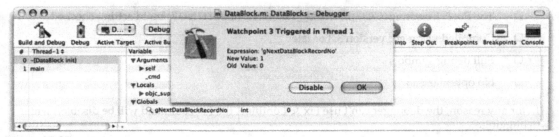

Figure 15-27

You can choose to acknowledge the event and leave the watchpoint set, or disable the watchpoint by clicking the Disable button. Watchpoints are automatically deleted whenever your application exits the context where the watchpoint variable exists. Watchpoints are not retained between debug sessions.

To remove a watchpoint, select the variable being watched and choose Debug⇨Variables View⇨Watch Variable again to remove the check mark.

Changing Data and Code

So far, this chapter has taken a rather passive approach to debugging. You've viewed code and variables in countless ways, but you haven't actually changed anything. But Xcode lets you alter both data and code, while your application is executing. This can be a huge timesaver when you're debugging. You can change the values of parameters to test specific cases, or correct a value that was miscalculated and continue testing.

Changing variables values is easy. Select a primitive variable and choose the Edit Value command from either the Data⇨Variables View menu or the Control-/right-click contextual menu in the variables pane. You can also double-click the value of the variable right in the variables pane. Edit the value and press Return. The only acceptable forms are decimal, octal (beginning with a zero), or hexadecimal (beginning with 0x). To enter a character you need to translate that character into a decimal or hexadecimal value. The Code Table view of the system's Character Palette is particularly useful in looking up character code values.

If the variable is a pointer, you can change the address of the pointer or you can expand the variable and Xcode allows you to change any primitive values that the pointer points to.

The Magic Fix

It's simple enough to poke a new value into a variable and continue executing. But what if the code itself is incorrect? Xcode allows you to fix that too.

This bit of magic, and it really is something close to it, is a feature called Fix & Continue. As the name implies, it enables you to recompile code in your application and continue debugging it *without restarting your program*. Use of this feature depends on some prerequisites. The debug version of your application must be built with the following:

❑   The Fix & Continue (GCC_ENABLE_FIX_AND_CONTINUE) build setting checked

❑   Compiled using gcc version 3.3 or later

❑   Full debug symbols

❑   No optimization

If, for any reason, the debugger can't use Fix & Continue, the Fix command will be disabled while debugging.

Using this feature is deceptively simple. Say, for example, you discover a bug in your source code while you're debugging. Listing 15-5 shows a common programming mistake: a loop with a missing increment statement.

Listing 15-5: Bad Loop

```
Token findOneToken( const char* s )
{
    while ( *s!='\0' && isspace(*s) )
        s++;

    Token token;
    token.word = s;
    token.length = 0;
    while ( *s!='\0' )
        {
```

```
            char c = *s;
            if (isspace(c))
                break;
            token.length++;
            }

        return (token);

    }
```

After stepping through the second loop a few times, it becomes obvious that it gets stuck because the statement `c = *s` should have been `c = *s++`.

To correct this code, simply edit the statement so that it reads `c = *s++` and choose Debug⇨Fix or click the Fix button in the debugger's toolbar. The source for this file is recompiled, the new code is loaded into your application's code space replacing the old version of findOneToken, and the program counter changes to point to the equivalent line in the new code.

If that was all that needed to be done, you could continue debugging the application. However, this code has another problem. The bug the char pointer s isn't being incremented, but the value of `token.length` is. If you let the code continue to run, the returned value of `token.length` would be wrong. There are two ways of addressing this. The first would be to use the variables pane and simply edit the value of `token.length`, setting it back to 0. Another way is to alter the program counter so that the program continues executing at a different location in the code. Here the PC indicator is being dragged back up to the `token.length = 0` statement so that the entire second loop starts over from the beginning (see Figure 15-28).

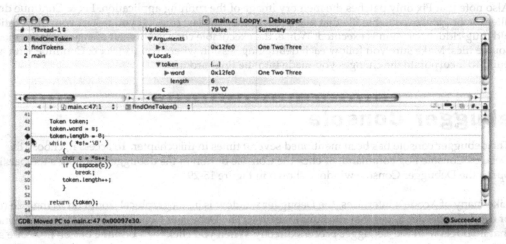

Figure 15-28

When the execution is continued, the program starts again at the top of the (now bug-free) loop, reinitializes `token.length` to 0, and executes correctly.

Magic Fix Limiations

Fix & Continue does have some limitations. Here are a few:

- ❑ You cannot redefine `typedef` variables, data structures, classes, or function arguments.
- ❑ You cannot redefine the automatic variables on the stack frame.
- ❑ You cannot redefine global data variables.
- ❑ You cannot make any change to your application's resources, such as icon or NIB files.
- ❑ You cannot fix a bad reference to a function by renaming the function.

In short, you can make any change that alters *only* the executable code of one or more functions. You can't make a fix that alters the data types or linkages that are, or could be, used anywhere else in the application.

There are a couple of other caveats about how Fix & Continue works that you should be aware of. Fix & Continue replaces the code of a function that was executing and changes the current program counter so that execution continues in the new code. However, it does not change the program counter in any other stack frame. Let's say that Function A calls Function B. If you stop the program in Function B and fix Function A, when Function B returns it will return to the *old* Function A, not the corrected one. The corrected Function A won't be called until something else calls Function A again.

Fix & Continue only compiles and replaces the in-memory image of a single file. If you make changes in several files, you will need to perform a Fix & Continue on each one.

Also note that Fix only patches the memory image of the running application. Fix & Continue does not alter the original executable file that was produced by the last build. If you restart your application the old (bug-ridden) version is executed. Worse, the executable code is now out of sync with the modified source files. Make sure you follow each debugging session where you use Fix & Continue with a new build to incorporate the changes you made into the final product.

Debugger Console

The debugger console has been mentioned several times in this chapter. To access it, choose the Debug⇨Console Log command, or click the Console button in the debugger window's toolbar. This opens the Debugger Console window, shown in Figure 15-29.

Like many of Xcode's interfaces, the Debugger window is just a graphical front-end to the gdb (or Java, or AppleScript) debugger that runs underneath it. The Debugger Console window is a shell window that interacts with the debugger process directly. When you click the Continue button in Xcode's Debugger window, Xcode just sends a `continue` command to gdb. Any information that gdb outputs is visible in the Debugger Console window.

If you are having problems with the debugger, the Debugger Console window is the first place to look. Problems setting breakpoints, resolving symbols, or evaluating expressions are logged there.

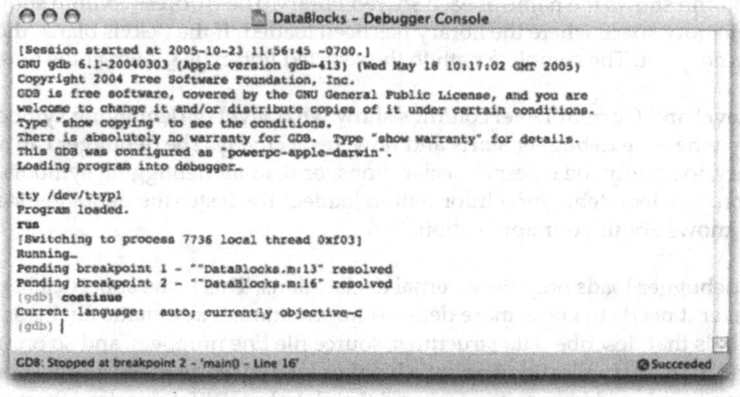

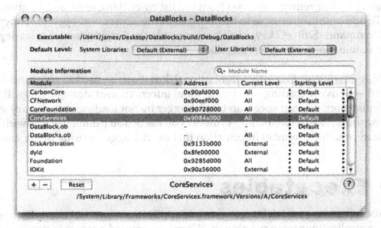

Figure 15-29

More interesting is that the Debugger Console window is a fully interactive terminal window. Open this window and you can type commands directly into the debugger. The debugger provides many features that are not available through the graphical interface provided by Xcode. Of course, this requires an understanding of the gdb and Java debugger commands and their syntax. You can learn the basics by entering the help command at the (gdb) or JavaBug> prompt. The AppleScript debugger has no inter-active commands.

Shared Libraries

One miscellaneous debugger tool is the shared library window, shown in Figure 15-30. Opened with the Debug⇨Tools⇨Shared Library command, it shows the status of the shared libraries that your application is linked to. Most of the information here concerns how many of the debugging symbols for each library have been loaded into the debugger.

Figure 15-30

The Module column shows the name of each shared library. The Address column shows the address in the application's memory space where the library has been loaded. If the field is blank, the library has not been loaded into memory yet. The complete path to the selected library is shown at the bottom of the window.

The Starting Level and Current Level columns show what level of debugging symbols should be loaded for each library when the debugger starts and now, respectively. The debugger can avoid loading symbols for a library, load only the external declarations, or read all debugging symbols including source file line information. The less debugging information loaded, the faster the debugger starts up and runs—and the less it knows about your application.

Normally, the debugger loads only the external declarations. This is the superficial information about the library. Whenever it needs to know more detailed information, it automatically loads any remaining debugger symbols that describe data structures, source file line numbers, and so on. You can watch this process at work. Start an application and set a breakpoint very early in the application, like at the first line of main(). Open the shared library window and the global variables window. Start looking through the libraries in the global variables window. As you browse each library for global variables, the status of the loaded symbols in the shared library window changes from None or External to All as you force the debugger to load additional debugging symbols for each library—debug symbol information that the debugger needs to display the global variables in each library.

You can manually load the symbols for a library into memory by changing the setting in the Current Level column. The change occurs immediately. The Starting Level column determines what the Current Level column will be set to when the library is initially loaded. You can set this to a particular level or use the Default setting. If set to Default, the level used will either be the Default Level for System Libraries or User Libraries, as appropriate, set with the two global pop-up menus at the top of the window. The default level of External is known as "lazy" symbol loading. Like ZeroLink, the object is to get your application running in the debugger as quickly as possible by loading only the minimal amount of information and worrying about the details later. You can disable Lazy Symbol Loading in the Debugger pane of the Xcode preferences. Disabling Lazy Symbol Loading changes the User Libraries default from External to All.

The Reset button at the bottom sets the Starting Level of all libraries to Default.

You can manually add or remove libraries from the list by clicking the + and - button at the bottom of the window. To add a library, browse to the location of the library and open it. Remember that in the file browser, the Command+Shift+G key combination opens the Go To window, allowing you to enter a path to normally invisible directories like /usr/lib.

The shared libraries window is mostly informational, but it can be used to give hints to the debugger telling it to load—or avoid loading—debug symbol information at strategic times. If you are debugging a very large application, this can speed up the debugger by not loading unnecessary symbols or speed up your debugging workflow by preloading symbols you need. You cannot use this window to force libraries to load or unload or to force symbol information that the debugger is using out of memory.

Custom Executables

So far you've been running and debugging simple applications without much thought to the environment that those applications were running in. When you created a target to produce your application, Xcode also created a matching product and an executable. The executable, which appears in the

Debugging

Executables smart group of the Groups & Files pane, defines the execution environment for your application. It defines what binary program will be executed when it is launched, what parameters and environment variable will be passed to it, and what its I/O file descriptors will be attached to. You can customize the environment settings of an executable created by Xcode, or you can create your own.

You may want to customize or create a custom executable for several reasons. For example:

❑ You need to pass command-line parameter to the process when it is started.

❑ You need to set environment variables for the process, or choose a different working directory before the process is started.

❑ You want to redirect the input or output of the tool to something other than the run or debug console windows.

❑ You need to debug an executable that Xcode didn't produce or for which Xcode doesn't automatically create a product and executable, such as a program produced by an external build process.

❑ Your executable is launched via a script or some other process.

❑ The project you are developing is a plug-in or a framework that can't be executed on its own. You need to launch an application that will load the plug-in and exercise it.

General Settings

Open the Info window for an existing executable, or choose the Project➪New Custom Executable command to create a new one. The General tab of the executable's Info window, shown in Figure 15-31, controls the environment for that executable when it is run.

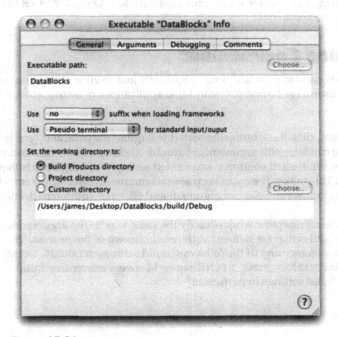

Figure 15-31

The Executable Path option is the path, relative to the build product's directory, to the program that will be launched when the executable is started. Normally this is the binary application produced by your target. Change this if you want a different program executed instead. An example would be a UNIX program that is started by a shell script. The script checks the state of the program, gathers configuration information, and so on, before launching the binary program with the correct environment and command switches. If your product is started by such a script, enter the path to the script here.

At the bottom of the window is the current or working directory that will be set before the executable is launched. This is important to some executables that expect to find resources or perform work on files relative to the current directory. Normally this is set to the build directory for the product. That is, the current directory will be the same directory that contains the executable. The build product directory will change depending on which build configuration is active. You can alternatively choose the project directory or a custom directory. Enter the custom directory path, or click the Choose button to browse for a folder.

The Use Suffix When Loading Frameworks option passes a special flag to the dynamic linker. It tells the system's runtime library loader to search for alternate versions of framework libraries. Many libraries are provided in alternate versions designed to aid in debugging or profiling. They may include additional integrity checks or log informational messages to the system log that are useful during development. When set to No, the loader links your application to the standard system libraries.

The Use For Standard Input/Output option determines where the stdout, stdin, and stderr file descriptors will be connected when the executable is launched. The Pseudo terminal connects your application to the run or debug console you've been using throughout this chapter. The Pipe choice is only useful for remote debugging, as described later. The System Console choice directs the program's output to the system console. Macintosh applications launched by the user, and command-line programs launched without a shell, normally have their output redirected to the system console log. You can review the system console log using the Console utility provided with Mac OS X. When set to the System Console choice, stdin is connected to null.

Arguments and Environment

Use the Arguments pane to pass additional arguments and environment variables to your program. This can be extremely useful for testing command-line applications or setting special features of the runtime system.

To add an argument, click the + button beneath the Arguments pane and type in the argument value (see Figure 15-32). You can later edit arguments by double-clicking their values and reordered them by dragging. The check box in the left column is an enabled setting. Only arguments that are enabled are passed to the executable. This makes it easy to keep several commonly used arguments in the list and quickly select just the ones you want. Select an argument and click the - button to delete it entirely.

The environment variables pane works exactly the same way as the arguments, except that this pane defines named variables that are defined in the environment of the process. The values of environment variables can also reference any of the following build settings: SYMROOT, SRCROOT, OBJROOT, BUILT_PRODUCTS_DIR, and TARGET_TEMP_DIR. (Chapter 14 covers referencing build setting in general and the meaning of these build settings in particular.)

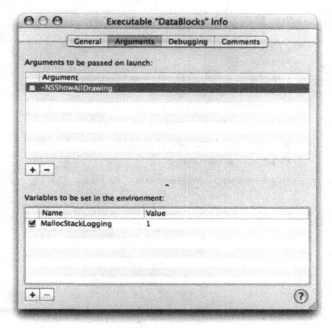

Figure 15-32

Debugging

The Debugging pane, shown in Figure 15-33, controls additional settings that affect the execution environment of your program when you launch it under the control of the debugger. The When Using option controls which debugger Xcode will start to debug your application. The debugger chosen must be capable of debugging the kind of application that the executable produces. The Java debugger cannot debug a binary executable. Xcode sets this appropriately for executable products produced from targets. For custom executables, you need to tell Xcode which debugger is appropriate.

The Use For Standard Input/Output option controls the connections to the program's I/O. You may want to set this to System Console if the output of the program is obscuring the output of the debugger itself in the Debugger Console window. It is also possible to distinguish between the output of the debugger and your program by coloring their text differently in the Debugger Console window. (See the Debugger pane settings in the Xcode preferences.) If you are doing remote debugging, this option must be set to Pipe.

The next two options configure the gdb debugger for remote execution. The "Remote Debugging" section in this chapter explains how to configure a program for remote debugging.

The Start Executable After Starting Debugger option automatically starts your application running as soon as the debugger is loaded. Normally this is checked, but you may not want this to happen. Turning this option off launches the debugger, but performs no further action. This permits you the opportunity of making special adjustments in the debugging environment, such as setting breakpoints, before the program starts running. You can even use the debugger command to attach to an already running instance of your application, rather than launching a new one.

Figure 15-33

The Break on Debugger() And DebugStr() option sets the USERBREAK environment variable before your application is started. The presence of this environment variable causes the Debugger() and DebugStr() functions defined in Core Services to send a SIGINT signal to your program if either of these functions are called. Normally, calls to these functions do nothing. When running under the debugger, a SIGINT signal suspends your program just as if it hit a breakpoint. This option only sets this environment variable when the executable is launched for debugging. To have it set all of the time, set the USERBREAK environment variable to 1 in the Arguments pane.

The Auto-Attach Debugger on Crash option causes the debugger to attach to the executable's process should it crash. This is equivalent to stopping your executable immediately after it crashes, but before the process is terminated, and issuing the Debug➪Attach command.

The Additional Directories to Find Source File In pane lists the paths to where the debugger can find the source file used to build the executable being debugged. Normally you don't need to add anything here because Xcode automatically searches all of the source directories in your project. However, if you have included source files outside your project or the executable was built from source files that Xcode doesn't know about (files in an externally built target, for instance), add those directories here. You can click the + button and type in the path, or drag a folder from the Finder and drop it into the list.

Selecting an Executable

The active executable that you select using the Project➪Set Active Executable menu is the executable that will be launched when you choose any of the Run or Debug commands. This is typically the product produced by the active target, but it doesn't have to be. After selecting a target, you can change the active executable to an executable produced by another target or to a custom executable that you've created.

When you switch targets, Xcode examines the active executable. If the active executable is the one created for the product produced by the current target, and the target you are switching to produces an executable product, the active executable is changed to match the new active target. For most projects, this means that the active executable will "follow" the active target as you change between them. However, if you have targets that don't produce an executable, or have created and made custom executables active, changing the target may not change the executable. You need to be especially watchful if you have created aggregate targets. An aggregate target that builds both a client and server application will not select an active executable when you make that target active. You must specify which executable, the client or the server, needs to be launched when you choose Run or Debug.

Debugger Preferences

You can use the Debugger pane of the Xcode preferences, shown in Figure 15-34, to configure a few common debugging features.

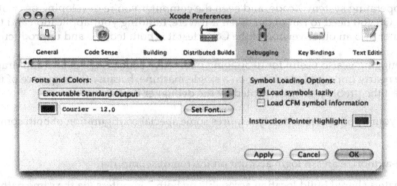

Figure 15-34

On the left are the Font and Color preferences. Select a category of text from the pop-up menu, and then change the font, style, and color of the font using the Set Font button. With these settings, you can alter the appearance of text that appears in the run and Debugger Console windows. This makes it possible, or at least easier, to differentiate between the text output by the debugger and the text output by your program. By default, Xcode colors the debugger's prompt and bolds the text sent to the debugger. All output appears the same.

Symbol Loading Options has two choices. Load Symbols Lazily controls the default level of symbols that load when modules and dynamic libraries are loaded into memory. Enabling lazy loading causes only the minimal amount of debug information to be loaded for each module initially, deferring the loading of more complete symbol information until it's needed. Turning it off causes the debugger to immediately load everything it knows about every library loaded into memory. This makes starting the debugger slower, but makes more complete debug information available. See the "Shared Libraries" section for more details.

Load CFM Symbol Information causes the debugger to load debug information from older Code Fragment Manger (CFM) binaries. Unless you are debugging an old CFM built binary, there is no reason to turn this on. Note that Xcode will not produce CFM executables.

The Instruction Pointer Highlight color is the color used to highlight the currently executing line of source code in the debugger. If you prefer to see a different color, click the color well or drag a color into the color well to change it.

Remote Debugging

The gdb debugger supports remote debugging. The debugger runs on one computer, while your application runs on a different computer. What actually happens is that another copy of the debugger is started on the remote computer along with your program, and the two debuggers communicate via a network connection. The remote instance of the debugger transmits all of the pertinent information about your application to the local debugger so you can see what's going on. Commands issued to the local debugger are, similarly, forwarded to the remote debugger for execution.

Remote debugging permits you to test your application in an environment different from that of your development system. A typical requirement is the need to debug your application using an earlier version of the operating system. Xcode, and even the computer you're developing on, may not be compatible with the OS you need to run under. Even if it were, building your application and then rebooting your computer into an older version of the OS to test it is both tedious and unproductive.

Remote debugging is also useful for debugging interactive code. Video games and drag-and-drop handlers can be nearly impossible to debug on a single machine, because the sequence of user events needed to test the problem are interrupted by the debugger itself.

Debugging your application remotely requires some special configuration of both computers. To wit, you must:

❑ Pre-authorize an ssh login account on the remote computer.

❑ Create a shared build location accessible by both computers via the same path.

❑ Configure the executable for remote debugging.

Remote debugging works through the Secure Shell (ssh) remote login facility built into Mac OS X. ssh provides secure communications paths using a public-key encryption system. The primary reason for using ssh for remote debugger communications is not security (although it's valuable if you need that), but the basic nature of ssh requires that a secure connection between the local and the remote computer be established first. This requires authentication. Normally this is done interactively using a password. For debugging, this is awkward. You need a pre-authorized login on the remote machine so that the local computer can connect directly to the remote computer without any human intervention.

You create pre-authorized ssh logins by manually generating and exchanging parts of a public/private key pair. (If you are curious, a typical ssh login authenticates a user and then spontaneously generates a temporary public/private key pair for that session. Pre-creating a public/private key pair skips both of these steps.) To create a pre-authorized login on the remote computer, follow these steps (the commands you would enter are in bold):

1. On the local computer, open a Terminal window and generate an RSA public/private key pair using the ssh-keygen tool:

```
local:~ james$ ssh-keygen -b 2048 -t rsa

Generating public/private rsa key pair.
```

```
Enter file in which to save the key (/Users/james/.ssh/id_rsa):
Enter passphrase (empty for no passphrase):
Enter same passphrase again:
```

Press Return when Xcode asks for a file name. This uses the default RSA file name for your account. If Xcode asks to overwrite the file, answer with a **y**. Enter a pass phrase or press Return to leave it blank. (A blank pass phrase is less secure, but is still acceptable and more convenient in a low-security environment.) Confirm the pass phrase by entering it again. If you are successful, a new private key is written to ~/.ssh/id_rsa and your public key is written to ~/.ssh/id_rsa.pub, as follows:

```
Your identification has been saved in /Users/james/.ssh/id_rsa.
Your public key has been saved in /Users/james/.ssh/id_rsa.pub.
```

2. On the remote computer, make sure Remote Login is enabled in the Sharing pane of the System Preferences. This allows ssh connections from other computers. Log into the remote computer using the account you plan to debug under. In this example, I'm logging into the computer whiterabbit using a special account I created just for testing. Use the account name and address of your remote computer in place of test and whiterabbit.local.

```
local:~ james$ ssh test@whiterabbit.local
Password:
Last login: Wed Sep 21 15:39:42 2005
Welcome to Darwin!
whiterabbit:~ test$
```

This verifies that the network connection works and that the remote computer is configured to accept ssh remote logins.

3. You now need to transfer the public key you just generated to the remote computer. One way is to use ssh's file transfer capability to send the id_rsa.pub file to the remote computer. Open a second Terminal window (you still have more work to do in the remote shell you just connected to, so leave that alone for the moment) and enter the following command:

```
local:~ james$ scp ~/.ssh/id_rsa.pub test@whiterabbit.local:development_rsa.pub
Password:
id_rsa.pub                                    100% 1123     1.1KB/s   00:00
```

Again, supply the password of the remote account and substitute the correct account name and computer address. This command copies the id_rsa.pub file from the local .ssh directory into the development_rsa.pub file in the home folder of the remote computer.

4. Return to the Terminal window with the ssh shell session on the remote computer. Use the ls command to verify that the development_rsa.pub file was transferred.

5. You now need to append the public encryption key in the development_rsa.pub file to the list of authorized computers for this account. To do this, use the following commands:

```
whiterabbit:~ test$ mkdir ~/.ssh
whiterabbit:~ test$ cat development_rsa.pub >> ~/.ssh/authorized_keys
whiterabbit:~ test$ rm development_rsa.pub
whiterabbit:~ test$ chmod go-rwx ~/.ssh/authorized_keys
```

The .ssh directory and authorized_keys file may already exist, in which case you don't want to overwrite them. You just want to append the new key to the existing file. This is a text file, so it

411

can also be edited using nano or your favorite text editor. The last two commands delete the public key file that was transferred and rescind all non-user access to the authorized_keys file for security purposes.

6. The remote computer is now pre-authorized to accept secure connections from your current account on the local computer to the account you just configured on the remote computer. Verify this by logging out of the current remote session and connecting again, like this:

```
whiterabbit:~ test$ exit
logout
Connection to whiterabbit.local closed.
local:~ james$ ssh test@whiterabbit.local
Enter passphrase for key '/Users/james/.ssh/id_rsa':
Last login: Tue Oct 25 09:49:46 2005 from marchhare.local
Welcome to Darwin!
whiterabbit:~ test$
```

This time, ssh prompted for the pass phrase used to generate the key, not for the password of the test account on the local computer. If successful, then you know that ssh used the key for this computer to connect to the test account on the remote computer. If you want to change any of these variables in the future — you want to connect from a different development machine or from a different account or to a different account — you must repeat these steps.

The next step is to create a shared build location accessible to both computers. Both the development and remote computer must have direct access to the entire build folder containing both the final product as well as all intermediate build files. More importantly, the UNIX path to the folder must be identical on both computers. There are three easy ways of accomplishing this.

The first, and probably simplest, solution is to employ a third-party file server. Create a build folder on a file server separate from your local or remote computer. (The "Build Locations" section in Chapter 14 discussed different ways of relocating your project's build folder.) You can now mount the build folder on both the local and remote computer using the same path.

The second is a hybrid approach. Configure your project to build to a local folder in a common, publicly accessible folder like /Users/Shared/Projects/DistantBugs. Turn on the file sharing services of OS X and connect to it from the local machine. Now create a symbolic link on the remote computer so that the build folder can be reached on both machines using the same path. You must use the command-line tools to create symbolic links. The following example mounts the main volume of a development system (Griffin) as a network volume on a remote computer, and a symbol link is created in the remote computer's Shared folder that links to the same folder on the development system:

```
ln -s /Volumes/Griffin/Users/Shared/Projects /Users/Shared/Projects
```

Now, any build folders that are created in the development computer's /Users/Shared/Projects folder will appear at the same location in the remote computer's file system.

The third method of getting both computers access to the same build folder would be to simply copy the entire build folder to the remote computer. For a one-shot test, this might be the easiest solution. However, if you were constantly rebuilding the project, this would be both inconvenient and inefficient. You could automate the process by creating a target script phrase to copy the contents of the build folder to the remote computer. If you decide to go this route, use a utility like rsync to quickly transfer only the portions of the build folder that change after each build. Remember that the location of the copy must reside at the same location as the original or at least have an equivalent UNIX path.

The last step in this process is to configure Xcode to start the debugging session remotely. This is done in the Debugging pane of the executable's Info window (previously shown in Figure 15-33).

Check the Debug Executable Remotely Via SSH option. When you do this, the Standard Input/Output option changes to Pipe. Leave it that way. This choice must be set to Pipe for remote debugging to work.

Start your debugging session as you normally would. The first time you do, Xcode asks for your pass phrase to decode the private key you generated earlier, as shown in Figure 15-35. Once it has your private key, it connects to the remote computer and starts the debugging session. After this point, debugging your application remotely isn't significantly different from debugging it locally.

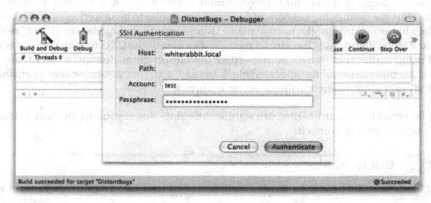

Figure 15-35

If anything goes wrong—problems connecting to the remote computer, accessing the product on the remote computer, or starting the debugger—consult the debugger console window for clues. Both the ssh client and the debugger output copious diagnostics messages while connecting and getting set up. Anything that goes wrong should be documented there.

Debugging Aides

There are a number of miscellaneous tools and features scattered around the debugger, Xcode, and the operating system itself that will help you find bugs in your code. The "Custom Executables" section covered loading the debug variant of frameworks and enabling Debugger() and DebugStr() calls. The following sections describe a few more Xcode facilities.

Catching a Catch

The Debug menu contains two commands: Stop On C++ Catch and Stop On C++ Throw. Both enable an implied breakpoint whenever a C++ function catches or throws an exception, respectively. You can enable or disable these built-in breakpoints at any time during your debugging.

If you are programming Objective-C and want to catch exceptions thrown by the NSException class, set a symbolic breakpoint at -[NSException raise].

Stopping for Debugger() and DebugStr()

The Debug⇨Stop on Debugger()/DebugStr() command sets an implied breakpoint whenever your application calls the `Debugger()` or `DebugStr()` commands. Normally these function calls are ignored. The command in the Debug menu enables this feature for all of the executables in your project. If you want to have `Debugger()` and `DebugStr()` break only in certain executables, disable the menu item and enable the feature for selected executables in the Debugger pane of the executable's Info window.

Guard Malloc

A very useful debugging feature for C programmers is the Guard Malloc library. Enabling this option before you start the debugging session causes your executable to be linked against the Guard Malloc (libgmalloc) library instead of the normal malloc routines provided by the standard C runtime library. The Guard Malloc library uses the virtual memory features of the CPU to map every block of memory allocated using malloc into its own address space. If your program attempts to access any data outside the immediate boundaries of the allocated block, an EXC_BAD_ACCESS error occurs, crashing your program at the exact point where the illegal access occurred.

It should be noted that Guard Malloc can significantly slow down your application. But the additional execution time is usually worth it.

Try It Out   Guard Malloc

Open the OutOfBounds project, or create a standard command-line project with the following code:

```
int main (int argc, const char * argv[])
{
    unsigned char* random_data = malloc(64);// allocate 64 bytes of data
    unsigned b, c;

    b = random_data[63];    // access the 64th byte of data in the block
    c = random_data[64];    // access the 65th byte of data in the block
    return (int)(b&c&0);    // this program will never get to this statement
                            //  if the Guard Malloc feature is enabled

}
```

Now follow these steps:

1. Set the build configuration to Debug.

2. Build and Debug the application. The application runs and exits without errors:

```
[Switching to process 11696 local thread 0xf03]
Running...

Debugger stopped.
Program exited with status value:0.
```

3. Choose Debug⇨Enable Guard Malloc.

4. Run the program in the debugger again. This time, the debugger halts the program as shown in Figure 15-36.

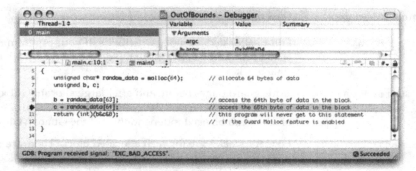

Figure 15-36

How It Works

Guard Malloc allocates every block of memory in its own private address space surrounded by "invalid" memory addresses. Any attempt to access the memory immediately before or after the contents of the data block results in an invalid memory exception, which the debugger catches. The random_data[63] statement accessed a byte within the block of data allocated by the malloc() call. random_data[64], however, accessed one byte beyond the end of the block and caused an invalid address exception.

All of a block's memory space is invalidated when the block is freed. Attempts to access the data *in* a block *after* it has been released will also be caught.

Debug Variables

Debug variables are either environment variables or preference property values that invoke special behavior in the libraries and frameworks and are useful for debugging. (There is also a wide range of debugging support functions that your application can call directly, but a discussion of those is beyond the scope of this book.)

Environment variables can be set using the Arguments pane of the executable's Info window. Preference values can be set using the defaults command-line tool. You can read the man page on the defaults tool for the details of setting user default values, but here's a simple example:

```
defaults write com.my.SimpleApp NSShowAllViews YES
```

The com.my.SimpleApp file is the user preferences file associated with the application. By default, this is the Identifier set in the target's Properties pane. The command sets the NSShowAllViews property to YES, which causes the AppKit framework to draw a colored border around every NSView. Setting property values only works for Carbon and Cocoa applications that use the user defaults framework.

The following table describes a few environment variables useful for C programming.

Environment Variable	Description	
MallocScribble	Fills deallocated memory with 0x55s. If your program reads the data again, it should be obvious in the debugger that the data is from a stale block.	
MallocGuardEdges	Adds guard pages before and after large allocation blocks. This will catch attempts to access data well beyond the edge of each allocated block. It can be used independently of the Guard Malloc library.	
MallocStackLogging	Logs the stack state for each allocated block. There are tools that will read this log and assist you in debugging memory allocation problems, especially memory leaks.	

If you think you have a problem with loading dynamic libraries, try some of the environment variables described in the following table.

Environment Variable	Description
DYLD_IMAGE_SUFFIX	Searches for libraries with this suffix first. Use this to load alternate variants of libraries. A lot of the system libraries include debug versions that can be loaded by setting the suffix to _debug.
DYLD_PRINT_LIBRARIES	Logs the names of each library, as it is loaded. If you think you're loading the wrong dynamic library set this variable to 1.
DYLD_PRINT_LIBRARIES _POST_LAUNCH	Logs the names of loaded libraries, but it only starts logging after your application has started executing. This avoids logging a lot of the core libraries.
DYLD_PREBIND_DEBUG	Logs pre-binding diagnostics information about your application.

If you're debugging memory leak or retain/release problems in Cocoa, consider setting some of the environment variables described in the following table.

Environment Variable	Default	Description
NSZombieEnabled	NO	If this is set to YES, NSObjects are "zombified" instead of being deallocated. A zombie object has all of its message handlers replaced with a call that will break into the debugger. This will catch an attempt to send a message to an object that has already been released and deallocated.
NSDeallocateZombies	NO	Set this to YES and the memory for zombie objects will actually be released. The NO setting is the safest, but can result in memory leaks that themselves may cause your application to misbehave.

Environment Variable	Default	Description
NSHangOnUncaughtException	NO	Normally an uncaught NSException will cause a Cocoa application to terminate. Set this variable to YES and it will simply hang instead, allowing you to break into it using the debugger and examine its state.
NSEnableAutoreleasePool	YES	Setting this value to NO defeats the functionality of auto-release pools. Use this if you want to keep around all of the objects that an auto-release pool would normally release.
NSAutoreleaseFreedObject CheckEnabled	NO	This is a very handy setting for finding double-release bugs. Setting this variable to YES will cause the auto-release pool to log an error message if the pool contains an object that has already been released.
NSAutoreleaseHighWaterMark	0	This is a useful diagnostics tool to check for situations where you are putting an excessive number of objects into an auto-release pool. Set it to a number other than 0 and the system will log a warning whenever more than that number of objects have been added to the pool.
NSAutoreleaseHighWater Resolution	0	Use this setting to log a warning message for every *N* number of objects above the high water mark level. The high-water mark level emits a single warning when the number exceeds that value. This setting emits a warning for every increment. Setting the high-water mark to 1000 and the resolution to 50 would log a message when there were 1000, 1050, 1100, 1050, . . . objects in any auto-release pool.

The two preference settings described in the following table are useful when you're debugging an AppKit application that is having drawing or layout problems. You must set preferences in the preference file of the application before you launch it.

Preference Key	Description
NSShowAllViews	Define this preference and set it to YES and the AppKit window manager will draw a colored border around each NSView in the application. This makes it very easy to see spacing and layout problems.
NSShowAllDrawing	Define this preference and set it to YES and AppKit will draw a colored rectangle before drawing each NSView. This makes it very easy to see what components in your windows are drawing, when, and in what order. Also check out the various Quartz Debug features.

This is just the tip of the iceberg. There are literally hundreds of variables, system calls, and development tools to help you track down and debug your application. Most are collected and maintained in Apple technical note number 2124, "Mac OS X Debugging Magic," which you can read at `http://developer.apple.com/technotes/tn2004/tn2124.html`.

Summary

You should now have at your disposal a cornucopia of tools and techniques for isolating, trapping, examining, and correcting any aberrant behavior in your application. You are likely to spend a lot of time using the debugger. Knowing how to harness the debugger's capabilities can save you hours of time and wasted effort.

Getting your application to build and execute correctly may be all you intended to accomplish. For some applications, even this isn't the end of the development process. You may not be satisfied simply that your application merely runs. You want it to run *fast* — and that is the subject of the next chapter.

Performance Analysis

Whether it's a rollercoaster ride or a visit to the dentist, a lot of times you just want things to go faster—and the applications you build with Xcode are no exception. Speeding up an application entails finding and eliminating inefficient code, making better use of the computer's resources, or just thinking differently. Neither Xcode nor I can help you with the last one. Sometimes the most dramatic improvements in a program are those that come from completely rethinking the problem. There are, sadly, no developer tools to simulate your creativity.

The more mundane approaches are to reduce the amount of wasted effort your application expends and to harness more of the computer system's power. To do that you first need to know where your application is spending its time and learn what resources it's using. In other words, to make your application run faster, you need to know what's slowing it down. This is a process known as performance analysis. And for that, Xcode offers a number of very powerful tools.

Xcode's performance analysis tools are strictly for native binaries and Java. To my knowledge, there are no performance analysis tools for AppleScript.

This chapter covers the four performance analysis tools that you can launch directly from within Xcode: Shark, Sampler, MallocDebug, and ObjectAlloc. The Developers tools CD that you used to install Xcode contains many other specialized tools for helping you identify and optimize your application. There is a brief round-up of these tools at the end of this chapter.

Performance Basics

The term *performance* means different things to different people. This chapter concentrates on the simplest and most direct kind of performance enhancement: getting an algorithm in your application to run in an acceptable amount of time. In general, this means getting your program to work more efficiently, and therefore finish sooner. But in the real world, this is too narrow of a definition, and performance solutions are sometimes counterintuitive. A graphics application that draws a placeholder image, and then starts a background thread to calculate successively higher resolution versions of the same image, might actually end up drawing that image two or three times. Measured both by the raw computations expended and by clock time, the application is doing much more work and is actually slower than if it had simply drawn the final image once. But from the user's perspective, the *perceived performance* of the application is better. It appears to be more responsive and useable, and therefore provides a superior experience. These are the solutions that require you to think "different," not just think "faster."

When considering the performance of your application, keep the following principles in mind:

❑   Only fix performance problems that need fixing.

❑   You are a very poor judge of how much time it will take code to execute.

❑   Combining the first two principles, you probably have no idea what or where your performance problems are.

❑   Set performance goals for your program and take benchmarks *before* starting any performance enhancements. Continue making, saving, and comparing benchmark results throughout your development.

The first principle is key. Don't try to optimize things that don't need optimizing. Write your application in a straightforward, well-structured, easily maintained, and robust manner. Run it and test it. If, and only if, it runs unacceptably slow should you even consider trying to speed it up. You might be taking a simple four-byte integer, turning it into a string object, stuffing that into a collection, serializing that collection into a data stream, and then pushing the whole mess into a pipe — whereupon the entire process is promptly reversed. You might recoil in horror at the absurd inefficiency used to pass a single integer value. But computers today are mind-numbingly fast. All that work, over the lifetime of your application, might ultimately consume less CPU time than it takes you to blink. In addition, optimization makes more work for you now and in the future. Optimized code is notoriously more difficult to maintain. This means that future revisions to your project will take longer and you run a higher risk of introducing bugs. Don't fix what ain't broke.

Closely released to this first principle is don't assume you can write something that's faster than the system. Use the system tools, collection, and math classes that you have available to you. Only if those prove to be a burden should you consider abandoning them. You might think you can write a better sorting routine, but you probably can't. Many of the algorithms provided by Apple and the open source software community have been finely tuned and tweaked by experienced performance engineers who are a lot smarter than you or I.

Modern computer languages, libraries, and hardware are both complex and subtle. It is very difficult to guess, with any accuracy, how much time a given piece of code will take to execute. Gone are the days where you could look at some machine code, count the instructions, and then tell how long it would take the program to run. Sure, sometimes it's easy. Sorting a hundred million of anything is going to take some time. But those kinds of hot spots are the exception, not the rule. Most of the time the performance bottlenecks in your application occur in completely unexpected places.

Combining the first two principles, you can distill this simple rule: Don't try to guess where your performance problems are. If you have a performance problem, let the performance analysis tools find them for you.

The last bit of advice is to keep some perspective. Know what the performance goals of your application should be before you even begin development. Your goals can be completely informal. You may simply want your application to "feel" responsive. If it does, then you're done. Most of the time you will not need to do any performance analysis or optimization at all.

If the application seems non-responsive, then begin by measuring its performance before you try to fix anything. If you accept the earlier principles, then this is a prerequisite: You must measure the performance of your application before you can begin to know where its problems are. But even if you already know, you should still benchmark your application first. You can't tell how much (or if) progress has been made if don't know where you started from.

Continue this process throughout the lifetime of your application. Applications tend to get heaver and slower over time. Keep the benchmarks you took when you first began, and again later after optimization. Occasionally compare them against the performance of your application as you continue development. It's just like leaving a set of scales in the bathroom.

Preparing for Analysis

Most of the performance analysis tools, especially ones that analyze the code of your application, need debug symbol information. They also need to analyze the code you plan to release, not the code you are debugging. If you've been building and testing your application using the debugger (covered in Chapter 15), then you probably already have a build configuration for debugging. The debugger needs debugging symbols on and all optimization turned off. Your released application should be fully optimized and free of any debugger data. Performance analysis sits right between these two points. It needs debugging symbols, but it should be fully optimized. Without the debugging symbols, it can't do its job. And there's no point in profiling or trying to improve un-optimized code.

Create a build configuration specifically for profiling by doing the following:

1. In the Configurations pane of the project's Info window, duplicate your Release build configuration, the configuration used to produce your final application. Name the new configuration **Performance**.

2. In the Performance configuration for all of your targets and/or the project, turn on Generate Debug Symbols. Turn off Strip Debug Symbols From Binary Files.

Switch to this build configuration whenever you need to do performance analysis and enhancements. If you change the code generation settings in your Release configuration, remember to update your Performance configuration to match.

For Java projects, just use your Debug configuration.

Shark

Shark is the preeminent performance analysis tool in Xcode. Shark can be used on its own in a variety of modes, but you're going to start it directly from within Xcode. First, build your target using your performance build configuration. From the Debug menu, choose Debug⇨Launch Using Performance Tool⇨Shark.

If your menu looks like the one in Figure 16-1, then Shark isn't installed. Despite its power and usefulness, Shark is not included in the default installation of the Xcode Development Tools. If you don't have Shark, locate and open the CHUD.pkg installer package. You will find it in the Packages folder of your

Developer Tools installation image or DVD. Alternatively, download the latest CHUD installer from Apple 's Developer Connection at http://developer.apple.com/tools/download/. The CHUD package includes a wide range of performance and hardware analysis tools, Shark being but one.

> Officially, CHUD stands for Computer Hardware Understanding Development. I can only speculate at what prompted the performance tools development team to concoct such a tortured acronym.

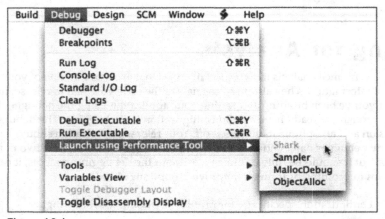

Figure 16-1

When Xcode starts Shark, it tells Shark which executable to analyze and starts them both running. This dialog box is shown in Figure 16-2. Before beginning analysis, you can choose to modify the command-line parameters or environment variables passed to your application. This example passes the "150000" parameter to the program for testing. The menu disclosure triangle to the right of the arguments field keeps a history of recently used argument lists.

The other window in Figure 16-2 is Shark's control window. It determines what kind of analysis will be performed, on what, and when. You will typically want to perform a Time Profile analysis. Shark can perform many different kinds of analyses, but only a few make sense when you're launching a single process from Xcode. If the selected analysis isn't the one you want, cancel the launch process, change the profile type, and quit Shark. Switch back to your project and launch it using Shark once more.

To profile a Java application, you should choose one of the Java specific analysis modes in Shark and must pass the -XrunShark argument to the Java command that launches your program. The easiest method of accomplishing this is to add a -XrunShark argument in the Arguments pane of the executable's Get Info window. You might want to create a custom executable just for Shark profiling, or just disable this argument when you are done.

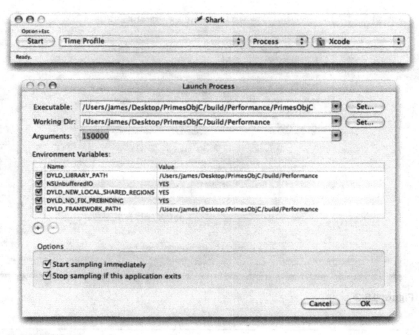

Figure 16-2

Java and Xcode have had an on-again, off-again romance. There are some combinations of the Java runtime and Xcode analysis tools that don't work well together, if at all. Consult the Java release notes or inquire on the Xcode-users discussion list if you are having problems.

Profile View

Your program runs while Shark is analyzing it. Shark stops its analysis after your program has terminated, when you stop it yourself using the Stop button, or when Shark's analysis buffer fills up — typically in about 30 seconds. Shark then presents its profile of your application's performance (see Figure 16-3).

The figure shows the Tree (Top-Down) view of your application's performance. The columns Self and Total show how much time your program spent in each function of your application. The Self column records the amount of time it spent in the code of that particular function. The Total column calculates the amount of time spent in that function and any functions called by that function. The organization of the tree view should be obvious, as it parallels the calling structure of your application. Every function listed expands to show the functions that it called and how much time was spent in each.

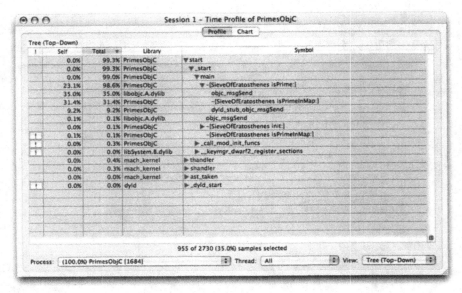

Figure 16-3

The compiler's optimization can confuse Shark as well as the debugger. Take the following code as an example.

```
main()
    calc();
}

int calc( )
{
    return (subcalc());
}

int subcalc( )
{
    return (x);
}
```

The compiler may convert the statement return (subcalc()) into a "chain" rather than a function call. It might pop the existing stack frame before calling subcalc, or jump to subcalc() and let it use the stack frame for calc(). Either way, it has avoided the overhead incurred by creating and destroying stack frames. But when Shark examines the stack, it thinks that main called subcalc directly, and it includes subcalc in the list of functions called by main.

Change the View menu in the lower-right corner to Heavy (Bottom-Up). This inverts the tree. Each item is now the amount of time spent executing the code within each function. This does not include any time spent in functions that this function might have called. When you expand a function group, you see the list of functions that called that function. The times for each break down the amount of time spent in that function while being called from each of the calling functions listed.

The tree view gives you a bird's-eye view of where your application is spending its time, starting with the first function called (where it spends all of its time), and subdividing that by the subroutines it calls, the subroutines called by those subroutines, and so on. The heavy view determines which functions use up the most of your program's CPU time. This view works backward to determine what functions caused those heavily used functions to be called, and how often. Use the View menu and choose to see both views simultaneously, if you prefer.

You can use this information in a variety of ways. The typical approach is to use the heavy view to see which functions use the most time. Those are prime candidates for optimization. If you can make those functions run faster, anything that calls them will run faster too. Both the heavy and tree views are also useful for finding logical optimizations. This usually entails reengineering the callers of heavy functions so that they get called less often or not at all. Making a function faster helps, but not calling the function in the first place is even quicker.

At the bottom of the window are the Process and Thread selections. These two menus enable you to restrict the analysis to a single process or thread within that process. Set one of these menus to something other than All, and only samples belonging to that thread or process are considered. Because Xcode launched Shark for our particular application, there is only one process. If the application you launched runs in multiple threads, select the thread you want to analyze. The status line above these two controls displays the number of samples being considered.

Statistical Sampling

At this point, you might be wondering how Shark obtained all of this information. Shark is one of a class of tools know as samplers. Shark interrupts your application about a thousand times every second and takes a (very) quick "snapshot" of where it is. After your program stops, or Shark's snapshot buffer fills up, it combines all of the samples to produce a statistical picture of where your program spends its time.

Think of trying to analyze the habits of a firefly. You set up a high-speed camera in the dark and film the firefly as it flies around. After you've got several thousand frames, you could composite all of those frames into a single picture like a single long exposure. Points in the picture that are very bright are where the firefly spent most of its time, dimmer spots indicate places where it visited briefly, and the black portions are where it never went at all. This is exactly what the heavy view shows — the accumulated totals of every snapshot where Shark found your application in a particular function at that moment.

The word "statistical" is important. Shark does not trace your program nor does it rigorously determine exactly when each subroutine was called and how long it took to run. It relies entirely on taking thousands of (essentially) random samples. Functions that execute very little of the time may not even appear. Shark can only be trusted when it has many samples of a function — which is perfect, because you're only interested in the functions that take up a significant amount of time. The ones that don't aren't worth optimizing.

Try It Out   Optimize a Class Using Shark

You'll be using the Roller project. Roller contains a rolling checksum class. Rolling checksums are used by utilities like rsync to calculate the checksums of a block of data at every offset within a file. In other words, after it calculates a checksum for bytes 0 through 99, it can quickly calculate the checksum for bytes 1 through 100, then 2 through 101, and so on.

Even though the algorithm is hundreds of times faster than the brute-force approach of recalculating the checksum for every offset from scratch, it is still a computationally intensive process that begs for optimization. Here you will use Shark to analyze the checksum algorithm, and then see if its performance can be improved.

The Roller project is a test harness. It exists solely to test the performance of the RollingChecksum class. Test harnesses make this kind of performance testing easier because you can quickly build, run, and test just the code you want to analyze. It is assumed that RollingChecksum is part of a larger application that you've already profiled to determine that RollingChecksum is taxing its performance. You can optimize RollingChecksum here, and then return to working on the larger project. Follow these steps:

1. Open the Roller project. Make the Performance build configuration active. Build the application.

2. Choose Debug⇨Launch Using Performance Tool⇨Shark. At the launch dialog box, click OK. The application runs. Shark performs its analysis after the program terminates, or 30 seconds has elapsed. The profile should look something like Figure 16-4.

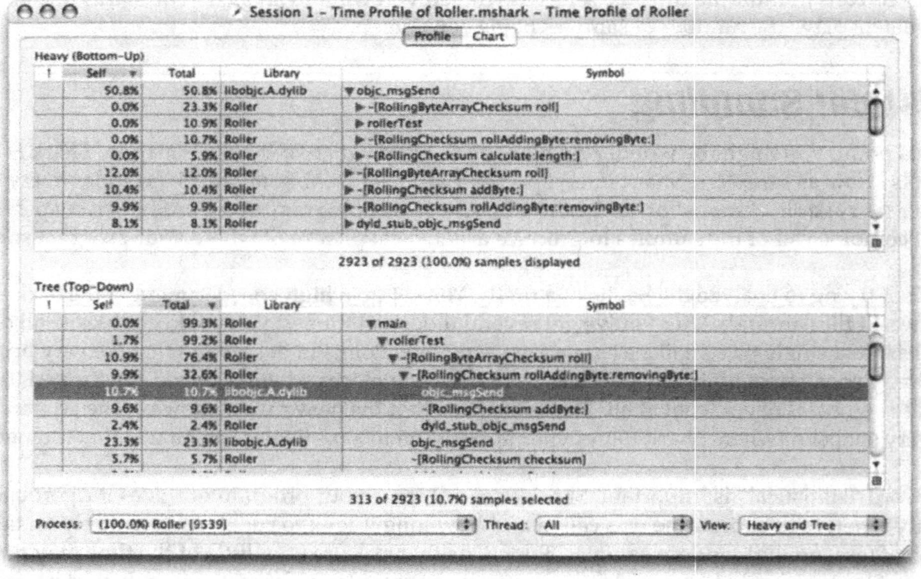

Figure 16-4

3. Review the profile and look for hot spots where the application is spending a lot of time. In this example, the program took 2.92 seconds to execute (2923 samples at 1ms/sample). 50.8% of that time was spent in `objc_msgSend`.

4. Edit the RollingChecksum.h file. Change the line that defines SHARK_OPTIMIZED from a 0 to a 1. The line should look like this:

```
#define SHARK_OPTIMIZED 1  // Compile optimization attempts
```

5. Build and profile the code again.

How It Works

With the SHARK_OPTIMIZED macro set to 0, the project compiles the original code for the class. This was simple, straightforward, Objective-C code to calculate rolling checksums.

In the first analysis, you discovered that the `objc_msgSend` function was consuming almost 50% of you applications time. So what is `objc_msgSend` and why it is getting called so much? This is the low-level routine that dispatches an Objective-C message to an object. It is called whenever a message is sent to an object, like this:

```
[someObject aMessage]
```

Normally the overhead of sending messages is trivial. But on computationally intensive code like this, the overheard becomes significant.

Now, you don't want to abandon my Objective-C class and rewrite everything as static C functions. So how do you eliminate the overhead associated with sending messages? The answer lies in the Objective-C runtime library. The `methodForSelector` method looks up and returns the address of the message handler for that object. You retrieve the function addresses for three critical routines once, and then call the functions directly — completely bypassing `objc_msgSend` each time. Using this technique completely defeats the dynamic nature of Objective-C message dispatching; but this is not a feature of Objective-C that your class uses and is just getting in the way of your program's efficiency.

In steps 4 and 5, you change the preprocessor constant to 1. This causes the code for your first optimization attempt to be compiled instead. In this version, the constructor for the RollingChecksum class caches the functions pointers to its `checksum`, `addByte`, and `rollAddingByte` methods. It keeps these in private instance variables. Internal calls to `checksum`, `addByte`, and `rollAddingByte` are replaced with direct function calls using the function pointers. The `rollTest` function also caches the single entry point into the object that it uses repeatedly. Note that you haven't altered the external definition of the class in any way. It is still functionally identical to the previous class.

Profiling the revised application, Shark now tells us that the process finished in 0.79 seconds (794 samples), as shown in Figure 16-5. Your class is already running 370% faster than it was. Looking at the heavy view, you can see that `objc_msgSend` isn't even listed anymore. Its impact on the program's performance has completely fallen off the map and is now negligible.

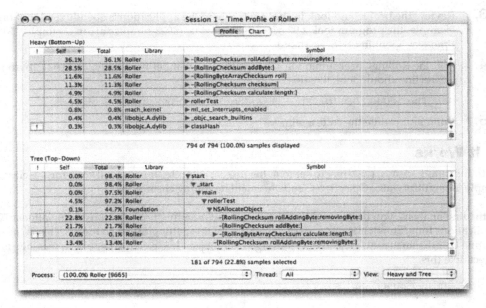

Figure 16-5

Code View

The profile view is useful for identifying the functions that are candidates for optimization. But what in those functions needs optimizing? Double-click any function name and Shark switches to a code view of that function (see Figure 16-6).

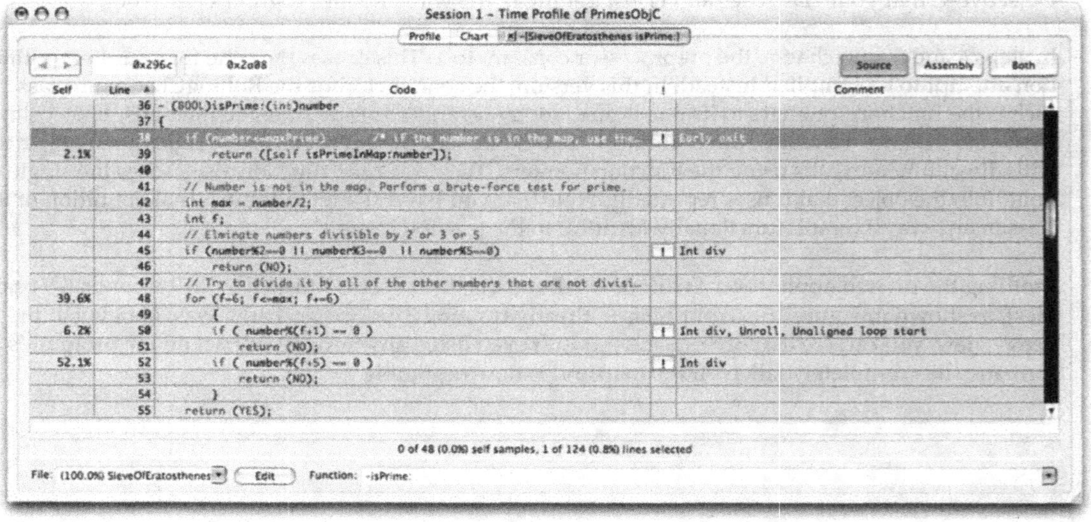

Figure 16-6

The code view shows the amount of time your application spent in each line of your function. Or, to put it more precisely, it shows the percentage of time that it found your application at that line of source code when it captured a sample. Source view requires that you compiled your application with full debug information, and that information was not stripped from the executable. If there is no debug information available, you'll see the machine code disassembly of the function instead. If you really want to get into the nitty-gritty details of your code, change the listing to show the machine code, or both the machine and source code side-by-side, using the buttons in the upper-right corner.

Shark highlights the "hot spots" in the code by coloring heavily used statements in various shades of yellow. This shading continues into the scrollbar area so you can quickly scroll to hot spots above or below the visible listing. Even though the window will scroll through the entire source file that contains the function you are examining, only the statistics and samples for the function you selected are analyzed. If you want to scrutinize samples in a different function, return to the Profile tab and double-click that function.

The truly amazing power of Shark is really becomes evident in the code view. Shark analyzes the execution flow of your code and makes suggestions for improving it. These suggestions appear as advice buttons — small square buttons with exclamation points — throughout the interface. One is shown in Figure 16-7. Click an advice button and Shark pops up a bubble explaining what it found and what you might do to improve the performance of your code.

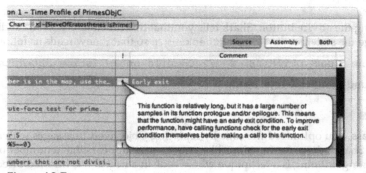

Figure 16-7

The advice feature is quite sophisticated. The suggestions are not merely canned responses to common code patterns. Many require the analysis of code flow, instruction pipelining, and caching features of various processors. Shark can recognize when you are dividing where you might be better of with a bit shift instead, or where loops should be unrolled, aligned, and so on. It's like having a CPU performance expert in a box.

Try It Out   Use Shark Advice

Open the Roller project once again, and then follow these steps:

1. Make the Performance build configuration active. Build the application.

2. Choose Debug⇨Launch Using Performance Tool⇨Shark. In the launch dialog box, click OK. The profile should look something like it did before in Figure 16-5.

3. Looking at the profile, you see that some 11% of the time is spent in the Checksum method. Double-click the Checksum function to see its code, as shown in Figure 16-8.

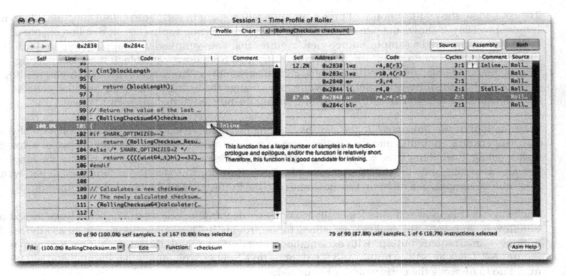

Figure 16-8

> **4.** Clicking the advice button, Shark tells you that this function is a good candidate for inlining. Change the statement in RollingChecksum.h so that it now reads as follows:
>
> ```
> #define SHARK_OPTIMIZED 2  // Compile optimization attempts
> ```
>
> **5.** Build and profile the code again.

How It Works

On your last pass, you optimized the code by replacing Objective-C messages with direct function calls. Looking at the Shark advice for functions like Checksum, it appears that a number of functions are candidates for inlining. Inlining is a technique where code in a function is inserted directly in the function that would call it, rather than calling the subroutine to do the same work and returning. The disadvantage to inlining is that is generates more code. But this is sometimes far better than the overhead that would be incurred by calling a subroutine.

I decide to experiment with inlining a few critical functions. Because Objective-C has no inline capabilities, I roll my own by creating three pre-processor macros: RollingChecksum_Result, RollingChecksum_Add(byte), and RollingChecksum_Roll. Each macro expands to the code implemented in the checksum, addByte, and rollAddingByte methods. I remove all of the code to obtain and cache the function addresses I put in before, and replace all of these with the appropriate macro. Now, functions like roll don't make any function calls at all. It duplicates all of the functionality of the rollAddingByte, addByte, and checksum methods itself and then returns.

After replacing all of the function calls with macros that expand to the same code, the application is built and profiled again, as shown in Figure 16-9. This time it runs in approximately 0.42 seconds (423 samples). The RollingChecksum class is now 700 percent faster than it was when you began. And you've done this without making any changes to the external definition of the class. The improved class is a drop-in replacement for the old one—just much faster.

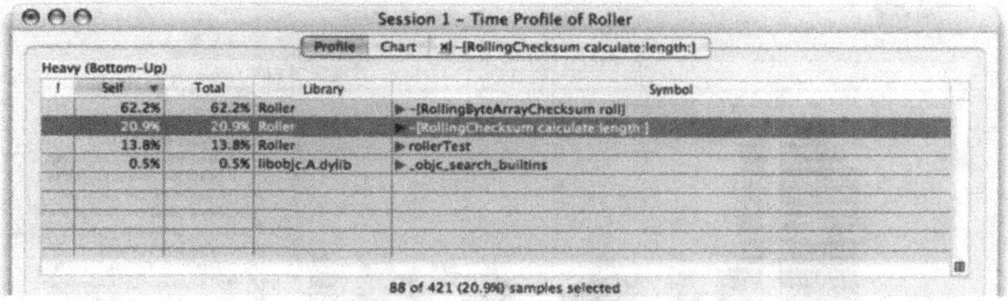

Figure 16-9

You could continue to try to optimize the class, but the effort will become greater and the rewards less. This is the point of diminishing returns where you are best off stopping, returning to the primary application, and looking for some other routines to optimize. If the Checksum calculations were consuming 50 percent of the application's processor time before, the new improved version should now only consume 12 percent. This has probably shifted the "hot spot" in the application to some other set of routines.

Every time you open a new code view, it creates another tab at the top of Shark's analysis window. You can switch back and forth between these tabs, or close a tab by clicking the small *x* button to the left of the tab's title.

Stack View

At the top of Shark analysis window is a tab control. When you switch to Chart, the view changes from the accumulated statistics to a temporal graph of your program's execution (see Figure 16-10). The table at the bottom are the samples taken by Shark — essentially the frames of the movie. The chart above it depicts the stack depth at each sample. Clicking a sample in the list or at the same horizontal location in the chart highlights its corresponding sample and displays the calling stack that was active at that moment in the program's execution. Using the right and left or up and down arrow keys, you can literally "scrub" back and forth through the execution of your application. When you select a function name in the chart or the stack frame list, Shark highlights the duration of every function executing at that moment. You can see in the chart not only how long it took for the selected function to run but how long functions that called that function ran.

The graph can be quite dense, depending on how many samples you have. Use the slider bar at the left to magnify the graph, and then scroll to the right and left through it using the horizontal scrollbar. You can hide the stack frames to see more of the chart by clicking the small join-pane button in the lower-right corner of the chart. Click it again to reveal the stack frames once more.

The squiggly lines between samples indicate a thread switch. The samples after the line are code executing in a different thread than the previous sample. As with the Profile view, you can choose to restrict the graph to just those samples from a single process or thread.

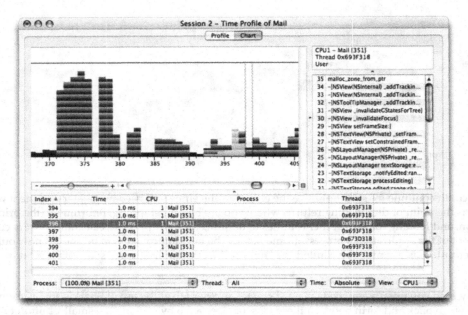

Figure 16-10

Refining the Analysis

Shark has a number of controls for refining what samples you choose to analyze and how. To see these controls, open the advanced settings drawer using the command View⇨Show Advanced Settings (Command+Shift+M). The advanced settings for the profile and chart views are shown in Figure 16-11.

The Callstack Data Mining section applies to all views and adjusts what samples are included and how they are accounted for. The Charge System Libraries to Callers option adds the time spent in system library calls to the function that called it. Similarly, the Charge Code Without Debug Info To Callers accumulates the time spent in calls compiled without debug information to the caller. Use these options when you want to assume that you can't optimize any of the system library code or code that you didn't write (and have no debug information for). This simplifies the profile and lets you concentrate on locating hot spots in your code.

Another simplification is to set the Hide Weight to something larger than 0. This simply ignores functions that don't have at least that many number of samples. Use this option to ignore functions that account for a very small portion of your application's runtime, allowing you to focus on the ones that take up a lot.

Flatten Recursion treats a function call to itself the same as two successive calls to the same function. For heavily recursive algorithms, this can greatly simplify the profile tree. Flatten System Libraries does the same thing for library calls. It allows you to ignore the complexities the system libraries under the assumption that you can't do anything about them anyway. Remove Supervisor Callstacks ignores any samples that occur in the kernel (supervisor) state. This includes interrupt handling.

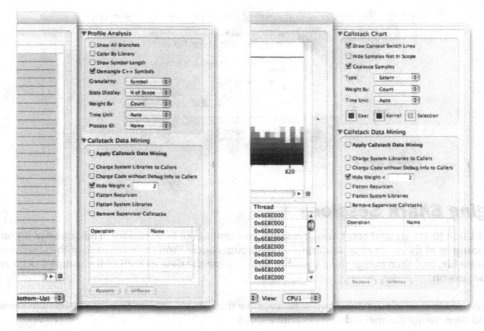

Figure 16-11

The Profile Analysis and Callstack Chart panels let you customize the display of the profile and chart views, respectively. You can color function calls by the library that they are in, demangle C++ function names, change how the time and sample units are displayed, and change the color of the chart. Play with these settings to get the display features you prefer.

Saving and Comparing Shark Sessions

The beginning of the chapter explained that it's important to keep track of your progress as you optimize your program. You will also want to review the performance of your application in the beginning, and compare that to what it is now.

Shark includes two functions for accomplishing this. The Save (Command+S) and Save As (Command+Shift+S) commands save the sample data in a file for later perusal. When you save a Shark session, it presents the dialog box shown in Figure 16-12. If you choose to embed the source file information, you'll be able to browse the code view with the original source at a later date. If you strip the information, you will have all of the statistical data but won't be able to examine code listing that include source (unless the original source is still available when you load the session). To load an old session, open the session file from the Finder or use Shark's File⇨Open or File⇨Open Recent command.

You can also have Shark compare two sessions. Choose the File⇨Compare (Command+Option+C) command and open two Shark session files. Shark presents a single profile browser showing the changes in the profile values instead of absolute values for each function.

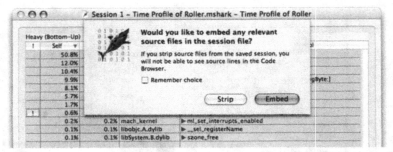

Figure 16-12

Merging Shark Sessions

In addition to saving and comparing sessions, you can merge two sessions. This is useful if you made two samples of the same code under different circumstances. You can save each of these sessions as a separate file, and then merge them together and analyze the data as if all of the samples occurred in a single session.

If you need to merge more than two sessions, save the merged session (it becomes its own session), close it, and then merge the merged session with a third.

Tip of the Iceberg

This introduction to Shark only scratches its surface. Full documentation for Shark is available within the application itself in the Help menu. There is a user's guide, profiling and data mining tutorials, as well as interactive processor instruction references.

Shark can analyze multiple processes and applications that are no longer responding. It can collect data from remote computers. You can control its sampling from within your application, the keyboard, or using command-line tools. It can debug memory bandwidth issues, processor cache hits, and virtual memory paging. Read the documentation for a complete description of all of these features. If you still have questions, consider joining the Performance Analysis and Optimization mailing list (PerfOptimization-dev) at `http://lists.apple.com/`.

Sampler

Before Shark, there was Sampler. Both are included with the Developer Tools. Sampler performs the same function as Shark, but it has fewer capabilities and options. If the interface to Shark overwhelms you, you might try Sampler instead. Sampler's stack depth display, which is similar to Shark's chart function, is shown in Figure 16-13.

It's useful to note that Sample and Shark use different technologies to obtain their samples. What Shark may fail to reveal, Sampler might, and vice versa. You'll find documentation for Sampler in its Help menu.

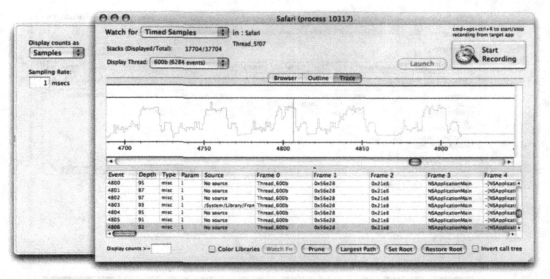

Figure 16-13

MallocDebug

The MallocDebug tool is launched exactly the same way as Shark or Sampler. Build your application and choose Debug⇨Launch Using Performance Tool⇨MallocDebug. MallocDebug is more of a debugging tool than strictly a performance analysis tool, but the two activities are closely related. Problems like memory leaks usually start out as performance problems before they become debilitating program flaws.

MallocDebug, as its name suggests, uses the special debug malloc library discussed in the Chapter 15. You do not have to build your application with the Debug⇨Guard Malloc option selected. MallocDebug launches your application with special environment settings that cause it to link to the debug malloc libraries.

Command-line tools that are statically linked to the malloc libraries do not work with MallocDebug. MallocDebug can only work with applications that dynamically link to the runtime libraries. See the documentation in Help⇨MallocDebug Help for how to use MallocDebug with statically linked programs.

MallocDebug is a "live" analysis tool, unlike Shark and Sampler that are "post-mortem" tools. MallocDebug shows you a snapshot of all of the memory blocks allocated by your application. You can update the picture by pressing the Update button, shown in Figure 16-14. After your application exits, the information in MallocDebug is lost.

The multi-column view shows the calling tree of your application. Each branch in the tree contains the functions that the selected function called. Work down into the tree and MallocDebug will list the memory block allocated by that function in your program. It shows the address, size, and zone the block was allocated in.

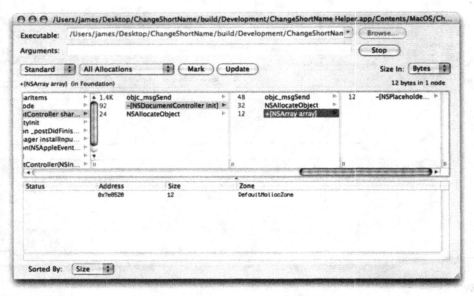

Figure 16-14

Double-click a block and you can see its actual data content in memory (see Figure 16-15).

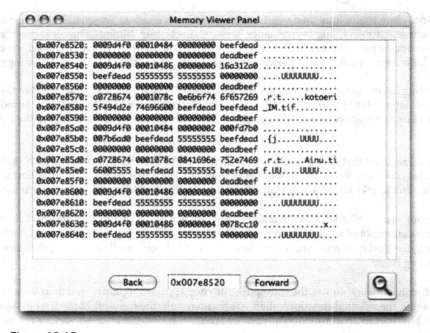

Figure 16-15

The tree display has three modes, which are described in the following table.

Display Mode	Description
Standard	Calling tree. Each column lists the functions called. Select a function and the next column lists the functions it calls. The values listed for each function are the accumulated amount of data allocated by that function and every function that function called.
Inverted	Shows the leaf functions that allocated the memory. Select a leaf function, and the next column lists the functions that called that function.
Flat	A flat list of every function in your application that allocated memory.

Next to the display modes is a menu of modes that control what memory blocks are listed. The content modes are described in the following table.

Content Mode	Description
All Allocated	Lists all memory blocks allocated. This is the default mode.
Allocations From Mark	Lists only those memory blocks that have been allocated since the last time you clicked on the Mark button. This marks all existing blocks as "old" and any blocks allocated after that as "new." Use this to diagnose memory allocated by a particular command in your application by clicking the Mark button, executing the code of interest, and then clicking on the Update button. Examine what blocks were allocated between those two points.
Leaks	MallocDebug has a conservative leak detector. The leak detector scans the address space of your application looking for any data that might be a pointer to each memory block that's allocated. It pares down the list to just those blocks for which it could *not* find data that could be interpreted as a valid pointer to those blocks. This is by no means foolproof. But if MallocDebug does list a block as having been leaked, there's a good chance that it has.
Overruns/Underruns	Like the Guard Malloc feature, this function looks for blocks that it suspects have had data written outside the boundaries of the block. Again, this isn't a definitive indictment, but you should carefully review all code that deals with any overrun or underrun blocks listed.

Pruning

When you're trying to debug memory block allocation problems, you can't see the trees for the forest. There may be thousands of block allocations that have nothing to do with the part of the program you're trying to analyze. Use MallocDebug's Prune commands, described in the following table, to simplify the display. These are found in the Prune menu.

Prune Command	Description
Prune Selection	Choose any function in the display and choose Prune⇨Prune Selection. Every instance of that function, anywhere in the tree, is deleted—hiding all of the memory blocks allocated by that function and any function it calls. For example, to ignore all of the memory blocks allocated by the Objective-C objc_msgSend function, select any instance of it in the tree and choose Prune Selection.
Prune Path	Similar to Prune Selection, but it only removes the one branch of the call tree that's currently selected. For example, if you select objc_msgSend in a sublist of functions and choose Prune Path, it will hide only the blocks allocated by objc_msgSend when it was called from this specific function. Blocks allocated by other calls to objc_msgSend in other functions are still listed.
Prune Not In This Library	Removes all blocks in the display that were not allocated by calling the currently selected function or any other function in the same library. This is useful for narrowing the display to only those blocks allocated by a particular library.
Prune Zone	This works with the Zone inspector, as shown in Figure 16-16. Select a zone and choose Prune⇨Prune Zone. All blocks in that zone are removed from the display.
Unprune	Resets all previous prune commands. This restores all allocated block to the display.

Every block of memory is allocated in a zone. You can display the zones with the Zones Inspector window, shown in Figure 16-16. Choose Tools⇨Zone Inspector to open the window.

Figure 16-16

The MallocDebug documentation contains additional information and debugging tips. Choose the different topics in MallocDebug's Help menu for more information.

ObjectAlloc

ObjectAlloc keeps track of objects and memory blocks allocated using the Core Foundation memory management routines. This is a very powerful tool for tracking down retain and release problems. You can use it to analyze the allocation of data and objects for any Core Foundation or Objective-C application. Although it's conceptually similar to the MallocDebug tool, ObjectAlloc takes a different approach. ObjectAlloc populates its lists and charts with the actual blocks and objects, not the functions that allocated those blocks. This is extremely useful for seeing how much and what kinds of objects are being created and destroyed. You can dig down into the data and find out not only where in the code an object was allocated, but also the history of where it has been retained and released.

The ObjectAlloc tools work as both a live monitoring and a postmortem analysis tool. While your application is running, it animates a histogram of all of the different sizes of memory blocks and objects that exist in your application while it is running. After your application stops, you can use the controls at the top of the window, shown in Figure 16-17, to rewind and replay the history information like a movie.

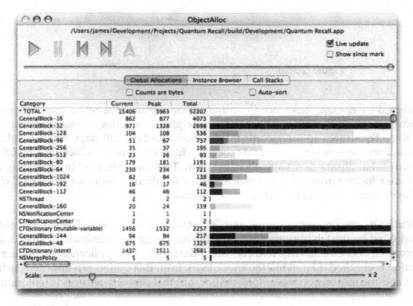

Figure 16-17

The controls in the upper-left corner work like a tape recorder. Press the play button to start recording. While you are recording, the play button turns into a stop button and the pause button is enabled. When you click the pause button, recording is suspended, and the pause button turns into a resume button. Click the stop button and the process is terminated. When the process ends, for any reason, recording is finished. The next two buttons and the slider below them let you step one sample forward or backward or slide to any point in the program's history. While you're "scrubbing" through the history, all of the allocation information and charts are updated. Use the history controls to revisit the state of your application at any point in the past.

While the process is running, the mark button — the upward pointing button on the right — sets a marker in the recording. By checking the Show Since Mark option on the right, you can limit the display to only those blocks and objects that were created after that point in the program.

When you press the record button to start the process, ObjectAlloc presents a dialog box that determines what information it will capture. This dialog box, shown in Figure 16-18, has three options and a field where you can add arguments to the executable when it is launched.

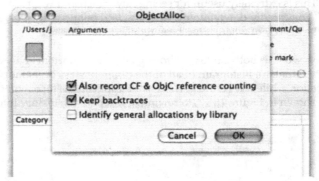

Figure 16-18

The Also Record CF & ObjC Reference Counting option captures the retain count of each object and Core Foundation memory block. This can be extremely helpful in isolating unbalanced retain and release bugs. The Keep Backtraces option records information about the call stack when each block was allocated. You will normally want to leave this checked. Identify General Allocations By Library separates data blocks by what library they were allocated from. This can be helpful in separating the data blocks that your code allocates from the data block allocated by library routines. Objective-C objects are always listed by their name and are not affected by this option.

After you click OK, the process is started and ObjectAlloc goes to work. The main display has three modes, controlled by the tab buttons just below the recording and playback controls: Global Allocations, Instance Browser, and Call Stacks. All three can update while the application is running if the Live Update option is checked. Removing the check mark from this option can improve performance of your application and the responsiveness of ObjectAlloc, but this severely reduces its entertainment value.

Global Allocations

The Global Allocation tab, previously shown in Figure 16-17, displays a histogram of the objects and data blocks allocated in your application. Data blocks are grouped into categories of similarly sized blocks. Internally, data block sizes are rounded up to the next 16-byte boundary, so all requests for a data block between 17 and 32 bytes long appear in the GeneralBlock-32 group. Objective-C objects are always listed by class name.

The Current column lists the number of objects in that category that currently exist in the application. The Peak column shows the largest number of objects that have ever existed at any one time. The Total column shows the total number of objects of this category that have been created since the application began.

The histogram on the right shows the same information in a graph. The length of each bar shows the total number of objects created. The shading of the bar changes at the peak and current levels. You can adjust the scale of the chart with the slider at the bottom of the window.

You can sort the objects by name or any of the summary values by clicking the title of any column in the table. While the application is running, all of these values are continuously updated and animated (assuming the Live Update option is checked). Check the Auto-sort option and the table will be continuously resorted using the column of your choice. The Count As Bytes option changes the numeric values and the chart scale from a count of blocks and objects to the count of bytes occupied by those blocks and objects.

History Graph

Double-click an object category in the global allocations graph and ObjectAlloc opens a chart window that displays the number of objects of that type that have existed over time (see Figure 16-19). The horizontal line across the top is the peak number of objects that have ever existed. Click and drag across the graph to select a portion of it. The sample numbers that encompass the selection portion are displayed in parentheses.

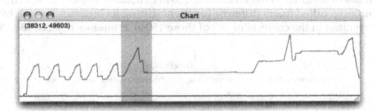

Figure 16-19

Instance Browser

The Instance Browser tab, shown in Figure 16-20, lets you examine the individual objects within a category. Select an object category in the left column, and the next column lists the addresses of every object of that type. The Current and Total radio buttons control whether the list contains only objects that are currently allocated in the application or every object that was ever created. Objects are listed in the order that they were created. Selecting an object displays its history in the third column. This column can be used to explore what routine allocated this object and when. It also tells you what function freed the object. If you enabled CF & ObjC Reference Counting when you began recording, it also lists every place this object was retained, released, or auto-released. Click an event in the history column and the Event Inspector window opens, displaying the details of event, as shown on the right in Figure 16-20. This includes the time the object was created, its size, and the thread and backtrace of the code that allocated it. The latter will only be present if you elected to capture backtraces. If a function can be correlated to your source code, that location is shown as a hyperlink. In the previous example, clicking the main.m:25 link opens your source code at that line in Xcode.

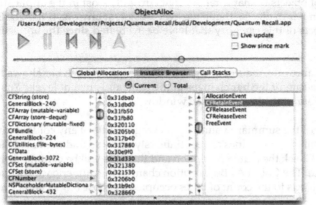

Figure 16-20

Call Stack

The Call Stacks display is where you can trace the origin of objects by function call. Select an object category and expand its calling tree. In the example shown in Figure 16-21, you can see that the call to NSApplicationMain resulted in the creation of 15040 CFNumber objects, of which 940 still exist. NSApplicationMain called many different functions during its lifetime. The call to [NSBundle mainBundle] resulted in the creation of 368 of those 15040 CFNumber objects, 23 of which still exist.

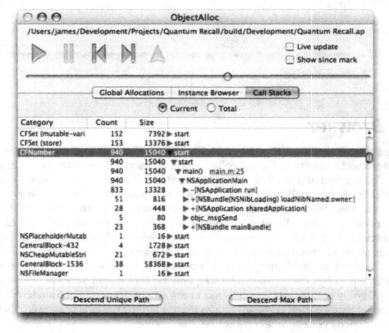

Figure 16-21

The Descend Unique Path button expands the selected function tree to the deepest function shared by each object's function call stack. In other words, it finds the top function in the tree where the calling tree begins to branch out. The Descend Max Path button expands the tree along the path of the deepest recorded call stack.

Other Performance and Analysis Tools

The four applications that this chapter has introduced you to thus far are the most useful when you're profiling or debugging applications from within Xcode. But these are by no means the only tools you have. The Developer and CHUD tools supplied by Apple include a host of other debugging and analysis tools. The following table describes some others you may find useful.

Tool	Description
OpenGL Profiler	If your application uses OpenGL, this program will trace and profile the OpenGL calls it makes.
Quartz Debug	A Swiss Army Knife of useful features for visualizing and tracking down drawing bugs.
Saturn	Saturn is a function call profiler. It records the number of times functions and events are sent and displays the results graphically. This tool is more definitive than Shark in determining what functions have been called, and how often.
MONster	Gathers general statistics about the efficiency of the processor. It records metrics such as memory bandwidth utilization, cache hits and misses, and the average number of cycles per second the CPU successfully executed.
BigTop	A nicer and more full-featured version of the UNIX top command.
Spin Control	Samples programs that have stopped responding to user events (when the system changes the cursor to the spinning Technicolor pizza of death). Leave this application running and it will automatically start sampling whenever an application becomes unresponsive. Shark has a similar feature.
Thread Viewer	Graphically displays the activity of threads in a process. Thread Viewer also draws a graphical history of thread execution.
heap	This is a command-line tool for examining malloc-allocated blocks in a process.
leaks	Another command line tool, this performs leak check on a process. It is similar to MallocDebug, but the algorithm used is different. This tool may identify problems where MallocDebug won't and vice versa.
vmmap	A command-line tool for analyzing the address space and virtual memory usage of a process.

There are scores of other tools. See the "Performance Overview" document for more details, general guidelines for performance measurement and tuning, and links to additional tools and documentation. You can find all of this in the "Performance" section of the Reference Library in Xcode's documentation window.

Summary

Xcode integrates with some powerful performance, profiling, and memory analysis tools. This goes well beyond just stepping through your code looking for logic mistakes. It means analyzing how much memory is allocated, when, and who's cleaning it up. It means taking a look at what functions your application is calling, how often, and how much time that takes. All of these tools are here to give you a different perspective into how your application behaves, and hopefully provide some insight into what you can do to make it better.

The next chapter explores yet another approach to finding and eliminating bugs from your application: Don't write those bugs in the first place. This might seem like a ridiculous statement, but unit testing strives to accomplish just that.

Exercise

Using the Shark and the techniques you've learned in this chapter, try your hand at optimizing the SlowPrimes project. This project contains a simple command-line tool that counts the prime numbers between 2 and a test value using a combination of algorithms. The first is a map of known prime numbers built using the Sieve of Eratosthenes technique. If a prime number is outside of that map, the tool performs a brute-force test by attempting to divide the prime by all smaller numbers.

The program has a limit on the size of the prime numbers map and the number of primes to test. The defaults are 100,000 and 120,000, respectively. You can change these in the source file or by passing alternate values to the program as command-line arguments.

Follow these steps:

1. Open the SlowPrimes project and set the active build configuration to Performance.
2. Build the application and profile it with Shark.
3. Make it run faster.

Unit Testing

Unit tests are instrumental in maintaining the integrity of your code. Unit testing is a way of validating the runtime behavior of your code at build time. In addition to writing your application's classes, you also write one or more *unit tests* that exercise those classes and verify that they perform as expected. These tests are not part of your application and live in a separate unit test bundle. You can elect to have these tests performed on your code whenever you build your product, insuring not only that your code compiles and links but that it behaves correctly as well.

Unit testing is a fundamental part of Test Driven Development (TDD), a development philosophy popularized by the Extreme Programming movement. In TDD, you develop the test for your function or class first; and then write your function to meet the expectations of the test. In essence, this is what rigorous designers have done for years. They first develop a detailed specification of exactly what a function should do, write the function, and then verify that the function behaves as designed. The quantum leap provided by unit tests is that the "specification" is now an automated test that verifies the design goals of the code rather than a paper description that must be interpreted and verified by the programmer or quality assurance engineer. Because the test is automated, it can be run every time the application is built, ensuring that every function still conforms to its specification and immediately alerting the developer if it does not.

Whether you subscribe to the principles of Extreme Programming or not, unit tests provide a powerful tool for avoiding things like "forgotten assumption" bugs. The typical scenario goes like this: You develop a complex application. You then decide to add a new feature to some core class. You make the change in what you think is a completely transparent manner only to discover that some other part of your application fails miserably. This invariably is a result of one of two problems. Either you inadvertently introduced a bug into the core class, or you forgot about an assumption made by the client code that uses the class. Unit tests can help avoid both of these pitfalls.

Xcode supports unit testing of C/C++ and Objective-C applications using two different technologies. Although the concepts and initial steps are the same, most of the details for creating and using unit tests differ for the two languages. After you get past the basics, skip to either the Objective-C or C++ section, as appropriate, for integrating unit tests into your application.

How Unit Tests Work

Unit tests are little more than code, which you write, that exercises the classes and functions in your project. You are entirely responsible for determining what and how your code is tested. Your tests are compiled into a unit test bundle, which is produced by a unit test target added to your project. To run the tests, all you do is build the unit test target. The target first compiles your tests. It then runs a special build script phase that loads your test code, runs all of the tests, and reports the results. If any of your tests fail, the build process reports these as errors and stops. Listing 17-1 shows the build log from a project with unit tests.

Listing 17-1: Unit Test Build Log

```
Test Suite '/Users/james/PrimesObjC/build/Debug/PrimesToolTest.octest(Tests)'
started at 2005-11-08 12:58:42 -0700
Test Suite 'SieveOfEratosthenesTests' started at 2005-11-08 12:58:42 -0700
Test Case '-[SieveOfEratosthenesTests testInvalidNumbers]' passed (0.000 seconds).
Test Case '-[SieveOfEratosthenesTests testMapEdges]' passed (0.000 seconds).
Test Case '-[SieveOfEratosthenesTests testNonPrimes]' passed (0.000 seconds).
Test Case '-[SieveOfEratosthenesTests testPrimes]' passed (0.287 seconds).
Test Suite 'SieveOfEratosthenesTests' finished at 2005-11-08 12:58:42 -0700.
Passed 4 tests, with 0 failures (0 unexpected) in 0.287 (0.353) seconds
```

Unit test bundles are part of the build process. The code associated with unit testing is compiled into the unit test bundle and should never be included in your final product.

Preparing for Unit Tests

There are four basic steps to adding unit tests to a project:

1. Create a unit test target.
2. Configure the target and your application for unit tests.
3. Write some tests.
4. Integrate the tests into your development workflow.

How you approach each step depends on a number of decisions. The biggest decision is whether to create *independent* or *dependent* unit tests. Each has its own advantages and disadvantages. The one you choose will determine how you configure your unit test target, your application target, and how your tests can be integrated into your development workflow.

> Don't confuse "dependent unit test" with "target dependencies." Although a dependent unit test target typically depends on its subject target, the term "dependent" has to do with the fact that unit test bundle is not self-contained. Both dependent and independent unit tests may depend on other targets, or not.

Independent Unit Tests

Independent unit tests are the simplest to create and use, but they have a couple of profound drawbacks. An independent unit test bundle includes both the tests and the code to be tested. All are compiled and linked into the unit test bundle. At build time, the bundle is loaded and all of the tests are executed.

The advantage to independent unit tests, and where it gets its name, is that the target and unit test bundle are entirely self-contained. All of the code to be tested is compiled by the target. That is, the target is *independent* of any other applications or products that your project produces. In fact, the code doesn't even need to be compiled elsewhere. You could, conceivably, create a project that only tested code and produced no products whatsoever.

The disadvantage is that the code being tested is compiled separately from the same code that gets compiled when your application is built. One consideration is the fact that the code could be compiled differently for the unit test bundle and the application. Build-setting differences between the unit test target and your application's target could easily cause subtle differences in the code the compiler produces, which means that your tests are not actually testing the same code that will run in your application. For most code, this probably won't matter. But a difference in, say, the signedness of character variables, optimization, or the size of enums could cause your tests to miss bugs in your application's code or fail tests that should pass. If you are rigorous, or just paranoid, you'll want to test the actual code that your final application will be executing—not just a reasonable facsimile.

The other, potential, disadvantage to recompiling all of the same code is that it takes time. All of the code you intend to test will have to be compiled twice—once for the application and again for the unit test bundle. If your code base is large, or it depends on a lot of other code that must be compiled, then compiling everything twice will slow down your builds.

Dependent Unit Tests

Dependent unit tests perform their tests on the actual code produced by your product. A dependent unit test bundle contains only the test code. When it comes time to perform your unit tests, the program or library that your project produced is loaded into memory along with the unit test bundle. The references in the unit test bundle are linked to the actual classes and functions in your application and then executed. The unit test bundle *depends* on another product to accomplish its purpose.

As you might guess, there's more than just a little slight of hand involved here. The unit test framework uses two techniques, depending on what kind of product you're testing. The method used to test libraries, frameworks, and independent unit tests is pretty straightforward. The unit test target executes a testing program that loads the unit test bundle (containing the test code and possibly some code to be tested) along with any dynamic libraries or frameworks that need testing. The tests are executed and the testing utility exits.

Testing an application is decidedly more bizarre. The unit test target runs a script that launches the actual executable produced by your project. Before the executable is started, several special environment variables are configured. These settings are picked up by the system's dynamic library loader and cause it to alter the normal sequence of binding and framework loading that occurs at runtime. The settings instruct the loader to first load a special unit test framework into the application's address space. This process is known as "bundle injection." The testing framework causes your unit test bundle to also be loaded into memory. Initialization code in your unit test bundle intercepts the normal execution of the application, preventing it from running normally. Instead, the unit test bundle's code links directly to the functions defined in the application and executes all of the tests. It then forces the application to terminate.

However convoluted, the beauty of this process is that your unit tests will test the actual, binary, code of your application; the same code that will run when your application launches normally. The disadvantage is that this process is complex and requires a number of concessions from your application. Mostly these are restrictions on how your application is built. In the case of some C/C++ applications, you are also required to add code to your application to support dependent unit testing.

Target Dependencies

Unit tests are part of the build process. Target dependencies are used to integrate unit tests into your development workflow.

Dependent unit test targets must depend on the target, or targets, that produce the products they test. Otherwise, there is no guarantee that the tests will be performed on up-to-date code. If you want unit tests run every time you build your product, set the active target to the unit test target and the executable to the results of the product target. Now, every time you build, the application is built followed by a run of all of the unit tests. The build will only be successful if both the build and the unit tests pass muster. Similarly, if you have complex target dependencies or aggregate targets, each of those targets should be dependent on the unit test target for each subproduct. As each subtarget is built, its unit tests are run and verified before the build continues with the next target.

Using this arrangement means that you can easily ignore unit tests by building just the product target, or making another target dependent on the product target directly. In a project with many product targets you could, for example, create two aggregate targets: one that depends on all of the product targets for "quick" builds and a second that depends on all of the unit test targets for "full" builds.

Because independent unit tests are self-contained, they do not need to be dependent on any other targets to ensure their integrity. All of the code that needs to be tested will be compiled when the target is built. This frees you to create target dependencies that fit your development style and needs. If you make your application target dependent on the unit test target, then every time you build your application, Xcode will first build and run all of the unit tests. If you make the unit test target dependent on your application target, then you have the choice of just building your application or building your application and running all of your unit tests. If you make no target dependencies, then you can individually select whether to build your application or just run the unit tests.

Adding a Unit Test Target

The first step to adding unit testing to a project is to create a unit test target. Choose Project⇨New Target and choose either the Carbon Unit Test Bundle to test a C/C++ product or the Cocoa Unit Test Bundle to test an Objective-C product, as shown in Figure 17-1.

Give the target a name and select the project it will be added to. Choose a name that reflects that subject of the test. For example, if you were writing tests for a target named HelperTool, you might name the unit test target HelperToolTests.

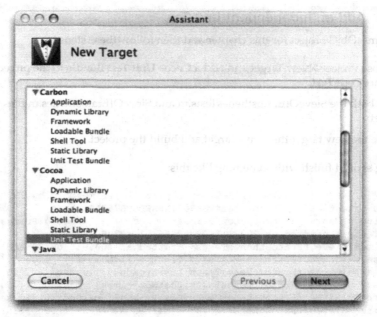

Figure 17-1

Xcode creates a new unit test target and adds it to your project. You now need to configure it properly and populate it with tests. How you configure your unit test target depends on what kind of unit test it is and what kind of product it tests.

> You might be anxious to try out your new unit test target, but you can't until it is configured and you have added at least one test. A unit test bundle will fail to function properly if it doesn't contain any tests. The "Creating a Unit Test" section, later in this chapter, tells you how to add tests to a unit test bundle.

Configuring an Independent Unit Test

Independent unit tests require no special configuration. All you need to do is include the source code for both the tests and the code to be tested. The compiler build settings for the target should match those of your product target as closely as possible, so that the code produced when you're compiling the source files for the unit test target is equivalent to the code that will be compiled into your final product.

Add the source files to the target by dragging them into the Compile Sources phase of the unit test target, or by opening their Info window and adding them to the unit test target in the Targets tab. You can add the source for the actual tests in a similar manner (if the tests already exist), or by adding them to the unit test target when you create them. The section "Creating a Unit Test" provides the details of writing and added a new test.

Try It Out   **Add an Independent Unit Test**

Open the PrimesObjC project for this chapter and then follow these steps:

1. Choose Project⇨New Target and add a Cocoa Unit Test Bundle to the project. Name the target **PrimesCodeTest**.

2. Add both the SieveOfEratosthenesTests.m and SieveOfEratosthenes.m files to the new unit test target.

3. Make the new target the active target and build the project.

The build log should finish with something like this:

```
/bin/sh -c "\"/Users/james/PrimesObjC copy/build/PrimesObjC.build/Debug/
PrimesBenchTest.build/Script-1A249C89091D6AED00B763AB.sh\""
Test Suite '/Users/james/Desktop/PrimesObjC copy/build/Debug/PrimesCodeTest.
octest(Tests)' started at 2005-11-09 09:56:51 -0700
Test Suite 'SieveOfEratosthenesTests' started at 2005-11-09 09:56:51 -0700
Test Case '-[SieveOfEratosthenesTests testInvalidNumbers]' passed (0.000 seconds).
Test Case '-[SieveOfEratosthenesTests testMapEdges]' passed (0.000 seconds).
Test Case '-[SieveOfEratosthenesTests testNonPrimes]' passed (0.000 seconds).
Test Case '-[SieveOfEratosthenesTests testPrimes]' passed (0.280 seconds).
Test Suite 'SieveOfEratosthenesTests' finished at 2005-11-09 09:56:51 -0700.
Passed 4 tests, with 0 failures (0 unexpected) in 0.281 (0.348) seconds

Test Suite '/Users/james/Desktop/PrimesObjC copy/build/Debug/PrimesCodeTest.
octest(Tests)' finished at 2005-11-09 09:56:51 -0700.
Passed 4 tests, with 0 failures (0 unexpected) in 0.281 (0.348) seconds
```

How It Works

An independent unit test target contains both the test code (which was already written for you in SieveOfEratosthenesTests.m) and the code to be tested (in SieveOfEratosthenes.m). You created a unit test bundle and added both the code and test code to the target. Building the target compiled the code and ran the tests.

Configuring a Dependent Unit Test

A dependent unit test needs to know where to load the application or libraries to be tested.

For applications, you accomplish this by setting the Bundle Loader (BUNDLE_LOADER) and Test Host (TEST_HOST) build settings. These should both be set to the executable you want to test. Follow these steps to quickly set both values:

1. In the Info window of the unit test target, select the Build tab. Choose All Configurations. Arrange the windows so that Groups & Files list in the project window and the Info window are both visible. Expand the Products group in the project source group.

2. In the target's Info window, choose the Unit Testing collection from the Collection pop-up menu. Find the Test Host setting and double-click its value field to edit it. Drag the icon for the executable product to be tested from the Products group into the value field of the Test Host setting. Xcode inserts the full path to the executable. For application bundles, you need to expand the product to locate the application's binary executable inside the `Contents/MacOS` folder of the bundle. This requires that you have successfully built the product. The path to the bundle itself (the folder with the extension `.app`) is not an executable.

3. Select the beginning of the path that represents the build location for the current build configuration. Typically this is `/path-to-project-folder/build/build-configuration-name/`, but it may be different if you have altered the default build locations. Replace this portion of the path with the `$(BUILT_PRODUCTS_DIR)` macro. In a project that produces a simple command-line executable, the final Test Host path will look like `$(BUILT_PRODUCTS_DIR)/ProgramName`. For a bundled Cocoa or Carbon application, the Test Host path will look something like `$(BUILT_PRODUCTS_DIR)/AppName.app/Contents/MacOS/AppName`.

4. Choose the Linking collection from the Collection pop-up menu. Locate the Bundle Loader setting and double-click its value field to edit it. Enter **$(TEST_HOST)** as its value. This sets the `BUNDLE_LOADER` build setting to the same value as the `TEST_HOST` setting.

The Bundle Loader setting tells the linker to treat the executable as is if were a dynamic library. This allows the tests in the unit test bundle to reference the classes and functions defined in your application without producing link errors.

The Test Host setting tells the unit test target's script phase the executable that will initiate testing. When testing an application, it is the application that gets loaded and launched. The injected testing framework and bundle intercepts the application's normal execution to perform the tests.

Testing Libraries and Frameworks

When you're constructing a unit test to test a dynamic library or framework, leave the Bundle Loader and Test Host settings empty. This is because the "program" to be loaded for testing will be the unit test bundle itself. If the Test Host setting is blank, the script launches the `otest` (for Objective-C) or `CPlusTestRig` (for C/C++) tool instead. The testing tool loads the unit test bundle and runs the tests it finds there, with the assumption that the unit test bundle either contains (in the case of independent tests) or will load (in the case of dependent tests for libraries and frameworks) the code to be tested.

For dependent unit tests that test libraries or frameworks, the unit test bundle *is* the client application. Configure your unit test bundle exactly as you would an application that uses those libraries or frameworks, adding the frameworks to the target and including whatever headers are appropriate to interface to them. The dynamic library loader takes care of resolving the references and loading the libraries at runtime.

Preparing Your Application

There are a few concessions required of applications being tested by dependent unit test bundles. You must make these changes in the target that produces your application, not the unit test target. These requirements do not apply to independent unit tests or when you're testing dynamic libraries or frameworks.

Open the Info window for the application target and choose the Build tab. Choose All Configurations and set the following:

❑ In the Linking collection, set ZeroLink to off (uncheck the box).

❑ If your project is a C++ program, choose the Code Generation collection in the group of the compiler you are using. Find the Symbols Hidden By Default setting and turn it off (uncheck the box).

ZeroLink must be turned off for your application. The ZeroLink technology is incompatible with the techniques used to intercept the application at runtime. The Symbols Hidden By Default option must be disabled for C++ applications so that all of the classes and functions defined by your application appear as external symbols. The unit test target must link to the symbols in your application, so these symbols must all be public. Objective-C tests are all resolved at runtime by introspection, so they don't require any public symbols at link time.

Try It Out   **Add a Dependent Unit Test**

Open the PrimesObjC project for this chapter and then follow these steps:

1. Choose Project⇨New Target and add a Cocoa Unit Test Bundle to the project. Name the target **PrimesToolTest**.

2. Make the PrimeToolTest target dependent on the PrimesObjC target.

3. Add just the SieveOfEratosthenesTests.m source file to the new unit test target.

4. Follow the steps to configure the unit test target as a dependent test, setting the BUNDLE_LOADER and TEST_HOST build settings to **$(BUILT_PRODUCTS_DIR)/PrimesObjC**.

5. Follow the steps to configure the PrimesObjC target so that it produces and application compatible with unit testing.

6. Make the new target the active target and build the project.

The build log should finish with something like this:

```
Test Suite 'All tests' started at 2005-11-09 10:07:17 -0700
Test Suite '/System/Library/Frameworks/SenTestingKit.framework(Tests)' started at
2005-11-09 10:07:17 -0700
Test Suite 'SenInterfaceTestCase' started at 2005-11-09 10:07:17 -0700
Test Suite 'SenInterfaceTestCase' finished at 2005-11-09 10:07:17 -0700.
Passed 0 tests, with 0 failures (0 unexpected) in 0.000 (0.000) seconds

Test Suite '/System/Library/Frameworks/SenTestingKit.framework(Tests)' finished at
2005-11-09 10:07:17 -0700.
Passed 0 tests, with 0 failures (0 unexpected) in 0.000 (0.000) seconds

Test Suite
'/Users/james/Desktop/PrimesObjC/build/Debug/PrimesToolTest.octest(Tests)' started
at 2005-11-09 10:07:17 -0700
Test Suite 'SieveOfEratosthenesTests' started at 2005-11-09 10:07:17 -0700
Test Case '-[SieveOfEratosthenesTests testInvalidNumbers]' passed (0.000 seconds).
Test Case '-[SieveOfEratosthenesTests testMapEdges]' passed (0.000 seconds).
Test Case '-[SieveOfEratosthenesTests testNonPrimes]' passed (0.000 seconds).
Test Case '-[SieveOfEratosthenesTests testPrimes]' passed (0.276 seconds).
Test Suite 'SieveOfEratosthenesTests' finished at 2005-11-09 10:07:17 -0700.
Passed 4 tests, with 0 failures (0 unexpected) in 0.277 (0.349) seconds

Test Suite '/Users/james/Desktop/PrimesObjC/build/Debug/
PrimesToolTest.octest(Tests)' finished at 2005-11-09 10:07:17 -0700.
Passed 4 tests, with 0 failures (0 unexpected) in 0.277 (0.349) seconds

Test Suite 'All tests' finished at 2005-11-09 10:07:17 -0700.
Passed 4 tests, with 0 failures (0 unexpected) in 0.277 (0.351) seconds
```

How It Works

A dependent unit test target contains only the test code (which was already written for you in SieveOfEratosthenesTests.m). You configured the unit test bundle to link against and load the `PrimesObjC` executable, which contains the code to be tested. When you built the unit test target, the dependent PrimesObjC target was first built and its executable product was launched. The testing framework intercepted the application's normal execution, loaded the unit test bundle into memory, and ran all of the tests. The tests were successful and the build finished.

Creating a Unit Test

In principle, creating a unit test is simple. Here are the basic steps:

1. Create a unit test class and add its source file to the unit test target.

2. Add test methods to the class.

Each class that you create defines a group of tests. Each class can contain as many different tests as you desire, but should contain at least one test. How you organize your tests is entirely up to you, but good organization practices dictate that a test class should limit itself to testing some functional unit of your code. It could test a single class or a set of related functions in your application.

Each test should perform its test and return when done. Macros are provided for checking the expectations of the test and reporting test failures. A test is successful if it completes all of its tests and returns normally. An example test is shown in Listing 17-2.

Listing 17-2: Sample C++ Unit Test

```
void SieveOfEratosthenesTests::testPrimes( )
{
    // Test a number of known primes
    static int knownPrimes[] = { 2, 3, 5, 11, 503, 977, 12347, 439357, 101631947 };

    SieveOfEratosthenes testSieve(UNIT_TEST_MAX_PRIMES);
    for (size_t i=0; i<sizeof(knownPrimes)/sizeof(int); i++)
        {
        int prime = knownPrimes[i];
        CPTAssert(testSieve.isPrime(prime));
        }
}
```

In this example, the `testPrime` function defines one test in the SieveOfEratosthenesTests class. The test creates an instance of the SieveOfEratosthenes class, and then checks to see that it correctly identifies a series of numbers known to be prime. If all of the calls to `testSieve.isPrime()` return `true`, the test is successful. The `testPrimes` object is destroyed and the function returns. If any call to `testSieve.isPrime()` returns `false`, the `CPTAssert` macro signals to the testing framework that the test failed.

Inter-test Initialization

If a group of tests (defined as all of the tests in a TestCase class) deal with a similar set of data or environment, the construction and destruction of that data can be placed in two special methods: setUp and tearDown. The setUp method is called before each test is started, and the tearDown method is called after each test is finished. Override these methods if you want to initialize values or create common data structures that all, or most, of the tests will use. The typical use for setUp and tearDown is to create a working instance of an object that the tests will exercise, as illustrated in Listing 17-3. The test class defines a single instance variable that is initialized by setUp and destroyed by tearDown. Each test is free to use the object in the instance variable as the subject of its tests.

For Objective-C tests, the methods your test class should override are -(void)setUp and -(void)teardown. For C/C++ tests, the functions to override are void TestCase::setup() and void TestCase::tearDown().

Listing 17-3: Objective-C Unit Test Using setUp and tearDown

SieveOfEratosthenesTests.h
```
#define UNIT_TEST_MAX_PRIMES  100000  /* size used during unit testing */

@interface SieveOfEratosthenesTests : SenTestCase
{
    SieveOfEratosthenes* testSieve;
}
```

SieveOfEratosthenesTests.m
```
@implementation SieveOfEratosthenesTests

- (void)setUp
{
    testSieve = [[SieveOfEratosthenes alloc] init:UNIT_TEST_MAX_PRIMES];
}

- (void)tearDown
{
    [testSieve release];
    testSieve = nil;
}

- (void)testInvalidNumbers
{
    // These should all return NO
    STAssertFalse([testSieve isPrimeInMap:-1],@"-1 is not a prime number");
    STAssertFalse([testSieve isPrimeInMap:0],@"0 is not a prime number");
    STAssertFalse([testSieve isPrimeInMap:1],@"1 is not a prime number");
}
```

The setUp and tearDown methods are called before and after every test. This allows tests to perform destructive tests on the object (tests that alter the object's state), because the object will be destroyed at the end of the test and recreated anew before the next test is run.

Unit test classes have standard constructor and destructor methods. *Do not use the constructor to create test data.* If your test structures are expensive to create and destroy, you may be tempted to create them in the constructor and let them persist for the duration of the test class. Don't do this. Instead, consider making a single test that creates the expensive object and then calls a series of subtests itself. Even turning the setUp method into a factory that creates a singleton object when called the first time may prove to be futile, as some testing frameworks create a separate instance of the test class for each test.

Because so many of the minor details of creating tests for Objective-C and C/C++ differ, the steps for creating your own tests have been separated into the following two sections.

Objective-C Tests

To create an Objective-C test class and add it to a unit test target, start by selecting the File⇨New File command. The new file assistant presents a list of new file templates. Choose the Cocoa Objective-C Test Case Class (see Figure 17-2).

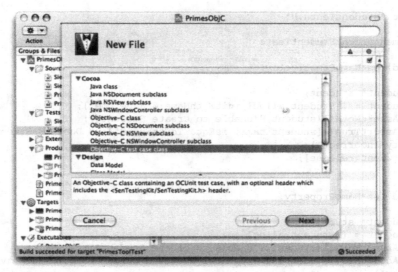

Figure 17-2

Click the Next button and give the test case class and file a name. The name should be descriptive of its purposes, such as StudentTests for a set of tests that validate the Student class. Make sure you create a matching .h file, select the working project, and add the test to the desired unit test target. Also make sure you don't include the test class file in any other target. Click the Finish button.

Xcode creates a skeletal test class definition and implementation, as shown in Listing 17-4. All of your test classes for Objective-C must be direct subclasses of the SenTestCase class.

Listing 17-4: Example Objective-C Test Case

```
#import <SenTestingKit/SenTestingKit.h>

@interface StudentTests : SenTestCase {

}

@end
```

Xcode has created the framework for your class and has already added it to your unit test target. The only thing you need to do now is to write one or more test methods. Each test method must return void and must not take any parameters, and its name must start with the word "test" in lowercase. An example of two such tests is shown in Listing 17-5.

Listing 17-5: Example Objective-C Tests

```
#import "StudentTests.h"

@implementation StudentTests

- (void)testNameConstructor;
{
    Student* student;
    student = [[Student alloc] initWithName:@"Jane Doe"];
    STAssertNotNil(student,@"Unable to create Student");
    STAssertTrue([[student name] isEqualToString:@"Jane Doe"],@"Student name
property incorrect");
    [student release];
}

- (void)testNameProperty;
{
    Student* student;
    student = [[Student alloc] init];
    STAssertNotNil(student,@"Unable to create Student");
    STAssertNil([student name],@"Newly created Student should not have a name
property");
    [student setName:@"Test"];
    STAssertTrue([[student name] isEqualToString:@"Test"],@"Student name property
incorrect");
    [student release];
}

@end
```

Amazingly, you are all done. The introspective nature of Objective-C allows the unit test framework to automatically discover all classes that are subclasses of SenTestCase in the bundle and then find all void methods that begin with the name "test." The unit test framework creates your test object and then executes each test one at a time.

Objective-C Test Macros

When you write your test, you will employ a set of macros to evaluate the success of each test. If the assertion in the macro fails to meet the expectation, the test fails and a signal with a description of the failure is passed back to the unit test framework. Test failures appear as an error in the build log.

Each macro accepts a description of the failure. The description argument is a Core Foundation format string that may be followed by a variable number of arguments, à la NSLog(description,...) or -[NSString stringWithFormat:format,...]. The unit test macros available are listed in the following table. The STFail macro unconditionally records a failed test. Use it in a block of code where the program flow has already determined that a failure has occurred. All of the other macros are assertion macros. The test is successful if the parameters meet the expectations of the assertion. If they do not, a failure is recorded using the description constructed using the format string (@"..." in the table) and the remaining arguments.

Unit Test Assertion Macro	Description
STFail(@"...",...)	This is the basic macro for unconditionally recording a test failure. This macro always causes the described failure to be recorded.
STAssertTrue (expression,@"...",...)	The test is successful if the statement expression evaluates to YES. Otherwise, a description of the failed test is logged.
STAssertFalse (expression,@"...",...)	The test is successful if the statement expression evaluates to NO.
STAssertNil(reference,@"...",...)	The test is successful if the statement reference evaluates to nil.
STAssertNotNil (reference,@"...",...)	The test is successful if the statement reference evaluates to something other than nil.
STAssertEquals (left,right,@"...",...)	The test is successful if the numeric value of statement left equals the numeric value of statement right. Both statements must evaluate to the same primitive type. That is, they must both be long int, float, and so on. You may cast them if necessary. If the values are not the same type or value, the test fails.
STAssertEqualsWithAccuracy (left,right,accuracy,@"...",...)	The test is successful if the absolute difference between the numeric value of the left statement and the numeric value of the right statement is equal to or less than the value of accuracy. Both left and right must evaluate to the same primitive type. If the values differ by more than accuracy or are not the same type, the test fails.

Table continued on following page

STAssertEqualObjects (left,right,@"...",...)	The test is successful if the object reference in the left statement is equal to the object reference in the right statement, according to the [left isEqual:right] method. Both object references must be of the same type and the isEqual method must return normally with a Boolean result. If the object references are not the same type, the isEqual method returns NO, or the isEqual method throws an exception, the test fails.
STAssertThrows (statement,@"...",...)	The test is successful if statement causes an exception to be thrown.
STAssertThrowsSpecific (statement,class,@"...",...)	The test is successful if statement causes an exception of the class class to be thrown.
STAssertThrowsSpecificNamed (statement,class,name,@"...",...)	The test is successful if the statement causes an exception of class with the name exception name to be thrown.
STAssertNoThrow (statement,@"...",...)	The test is successful if statement does not causes an exception to be thrown.
STAssertNoThrowSpecific (statement,class,@"...",...)	The test is successful if statement does not cause an exception of class to be thrown. Note that the test is still successful if the statement causes some other class of exception to be thrown.
STAssertThrowsSpecificNamed (statement,class,name,@"...",...)	The test is successful if statement does not cause an exception of class with the name exception name to be thrown.

After you have added your tests, you are ready to build the unit test target.

C++ Tests

To create a C++ test class and add it to a unit test target, start by selecting the File⇨New File command. The new file assistant presents a list of new file templates. Choose the Carbon C++ Test Case (see Figure 17-3).

Click the Next button and give the test case class and file a name. The name should be descriptive of its purposes, such as StudentTests for a set of tests that validate the Student class. Make sure you create a matching .h file, select the working project, and add the test to the desired unit test target. Also make sure you don't include the test class file in any other kind of target. Click the Finish button.

> Even if your application is written in pure C, the C/C++ testing framework still requires C++ objects to define and drive the test process. Write your tests by creating the appropriate C++ class. The test member functions you add can then call your application's C functions.

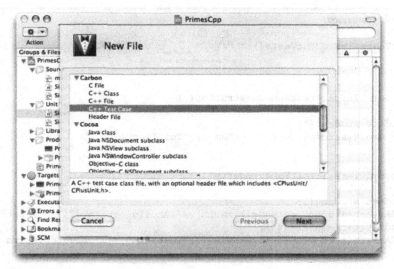

Figure 17-3

Xcode creates a skeletal test class definition and implementation, as shown in Listing 17-6. All of your test classes for C++ must be direct subclasses of the TestCase class.

Listing 17-6: Example C++ Test Case

```
#include <CPlusTest/CPlusTest.h>

class StudentTests : public TestCase {
public:
    StudentTests(TestInvocation* invocation);
    virtual ~StudentTests();
};
```

Xcode has created the framework for your class and has already added it to your unit test target. The only thing you need to do now is to write one or more test methods. Each test method must return void and must not take any parameters. Unlike Objective-C, C++ test method names do not have to conform to any naming convention. But it is more readable if you retain the habit of starting each method name with "test." An example of two such tests is shown in Listing 17-7.

Listing 17-7: Example C++ Tests

```
#include "StudentTests.h"

StudentTests::StudentTests(TestInvocation *invocation)
    : TestCase(invocation)
{
}
```

(continued)

Listing 17-7: *(continued)*

```
StudentTests::~StudentTests()
{
}

void StudentTests::testNameConstructor( )
{
    Student student("Test");
    CPTAssert(strcmp(student.getName(),"Test")==0);
}

void StudentTests::testNameProperty( )
{
    Student student();
    CPTAssert(student.getName()==NULL) // should not have a name yet
    student.setName("Test");
    CPTAssert(strcmp(student.getName(),"Test")==0); // should return new name
}
```

C++ Test Registration

C++ does not include the kind of introspection that Objective-C uses to discover the test classes and methods that you've defined. Consequently, you must tell the C++ unit test framework exactly what tests you've defined. This is accomplished by registering the tests using static constructors, as shown in Listing 17-8.

Listing 17-8: C++ Test Registration

```
StudentTests
studentTestsNameConstrutor(TEST_INVOCATION(StudentTests,testNameConstructor));
StudentTests
studentTestsNameProperty(TEST_INVOCATION(StudentTests,testNameProperty));
```

For every test you want run, you must create an instance of your test class, passing a TestInvocation object to its constructor. The unit test framework provides a TEST_INVOCATION macro, which creates an instance of the TestInvocation class for you. The parameters are the name of your TestCase subclass and the method name of the test function. You can give the static variable any name you want, but it is more readable if you give it a name that describes the test. Remember that these object names are public, so generic names like test1 are likely to collide with similar names from other TestCase classes.

Each object instance is constructed when the application starts up. The constructor for the TestCase class registers the test with the unit test framework. Thus, as soon as the application is ready to run, all of the tests that you've defined have been registered and are ready to run as well.

C++ Test Macros

When you write your test, you will employ the CPTAssert macro to evaluate the success of each test. If the argument to the macro evaluates to a non-zero value, then the test was successful. If not, the test and a signal with a description of the failure is passed back to the unit test framework. Test failures appear as an error in the build log. Examples of using CPTAssert were shown in Listing 17-7.

C++ Test Execution

In addition to registering the tests, a C/C++ application being tested by a dependent unit test needs to invoke the unit tests at the appropriate time. Unlike an Objective-C application, C applications can't be automatically intercepted to prevent their normal execution. You need to add code to the application to run the tests and exit, but only if the application is being run for the purposes of unit testing.

For command-line applications, this is simply a matter of inserting some code into your main() function. You insert this code at the point in your application where whatever initialization is required to unit test your application has been performed, but before the application actually starts running. Assuming your application has no special initialization, the example in Listing 17-8 shows what you need.

Listing 17-9: Unit Test Hook for main()

```
#ifndef UNIT_TEST_SUPPORT
#define UNIT_TEST_SUPPORT   1   /* compile support for C/C++ unit tests */
#endif

#if UNIT_TEST_SUPPORT
#include <CPlusTest/CPlusTest.h>
#endif

int main (int argc, char * const argv[])
{
#if UNIT_TEST_SUPPORT
    TestRun run;
    // Create a log for writing out test results
    TestLog log(std::cerr);
    run.addObserver(&log);
    // Get all registered tests and run them.
    TestSuite& allTests = TestSuite::allTests();
    allTests.run(run);
    // If the TestSuite ran any tests, log the results and exit.
if (run.runCount())
        {
        // Log a final message.
        std::cerr << "Ran " << run.runCount() << " tests, " << run.failureCount()
<< " failed." << std::endl;
        return (0);
        }
    // Otherwise, run the application normally.
#endif
...
```

The code creates a TestRun object, gets all of the registered tests, and then runs them. In a dependent unit test, the registration code for the tests exists in the unit test bundle. Unless the unit test bundle was loaded and initialized before the startup code called main(), there will be no tests to run. In this case, the application assumes that it is running in the absence of the unit test bundle, falls through, and executes normally. If tests are registered and run, then the code reports the success or failure of those tests and exits immediately.

> The definitions of the TestRun, TestLog, TestSuite, and related classes are included
> in the special unit testing framework that was added to your system when you
> installed the Xcode Developer Tools. These classes do not normally exist in a stan-
> dard installation of Mac OS X, and your application will fail to start without them.
> *Do not include this testing code in your final application.* Ensure that the release
> build of your application is devoid of any references to the unit testing classes and
> framework. Using the previous example, the Release build configuration of this pro-
> ject could define the UNIT_TEST_SUPPORT=0 preprocessor macro to ensure that no
> unit test code was compiled in the final version.

For Carbon applications, you can intercept the start of program execution far more elegantly. Any technique that runs the unit tests after initialization, but before regular program execution, is acceptable.
However, the dynamic nature of the Carbon event loop allows your unit testing bundle to intercept the
execution of the application without making any changes to the application itself. Listing 17-10 shows
how to use a Carbon timer to accomplish this. This code should be added to the unit test target.

Listing 17-10: Unit Test Hook for Carbon Application

UnitTestRunner.h
```
#include <Carbon/Carbon.h>

class UnitTestRunner
{
private:
    EventLoopTimerUPP timerUPP;
    EventLoopTimerRef timerRef;

public:
    UnitTestRunner();
    virtual ~UnitTestRunner();

protected:
    static void testTimerFired(EventLoopTimerRef timer, void* userData);
    void runTests(EventLoopTimerRef timer);
};
```

UnitTestRunner.cpp
```
#include <CPlusTest/CPlusTest.h>
#include "UnitTestRunner.h"

UnitTestRunner installTimer;    // static constructor to create timer

UnitTestRunner::UnitTestRunner() : timerUPP(NULL), timerRef(NULL)
{
    // Get the UPP for the static bridge method.
    timerUPP = NewEventLoopTimerUPP(UnitTestRunner::testTimerFired);
    (void)InstallEventLoopTimer(GetMainEventLoop(),0,0,timerUPP,this,&timerRef);
}

UnitTestRunner::~UnitTestRunner()
```

```
    }
        // Destroy the timer
        if (timerRef != NULL)
            {
            RemoveEventLoopTimer(timerRef);
            timerRef = NULL;
            }
        if (timerUPP != NULL)
            {
            DisposeEventLoopTimerUPP(timerUPP);
            timerUPP = NULL;
            }
    }

    // Static method to bridge the call to the local instance.
    void UnitTestRunner::testTimerFired(EventLoopTimerRef timer, void* userData)
    {
        ((UnitTestRunner*)userData)->runTests(timer);
    }

    void UnitTestRunner::runTests(EventLoopTimerRef timer)
    {
        if (timer == timerRef)
            {
            // We're done with the timer
            RemoveEventLoopTimer(timerRef);
            timerRef = NULL;
            // Creat the test run
            TestRun run;
            // Create a log for writing out test results
            TestLog log(std::cerr);
            run.addObserver(&log);
            // Get all registered tests and run them.
            TestSuite& allTests = TestSuite::allTests();
            allTests.run(run);
            // If tests were run, log the results and terminate the application
            if (run.runCount())
                {
                // Log a final message.
                std::cerr << "Ran " << run.runCount() << " tests, " <<
    run.failureCount() << " failed." << std::endl;
                QuitApplicationEventLoop();
                }
            // Else, fall through and continue running the application
            }
    }
```

The static constructor for installTimer causes an instance of this object to be created during the initialization of your application. Because the constructor is part of the code in the unit test, the UnitTestRunnier object is only created when your application is running in the presence of the unit test bundle. The class creates a timer with a 0 interval and registers it with the Carbon event manager. As soon as the application has performed its basic initialization and the event loop is ready to run, the timer fires. The methods in the class catch the timer event and run the unit tests, forcing the application event loop to exit if unit tests were performed.

In the absence of the unit test bundle, there is no constructor, no timer object is created, and your application starts running normally. The beauty of this scheme is that it requires no modification to your application. There is no possibility of accidentally producing a version of your application that contains any unit test support, and you can test the final application binary you intend to release.

Debugging Unit Tests

Who watches the watchers? Sometimes a unit test, designed to keep your application free of bugs, has bugs itself. When this occurs, you need to bring the power of the debugging tools to bear on the unit test code, rather than your application. The problem is that unit tests run during the build phase, not the debug phase, of the Xcode environment. The tests themselves are never the target of a Debug or Run command, and you have the added catch-22 of trying to build an application whose unit tests fail.

Debugging Dependent Unit Tests

To debug dependent unit tests for an application requires that you reverse the normal order of targets and trick the application target into running your unit tests instead of executing your application normally. Here's how:

1. Remove the application target dependency from the unit test target. Add the unit test target as a dependency for the application. This reverses the normal dependency between the unit test and the target.

2. Disable the run script phase of the unit test target. Expand the dependent unit test target and double click on the final run script phase. Edit the script by adding an `exit` command at the beginning, essentially disabling the script (Figure 17-4).

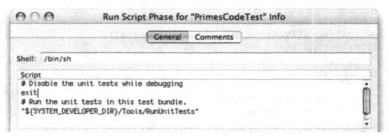

Figure 17-4

3. Double-click the executable for the application. Select the Arguments tab. If this is an Objective-C application, add the argument `-SenTest All`.

4. In the environment variables pane, add a `DYLD_INSERT_LIBRARIES` variable and set its value to `/System/Library/PrivateFrameworks/DevToolsBundleInjection.framework/DevToolsBundleInjection`. Add a `XCInjectBundle` variable and set it to `$(BUILT_PRODUCTS_DIR)/unit-test-bundle-name.octest`. If this is a C++ testing bundle, the extension will be `.cptest` instead of `.octest`.

5. Your application executable should now look like the one in Figure 17-5. Set your active target to your application's target, the active executable to your application, and your build configuration to Debug.

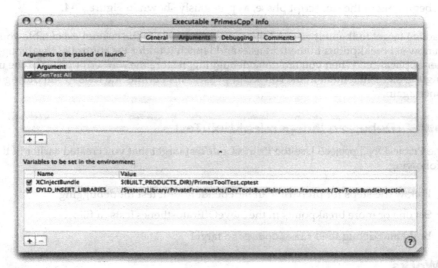

Figure 17-5

Now build and debug your project. The application target causes the unit tests target to build, but not run (because you disabled the unit test's run script). Xcode then launches the executable under the control of the debugger. The environment variables trick the application executable into acting as if it were being run for the purposes of unit testing. The system loads the unit test bundle and executes the tests, allowing you to set breakpoints in the unit test source and debug them. When you are done debugging your unit tests, reverse the entire process, as follows:

1. Reverse the dependencies so that the unit test target once again depends on the application target.

2. Remove or comment out the exit statement at the beginning of the unit test's run script phase.

3. Disable the special arguments and environment variables in the application's executable by removing the check mark next to each one.

Debugging Independent Unit Tests

Debugging independent tests requires that you create an executable from the unit test bundle so that the debugger knows how to launch it under its control. The executable is actually the test harness utility and its arguments tell it what unit test bundle to load and execute. Follow these steps to create the executable:

1. Create a custom executable. Give it the same name as your independent unit test target. (The "Custom Executables" section provided the details.)

2. Set the executable to /Developer/Tools/otest for Objective-C unit test bundles, or /Developer/Tools/CPlusTestRig for C++ unit test bundles.

3. In the Arguments tab, add the `$(BUILT_PRODUCTS_DIR)/name-of-unit-test.octest` argument for Objective-C bundles. The bundle extension will be `.cptest` for C++ bundles.

4. Disable the unit tests in the independent unit test target by adding an `exit` statement to the beginning of the run script phase, as previously shown in Figure 17-4.

Set the active target to the unit test and the active executable to the custom executable you just created. You can now set breakpoints in the unit tests and launch it under the control of the debugger just like any other application. When you are done debugging, restore the run script phase of the unit tests by removing the `exit` statement in the run script phase. This permits the tests to run during the build phase once again.

Try It Out   **Debug an Independent Unit Test**

Open the PrimesObjC project. Use the PrimesCodeTest target that you created earlier in this chapter and do the following:

1. Follow the steps for preparing an independent unit test for debugging.

2. Set one or more breakpoints in the SieveOfEratosthenesTests.m file.

3. Build and debug the `PrimesCodeTest` target.

How It Works

Creating a custom executable for the target allows Xcode to launch the unit test bundle as an application under the control of the debugger. After it has launched, debugging the unit testing code is no different that debugging application code.

Summary

Unit tests can be powerful allies. They permit you to codify the behavior of your code and integrate the validation of that behavior directly into the build process. Incorrect handling of a parameter value, or the failure to throw an exception under certain circumstances, is now as easily caught as syntax errors in your source code.

Effective use of unit testing is a discipline, encompassing a variety of philosophies and a broad range of styles and techniques. If you are serious about integrating unit testing into your development, you should get a good book on test-driven design or extreme programming.

Exercise

Open the Roller project for this chapter. In it you will find a copy of the Roller project you used in the Chapter 16. Write a unit test to verify the functionality of the RollingChecksum class. You will be particularly interested in knowing that the rolling checksum is correctly calculated for each offset within an arbitrary test data buffer.

Sharing Source

Software development has always been characterized as a rather solitary vocation. However, the stereotype of a single programmer working into the wee hours of the night, isolated in a basement or attic room, is now mostly the purview of fiction writers. Most modern development is done in teams — even when those teams are scattered across the globe and connected only by the Internet. Members of a team need ready access to the assets of projects they are working on. They need to collaborate on changes and distribute their work to other team members.

Software projects themselves may also need to share resources. A suite of applications developed for a single corporation might need to include a common set of graphics, or share a set of preprocessor definitions. It's impractical to put all of the applications into a single project, and (as you saw in Chapter 5) source file references outside the project folder can be problematic.

Closely related to the subject of sharing source files is the concept of "source control management" (SCM). Source control management systems store and track the changes made to source files over time. It is usually the basis of a collaboration system among multiple developers, acting as a mediator between developers, arbitrating changes, and communicating those changes to others. But individual developers have come to appreciate the discipline, security, and accountability that source control systems bring to their development. Even if you are a single programmer working on a single project, you may still want to set up a source control system.

Source control is used for many, if not most, open source projects. If you want to participate in an open source project, you'll want to "plug" your Xcode project directly into the source control system used by that project. After it is configured, you'll be able to browse the comments and revisions for the project right in the Xcode interface. You can see what new files are available and immediately update your local copy to stay in synchronization.

Xcode provides two facilities for sharing source files between projects and developers: shared source trees and source code management.

Source trees define folder locations where shared source files reside. There is no restriction on where these locations are or how the source files located there are maintained. An earlier chapter mentioned a suite of application projects that all need to include the same corporate artwork. A source tree folder could be defined for those graphic files. Any number of projects can reference those source files relative to that source tree's location. Changing the location of the source tree changes all of the references in all of those projects simultaneously. For example, if the graphics art department sends you a new CD with updated artwork, all you have to do is pop the disc in the CD-ROM drive, point that source tree to a folder on the CD, and rebuild your projects. Source tree locations are defined individually for each user, so a different programmer can use the same project with source tree locations specific to their environment.

Source control, often referred to as version control, is the principle method of sharing source files among a group of developers. It provides three important services. The first service is that it stores the master copy of all source files in a central repository. Changes made to a source file by one developer are sent back to the central repository, where those changes can then be distributed to other developers. This allows multiple developers to work on the same project files in a rational manner. The second service is that it also provides a degree of security, protecting against accidental damage to project files and providing a point for centralized backups. The third service is that source control systems keep a record of all changes made to a project over time. Developers can quickly see exactly what has changed in each file, and review comments made by the programmer that explain why. Source control can also be used like a time machine. You can reconstruct the state of a project at any point during its lifetime. You don't need to archive a copy of your entire project at every point in its development. For example, if you're working on version 1.6 of your application, but suddenly need to debug version 1.2, simply query the source control system for a copy of your project as it existed on the day you finished version 1.2.

Source trees and source control serve different needs and each is designed to solve a different problem. Some aspects overlap, but generally they complement each other. They can be used independently or in combination. What source file sharing and control techniques you employ will depend entirely on your needs and work environment.

Source Trees

A source tree is a named path to a folder on your system. A tree consists of a symbolic name, a display name, and the path to the tree's location on your system. Any source file reference in a project can be relative to a source tree location. The location of the tree is independent of the location of the project folder. For example, if you define a source tree named "buttons" and set it to the location /Users/*yourname*/Development/Common/Buttons, any project that has a source reference relative to the buttons source tree will look for that file in the Buttons folder inside your local Development folder. If you move that folder, or decide to use a different folder, you simply redefine the buttons source tree and every source file reference based on that tree changes.

The "your" in "the source trees on your system" is important. Source trees are defined individually for each user account. For someone else to use a project that references files in the buttons source tree, they must also have defined a source tree named "buttons." It doesn't have to have the same display name or be the same path, but it does have to have the same symbolic name. In fact, it makes sense that it wouldn't have the same path—another developer wouldn't have access to your /Users/*yourname* directory.

The source trees defined for your account are global to all Xcode projects that you open. Consider this when deciding on a name for your source tree.

Define a Source Tree

Open the Source Tree tab of the Xcode Preferences, shown in Figure 18-1.

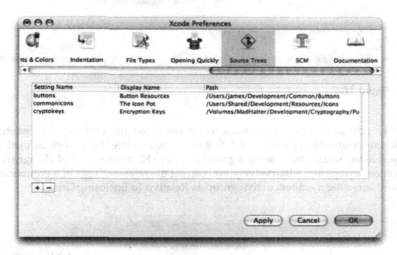

Figure 18-1

Click the + button below the list to define a new source tree. Give it a symbolic name or key, a display name, and a path where the tree can be accessed on your system. The display name is the title of the source tree as it will appear in all of your project windows and dialog boxes. You will rarely see the tree's symbolic name anywhere outside the Source Tree tab of the Xcode Preferences. To delete a tree, select it in the list and click the - button.

Source Tree References

After you've defined a tree, use it to reference source files in your project. The source trees you've defined automatically appear in all dialog boxes that add an existing file, folder, or framework to your project, as shown in Figure 18-2.

Figure 18-2

Source trees also appear in the reference section of every source file's Info window, as shown in Figure 18-3. You can make any source file's path type relative to any source tree that you've defined. If you are reorganizing a project to use source trees, select a group of source file references and change their reference type to new source tree as a group. Alternatively, you can set the reference type of a group folder to that of a source tree, and leave the members of that group as Relative To Enclosing Group.

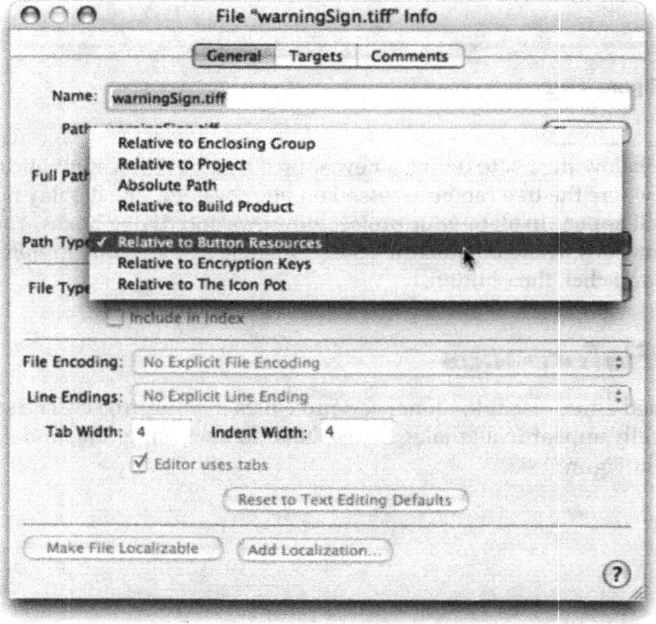

Figure 18-3

If you open a project that references a source tree that is not defined on your system, Xcode will attempt to locate the file at the same path it used the last time that tree was defined. If this path is wrong, the file will turn red, indicating that it cannot be located. Define the required source tree, close, and reopen the project to resolve the reference.

To redefine your source trees, close all projects, redefine your source trees, and open the projects again. Xcode resolves the source file paths using the new source tree locations.

Source Control

Source control systems work by storing the master copies of your project files in a separate repository. A repository is a database of files. A repository might be on the same file system or on a remote system. You might access a repository using direct file access or by sending requests over a network to a source control server. Regardless of the implementation, you interact with the source control system using a source control client.

When you want to work with a file, you request that the client *check out* a file from the repository. The copy of the file you checked out is called the *working copy*. If you make changes to the working copy, you later *check in* the file to record those changes in the central repository. After the changes have been recorded, other developers can check out the file to incorporate your changes into their working projects. You can also compare your working copy with other versions in the repository to see exactly what has changed. You also have the option of checking out an earlier version of any file and using it instead (maybe because you don't like the changes made by another developer).

Xcode has integrated support for three major source control systems: Concurrent Versions System (CVS), Subversion, and Perforce. CVS is the reigning king of open source control systems and comes bundled with OS X. You can get more information about CVS at http://www.nongnu.org/cvs/. Subversion is the heir apparent and is poised to replace CVS as the preferred source control system. Perforce is a commercial source control system available from Perforce Software Inc. If you need a full-featured, and reasonably priced, source control management system, you'll want to check out Perforce at http://perforce.com/perforce/products.html.

This chapter concentrates on setting up Subversion and configuring Xcode to use it. Subversion was chosen for this book over CVS and Perforce for two reasons. It is in many ways superior to CVS and it costs much less than Perforce (it's free). However, Subversion is not pre-installed in Mac OS X but that's a trivial problem to solve.

> **Setting up and using any of these systems to their full potential is not trivial. The instructions in this chapter are the bare minimum required to install, configure, and start using a source control system. Although tightly integrated and convenient, the commands available through Xcode barely scratch the surface of what you can do with a modern source control system. Entire books have been written about CVS and Subversion. If you are serious about integrating source control into your projects, or need to set up source control for a group of developers, you should explore the literature and documentation. The book *Version Control with Subversion* is available at** http://svnbook.red-bean.com/. **You can purchase a printed copy of the book, or download the electronic version for free.**

Installing the Subversion Client

The first step to using Subversion is to install it. If you plan to use a different source control system, then follow its installation instructions — assuming it's not already installed. The principle steps involved in configuring and using any of the source control systems with Xcode are the same, except for minor differences in the syntax of the client commands. Refer to the documentation for CVS or Perforce if you are using those systems instead. Subversion is intended to be "command-for-command" compatible with CVS in most cases, so the syntax differences between these two systems will be minimal. Perforce uses its own syntax and you should refer to the Perforce documentation for the equivalent commands.

Most source control systems are distributed in separate client and server packages. The Subversion client package installs the tools necessary to access local repositories stored on your computer's file system and to communicate with a remote repository server. This chapter will explain how to share a repository between multiple users on the same system and also how to set up a repository server suitable for access by remote users via a network. But to get started, take a look at how you create a local repository accessible to your user account. Ultimately, it doesn't matter that much how your source control system is installed and configured. After you have it set up, using source control from within Xcode is essentially the same for all systems and implementations.

The easiest and quickest way of installing the Subversion client is to install the binary client package for OS X. For alternate methods of installing Subversion, see the "Installing a Subversion Server" section, later in this chapter. For now, follow these steps to install the OS X binary client package:

1. Go to the Subversion home page at `http://subversion.tigris.org/`.

2. Locate the Downloads section. Find the pre-built client binary installer package for Mac OS X. At the time this book was written, this was being maintained at `http://metissian.com/ projects/macosx/subversion/`.

3. Download the disk image, open it, and double-click the installer package. This is a standard Mac OS X installer package. It places all of the binaries and supporting libraries in their correct location.

4. If you have not already done so, modify your shell environment to include /usr/local/bin in the command search path. For bash, add the following command to either your local `~/.bash_profile` or the global `/etc/profile` script.

   ```
   PATH="$PATH:/usr/local/bin"
   ```

   If you are using tcsh, add the following to your local `~/.tcshrc` or the global `/etc/csh.cshrc` script.

   ```
   set path = ( $path /usr/local/bin )
   ```

These instructions assume that the Subversion installer installed the Subversion tools in /usr/local/bin. Different installers use different locations, so refer to the ReadMe file that came with the installer or package for the correct path.

Open a new Terminal window and test your installation by issuing the following command.

```
svn cat http://svn.collab.net/repos/svn/trunk/README
```

This command fetches the current README file from the Subversion project repository at svn.collab.net and echoes it to the Terminal window (this requires Internet access). If it worked, then the Subversion client is installed and is capable of accessing a remote source control repository. If you don't have Internet access, just try the `svn help` command.

Creating a Repository

You now need to create a local repository. The following command creates an empty repository named Subversion in your Documents folder:

```
svnadmin create ~/Documents/Subversion
```

> You are free to create this repository in any local folder that your account has access to, but you will have to adjust the paths in the subsequent examples accordingly.

You are now ready to start storing and using your Xcode projects under source control.

Adding a Project to Source Control

To begin managing a project using source control requires the following three steps:

1. Add the project files to a source control repository.

2. Check the project out from the repository to create a working copy.

3. Configure the project to use source control.

The second step is critical. When you check out a project from a repository, the source control client creates invisible files that contain information about the repository it came from, the status of the files in the repository, and so on. Unless these invisible files are present, Xcode cannot integrate the project into source control.

Xcode does not provide any facility to add a project to a repository or to check out an entire project from a repository. You can easily see that this is a chicken-and-egg problem—how can Xcode check out a project before it's been initially checked out and configured to use that repository? You will have to use the source control client to perform the initial check-in and to obtain the first working copy. After the project has been checked out and configured, Xcode can add, remove, update, and refresh any of the project files. Except for more advanced source control functions, the initial check-in and check-out will be your only use of the command-line tools.

To add a project to a repository, as outlined earlier, follow these steps.

1. Close the project.

2. Delete its local build folder and/or any products or other intermediate build files produced by the project that are inside the project folder.

3. Use the source control client to add the entire project folder to the repository.

When you're checking in a new project, first close the project and delete its local build folder. *Do not check in a project's build folder into source control.* Only source files and the project document package itself should be in source control. Intermediate build files and products should never be checked in. Some developers like to store copies of finished products in source control for easy retrieval. If you do that, do it in a different location in the repository. Don't include those files in the project folder.

Now that your project is in source control, you need to check it back out again:

1. If you plan to continue using the project in its current location, move the project folder to the trash or rename it and put it a safe location until you have verified that you can check it back out from the repository.

2. Check out the entire project folder from source control. Open the project and verify that it contains all of the necessary source files and functions as expected. Consider comparing the files you just checked out with the originals using a diff such as the FileMerge utility. FileMerge is briefly described later, in the "Comparing Revisions" section.

3. You can now delete the original copy of your project.

Configuring a Project for Source Control

The last step is to configure the project to use source control. Open the Info window for the project group, or choose the Project⇨Edit Project Settings command. Towards the bottom of the General tab, you will see the SCM options, as shown in Figure 18-4.

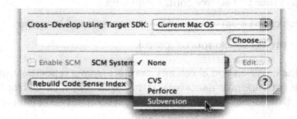

Figure 18-4

First, select the source control system you are using from the SCM System pop-up menu. In the example shown in Figure 18-4, Subversion is selected as the source control system. To the right of the SCM System menu is an Edit button. Click it to verify the location and name of the source control client you installed, as shown in Figure 18-5. As mentioned earlier, where your source control client tool resides may vary depending on how you choose to install it. If you are using CVS or Perforce, you will have other options to configure. These may include security, account, and server configuration parameters. Refer to the CVS or Perforce documentation for the values you need to configure.

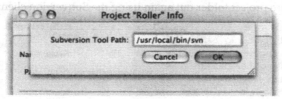

Figure 18-5

Next, check the Enable SCM option to turn on source control for this project. Xcode uses the client tool you just configured to access the source control management system and places all project files that were checked out of the repository under source control.

Try It Out   Put a Project in Subversion

Put the Roller project under the control of Subversion as follows:

1. If you haven't already, create a local Subversion repository. Open a Terminal window and enter the following command.

```
svnadmin create ~/Documents/Subversion
```

2. Make sure the Roller project is not open in Xcode. Open the project folder and trash its build folder.

3. Open a new Terminal window and cd to the folder that contains the Roller project folder (do not cd into the Roller project folder itself):

```
cd ~/Development/Projects
```

4. Add (import) the unmanaged project folder and all of its documents into the local repository using the following command. Note that the -m argument specifies a comment that will be recorded with this action in the repository. It should be something descriptive and explanatory, like -m 'Initial check in of Roller project'. You're using "Hello" here only for brevity. If you omit this argument, svn prompts you for a comment using the shell's default editor.

```
james$ svn import -m "Hello" Roller file:///Users/james/Documents/Subversion/Roller
Adding         Roller/RollingChecksum.h
Adding         Roller/RollingByteArrayChecksum.h
Adding         Roller/RollingChecksum.m
Adding         Roller/Roller_Prefix.pch
Adding         Roller/RollingByteArrayChecksum.m
Adding         Roller/Roller.m
Adding         Roller/Roller.xcodeproj
Adding         Roller/Roller.xcodeproj/james.model
Adding         Roller/Roller.xcodeproj/james.pbxuser
Adding         Roller/Roller.xcodeproj/project.pbxproj
Adding         Roller/Roller.1

Committed revision 1.
```

5. Drag the existing Roller project folder to the Trash.

6. Check the entire project folder out again using the Subversion client:

```
james$ svn checkout file:///Users/james/Documents/Subversion/Roller Roller
A    Roller/RollingChecksum.h
A    Roller/RollingByteArrayChecksum.h
A    Roller/RollingChecksum.m
A    Roller/Roller_Prefix.pch
A    Roller/RollingByteArrayChecksum.m
A    Roller/Roller.m
A    Roller/Roller.xcodeproj
A    Roller/Roller.xcodeproj/james.model
A    Roller/Roller.xcodeproj/james.pbxuser
A    Roller/Roller.xcodeproj/project.pbxproj
A    Roller/Roller.1
Checked out revision 1.
```

7. Open the project and build it.

8. Open the project's Info window by choosing the Project⇨Edit Project Settings command. In the General tab, change the SCM System to Subversion, edit the tool's path to /usr/local/bin/svn (or whatever is appropriate for your installation), and enable SCM.

How It Works

You created a local Subversion repository in your Documents folder and added the Roller project folder to it. You then discarded the unmanaged Roller project and replaced it with a working copy of the Roller project checked out from the repository.

The working copy of the project was then configured to use the Subversion source control system directly.

Use this project to explore Xcode's SCM interface in the next section.

> The example given here checks the project folder directly into the root of the Subversion repository. While this is sufficient for the purposes of this chapter and possibly sufficient for your needs as well, you might want a different organization.
>
> The book *Version Control with Subversion* explains how to manage branches and create tagged versions of your project using a structure of subdirectories within the repository. Read through the basics of source control for your chosen SCM before setting up your repository for actual use.

Source Control Interface

Interaction with source control in Xcode is done primarily through the commands in the SCM (Source Control Manager) menu and the SCM tab in various Info widows. File specific commands apply to either the selected file or group of files in the project window, or to the currently active editor pane. This chapter refers to selecting a file before executing one of the SCM commands. It's implied that the same command would apply equally to the file in the active source file editor pane.

As soon as you enable source control for a project, a new SCM tab appears in the project's Info window, as shown in Figure 18-6. A similar SCM tab appears in the Info window of all project source files that are under source control.

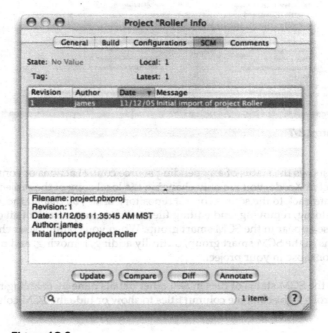

Figure 18-6

The State field shows the current status of the project document or source file. This tells you if the file is up-to-date (that is, it is the same as the most recent version of the file stored in the repository), if it has been modified locally, if it needs to be updated, and so on. The Local field is the version of the file that you last checked out of the repository, and the Latest field is the most recent version stored in the repository.

Below the file's status is the list of revisions. Each revision has a number, an author, a date, and a comment. Select one to show the full details of the revision in the lower pane of the window.

Use the four buttons below the detailed description to update or see the annotation view of a selected revision in the list. You can select one revision in the list and compare or diff it against the working copy of the file, or you can select two revisions in the list and compare them to each other. All of these commands are explained later in this chapter.

SCM Smart Group

Expanding the SCM smart group in the Groups & Files pane displays the pending source control operations for the project, as shown in Figure 18-7. The details pane for the SCM smart group displays an additional source control status column — the left column, next to the document icons shown in Figure 18-7.

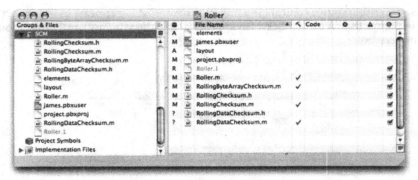

Figure 18-7

The SCM column shows the status of any pending source control actions or conflicts. When you make changes to a project in Xcode, you are only changing the local copy of the project. None of the changes you make propagate back to the source control repository until you *commit* those changes. As you work on the project — adding, removing, and editing files — Xcode keeps track of all of the changes that you've made. These appear in the SCM smart group. When you commit your changes, Xcode executes the pending actions in the SCM smart group, dutifully adding, removing, and modifying files in the repository to mirror those in your project.

You can also view the SCM status of files in any other details pane by enabling the SCM column (see Figure 18-8). Control-/right-click the column titles to show or hide the SCM column.

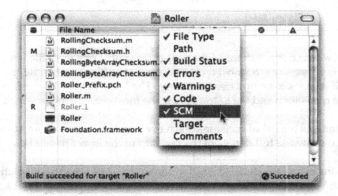

Figure 18-8

The SCM column contains a single character that indicates the status or pending SCM operation of each file, as described in the following table.

SCM Status	Description
(blank)	The file is up-to-date. It is the same file as the latest version in the repository. You have not modified it, nor are there any newer versions available to be checked out.
M	The file has been modified locally. The changes will be written to the repository the next time the file is committed.
U	The file needs updating. The file has not been modified locally, but the repository now contains a newer version of the file than the one you have checked out.
C	The modifications to the file are in conflict. There is a newer version of this file in the repository *and* you have modified the local copy of the file. This usually occurs when two or more developers are making changes to the same file simultaneously. The "Resolving Conflicts" section tells you how to merge your changes which those in the repository.
A	The file will be added to the repository. The file is not currently in the repository, but you have instructed Xcode to add it the next time you commit this project.
R	The file will be removed from the repository. You have deleted (or renamed) the local file. The next time you commit the project, the corresponding file in the repository will also be deleted.
?	The repository has no information about this file. This is usually because it is a new file that hasn't yet been added to the repository.
- (dash)	The file is in a directory that does not exist in the repository. When you're adding folders to your project, you first add them to the repository using your source control client. After the enclosing folder is added, you can add files to the repository using either Xcode or your client tool.

Choose the SCM⇨Refresh Entire Project to update the SCM status of every file in your project.

Double-clicking the SCM smart group or choosing the SCM⇨SCM Results (Command+Shift+V) command opens the SCM results window, shown in Figure 18-9.

This window shows the same information as the details pane of the SCM smart group, just in a separate window. In the lower-right corner of the window is a small log button. Click it to show the SCM transaction log, as shown on the right in Figure 18-9. The log shows the commands issued to, and the results from, the source control client used for this project.

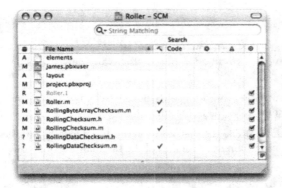 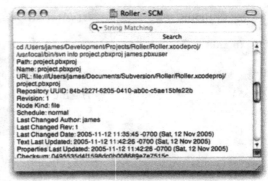

Figure 18-9

Committing Changes

No change occurs in the repository until you commit it. You can commit all changes made to a project by choosing the SCM⇨Commit Entire Project command. Alternatively, you can select individual files in a source group or details pane and commit just a subset of files using the SCM⇨Commit Changes command. You can only commit pending actions, such as Add, Modify, or Remove. Files that display no status or a conflict status cannot be committed because Xcode doesn't know what to do with them. First tell Xcode what to do with the file, and then commit the change.

Committing individual files is usually safe, as long as you are sure the changes being checked in will be valid in the absence of other changes that you have yet to commit. Whenever a commit includes the addition or removal of files, you must be very careful to commit those actions along with the corresponding changes made to the project document. The safest action in this situation is to commit the entire project. The "SCM and the Project Document" section will provide an explanation for this.

> In general, your goal when checking in changes should be to maintain the integrity of the project in the repository. If you make changes in two files that depend on each other, check both of those files in together. If you don't you'll have a version of the project in the repository that won't build because a change made to a source file was checked in, but the matching change made in its header file was not. Some source control systems, such as Subversion, guarantee *atomic* updates. That is, all of the changes being checked in will be stored in the repository or none of them will. There is no grey area, where some of the changes were stored but others failed. The documentation for your chosen SCM system should explain what actions are atomic and how this might affect the repository. Regardless, get into the habit of committing complete changes that leave the project in the repository in a useable condition.

When you commit a change, Xcode prompts you for a comment (see Figure 18-10). You should be descriptive and complete. The comments you enter will be attached to every transaction required to complete the commit. Source control comments are another form of documentation. The modifications made in your project are only comprehensible if you explain what you changed and why, both clearly and accurately.

480

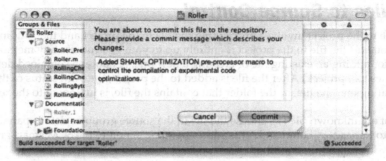

Figure 18-10

Saving Before Committing

In the SCM tab of the Xcode preferences window (shown later in Figure 18-17) is an option to Save Files Before SCM Operations. Normally this is checked, causing Xcode to save all open files before performing any SCM command. This avoids the unpleasant occurrence of committing a file without all of the changes that have been made to it. In most cases, you should leave this option checked, but you may turn if off if you ever need to perform SCM commands without forcing files to be saved first.

Discarding Changes

If, for whatever reason, you decide to abandon the changes that you've made to a file, you can discard them and revert to the version you originally checked out from source control. This is not necessarily the latest version of the file in the repository — it is the revision of the file you last checked out or updated to. This is also referred to as the *base* revision of your file. When you discard changes to a file, Xcode presents the warning dialog box shown in Figure 18-11.

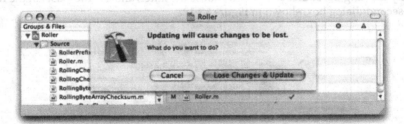

Figure 18-11

You can't discard changes by simply checking out a different revision of the file (as discussed in the "Updating Files" section). Xcode won't overwrite your local file with a revision from the repository until you explicitly discard your changes. This prevents Xcode from accidentally wiping out hours, if not days, worth of work. If you do try to update a modified file, you will only end up changing the base revision associated with that file. This action will either associate the file with the latest revision (containing as-yet uncommitted changes), or it will put the file in conflict mode. The "Resolving Conflicts" section explains how to merge conflicting changes.

Adding Files to Source Control

Adding a file to the project involves first adding the file to the project and then adding it to the repository. How you add the file to the project is entirely up to you. You can use any method discussed in the book so far for adding an existing file or creating a new one. (Chapter 5 contained detailed instructions on adding files to a project.) After the file is added to the project, the SCM status of the file may be ?, -, or blank, indicating that the file, or the folder that contains the file, is unknown to the repository.

In the case of an unknown file (?), choose the file in the source group or details pane and choose the SCM⇨Add to Repository command. This adds a pending action to the SCM smart group to add that file the next time the project is committed.

If the files exist in a folder that is not in the repository, use your SCM client tool to either add that folder or both the folder and the files to the repository. If you add just the folder, the status of the files will change from - to ?. You can now use Xcode to add the files to the repository.

A more reliable, and quicker, method (because it only requires a single command) is to use the import command of your SCM client to create the folder in the repository and add all of the new source files simultaneously—just as you did when you added the original project folder. Here is an example of adding a subfolder, and all of the source files it contains, to an existing project folder using Subversion:

```
svn import Roller/Data file:///Users/james/Documents/Subversion/Roller/Data
```

Whenever you manually alter the repository using the client tool, choose SCM⇨Refresh Entire Project to update Xcode's status of the repository.

Deleting Files under Source Control

Deleting a file requires that you remove it from both the project and the source control repository. When you delete a file reference from a project, Xcode gives you the option of removing just the file reference or physically deleting the source file. If you choose the latter, and the file exists in the repository, Xcode presents a second dialog box, shown in Figure 18-12.

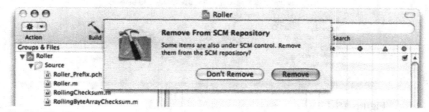

Figure 18-12

If you choose to remove the file, a repository remove action is added to the SCM smart group and the file is removed from the repository the next time the project is committed. If you choose not to remove the file, the file is deleted locally but remains in the repository. If you choose to remove the repository file as well, the project displays a grey (disabled) reference to the file in the project, indicating a reference to a file that has been deleted. After the action has been committed and the file in the repository has been removed, the phantom reference to the deleted file will disappear.

Renaming Files under Source Control

Renaming a file in a source control repository consists of removing an existing file and adding a new file with a different name. When you rename a source file in Xcode, it presents the dialog box shown in Figure 18-13.

Figure 18-13

If you choose to rename the file in the repository, Xcode creates two SCM actions. The first action removes the old file and the second action adds the same file back into the repository with its new name. Commit these two actions together to complete the rename.

Updating Files

When a newer version of a file exists in the repository, Xcode displays a *U* as the SCM status for the file. This indicates that you must update this file if you want the latest version.

If you want retrieve the latest version of a file, select one or more files in the project window and choose the SCM⇨Update To⇨Latest (Command+Shift+L) command. This checks out the most recent version of the files from the repository, replacing your working copies.

You can also retrieve an earlier version of a file. Select a single file and choose the SCM⇨Update To⇨Revision command. This presents a sheet, similar the one shown in Figure 18-14, listing the history of the file. Highlight the revision of the file you want to retrieve and click the Update button.

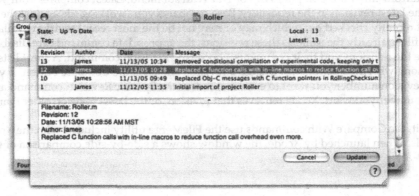

Figure 18-14

You can also update (check out) multiple files at or near a specific revision using the SCM⇨Update To⇨Specific Revision command. Enter the desired revision number into the dialog box and click the Update button. Xcode checks out either that specific revision of the file, or the most recent revision that is older than that revision. For example, assume there are two files in the repository. File A has revisions 1, 3, and 5. File B has revisions 1, 2, 4, and 6. If you update both to specific revision 4, Xcode checks out revision 4 of file B and revision 3 of file A.

When you revert to an older revision of a file, the SCM information about that file may revert as well. This depends on which source control system you are using. If it does revert, then the file's SCM history appears to be current when it isn't, listing only the revision information up to the revision you retrieved. The file does not display a *U* indicating that a newer version of the file is available. Use the SCM⇨Refresh Entire Project command to fetch the latest SCM information from the repository. The information about the more recent versions of the file reappears and the file status changes to *U*.

You can bring an entire project up-to-date by selecting the project group in the Groups & Files pane of the project window and choosing the SCM⇨Update To⇨Latest (Command+Shift+L) command or by choosing the SCM⇨Update Entire Project command. Xcode retrieves the most recent revision of the project document and every file in the project.

> Whenever you update the project document itself, close the project and reopen it. Changes made to the project document by updating will not be "seen" by Xcode until it is forced to reread the project document.

Comparing Revisions

You can compare the files in your project with other revisions using the SCM⇨Compare With and SCM⇨Diff With commands. The Compare With commands employ a graphical utility to compare, and possibly merge, the differences between the two files. The Diff With commands use the UNIX diff tool to compare the files.

Choose the file you want to compare, and then choose the Latest, Base, Revisions, or Specific Revision... command from either the Compare With or Diff With submenu. Latest compares your working file against the latest revision in the repository. Base compares your working file against the revision that you most recently checked out, which may or may not be the most recent revision available. If your working file is already the same as these revisions, the appropriate commands are disabled. If you want to browse the revisions and their comments, choose the Revision command. A sheet lists the revisions of the file along with their comments. Choose a revision and click the Compare button. If you know the specific revision number you want to examine, choose the Specific Revision command and enter the revision number you want. Xcode retrieves that revision, or the latest revision older than that revision.

By default, the Compare With commands use the FileMerge utility included with the Xcode development tools. When launched by Xcode, the window shows a side-by-side comparison of the two files (see Figure 18-15).

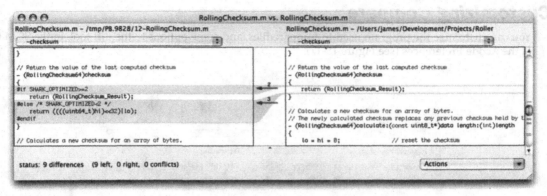

Figure 18-15

The windows graphically illustrate the changes made between the two files. In the example shown in Figure 18-15, four lines were removed from the working source file (on the right) that were present in the latest revision of the file in source control (on the left). Scroll through the file to see other differences, or use the Find⇨Go To Next⇨Difference (Command+Down Arrow) and Find⇨Go To Previous⇨Difference (Command+Up Arrow) commands. The window may have a third pane at the bottom, which shows a merged copy of the two files. To hide this pane, use the pane divider. The "Resolving Conflicts" section discusses how to merge files.

The Compare With commands gives you one additional command not available in the Diff With submenu. SCM⇨Compare With⇨File enables you to select an arbitrary file and compare it with your working source file.

If you use one of the Diff With commands, Xcode opens a text window that displays the output of the diff command (see Figure 18-16).

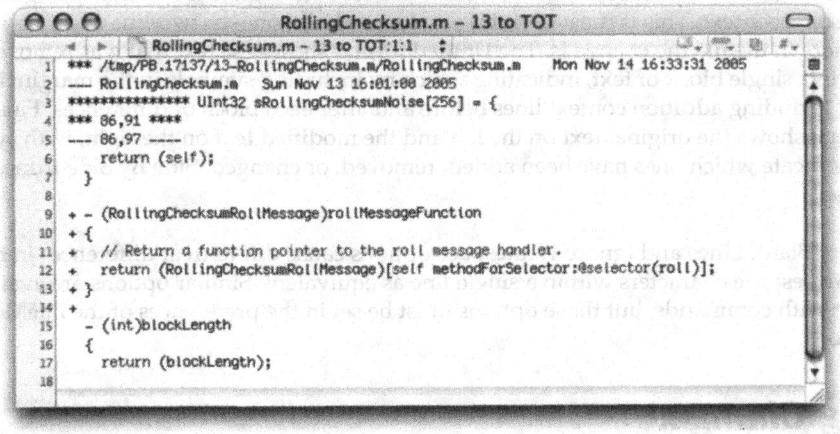

Figure 18-16

485

Customizing Compare

You can customize the program used to compare files, and some options to the diff tool, in the SCM tab of the Xcode Preferences (see Figure 18-17).

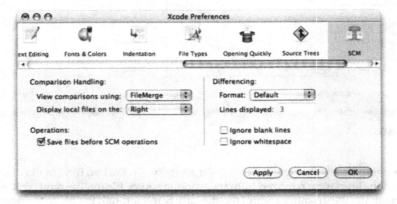

Figure 18-17

The Comparison Handling options select the application to be used to compare files. The choices are FileMerge, BBEdit, and Other. BBEdit requires that the BBEdit application is installed. The Other option prompts for an application that will perform the comparison. The Display Local File On The option selects whether your working file is displayed in the right or the left pane or window of the comparison application.

For diffs, you have a choice of formats and what whitespace to ignore. The Format choices are Default, Contextual, Side By Side, and Unified. Default uses diff's default format, which outputs each difference as blocks of text—a "before" block and an "after" block. The Contextual format is the same, except that it includes a number of additional lines before and after each region of text that changed to give the changes some context. This is most useful if you have a lot of one- or two-line changes and it's difficult to tell where in the file the change is. The Unified format shows the text that was removed, added, and changed in a single block of text, indicating which by including symbols in the margin. It too has the option of including addition context lines before and after each block of differences. Finally, the Side By Side format shows the original text on the left and the modified text on the right, with symbols between them to indicate which ones have been added, removed, or changed. Side By Side truncates long lines to fit the display.

The Ignore Blank Lines and Ignore Whitespace options cause diff to treat differences in blank lines or runs of whitespace characters within a single line as equivalent. Similar options are available for the Compare With commands, but those options must be set in the preferences of the FileMerge and BBEdit applications.

Merging Changes

The file comparison and merge utilities can also be used to combine the differences between two files. This is useful in a number of situations. One of the very liberating aspects of working with a source control system is the freedom to make experimental changes to your code. If you decide that you don't like the changes, you can compare your working copy with an earlier version of your source code stored in the repository. The file comparison utilities let you "undo" your changes by selectively moving blocks of code from the earlier version back into your working one. This is a much more surgical correction than merely discarding all of the changes in a file.

Both the FileMerge utility and BBEdit's compare files function place both old and new versions of the file on the screen side by side. Both highlight the blocks of text that differ between the two. For each difference, you can choose whether to keep it as it is or revert to the alternative version in the other file.

The FileMerge utility does this with a merged file pane at the bottom of the window. The merged file contains all of the common elements of both files and the selected blocks of text from either the right or left file pane. To create the merged version, select each difference and decide if you want to keep the version in the left file, the right file, neither, or both using the Actions pop-up menu. When you are finished, save the file as a new document, or replace one of the existing files with the merged version.

BBEdit works a little differently. In BBEdit there is no third file. It presents the two files in a separate editor windows (see Figure 18-18). A third window displays the list of differences between the two. Select a difference to highlight the corresponding regions in both files. From the differences window, you can replace the block in either file with the contents of the other using the Apply To New or Apply to Old button. When you are done, save the modified files back to their original locations, or use the File⇨Save As command to save the changes to a new file.

Figure 18-18

Viewing Annotations

Another way of seeing how a file has evolved is to look at its annotation view. Select a file and choose a command from the SCM⇨Get Annotations For submenu. The choices are Latest, Base, Revision, or Specific Revision. You can also select a revision of a file in the SCM tab of the Info window for the files and click the Annotate button.

The annotated listing of a file, shown in Figure 18-19, displays the revision number in which each line was added and the author of that line. In this example, you can see that the typedef for RollingChecksumRollMessage was added by deborah in revision 14 of the file. The in-line macros were added by james in revisions 12 and 13. The rest of the file was from the original when james first checked it in. Annotated listings do not show lines that have been removed, nor do they show the pervious versions of lines that have been altered.

```
● ● ●                    Annotations for RollingChecksum.h
◀ ▶   Annotations for RollingChecksum.h:1:1  ⬍   <No selected symbol>  ⬍
11    1    james // The data checksum scalar type
12    1    james typedef uint64_t RollingChecksum64;           // rolling checksums are 64 bit unsigned integers
13    1    james
14   14    deborah // Typedef of function pointer to call the roll method
15   14    deborah typedef RollingChecksum64 (*RollingChecksumRollMessage)(id,SEL);
16   14    deborah
17   14    deborah
18    1    james // The RollingChecksum object is used simply to calculate an Adler-like 32-bit checksum for a b
19    1    james // It does not contain the data, or any reference to it.
20    1    james
21    1    james extern UInt32 sRollingChecksumNoise[256];
22    1    james
23   13    james // In-line macros used for common operations
24   12    james #define RollingChecksum_Result             (((((uint64_t)hi)<<32)|lo)          /* return as a 64-
25   12    james #define RollingChecksum_Add(byte)          hi += ( lo += sRollingChecksumNoise[byte] )
26   12    james #define RollingChecksum_Roll(out,in,length)   lo -= sRollingChecksumNoise[out];          \
27 ◀
```

Figure 18-19

Resolving Conflicts

When a newer revision of a file appears in the repository, and you have modified that same file locally, the SCM status of the file changes to C to indicate a conflict. Before committing your version of the file, you need to join it with the latest revision checked into the repository to add, combine, or discard the changes made by the other developer with yours — or not.

When a conflict occurs, you have two choices. You can abandon the changes that you've made, replacing them wholesale with the changes made in the latest revision of the file. To abandon your changes, select the conflicting file and choose SCM⇨Discard Changes.

The other choice is to manually merge your changes with the ones checked into source control. Select the file and choose the SCM⇨Update To⇨Latest (Command+Shift+L) command. Instead of overwriting your changes with the latest revision of the file in the repository, which is what you might expect, your version and the latest version of the file are combined. The sections of the file that are different are noted by comments (see Figure 18-20). The SCM status for the file changes to a green C, indicating that the file is in conflict resolution.

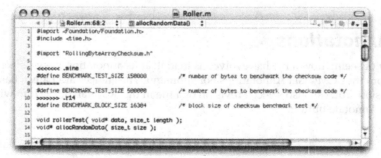

```
● ● ●                              m Roller.m
◀ ▶   Roller.m:68:2  ⬍   allocRandomData()  ⬍
1   #import <Foundation/Foundation.h>
2   #include <time.h>
3
4   #import "RollingByteArrayChecksum.h"
5
6   <<<<<<< .mine
7   #define BENCHMARK_TEST_SIZE 150000        /* number of bytes to benchmark the checksum code */
8   =======
9   #define BENCHMARK_TEST_SIZE 500000        /* number of bytes to benchmark the checksum code */
10  >>>>>>> .r14
11  #define BENCHMARK_BLOCK_SIZE 16384        /* block size of checksum benchmark test */
12
13  void rollerTest( void* data, size_t length );
14  void* allocRandomData( size_t size );
15
16 ◀
```

Figure 18-20

Edit the file, removing or combining the differences, until you have successfully integrated your changes with those of the other developer. If you are using Subversion, choose the SCM⇨Resolved command to let the repository know that you are done merging the changes.

You can now commit your combined changes, creating a new revision that contains the changes from both versions. When you commit your merged file, document your changes and the fact that these were combined with changes from the previous revision.

Going Offline

At some point, you may find yourself working on a project without access to the source control system or repository from which it was checked out. For example, you might have moved the project to another computer, or are using it on portable and are no longer in contact with your source control server.

You can temporarily disable SCM control of your project using the SCM⇨Go Offline command. This disables most SCM menu commands and the SCM status column. History and revision information that Xcode has already obtained for files is still available, but none of the commands that operate on those revisions will function.

When you are back in touch with the source control repository, restore SCM functionality by choosing the SCM⇨Go Online command.

SCM and the Project Document

The project document requires some special handing when a project is under the control of a source control system. The project document is a package containing several files. The project.pbxproj file contains the structure and common settings of the project document bundle. This includes source file references, target definitions, and build settings. If you change any of these values, the project.pbxproj file appears in the SCM smart group as a modified file (see Figure 18-21). The changes made to the project won't be stored in the repository until you commit this file.

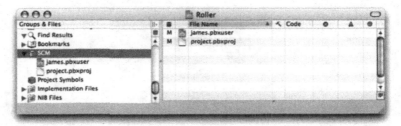

Figure 18-21

Each user has a personalized settings file in the project document package. The name of the file is the user's UNIX account name with the extension .pbxuser. Settings such as the appearance of windows, breakpoint locations, debugger options, and many other personalized touches are stored individually for each user. Whether you store these files in source control or not is entirely up to you. If you do not, checking out the project on another system using the same account will forfeit these settings. This may, or may not, be desirable to you.

Here are some points to keep in mind:

- ❑ Whenever you add, remove, or rename files in a project, commit the changes to the project document and *all* of the add and remove actions simultaneously. This will avoid the situation where the project has file references that are out of synchronization with the list of files in the repository.

- ❑ Whenever you update the project document files from the repository, close the project and reopen it from the File➪Recent Projects menu. Replacing the project document on disk does not force Xcode to reread the project settings in all cases. Closing the project and reopening it does. After you update a project document, you may get a warning that the project file has changed. Choose the option to reread the document from disk.

- ❑ To make the most of personal settings in the .pbxuser files, make sure all of the developers working on a project have distinct account names. If you work on a project from different systems, use the same account name on both or you will be treated as a different developer.

Summary

Source control management allows Xcode to become a member of a community. It also provides important tools for tracking, auditing, documenting, and protecting your hard work. Source trees let projects share common assets, maximizing their reuse, in a manner that won't break your projects when they're moved to another location or environment. Together, source control management and source trees allow you to benefit from the value of work that has already been done, and the work of your colleagues, in a portable and interactive manner.

The final chapter turns to what many consider to be an endless source of joy and entertainment: tweaking obscure options and settings in Xcode, customizing it to suite your every whim.

Customizing Xcode

Apple is famous for developing spare and elegant software solutions. Rare indeed is the Apple application that suffers from "featurosis" — a malady of ever-expanding specialized features that eventually smother an application in an incomprehensible maze of commands and options. But developers are not consumers. Developers are professionals that expect, nay demand, that almost every aspect of the tools they use be under their control; to alter, repurpose, and tweak as they see fit. I have personally worked with a developer who, dissatisfied with the warnings produced by a compiler, downloaded its source code, corrected the perceived flaw, and built his own personalized version to use. Although the wisdom of his actions are debatable, the spirit of "if you don't like the way it works, build your own" runs deep and strong through the developer community.

For this reason, Xcode is a departure from most software produced by the engineering teams at Apple Computer. Xcode has a dizzying array of customizable options, as witnessed by the monstrous Xcode Preferences window. Using the Xcode interface, you can completely customize the keystrokes used to invoke every Xcode command and motion. The extensive set of build settings enable you to specify any of the innumerable switches passed to compilers, linkers, and other tools employed by Xcode. You can completely reorganize the build process, and even assume complete responsibility for it. You are free to use a different text editor. You can even alter seemingly inconsequential interface details, such as the highlight colors used by the debugger.

Surprisingly, the list doesn't stop there. There are scores of hidden and undocumented customizations in Xcode. Most are application settings that you can be alter by editing the Xcode preferences file, as discussed in this chapter. You'll also find out how to create your own templates and customize the Xcode application by adding your own commands.

> Most undocumented features are unsupported by Apple and the Xcode development team. I've tested every customization presented in this chapter, but that doesn't mean they will all work in future versions of Xcode. Customization features that turn out to be popular are often re-implemented and appear in future versions in a friendlier and better-supported form. Check the release notes for the feature you are looking for.

Xcode Preferences

If you came to this chapter looking for the meaning of a particular Xcode preference setting, most of them are discussed in the chapter that the setting applies to. For example, the options in the Code Sense tab are discussed in the "Code Sense" section in Chapter 6. To point you in the right direction, the following lists the tabs in the Xcode Preferences window and the chapter where those settings are explained.

Preference Tab	Chapter	
General	3 and 6	
Code Sense	6	
Building	14	
Distributed Builds	14	
Debugging	15	
Key Bindings	19	
Text Editing	6	
Font & Colors	6	
Indentation	6	
File Types	6	
Opening Quickly	6	
Source Trees	18	
SCM	18	
Documentation	9	

Also refer to the Xcode Preferences appendix in the online Xcode Help document. It contains an excellent summary of all of the preference panes in Xcode. Chapter 9 of this book also provides assistance in browsing the Xcode Help documents.

Key Bindings

The only preference tab not covered in the other chapters is Key Bindings. The Key Bindings tab, shown in Figure 19-1, allows you define the keystroke combination associated with just about every command and action that Xcode performs. You will also see that a few buried actions are inaccessible in Xcode's default configuration and can only be accessed by assigning them a key binding.

Key bindings are stored in sets. Use the Key Binding Sets pop-up menu to switch between any of the predefined sets that ship with Xcode, or any sets that you've defined. Choose a set and click the Apply or OK button, and the new bindings take effect immediately. If you want to create a new binding set, select a base set and click the Duplicate button. Give the key binding set a name, as shown in Figure

19-2. To delete the selected set, click the Delete button. You cannot edit or delete predefined sets. To customize one of the predefined sets, duplicate it and edit the new set. If you try to edit a predefined key binding set, Xcode offers to first duplicate the set.

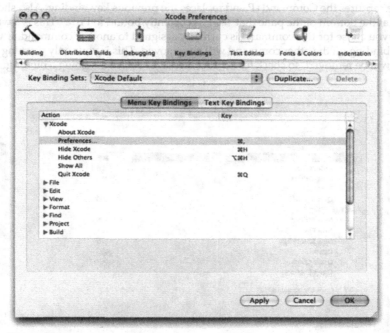

Figure 19-1

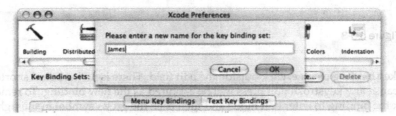

Figure 19-2

Menu Key Bindings

The Key Bindings pane has two sections: Menu Key Bindings and Text Key Bindings. Menu key bindings, previously shown in Figure 19-1, bind keyboard shortcuts with the items in the Xcode menus. Menus items that are created dynamically, such as the list of recently opened projects, cannot be bound by menu key bindings.

To edit a menu key binding, find the menu item in the hierarchy of menu groups and double-click its Key field. The menu item's current binding turns into an editable field (see Figure 19-3). This is not a normal text edit field. It captures any single keystroke or combination you press. To bind Command+P to the Xcode Preferences command, press Command+P on the keyboard. Instead of invoking the File⇨Print command, Xcode captures the Command+P and replaces the previous key binding. Also shown in Figure 19-3 is a warning at the bottom of the pane that "⌘-P is currently bound to Print" This is a warning that the key binding that you chose for this command is currently assigned to another command. If you accept this key binding, the binding on the other command will be removed. This is your only warning that a conflicting key binding will be removed, so check for conflict messages before assigning a binding.

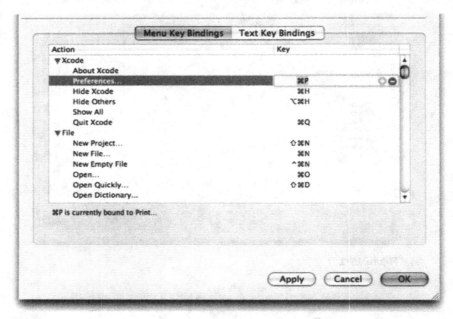

Figure 19-3

To accept a key binding change, click outside the edit field. There is no keyboard shortcut to accept a binding, because any keystroke you press will be captured as the new binding. To remove a key binding, double-click the binding to enter edit mode and then click the grey - symbol in the right portion of the edit field.

Traditionally, key bindings for menu items are Command key combinations. However, you are free to assign any keystroke combination you want to menu items. Existing examples are commands like Edit⇨Next Completion, which is bound to Control+., or Edit⇨Select Next Placeholder, which is bound to Control+/. Be judicious in these assignments — for example, assigning the Tab key to the Xcode⇨Quit command is *not* recommended.

Letter keys have no sense of case in key bindings. Command+A is one key combination, and Command+Shift+A is a different key combination. The state of the Caps Lock key has no influence on key bindings.

When editing key bindings, Xcode displays the symbols listed in the following table for special keys.

Symbol	Key
⌘	Command
⌥	Option
⇧	Shift
^	Control
←	Left Arrow
→	Right Arrow
↑	Up Arrow
↓	Down Arrow
⇥	Tab
⎋	Esc
⌫	Delete (backspace)
⌦	Delete (forward)
⇞	Page Up
⇟	Page Down
↖	Home
↘	End
↩	Return
⌤	Enter
Space	Space

Try It Out   **Redefine Command Keys for Debugger**

When debugging, I use the Step Over, Step Into, and Continue commands buttons a lot; sometimes hundreds of times while stepping through a loop or looking for a suspicious value. The default key combinations for these commands are Command+Shift+., Command+Shift+O, and Command+Shift+I. I find these key combinations awkward. Anything awkward multiplied a hundred times becomes down right annoying. I have an extended keyboard, which gives me lots of function keys.

Change the debugger commands to use function keys instead of the default mnemonic combinations as follows:

1. Open the Key Bindings tab of the Xcode Preferences. Duplicate the key bindings set you are using now. Give it a new name.

2. In the Menu Key Bindings table, find the Continue command and double-click its current binding (usually Command+Shift+.).

495

3. Press Control+F13 to change the binding. Click outside the field to set it.

4. Repeat steps 3 and 4, binding Step Into to Control+F15 and Step Over to Control+F14.

5. Click the OK button to adopt the new key bindings. When you're done, the menu bindings should look like the ones shown in Figure 19-4.

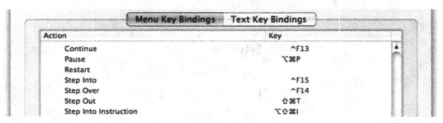

Figure 19-4

How It Works

Editing the menu key bindings changes the key combinations that Xcode uses for menu command shortcuts. You redefined the shortcuts for three commands in the Debug window, replacing the more traditional Command key combinations with Control+Function key combinations.

You can verify the change by examining the Debug menu itself. It should now look similar to the one in Figure 19-5.

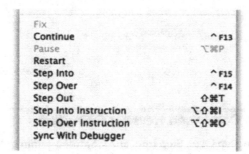

Figure 19-5

Text Key Bindings

Text key bindings are the bindings to the text editor and navigation actions built into Xcode. By altering the text key bindings, you can change the behavior of the Xcode text editor.

Editing a text key binding is almost identical to the procedure for editing menu key bindings (see Figure 19-6). The only significant difference is that you can assign multiple key bindings to the same action. Any of the key combinations listed will invoke that action.

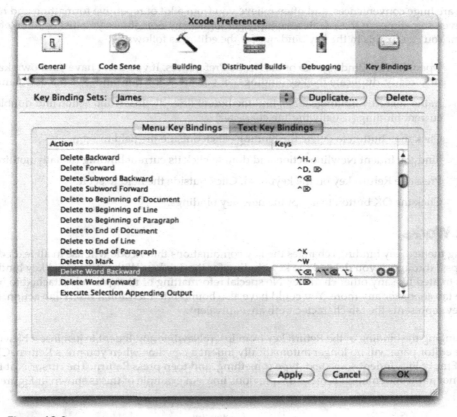

Figure 19-6

To alter a key binding, double-click the Keys field of the binding. Set the first, or replace the existing, key combination by typing the desired combination. To add additional key combinations to the same action, click the + button to the right side of the edit field, as shown in Figure 19-6. To delete a specific key combination, click the combination in the list to select it and then click the - button.

In the editor, any regular character key that is not assigned an action is inserted literally into the text (assuming the encoding of the document permits it).

Try It Out   Make Your Editor Less Friendly

The normal key bindings in the editor add some subtle nuances to what would normally be very mundane actions. Pressing the Tab or Return key in most text editors simply inserts a tab or return character into the text. But if you look at the key bindings for Xcode, you'll see that these keys are tied to the Indent Friendly Insert Tab and Insert Newline and Indent actions. Pressing the Tab or Return key does more than just insert a character. In the case of Tab, if you insert it at the beginning of a line, it inserts a tab character then jumps to the first non-whitespace character in the line. The Return key inserts a newline character, and then re-indents the new line to the same level as the previous line.

These are huge conveniences, and often relieve you from a lot of repetitive formatting and navigation. However, sometimes of these features simply get in the way. Sometimes you just want a Return to be a Return. You can fix this in the key bindings for the editor, as follows:

1. Open the Key Bindings tab of the Xcode Preferences. If you don't have your own key bindings set already, duplicate the key bindings set you are using now and give it a new name.

2. In the Text Key Bindings table, find the Indent Friendly Insert Tab action and double-click its current binding (usually the Tab character).

3. Click the - button to delete the binding. Click outside the field to set it.

4. Find the Indent Newline action and double-click its current binding (usually nothing).

5. Press the Return key on the keyboard. Click outside the field to set it.

6. Click the OK button to adopt the new key bindings.

How It Works

Editing the text key bindings changes the key combinations that Xcode will use in all text editor panes. In steps 2 through 4, you deleted the key binding for the Tab key. Without a special key binding, the Tab key is treated like any other character. No special reformatting or navigation is attached to inserting a single tab character any more. You could have also bound it to the vanilla Insert Tab action. Because the Tab key represents the tab character, both are equivalent.

By changing the binding of the Return key from Insert Newline and Indent to just Insert Newline, a syntax-aware editor pane will no longer automatically indent a new line when you press Return. Choose File⇨ New Empty File, indent some text, type something, and then press Return. The cursor is at the first column, not at the indentation level of the previous line. An example of this is shown in Figure 19-7.

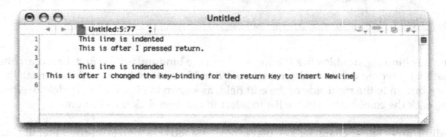

Figure 19-7

Well, that's the theory at least. If you try this out on a source code file, you may find that text is still automatically indented when you press Return. Check your settings in the Indentation tab of the Xcode Preferences. You probably have Return checked in the list of Automatically Indented Characters. The syntax-aware indentation logic and key-binding actions operate independently of each other. Turn that option off, and a Return key will be just a return.

You can also use the "naked" Inset Newline and Insert Tab actions to insert an unadorned return or tab character by binding it to something other than a simple return or tab character. Try this: Leave the original bindings alone, bind Insert Newline to Shift+Return, and bind Insert Tab to Shift+Tab. Now you have the choice of inserting a "friendly" or "raw" return or tab using the Shift key.

Key bindings are global, and both the menu key bindings and text key bindings share the same table. A key combination can only be assigned to a single menu command or editor action. Keep this in mind when you're assigning non-Command key combinations to menu commands and vice versa.

Key bindings are stored by name in your local ~/Library/Application Support/Xcode/Key Bindings folder. You can exchange key binding files with other users if you like. Quit Xcode, install a new key bindings file, launch Xcode, and select the new binding in the Key Bindings Sets pop-up menu.

Expert Preferences

You set Xcode's so-called "expert" preferences by directly altering the settings in the preferences file for the Xcode application. This file is named com.apple.Xcode.plist and is located in the Preferences folder of your home Library folder. There are two simple ways of changing these settings. However you alter them, you must remember that the Xcode application should not be running when you change them. First quit the Xcode application, make the change, and then launch Xcode again.

The first method is to use the `defaults` command from a Terminal window. The syntax for setting a value in the Xcode preferences is as follows:

```
defaults write com.apple.Xcode key value
```

The `write` command tells the defaults command to set a value in the file. The last two arguments specify the symbol and value it will be set to. (Refer to the man page for the `defaults` command for more options.) For example, the drag-and-drop delay used by Xcode's text editor can be adjusted by setting the value for the NSDragAndDropTextDelay key. The command to set this value to 500 (milliseconds) is as follows:

```
defaults write com.apple.Xcode NSDragAndDropTextDelay 500
```

The second method is to use the Property List Editor application included with the Xcode development tools. Figure 19-8 shows setting the same value by editing the com.apple.Xcode.plist property list file. Remember not to open the file until *after* you have quit the Xcode application. The Property List Editor makes setting complex values, like dictionaries and numeric types, much easier.

The following tables list some of the more useful expert preferences settings, grouped by subject. You can find a complete list by choosing the Help⇨Show Expert Preferences Notes command. These hidden settings change from one version of Xcode to the next, so review this list, or consult the release notes if you can't find what you're looking for here.

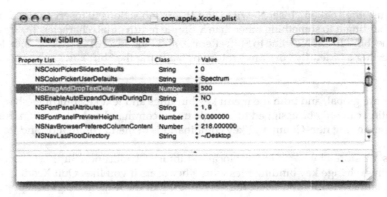

Figure 19-8

Projects and Files

The following table lists the projects and files settings.

Setting	Default	Description
PBXCustomTemplate MacroDefinitions	(none)	A dictionary of values used to replace variables in project and file templates. The "Who's __MyCompanyName__?" section of Chapter 4 provides an example of setting a template value using this setting.
PBXDontWarnIf ProjectSaveFails	No	Setting this to Yes suppresses Xcode's warning that there were problems saving the project documents. Project documents are constantly being updated, and Xcode warns you if the file cannot be written. This occurs repeatedly if you have no write access to the document, such as a project on a CD-ROM.
PBXPreservePosix PermissionsOnSave	Yes	If set to Yes, Xcode tries to restore the POSIX file permissions whenever it saves a file. You may want to change this to No if you are writing project files to a non-native or networked file system.
NSRecentDocumentsLimit	10	The maximum number of projects to keep in the File⇨Recent Projects menu.

Editing

The following table lists the editing settings.

Setting	Default	Description
NSDragAndDrop TextDelay	500	The delay, in milliseconds, that you must hold the mouse button down without moving it before a click in a text selection becomes a text drag. If you are constantly selecting instead of dragging text, reduce this delay. Increase it if you find yourself dragging text when you wanted to select it. Set the delay to 0 or a negative number to disable text dragging altogether.
PBXIndentOnPaste	Yes	Normally, when you're pasting text into a syntax-aware editor pane, Xcode automatically re-indents the text. If you find this annoying, change this setting to No and pasted text will be inserted literally. You can always manually re-indent the text using the Format⇨ Re-Indent command.
PBXBeepOnNoMatching Brace	Yes	Set this to No to suppress Xcode's habit of playing the system "beep" sound when it can't find a matching brace. The editor looks for matching braces whenever you type a closing brace or parentheses, or if you double-click a brace or parentheses.
XCShowUndoPast SaveWarning	Yes	Xcode warns you whenever you are about to undo a change that occurred before the point where a file was last saved. If you find this warning annoying, change this setting to No.
XCColorUnknown Languages	No	The Xcode editor normally provides syntax coloring only for file types that it understands. Setting this to Yes will cause text that appear to be comments (lines beginning with #, text between /* . . . */, and so on) to be colored in any text file.
XCSelectToInside MatchingQuotes	Yes	Doubling-clicking a single or double-quote in the Xcode editor causes it to select the entire string by finding and selecting all text up to and including the matching quote. Set this to No and Xcode will not try to auto-select quoted strings.
XCScrollToEndOf MatchingBrace	Yes	When you double-click a quote, brace, or parenthesis, Xcode scrolls so that the matching brace is visible in the editor pane. Set this to No to leave the scroll position alone.

Table continued on following page

Setting	Default	Description	
XCMatchIndentWith LineAbove	Yes	When Syntax-Aware Indenting is disabled, or when you're editing a non-syntax-aware source file type, this setting still causes auto-indenting of a new line to the same level as the previous line. Setting the value to No disables auto-indenting of new lines, even when you're using the Insert Newline And Indent action.	
XCSmartInsertDelete Enabled	No	Set this to Yes and Xcode will try to be "smarter" about how it inserts and deletes spaces around words when inserting and deleting within a source file.	
XCShowNonBreaking Space	Yes	Xcode normally displays a non-breaking space (Unicode 0x00A0) as a dot (•). Change this setting to No and non-breaking spaces will display as whitespace.	
XCShowControl Characters	Yes	Xcode normally displays control characters that it finds in text files as an inverted question mark (¿). Change this setting to No and control characters in editor panes will be invisible.	

Functions Menu

The following settings control what kinds of items are included in the functions menu of the editor pane's navigation bar. The Show Declarations setting in the Code Sense tab of the Xcode Preferences controls the inclusion of function and method definitions. To include, or exclude, other types of items from the menu change these settings to Yes or No as desired.

Setting	Default	
PBXMethodPopupIncludeMarksDefault	Yes	
PBXMethodPopupIncludeClassDeclarationsDefault	Yes	
PBXMethodPopupIncludeClassDefinitionsDefault	Yes	
PBXMethodPopupIncludeMethodDeclarationsDefault	Yes	
PBXMethodPopupIncludeMethodDefinitionsDefault	Yes	
PBXMethodPopupIncludeFunctionDeclarationsDefault	Yes	
PBXMethodPopupIncludeFunctionDefinitionsDefault	Yes	
PBXMethodPopupIncludeTypesDefault	Yes	
PBXMethodPopupIncludeDefinesDefault	Yes	
PBXMethodPopupIncludeWarningsDefault	No	

Building

The following table lists the building settings.

Setting	Default	Description
BuildSystemCacheSizeInMegabytes	1024	The "trim" size of the pre-compiled headers cache. Precompiled headers are cached and reused whenever possible. If the size of the cache is larger than this value in megabytes, Xcode deletes the oldest precompiled headers to recover disk space. Note that this happens only once, when the Xcode application is first launched. Setting this value to 0 disables this check, allowing the cache to grow unabated. Also see the BuildSystemCacheMinimumRemovalAgeInHours setting.
BuildSystemCacheMinimumRemovalAgeInHours	24	This is the number of hours a precompiled header must have been in the cache before it can be removed. Even if the BuildSystemCacheSizeInMegabytes setting tells Xcode it's time to delete old headers in the cache, headers that are younger than this setting will never be removed; even if the means not trimming the cache down to the requested size.
PBXBuildSuccessSound	(none)	Set this to a path of a sound file you want played when a build is successful.

Table continued on following page

Setting	Default	Description
PBXBuildFailureSound	(none)	Set this to a path of a sound file you want played when a build fails.
PBXNumberOfParallelBuildSubtasks	0	The number of parallel tasks the build system will try to keep running while building. If set to 0, the build system uses the number of processors installed in your computer. Set this to a number greater than the number of processors if your builds are I/O bound. Reduce the number to keep Xcode from using all available CPU resources.
PredictiveCompilationDelay	30	The number of seconds before a predictive compile is performed. If a source file in an editor pane hasn't been modified for a while, Xcode attempts to compile it in the background. Increase this delay if background compilation is using too many resources, or reduce it to be more aggressive. This feature requires that predictive compilation is enabled in the Xcode Preferences. Xcode ignores this setting if you try to set it lower than 10.
UsePerConfigurationBuildLocations	Yes	Build locations are normally separated into subfolders by build configuration. This avoids the need to rebuild the entire project when switching build configurations, but uses considerably more disk space. Set this to No, and the build products of different build configurations will be written to the same folder.

Distributed Builds

The following table lists the distributed builds settings.

Setting	Default	Description
XCMaxNumberOfDistributedTasks	25	The maximum number of tasks to distribute to other computers when you're using distributed builds.
XCDistributedBuildsVerboseLogging	No	Change this setting to Yes to enable diagnostic messages from the distcc tool. If you are having problems with distributed builds, these messages may provide some insight as to why.
DistributedBuildsLogLevel	0	Controls the amount of detail produced by Xcode's distributed build manager. This is useful for debugging distributed build problems. The value must be 0, 1, or 2.

Debugging

The following table lists the debugging settings.

Setting	Default	Description
XCAutoClearRunDebugStdIOLogs	No	Set this to Yes and Xcode will clear the run, debug, and standard I/O windows at the beginning of each debugging or run session. Normally, Xcode preserves the results of the previous run or debug session, allowing the output of those to accumulate until you quit Xcode or manually clear the log windows with the Debug⇨Clear Logs command.
PBXGDBPath	/usr/ bin/gdb	The path to the gdb debugger. Change this setting to use an alternate version of the gdb debugger.

Table continued on following page

Setting	Default	Description
PBXGDBDebuggerLogToFile	No	If you think you need to debug the communications with the debugger, change this setting to Yes. This causes Xcode to log all communications between Xcode and the gdb tool to a file in /var/tmp/ folders/uid/Temporary Items. The name of the file is determined by the PBXGDBDebuggerLogFileName setting. If you are having problems with the debugger, Apple requests that you include this log file in any bug reports.
PBXGDBDebuggerLogFileName	(none)	If left undefined, the name of the debugger log file will be XCGDB-*name-pid*, where *name* is the name of the executable and *pid* is its process ID. Setting this to a fixed value causes the log to be written to the same file for every debug session, overwriting any previous file. This setting requires that PBXGDBDebuggerLogToFile is set to Yes to have any effect.

Source Code Management

The three path settings hold the default path to their respective source control client tool. Changing this setting for Xcode can save you the trouble of editing the path in every new project you configure for source control. (Chapter 18 explained how to configure source control for a project.) Changing this setting will not alter the path of any project that has already been configured.

Setting	Default	Description
PBXCVSToolPath	/usr/bin/ ocvs	The default path to the CVS client tool.
PBXPerforceToolPath	/usr/local/ bin/p4	The default path to the Perforce client tool.
XCSubversionToolPath	/usr/local/ subversion/ bin/svn	The default path to the Subversion client tool.
XCSMLogSize	500	The maximum amount of text (in K) that will be kept in the SCM log, which can be viewed in the SCM Results window.

Documentation

The following table lists the documentation setting.

Setting	Default	Description
XCDocWindowSharesGlobalFindString	Yes	When this is set to Yes, the search field for the help window automatically picks up the value of the global find string. This is a system-wide resource shared by Xcode's find windows and other find-savvy applications. If you make a search in Mail, for instance, switching to Xcode automatically picks up the last term you searched for. Change this setting to No to suppress this behavior.

Try It Out   **Enable the Auto Clear Logs Setting**

I am rarely interested in the program output of older debug or run sessions. On the rare occasion that I am, I will save the program output that I want to preserve to a clipping file. Consequently, I prefer Xcode to clear the run, debug, and I/O log windows whenever I start an executable. Follow these steps to enable that feature in Xcode.

1.   Quite the Xcode application.

2.   Open a Terminal window and execute the following command:

```
defaults write com.apple.Xcode XCAutoClearRunDebugStdIOLogs Yes
```

3.   Launch Xcode and open any project that you can run.

4.   Open the run log window (Debug⇨Run Log) and run the program. Run it again.

How It Works

Xcode has a wealth of named properties that are used to customize its behavior. Many of these are adjustable using the user interface, and all are stored in its preferences file. Xcode (and actually any Cocoa application) uses the value set in a preferences file if one is present there. Using the `defaults` tool, you set or altered the value of the XCAutoClearRunDebugStdIOLogs property in the preferences file. When Xcode was launched again, it read the value of this property and used that setting (Yes) instead of its internal default value (No).

With this property set to Yes, the contents of the run log are cleared whenever you run or debug an application. Running the application in step 4 outputs information to the run log window. Issuing the Run command again first erased the contents of the window before rerunning the application.

Templates

Although this is not officially documented, it is easy to customize Xcode by adding your own project and file templates. Templates are installed in the File Templates and Project Templates folders found in the system-wide /Library/Application Support/Apple/Developer Tools folder. You can customize the existing one or add your own here, or create private templates for your personal development in your local ~/Library/Application Support/Apple/Developer Tools folder. All of the templates found in either location are merged to form a single list of templates when you create a new project or file.

The hierarchy and names of the subfolders within the templates folder determine the grouping and order of the templates that will appear in the new file or project assistant. The easiest way to see this is to compare the file structure of a template folder with the new file assistant, shown in Figure 19-9.

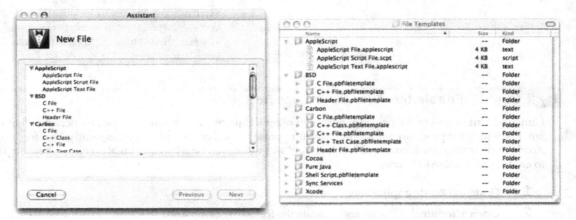

Figure 19-9

You can group your templates however you want, simply by placing them into a subfolder of related templates.

File Templates

File templates can be a single file or a file template bundle. The simplest way to add a file template is to place a plain document file in the File Templates folder. The next time you start Xcode and use the File⇨ New File command, the name of the file appears in the list. Select it and Xcode reads the file and use its contents to fill in your new file.

File template bundles are a little more sophisticated. File template bundles are not *real* bundles, but are folders that mimic the bundle structure. A file template bundle has an extension of .pbfiletemplate. The name of the folder is the name of the template, as it will appear in the new file assistant. Inside the folder is a TemplateInfo.plist file and one or two document files. TemplateInfo.plist contains a number of properties, described in the following table.

Property	Description
MainTemplateFile	This property is required. It is the name of the primary template file in the bundle.
CounterpartTemplateFile	This property is the name of a companion file that can be created by the template. This property is optional. If present, Xcode displays a check box option in the new file dialog box that asks if the user wants to create the companion file at the same time they create the main file.
Description	Text that describes the template. This description appears in the lower pane of the new file assistant when the user selects this template in the list. This property is optional, but highly recommended. If omitted, Xcode displays "No description available."

Create the template file or template bundle, name it appropriately, and place it in the File Templates folder or in a subfolder if you want it to be in a group of templates. Relaunch Xcode and your new template appears in the new file assistant.

Template Macros

Templates can contain variable names that are replaced with a value when the template is read. The macro names are surrounded double-angle quotes («*NAME*»). The following table lists the macro variables defined by Xcode when a file template is read.

> The double-angle quote characters, which are Unicode characters 0x00AB and 0x00BB respectively, require that the file be encoded correctly. "Correctly" being defined as whatever Xcode expects the encoding to be. Open the template file in Xcode. If the double-angle quotes appear as one or two strange characters, then the encoding is mismatched. First note the current encoding. Now, try switching to a different encoding using the Format⇨File Encoding menu and choose the Reinterpret option. If the double-angle quote characters appear correctly, you've discovered their encoding. Switch back to the original encoding, this time choosing the Convert option, and save the file. You can type these characters using Option+\ and Option+Shift+\ on a U.S. Standard keyboard. If you are using a different keyboard layout, you may have a different key combination. Refer to the system's Keyboard Viewer palette if you have difficulty finding them, or use the system's Character Palette to insert the characters directly.

Macro	Example	Description
DATE	11/17/05	Today's date, short format.
YEAR	2006	The year.
FILENAME	My File.txt	The complete name of the new file.
FILEBASENAME	My File	The file name given to the file by the user, without its extension.
FILEBASENAMEASIDENTIFIER	My_File	The base file name, suitable for use as a language identifier. The same as FILEBASENAME, but with all non-alphanumeric characters replaced with underscores.
FULLUSERNAME	James Bucanek	The current user's full account name.
PROJECTNAME	Tom & Jerry	The name of the project.
PROJECTNAMEASIDENTIFIER	Tom___Jerry	The name of the project, suitable for use as a language identifier. The same as PROJECTNAME, but with all non-alphanumeric characters replaced with underscores.
PROJECTNAMEASXML	Tom & Jerry	The name of the project encoded using XML entities to escape any special characters.
USERNAME	james	The current user's UNIX account name.
UUID	89E2FBF6-9B88-40EB-BFCF-4550CA9F54CA	A Universally Unique Identifier. This value will be different every time.
ORGANIZATIONNAME	Genius, Inc.	A common macro defined in the expert preferences.

The UUID value is interesting and might be useful if the documents you are creating need to be managed by a database or identified in some fashion.

Xcode doesn't define the ORGANIZATIONNAME macro. It is a common macro added to the PBXCustomTemplateMacroDefinitions dictionary, but it is not required. You can define and use any macro value defined in the PBXCustomTemplateMacroDefinitions setting in your template.

The PROJECTNAME and related macros are defined for project templates or if the file is being added to a project. If you create new file using a template but select "none" as the project to add it to, these variables are replaced with nothing. In fact, any undefined or unrecognized macro name is replaced with nothing in the new file.

Try It Out — Create a Custom File Template

Follow these steps to create a custom file template that generates an empty XML document used to create test items, linked to a matching cascading style sheet (SSH):

1. Create a new folder named **Styled Test Item.pbfiletemplate**.

2. Inside that folder, create two UTF-8 encoded text files named **item.xml** and **item.css**. The files should look like those in Listing 19-1.

Listing 19-1: Test Item Template Files

item.xml
```xml
<?xml version="1.0" encoding="utf-8"?>
<?xml-stylesheet href="«FILEBASENAME».css" type="text/css"?>
<!--
    Created «DATE» by «FULLUSERNAME»
    Copyright «YEAR» «ORGANIZATIONNAME», all rights reserved
-->
<item name="«FILEBASENAMEASIDENTIFIER»"
    uuid="«UUID»"
    author="«USERNAME»"
    created="«DATE»">
</item>
```

item.css
```css
/* «FILENAME» */
/* Created «DATE» by «FULLUSERNAME» */
/* Copyright «YEAR» «ORGANIZATIONNAME», all rights reserved */

BASE { /* ... styles go here ... */ }
```

3. Create a new TemplateInfo.plist file inside the template bundle folder. Use the Property List Editor utility to set the properties to those shown in Figure 19-10.

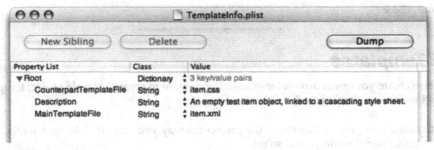

Figure 19-10

4. Locate, or create if necessary, the local ~/Library/Application Support/Apple/Developer Tools/File Templates folder. Inside that folder, create a new folder named **XML** and drop the Styled Test Item.pbfiletemplate template bundle inside that.

5.　Quit Xcode. Relaunch Xcode and choose the File↑New File command.

6.　Give the file a name of **Questions.xml**, and create it and its companion CSS file.

How It Works

In steps 1 through 4, you created a file template bundle and installed it for use by Xcode. After Xcode is relaunched, the new template appears in the new file assistant, as shown on the left in Figure 19-11.

Figure 19-11

In step 6, Xcode is offering to create a companion .css file, shown on the right in Figure 19-11. This is because there is a CounterpartTemplateFile property defined in the TemplateInfo.plist file. The new files are created from the template with all of the template macros replaced with their current values (see Figure 19-12).

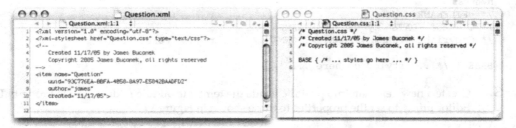

Figure 19-12

Project Templates

You can also create your own project templates. If you want to create a simple project template that gets duplicated verbatim when created, follow these steps:

1.　Create a new project. Configure the project the way you want it: Add source files, frameworks, targets, special settings, and so on.

2.　Close the project. Delete the build folder and any other intermediate files that might be in the project folder.

3.　Rename the project folder to the name of the template as you want it to appear in the new project assistant.

4. Move the project folder to a location in the Library/Application Support/Apple/Developer Tools/Project Templates where you want it to appear in the new project assistant list. This can be in the global /Library folder or in your local ~/Library folder. Create a new subfolder if you want a separate category for your template.

5. Quit Xcode. Relaunch Xcode and create a new project using your template.

Project Templates with Macros

Simple project templates are easy, but boring. What you really want is a project template like the ones that ship with Xcode. These include files, class names, and project settings that magically alter themselves to match the name of the project you just created.

Making a template that will customize itself is considerably trickier. How much of your project gets dynamically configured depends on how much work you want to put into it. The key to configuring a self-customizing project template is to create a TemplateInfo.plist file and embed that in your project document package. The TemplateInfo.plist file should contain three properties: Description, FilesToMacroExpand, FilesToRename, as described in the following table.

Property	Type	Description
Description	String	This optional property is a string that describes the template. This description appears in the lower pane of the new project assistant window when a user selects this template from the list.
FilesToRename	Dictionary	This optional property is a list of key/value pairs. Each pair consists of the name of the original file in the project and the name it should be renamed to when the new project is created.
FilesToMacroExpand	Array	This optional property is a list of file name paths, relative to the new project folder, of the files that should be scanned for replicable template macro names.

You should definitely supply a description string. It makes the template more pleasant to use, and is useful for debugging (explained later).

The FilesToRename property is a translation table that renames certain files in the project as the project template is being duplicated. The values in this dictionary can include template macros, which allow you to give files in your project dynamic names. In the example shown in Figure 19-13, the Template_Prefix.pch file in the project template will be renamed to «PROJECTNAME»_Prefix.pch. PROJECTNAME will be replaced with whatever filename was given to the new project by the user.

You can use any of the template macros listed previously in the "Template Macros" section in the project document or in the source files of your project template. The files in the project document package are automatically scanned for template macro names. This is how the macro names in the TemplateInfo.plist file are expanded. Also scanned is the project.pbxproj document. Thus, any build settings in the project that contains a template macro name will be replaced. This allows you, for example, to set the Prefix Header build setting to «PROJECTNAME»_Prefix.pch so it will match the name of the renamed Template_Prefix.pch file in the new project.

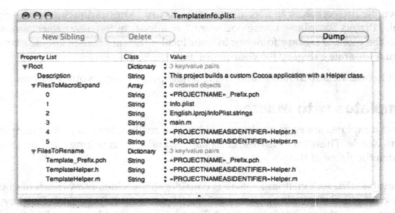

Figure 19-13

Other files in the project are not automatically scanned for template macro names. To replace template macro names in any other files requires that you add its path to the FilesToMacroExpand property. The names in the list are the files in the new project, not the template, so if you want to process a file that you've also renamed, use the name the file was changed to—which itself will probably involve template macros.

In the example previously shown in Figure 19-13, the «PROJECTNAMEASIDENTIFIER»Helper.h files are scanned for template macros. The original file in the TemplateHelper.h template looks like this:

TemplateHelper.h
```
//
//   «PROJECTNAMEASIDENTIFIER»Helper.h
//   «PROJECTNAME»
//
//   Created by «FULLUSERNAME» on «DATE».
//   Copyright «YEAR» «ORGANIZATIONNAME». All rights reserved.
//

#import <Cocoa/Cocoa.h>

@interface «PROJECTNAMEASIDENTIFIER»Helper : NSObject
{

}

@end
```

Not only will the file be renamed to match the project, but the class it defines will also get a matching name.

File References in Project Templates

The FilesToRename property renames files in the project folder. The macro replacement can be used to generate names dynamically in files and project properties. Unfortunately, these two mechanisms don't work closely with each other or with the project itself. The FilesToRename property just renames files. It doesn't alter or fix up any of the project references to those files. If nothing else is done, the project will contain bad references to the original files. To fix this, you have to manually insert template macros into the project.pbxproj file. You can do this in Xcode or the Property List Editor by temporarily giving the project.pbxproj file an extension of .xml or .plist, or you can use another text editor like BBEdit.

> If you edit template property files with BBEdit, make sure you use the correct encoding. Property list files typically have an encoding of UTF-8. If you open one of these files using ASCII encoding, the double-angle quote characters will not be encoded correctly. Use BBEdit's File⇨Reopen Using Encoding⇨Unicode command to reinterpret the file as UTF-8.

You'll have to find and replace the file name paths in the property files by hand, as there is no facility for entering these dynamic names in the Xcode interface. The format for the project document file is not intended to be "user friendly." Nevertheless, it's pretty safe to search for the file names you want to make dynamic and replace them with template macros. Just be careful not to make any other structural changes in the file, or you'll likely end up with a corrupted project document.

For example, here's a fragment of a project.pbxproj file that contained references to the TemplateHelper.h, TemplateHelper.m, and main.c source files:

```
1AAE3664092E3E8C00412C87 /* TemplateHelper.h */ = {isa = PBXFileReference;
fileEncoding = 4; lastKnownFileType = sourcecode.c.h; path =
«PROJECTNAMEASIDENTIFIER»Helper.h; sourceTree = "<group>"; };

1AAE3665092E3E8C00412C87 /* TemplateHelper.m */ = {isa = PBXFileReference;
fileEncoding = 4; lastKnownFileType = sourcecode.c.objc; path =
«PROJECTNAMEASIDENTIFIER»Helper.m; sourceTree = "<group>"; };

29B97316FDCFA39411CA2CEA /* main.m */ = {isa = PBXFileReference; fileEncoding = 4;
lastKnownFileType = sourcecode.c.objc; path = main.m; sourceTree = "<group>"; };
```

The file has been edited so that the first two source file names are now altered dynamically to match their renamed versions in the new project.

Problems with Project Templates

Template project problems can be difficult to isolate, because there are no overt errors or warnings produced by Xcode to tell you that something is wrong.

The first thing to check in your new template is that its description appears in the new project assistant window when you choose your template in the list. If it does not, then Xcode didn't read your TemplateInfo.plist file. Make sure the location, syntax, and encoding of the file is correct. You might find that the easiest way of doing this is to open the file using the Property List Editor and forcing the file to be resaved. The Property List Editor usually corrects any inconsistencies when it writes a new file.

If you have macros in source files that aren't being expanded, make sure they have been written using the default encoding expected by Xcode for that file type. Follow the steps for fixing the encoding in the earlier "Template Macros" section. Also double-check that you've added the file to the

FilesToMacroExpand property. If the file is one that gets renamed, make sure you specified its new name—not its original name—in the template.

Look at the system console log. Some problems encountered during template processing are logged here and may give you some clue as to what is wrong.

Last, but not least, study (or just copy) the Xcode templates that come pre-installed. They demonstrate a wide range of customizations. Learning how they work may illuminate what's not working in yours.

Project Template Portability

If you are creating project templates for your own consumption, you're pretty much done. However, if you want to create sophisticated templates to share with other developers, there are a couple of additional details you should consider.

You'll want to delete your user settings files from the project document package. These documents are stored inside the project document package and are named using your logged-in UNIX account name. Other users don't need these documents in their projects.

The Xcode templates are supplied as .pbproj documents, known as Project Builder Projects. These are the oldest form of project documents that Xcode can import. When a project template is read, Xcode automatically upgrades the project to the latest version and discards the original. If the developers you are giving these template to all have the same or later version of Xcode, then you don't need to worry about this. If you want to provide templates to users with earlier versions of Xcode, you will need to install the earliest version of Xcode you plan to support and create your templates using that version.

Target Templates

You may also find it useful to create custom target templates. These are the templates used by the new target assistant when you're adding a new target to your project. Target templates are defined by the target template files found in the Library/Application Support/Apple/Developer Tools/Target Templates folder. A target template file is a property list fragment with an extension of .trgttmpl. There are several properties that must be set correctly for the target template to be functional. The important elements are the Class and ProductType properties. The easiest way to create a new target template is to copy a template file that creates the correct target type and edit its other properties. Listing 19-2 shows the target template file for a Cocoa application target.

Listing 19-2: Cocoa Application Target Template

```
{
    Class = Native;
    ProductType = "com.apple.product-type.application";
    Description = "Target for building an application that uses Cocoa APIs.";
    CustomBuildSettings = {
        INSTALL_PATH = "$(USER_APPS_DIR)";
        INFOPLIST_FILE = "«PRODUCTNAME»-Info.plist";
        OTHER_LDFLAGS = "-framework Foundation -framework AppKit";
        GCC_PREFIX_HEADER = "$(SYSTEM_LIBRARY_DIR)/Frameworks/AppKit.framework/
Headers/AppKit.h";
        GCC_PRECOMPILE_PREFIX_HEADER = YES;
        PRODUCT_NAME = "«PRODUCTNAME»";
```

```
        PREBINDING = NO;
        GCC_GENERATE_DEBUGGING_SYMBOLS = NO;
        GCC_MODEL_TUNING = G5;
    };
    CustomProductSettings = {
        CFBundleExecutable = "«PRODUCTNAME»";
        CFBundleInfoDictionaryVersion = "6.0";
        CFBundleVersion = "1.0";
        CFBundleIdentifier = "com.yourcompany.«TARGETNAMEASIDENTIFIER»";
        CFBundleDevelopmentRegion = English;
        CFBundlePackageType = "APPL";
        CFBundleSignature = "????";
        NSMainNibFile = "MainMenu";
        NSPrincipalClass = "NSApplication";
    };
    BuildPhases = (
        {
            Class = Resources;
        },
        {
            Class = Sources;
        },
        {
            Class = Frameworks;
        },
    );
}
```

After you make a copy of the template file, edit the Description, CustomBuildSettings, CustomProductSettings, and BuildPhases properties. The CustomBuildSettings can define any build settings you want and can reference template macro values. The PRODUCTNAME and TARGETNAMEASIDENTIFIER template macros are defined while creating a new target and can be used to refer to the new target's name.

The CustomProductSettings are present for targets that produce an Info.plist file and contain a list of customized values that will appear in the Properties pane of the target's Info window.

The BuildPhases property lists the build phases for the new target. The possible BuildPhase types are Aggregate, Application, Bundle, CopyFiles, Frameworks, Headers, JavaArchive, Legacy, Library, Native, Resources, ShellScript, Sources, and Tool. Refer to other templates, or first create a target of the desired type and add your desired phases to it, to ensure that the target can accept a particular build phase type. You should not include a build phase in a target type that does not normally accept that build phase type.

Name your target template file and place it where you want it to reside inside the Target Templates folder. Relaunch Xcode to use the new template.

Custom Scripts

You can use scripts to augment the menu commands available in Xcode. Scripts contain custom code and instructions that are executed when its corresponding menu item is chosen. Each script file is an executable text file with a "she-bang" (#!) line specifying the interpreter to use. You can write your scripts using a shell language, perl, python, awk, or any other interpreter you want.

> Although the script is in the form of an executable file, you cannot substitute a binary executable. The file must be a text file encoded using UTF-8. However, there is nothing stopping a script from launching another binary executable or script. For example, a custom script could start an AppleScript using the `osascript` tool.

Xcode preprocesses script files before they are executed. Scripts contain additional properties and commands that enable them to communicate with the Xcode application — in a fashion. Because of the subtle differences between regular executable scripts and custom Xcode scripts, the following sections use the term "custom script" to indicate an executable script designed to be run by Xcode, and employing special syntax that enables the two to cooperate.

The StartupScript

When Xcode starts, it looks for a custom script named StartupScript. It first looks in your local ~/Library/ Application Support/Apple/Developer Tools folder. If it doesn't find one there, it looks in the system's /Library/Application Support/Apple/Developer Tools folder. Xcode executes the first one it finds and ignores any others. This script is itself a custom script that can employ any of the special custom script extensions explained later.

StartupScript is responsible for performing whatever initial customizations you want, which includes adding your custom menu items to the Xcode menus. In the absence of your own local StartupScript script, Xcode provides a robust and intelligent StartupScript installed in the /Library/Application Support/Apple/Developer Tools folder. Xcode's default startup script looks for a local ~/Library/ Application Support/Apple/Developer Tools/Scripts folder or a global /Library/Application Support/ Apple/Developer Tools/Scripts folder. It takes the first one it finds and uses the files and subfolders in that folder to automatically create a hierarchy of custom menu items. You can see this at work by comparing the structure of the Scripts folder installed with Xcode with the User Scripts menu that appears in the Xcode application, both of which are shown in Figure 19-14.

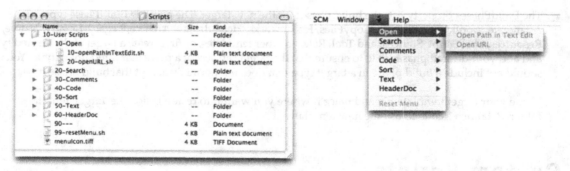

Figure 19-14

All of this automatic menu construction is done by the default StartupScript that was installed with Xcode. If you create your own local StartupScript, none of these menus are created unless your script also creates them. If you want to augment the functionality of the original StartupScript, copy it into your local ~/Library/Application Support/Apple/Developer Tools folder, and then make whatever modifications you want. Note that the supplied StartupScript is written in Perl.

> You cannot write a local StartupScript that "calls" the default one. Xcode prepro-
> cesses custom scripts before they are run, and only the scripts started by Xcode are
> preprocessed. Trying to execute another custom script will, most likely, fail if it uses
> any of the special variables or commands specific to custom scripts.

Unless you have very special needs, it's unlikely that you will outgrow the StartupScript provided by Xcode. Start your customizations by adding custom script items to the Scripts menu. Only if that solution proves to be inadequate should you tackle the job of rewriting or replacing the StartupScript provided by the Xcode tools.

The Default StartupScript

The StartupScript provided by the Xcode tools scans either the ~/Library/Application Support/Apple/Developer Tools/Scripts folder or the global /Library/Application Support/Apple/Developer Tools/Scripts folder for custom menu command scripts. If you have a local Scripts folder, Xcode scans that one and ignores the global one entirely. If you want to modify the custom script menus, copy the entire Scripts folder into your home folder and make your modifications there.

The StartupScript looks for the following four kinds of items in the Scripts folder:

- ❏ Custom script files
- ❏ Submenu folders
- ❏ Menu separator item files
- ❏ Custom menu icon files

Except for custom menu icon files, all files and folders in the Scripts folder must follow a strict naming convention. The file or folder name must begin with a decimal number followed by a hyphen. Any file or folder that does not begin with a number and hyphen is ignored. The order of items in the menu and submenus are determined by the value of the number at beginning of each item's name — smaller numbers appear before larger ones in the menu. Refer back to Figure 19-14 for an example.

A custom script file contains a custom script. By default, the presence of a custom script file inserts a single menu item with the name of the script in the menu. The menu item executes the script when chosen in the Xcode application. Custom script files can, however, contain special tokens that can override the name of the menu item, give the menu item a keyboard shortcut, or even define multiple menu items. A custom script file should have an appropriate extension. If it is a shell script, it should have an extension of .sh, a Perl script should have an extension of .pl, and so on.

A folder that begins with a number and hyphen creates a submenu of custom script items. The name of the submenu is the name of the folder (without the numeric prefix and hyphen). All of the items in the subfolder are recursively scanned to populate the submenu with custom script items or even sub-submenus. The subfolders in the Scripts folder create the top-level menus in Xcode's menu bar. To create additional menus in the menu bar, add custom submenu folders to the Scripts folder. You should not put custom scripts or separator files in the menu bar (Scripts folder).

A menu separator file is a dummy document used to insert a menu separator (grey divider line) into a menu. This is useful to visually group related commands. The file name must consist of a number and three hyphens. The contents of the file are ignored, but should probably be empty to avoid any confusion about its purpose.

A custom menu icon file must be named menuIcon.tiff and is the only item that doesn't follow the menu item naming convention. If a custom menu icon file is found in a submenu folder, the icon is used in place of the submenu's name. The file must contain a TIFF image usable by the Cocoa menu framework. Look in the 10-User Scripts folder previously shown in Figure 19-14. The menuIcon.tiff file in this folder is what gives the User Scripts menu in the menu bar its distinctive script icon. Without it, the menu would have a menu title of User Scripts.

Anatomy of a Custom Script

A custom script is, above all else, an executable script file. The first line of the file must be a "she-bang" line that informs the system the application that will be used to interpret the script. The first line of a bash script would be as follows:

```
#! /bin/bash
```

The file must be encoded using UTF-8 or an encoding that is compatible with UTF-8. UTF-8 is a superset of the plain ASCII encoding, so any interpreter that requires ASCII source will be compatible.

A custom menu script can contain special tokens that enable it to interact, in a fashion, with the Xcode application. These consist of menu script definitions and custom script variables. Custom script tokens are surrounded by the character sequences %%%{ and }%%%. An example is the PBXKeyEquivalent definition. This menu script definition specifies a keyboard shortcut for the custom script's menu item. To set the keyboard shortcut for the script, include the text %%%{PBXKeyEquivalent=@~R}%%% in the script.

Menu script definitions pass values and settings to Xcode. Custom script variables retrieve values from Xcode. The next two sections explain how to use menu script definitions and custom script variables.

Scripts can also call a number of utilities provided by the Xcode tools framework. These are executable programs and scripts that can be called by your custom script. See the "Script Helpers" section for the script utilities you can use.

Menu Script Definitions

Menu script definitions generally have the form %%%{name=value}%%%, where name is the name of the property you want the script to declare and value is the value of that property. Xcode interprets and absorbs these values when the file is preprocessed — prior to being executed. This is how scripts communicate values and options to Xcode. Because this happens during the script's preprocessing phase, you cannot use these declarations programmatically within your script. During preprocessing, the menu script definitions are removed. So it really doesn't matter where these tokens appear in the file; they won't be there when the script begins execution. For safety and readability, place menu script definitions in a comment, like this:

```
# %%%{PBXKeyEquivalent=@~$R}%%%   Set shortcut to Command+Option+Shift+R
```

PBXName

The PBXName=title definition specifies the title of the script's menu item. If this definition is omitted, the name of the item is the file name of the custom script. For example:

```
%%%{PBXName=Run Me}%%%
```

PBXKeyEquivalent

The PBXKeyEquivalent=key-combination definition specifies a keyboard shortcut for the menu item. If this definition omitted, the menu item will have no keyboard shortcut. Make sure you don't use a shortcut that is already assigned to another menu item. Use the Key Bindings tab in the Xcode preferences to experiment with key combinations and check for collisions.

The key-combination is a single letter or number plus any combination of the modifiers found in the following table.

Character	Menu Shortcut Modifier
@	Command
~	Option
^	Control
$	Shift

For example, to set the keyboard shortcut for a script's menu item to Command+Option+Shift+R, use the definition %%%{PBXKeyEquivalent=@~$R}%%%.

PBXInput

Custom scripts can obtain the contents of the current text selection of the active editor pane, or its entire contents. To do either, the script must declare a PBXInput=source definition to declare which it wants. If the declaration is missing, it is assumed to be None. The text chosen will be available on the script's stdin file when executed. To process the text, the script should read from stdin. The value of source must be one of those listed in the following table.

Source	Description
None	No input is desired. There will be no data in stdin. This is the default.
Selection	The current text selection in the active editor pane will be readable on stdin.
AllText	The entire contents of the active editor pane will be readable on stdin.

An alternative way of accessing the contents of the active file or text selection is to use the PBXSelectedText or PBXAllText script variables. See the Custom Script Variables section for the definition of these variables.

PBXOutput

Custom scripts can elect to output text, appending to or replacing text in the active editor pane. How text output by your script is treated is controlled by the PBXOutput=destination definition. If this definition is omitted, the output of your script is ignored. The value of destination must be one of the following.

Output	Description
Discard	The output of the script is discarded. This is the default.
ReplaceSelection	The output of the script replaces the current selection in the editor pane.
InsertAfterSelection	The output of the script is inserted into the active file immediately following the current selection or insertion point.
ReplaceAllText	The output of the script replaces the contents of the entire editor pane.
AppendToAllText	Appends the output of the script to the end of the editor pane.
SeparateWindow	Opens a new editor window and writes the output of the text to it. The original source file is not affected.
Pasteboard	Transfers the output of the script to the clipboard. The original source file is not affected.

PBXIncrementalDisplay

When a script outputs text (see PBXOutput), the text is normally buffered and inserted all at once into the editor pane or window receiving the new text. If your script performs a particularly lengthy procedure, you may want to the text to appear incrementally as the script works. To enable this feature, include the PBXIncrementalDisplay=Yes definition in your script. Setting the definition to No, or omitting it, results in the normal behavior.

PBXArgument

Fixed arguments can be passed to your script by adding any number of PBXArgument=argument definitions to your script. Each argument declared is added to the standard command-line argument list of the script when is it executed. This is particularly useful when combined with the PBXNewScript definition.

PBXNewScript

This definition declares the start of a new menu item. Use this definition to define multiple menu items in the same custom script file. Any menu script definitions that follow this one will apply to the new menu item. All menu items defined by this script share the same script. That is, all of the items in the menu will run the same script, but the menu script definitions for each menu item will be different.

This is particularly powerful when combined with the PBXArgument, PBXInput, and PBXOutput definitions.

Define Four Commands with a Single Script

Create a custom script that will add four new commands to the Xcode interface. Each command inserts the
date, time, and currently logged-in user ID into the active editor pane. There are two variations, resulting in
four possible commands. The date inserted can be in the local time zone or in universal (GMT) time. The
text can be inserted before or after the current selection.

Follow these steps:

1.   Create a new text file named **90-insertTimestamps.sh** and place it in the 30-Comments folder of
Xcode's default Scripts menu. The contents of the script are in Listing 19-3.

Listing 19-3: Custom Script with Four Commands

```
90-InsertTimestamps.sh
#! /bin/bash
#
# Insert a date/time stamp and a user name comment,
# either before or after the current selection,
# in either local or universal time.
#
# (first menu item)
# Append Timestamp
# %%%{PBXName=Append Timestamp}%%%
# %%%{PBXInput=None}%%%
# %%%{PBXOutput=InsertAfterSelection}%%%
#
# (second menu item)
# %%%{PBXNewScript}%%%
# Append GMT Timestamp
# %%%{PBXName=Append GMT Timestamp}%%%
# %%%{PBXInput=None}%%%
# %%%{PBXOutput=InsertAfterSelection}%%%
# %%%{PBXArgument=-u}%%%
#
# (third menu item)
# %%%{PBXNewScript}%%%
# Insert Timestamp
# %%%{PBXName=Insert Timestamp}%%%
# %%%{PBXInput=Selection}%%%
# %%%{PBXOutput=ReplaceSelection}%%%
#
# (forth menu item)
# %%%{PBXNewScript}%%%
# Insert GMT Timestamp
# %%%{PBXName=Insert GMT Timestamp}%%%
# %%%{PBXInput=Selection}%%%
# %%%{PBXOutput=ReplaceSelection}%%%
# %%%{PBXArgument=-u}%%%

# output the current date, time, and user
echo -n " $(date $1) ($USER) "

# include the contents, if any, of the selected text
cat -
```

2. Quit Xcode and relaunch it.

3. Open a text file, select some text, and try out your new commands.

How It Works

Adding an appropriately named script file to the Scripts folder caused StartupScript to add your script to the Xcode user scripts menu.

The script declares four different commands: one that is implied, and three more using PBXNewScript declarations. The menu script definitions are associated with either the implied menu item, or the most recent PBXNewScript definition found in the file. All four menu items will execute the same script, but each gets declared with a different set of definitions. These differing definitions cause the script to be called with different arguments and different settings for PBXInput and PBXOutput.

The insertion of a local versus GMT time is controlled by passing, or omitting, a -u argument to the script. This argument is passed on to the date command. When this argument is present, it causes date to output a universal date and time rather than a local one.

The PBXInput and PBXOutput definitions are used to control whether the output of this script is inserted before or after the current text selection. The script outputs its date stamp and user ID, and then appends whatever text it finds on stdin using the cat - command. When the script is run with PBXInput=None and PBXOutput=InsertAfterSelection, there is no text in stdin so the cat command does nothing. The output selection causes the results of the script, in this case just the timestamp, to be inserted after the selected text. When run with PBXInput=Selection and PBXOutput=ReplaceSelection, stdin contains the contents of the current selection and the output of the script replaces the entire selection. But because the output now includes the original selection (from stdin), the effect is the insertion of the timestamp before the selected text.

Custom Script Variables

Custom script variables use the same syntax as menu script definitions, but instead of being removed from the script during preprocessing, they are replaced by the value of the variable. Again, this substitution happens prior to the beginning of script execution, so treat these variables as constants in your script. Here's an example that uses the PBXSelectionLength variable that contains the number of characters in the user's current text selection when the script is executed:

```
if [ %%%{PBXSelectionLength}%%% == 0 ]; then echo "No Selection"; exit; fi
```

If the value of PBXSelectionLength is 8, the actual line of text in the script that is executed by the interpreter is as follows:

```
if [ 8 == 0 ]; then echo "No Selection"; exit; fi
```

PBXSelectedText and PBXAllText

The PBXSelectedText and PBXAllText variables expand to the contents of the current text selection or the contents of the entire editor pane. You can use these variables instead of, or in addition to, the PBXInput definition.

These can be rather dangerous to use in a script. They are replaced, verbatim, with the contents of the selection or file. There is no protection from special characters that might be inappropriate at this location in your script. Use of these may even result in portions of the selected text or file from being executed as part of the script. For example, the following shell statement appears harmless, but it will cause the script to fail with a syntax error if the currently selected text contains a double quote character:

```
SELECTION="%%%{PBXSelectedText}%%%"
```

One way to avoid this kind of problem in the shell is to use a "here document" like this:

```
cat << END_OF_SELECTION
%%%{PBXSelectedText}%%%
END_OF_SELECTION
```

PBXTextLength, PBXSelectionStart, PBXSelectionEnd, and PBXSelectionLength

These four variables, described in the following table, report the number of characters in the file or current text selection and the index into the current document where the text selection begins and ends.

Variable	Description
PBXTextLength	The number of characters in the active editor pane.
PBXSelectionLength	The number of characters in the current text selection. This will be 0 if the text selection is an insertion point.
PBXSelectionStart	The position within the editor pane where the current text selection or insertion point begins.
PBXSelectionEnd	The position within the editor pane where the current text selection ends.

PBXSelection

The PBXSelection variable is replaced by a special marker. This marker — some obscure sequence of characters — is used in conjunction with the PBXOutput definition to control what portion of the output will be selected, or where the insertion cursor will be, in the new text. Including one PBXSelection marker in your script's output causes the insertion point to be placed at that position. Including two PBXSelection markers causes everything between the two to be selected. Listing 19-4 shows a custom script that inserts a HeaderDoc comment.

Listing 19-4: Controlling Text Selection

```
92-insertHeaderDoc.sh
#! /bin/bash
# %%%{PBXName=Insert HeaderDoc}%%%
# %%%{PBXInput=None}%%%
# %%%{PBXOutput=InsertAfterSelection}%%%

cat << END_OF_HEADERDOC
```

(continued)

Listing 19-4: *(continued)*

```
/*!
    @class      %%%{PBXSelection}%%%Class%%%{PBXSelection}%%%
    @abstract
    @discussion
    */
END_OF_HEADERDOC
```

The two selection markers in the text sent to stdout are caught by Xcode and used to establish a new text selection (see Figure 19-15).

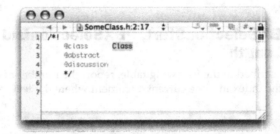

Figure 19-15

Script Helpers

Xcode, or more precisely the Xcode developer tools framework, provide a number of utility programs that can be called by a custom script to programmatically interact with Xcode and the user.

These tools are in a framework bundle added by the Xcode Developer Tools installer. To execute the tools, you must use the path supplied in the PBXUtilityScriptsPath custom script variable. The following script demonstrates using the PBXUtilityScriptsPath variable to execute the AskUserForExistingFileDialog tool:

```
TOOLSPATH='%%%{PBXUtilityScriptsPath}%%%'
"${TOOLSPATH}"/AskUserForExistingFileDialog "Choose a text file"
```

Prompt for a String

The AskUserForStringDialog tool prompts the user for some text, which they can enter interactively via a dialog box. The single, optional, argument specifies the default text value that will appear in the dialog box when it is opened. The text entered by the user is returned via stdout. The following example bash script prompts for a user name, supplying the current account's short name as a default, and captures the results in the variable NEWNAME:

```
NEWNAME="$('%%%{PBXUtilityScriptsPath}%%%/AskUserForStringDialog' ${USER})"
```

Ask for an Existing File or Folder

AskUserForExistingFileDialog and AskUserForExistingFolderDialog prompt the user to select an existing file or folder, respectively. Each takes a single, optional, prompt argument that will be visible in the dialog box. The path to the selected file or folder is returned via stdout. If the user clicks the Cancel button in the dialog box, the return value is empty. You have no control over the type of file the user can select. The dialog box displays, and allows the user to choose, invisible files and folders.

Prompt for a New File

The AskUserForNewFileDialog tool prompts the user to choose a file name and location for a new file. The path to the new file is returned via stdout. The tool takes two, optional, arguments. The first is a prompt string that will be visible in the dialog box. The second is a default file name for the new file. To specify a default file name but no prompt, pass an empty prompt like this:

```
'%%%{PBXUtilityScriptsPath}%%%/AskUserForNewFileDialog' "" New.txt
```

Ask for an Application

AskUserForApplicationDialog presents the user with an application picker dialog box. This dialog box, shown in Figure 19-16, enables the user to choose an application known to launch services, or browse the file system in search of an unknown one. The tool returns the full path to the application's program file or bundle folder, as appropriate.

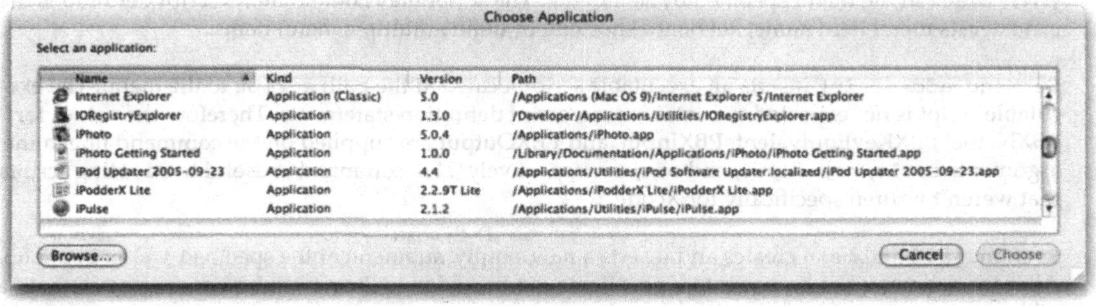

Figure 19-16

The command takes two, optional, arguments. The first is the title used for the dialog box, normally "Choose Application." The second argument is a prompt string, normally "Select an application."

Altering the Xcode Menus

The last, and most complex, script helper is the SetMenu tool. This tool allows custom scripts to add or remove menu items from the Xcode menu. The StartupScript script supplied with Xcode uses this tool extensively to build the hierarchy of custom script menu items. There are six different ways of calling the SetMenu tool:

❑   SetMenu add scriptfile script index [menupath ...]

❑   SetMenu add script script title key input output [menupath ...]

❏   `SetMenu add submenu title index [ menupath ... ]`

❏   `SetMenu add separator index [ menupath ... ]`

❏   `SetMenu remove item index [ menupath ... ]`

❏   `SetMenu remove all [ menpath ... ]`

All of the commands use a similar syntax. The `menupath` arguments are a variable number of arguments that specify the location in the Xcode menu tree where the `SetMenu` tool will perform the requested action. If omitted entirely, the action will occur in the menu bar. To specify a specific menu in the menu bar, pass one parameter with the name of that menu. To specify a submenu, pass two parameters: the name of the top-level menu and the name of the submenu. Extend this as required to address submenus of submenus.

An `index` parameter specifies a position within a menu (the one specified by the `menupath` arguments). A non-negative number addresses the nth item in the menu, counting from the top item, and starting from 0. Thus, 0 specifies the top-most item in the menu, 1 the second, and so on. Negative numbers count backwards from the bottom-most item, starting at –1. –1 specifies the last item in a menu, –2 the second to the last item, and so on. When you're inserting new items, the item is inserted above the indexed item when you're using non-negative indexes and below the item when you're using negative indexes. An index of 0 inserts before the first item, an index of –1 at the end.

`SetMenu add scriptfile` inserts a custom script file located at the path `script` to the menu at the given `index` in the menu specified by `menupath`. The script may contain menu script definitions that can alter its menu item name, keyboard shortcut, or define multiple menu items.

`SetMenu add script` inserts an executable script located at the path `script` to the menu. The executable script is not expected to contain menu script definition statements. Therefore the values for PBXName, PBXKeyEquivalent, PBXInput, and PBXOutput are supplied on the command line in the arguments `title`, `key`, `input`, and `output` respectively. This command is useful to adopting scripts that weren't written specifically for Xcode.

`SetMenu add submenu` creates and inserts a new, empty, submenu at the specified `index` in `menupath`. After the submenu has been created, new items can be added to the new submenu using `SetMenu add` with a `menupath` that includes the new submenu's `title`.

`SetMenu add separator` adds a separator item to the menu.

`SetMenu remove item` removes a single custom menu item.

`SetMenu remove all` deletes all menu items and submenus contained by the given menu path.

AppleScript

In addition to the many ways in which Xcode can run automated scripts, the Xcode application itself can be driven programmatically using AppleScript. Open the AppleScript dictionary for Xcode, shown in Figure 19-17, and you will find a rich and complex set of objects and command to work with.

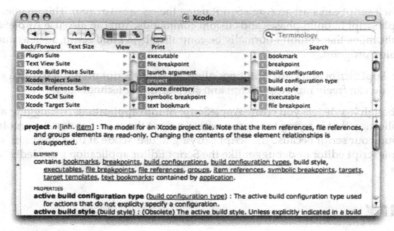

Figure 19-17

Closely related to AppleScript are Automator actions. Xcode includes several Automator actions, shown in Figure 19-18, that allow Xcode processes to be integrated into Automator workflows.

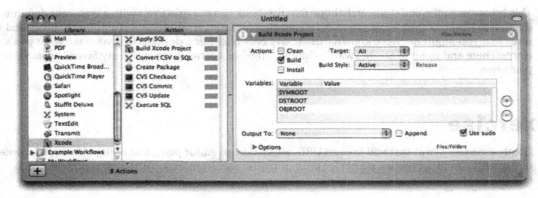

Figure 19-18

Although you can build a project using the `xcodebuild` tool, that's about all you can do with it. AppleScript provides the ability to automate Xcode by accessing the data and structures within projects and the Xcode application itself. For example, your company may have a set of target settings that need to be uniform across multiple projects. You can quickly write an AppleScript program to quickly check, and possibly correct, those properties in dozens of projects containing potentially hundreds of individual settings. Or maybe you just like your windows stacked up in certain way. The possibilities are almost endless.

AppleScript programming is beyond the scope of this book, but here are a few tips for using AppleScript with Xcode:

- ❏ A shell script can start an AppleScript using the `osascript` tool. This enables you to utilize AppleScript in build phases and custom commands. You can also use AppleScript to integrate applications that couldn't normally be controlled by a build script, such as audio or image conversion program.

- ❏ The AppleScript Standard Additions allow an AppleScript program to run a shell script, meaning you can freely mix AppleScript and shell scripting technologies.

- ❏ Although Xcode lets you create AppleScript Studio applications, debugging an AppleScript application that is trying to interact with Xcode at the same time can be problematic. If you can't debug your script because the script is trying to use Xcode at the same time, switch to another AppleScript editor or debugger like the Script Editor application included with Mac OS X.

Summary

In earlier chapters, you learned to customize your project and how it is built. In this chapter, you learned to customize your Xcode environment beyond the many options already exposed in the Xcode Preferences window. You can set invisible features, add your own processing scripts to any editor pane, and develop your own file, project, and target templates to make repetitive tasks in Xcode easier and more productive.

This brings us to the end. I sincerely hope that this book has provided you with a well-rounded introduction to Xcode, a clear explanation of its core concepts, and an appreciation of those facilities and features that you might not have known existed. My only remaining desire is that you take what you've learned here and use it to create award-winning, bug-free, software for one of my favorite computer platforms.

Exercise

Create a custom script that will take an URL, selected in an editor pane, and replace it with the contents of that URL. You'll get bonus points for prompting the user to enter the URL if the text selection is empty.

Exercise Answers

Chapter 3

Exercise Solution

Your customized project should look something like the one in Figure A-1.

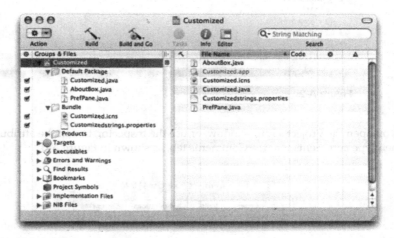

Figure A-1

In step 2, you can create a new Source group, name it **Default Package**, and then move the three source files into it by dragging. Or you can select the three files and use the File⇨Group command to do both in one step.

In steps 4, 7, and 8 you can use either the menu commands in the File and View menus, or you can use the contextual menu accessed by Control-/right-clicking the group or column title.

In step 5, you have to use the contextual menu to hide the group. The Preferences menu that selects which groups are visible is not available from any of the main menus (unless you also remembered that Deleting a Smart group is equivalent to hiding it).

Chapter 4

Exercise Solution

In step 1, you use the new project assistant to create a project based on the Java Tool template, found in the Java group. It should look something like the project in Figure A-2.

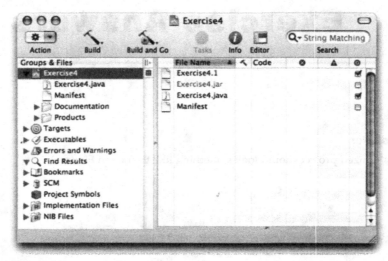

Figure A-2

In step 2, you open the Project's Info window, or use the Inspector, to edit the attributes of the project. You can then type comments into the Comments tab, as shown in Figure A-3.

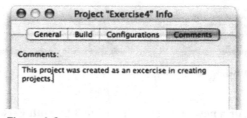

Figure A-3

The project created by the template is complete and ready to run. Selecting the Build⇨Build and Run command produces the following output:

```
Hello World!

java has exited with status 0.
```

Chapter 5

Exercise Solution

There are a variety of ways you can accomplish this exercise. In the end, you should have a project that looks like the one in Figure A-4.

Figure A-4

In step 1, you can create a new project outside the existing MakeMe folder. Or you can be clever and edit the path of the new project so that the project document is created in the existing MakeMe folder.

To create the Source folder in step 2, you can create a Source folder in the Finder and a Source group in the project, and then use an Info window to set the folder of the group. To save a little work, you can create the Source group first and then use the New Folder button in the Info window to create and set the folder in one step.

You can add the existing source files to the project by dragging them into the Source group or using the Add to Project command. If the source files are still in a separate folder, you can use the Copy option to copy them to the Source folder at the same time.

If you are thinking ahead, you can accomplish all of the tasks in step 2 by starting in the Finder: Creating the Source folder first, moving or copying the source files into the new folder, and then dragging the folder into the project window, thus creating the Source group and all of the source items at once.

Step 3 is the most obvious. Select the Source group, choose File⇔New File, pick one of the C++ file templates, and name the files **Application**.

Appendix A

Chapter 7

Exercise Solution

The essence of this problem is that maxPrime is both a parameter of the init method and an instance variable of the SieveOfEratosthenes class. You want to change the occurrences of the parameter without altering the occurrences of the instance variable. There are two obvious ways of accomplishing this quickly. The first is to use the single file find window and search for maxPrime (Textual, Whole Word) and replace it with largestPrime. If the search finds an occurrence of the parameter value, use the Replace & Find button to replace it and find the next occurrence. If the search finds an occurrence of the instance variable, use Next to leave it alone. Repeat this procedure on each source file that contains a reference to the parameter value.

The more direct solution is to use the project find window. Again using a search term of maxPrime and a replacement text of largestPrime, perform a whole word search on all files in the project. Then simply select the matches that correspond to the parameter value in the results list and click the Replace button (see Figure A-5).

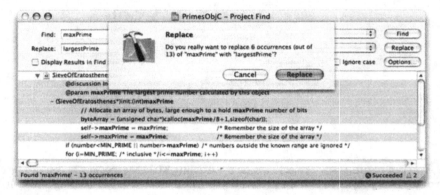

Figure A-5

Make special note of the assignment line that is listed twice. The first line found the instance variable, and the second line found the parameter value. By selecting only the second line, you replace one occurrence of the pattern on that line, leaving the other one unchanged.

Rewriting the comments is a little trickier. Probably the most robust method is to use the regular expression /*(.*)\s**/[\t]*$ and replace it with //\1. Let's break this down one expression at a time:

❑ /* finds the opening /* delimiter of a C style comment. Note that the asterisk is escaped so that it isn't interpreted as an operator.

❑ (.*) matches the contents of the comment (which can be anything), and captures it in a replacement variable.

❑ \s*/* finds the closing delimiter, and also matches any white space that might be between the end of the comment and the */. This is really being extra neat, as this omits any trailing white space from the parenthesized pattern that captured the comment itself. You don't need the \s* expression, but your C++ comments will have trailing white space without it.

❑   `[\t ]*$` is the expression where you get extra credit, and demonstrates some of the potential pitfalls when you're constructing regular expressions. `[\t ]*` matches any number of space or tab characters that might follow the comment and `$` requires that the pattern matches only at the end of a line. Omitting either of these will cause problems. The `$` is critical; otherwise, the pattern could match comments in the middle of a line, effectively commenting out anything following the comment. This would, for example, break the code in the two nested for loops. `[\t ]*` catches C style comments that have trailing tab or space characters. Avoid using the simpler `\s*` expression, because `\s` also matches the end-of-line character (which is also considered to be white space). Replacing the end-of-line character joins the line with the next one, commenting out the next line as well. The two expressions, taken together, catch all C style comments at the end of a line, with no significant code between the end of the comment and the end of the line.

❑   `//\1` replaces the entire C style comment with a C++ style comment that contains the text matched by the `(.*)` expression. Any trailing white space, either in or after the C comment delimiter, is neatly stripped off.

Chapter 10

Exercise Solution

In step 1, select the new `NSTableView` objects and use Layout⇨Make Subview of⇨Split View to nest the two tables inside a split view. To make the layout function nicely, set the internal "springs" in the Size panel of the `NSSplitView` object so the entire subview resizes when the window does.

In step 2, add the check box button simply by dragging from the objects palette into the window. You can double-click the text or use the Inspector palette to change its title.

In steps 3 and 4, you can follow the manual procedure for defining the two classes, their outlets, and actions. But you get bonus points if you use the Classes⇨Read Files command. The declarations of these classes include the `IBOutlet` and `IBAction` keywords, so Interface Builder can construct their class definitions automatically.

The remaining steps consist of making the necessary connections between the objects for the application to work:

❑   Control-drag from the ListController to each of the two NSTableView objects, setting the dateOrderList and alphabeticList outlets.

❑   Control-drag from each NSTableView to a separate ListDataModel object, setting the dataSource outlet.

❑   Control-drag from each ListDataModel to ListController, setting both to the single instance of the ListController object.

❑   Control-drag from the NSButton to ListController and choose to send the showHideSoloFlights action.

The outlets in the `ListController` object enable it to access the two `NSTableView` objects, so it can cause them to redraw when the state of the "Solo-Flights Only" check box is altered. Each `NSTableView` is connected to its dataSource object, which is what provides the data to display. Your data source objects need a reference back to the single `ListController` object. The `ListController` has the actual data and knows how it should be filtered. Finally, the `NSButton` must know to fire the showHideSoloFlights message whenever it is changed.

Running the final application should produce the results shown in Figure A-6. On the left is the working application. On the right is the Instances pane showing the connections between the `ListController` object and the two `NSTableView` objects.

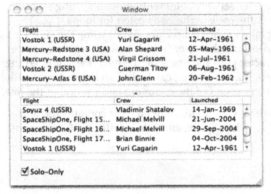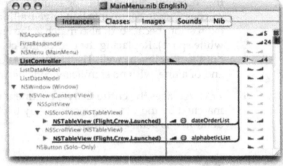

Figure A-6

Chapter 13

Exercise Solution

The first step to completing this project is to create the target to build the `primetest` command-line tool. You should have created a new target named **primetest** based on the BSD Shell Tool target template. You can name the target something else, but then you have to edit the product name so that it is **primetest**.

After the target is created, the primetest.c file needs to be added to the Compile Sources phase of the primetest target. The two simplest ways of accomplishing this are to either open the Info window for the primetest.c file and check the primetest target in the Targets tab, or drag the primetest.c file in the Groups & Files list directly into the Compile Sources phase of the target.

The finished product of the primetest target needs to be included in the Resources folder of the Primer application bundle. You accomplish this by adding the primetest product reference, found in the Products source folder, into the Copy Bundle Resources phase of the Primer target. Just like primetest.c, you can either use the Targets tab of the Info window to add the primetest product to the Primer group, or simply drag the product into the Copy Bundle Resources phase. The Info window works because the Copy Bundle Resources phase is the first phase that accepts arbitrary files. If other phases accepted the file type being added, then you would have to use the drag-and-drop method to specify the phase you wanted the file added to.

Before the Primer target can be built, you must ensure that the primetest target is built. Otherwise, the Copy Bundle Resources phase has no primetest binary file to copy into the application's bundle. You can open the Info window for the Primer target and add the primetest target to its dependencies in the General tab. Alternatively, you can simply drag the primetest target into the Primer target.

When all of this is done, the project should look something like the one in Figure A-7.

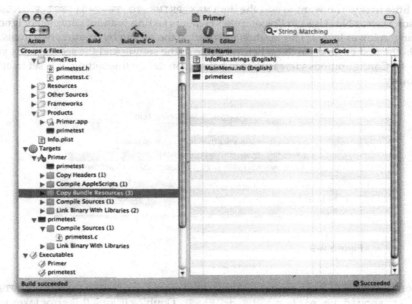

Figure A-7

Building and the running the application should produce the results shown in Figure A-8.

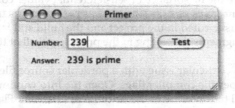

Figure A-8

Chapter 14

Exercise Solution

In step 1, go to the Configurations pane of the project's Info window and create a new build configuration by copying the Debug configuration.

To change the optimization setting in step 2, open the BuildPrimes Info window, select the Build tab, and choose the Performance configuration. Change the Optimization Level by clicking its value. While there, click the + button and define the TEST_PRIMES setting. Switch to the Debug configuration and repeat, using a different value. If you are clever, you can copy the setting after it is defined in the Performance configuration, switch to Debug, paste it in, and then edit just its value.

Step 4 is a little tricky. You want to add the item MAX_PRIME_TO_TEST=$(TEST_PRIMES) to the Preprocessor Macros Not Used in Precompiled Headers setting without completely ignoring the value of this setting in lower layers. The solution is to define the setting by creating two items, as shown in Figure A-9. The first expands to the inherited value of the setting and the second adds your customization. If the All Configurations view is chosen before you define this setting, it is set in all configurations simultaneously.

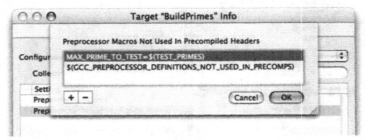

Figure A-9

The build of the project fails. The compiler throws the error #error The symbol BRUTE_TEST is not defined; It should be either TRUE or FALSE. Double-clicking this error takes you to the #error directive in the source code where you see that the programmer has decided that this preprocessor symbol is not optional. The solution, in step 6, is to define the BRUTE_TEST preprocessor symbol for all compilations. You do this in the project layer by editing the Preprocessor Macros Not Used in Precompiled Headers setting to include the statement BRUTE_TEST=TRUE or BRUTE_TEST=NO as appropriate for each configuration. This is where the importance of self-referential values comes into play. If you had just defined our preprocessor macro as MAX_PRIME_TO_TEST=$(TEST_PRIMES) in step 4, then that setting overrides the setting you just created in the project and the build still fails. By adding the self-reference, the setting in the targets augments the setting in the project, and all of the macros get defined correctly.

In step 8, you want to fix a particular issue with a particular source file. One solution (besides recoding the function) is to use the per-file compiler flags. Open the Info window for the SieveOfEratosthenes.m source file and in the Build tab enter **-w** in the Additional Compiler Flags field. This switch disables all compiler warnings. This is probably overkill, but it's just a demonstration. Rebuild the project, and the warnings for this file (but not any other files) are suppressed.

Finally, the build succeeds. You now want to build the release version. Switch the active build configuration to rebuild and build again. The compilation produces an error. The problem is that you've defined a pre-processor macro that itself depends on the TEST_PRIMES build setting. But you never defined a value for TEST_PRIMES in the Release configuration, so the value is empty and the code is incomplete.

You could define a value for TEST_PRIMES, but this setting was really created for use in the Debug and Performance configurations and shouldn't exist in the Release configuration. The correct solution is to *not* define the MAX_PRIMES_TO_TEST macro in the Release configuration. Go back to the target build configuration and delete the Preprocessor Macros setting for this target. The value reverts to the value set in the project settings.

You still get a warning when you build again. This time, you discover that the programmer wants to warn you if the MAX_PRIME_TO_TEST macro is undefined. If you had disabled all warnings in your project in step 8, you would have missed this one. In this case, you simply disagree with the programmer, and comment out the line. Building again produces a finished, optimized, error, and warning-free build.

Chapter 16

Exercise Solution

There is no "right" answer to this exercise. It should be a personal challenge to optimize the performance of this application until it is acceptable to you.

The project source already contains a number of attempts at improving the program's performance. You can choose to compile different blocks of code by editing the #if 0 statements. Choose an alternative block of code, build, and profile the application again. You should have at least tried the following:

❑   Profile the program without making any changes and save the results as your baseline.

❑   Try the alternative blocks of code already in the source and profiled their performance.

❑   Try comparing the results of one profile with another.

❑   Experiment with changing the values of the map size and test value.

❑   Make your own attempt at improving the program's performance.

Chapter 17

Exercise Solution

There are many ways of approaching this problem. Here is the one possibility:

1.   Create a RollingChecksumTests unit test target.

2.   Create a RollingChecksumTest.m source file using the Objective-C Test Case Class template.

3.   Add the following test to the unit test class:

```
//
//  RollingChecksumTests.m
//  Roller
//
//  Created by James Bucanek on 11/9/05.
//  Copyright 2005 James Bucanek. All rights reserved.
//

#import "RollingChecksumTests.h"

#import "RollingByteArrayChecksum.h"

@implementation RollingChecksumTests

- (void)setUp
```

```
    {
        // Allocate a block of memory and fill it with random integers
        randomDataBlock = malloc(BENCHMARK_TEST_SIZE);
        randomDataLength = BENCHMARK_TEST_SIZE;

        // Fill the block with random data
        srandom(time(NULL));
        if (randomDataBlock!=NULL)
            {
            long* r = (long*)randomDataBlock;
            int ints = randomDataLength/sizeof(long);
            while (ints--)
                *r++ = random();
            }
    }

- (void)tearDown
    {
        free(randomDataBlock);
        randomDataBlock = NULL;
        randomDataLength = 0;
    }

- (void)testRollingChecksum
    {
        // Verify that the rolling checksum method correctly calculates the checksum
        // at every offset within the data buffer. Verify this by spot checking the
        // checksum generated by the rolling checksum method with the
        // checksum produced by recalculating the checksum at that offset.

        // It's too time consuming to check every single offset, so check the offsets
        // in a Fibonacci series.
        int fib0 = 0;
        int fib1 = 1;
        int offset;
        int endOffset = randomDataLength-BENCHMARK_BLOCK_SIZE;

        // Create a rolling byte array checksum object and calculate
        // This calculates checksum for the initial offset
        RollingByteArrayChecksum* checksum = [[RollingByteArrayChecksum alloc]
initWithBytes:randomDataBlock length:BENCHMARK_BLOCK_SIZE];
        // Create a 2nd checksum object to recalculate checksums for comparison.
        RollingChecksum* checksumChecker = [[RollingChecksum alloc] init];

        for (offset=0; offset<endOffset; offset++)
            {
            if (offset==(fib0+fib1))
                {
                // We hit a checkpoint offset.
                // Recalculate the checksum at this offset from scratch and compare
                // that with the checksum reported by the rolling checksum object.
                RollingChecksum64 rollingChecksum = [checksum checksum];
                RollingChecksum64 check = [checksumChecker
calculate:randomDataBlock+offset length:BENCHMARK_BLOCK_SIZE];
```

```
            STAssertEquals(check,rollingChecksum,
                        @"Checksum calculated at offset %d does not match the
checksum produced by the rolling checksum",
                        offset);
        // Advance to the next Fibonacci number
        int fib2 = fib0+fib1;
        fib0 = fib1;
        fib1 = fib2;
        }
    // Roll to the next checksum
    [checksum roll];
    }

    [checksumChecker release];
    [checksum release];
}

@end
```

4. Build a `RollingChecksumTests` target to verify the functionality of the RollingChecksum and RollingByteArrayChecksum classes.

Chapter 19

Exercise Solution

Listing A-1 shows a custom script that will take the current selection in an editor pane, treat is as an URL, and replace it with the contents of that URL. The URL is fetched using the curl tool.

Listing A-1: 10-insertURL.sh

```
#! /bin/bash
# %%%{PBXName=Insert Contents of Selected URL}%%%
# %%%{PBXInput=Selection}%%%
# %%%{PBXOutput=ReplaceSelection}%%%

# copy the selection to a temporary file
# we do this because we might need it twice
URLFILE=`mktemp /tmp/insertURL.XXXXXX`
cat - > ${URLFILE}

if [ %%%{PBXSelectionLength}%%% == 0 ]
then
    URL="$('%%%{PBXUtilityScriptsPath}%%%/AskUserForStringDialog' 'http://')"
else
    # try to do some modest sanity checking by filtering the selection
    # through grep, extracting only the URL from the text selection
    URL="$(egrep --only-matching '[-+a-zA-Z]+://[^"]+' ${URLFILE})"
fi

# run the curl tool,
```

(continued)

Listing A-1: *(continued)*

```
if curl --silent "${URL}"
then
    # curl was successful; the output has already replaced the selection
    echo -n
else
    # curl failed.
    # log the error to the system console for debugging
    logger "$0: curl returned status of $?"
    # Replace the selection with the original value
    cat ${URLFILE}
fi

# cleanup
rm ${URLFILE}
```

The file is saved in the /Library/Application Support/Apple/Developer Tools/Scripts/10-User Scripts/80-URLs folder. This creates a new URLs submenu in the User Scripts menu, containing the single new custom script command.

Quit Xcode, relaunch it, open a text editor pane, select a URL, and choose the new User Scripts⇨URLs⇨ Insert Contents of Selected URL command. If successful, the URL is replaced by its contents. If not, the system.log file records the error returned by the curl tool.

Project Templates

Xcode includes numerous project templates. Choosing the right template when you're creating a new project can go a long way in getting your project going in the right direction.

Both the new project assistant and the Xcode documentation include short descriptions of each template — too short, in my opinion. For example, the CoreFoundation Tool template is described as "A tool that links against the Core Foundation library." That's all well and good if you know what the Core Foundation library is or how it differs from the Core Services library and the Foundation framework. While the descriptions of the templates in this appendix are brief, you should find them substantially more enlightening than the descriptions found in the new project assistant.

If you have jumped here from Chapter 4, some of the terminology and concepts described here, like External Targets and NIB files, might not make sense yet. Don't worry. You can fix your project later if you make a less-than-optimal choice to begin with. And don't be afraid to just start a new project and import the work you've already done from a previous project. This can often be much more expedient than trying to fix a project that needs significant reorganization.

The templates here are those found in Xcode version 2.2. However, the Xcode team at Apple never rests. Don't be surprised to find new or improved templates in the version of Xcode that you are using.

Empty Projects

Listed in the following table are the top-level project templates, and are as close to an empty project as you can get. If what you want to build isn't even close to any of the more specific categories listed later, choose one of these and customize it to your needs.

Template	Description
Empty Project	This means just what it says. The project created will have no source files, groups, or targets. It defines Debug and Release build configurations, with only one setting defined (strip symbols in Release build).
External Build System	Use this template if you want to build your project using the standard Unix make tool. Normally, Xcode uses its own make tool for building targets, but any project can include an External Target that uses /bin/make instead. This template defines no source files and a single External Target. This is a good choice for wrapping the Xcode IDE around an existing project that is already being built and maintained using make.

Action

These are the project templates to use if you want to develop an Automator Action. Actions are steps that can be added to an Automator workflow. You can learn more about programming Automator Actions at http://developer.apple.com/documentation/AppleApplications/Conceptual/AutomatorCon cepts/.

Template	Description
AppleScript Automator Action	This template creates the basic framework for an Automator action implemented using AppleScript. An on run handler is defined in main.applescript, which does nothing but return the input of the action, along with a NIB file containing the empty view of the action's user interface. An Info.plist file defines all the attributes needed to identify the finished package as an Automator action, along with an InfoPlist.strings file containing placeholders for the Automator messages that your action should define. The project also includes an external reference to the system's AppleScriptKit scripting definition guide (sdef file), but this file is not included in the final product.
Cocoa Automator Action	This template creates the same NIB and Info.plist files as the AppleScript template. But instead of a functionless AppleScript handler, it predictably creates an Objective-C class file, header, and precompiled header. The target is linked to the Cocoa and Automator frameworks. References to the Foundation and AppKit frameworks are also defined, but not included in the target.
Shell Script Automator Action	Almost identical to the Cocoa Action template, the Shell Script template creates a single main.command shell script file instead of the Objective-C source files. Inexplicable, it also includes the Cocoa and Automator frameworks.

Application

Modern graphical applications are the most complex, technologically intensive, constructions that the majority of software developers will ever work on. Ironically, they are also the project that most developers want to start with. The engineers at Apple want to make it easy to create fully functional applications, so a lot of work has gone into the templates listed in the following table. Each one immediately produces a full-fledged, launchable application complete with standard menus, document and window management, clipboard handling, Special Characters palette, connections to Services, and even a working About This Program window. About the only thing it doesn't include is, of course, the code and resources to make your application do what you want it to do.

Template	Description
AppleScript Application	This template creates a Cocoa-based application that uses the AppleScript programming language, commonly referred to as an AppleScript Studio application. The project includes a tiny Cocoa wrapper in main.m that initializes the Cocoa and AppleScript frameworks, which in turn start the application contained in the .applescript file. You can also extend an AppleScript Studio application with C and Objective-C code. The MainMenu.nib file doesn't define an action for the About This Application item, and the template does not include a Credits.rtf file. So if you want an About window, you'll have to create it yourself. Read more about AppleScript applications at `http://www.apple.com/applescript/studio/`.
AppleScript Document-based Application	This template is like the AppleScript application, but with the addition of Document.applescript and Document.nib files. These two files work together to read, write, and display the document files used by your application. This template includes a handler for the About This Application window and a Credits.rtf file.
AppleScript Droplet	A minimalist version of the AppleScript template, the Droplet template creates an AppleScript Studio application with no user interface to speak of. Most droplets are intended to process documents that are "dropped" on them and then immediately quit, with little or no interaction with the user. The Application.applescript file contains an `on open` handler, which are invoked when the documents are dropped on the application.
Carbon Application	The Carbon template defines a pure Carbon application. Carbon is the C interfaces to Aqua and the legacy support for applications written using the APIs in Mac OS 9 and earlier. Use this template if you are porting an application from OS 9 to OS X, or you want to create native applications using only C or C++. The main.c file includes a skeletal application that loads the main.nib file, creates the application's window, and starts the main event loop. See `http://developer.apple.com/carbon/` for more information about Carbon applications.
Cocoa Application	Cocoa is the preferred application development technology for Mac OS X. It is based on the Objective-C programming language. The Cocoa framework is the Objective-C interfaces to Aqua and most other Apple technologies. If OS X has a "native" development environment, Objective-C and Cocoa are it. A few technologies are only available using Cocoa interfaces. The Cocoa template creates a minimal Cocoa application. The only functional part of the project is the main.m file which does nothing but create and start the generic `NSApplication` object. It does provide generic handling of the About This Program menu item, but it does not include a Credits.rtf file.

Table continued on following page

Template	Description
Cocoa Document-based Application	This template creates a more full-featured, document-centric Cocoa application. It defines a MyDocument.nib file that contains an empty document window, paired with an empty implementation of the MyDocument class. An instance of the MyDocument class is already defined in the NIB and is connected to the window. The class is associated with the bogus???? document type in the project attributes. You will want to edit the document type in the Properties tab of the application target.
Cocoa-Java Application	Mac OS X includes an extensive bridge between the Java programming language and the Objective-C APIs defined in the Cocoa framework. These Java proxy objects make it possible to use most of the Cocoa and Foundation frameworks as though they had been written in Java. If you need to create a native Cocoa application and prefer, or require, the Java programming language, create a Cocoa-Java application. The template sets up a Cocoa application whose native executable is the Cocoa-Java stub. This stub application creates a Java runtime, that loads and starts the Java classes which constitute the application. Read more about mixing Java and Cocoa at http://developer.apple.com/documentation/Cocoa/Java-date.html. Apple has recently announced that it will no longer be updating in the Cocoa-Java bridge beyond Mac OS X 10.3, so the future of this technology is murky.
Cocoa-Java Document-based Application	This template creates a Cocoa-Java application that includes a MyDocument.nib file containing a window connected to the MyDocument.java class. Like its native Cocoa counterpart, these are associated with the ???? document type.
Core Data Application	The Core Data template creates a native Cocoa application with a twist. Mac OS X 10.4 (also known as Tiger) includes a built-in database technology called Core Data. This allows any application to quickly and easily interface with complex databases. The application created by the Core Data template loads and maintains objects defined by the data model in the project's DataModel.xcdatamodel file. An application delegate class is included that handles all of the details of loading and keeping the data objects in synchronization with the database. By default, the database is SQLite. You can learn more about Core Data at http://developer.apple.com/macosx/coredata.html.
Core Data Document-based Application	This template sets up a Core Data application that uses the Cocoa document architecture. A little more abstract than the Core Data template, this template assumes that you use Core Data to obtain, or augment, the contents of documents. This is still a file-based application, so if the concept of a "document" is not a file, you have some work to do. An empty MyDocument.xcdatamodel data model file is included, but is not connected to anything.
Core Data Document-based Application with Spotlight Importer	A slight variation of the Core Data Document-based template, this template creates a document-based Cocoa application that has an imbedded Spotlight Importer plug-in. This plug-in, which is registered for each type of document the importer supports, is compiled and imbedded inside the application package. Developing Spotlight Importers is described in http://developer.apple.com/documentation/Carbon/Conceptual/MDImporters/. Also read the Importer Read Me.txt file included in the project.

All of these templates produce an application based on Apple's Aqua interface. Because of this, there are a number of commonalities among all of the application templates:

All of the application templates create a MainMenu.nib file. MainMenu.nib contains definitions for the standard menus (Application, File, Edit, Window, and Help) and is set to load when the application launches. The only exception is the Carbon template, which creates a main.nib file containing menu definitions only for Application, File, Edit, and Window.

If the template is one of the document-based varieties, the project includes an additional NIB file named MyDocument.nib (or in the AppleScript application, just Document.nib). MyDocument.nib is loaded each time a new document window needs to be created. Non-document-based projects also define a single window, but in their MainMenu.nib file. It is assumed that if your application is not document-based (with new document windows being created for each file it opens like TextEdit), then it probably uses a single interface window (like iTunes or Disk Utility) that is displayed when the application launches.

Almost all of these projects produce an application contained in a package (a folder that acts like a document in the Finder). An appropriately populated Info.plist file is included that identifies the package as an application, its name, version, and other generic information. Info.plist identifies the MainMenu.nib file as the one to load when the application launches. It also contains the attributes appropriate to the specific technology your application is based on. For instance, all of the projects based on the Cocoa framework contain an NSPrincipalClass value, which identifies the class of the main application object created by NSApplicationMain(). Document-based templates also define a list of document type associations, filled with the single invalid document type of ????.

Most of the templates include a Credits.rtf file, which is displayed by the default About This Application window handler. Unless you plan to implement your own, just edit this file to alter the contents of your application's About window.

Bundle

Bundles are packages (a file system directory that acts as a single document) that store a collection of executable code and resources. Applications, plug-ins, installers, are all packaged as bundles.

All bundles adhere to a basic structure. The package folder contains a subfolder named Contents. Inside that is an Info.plist file that describes the type and various properties of the bundle. Also in the Contents folder is a MacOS "architecture" folder that contains code suitable for execution on the Mac OS, and a Resources folder that contains whatever auxiliary support files the bundle needs.

Standard bundle types, like Cocoa applications, have Info.plist attributes that are defined by Apple. Developers are free to define their own extensions to the basic bundle structure. You can learn more about bundles at http://developer.apple.com/documentation/CoreFoundation/ Conceptual/CFBundles/.

The templates listed in the following table set up a project that produces a bundle conforming to one of three basic bundle types: Carbon, Code Fragment Plug-in, or Cocoa. Use these templates if you need to produce a bundle that isn't already defined by one of the other, more specific, templates — such as a Cocoa application or an Automator Action. For instance, if you were writing a plug-in for a third-party audio processing system, and the plug-in for that application is bundled Objective-C code, the Cocoa bundle template would probably be the place to start.

Template	Description
Carbon Bundle	This template creates a minimal bundle containing a single C executable. The main.c in the template doesn't contain any code, not even an empty main(). The CSResourcesFileMapped bundle property is defined to use mapped resources. Resources are separate files in the Resources folder, rather than resource objects in the resource fork of the executable.
CFPlugin Bundle	Also a minimal template, the CFPlugin template contains no code files. Its Info.plist does include the skeletal definitions for declaring the CF plug-in types, factories, unload functions, and other items needed by the Code Fragment Manager.
Cocoa Bundle	The Cocoa bundle template, like the others, produces an empty bundle package. It contains no source files and produces no code. It does declare an NSPrincipalClass property in the Info.plist file, which can be set to specify the main Objective-C class that your bundle uses.

All of these templates produce a product with the basic bundle structure (Contents folder, Info.plist file, Resources folder). The different flavors vary mostly in what additional attributes are included in the Info.plist file and what programming language is assumed.

Command-Line Utility

From simple text parsers to file servers, this is the domain of the command-line utility. Although the scope of such a project may be complex, the output isn't. The templates listed in the following table all set up projects that will produce a single binary executable file. The only difference between them is the programming language of choice, and what libraries and frameworks the program will be linked to.

Template	Description
C++ Tool	This template creates a simple command line program written in C++ and linked to the standard C++ runtime library.
CoreFoundation Tool	The CoreFoundation template creates a command line program written in C and linked to the CoreFoundation framework. These are the C interfaces to the core of the Mac OS operating system. Although the interfaces are in C, many of the concepts and structures of the Core Foundation framework are object-oriented and parallel many of the classes in the Foundation framework. Core Foundation includes the Core Services framework, plus some additional higher-level services such as XML parsing and communication ports. Use this template if you need to create a command-line utility that uses APIs in the CoreFoundation framework.

Template	Description
CoreServices Tool	Like the CoreFoundation template, the CoreServices template creates a command line program written in C. But instead of being linked to CoreFoundation, it is linked to the more primitive CoreServices framework. Core Services consists of basic memory management, task and process control, strings, collections, and other programming primitives. This is a good choice for a Mac OS native program that has no user interface or dependence on more complex services.
Foundation Tool	This template creates a command-line program written in Objective-C and linked to the Foundation framework. The Foundation framework is an object-oriented framework that forms the core of the Cocoa framework. It contains all of the primitive Cocoa classes (NSString, NSArray) but none of the higher application classes like NSApplication or NSWindow. Note that you can link a command-line tool to the Cocoa framework if you need access to image manipulation or other application-centric classes, even if your program doesn't create an Aqua interface. Although it is assumed that the program will be written in Objective-C, you are free to intermix C and C++ code as well.
Standard Tool	A project with this template creates a command-line program written in C and linked to the standard Unix C library.

In the grand tradition of Unix program development, all of these templates create a command that outputs "Hello, World!" to the console. Each also includes a source file with the helpful comment "insert code here."

As a perk, these templates also define a man page source file that will document your command tool using man. Assuming that you are creating a user command, the man page file has the suffix .1 that places it in the first section of the man pages. If your documentation belongs in a different section, renumber the suffix as appropriate.

Dynamic Library

Dynamic libraries contain common functions, classes, and variables that can be reused by multiple applications. The name reflects how the linkages between the references to the code in the application, and the actual code in the library, are resolved. Applications that use code in dynamic libraries include the name of the library, and the names of the routines in that library, that they intend to call. When the application is actually launched, the operating system locates the library and the finds the routines the application needs. The library is loaded into memory and the two are "dynamically linked." After this occurs, the application can directly call the routines in the library as though they had been compiled into the application.

The principle feature of dynamic libraries is that this linking does not occur until the application is actually run. The code in the library can be updated, or augmented, without altering the application in any way. The next time the application is run, it dynamically links to the new routines in the updated library. You can read more about dynamic libraries at http://developer.apple.com/documentation/ DeveloperTools/Conceptual/DynamicLibraries/index.html. For contrast, see the Static Library templates.

The Dynamic Library templates, listed in the following table, are all pretty simple. They create a project with no source code and a single target that produces a dynamic library. All of these targets create the same type of .dylib library. The only significant differences between them are the assumptions about what *other* libraries the library being produced will be linked to. If you need to link to other libraries, just start with whichever template meets your base requirements and add the additional libraries or frameworks you require.

Template	Description
BSD Dynamic Library	This template produces a dynamic library, but contains no source or linkages to any other libraries. It is suitable for dynamic libraries containing C (or C++) code that only use the standard C runtime libraries.
Carbon Dynamic Library	The Carbon template produces a dynamic library suitable for C development. The code in the library is, itself, linked to the Carbon framework, allowing the code to use any of the Carbon APIs. As a convenience, a precompiled header containing all of the Carbon headers is included.
Cocoa Dynamic Library	The Cocoa template is like the Carbon template, but it links to the Cocoa framework instead. References are also included to the AppKit, CoreData, and Foundation frameworks, but these are not included in the target. If your code needs more than what is in the Cocoa framework, you can easily add the AppKit or CoreData framework to the target. If the entire Cocoa framework is overkill, you can replace it with just the Foundation framework in a similar manor. This template is suitable for Objective-C development.

Framework

A framework is a collection of dynamic libraries, header files, images, data files, and other resources. Even more elaborate, frameworks can be containers for a collection of other frameworks. These are called *umbrella* frameworks. The bulk of the Mac OS X operating system is organized into frameworks. You can see the frameworks provided by the operating system by browsing the /System/Library/Frameworks folder.

If you need to create dynamic libraries that will be used by other developers, you should provide not just the code in the library but also header files, documentation, and other information on how to access it. You might also be producing several dynamic libraries that need to be kept together. Or, your dynamic libraries might need other resource files such as images, NIB files, or help documents. All of these are good reasons to package your dynamic libraries into a framework.

Like applications, frameworks are packaged as bundles. Both of the templates listed in the following table produce a framework bundle that contains an Info.plist file which describes the contents of the bundle, and MacOS and Resources folder for auxiliary files. Frameworks are also intended to be versioned. If you radically alter the structure or definitions of a framework, applications that were compiled for the older version of the framework will stop working. To address this, a framework package can contain multiple versions of itself. The different versions can be found in the Versions folder of the package, alongside a symbolic link named "Current" that points to the folder containing the default version of the framework. You can read more about frameworks and how they are structured at `http://developer.apple.com/documentation/MacOSX/Conceptual/BPFrameworks/index.html`.

Template	Description
Carbon Framework	The Carbon template produces a framework suitable for C development. The code in the framework is linked to the Carbon framework. There is a main.c file, but it contains no code.
Cocoa Framework	The Cocoa template produces a framework suitable for Objective-C development and is linked to the Cocoa and Core Data frameworks. It contains no source code at all.

One quirk of framework packages is that they are not opaque. Unlike other bundles and packages, the Finder does not hide the contents of the framework structure. You are free to browse their contents in the Finder.

Java

Mac OS X comes pre-installed with a world-class implementation of the Java runtime system, originally developed by Sun Microsystems. Installing the Xcode developer tools also installed the complete Java SDK. Xcode also throws in a copy of Ant, a Java-based make and deployment tool. And as if that weren't enough, Apple engineers have developed a suite of technologies that allow Java to directly access most of the C and Objective-C code in the Mac OS X frameworks. For pure-Java developers, Apple has also spent considerable time and effort making the cross-platform Swing and AWT environments Mac-friendly — so Java applications written using these technologies don't look and act like Frankenstein's monster.

Apple has gone to heroic efforts to make Java a first-class citizen in Mac OS X. But there are fundamental differences between Java and the Objective-C technologies that OS X is built on. The vast majority of Objective-C classes are available directly to Java programs. Xcode integrates with the Java debugger, and provides source level formatting and auto-completion. The entire suite of JavaDocs is included in Xcode's help system.

Yet, the Java documentation isn't quite as easy to navigate as Objective-C's. The Java debugger isn't quite as full-featured as gdb. Code Sense isn't quite as nice as the code completion or reformatting tools in a Java IDE like Eclipse. And the Interface Builder doesn't create Swing user interfaces the way Sun's Java Studio does.

So Java in Xcode isn't the best development experience that you'll ever encounter. But it is more than adequate for simple projects. And if you are developing Java programs that use Cocoa objects or other Apple specific technologies, it's the only IDE that lets you do this seamlessly. So even if it's not the best at everything, Xcode is often the best choice for your Java development needs.

You can read more about Apple's support for Java technologies at `http://developer.apple.com/java/`.

The Java templates are grouped in the following table by their common use of Java, rather than by the purpose of the template. Consequently, the Java templates are a wildly varied bunch broadly paralleling the major categories of other templates. Some of these projects use Ant.

Template	Description
Ant-based Application Jar	Like the External Build System template described at the beginning of this appendix, Xcode also has the ability to use other make-like tools for building products. For Java developers, Xcode provides built-in support for using Ant http://ant.apache.org/. The Ant-based Application Jar project creates a project containing no source and a single External target that invokes the Ant tool to build the project. A functional Ant build.xml file is included that defines targets for install, clean, compile, jar, and run. The build.xml file also defines locations for src, lib, bin, and dist folders, but only the src folder is actually created.
Ant-based Empty Project	This template creates a truly empty Ant-based project. The project will have a single External target, but includes no source or build.xml file. This would be a good choice if you wanted to wrap Xcode around a project already being built using Ant.
Ant-based Java Library	Like the Ant-based Application Jar, this template creates a project with no source and a simple build.xml file. In this project, the jar target of the build.xml file creates a JAR file from whatever files are in the bin directory after the compile target runs, and writes the new JAR to the dist folder.
Ant-based Signed Applet	This target sets up the Ant build.xml file with additional targets and attributes suitable for producing and deploying a signed applet. The gen-key and jar targets generate a signed applet JAR, which includes the Manifest file. An HTML file that loads the applet is included, and can be opened using the run target. An install target is also included that can be customized to deploy the applet's JAR to an FTP site.
Ant-based Web Start Application	This template creates an Ant project that builds and deploys a Web Start application. A functional JNLP file is created, along with an HTML file that will start the application. Like the Ant-based Signed Applet, targets are provided that sign the application JAR file, deploy it to and FTP server, or run it locally using the HTML document.
Java AWT Applet	The Java AWT Applet template creates a single Java source file containing a skeletal AWT applet and an example1.html file that will load and run the applet in the default web browser. The target is an Xcode Tool target. Java files are compiled and assembled into a JAR file by Xcode's build-in make facilities. This is suitable for cross-platform development of AWT applets.
Java AWT Application	This template creates a full-featured AWT application. It includes three sources file. The main Java source file includes a complete AWT application class, which creates the standard File and Edit menus, and opens an empty window, along with code to display About and Preferences windows. Handlers are defined and connected to all of the menu items, although most of the handlers are stubs that do nothing but output the command selected to the console. Use this template if you must create a cross-platform AWT application. AWT is not well supported on the Mac OS X, and Apple encourages Java developers to migrate to Swing applications whenever possible.

Template	Description
Java JNI Application	JNI (Java Native Interface) is the means by which a Java application can directly interface to C and other code. If you need to call your own C code from a Java application or tool, this template will create a project with all of the prerequisites for accomplishing that. The project includes a JNIWrapper.java file that demonstrates calling a C function with a parameter and retrieving the results as a Java String. You should rename both the calling class and the C function name, but the technique is clearly demonstrated and should be easy to modify. The build portion of this project is complicated and consists of several targets. To build a JNI application requires the Java application and the C code, and the JNI "glue" between the two is built separately using different compilers, linkers, and tools.
Java Swing Applet	This template is almost identical to the Java AWT Applet, except that the skeletal applet defined in the Java source file extends from the JApplet class, instead of the Applet class. An example1.html file is provided for testing your applet in the local browser.
Java Swing Application	This template creates a fully functional Java Swing application, complete with menus, stub handlers, and About and Preferences windows. The code also demonstrates using localized strings from a Java bundle. (Don't confuse Java bundles with Mac OS X bundles — same name and similar concept, but completely different technology.) Unlike the other Java templates, projects created with this one produce a Cocoa application bundle, not a cross-platform JAR file. Although the JAR file found inside the Java folder of the package is a standard JAR application file, the bundle is actually a native Cocoa application that contains a small stub executable (Java Swing Application) that starts up the Swing application and provides many Mac OS X-friendly features. In this respect, it is very similar to the Cocoa-Java Application template in the Applications group. The template also includes a generic .icns file in the package and an Info.plist file, if you want to customize the icon your application gets.
Java Tool	Projects created with this extremely simple template produce a simple JAR file from Java source. The single source files includes the prerequisite `public static void main (String args[])` method for invoking a Java class from the command line. Like its kin in the Command-Line group, it also includes a man page template for documenting your tool.

Kernel Extension

Kernel Extension templates, listed in the following table add functionality to the Darwin kernel — the very foundation of the OS X operating system. Writing kernel extensions is a technically demanding, and hazardous, task. Mistakes usually crash the entire system. You can learn more about writing kernel extensions at `http://developer.apple.com/documentation/Darwin/Kernel-date.html`.

Template	Description
Generic Kernel Extension	This template produces a KEXT (Kernel Extension) bundle. The Info.plist file identifies the bundle type, version, and name. The included C source file defines the two standard _start() and _stop() entry points.
IOKit Driver	An IOKit Driver is a special kind of kernel extension that provides IO services for hardware devices. IOKit drivers are how all OS X applications communicate with peripherals. If you are developing hardware for Macintosh computers that does not communicate through any of the standard IO channels (USB, FireWire, Ethernet, and so on), you many need to write an IO driver. The IOKit Driver template creates an empty C++ (drivers are written in C++) source file and header. The Info.plist file identifies the bundle as a kernel extension, with additional attributes that provide information about the devices the driver interfaces with. You can browse various device driver development documents at http://developer.apple.com/documentation/Darwin/Device Drivers-date.html.

Loadable Bundle

If you have this group of templates, then it means that you've upgraded from an older version of Xcode. The two templates in this group are essentially identical to the Bundle templates described earlier. The only difference is that these templates include an empty source file. Using these, instead of the templates in the Bundle group, will do no harm.

Standard Apple Plug-ins

The "Bundles" section mentioned that there are many bundle types defined by Apple. The following table lists the lion's share of those bundles. If you want to develop an Address Book Action or a Screen Saver, you must create a project that produces the correct kind, and form, of bundle. And that's exactly what the templates in this group do.

Template	Description
Address Book Action Plug-in for C	This template produces an Address Book Action bundle (see http://developer.apple.com/documentation/UserExperience/Conceptual/AddressBook/index.html) written in C. The main.c file has the required ABActionRegisterCallbacks() function, which returns pointers to stub functions. The code is linked to the AddressBook and CoreFoundation frameworks.
Address Book Action Plug-in for Objective-C	This template produces an Address Book Action bundle developed using Objective-C, and linked to the AddressBook and Cocoa frameworks. Instead of the callbacks used in the C version, this project defines an Objective-C class with specific methods for you to customize. It also creates a precompiled header that includes all of the definitions in the AddressBook and Cocoa frameworks.

Template	Description
AppleScript Xcode Plug-in	The Xcode IDE itself can be extended using plug-ins, and this template creates an Xcode plug-in written using the AppleScript language. A project from this template builds a Cocoa bundle that includes a stub executable (AppleScript Xcode) that starts the plug-in. In this respect, it is very much like an Apple-Script Studio application. The AppleScript source file defines the required on `plugin loaded` handler.
IBPalette	Like Xcode, Interface Builder is modular and can be extended using plug-ins. Interface Builder plug-ins are complex, producing both a plug-in bundle and a framework. See the "Custom Objects" section, towards the end of Chapter 10, for more details.
Image Unit Plug-in for Objective-C	Core Image is Apple's newest interface to its amazing suite of image generation and display technologies. This architecture can be extended using Image Unit Plug-ins. This template creates a project that produces an Image Unit bundle. It creates an Object-C class containing a single method, `-(BOOL)load:(void*)host`, along with a sample MyKernelFilter.cikernel file. The code is linked to the Foundation and QuartzCore frameworks. You can find information about programming with Core Image and how it is extended at `http://developer.apple.com/documentation/GraphicsImaging/Conceptual/CoreImaging/index.html`.
Installer Plug-in	An Installer Plug-In lets a developer customize the user interface presented by the Installer application. When and why you would use in the Installer to distribute your application is discussed at `http://developer.apple.com/documentation/DeveloperTools/Conceptual/SoftwareDistribution/index.html`. The project created with this template produces a Cocoa bundle that includes a NIB file that defines the custom view that the Installer will insert. An Objective-C class is defined that is a subclass of the InstallerPane class, and contains a default implementation of the `- (NSString *)title` method. An instance of the class is connected to the custom NSView in the NIB.
Metadata Importer	Metadata Importers decode the content of data files, extract the metadata values that would be of interest to users trying to locate those files, and returns that information to the Spotlight system. Use this template if you need to create a standalone Spotlight importer. The project produces a Metadata Importer bundle written in C and linked to the CoreServices and CoreFoundation frameworks. Implement your metadata importer in the GetMetadataForFile.c source file. Do not modify main.c, as it contains glue code for the Code Fragment Manager. The Core Data Document-based Application with Spotlight Importer template shows an example of a project that embeds a metadata importer directly into an application package. You may want to consider taking this approach with your application, rather then creating a standalone importer. The "Spotlight Importer Programming Guide" at `http://developer.apple.com/documentation/Carbon/Conceptual/MDImporters/index.html` has more information about developing metadata importers.

Table continued on following page

Template	Description
PreferencePane	Every part of the System Preferences pane is actually a plug-in. If you need to create your own System Preferences pane, use this template to get started. It creates a project that produces a Preference Pane package, suitable for dropping into your ~/Library/PreferencePanes folder. The NIB file created by the template contains the NSWindow that your preference pane presents to the user, and is connected to an instance of the NSPreferencePane class. An icon file is also included, which you will want to customize so your preference pane has a distinct look in the System Preferences window. Browse `http://developer .apple.com/documentation/UserExperience/Conceptual/Preference Panes/index.html` for articles on how to program Preference Panes.
Screen Saver	Screen Savers (formerly Screen Effects) are bundles that implement a screen saver when the system, or maybe just the user, is idle. The interface for Screen Saver plug-ins is Objective-C. The template creates a new subclass of the ScreenSaverView class and implements the required methods. If you want to use some other language, it is very easy to mix in C or C++ with Objective-C. The code is linked, by default, against the Cocoa and ScreenSaver frameworks. Look at the documentation for the ScreenSaverView class for what methods to implement. Starting at `http://developer.apple.com/ documentation/MacOSX/Conceptual/OSX_Technology_Overview/index .html`, locate the "Software Development Overview" section, and then find the section on Screen Savers.
Sherlock Channel	This template produces a Sherlock Channel. Sherlock is no longer supported, and has been largely replaced by Widgets in Mac OS X 10.4 Sherlock channels are described at `http://developer.apple.com/documentation/ AppleApplications/Conceptual/Sherlock/index.html`
Sync Schema	iSync enables you to synchronize user data (contacts and appointments) with external devices (cell phones, PDA, and so forth). If you want to synchronize your user data with a device not already supported by iSync, you need to create a Sync Schema plug-in. The project created by the Sync Schema template contains Schema-strings.m and Schema-strings.h files that define certain statically defined NSStrings used to identify the plug-in. It also includes an image for your plug-in. It doesn't define source files, so you will have to add those. Your code is linked against the Objective-C Foundation framework. Sync Schema Plug-ins are discussed in the "Sync Services Programming Guide" at `http://developer.apple.com/documentation/Cocoa/Conceptual/Sync Services/index.html`.

Static Library

Static libraries are essentially the opposite of dynamic libraries. Static libraries are collections of code that other programs can link to. Unlike dynamic libraries, the code in static libraries is physically inserted into the program when it is linked to the library — just as if the program contained the source in the library. The program is self-contained, having its own copy of the code in the library and not dependent on the original library to execute.

The templates for static library, listed in the following table, have the same form as the dynamic library templates. Each differs only in what programming language the library is written in and what libraries the code links to. Note that code in a static library can still contain linkages to code in a dynamic library. If a program links to code in a static library that makes references to routines in the Cocoa framework, that program will be dependent on the Cocoa framework to load and run.

Template	Description
BSD Static Library	This template produces a static library, but contains no source or linkages to any other libraries. Suitable for static libraries containing C (or C++) code that only use the standard C runtime libraries.
Carbon Static Library	The Carbon template produces a static library suitable for C development. The code in the library is, itself, linked to the Carbon framework, allowing the code to use any of the Carbon APIs. As a convenience, a precompiled header containing all of the Carbon headers is included.
Cocoa Static Library	The Cocoa template is like the Carbon template, but it links to the Cocoa framework instead. References are also included to the AppKit, CoreData, and Foundation frameworks, but these are not included in the target. If your code needs more than what is in the Cocoa framework, you can easily add the App-Kit or CoreData framework to the target. If the entire Cocoa framework is overkill, you can replace it with just the Foundation framework in a similar manner. This template is suitable for Objective-C development.

WebObjects

If you chose to install the optional WebObjects development package when you installed Xcode, a group of WebObjects templates will also be listed in the new project assistant window. WebObjects is Apple's award-winning web application server, and is an amazing piece of technology. I have had the pleasure of using WebObjects for two large web-based projects, and they were the most pleasurable and productive web development experiences I've ever had.

WebObjects is well beyond the scope of this book. Even a brief description of the WebObjects templates is pointless. If you're doing WebObjects development and understand the deployment differences between a two-tier Cocoa-Java client and a three-tier Java Swing client, then you don't need a paragraph explaining what these templates create. And if you're not, well, it's a waste of space.

You can learn more about WebObjects and Enterprise Objects at http://developer.apple.com/webobjects/. You should also take one of the online training courses or one the training workshops if one is available in your area.

Index

D